Peter Schäfer

The Origins of Jewish Mysticism

Peter Schäfer

The Origins of
Jewish Mysticism

Princeton University Press
Princeton and Oxford

Peter Schäfer is the Ronald O. Perelman Professor of Jewish Studies and Professor of Religion at Princeton University. His books include *Jesus in the Talmud* and *Mirror of His Beauty: Feminine Images of God from the Bible to the Early Kabbalah* (both Princeton). He received a Distinguished Achievement Award from the Andrew W. Mellon Foundation in 2007.

Copyright © 2009 by Mohr Siebeck, Tübingen, Germany

Original cloth edition published by Mohr Siebeck in 2009

First paperback printing by Princeton University Press in 2011

Paperback published by Princeton University Press, 41 William Street, Princeton, New Jersey 08540

In the United Kingdom: Princeton University Press, 6 Oxford Street, Woodstock, Oxfordshire OX20 1TW

press.princeton.edu

Cover illustration: *Ezekiel, Vision of Shekinah.* Detail of historiated initial and surrounding text from an English Bible, ca. 1270s. Robert Garret Collection of Medieval and Renaissance Manuscripts No. 28. Courtesy of Manuscripts Division, Department of Rare Books and Special Collections, Princeton University Library.

Library of Congress Cataloging-in-Publication Data

Schäfer, Peter, 1943–
   The origins of Jewish mysticism/Peter Schäfer.
      p.   cm.
   Includes bibliographical references and index.
   ISBN 978-0-691-14215-9 (pbk. : alk. paper)
   1. Mysticism—Judaism—History. 2. Bible. O.T. Ezekiel—Criticism, interpretation, etc. 3. Ethiopic book of Enoch. 4. Mysticism in rabbinical literature. 5. Merkava. I. Title.
   BM526.S2825 2009
   296.7′12—dc22   2009015049

British Library Cataloging-in-Publication Data is available

Typeset by Martin Fischer in Tübingen, Germany

Printed on acid-free paper. ∞

Printed in the United States of America

10 9 8 7 6 5 4 3 2 1

Margarete Schlüter

In memoriam

Contents

Acknowledgments   XI

Abbreviations XIII

Introduction   1
Mysticism   1
Jewish Mysticism   9
   1. Phases of Jewish Mysticism   9
   2. Unio mystica   17
Origins   20
The Origins of Jewish Mysticism   23

Chapter 1. Ezekiel's Vision: The Cosmos as Temple   34

Chapter 2. Enoch and His Circle: Ascent to Heaven   53
The Book of the Watchers (1 Enoch 1–36)   53
The Testament of Levi   67
Similitudes of Enoch (1 Enoch 37–71)   72
2 Enoch   77

Chapter 3. Enoch's Companions: From the Community
to the Individual   86
Apocalypse of Abraham   86
Ascension of Isaiah   93
Apocalypse of Zephaniah   99
Apocalypse of John 103

Chapter 4. Qumran: Communion with the Angels 112

A Community of Priests 113
Communion with the Angels in the Holy War 116
Liturgical Communion with the Angels 122
The Songs of the Sabbath Sacrifice 130
The Self-Glorification Hymn 146
Summary 151

Chapter 5. Philo: The Ascent of the Soul 154

Philo's Concept of God 155
Body and Soul, Senses and Mind 160
The Soul's Vision of God 164

Chapter 6. The Rabbis I: Approaching God through Exegesis 175

Reading and Expounding the Torah 176
The Cycle of Seven Stories 185
    1. Yohanan b. Zakkai and Eleazar b. Arakh: Teacher and Student 186
    2. Chain of Transmission 195
    3. Four Entered a Garden 196
    4. Parable of the King's Garden 203
    5. Parable of the Middle Course 206
    6. Ben Zoma and Creation 207
    7. Creation 209
Summary 210

Chapter 7. The Rabbis II: The Merkavah in Context 214

Yerushalmi 214
Bavli 222

Chapter 8. The Merkavah Mystics 243

Hekhalot Rabbati 244
    1. The Gedullah Hymns 245
    2. The Qedushah Hymns 254
    3. The Ten Martyrs Narrative 256
    4. The Apocalypses 257

5. Qedushah Hymns and Hymns of Praise 259
6. The Ascent Accounts 268
Hekhalot Zutarti 282
1. §§ 335–374: Ascent Accounts 283
2. §§ 375–406: Metatron 294
3. §§ 407–427: The Test of the Mystic and His Ascent 298
4. §§ 489–495: The Book of the Mysteries of the Divine Names 304
5. §§ 498–517: The Magic of the Name 305
Shi'ur Qomah 306
3 Enoch 315
1. Ishmael's Ascent 316
2. Enoch Is Metatron 318
Summary 327

Chapter 9. Conclusions 331

Ezekiel and the Ascent Apocalypses 331
Hekhalot Literature 339
Qumran 348
The Rabbis 350
Philo 352
Mysticism 353

Bibliography 357
Source Index 373
General Index 391

Acknowledgments

This is a book that I have been working on for several years. I started the actual writing in 2002–2003, during my sabbatical at the Historisches Kolleg in Munich, but when I returned to Princeton, more pressing issues came to the fore. Among other things, I was captivated by the subject of the relationship between Judaism and the emerging Christianity in the first centuries CE and couldn't stop thinking about what finally became my book, *Jesus in the Talmud* (published in 2007 by Princeton University Press). I kept working on the mysticism manuscript, but it wasn't until my next sabbatical at the Wissenschaftskolleg/Institute for Advanced Study at Berlin in 2007–2008 that I found the congenial atmosphere that enabled me to finish the book.

This book in a way summarizes my views on early Jewish mysticism. I spent many years working on this subject, mainly on what is generally called the first full-fledged manifestation of Jewish mysticism, Merkavah mysticism. In recent years, however, the question of what happened before Merkavah mysticism has become ever more acute. We speak about the Kabbalah, a phenomenon emerging in twelfth-century Europe, as the epitome of Jewish mysticism, and we regard Merkavah mysticism as some earlier form of Jewish mysticism that, to be sure, does not fall under the category of Kabbalah proper – but what, then, about the period before Merkavah mysticism? Can we rightfully and sensibly speak of Jewish mysticism as a uniform and coherent phenomenon that started some time in antiquity (in the Hebrew Bible, even?) and that later developed into what would become Merkavah mysticism and ultimately the Kabbalah? Many scholars have dealt with Merkavah mysticism and its ramifications for classical rabbinic Judaism – in fact, this field has become one of the most vibrant areas of Jewish studies in the past thirty years – as well as with the origins of the Kabbalah in the Book Bahir, but very few have paid full attention to the evidence of the Hebrew Bible, the apocalyptic literature, Qumran, and Philo. It is this gap between the Hebrew Bible and Merkavah mysticism that the present book wishes to address in a systematic and reflective manner.

I have to thank many friends and colleagues who accompanied me on my long way up to this juncture. Martin Hengel has never stopped encouraging me and giving me his wise counsel. My Princeton colleague Martha Himmelfarb took the trouble of reading the entire manuscript and sharing with me her extraordinary knowledge of the apocalyptic and Qumranic literature. Another Princeton colleague, Simeon Chavel, gave me a critical reading of the chapter on Ezekiel and patiently answered my questions. My former student Maren Niehoff, now at Hebrew University, was kind enough to read the chapter on Philo and to offer her critique. My former student Ra'anan Boustan (Abusch), now at UCLA, drew my attention to some important literature. The readers who evaluated the manuscript for the publisher gave me invaluable advice. I am particularly grateful to the reader who graciously revealed his identity, my esteemed colleague Philip Alexander; although we disagree on certain issues (a fact of which I make no secret in my book), he not only subjected the manuscript to a meticulous reading but offered the most generous and constructive critique, a treatment an author can only dream of. I have taken many of his suggestions to heart, and I hope he will forgive me when occasionally I have stubbornly insisted on my viewpoint. Ultimately he may well be right in his judgment that we are much closer to each other than it appears.

I thank Kevin McAllen, the Wissenschaftskolleg's ingenious English-language editor, for style editing the entire manuscript. We spent many hours discussing the minutiae and mysteries of the English language, and he sometimes even generously accepted when I refused to follow his suggestion. Baru Saul, my irreplaceable assistant, patiently and efficiently took part in all the various stages of the manuscript preparation. Marjorie Pannell carefully and perceptively copy edited the entire manuscript. Baru Saul and Maria denBoer kindly prepared the Source Index and the General Index respectively.

It is with deep sadness and sorrow that I dedicate this book to Margarete Schlüter, who passed away on November 2, 2008, at the age of sixty-one. Margarete Schlüter was my very first Ph.D. student, served many years as my colleague at the Berlin Institute of Jewish Studies, and became the successor of my teacher Arnold Goldberg at the University of Frankfurt. She was a dedicated teacher and scholar who devoted her life to the development and consolidation of Jewish studies in Germany. *Tehe nafshah tzerurah bi-tzror ha-hayyim.*

Abbreviations

Abr.	De Abrahamo
ad loc.	ad locum
Adv. haer.	Adversus haereses
AHDL	Archives d'histoire doctrinale et littéraire du moyen âge
Ant.	Antiquitates
b	Babylonian Talmud (Talmud Bavli)
b.	ben ("son of")
Bar.	Baruch
BCE	before the Christian Era
BJRL	Bulletin of the John Rylands Library, University Library Manchester
Cant.	Canticum Canticorum (Song of Songs)
CBQ	Catholic Biblical Quarterly
CBR	Currents in Biblical Research
CE	Christian Era
ch.	chapter
chs.	chapters
Cher.	De Cherubim
Chron.	Chronicles
Conf.	De Confusione Linguarum
Cong.	De Congressu Eruditionis Gratia
col.	column
cols.	columns
Cor.	Letter to the Corinthians
Dan.	Daniel
Deut.	Deuteronomy
DSD	Dead Sea Discoveries
Eccl.	Ecclesiastes
Ebr.	De Ebrietate
En.	Enoch
Ex.	Exodus
Ezek.	Ezekiel
FJB	Frankfurter Judaistische Beiträge
fol.	folio
Fug.	De Fuga et Inventione

Gal.	Letter to the Galatians
Gen.	Genesis
Gig.	De Gigantibus
GRBS	Greek, Roman and Byzantine Studies
Hab.	Habakkuk
Heb.	Letter to the Hebrews
Her.	Quis Rerum Divinarum Heres Sit
Hos.	Hosea
HTR	Harvard Theological Review
HUCA	Hebrew Union College Annual
Isa.	Isaiah
JAOS	Journal of the American Oriental Society
JBL	Journal of Biblical Literature
Jer.	Jeremiah
JH	Jewish History
JJS	Journal of Jewish Studies
Jos.	Joshua
JPS	Jewish Publication Society
JQR	Jewish Quarterly Review
JSJ	Journal for the Study of Judaism
JSQ	Jewish Studies Quarterly
l.	line
Leg. All.	Legum Allegoriarum
Lev.	Leviticus
Lk.	Luke
LXX	Septuagint
m	Mishna
Macc.	Maccabees
Mal.	Malachi
MGWJ	Monatsschrift für die Geschichte und Wissenschaft des Judentums
Mig.	De Migratione Abrahami
Mk.	Mark
Mos.	De Vita Mosis
Ms.	Manuscript
Mss.	Manuscripts
Mt.	Matthew
Mut. Nom.	De Mutatione Nominum
n.	note
nn.	notes
Nah.	Nahum
NRSV	New Revised Standard Version
Num.	Numbers

Op. Mund.	De Opificio Mundi
OTP	The Old Testament Pseudepigrapha
Phil.	Letter to the Philippians
Plant.	De Plantatione
Post.	De Posteritate Caini
Praem.	De Praemiis et Poenis
Prov.	Proverbs
Ps.	Psalms
Q.E.	Quaestiones et Solutiones in Exodum
QS	Qiryat Sefer
Quod Deus	Quod Deus Immutabilis Sit
R.	Rabbi
RdQ	Revue de Qumran
Rev.	Revelation
RSV	Revised Standard Version
Sac.	De Sacrificiis Abelis et Caini
Sam.	Samuel
Sap. Sal.	Sapientia Salomonis
SBL.SPS	Society of Biblical Literature, Seminar Paper Series
Sir.	Jesus Sirach
Som.	De Somniis
Spec. Leg.	De Specialibus Legibus
t	Tosefta
ThZ	Theologische Zeitschrift
TJ	Targum Jonathan
v.	verse
vv.	verses
VT	Vetus Testamentum
y	Jerusalem Talmud (Talmud Yerushalmi)
Zech.	Zechariah

Introduction

A book with the provocative title *The Origins of Jewish Mysticism* requires some comment on the terminology used. I will begin with the term "mysticism" in general, then discuss the implications of the modifier "Jewish" – the phases of Jewish mysticism and the viability of the notorious concept of mystical union (*unio mystica*) – continue with remarks on the quest for the "origins" of Jewish mysticism, and conclude by elaborating the principles that will guide me through my inquiry and outlining the book's structure.

Mysticism

Any attempt to define mysticism in a way that allows the definition to be generally accepted is hopeless. There is no such thing as a universally recognized definition of mysticism, just as there is no such thing as a universally recognized phenomenon of mysticism or notion of mystical experience. In fact, there are almost as many definitions of the term as there are authors – if the authors even bother to define the object of their study at all. Mystical experiences differ greatly from culture to culture; the particular cultural and religious conventions within which a "mystic" lives make his or her mystical experience culturally specific. This becomes immediately clear from the very use of the words "mysticism" or "mystic," which derive from the Greek root *myein*, meaning "to shut the eyes"; accordingly, the *mystikos* is someone who shuts his or her eyes in order to shut out the mundane world and experience other realities. Hence the derivative *myeō*, "to initiate into the mysteries," and more frequently the passive *myeomai*, "to be initiated." More specifically, the *mystēs* is the one who is initiated into the Greek mystery cults and who participates in secret rituals that dramatize certain myths (such as the mystery cult at Eleusis, as early as the seventh century BCE). The *mystikos* or the *mystēs*, therefore, is connected to the "mysteries" of these mystery cults; that is, the word acquires also the coloration of secrecy and privacy.

No one today would claim that this very specific meaning of initiation into mystery cults prevailed as a common denominator in all or even many later manifestations of mysticism – although, to be sure, the notion of "secrecy" and "mystery" remained an important aspect of what might be dubbed "mysticism."

Hence, despite its explicit connection with ancient mystery cults, "mysticism" is, in modern scholarly terminology, not an emic but an etic term, that is, a term that was not actually used by the people who practiced mysticism (clearly not in antiquity) but was invented by modern scholars in order to define and classify certain religious experiences. In this respect, "mysticism" is akin to that other notoriously problematic term, "magic" – a term that some scholars want to exorcize from the politically correct scholarly vocabulary.[1]

Nevertheless, if we look at certain definitions of mysticism in handbooks of religion or in popular dictionaries, we encounter some striking common features.[2] Take, for example, the following definitions in the German *Brockhaus Enzyklopädie* and in the British *Oxford English Dictionary*. The *Brockhaus* runs as follows:

> Mysticism [the original Greek *myeomai* translates as "to be initiated," literally "to have one's eyes and mouth closed"], a structural form of religious experience and life in which the *unio mystica* – an intrinsically experienced unification (*Einung*) of the human self with the divine reality – is achieved.[3]

---

[1] See, e. g., Philip Alexander, "Response," in Peter Schäfer and Joseph Dan, eds., *Gershom Scholem's Major Trends in Jewish Mysticism: 50 Years After* (Tübingen: J.C.B. Mohr [Paul Siebeck], 1993), p. 82; Marvin W. Meyer and Richard Smith, eds., *Ancient Christian Magic: Coptic Texts of Ritual Power* (San Francisco: HarperCollins, 1994), pp. 4 ff. On the problems resulting from such an approach, see Henk S. Versnel, "Some Reflections on the Relationship Magic-Religion," *Numen* 37 (1991), pp. 177–197, and Yuval Harari's recent attempt to go beyond a pragmatic use of the category "magic" (see his "What Is a Magical Text? Methodological Reflections Aimed at Redefining Early Jewish Magic," in Shaul Shaked, ed., *Officina magica: Essays on the Practice of Magic in Antiquity* [Leiden: Brill, 2005], pp. 91–124). Using the notion of "family resemblance" and resorting to the "partial resemblance" of certain phenomena, he tries to avoid any essentialist or substantialist definition of "magic" (as opposed to "religion"). I wonder, however, how sentences such as "The density of the web of partial resemblance ties is what determines whether they are definitely [!] more or less magical or religious. ... The web of partial resemblance creates a fabric, varying in its density, in which religious and magic phenomena [!] are tied together" (ibid., p. 115) avoid relapsing into the essentialist mode.

[2] It is by no means my goal here to attempt an even approximate account of the major definitions suggested by historians of religion; I merely give some examples that I find instructive. For further information, see, e. g., the "classic" contributions by William James, *The Varieties of Religious Experience: A Study in Human Nature* (London: Longman, Green), 1902 (esp. pp. 366 ff.); Evelyn Underhill, *Mysticism: A Study in the Nature and Development of Man's Spiritual Consciousness*, 12th ed. (London: Methuen, 1930, repr. 1967 [first published 1911]); Rufus M. Jones, *Studies in Mystical Religion* (London: Macmillan, 1909, repr. 1923); idem, *New Studies in Mystical Religion* (London: Macmillan, 1927); Emily Herman, *The Meaning and Value of Mysticism* (London: Clark, 1922); Louis Dupré, "Mysticism," in Mircea Eliade, ed., *The Encyclopedia of Religion*, vol. 10 (London: Collier Macmillan, 1987), pp. 245–261.

[3] *Brockhaus Enzyklopädie in Zwanzig Bänden*, vol. 13 (Wiesbaden: F.A. Brockhaus, 1971), p. 141. The German version reads: "Mystik [zu grch. myeomai 'eingeweiht werden'; eigentl. 'sich Augen und Mund schließen lassen'], eine Strukturform relig. Erlebens und Lebens, in der die unio mystica – die wesenhaft erfahrene Einung des menschl. Selbst mit der göttl. Wirklichkeit – erreicht wird."

This definition limns mysticism as an essential structure of religious life in which the *unio mystica* is attained, the unification of the human self with divine reality; that is, mysticism is a particular variety of religion having as its most prominent characteristic the *unio mystica.*[4]

The *Oxford English Dictionary* is more comprehensive but likewise emphasizes the mystical union of man and God. Here, the term "mysticism" captures

> [t]he opinions, mental tendencies, or habits of thought and feeling, characteristic of mystics; mystical doctrines or spirit; belief in the possibility of union with the Divine nature by means of ecstatic contemplation; reliance on spiritual intuition or exalted feeling as the means of acquiring knowledge of mysteries inaccessible to intellectual apprehension.[5]

The first sentence is not very helpful because the "opinions" and so forth of "mystics" or "mystical doctrines or spirit" only shift the problem from "mysticism" to "mystics" or "mystical": what then, pray tell, are "mystics," and what is "mystical"? Then comes the major characteristic, the "union with the Divine nature," obviously avoiding the word "God" and preferring instead the vague "Divine nature" and adding some important qualifications: ecstatic contemplation, exalted feeling, acquiring knowledge of mysteries as opposed to intellectual apprehension. "Ecstasy," "feeling," and "knowledge" are characteristics that play an important part in most definitions of mysticism. But it cannot be stressed enough: the ultimate goal according to this definition is the union of man with God. Some scholars even go so far as to boldly proclaim, "That we bear the image of God is the starting-point, one might almost say the postulate, of all Mysticism. *The complete union of the soul with God is the goal of all Mysticism.*"[6]

There is, however, one problem with this definition. Whether or not it fits a religion such as Judaism we will see, but what about religions that do not presuppose the existence of a transcendent God and the human soul, that is, religions

---

[4] Interestingly enough, this definition has become much less assertive – and loses the *unio mystica* – in the more recent nineteenth Brockhaus edition of 1991 (vol. 15, p. 268): "Mysticism [the original Latin *mysticus* translates as "mysterious," from the Greek *mystikós*], ... a multi-level phenomenon that is difficult to pin down and which in its various cultural manifestations is common to all religions. Mysticism designates the direct experience of a divine reality that transcends everyday consciousness and rational perception."

[5] *The Oxford English Dictionary*, 2nd ed., prepared by J. A. Simpson and E. S. C. Weiner, vol. 10 (Oxford: Clarendon Press, 1989), p. 176.

[6] William Ralph Inge, *Christian Mysticism: Considered in Eight Lectures Delivered before the University of Oxford* (London: Methuen, 1899, Appendix A), p. 339 (my emphasis in italics). Scholem refers to this appendix in his *Major Trends* (below, n. 10), p. 4, without giving the precise bibliographical details. Unfortunately, the appendix has disappeared in later editions of Inge's book, and one frustrated reader added (on p. 333 of the 1956 edition) the handwritten note, "What [expletive] happened to the famous Appendix?" On the concept of the mystical union in general, see Ileana Marcoulesco, "Mystical Union," in Mircea Eliade, ed., *The Encyclopedia of Religion*, vol. 10 (London: Collier Macmillan, 1987), pp. 239–245.

that are not based on the Hebrew Bible with its notion of human beings "in the image and likeness of God"? Hindu and Buddhist mysticism, for example, suggest that the world and nature are illusions and that the deepest and truest "unity" is achieved when awareness of the self and its connection with the world is annihilated, thus interrupting the fatal cycle of reincarnation. This kind of mysticism is called "acosmic" or "world-negating." Other religious systems prefer the mystical experience of a unity or oneness with nature instead of God, following the pantheistic idea that nature constitutes the Absolute behind and beyond all reality: God is everywhere and in everything, a notion that obviously challenges the concept of a personal God. A prominent example of a Christian mystic who expressed a pantheistic view of the oneness of nature and man's unity with nature is Meister Eckhart (1260–before 1328): "All that a man has here externally in multiplicity is intrinsically One. Here all blades of grass, wood and stone, all things are One. This is the deepest depth."[7]

Here mysticism is not the union or rather unity with the Absolute, let alone a personal God, but the awareness of the inherent unity of all beings. God is part of this unity because he is part of nature and nature is a part of God. The idea of a personal God as the goal of the mystic has become so remote that Meister Eckhart was suspected of being a pantheist and heretic, denying the essential difference between God and his creation.[8]

An outstanding example of mystical union with nature, a kind of "secular mysticism," is the famous poem *Tintern Abbey*, by William Wordsworth (1770–1850), that celebrated representative of the "romantic revolt" in England:

> […] For I have learned
> To look on Nature not as in the hour
> Of thoughtless youth, but hearing oftentimes
> The still, sad music of humanity,
> Nor harsh, nor grating, though of ample power
> To chasten and subdue. And I have felt
> A presence that disturbs me with the joyces
> Of elevated thoughts, a sense sublime
> Of something far more deeply interfused,
> Whose dwelling is the light of setting suns,
> And the round ocean, and the living air,
> And the blue sky, and the mind of man –

---

[7] Quoted in Rudolf Otto, *Mysticism East and West: A Comparative Analysis of the Nature of Mysticism*, trans. Bertha L. Bracey and Richenda C. Payne (New York: Macmillan, 1932 [repr. 1957, Meridian Books, New York]), p. 61.

[8] The archbishop of Cologne accused him of heresy, and in 1329 Pope John XXII declared some of Eckhart's propositions heretical and others suspicious of heresy. See Otto Karrer and Herma Piesch, eds., *Meister Eckeharts Rechtfertigungsschrift vom Jahre 1326: Einleitungen, Übersetzung und Anmerkungen* (Erfurt: Kurt Stenger, 1927); G. Théry, "Édition Critique des Pièces Relatives au Procès d'Eckhart Contenues dans le Manuscrit 33b de la Bibliothèque de Soest," *AHDL* 1 (1926–1927), pp. 129–268.

A motion and a spirit that impels
All thinking things, all objects of all thought,
And rolls through all things.[9]

In view of these difficulties – not only of those emerging from Eastern religions – modern scholars tend to suggest more nuanced definitions of mysticism. As my two prime examples I have chosen Gershom Scholem, the founding father of the academic discipline of Jewish mysticism, and Bernard McGinn, the eminent expert on Christian mysticism. In the introductory chapter of his *Major Trends in Jewish Mysticism* (first published in 1941), which bears the optimistic title "General Characteristics of Jewish Mysticism," Scholem asks, almost despairingly: "[W]hat is Jewish mysticism? What precisely is meant by this term? Is there such a thing, and if so, what distinguishes it from other kinds of mystical experience?"[10] To answer this question he first summarizes what we know about mysticism in general. He begins by praising "the brilliant books written on this subject by Evelyn Underhill[11] and Dr. Rufus Jones" and by quoting Jones's definition of mysticism in his *Studies in Mystical Religion*: "I shall use the word mysticism to express the *type of religion which puts the emphasis on immediate awareness of relation with God, on direct and intimate consciousness of the Divine Presence. It is religion in its most acute, intense and living stage.*"[12] Then Scholem moves back to what he calls Thomas Aquinas's brief definition of mysticism as *cognitio Dei experimentalis* – a knowledge of God through experience.[13] The latter in particular, he argues, is guided by the biblical verse Psalms 34:9: "Oh taste and see that the Lord is good." The tasting and seeing of God is what "the genuine mystic desires ... determined by the fundamental ex-

---

[9] William Wordsworth, "Tintern Abbey," in *The Pedlar. Tintern Abbey. The Two-Part Prelude*, ed. with a critical introduction and notes by Jonathan Wordsworth (Cambridge: Cambridge University Press, 1985), pp. 37 f., l. 89–103.

[10] Gershom Scholem, *Major Trends in Jewish Mysticism* (New York: Schocken, 1974 [repr.]), p. 3.

[11] See above, n. 2.

[12] Jones, *Studies in Mystical Religion*, p. XV (Jones's emphasis).

[13] Scholem quotes Aquinas according to Engelbert Krebs, *Grundfragen der kirchlichen Mystik dogmatisch erörtert und für das Leben gewertet* (Freiburg: Herder, 1921), p. 37. Apparently Scholem did not bother to check the original context of the quotation from Thomas, because there (Summa theologiae II.2, quaestio 97, art. 2 arg. 2) it belongs to the question as to whether or not it is a sin to tempt God, and has nothing to do with mysticism. In his refutation of the premise that "it is not a sin to tempt God," Thomas distinguishes between two kinds of knowledge of God's goodness (*bonitas*) or will (*voluntas*), one speculative (*speculativa*) and the other affective or experiential (*affectiva seu experimentalis*). It is through the latter knowledge that a human being "experiences in himself the taste of God's sweetness (*gustum divinae dulcedinis*) and complacency in God's will (*complacentiam divinae voluntatis*)," and it is only in this affective-experiential way that we are allowed, according to Aquinas, to prove God's will and taste his sweetness. In quoting Aquinas, Krebs focuses solely on the experience of God's goodness or sweetness and completely suppresses the connection with God's will.

perience of the inner self which enters into immediate contact with God or the metaphysical Reality."[14]

Both definitions serve Scholem, however, in rejecting two of their major presuppositions. The first is the notion of *unio mystica*, the mystical union of the individual with God. This term, he posits, "has no particular significance" in mysticism in general and in Jewish mysticism in particular: "Numerous mystics, Jews as well as non-Jews, have by no means represented the essence of their ecstatic experience, the tremendous uprush and soaring of the soul to its highest plane, as a union with God."[15] He briefly refers to the very different experiences of what he labels the earliest Jewish mystics of talmudic times (in his terminology, the "old Jewish Gnostics") and the latest offshoot of Jewish mysticism, the Hasidim of Eastern Europe, and concludes: "And yet it is the same experience which both are trying to express in different ways."[16]

The second rather useless presupposition, according to Scholem, is the assumption that "the whole of what we call mysticism is identical with that personal experience which is realized in the state of ecstasy or ecstatic meditation. Mysticism, as an historical phenomenon, comprises much more than this experience, which lies at its root." So, although within certain strands of mysticism we do find mystical union and ecstasy – the two most cherished elements of many modern definitions of at least Jewish, Christian, and Islamic mysticism – they are useless as parameters in defining both mysticism and Jewish mysticism alike. What remains is mysticism as a historical phenomenon, to be described and analyzed within the framework of other religious phenomena and in different and changing historical contexts: "The point I should like to make," Scholem concludes, "is this – that there is no such thing as mysticism in the abstract, that is to say, a phenomenon or experience which has no particular relation to other religious phenomena. There is no mysticism as such, there is only the mysticism of a particular religious system, Christian, Islamic, Jewish Mysticism and so on."[17] Definitions, in the end, prove to be futile.

Finally, in Scholem's view, there is still yet another danger lurking in the all-too-sweeping definitions of mysticism: they confuse religion with mysticism and

---

[14] Scholem, *Major Trends*, p. 4.

[15] Ibid., p. 5. It is therefore simply wrong to maintain, as Elliot Wolfson does, that "the mystical experience, according to Scholem, involves a direct and intimate consciousness of the divine Presence that, in the most extreme cases, eventuates in union with God" and that "from Scholem's own standpoint the vast majority of Jewish mystical sources fall somewhat short of the ideal that he himself set up, which involves unitive experience" (Elliot Wolfson, "Mysticism and the Poetic-Liturgical Compositions from Qumran: A Response to Bilhah Nitzan," *JQR* 85 [1994], p. 191). Scholem set up no such ideal but stated explicitly and unequivocally that the term *unio mystica* "has no particular significance" for many mystics, "Jews as well as non-Jews."

[16] Scholem, *Major Trends*, p. 5.

[17] Ibid., pp. 5 f.

conclude that *"all* religion in the last resort is based on mysticism," a mistake for which he quotes Rufus Jones's definition as a prime example that he does not want to repeat.[18] Instead he favors an evolutionary model of religion in three stages, of which only the third and last stage witnesses the birth of mysticism. The first stage is that of a naïve harmony between man, universe, and God and where there is no need for ecstatic meditation. The second stage may be called the classical stage in the history of a religion, in which religion becomes institutionalized and is characterized by a vast abyss between God and man. Yet it is at this stage – "more widely removed than any other period from mysticism and all that it implies"[19] – that mysticism is born. Borrowing a turn of phrase from Nietzsche,[20] it is the birth of mysticism out of the spirit of the institutionalized and classical form of religion, a form and period of religion, moreover, that may be labeled romantic.[21] At this stage, all religious concepts (above all the ideas of creation, revelation, and redemption) "are given new and different meanings reflecting the characteristic feature of mystical experience, the direct contact between the individual and God."[22]

If we now turn to McGinn's definition of mysticism, we discover a number of important points of agreement with Scholem, but also points of agreement with other, more general definitions that Scholem ultimately rejects. McGinn aims at a broad and flexible definition of mysticism and discusses it under three headings in the "General Introduction" to his monumental *The Foundations of Mysticism*:[23]

1. Mysticism is always a part or element of *religion*. All mystics believed in and practiced a religion (Christianity, Judaism, Islam, Hinduism), not "mysticism"; that is, mysticism is a subset of religion, part of a wider historical whole. Even when it reaches a level of explicit formulation and awareness, it remains inseparable from the larger whole, never becoming independent of religion.

2. Mysticism is a *process* or *way of life*. The goal of the mystic (whatever this is) shall not and cannot be isolated from the life of the individual. The individual is part of a community, and this relationship between individual and community also needs to be determined in any proper evaluation of the individual's mysticism.

3. Mysticism is an attempt to express a direct or immediate *consciousness* of the *presence of God*. This is the most important part of McGinn's definition. He is very careful in his choice of words, in particular "consciousness" and "pres-

---

[18] Ibid., pp. 6 f. (my emphasis).
[19] Ibid., p. 7.
[20] Friedrich Nietzsche, *Die Geburt der Tragödie aus dem Geiste der Musik* (Leipzig: E. W. Fritzsch, 1872).
[21] Scholem, *Major Trends*, p. 7.
[22] Ibid., p. 9.
[23] Bernard McGinn, *The Foundations of Mysticism*, vol. 1: *The Presence of God: A History of Western Christian Mysticism* (London: SCM Press, 1992), pp. XI ff.

ence." "Presence" is a deliberate substitute for "union," a word that McGinn finds rather problematic:

> If we define mysticism in this sense [as some form of union with God], there are actually so few mystics in the history of Christianity that one wonders why Christians used the qualifier "mystical" so often (from the late second century on) and eventually created the term "mysticism" (first in French, "la mystique") in the seventeenth century.[24]

Because "union" might not be the most suitable category for an understanding of mysticism and because there were several, perhaps even many, understandings of union with God, McGinn suggests expanding the notion of union and finds the

> term "presence" a more central and more useful category for grasping the unifying note in the varieties of Christian mysticism. ... From this perspective, it comes as no surprise that union is only one of the hosts of models, metaphors, or symbols that mystics have employed in their accounts. Many have used it, but few have restricted themselves to it. Among the other major mystical categories are those of contemplation and the vision of God, deification, the birth of the Word in the soul, ecstasy, even perhaps radical obedience to the present divine will. All of these can be conceived of as different but complementary ways of presenting the consciousness of direct presence.[25]

The other term in the third part of his definition, "consciousness," is a deliberate substitute for "experience," a word that he finds imprecise and ambiguous:

> The term mystical experience, consciously or unconsciously, also tends to place emphasis on special altered states – visions, locutions, rapture, and the like – which admittedly have played a large part in mysticism but which many mystics have insisted do not constitute the essence of the encounter with God. Many of the greatest Christian mystics [...] have been downright hostile to such experiences, emphasizing rather the new level of awareness, the special and heightened consciousness involving both loving and knowing that is given in the mystical meeting.[26]

From these quotations we can easily see that McGinn and Scholem[27] agree most with regard to what is summarized under (1): mysticism as part of a concrete historical religion. Also (2) would certainly find Scholem's approval (although he does not dwell on this particular aspect when discussing the problem of defi-

---

[24] Ibid., p. XVI.

[25] Ibid., p. XVII.

[26] Ibid., pp. XVII f.

[27] Interestingly enough, the recent definition of mysticism by Philip Alexander, a Jewish studies scholar, comes very close to that of McGinn. Alexander suggests that the following three characteristics are shared by most concrete mystical traditions (*Mystical Texts: Songs of the Sabbath Sacrifice and Related Manuscripts* [London: T. & T. Clark International, 2006], p. 8): (1) mysticism arises from the religious experience of a transcendent divine presence; (2) the mystic enters a close relationship with this divine presence that can be described in theistic systems as "communion" and in pantheistic systems as "union"; and (3) mysticism always requires a *via mystica*.

nition). As for (3), however, this is more complicated. Scholem and McGinn share the reluctance of granting the notions of *unio mystica* and personal experience too much sway in any definition of mysticism, but I do not think that Scholem would approve of McGinn's substitute, the consciousness of direct divine presence. For this comes surprisingly close to Jones's definition ("direct and intimate consciousness of the Divine Presence"), which Scholem rejects as too general because it blurs the distinction between "religion" and "mysticism." But Scholem has made things a bit too easy for himself by failing to suggest an alternative and instead contenting himself with the emphatic statement: "I, for one, do not intend to employ a terminology [such as used by Jones] which obscures the very real differences [between "religion" and "mysticism"] that are recognized by all, and thereby makes it even more difficult to get at the root of the problem."[28]

Jewish Mysticism

"Jewish mysticism" is obviously a subset of "mysticism," and it will be useful to continue with Scholem and to see how he delineates the former within the framework of the latter. The main bone of contention seems to be the nature of that "fundamental experience" encountered by the mystic in his relationship with the divine, in particular whether it can or cannot be subsumed under the category of "mystical union." Before we go into such detail, however, it is necessary to examine first how Scholem (and his successors) define and describe Jewish mysticism historically, that is, as a historical manifestation within the larger context of the Jewish religion.[29]

1. Phases of Jewish Mysticism

Since, according to Scholem, mysticism arises out of the classical stage of a given religion, it will come as no surprise that for him, Jewish mysticism begins with the talmudic period and continues, with many variations, up to the present day. At least this is what he asserts in his introductory chapter, "General Characteristics of Jewish Mysticism."[30] In the second chapter of *Major Trends*, the chapter dealing with Merkavah mysticism (the first full-fledged system of Jewish mysticism), he is more generous and grants the first phase of Jewish mysticism

---

[28] Scholem, *Major Trends*, p. 7.

[29] For a useful overview, see Philip S. Alexander, "Mysticism," in Martin Goodman, ed., *The Oxford Handbook of Jewish Studies* (Oxford: Oxford University Press, 2002), pp. 705–732.

[30] Scholem, *Major Trends*, p. 18: The uninterrupted mystical chain leads from the talmudic hero Rabbi Aqiva to the "late Rabbi Abraham Isaac Kook, the religious leader of the Jewish community in Palestine and a splendid type of Jewish mystic."

its beginnings in the first century BCE, thus clearly predating the talmudic period.[31] He opens this chapter with the programmatic statement:

> The first phase in the development of Jewish mysticism before its crystallization in the
> mediaeval Kabbalah is also the longest. Its literary remains are traceable over a period
> of almost a thousand years, from the first century B. C. to the tenth A. D., and some of
> its important records have survived.[32]

Here we learn in two sentences many important (and some problematic) things.
First, there are several phases of Jewish mysticism that are bound together by
the term "mysticism." The first of these phases is Merkavah mysticism, that
peculiar mystical movement that, as we will soon discover in greater detail, re-
volves around the divine throne in heaven. This is clear enough and can hardly
be contested. Second, Scholem distinguishes between "Jewish mysticism" and
"Kabbalah": Jewish mysticism begins in antiquity, but it somehow "crystallizes"
in what is called "Kabbalah" in the Middle Ages. "Kabbalah" seems to be the
epitome of Jewish mysticism, but Scholem does not bother to explain why the
manifestation of mysticism before the Kabbalah is just "mysticism" and mysticism's medieval strand "Kabbalah" proper – yet he nevertheless calls his book
Major Trends in Jewish Mysticism. When in 1962 he published a book in German titled *Ursprung und Anfänge der Kabbala*,[33] he took for granted that distinction between "Jewish mysticism" and "Kabbalah."[34]

Third, and most important for our purpose, the boundaries in both directions
(forward and backward in time) of the first phase of Jewish mysticism are less
obvious. Whereas Scholem's strategy for extending the first phase into the tenth
century is clearly an attempt to narrow the gap between his first and second
phases, Merkavah mysticism and Hasidism in medieval Germany (approxi-
mately 1150–1250 CE), he remains remarkably vague with regard to the beginning of the first phase. Although he has declared that the first phase, Merkavah
mysticism, begins in the first century BCE, he is reluctant to put it into its full
historical context. "It is not my intention here," he states at the outset,

---

[31] Whether the first century BCE belongs to the "classical" period of Judaism is another
issue, but it is certainly part of the "institutionalized" form of the Jewish religion – the other
characteristic of Scholem's definition of the "romantic period" out of which Jewish mysticism
emerged.

[32] Scholem, *Major Trends*, p. 40.

[33] Berlin: Walter de Gruyter, 1962. English translation *Origins of the Kabbalah*, ed. R. J.
Zwi Werblowsky, trans. Allan Arkush (Philadelphia: Jewish Publication Society; Princeton, NJ:
Princeton University Press, 1987).

[34] The first sentence of the first chapter reads: "The question of the origin and early stages
of the Kabbalah, that form of Jewish mysticism and theosophy that appears to have emerged
suddenly in the thirteenth century, is indisputably one of the most difficult in the history of the
Jewish religion after the destruction of the Second Temple" (*Origins*, p. 3). At least we get the
additional information here that the Kabbalah would appear to have emerged "suddenly" out
of the common ground of Jewish mysticism.

to follow the movement [of Merkavah mysticism] through its various stages, from its early beginnings in the period of the Second Temple to its gradual decline and disappearance. ... I do not, therefore, intend to give much space to hypotheses concerning the origins of Jewish mysticism and its relation to Graeco-Oriental syncretism, fascinating though the subject be. Nor am I going to deal with the many pseudepigraphic and apocalyptic works such as the Ethiopic book of Enoch and the Fourth Book of Ezra, which undoubtedly contain elements of Jewish mystical religion. Their influence on the subsequent development of Jewish mysticism cannot be overlooked, but in the main I shall confine myself to the analysis of writings to which little attention has hitherto been given in the literature on Jewish religious history.[35]

Despite this restrained attitude toward the earlier manifestations of Jewish mysticism before the appearance of Merkavah mysticism in the technical sense of the term, Scholem is convinced that "subterranean but effective, and occasionally still traceable, connections exist between these later [Merkavah] mystics and the groups which produced a large proportion of the pseudepigrapha and apocalypses of the first century before and after Christ"[36] and that "the main subjects of the later Merkabah mysticism already occupy a central position in this oldest esoteric literature, best represented by the book of Enoch."[37] So he ultimately (and boldly) concludes that we can actually delineate three stages of Merkavah mysticism, that first phase of Jewish mysticism, namely

1. "the anonymous conventicles of the old apocalyptics";
2. "the Merkabah speculation of the mishnaic teachers who are known to us by name"; and
3. "the merkabah mysticism of late and post-Talmudic times, as reflected in the literature which has come down to us [Hekhalot literature]."[38]

Unfortunately, Scholem not only eschews any substantial treatment of the "apocalyptic stage" of Merkavah mysticism – let alone that he does not make an attempt to prove the historical connection between the alleged Merkavah speculations of the "old apocalyptics" and the Mishnah teachers of rabbinic Judaism or the Merkavah mystics presented in the Hekhalot literature – in his description he leaves his second stage almost completely out, his chapter on Merkavah mysticism drawing solely on the Hekhalot literature (although he was convinced, and became ever more so in his later writings, that the heroes of Hekhalot literature – most prominent among them R. Ishmael and R. Aqiva – were identical

---

[35] Scholem, *Major Trends*, p. 40.
[36] Ibid., p. 42.
[37] Ibid., p. 43.
[38] Ibid. On Scholem's approach, see also the very useful summary by Martha Himmelfarb, "Merkavah Mysticism since Scholem: Rachel Elior's *The Three Temples*," in Peter Schäfer, ed., *Wege Mystischer Gotteserfahrung: Judentum, Christentum und Islam / Mystical Approaches to God: Judaism, Christianity, and Islam* (Munich: Oldenbourg, 2006), pp. 19–22.

with the famous rabbis as we know them from the rabbinic literature).[39] So all that in fact remains of Scholem's three stages of the first phase is just the third and last stage.

This result is highly unsatisfactory, and scholars after Scholem have tried to fill the gaps. Whereas the second gap (the "rabbinic stage" of Merkavah mysticism) was effectively eliminated by David Halperin in his thorough analyses of the rabbinic Merkavah texts[40] – although, to be sure, other scholars are still convinced of a close relationship between the Merkavah speculations of the rabbis and the Merkavah mysticism of the Hekhalot literature[41] – the first gap (the "apocalyptic stage" of Merkavah mysticism, as Scholem defines it, and the relationship between the apocalypses and Hekhalot literature) was perceived more constructively and filled in with ever more details. Ithamar Gruenwald wanted to establish, along the lines of Scholem's taxonomy, an unbroken continuity between the early apocalypses and the Hekhalot literature,[42] but Martha Himmelfarb cautioned against too naïve an approach with regard to these two after all very different bodies of literature.[43] Most recently, Andrei Orlov, focusing on the Enoch-Metatron traditions, reopened the question and tried to resuscitate Scholem's approach despite its acknowledged shortcomings, which, he holds, were responsible for the shift in modern research from the apocalypses to the Hekhalot literature.[44] He accuses Halperin, me, and others of throwing out the baby with the bathwater and, in our predilection for the rabbinic and Merkavah mystical manifestations of early Jewish mysticism, not only of ignoring the earlier phases but even of blocking access to them:

> Despite the significant advance that the investigations of Schäfer, Halperin, and other opponents of Scholem's position brought to a better understanding of the conceptual world of the rabbinic and Hekhalot mystical developments, their works, in my judg-

---

[39] Scholem, *Major Trends*, pp. 42 f. (despite his somewhat twisted reservations there).

[40] *The Merkabah in Rabbinic Literature* (New Haven, CT: American Oriental Society, 1980); see also his *The Faces of the Chariot: Early Jewish Responses to Ezekiel's Vision* (Tübingen: J. C. B. Mohr [Paul Siebeck], 1988).

[41] See, e. g., Elliot R. Wolfson, *Through a Speculum That Shines: Vision and Imagination in Medieval Jewish Mysticism* (Princeton, NJ: Princeton University Press, 1994), pp. 121 ff.; April D. DeConick, "What Is Early Jewish and Christian Mysticism?" in eadem, ed., *Paradise Now: Essays on Early Jewish and Christian Mysticism* (Atlanta, GA: Society of Biblical Literature, 2006), pp. 3 f.

[42] Ithamar Gruenwald, *Apocalyptic and Merkavah Mysticism* (Leiden: Brill, 1980).

[43] Martha Himmelfarb, "Heavenly Ascent and the Relationship of the Apocalypses and the *Hekhalot* Literature," *HUCA* 59 (1988), pp. 73–100.

[44] Andrei A. Orlov, *The Enoch-Metatron Tradition* (Tübingen: Mohr Siebeck, 2005), p. 3: Scholem's inability to demonstrate textually the persistent presence of the matrix of early Jewish mysticism in the pseudepigraphic literature would later lead his critics to concentrate their studies mainly either on the rabbinic *ma'aseh merkavah* accounts or on the Hekhalot writings and to regard these literary evidences as the first systematic presentations of early Jewish mysticism.

ment, affected negatively the study of the premishnaic Jewish mystical testimonies. Their writings shifted the whole notion of early Jewish mysticism towards the rabbinic and Hekhalot documents and separated it from the early mystical evidence of Second Temple Judaism. The criticisms of Scholem's hypothesis have led to the refocusing of priorities in the study of early Jewish mysticism. The main focus of research has been transferred from pseudepigraphic evidence to the rabbinic *ma'aseh merkavah* and the Hekhalot writings in an attempt to show their conceptual independence from the early apocalyptic materials. The view that the Hekhalot tradition possesses its own set(s) of concepts and imagery, different from the conceptualities of the early apocalyptic mystical testimonies, should not however lead one to ignore the association of these texts with early Jewish mysticism. It is apparent that, despite its importance, the body of Hekhalot literature cannot serve as the ultimate yardstick for measuring all early Jewish mystical traditions.[45]

Much as I agree with Orlov's last sentence, I am at a loss with regard to his main critique. True, research on the Hekhalot literature and Merkavah mysticism has made some progress over the last twenty-five years or so, but I, for one, did not embark on a study of the Hekhalot literature in order to prove Scholem wrong and to demonstrate that the concepts and imagery of the Hekhalot traditions were distinct from those of the apocalypses (when I started my work on the Hekhalot manuscripts I couldn't have cared less about the apocalyptic literature). No doubt, publication of the *Synopse zur Hekhalot-Literatur* has triggered an avalanche of publications on Merkavah mysticism,[46] but I do not think that this has much to do with Scholem's failure to make a good case for his first stage of the first phase of Jewish mysticism.

Moreover, and even more important, it soon became clear that the gap in Scholem's presentation of the three stages of Merkavah mysticism was even larger than Scholem could have known when he wrote his *Major Trends*: still undiscovered were the Dead Sea Scrolls, which contain a number of texts – in particular the Hodayot (Thanksgiving Scroll) and the text that is now labeled Songs of the Sabbath Sacrifice – that, as scholars immediately observed, bear a striking resemblance to the Hekhalot literature. Although he later became aware

---

[45] Ibid., pp. 5f. See also James R. Davila, "The Ancient Jewish Apocalypses and the *Hekhalot* Literature," in DeConick, *Paradise Now*, pp. 105–125. Davila concludes that in his view, "a genetic relationship of some sort [!] between the descenders to the chariot and the ancient Enochic traditions and practitioners seems likely" (p. 123). Although he acknowledges the very late social context for the "descenders to the chariot" (namely, "Babylonia in the fifth to the seventh centuries CE"), he nevertheless believes that "at least in the case of the Enochic literature, a historical link [between the earlier Enoch traditions and Enoch-Metatron in the Hekhalot literature] does seem plausible" (p. 124).
[46] A very useful summary of the present state of scholarship can be found in Ra'anan S. Boustan, "The Study of Heikhalot Literature: Between Mystical Experience and Textual Artifact," *CBR* 6 (2007), pp. 130–160.

of these connections,[47] Scholem never took up the subject systematically.[48] Conspicuously, it is this gap (the Dead Sea Scrolls) within the first gap (prerabbinic apocalyptic literature) that has occupied scholars far more as a potential precursor of Merkavah mysticism than have the apocalypses.

The most ambitious attempt not only to fill the gaps in Scholem's taxonomy of early Jewish mysticism but also to give a comprehensive picture of Scholem's first phase, including the Dead Sea Scrolls and related literature, has been made by Rachel Elior. In a series of articles and in her book, *The Three Temples: On the Emergence of Jewish Mysticism*,[49] Elior programmatically claims to have taken up the legacy left by Scholem in his few remarks, thanks in large part to the publication of most of the Qumran library and our greater knowledge of the context of the writings preserved in this library.[50] It is hardly my intention here to give a full summary of her arguments – a difficult task, to be sure, not only because of the richness of the material but also because she often repeats and sometimes even contradicts herself – but the following observations seem to me important:[51]

1. Elior does not just deal with the Qumran literature (both the sectarian and nonsectarian works preserved in the Qumran library) but sees much of the Qumranic and related literature (including, in particular, the Enochic literature) as the reservoir from which the full picture of pre-Hekhalot mysticism emerges.

2. Like Scholem, she reconstructs three stages of early Jewish mysticism, but these stages are different from Scholem's, namely (1) Ezekiel's vision of the Merkavah in Ezek. 1; (2) the literature of the "deposed priests" of the Sec-

---

[47] Gershom Scholem, *Jewish Gnosticism, Merkabah Mysticism, and Talmudic Tradition* (New York: Jewish Theological Seminary, 1960, 1965), pp. 3 f., 29, 128.

[48] Not surprisingly, as Himmelfarb reminds us ("Merkavah Mysticism since Scholem," p. 22): the *editio princeps* of all the fragments of the Songs of the Sabbath Sacrifice appeared in 1985, three years after Scholem's death.

[49] Rachel Elior, *The Three Temples: On the Emergence of Jewish Mysticism* (Oxford: Littman Library of Jewish Civilization, 2004 [originally published in Hebrew, 2002, Magnes, Jerusalem]). Of the many articles (which often give a preview of what is said in the book or summarize the book's results) I mention only "From Earthly Temple to Heavenly Shrines: Prayer and Sacred Song in the Hekhalot Literature and Its Relation to Temple Traditions," *JSQ* 4 (1997), pp. 217–267; "The *Merkavah* Tradition and the Emergence of Jewish Mysticism: From Temple to *Merkavah*, from *Hekhal* to *Hekhalot*, from Priestly Opposition to Gazing upon the *Merkavah*," in Aharon Oppenheimer, ed., *Sino-Judaica: Jews and Chinese in Historical Dialogue* (Tel Aviv: Tel Aviv University, 1999), pp. 101–158; and "The Foundations of Early Jewish Mysticism: The Lost Calendar and the Transformed Heavenly Chariot," in Schäfer, *Wege mystischer Gotteserfahrung*, pp. 1–18. And see already Crispin H. T. Fletcher-Louis, *All the Glory of Adam: Liturgical Anthropology in the Dead Sea Scrolls* (Leiden: Brill, 2002), pp. 252 ff., the publication of which coincided with publication of the Hebrew edition of Elior's book.

[50] In "Foundations," p. 2, she explicitly connects herself with Scholem's brief remark in *Jewish Gnosticism*, p. 128, that refers to the Songs of the Sabbath Sacrifice.

[51] I refrain from giving full references in each case. For a thorough analysis of her work and a devastating critique of most of her major theses, see Himmelfarb, "Merkavah Mysticism since Scholem."

ond Temple who were forced to leave the defiled sanctuary and took refuge in Qumran, that is, the Qumran library in the fullest sense of the word; and (3) the Hekhalot literature.[52]

3. All these three stages are characterized by three absent Temples (hence the title of her book) and all the three literatures preserved in these three stages are the product of priestly circles (yes, also the Hekhalot literature).[53]

4. The Qumran library is not (or at least only to a certain degree) the library of the Qumran sectarians but "originated in the Temple library that was created and guarded for centuries by priests and prophets and was taken by the deposited priests when they were forced to leave the defiled sanctuary."[54]

5. Elior is not particularly forthcoming with regard to how she defines "mysticism," although, as Himmelfarb has observed, "a definition is implicit in her work and could be extracted with proper care."[55] In her 2006 article she gives the following definition: "Mysticism in the present context refers to literary traditions which assume the everlasting existence of transcendental heavenly counterparts of the ritual world of the Temple and the Levitical priesthood."[56] What she does not say in her brief definition but is clearly included is the presupposition that this "mysticism" constitutes itself in a peculiar relationship between the heavenly ritual of the angels and the ritual world of the earthly priests (priestly angels and angelic priests performing an angelic liturgy in a heavenly sanctuary that has replaced the destroyed or defiled Temple on earth).

Elior's taxonomy of early Jewish mysticism and her definition of this "mysticism" are quite surprising, to say the least, and we will see whether or not they are based on a fair picture of the evidence (however, I have serious doubts as to whether Scholem would have agreed with them). But they are, of course, in line with her main thesis, that early Jewish mysticism developed out of the priestly traditions that were collected in the Temple library and preserved in Qumran. Yet this is precisely the question that looms large with her schema and definition,

---

[52] Ezekiel does not serve as a separate stage in Scholem's taxonomy (although his vision is clearly also for Scholem the starting point of everything that would come later in Jewish mysticism), whereas Scholem's second stage (the rabbis) has disappeared in Elior. Scholem's first stage and Elior's second stage correspond (with the omission of Qumran in Scholem), as do both their third stages.

[53] In "Foundations," pp. 17 f., she reduces the schema to just "two chapters of Jewish Mysticism in late antiquity," namely (1) "the traditions centered on Enoch and the priestly library that have commenced in angelic teaching of divine knowledge and concentrated on the priestly solar calendar, the angels, the chariot and the sevenfold angelic liturgy which were written before the Common Era," and (2) "the Heikhalot and Merkabah literature, written after the destruction of the Temple and incorporating similar topics." This second chapter, as she explicitly states, "reflects the dialectical continuity with its priestly sources" (ibid.).

[54] Elior, "Foundations," p. 17.

[55] Himmelfarb, "Merkavah Mysticism since Scholem," p. 23.

[56] Elior, "Foundations," p. 3.

for both are bought at the great cost of unabashedly or naively (or both) harmonizing the sources in order to extract from them a common priestly ideology.[57] Obviously, according to Elior, there is no early Jewish mysticism outside the realm of priestly ideology,[58] or, to put it differently, all disenfranchised priestly ideology is "mystical."

Elior's sweeping pan-priestly approach has been met with much interest and approval, at least in certain scholarly circles. April DeConick in her essay "What Is Early Jewish and Christian Mysticism?" attests that Elior "has set forth the most comprehensive thesis that I am aware of" and approves of her premise that the priestly worldview or cosmology indeed informs the mystical discussions within early Judaism and Christianity.[59] Most recently, Philip Alexander, having subjected the Songs of the Sabbath Sacrifice to a fresh examination, categorically declares:[60]

> There *was* mysticism at Qumran. This mysticism arose not at Qumran itself but in priestly circles in Jerusalem, from where it was taken to Qumran and adapted to the community's particular needs. This mysticism was the historical forerunner of later Jewish Heikhalot mysticism, and should now be integrated into the history of Jewish[61] mysticism.[62]

Furthermore, and quite in contrast to Elior, Alexander is convinced that this "new" attempt to "trace Jewish mysticism firmly back to Second Temple times" contradicts the paradigm established by Scholem, who, in Alexander's words, "was reluctant to date the origins of Jewish mysticism much earlier than the third century CE."[63] I am not sure that this statement accurately reflects Scholem's point of view,[64] since, as we have observed, Scholem is much more sophisticated with regard to the prerabbinic stage of the first phase of Jewish mysticism.[65] We

---

[57] This is also one of Himmelfarb's main points; see her "Merkavah Mysticism since Scholem," pp. 24, 36.

[58] This claim becomes particularly difficult with regard to the Hekhalot literature because it presupposes that the bulk of this literature is of priestly origin – a very bold claim indeed. See the critique of Himmelfarb, "Merkavah Mysticism since Scholem," pp. 34 ff.

[59] April D. DeConick, "What Is Early Jewish and Christian Mysticism?" in eadem, *Paradise Now*, pp. 10 f.

[60] Interestingly enough, without explicitly mentioning Elior but instead emphasizing the connections with the earlier works of Johann Maier and Ithamar Gruenwald.

[61] And, as he later concludes, also of Christian mysticism: "These comments ... are surely sufficient to make at least a prima facie case that Qumran mysticism belongs somewhere in the genealogy of Christian as well as of Jewish mysticism" (*Mystical Texts*, p. 143).

[62] Alexander, *Mystical Texts*, p. VII (Alexander's emphasis); see also p. 137.

[63] Ibid., p. 136.

[64] Although, to be fair, Alexander is acutely aware of the fact that Scholem effectively ignored the earlier antecedents and increasingly concentrated on mysticism in a rabbinic milieu, as I have argued above as well.

[65] One needs much patience to fully understand and appreciate what Scholem says, not least because he is a master of the art of "give and take," that is, of developing his argument in a dialectical process rather than in linear progression.

will see whether or not our analysis of the Qumran sources – in particular the Songs of the Sabbath Sacrifice and the Self-Glorification Hymn – supports the thesis of Qumran as the primary source feeding early Jewish mysticism.

2. Unio mystica

Since the *unio mystica*, the mystical union of the adept with the divine, is regarded as the backbone of most definitions of mysticism (that is, in religions envisioning a personal God), and since Scholem was reluctant to give special weight to this distinctive feature, scholars have quarreled over its application to Jewish mysticism. Moshe Idel, one of the most fervent critics of Scholem, even goes so far as to accuse Scholem of implicitly, if not deliberately, suppressing in his vast research that particular strand of Jewish mysticism of which the mystical union is characteristic. Idel distinguishes between two major strands in Jewish mysticism, the theosophical-theurgical and the ecstatic. The former he defines as mythic or mythocentric, symbolic, theocentric, sefirotic (that is, designing the system of the ten Sefirot, the ten dynamic potencies within God), nomian (that is, centered on the Halakhah), canonical, exoterically open to all Jews, less mystical, and not interested in the union with God, whereas to the latter he deigns to grant the attributes anthropocentric, esoteric, sublime, anomian, individualistic, intended to induce paranormal experiences, mystical par excellence, and indeed aiming at the union with God.[66] Unfortunately for Idel, Scholem's verdict that "a total union with the Divine is absent in Jewish texts"[67] has been accepted by most modern scholars of both Jewish as well as general mysticism. Even worse, Idel holds, Scholem's emphasis on the theosophical type of Jewish mysticism and his neglect of the ecstatic type has led some scholars to conclude that Jewish mysticism, since it is devoid of the essence of mysticism, should not be called mysticism at all.[68] Ultimately, this negation in Jewish mysticism of the *unio*

---

[66] Moshe Idel, *Kabbalah: New Perspectives* (New Haven, CT: Yale University Press, 1988), pp. XI ff.; idem, "The Contribution of Abraham Abulafia's Kabbalah to the Understanding of Jewish Mysticism," in Peter Schäfer and Joseph Dan, eds., *Gershom Scholem's Major Trends in Jewish Mysticism: 50 Years After* (Tübingen: J.C.B. Mohr [Paul Siebeck], 1993), pp. 117–143.

[67] Idel, *Kabbalah: New Perspectives*, p. 59. Idel does not refer to Scholem's full discussion of the subject in the introductory chapter to *Major Trends* and in the chapter "Merkabah Mysticism and Jewish Gnosticism," but quotes only the following sentence from his chapter on Abulafia: "It is only in extremely rare cases that ecstasy signifies actual union with God, in which the human individuality abandons itself to the rapture of complete submersion in the divine stream. Even in this ecstatic frame of mind, the Jewish mystic almost invariably retains a sense of the distance between the Creator and His creature" (*Major Trends*, pp. 122 f.).

[68] Idel, *Kabbalah: New Perspectives*, pp. 59 f.; idem, "The Contribution of Abraham Abulafia's Kabbalah," pp. 133 ff. On Idel's problematic taxonomy, see also Peter Schäfer, "Ekstase, Vision und *unio mystica* in der frühen jüdischen Mystik," in Aleida and Jan Assmann, eds., *Schleier und Schwelle: Archäologie der literarischen Kommunikation V*, vol. 2: *Geheimnis und Offenbarung* (Munich: Fink, 1998), pp. 101 ff.

mystica as the core of mysticism, Idel concludes, assumes with Christian scholars like Carl Jung and Robert C. Zaehner (a well-known historian of religion of Scholem's generation) an overtly anti-Jewish bias. As a prime example of this bias Idel quotes Zaehner:

> If mysticism is the key to religion, then we may as well exclude the Jews entirely from our inquiry: for Jewish mysticism, as Professor Scholem has so admirably portrayed it, ... would not appear to be mysticism at all. Visionary experience is not mystical experience: for mysticism means, if it means anything, the realization of a union or a unity with or in something that is enormously, if not infinitely, greater than the empirical self. With the Yahweh of the Old Testament, no such union is possible. Pre-Christian Judaism is not only un-mystical, it is anti-mystical. ... [I]t is therefore in the very nature of the case that Jewish "mysticism" should at most aspire to communion with God, never to union.[69]

The Christian bias of the sentence about the "Yahweh of the Old Testament" is unmistakable, and Scholem would certainly not want to exclude Jewish mysticism from mysticism, but does this necessarily mean that Zaehner's distinction between "communion" and "union" is wrong (notwithstanding the question of whether or not one is inclined to call such a communion "mysticism")? After all, Philip Alexander, definitely not prone to anti-mystical attitudes, has recently made the very same distinction between "communion" (which he assigns to "theistic systems, which in turn are conscious of an unbridgeable ontological gap between the Creator and the created") and "union" (which he reserves for pantheistic systems).[70] In Idel's attempt to prove that the ecstatic type is the dominant strand in Jewish mysticism and that the striving for mystical union is therefore its predominant characteristic, one cannot avoid the impression that he is driven more than necessary by a zeal to turn almost everything Scholem wrote on its head. In any case, when we look for his proofs of the notion of a mystical union in the early phase of Jewish mysticism (Merkavah mysticism), we find remarkably little. Although he includes Merkavah mysticism in the ecstatic strand (because for him it is by nature "ecstatic"), his chapter, "*Unio Mystica* in Jewish Mysticism," in *Kabbalah: New Perspectives*[71] jumps immediately into the ecstatic Kabbalah proper[72] and does not deal with Merkavah mysticism at all,

---

[69] Robert C. Zaehner, *At Sundry Times: An Essay in the Comparison of Religions* (London: Faber and Faber, 1958), p. 171.

[70] Alexander, *Mystical Texts*, p. 8; see also above, n. 27.

[71] Idel, *Kabbalah: New Perspectives*, pp. 59–73. Fletcher-Louis, *All the Glory of Adam*, p. 3, declares simply – and simplistically – that Scholem's judgment regarding the place of *unio mystica* in Merkavah mysticism "has now been rightly rejected by those who have taken up his challenge that scholarship take Jewish mysticism seriously" and refers, as one of his major proofs, to precisely these pages in Idel's *Kabbalah: New Perspectives*. See now also William Horbury, *Herodian Judaism and New Testament Study* (Tübingen: Mohr Siebeck, 2006), p. 49, with n. 4.

[72] He is, however, convinced that certain conceptual structures of the (later) Kabbalah can be (re)discovered in pre-kabbalistic texts, in particular in the talmudic, gnostic, and Merkavah

except for a couple of sentences about the transformation of Enoch into Metatron, which falls for him under the category of a unitive experience.[73] Influenced mainly by Abulafia's peculiar kind of mysticism, Idel takes the idea of a Jewish *unio mystica* to the extreme.

Among contemporary scholars, Elliot Wolfson has made the most progress regarding a typology of the mystical experience that does not just include (alleged) ancient manifestations of Jewish mysticism but instead takes these ancient manifestations (apocalypses, Qumran sources, Hekhalot literature) as starting point of the inquiry.[74] Responding to a paper by Qumran scholar Bilhah Nitzan,[75] Wolfson finally gets to the root of the problem by stating that the modern scholarly tendency to focus on mystical union as the very essence of mysticism is informed by Neoplatonic ontology, namely, the assumption that "contemplation of God results in a form of union whereby the soul separates from the body and returns to its ontological source in the One. Insofar as the One is beyond intellect and being, the return to the One is depicted in figurative terms as a mystical merging of the soul in the Godhead."[76] This Neoplatonic model, he posits, is alien to the Jewish sources:

> The Jewish sources, beginning with the apocalyptic and Qumran texts, may provide a different model based not on *henosis*, but rather on the "angelification" of the human being who crosses the boundary of space and time and becomes part of the heavenly realm. ... The mystical experience in this framework involves as well a closing of the gap separating human and divine, not, however, by the return of the soul to the One, but rather by the ascension of the human into the heavens. ... In my opinion, the word "mysticism" should be used only when there is evidence for specific practices that lead to an experience of ontic transformation, i.e., becoming divine or angelic. Accordingly, it is inappropriate to apply the word "mystical" to the unison or harmony of human and angel if there is no technique or praxis that facilitates the idealization of a human being into a divine or angelic being in the celestial abode.[77]

Here we finally rid ourselves of the model of *unio mystica* as the ultimate litmus test for the quality of a mystical experience. Instead, now is introduced the notion of heavenly ascent as leading to an ontic transformation of the adept and resulting in his angelification or deification. According to this definition, Wolfson finds "mysticism" in the ascent apocalypses (which he does not discuss), the so-called Self Glorification Hymn from Qumran (but not in the Songs of the Sabbath Sacrifice) and, most prominently, in the Hekhalot literature. The advan-

---

mystical literature. He calls this approach "reconstructionalist"; see his *Kabbalah: New Perspectives*, pp. 32 ff.

[73] Ibid., p. 60.

[74] Wolfson, "Mysticism," pp. 185–202.

[75] Bilhah Nitzan, "Harmonic and Mystical Characteristics in Poetic and Liturgical Writings from Qumran," *JQR* 85 (1994), pp. 163–183.

[76] Wolfson, "Mysticism," p. 186.

[77] Ibid., pp. 186 f.

tage of this definition consists in the fact that it does not impose a terminology on the ancient texts that is alien to them (such as "mystical union") but takes the experience described in these texts as its starting point: the ascent of a human individual to heaven that is indeed seminal to the apocalypses and the Hekhalot literature (while being less so for the Qumran sources). Also, there can be no doubt that in some of these texts the individual undergoes a bodily alteration that transforms him into an angelic being. This is particularly true for the ascent apocalypses and probably also for the Qumranic Self Glorification Hymn, but the Hekhalot literature poses a problem. The prime example for the transformation of a human being into an angel, of course, is Enoch's metamorphosis into the highest angel Metatron. But Wolfson wishes to go much further. For him, the major Hekhalot texts involve not only an ascent of the adept to the heavenly realm and his participation in the heavenly liturgy; rather, "a critical part of the ascent experience is the enthronement of the *yored Merkavah*, either on the chariot itself or on a throne alongside the throne of glory"; and it is this enthronement of the adept "that transforms him into an angelic being, a transformation that facilitates his vision of the glory and the hypostatic powers of God that are active before the throne."[78] Through this ingenious move Wolfson manages to declare angelification an essential part of the Hekhalot literature as well. I discuss the textual basis for this interpretation in my concluding chapter.

Finally, in using the term "deification" alongside the term "angelification," Wolfson avails himself of another artifice. He never explains the two words but simply pretends they are both the same (employing them as a binomial and mostly connecting them with the innocent conjunction "or"). But are they really the same? True, human beings are sometimes transformed into angels, but does this also mean that they are "deified," that they become God? I suspect that Wolfson reaches his equation of angelification with deification by identifying the angels acting before God's throne with "hypostatic powers of God," thus placing God and his angels to a certain extent on an equal plane; hence, if the angels are in fact "hypostatic powers," then it makes little difference if the mystic is angelicized or deified. But are the angels really hypostatic divine powers – or could it be that Wolfson succumbs here to Neoplatonic categories alien to the apocalyptic, Qumranic, and Hekhalot literatures? This question and its implications are likewise discussed in my concluding chapter.

Origins

For Scholem, as we have seen, the rise of mysticism out of or rather within the husks of the institutionalized classical form of religion coincides with the ro-

---

[78] Ibid., p. 193.

mantic period of religion.[79] Hence, romanticism is the catalyst of mysticism: once romanticism breaks through the solidified forms of religious institutions, the mystical phase of religion is born. This phase, moreover, is characterized by a revival of mythical thought and therefore, to some extent, constitutes a return to the "old unity which [institutionalized] religion has destroyed, but on a new plane, where the world of mythology and that of revelation meet in the soul of man."[80] So, more precisely, mysticism brings religion back to its old mythical roots – roots that were covered by the agglomerating sediments of religion's institutionalization.

In his quest for the origins of mysticism, emerging at a certain point in space and time in the history of a given religion, Scholem reveals himself to be a true heir of evolutionary models within the history of religion, seasoned with a heavy dose of German romanticism. As to the former, he clearly presupposes a linear development, beginning with the innocent "childhood of mankind" in primordial mythical times[81] and ultimately culminating in mysticism as the highest form of religion (its conflicting tendencies notwithstanding).[82] As to the latter, his romantic tendencies, these are much more obvious in *Origins of the Kabbalah* than in *Major Trends*. It is in *Origins of the Kabbalah* that he tries to uncover the remote and mythical "origins" of the Kabbalah in the "oriental" Gnosis of the first centuries CE,[83] whereas in *Major Trends* he remains rather vague about the origins of Jewish mysticism, apart from the proposition that Jewish mysticism originated in the romantic period of Judaism. But as we have already seen, this description reveals a certain tension, to say the least, since it seems to presuppose two different origins: one of "Jewish mysticism" in general and another one of "Kabbalah" in particular (although, to be sure, Kabbalah remains part of Jewish mysticism).

So the quest for origins appears to be highly charged territory. If we disregard the tension between "mysticism" and "Kabbalah," mysticism, according to Scholem, can nevertheless be seen to emerge (despite its mythical roots in prehistoric times) from very real historical circumstances: it is the driving force that transforms institutionalized religion into something new, a higher and revitalized form of the religion under discussion. This dialectic between mysticism's mythic origins and its historical manifestation is obviously what Scholem tried to capture in the tricky German title of his book on the origins of the Kabbalah, *Ursprung und Anfänge der Kabbalah*; that is, literally, origins and beginnings

---

[79] Scholem, *Major Trends*, p. 8.
[80] Ibid.
[81] Ibid., p. 7.
[82] Ultimately seeing mysticism as a universal condition of humanity in Underhillian terms.
[83] See in more detail my *Mirror of His Beauty: Feminine Images of God from the Bible to the Early Kabbalah* (Princeton, NJ: Princeton University Press, 2002), pp. 218 ff.

(or early stages)[84] of the Kabbalah, with "beginnings" so conspicuously dropped from the title of the English translation.

But what does this mean for the Jewish religion? What is the institutionalized form of the Jewish religion out of which mysticism emerged? Scholem remains in this regard rather vague. In terms of the lowly spheres of chronology, as we have already seen, he wavers between the first century BCE and the talmudic period for the emergence of the first stage of Jewish mysticism; and with regard to the substance of the institutionalized religion he clearly has in mind rabbinic Judaism, which for him serves as the epitome of a halakhically oriented form of Judaism: only when the Halakhah becomes too rigid (this is the underlying premise) is it time for mysticism to break through and inaugurate a new era.

As has been observed by several scholars, this definition of rabbinic Judaism is in itself problematic.[85] To portray rabbinic Judaism as entrapped within the rigidity of the Halakhah and therefore in need of the liberating forces of mysticism smacks ominously of certain Christian prejudices. Also, if mysticism is a reaction to rabbinic Halakhah, one would expect the emergence of mysticism to occur at the peak of halakhic development (let's say with the appearance of the Bavli) and not at its beginnings (with the appearance of the Mishnah). But Scholem needs to have the early stage of rabbinic Judaism in the first two centuries as the hotbed of mysticism because R. Ishmael and R. Aqiva, the most important rabbis of tannaitic Judaism, also happen to be the heroes of Merkavah mysticism – although the first half of the second century CE can hardly be characterized as the epitome of rabbinic Judaism's halakhic obsession. Moreover, if the institutionalized religion of rabbinic Judaism triggers mysticism, how then can the "anonymous conventicles of the old apocalyptics,"[86] as Scholem puts it, be included as the first stage in his taxonomy of the first phase of Jewish mysticism? The ascent apocalypses were certainly not motivated by any particular halakhic considerations, and although Halakhah plays an important role in Qumran, no one would wish to classify the Qumran sect as a specific form of institutionalized Jewish religion (Scholem, for his part, makes no attempt to consider the Qumranic Halakhah).

Scholem's description of the origins of the earliest manifestation of Jewish mysticism is a tangle of contradictions. With his attempt to incorporate the pre-rabbinic apocalypses into nascent mysticism, he sensed something important. Yet he was reluctant to follow this intuition, not just, as he specifies (if not uses as an excuse), because "to do so would involve a lengthy excursion into historical and philological detail"[87] but first and foremost, I venture to say, because he was transfixed by his own definition of the origins of mysticism.

---

[84] "Early stages" is what the English translation uses for *Anfänge* in the first sentence of the first chapter of the book (Scholem, *Origins*, p. 3; see the full quotation above, n. 34).

[85] See the apt summary in Alexander, *Mystical Texts*, p. 137.

[86] Scholem, *Major Trends*, p. 45.

[87] Ibid., p. 40.

The Origins of Jewish Mysticism

Bearing in mind Scholem's grandiose but ultimately failed scheme, not to mention the attempts of his successors, it would seem futile to try to design a theoretical model of the origins of Jewish mysticism within the developing Jewish religion. The term "origins" as the mythical source from which something arises or springs out of the primordial past,[88] and which, to be sure, in due time substantiates itself under certain historical circumstances that, for their part, mark a crucial turning point in the history of the respective religion – this term "origins" has proven to be highly problematic. It will therefore come as no surprise that I will not be using the term in this sense. On the other hand, one cannot ignore the necessity of determining the historical conditions under which a certain phenomenon arises. After all, we start with the assumption that "mysticism" is not an ideal construct suddenly descended from heaven but a historical phenomenon that has established itself in space and time. So I will use the term "origins" in a much more modest sense, namely, as the beginnings of something that has subsequently been labeled "Jewish mysticism." And with "beginnings" I do not mean an absolute and fixed beginning at a certain place and time but a *process* that extended over a protracted period and was not bound to one particular place. Moreover, I do not envision this process to be linear and progressive; on the contrary, I expect it to materialize differently at different times and places, not in a linear development from A to B to C but as a polymorphic web or network of ideas that are not free-floating but manifest themselves in certain practices of individuals as members of certain communities. Whether these ideas can be tied together under a common denominator – for example, "mysticism" – or whether they ultimately fall apart into *disiecta membra*, scattered limbs, fragments of something that in fact never achieved unity, remains to be seen. But this common denominator, if one does indeed exist, can only be determined at the end of our investigation and not as some theoretical construct at its beginning. Hence, I will employ a heuristic model of inquiry, merely allowing the historical process to unfold instead of trying to prove something that has been established from the beginning, in the double sense of the beginning of my research and the beginning of the manifestation of the phenomenon.

The same is true for "Jewish mysticism," the other part of our investigation's taxonomy. I deliberately refrain from any preconceived definition of mysticism and use the word (in fictive quotation marks) only because it is the label that

---

[88] This is the definition of the word "origin" as given by *The Oxford English Dictionary*, vol. 7 (repr. Oxford 1961), p. 202. More precisely, "origin" denotes both the source from which something springs as well as the act of arising or springing; see *The Oxford English Dictionary*, 2nd ed., vol. 10, p. 933. The same is true for the German *Ursprung*, which literally means "that which rises or springs from something primordial"; see Jacob and Wilhelm Grimm, *Deutsches Wörterbuch*, vol. 11.3, ed. Karl Euling (Leipzig: Hirzel, 1936), cols. 2538–2545.

scholarly tradition has long attached to the texts I will be treating. But of course I keep in mind those definitions that have been suggested by scholars of mysticism in general and Jewish mysticism in particular, some of which have been discussed above. I make no secret of my reservations regarding the view that the *unio mystica* is the epitome of mysticism, including its Jewish incarnation, and I also make no secret of my preference for definitions that take as their starting point the literary evidence as it has been preserved to the present day. Indeed, I start with the assumption that it is our task to allow each set of texts and each community represented by certain texts to speak for themselves, to tell us what it is they find important and wish to emphasize. To be sure, the various texts and communities have not volunteered as subjects for this enterprise; rather, it is I alone who has decided which texts representing certain authors or communities to include in my inquiry. Yet this dilemma can hardly be avoided unless one wishes to cast such a wide net that the exercise becomes useless. That being said, with regard to the material basis of this study, I have not attempted to reinvent the wheel but rely entirely on the corpus of texts that has emerged in a long tradition of previous scholarship.

Hence, I ultimately and deliberately juggle two unknowns, "origins" and "mysticism." In analyzing certain core texts I attempt to capture and describe the "toponymy" and nomenclature of these texts on their own terms, but of course always with an eye to what they may or may not contribute to the question of "mysticism." I am aware of the vicious circle that such a pointedly pragmatic approach entails, but I believe there exists no other or better solution that at the same time avoids the risk of imposing a preconceived definition on the texts. As has already become clear with the term "origins," I am even prepared, as far as "mysticism" is concerned, to accept a result that declares it to be a category of no real use or meaning within the history of the Jewish religion and that ultimately pronounces it dead.[89]

My methodology arises from these clarifications. Taking the texts as my starting point, I am interested in methods that are most suitable not just for solving textual problems but also for bringing out what the texts themselves seek to convey. Accordingly, methods that do justice to the linguistic and historical parameters of a given text still seem to me most appropriate, and I am not afraid of resorting to the allegedly old-fashioned and outdated historical-critical method – a method that, in the post-Scholem era, serves as a scapegoat for almost everything that (supposedly) went wrong with Scholem's approach. This method, however, does not confine itself to philological exercises; on the contrary, it takes the historical circumstances surrounding the texts very seriously. It is concerned with locating the various phenomena under discussion in their historical contexts

---

[89] See Boaz Huss, "The Mystification of the Kabbalah and the Myth of Jewish Mysticism," *Pe'amim* 110 (2007), pp. 9–30 (in Hebrew). I return to this question in my concluding chapter.

and not just seeing them as free-floating entities beyond space and time. If this method is able to connect given phenomena diachronically, this does not necessarily presuppose a linear development of essentially the same "thing" – indeed, quite the opposite: it reckons with substantial changes over time that ultimately challenge the "identity" of the phenomenon. But in no way does it aim at a synchronic description of a phenomenon detached from space and time.

If one wishes to discover in my methodological preferences elements of what has been classified as the "phenomenological" approach, propagated by Moshe Idel and his followers, then so be it – to a certain extent. Idel defines this approach as follows:

> Thus, my approach uses phenomenology in order to isolate significant phenomena and only thereafter to elaborate upon the possible historical relationships between them. In other words my starting point is the unfolding of the phenomenological affinity between two mystical patterns of experience, preceding their historical analysis per se. Hence, the phenomenological approach also serves historical aims, although not exclusively.[90]

This statement is not as innocent as it sounds. To be sure, I am also interested in "significant phenomena" that may be related to "mystical patterns of experience," but, unlike Idel, who apparently knows from the outset what these phenomena are, I leave open the question as to what may or may not be judged mystical. Moreover, and most important, I do not believe that such "mystical patterns" can be discovered and delineated – let alone compared with each other – outside their respective historical contexts. Thus, I do not think that one can neatly distinguish between the isolation of "pure" mystical phenomena as such and their subordinated historical condition. Both belong together, and furthermore, both come before the next step, namely the evaluation of the possible historical relationship between related phenomena.

In fact, despite his rather moderate and modest definition, Idel's phenomenological approach runs the risk of dehistoricizing the phenomena it is looking at and establishing an ahistorical, ideal, and essentialist construct.[91] This becomes

---

[90] Idel, *Kabbalah: New Perspectives*, pp. XVIII f.

[91] The most recent example of this approach is Idel's *Ben: Sonship and Jewish Mysticism* (London: Continuum, 2007). It offers many new and creative insights, but methodologically it presents a breathtakingly ahistorical hodgepodge of this and that, quotations from many different periods and literatures, pressed into scholarly sounding categories such as "apotheotic" and "theophanic" but in fact lumped together by sentences like "Let me discuss now ...," "Let me/ us turn to ..." (the preferred phrase), "Interestingly enough," "I would like to now address," "In this context it should be mentioned," and so forth. Constantly arguing against the usual suspects who, in his view, impose a wrong and simplistic logic on the texts, in this book Idel has developed his method of leaps in logic and intuition to the extreme. For a critique of Idel's approach, see Lawrence Kaplan, "Adam, Enoch, and Metatron Revisited: A Critical Analysis of Moshe Idel's Method of Reconstruction," *Kabbalah* 6 (2001), pp. 73–119, and see furthermore Y. Tzvi Langermann's critique of Yehudah Liebes, below, n. 94.

even clearer if one takes into consideration the fact that, according to Idel, the historical-philological method favored by Scholem and his school of secular academics results in an unbalanced preponderance of the theosophical-theurgical strand of Jewish mysticism (as found, for example, in the Zohar and in the Lurianic writings), whereas Idel's phenomenological method is open to the on-going *living* experience of mysticism, including certain orthodox Jewish circles today.[92] Hence, what is ultimately at stake in Idel's version of the phenomenological method is mysticism as a timeless religious phenomenon that deserves not a "secular" historical analysis but a clarification of its practice. Idel's students went even further along this route and advocated a phenomenology that focuses on the universalistic aspects of the mystical experience (devoid of its historical constraints), on the mystical practice, and on its ramifications for our religious life today. In essence, this new approach uses academic scholarship and its results as building blocks for a new, postmodern mystical Jewish religion.[93]

It goes without saying that the extreme version of this approach must be reserved for practitioners of the Jewish religion – for how could a non-Jew contribute to this ultimate goal? – and thereby, in my view, deliberately abandons the realm of secular academic research in favor of a new theology, if not some New Age spirituality. If I, for one, feel excluded from such an enterprise – and indeed, prefer to be excluded – I nevertheless do not wish to judge the legitimacy of the enterprise. It may well have its place in the framework of some institutionalized versions of "Jewish thought" or "Jewish theology," but it should be aware of its exclusivity, and it cannot and must not pretend to be the most consequential and comprehensive approach to the Jewish form of mysticism in the post-Scholem era.[94]

---

[92] Idel, "The Contribution of Abraham Abulafia's Kabbalah," p. 131.

[93] See the illuminating review essay by Boaz Huss, "The New Age of Kabbalah Research: Book Review of Ron Margolin, *The Human Temple*; Melila Hellner-Eshed, *A River Issues Forth from Eden*; Jonathan Garb, *Manifestations of Power in Jewish Mysticism*," *Te'oriyah u-Viqqoret* 27 (2005), pp. 246–53 (in Hebrew). The use or rather misuse of the "phenomenological approach" in Vita Daphna Arbel, *Beholders of Divine Secrets: Mysticism and Myth in the Hekhalot and Merkavah Literature* (Albany: State University of New York Press, 2003), has been aptly criticized in Ra'anan S. Boustan's review in *JAOS* 125 (2005), pp. 123–126. Boustan rightly points out that Arbel completely ignores the long tradition of the phenomenology of religion school and instead favors a "spiritualizing psychological interpretation" of Merkavah mysticism that is "grounded in a fundamentally private, interior, and contemplative-meditative experience" (p. 124).

[94] For a devastating critique of the school of "Jewish thought" in Jerusalem – its neglect of history as a discipline and its exclusive reliance on "parallels" (*maqbilot*) – see Y. Tzvi Langermann, "On the Beginnings of Hebrew Scientific Literature and on Studying History Through 'Maqbilot' (Parallels)," *Aleph* 2 (2002), pp. 169–189. Reviewing Yehudah Liebes's *Torat ha-Yetzirah shel Sefer Yetzirah* (Jerusalem: Schocken, 2000), Langermann concludes that Liebes "merely juxtaposes the sources; rather than constructing arguments, he relies on innuendo. Although he sometimes explains why he believes that a certain parallel is or is not significant, Liebes applies no consistent method of analysis to the parallels adduced" (ibid., pp. 177 f.).

The scope of my inquiry in the chapters to follow is delimited on the one hand by the book of Ezekiel in the Hebrew Bible as the starting point, and on the other by the Hekhalot literature as the first unchallenged manifestation of Jewish mysticism. Therefore, I am not interested in illuminating the relationship between Jewish mysticism and Kabbalah, a problem that has been so inadequately addressed and even conspicuously glossed over by Scholem and his heirs. Kabbalah as a distinctly medieval phenomenon that presumably begins in the twelfth century CE in Provence and extends well into our present day remains outside the parameters of my survey. Rather, I focus exclusively on that early phase of Jewish mysticism that Scholem has divided into three stages, the earliest of which (Qumran and related literature) others have identified as the birthplace of Jewish mysticism.

I begin with the famous first chapter of the book of Ezekiel – Ezekiel's vision of the open heavens with the four creatures carrying God's throne and the "figure with the appearance of a human being" seated upon this throne (chapter 1). Ezekiel's vision sets the tone for the subsequent traditions: a fourfold relationship between and among a somehow accessible heaven, a human seer or visionary who has a vision, God as the object of this vision, and a revelation as the purpose of the vision. As to God, the object of the vision, the description goes remarkably far in Ezekiel's case. He sees a human-like figure that still bears little resemblance to an ordinary man. The figure's overwhelming impression is that of radiating fire: God's body is of human shape but its essence is fire. Yet the appearance of God, however veiled or revealed, is not an end in itself. I demonstrate that it conveys a message to Ezekiel and his community (the vision is complemented by, or rather climaxes in, an audition), namely, the message that God is still there, in heaven, although the Temple will soon be destroyed. God does not need the Temple – the whole cosmos is his Temple, as it once was in the time of the patriarchs.

The second chapter turns to those ascent apocalypses that revolve around the enigmatic antediluvian patriarch Enoch, who, according to the tradition, did not die a natural death but was taken up by God into heaven. The first and oldest Enoch narrative, derived from the biblical *Vorlage*, is that of the Book of the Watchers (1 Enoch 1–36: late third century BCE?), in which Enoch experiences a vision of God in heaven (ch. 14). Unlike his precursor Ezekiel, Enoch *ascends* to heaven, more precisely to the heavenly Temple, to see God on his throne; from now on the ascent becomes the predominant mode of human approach to the God who is enthroned in heaven. But Enoch only attains to the open door of the heavenly Holy of Holies from where he sneaks a peek – not at God but at

---

"Nevertheless it seems to me that Liebes' exclusive attention to *maqbilot* – along with his obliviousness to the limits of this method – stems from the relative neglect of the particular demands of historical writing" (ibid., p. 188). I thank Ra'anan Boustan for having drawn my attention to Langermann's article.

his raiment behind a veil of fire. And as with Ezekiel, the purpose of the exercise is not the vision as an individual experience but is an audition, in Enoch's case, God's revelation that the Watchers will be condemned forever. This critique of the Watchers, who have defiled themselves and brought evil upon the earth, includes, I will argue, an implicit critique of the (rebuilt) earthly Temple: since the Temple in Jerusalem has also been defiled, the heavenly Temple has become the complete and perfect counterpart to the earthly Temple. Ultimately, God no longer resides in the Jerusalem Temple but has withdrawn to his heavenly abode.

This Temple-critical motif continues with the Testament of Levi, the next apocalypse to be discussed in this chapter. It has nothing to do with Enoch, but in its oldest form (the Aramaic Levi document) it has been dated to the middle of the second century BCE and attributed to the same circles whence the Book of the Watchers originated. Again, the vision of God is not the primary goal of this narrative (in a very reduced form of a vision, Levi sees "the holy Temple and the Most High upon a throne of Glory") but rather the message conveyed by God: Levi is invested with the insignia of the priesthood, yet unfortunately, his successors will not live up to the task. They will corrupt the priesthood until God appoints a new eschatological priest whose priesthood will endure forever.

The Similitudes or Parables of Enoch (1 Enoch 37–71: late first century BCE/ turn of the era) and the Second Book of Enoch (first century CE) retell Enoch's ascent to heaven in the Book of the Watchers, but they add a new element that is alien to the earlier apocalypses: Enoch's transformation into an angel. Only hinted at in the Similitudes, this transformation plays a prominent role in 2 Enoch, where Enoch is stripped of his earthly clothes, anointed with holy oil, and dressed in heavenly raiment, clearly indicating his transformation from a human being into an angel. The angels, who make their first appearance as the companions and interpreters of the visionary during his heavenly journey in the Testament of Levi, become now the role model for the human hero, who aspires to be one of them, for it is only in angelic form that he can approach as close to God as he desires.

The third chapter also deals with ascent apocalypses, but now Enoch is replaced by a variety of heroes. The chapter begins with the Apocalypse of Abraham (after 70 CE), which still follows the older Temple-critical motif and lacks the explicit physical transformation of the seer. Instead, it grants the angel Iaoel, who accompanies Abraham on his journey, a God-like state, a kind of compensation for the fact that Abraham is not allowed to see God. However, the climax of Abraham's vision is his participation in the angelic liturgy, which may well imply his transformation into an angel. But again, this angelification of the seer is no mere end in itself: God reveals to Abraham the future history of Israel, with the desecration of the Temple and the necessity of its destruction at that history's center.

With the next apocalypse, the Ascension of Isaiah (early second century CE), we observe a decisive shift from the destiny of the community to that of the righteous individual. Isaiah, in ascending to heaven during his lifetime (like his predecessors) and in entering into a liturgical union (*unio liturgica*) with the angels, is himself transformed into an angel, the highest stage that a human being can achieve. But there remains a major difference between him as a member of the angelic company and the deceased righteous, who populate heaven together with the angels. In fact, the deceased righteous are superior to the angels (and hence to Isaiah in his present state) since only they can actually look at God, whereas the angels see him only vaguely. The ultimate transformation (into a deceased righteous) and vision (of God) is left to the last stage of Isaiah's human journey, when he returns to heaven as a deceased righteous. This last step is taken in the Apocalypse of Zephaniah (end of first century or beginning of the second century CE?), where Zephaniah's ascent to heaven is described as the last journey of the righteous soul to its place in paradise. God remains completely unseen – or else he got lost in the missing pages of the single remaining manuscript. Instead, as in the Apocalypse of Abraham, emphasized here is the God-like state of the highest angel (Eremiel).

The last ascent apocalypse to be included in my survey is the Apocalypse of John (written between 81 and 96 CE) because I regard it, despite its Christian provenance, as deeply indebted to the Jewish tradition. It has preserved many of the characteristics of its predecessors while transforming them into something intrinsically new. Here, the seer who undertakes the ascent recedes farthest into the background; his place is taken by the Lamb, Jesus Christ, who is the one at whom the revelation is directed and who is transformed – not just into an angel but into a divine power next to and of equal rank with God.

In chapter 4, I continue with the literature preserved in the Qumran community.[95] In retreating to the shores of the Dead Sea because of the pollution of the Jerusalem Temple, this community drives the Temple-critical motif to its extreme. Only they, the chosen remnant of Israel, achieve cultic purity as a priestly community that regards itself as living in communion with the angels. This communion can take place either on earth – when, during the eschatological battle between the "Sons of Light" and the "Sons of Darkness," the angels descend to earth in order to lead the holy warriors to their final victory (War Scroll) – or it takes place (presumably) in heaven, when, during their liturgical worship, the Qumran sectarians join their voices to the praise of the angels (Hodayot). I use the word "communion" here deliberately, since it must remain an open question as to whether or not the members of the community envision themselves, during their joint worship with the angels, as being transformed into angels. The same

---

[95] An earlier version of this chapter appeared as "Communion with the Angels: Qumran and the Origins of Jewish Mysticism," in Schäfer, *Wege mystischer Gotteserfahrung*, pp. 37–66.

is true, I will argue, for the hymns collected under the title Songs of the Sabbath Sacrifice. It is only in the so-called Self-Glorification Hymn that the hero of this text imagines himself to be elevated among the angels in heaven, that is, actually and physically to be transformed into an angel.

Contrary to the prevailing trend in research on Jewish mysticism (or even in Qumran scholarship) I contend that the vision of God plays a strikingly marginal role in the Qumran texts and much less of one than in the ascent apocalypses, where the vision at least is the goal of the ascent (although its details often remain rather vague). I demonstrate that in all of the analyzed texts, the visual aspect of the enterprise is almost completely neglected. The same is true also for the other important ingredient of the experience as described by Ezekiel and the ascent apocalypses – the ascent. In the Qumran texts there is no description of the ascent, be it of the community at large or of the individual that boasts of his elevation among the angels. I therefore do not see any basis for the claim that the Qumran community constitutes the incubator that hatched Jewish mysticism and that the Qumran literature finds its mystical completion in the Hekhalot literature.

With the fifth chapter treating Philo, we enter a completely new realm, the realm of a Jewish philosopher who was deeply imbued with the ideas of Plato and their Middle Platonic offspring. Now, for the first time in Jewish history and the history of the texts with their respective communities that we discuss, the biblical and postbiblical unity of body and soul has been abandoned in favor of a radical and constitutive separation between body and soul. The body is portrayed as the prison of the soul, while the latter, being of divine origin, longs for its release from this prison and a return to its place of origin. This Platonic concept has far-reaching consequences for our subject. I posit that Philo is by no means concerned only with the postmortem return of the human soul to its divine origin; he also holds that the souls of certain individuals (including his own) can undertake, during their lifetime, a "heavenly journey" that lifts the individual's soul up in a state of ecstasy and frenzy and transforms it into a kind of divine essence. If anywhere in the Jewish tradition it is here, I argue, that we encounter the idea of the divinization, yet not of the human being in his body and soul but solely of his soul (which, moreover, no longer remains "his" soul in the strict sense of the word but is replaced by a divine essence).

The complex and extensive rabbinic evidence of Ezekiel's Merkavah and related traditions are discussed in two chapters. The first of these, chapter 6, begins with the public exposition of Ezekiel 1 in the synagogue and with the famous restriction in m Hagigah 2:1 regarding the biblical subjects of forbidden sexual relations (Lev. 18/20), creation (Gen. 1), and the Merkavah (Ezek. 1). I demonstrate that the former is concerned with the public presentation and exegesis of the biblical text of Ezekiel, not with some kind of mystical experience, whereas the latter shifts the emphasis from the public realm of the synagogue to a private teacher-student relationship in which the "dangerous" biblical subjects of creation and the Merkavah in particular are perceived as an esoteric discipline reserved for the rabbinic elite. But there can be no doubt, in my view, that these rabbis understood the respective biblical texts as material for exegetical exercises and not for ecstatic experiences that aim at an ascent to the Merkavah in heaven.

The Mishnah's harsh restriction is illustrated by a cycle of seven stories that the Tosefta attaches to the Mishnah and that also appears in the Yerushalmi and the Bavli, albeit in different contexts and in a different sequence. I discuss these stories as separate units in the sequence in which they appear in the Tosefta, but in each case I compare the Tosefta version with the versions in the Yerushalmi and the Bavli, respectively. My analysis concludes that these seven stories, in the earliest form that we can reconstruct, focus not on a mystical experience but on the *exegesis* of what they call the "work of creation" (Gen. 1) and the "work of the Merkavah" (Ezek. 1) as an esoteric discipline. Unlike the authors of the ascent apocalypses, the rabbis seek their God not through an ascent to heaven but through exegesis. However, there are clear traces in some of the stories, particularly in the Bavli, that later editors tried to adapt them to the Merkavah mystical ascent experience.

Having discussed the seven Tosefta stories as separate and quasi-independent units, in my seventh chapter I turn to the structure in which they are presented in the two Talmudim; that is, I analyze the respective contexts in which the Yerushalmi and the Bavli processed them. I show that the Yerushalmi editor leaves no doubt as to his concern with the exegesis of problematic biblical passages and that he, within the array of such passages, seems to have placed more weight on the exposition of the work of creation than on the exposition of the work of Merkavah. Moreover, although he appears intent on softening the strict ruling of the Mishnah, he does not display any mystical-experience leanings in his exposition of the Merkavah. The Bavli editor also emphasizes his interest in the Merkavah as an exegetical discipline, but unlike his Yerushalmi colleague he could not help imposing on his exposition of the Merkavah elements that do indeed smack of "mystical" experience. I suggest that he received these elements from outside sources that were strong enough to compel him to include them. But it also becomes clear that he nevertheless felt obliged (as well as strong enough) to neutralize and rabbinize this in his view dangerous and unwelcome material.

With chapter 8, we finally tackle the Hekhalot literature, that is, the literature that for almost every scholar embodies the first climax of the fledgling mystical movement within Judaism: Merkavah mysticism. I again adopt a heuristic approach. Instead of choosing and reconstructing certain key concepts out of the voluminous and chronologically as well as stylistically and thematically disparate literary material, I follow the given sequence of some of the major Hekhalot texts (Hekhalot Rabbati, Hekhalot Zutarti, Shiʻur Qomah, and 3 Enoch) as they are preserved in the manuscripts and try to evaluate what they have to tell us about our subject in their own terms and within their respective context. What emerges is a highly complex and multilayered network of ideas that cannot and must not be reduced to the heavenly journey of the mystic and his climactic vision of God in the highest heaven. In its multifarious complexity, the Hekhalot literature offers us much more than just a report on the ascent of certain rabbis, and it is one of the goals of this chapter to capture this "more" and to put the ascent traditions in their appropriate frame of reference as presented by the editor(s) of the texts.

I demonstrate that in Hekhalot Rabbati we encounter a clear tendency to disappoint or even frustrate our expectation of the depiction of God on his throne (to be sure, an expectation cunningly fueled by the editor), wishing instead to impress us with endless and exhausting descriptions of the heavenly liturgy, of which the adept becomes part. But as I will argue, this strategy seems to be quite deliberate, since it is not a *unio mystica* that our editor wishes to convey but rather a *unio liturgica*, a liturgical union of the Merkavah mystic with God through his participation in the heavenly liturgy that surrounds God's throne. Moreover, and more important, I posit that this liturgical union is again, as in some of the ascent apocalypses, no end in itself; rather, within the narrative composed by the editor of Hekhalot Rabbati, it serves to convey the message that God continues to love his people of Israel on earth, even though the Temple is destroyed and the Merkavah mystic must undertake his dangerous heavenly journey to visit God on his throne in the heavenly Temple. It is this message that God wants the Merkavah mystic – the new Messiah – to bring down to his fellow Jews as the ultimate sign of salvation.

Quite in contrast to Hekhalot Rabbati, the text labeled Hekhalot Zutarti in some later manuscripts puts great emphasis on the magical use of the divine names. To be sure, in a certain layer of it we do find ascent traditions similar to those of Hekhalot Rabbati, but even these are adapted to the editor's main message, namely, that the ascent primarily results in neither a vision of God nor in the adept's participation in the angelic liturgy but in the knowledge of the divine names and their proper use. In addition, the communal orientation so conspicuous in Hekhalot Rabbati gives way to a much more individualistic or even egoistic approach in Hekhalot Zutarti, with R. Aqiva and his students as the heroes. And the angels – in Hekhalot Rabbati, primarily the guardians of the heavenly palaces and the guides of the worthy mystic – become the forces that are at the adept's disposal for the accomplishment of a successful magical adjuration.

Next follows a survey of the Shiʻur Qomah fragments preserved in the Hekhalot literature; that is, the traditions that assign God gigantic body dimensions to which hundreds of unintelligible names are attached. My analysis of the respective texts in the Hekhalot literature goes against the grain of the thesis inaugurated by Scholem and accepted by many scholars, namely, that the mystic's vision of the gigantic body of God serves as the climax of his ascent. Quite in contrast to this still prevalent trend in research, I hold that what is at stake here is not the dimensions of God's body but the knowledge of the appropriate names attached to the limbs of God's body and, consequently, the magical use of these names. Furthermore, I argue against the suggestion made by Scholem and others that the Shi'ur Qomah traditions are essential for the Merkavah mystical speculations, that they are a particularly old layer of the Hekhalot literature, and that they emerged out of the exegesis of the biblical Song of Songs. Finally, I compare the Shi'ur Qomah traditions in the Hekhalot literature with some related evidence that has been adduced from Jewish, Gnostic, and Christian sources, and I propose that it was originally angels in the Jewish tradition to whom gigantic dimensions were attributed. Only when the idea of vast angelic dimensions was usurped by the Christians did the (later) Jewish traditions – as they are preserved in the Shi'ur Qomah – transfer these gigantic dimensions to God and claim that they were suitable for God alone, and not for angels or other figures that might dispute God's position as the one and only God.

The last subsection of this chapter turns to the Third Book of Enoch (3 Enoch), in my view the latest offspring of Hekhalot literature. Here, the ascent of a rabbi (Ishmael) to the highest heaven recedes in importance; instead, the human being Enoch returns as the main hero of the text. In a way that is unparalleled in the ascent apocalypses as well as in other texts of the Hekhalot literature, Enoch is physically transformed into Metatron, the highest angel in heaven, and is assigned the unique title "Lesser YHWH." Against an increasingly fashionable trend in modern scholarship, I insist that we need to take the rather late date of 3 Enoch seriously and cannot connect Enoch's transformation into Metatron directly and monolinearly with early (pre-Christian) Jewish traditions – such as the hypostasized "Wisdom" and "Logos" or the "Ancient of Days" in Daniel with the "Son of Man" as his allegedly younger companion – in order to utilize Metatron for the reconstruction of an (early) "binitarian" Jewish theology. In contrast, I posit that Enoch's transformation into Metatron in 3 Enoch may well be a *response* to the New Testament's message of Jesus Christ as the divine figure second only to God who takes his seat in heaven "at the right hand" of God. Understood this way, Metatron, as the antagonist of Jesus, completes and ultimately concludes the movement of the Merkavah mystics. The human individual who ascends to heaven and returns from there with God's message to the people of Israel is replaced by a human-divine savior figure who, from his heavenly abode, intercedes on behalf of God's beloved people on earth.

Chapter 1

Ezekiel's Vision

The Cosmos as Temple

In 597 BCE the Babylonian King Nebuchadnezzar deported Jehoiachin, King of Judah, together with the royal establishment to Babylonia. Among the exiled was Ezekiel, son of Buzi the priest and himself a priest. Five years after his arrival in Babylonia, Ezekiel had a vision in which he was appointed prophet and ordered to console his fellow captives, to admonish them and announce the final downfall of Jerusalem, the eventual return from exile, and the time of salvation. The precise locale of the vision has been determined as the Chebar canal, apparently near the city of Nippur,[1] where the exile settlement Tel Aviv was located (Ezek. 3:15).[2]

Ezekiel is not the first prophet to be appointed such through a vision. His predecessor Isaiah had his famous vision of God "in the year that King Uzziah died" (Isa. 6:1), namely, the year 739 BCE, and Ezekiel's older contemporary Jeremiah, also a priest, received his first prophetical revelation in the thirteenth year of King Josiah (Jer. 1:2), the year 628 BCE. But whereas Isaiah's vision clearly took place in the Jerusalem Temple, and while Jeremiah was granted his many revelations in the land of Israel, Ezekiel is the first biblical prophet to be granted a vision and emerge a prophet outside the Holy Land. Foreign lands were regarded as unclean (Ezek. 4:13), and that God should have revealed himself to a newly appointed prophet outside the land of Israel created a problem. The explicit mention of the Chebar canal may well be an attempt to circumvent this problem: running water was considered to have a purifying effect (Lev. 15:13; Num. 19:17) and hence could compensate for the negative impact of the unclean foreign land. Already the Mekhilta, one of the earliest midrashic commentaries on the Bible, follows this line of argumentation and suggests that after the land of Israel was

---

[1] John William Wevers, *Ezekiel: Based on the Revised Standard Version* (London: Nelson, 1969 [repr. 1982, William B. Eerdmans, Grand Rapids, MI]), p. 43; Moshe Greenberg, *Ezekiel 1–20: A New Translation with Introduction and Commentary* (Garden City, NY: Doubleday, 1983), p. 40; Daniel I. Block, *The Book of Ezekiel: Chapters 1–24* (Grand Rapids, MI/Cambridge: William B. Eerdmans, 1997), p. 84.

[2] From which the name of the modern Israeli city Tel Aviv was taken.

chosen the Holy Land, God revealed himself to his prophets outside the land of Israel at a "place which was pure because of (running) water."[3]

Ezekiel's vision is the most elaborate vision of any prophet in the Hebrew Bible, becoming the role model that has shaped many visionary experiences in the Jewish and Christian traditions. This chapter is devoted to a close reading of Ezekiel 1. What is it precisely that Ezekiel saw, and how does the content of his vision relate to the biblical context in which it is embedded? What kind of experience does it entail? What is the message of the vision, and what is its function in the book of Ezekiel?

The book opens solemnly, dating and locating Ezekiel's decisive vision:[4]

> (1) It was in the thirtieth year in the fourth month on the fifth day of the month, as I was among the exiles by the Chebar canal, that the heavens opened (*niftehu ha-shamayim*), and I saw visions of God (*wa-'er'eh mar'ot elohim*). (2) On the fifth day of the month – that was the fifth year of King Jehoiachin's exile – (3) it happened (*hayoh hayah*) that the word of YHWH (*devar YHWH*) came to Ezekiel the priest, the son of Buzi, in the land of the Chaldeans by the Chebar canal, and the hand of YHWH (*yad-YHWH*) came upon him there.

Scores of scholars have dealt with the unevenness of this text (what is the thirtieth year; how does the fifth year of King Jehoiachin's exile refer to this; is v. 2 a gloss explaining or correcting v. 1, etc.),[5] but these details are of minor importance here. The chief message is that Ezekiel was among the exiles by the Chebar canal when the heavens opened and he saw visions (v. 1), which were accompanied by an audition (v. 3). Let us briefly look at these characteristics.

The phrase that introduces the whole experience, "the heavens opened,"[6] is unique in Ezekiel and in the Hebrew Bible[7] but becomes a common expression

---

[3] Mekhilta de-Rabbi Ishmael, pisha bo 1 (H. S. Horovitz and I. A. Rabin, eds., *Mechilta d'Rabbi Ismael* [Jerusalem: Bamberger and Wahrman, 1960], p. 3; Jacob Z. Lauterbach, *Mekilta de-Rabbi Ishmael*, vol. 1 [Philadelphia: Jewish Publication Society, 1933], p. 6). In Ezek. 3:22 f., however, it is a "valley" in which God reveals himself to Ezekiel (with no water mentioned). The Targum on Ezek. 1:1 has a different solution (which is also mentioned as a possibility in the Mekhilta): God would reveal himself to a prophet outside the land of Israel only after this same prophet had first received a revelation within the Holy Land. This, of course, goes against the plain meaning of the biblical text of Ezek. 1:1 f., but it is read into the pleonastic phrase (infinitive and finite verb) *hayoh hayah* in v. 2: the seemingly superfluous *hayoh* refers to a previous revelation within the land of Israel, whereas *hayah* refers to the actual vision in Babylonia. See also Rashi, ad loc. In Ezek. 8:3 f. and 40:2, Ezekiel is brought to Jerusalem and the land of Israel, respectively, probably to avoid this problem.

[4] The translation of the biblical text follows Greenberg, *Ezekiel 1–20*, pp. 37 f., though with some changes.

[5] Gustav Hölscher, *Hesekiel, der Dichter und das Buch: Eine literarkritische Untersuchung* (Giessen: A. Töpelmann, 1924), pp. 43 ff.; Greenberg, *Ezekiel 1–20*, pp. 8 ff., 39 f.; Block, *Ezekiel*, pp. 80 ff.

[6] The Hebrew word is *patah* in the Nif'al.

[7] Coming closest to our Ezekiel text is 2 Sam. 22:10, in which God "bends" (*wa-yet*) the sky and "comes down" (*wa-yerad*), mounts a cherub, and flies on its back (v. 11).

in the later Jewish tradition. Particularly instructive are 2 Baruch and the Testaments of the Twelve Patriarchs. 2 (Syriac) Baruch pretends that Baruch, the son of Neriah, received his first prophetic revelation in the very year in which King Jehoiachin was deported, thereby clearly connecting Baruch and his prophecy with Ezekiel (1:1); however, the book was in fact written after the destruction of the Second Temple, in the early second century CE. As in Ezekiel, the "word of the Lord came to Baruch," but it is much later in the book that the audition is accompanied by the vision of the open heaven: "And afterward it happened that, behold, the heavens were opened, and I saw, and strength was given to me, and a voice was heard from on high" (22:1).[8] More emphasis is placed on the open heavens in the Testament of Levi, where the priest Levi assumes the role of the prophet and is appointed by God to "tell forth his mysteries to men" and to "announce the one who is about to redeem Israel" (2:10).[9] Accordingly, "the heavens are opened" in front of him, and he is asked to enter (2:6). He sees a first and a second heaven and finally the uppermost (third?) heaven, where the "Holy Most High is sitting on the throne" (5:1).[10] When the redeemer, an eschatological (high) priest, appears at the end of time, "the heavens will be opened" again, "and from the temple of glory sanctification will come upon him" (18:6). Hence, as in Ezekiel, the open heavens function as the visionary tool of the prophet/priest, but they acquire here important additional meanings. First, the vision of the prophet is not solely limited to the earth: unlike Ezekiel, who remains earthbound and has no direct contact with the divine realm, Levi physically enters heaven. It is not God who moves downward from heaven to earth, but the prophet who leaves his position on earth and traverses the open heavens to see God in his place in heaven. Second, and even more far-reaching, the prophet is exchanged for the Messiah: the open heavens become the channel through which the Messiah receives the Spirit of God as the sign of his divine appointment and the tool of his mission of redemption. The same is true for the Testament of Judah, where the messianic "Star from Jacob" is announced: the "heavens will be opened upon him to pour out the spirit as a blessing of the Holy Father" (24:2).[11]

The New Testament continues both lines of the Jewish tradition, the open heavens as medium of the prophetic vision and as divine confirmation of the Messiah. Examples of the former are Acts 7:55 f. (Stephen sees "the heavens opened and the Son of Man standing at the right hand of God") and Acts 10:11 ff.

---

[8] The translation follows A. F. J. Klijn, "2 (Syriac Apocalypse of) Baruch," in *OTP*, vol. 1, pp. 621 ff.

[9] The translation follows H. C. Kee, *Testaments of the Twelve Patriarchs*," in *OTP*, vol. 1, pp. 782 ff.

[10] More on this in the next chapter.

[11] Very different from the prophetic-apocalyptic tradition is 3 Macc. 6:18: here God opens the gates of heaven to send down two angels, which threaten the king (Ptolemy IV Philopator) and his forces.

(the apostle Peter sees the heavens open and all kinds of unclean animals coming down, and he hears a heavenly voice calling upon him to slaughter and eat these animals).[12] The latter is most prominent in those passages describing Jesus's baptism in the Jordan and Stephen's stoning. After Jesus was baptized by John the Baptist and emerged from the water, "the heavens were opened and he saw the Spirit of God descending like a dove alight on him. And there came a voice from heaven saying, 'This is my beloved Son, in whom I take delight.'"[13] The open heavens and the descent of the Spirit of God, together with the heavenly voice quoting a patchwork of verses from the Hebrew Bible,[14] confirm Jesus as the Messiah. Similarly, when Stephen claims to see the heavens opened and the "Son of Man standing at the right hand of God," he manages to provoke his fellow Jews and is stoned to death, because he makes no less a claim than that Jesus, the Messiah, has been resurrected and returned to his hereditary place in heaven.[15]

In Ezekiel, the open heavens enable the prophet to see "visions of God," in other words, to make direct contact with the divine while still remaining on earth. Most scholars agree that these visions are not, strictly speaking, visions of the deity but rather a "divine vision," a supernatural vision (or supernatural visions) provided by God.[16] This becomes clear from the parallels in Ezek. 8:3 and 40:2, where Ezekiel is brought, by *mar'ot elohim*, to Jerusalem or the land of Israel, respectively; but nevertheless, as we will see, the climax of these visions is the vision of God himself. The effect of the divine vision on the prophet is expressed by the phrase "and the hand of the Lord came upon him," which is again peculiar to Ezekiel's experience from the very beginning of his prophecy.[17] It characterizes the prophet's physical rapture: he is grabbed by God, singled out from the other exiles and likely also transformed into a state of mind – or, in some cases, of body (in 8:3 and 40:1 f. the "hand" delivers him to some other place) – that enables him to perceive the vision.[18] Most scholars want to see here the echo of an extraordinary, paranormal and probably even ecstatic experience.[19] Finally, the text makes clear that the vision is accompanied by an auditory revelation:

---

[12] In Rev. 4:1 ff. (discussed in detail in chapter 3), the visionary sees a door open in heaven and hears a voice that invites him on up. Hence, Revelation combines the motifs of the open heavens and the ascent.

[13] Mt. 3:16 f.; cf. Mk. 1:10 f.; Lk. 3:21 f.; John 1:32–34.

[14] Gen. 22:2; Ps. 2:7; Isa. 42:1.

[15] Cf. also John 1:51.

[16] Greenberg, *Ezekiel 1–20*, p. 41; Block, *Ezekiel*, pp. 84 f.; but see Wevers, *Ezekiel*, p. 43.

[17] See Greenberg, *Ezekiel 1–20*, pp. 41 f. (it occurs only with earlier prophets but not with the other literary prophets).

[18] See also Ezek. 3:22, 8:1 (here "the hand of the Lord fell" upon Ezekiel), 40:1.

[19] Georg Fohrer, *Ezechiel*, mit einem Beitrag von Kurt Galling (Tübingen: J. C. B. Mohr [Paul Siebeck], 1955), p. 10, speaks of an "ecstatic state," Wevers, *Ezekiel*, p. 43, speaks of an "ecstatic vision," and Greenberg, *Ezekiel 1–20*, p. 42, speaks of a "trance."

"the word of the Lord came to Ezekiel," a clause that is exceedingly common in the book of Ezekiel but almost absent from the other literary prophets.[20]

What is it now precisely that Ezekiel sees? The vision proceeds in four stages. The first is the vision of the four enigmatic creatures (the *hayyot*):

> (4) As I looked, a stormy wind came from the north, with a large cloud and flashing fire, surrounded by a radiance (*nogah*); out of it – out of the fire – [appeared] something that looked like (*ke-'ein*) *hashmal*.[21] (5) Out of it the shape (*demut*)[22] of four creatures (*hayyot*) [emerged], and this was their appearance (*mar'ehen*): they had a human shape (*demut adam*), (6) but they had each four faces and four wings. (7) For legs, they had a straight leg,[23] and their feet were like a calf's foot.[24] They gleamed like (*ke-'ein*) burnished bronze (*nehoshet qalal*). (8) Human hands were under their wings on their four sides. As for the faces and the wings of the four of them, (9) their wings were joined one to another;[25] they did not turn around as they went, but each went straight ahead.[26] (10) [As for] the shape of their faces (*demut penehem*), [each had] the face of a man (*penei adam*) [in front]; but on the right the four of them had a lion's face (*penei arieh*), and on the left the four of them had a bull's[27] face (*penei shor*); and the four of them had an eagle's face (*penei nesher*) [at the back].[28] (11) And their faces[29] and their wings were spread out above; each of them had two [wings] joining each other, while two [wings] covered their bodies. (12) Each went straight ahead; wherever the spirit would go they went, without turning around as they went. (13) And the shape (*demut*) of the creatures, their appearance, was like[30] burning coals of fire, something with the appearance (*ke-mar'eh*) of torches it was, moving to and fro among the creatures. The fire had a radiance (*nogah*), and from it lightning flashed. (14) And the creatures darted to and fro with the appearance (*ke-mar'eh*) of sparks (*bazaq*).

This dramatic, textually highly complex narrative (sometimes corrupt and sometimes glossed by a later editor) can be summarized as follows. On a summer day[31] at the Chebar canal, Ezekiel suddenly experiences a strong wind from the north and sees a cloud with a bright, glowing center out of which fire flashes. The fire takes the form of four creatures, each with straight legs and four faces and

---

[20] Greenberg, *Ezekiel 1–20*, pp. 83 f.

[21] The etymology of this word (used only in Ezekiel) is unclear; it seems to indicate some kind of precious metal. The Septuagint and the Vulgate have *ēlektron/electrum*, "amber." Accordingly, Block, *Ezekiel*, p. 92, translates "the sparkle of amber."

[22] *Demut* can mean "form, shape, figure" as well as "likeness, semblance."

[23] Meaning either "unjointed" or simply "standing with legs straight, not in a crouching position"; see Greenberg, *Ezekiel 1–20*, p. 44.

[24] Greenberg, *Ezekiel 1–20*, p. 44: round, that is, lacking orientation.

[25] The upper set of their wings touched each other.

[26] Lit. each went in the direction of their faces.

[27] Or "ox's."

[28] The Hebrew text has neither "in front" nor "at the back," but this can be easily inferred: an observer would see the human face looking at him, flanked by a bull's face to the left and a lion's face to the right; the eagle's face would then be left for the back of the creature.

[29] "And their faces" does not make any sense here; it is missing in the Septuagint.

[30] The Septuagint has: "and amidst the creatures there was something looking like. ..."

[31] The "fourth month" seems to be the month of June or July.

four wings. Their bodies and their hands are human, but of their four faces only one is human; the others are of a lion, a bull, and an eagle. Of the four wings, two cover their bodies and two are spread out, touching the wings of their companions. The creatures move in any direction they wish, in perfect harmony and unity, and never turn around, since they always face the direction in which they move. In addition to the movement of the creatures, there is another, torchlike fire among the creatures[32] that possesses a movement of its own and from which lightning flashes.

The four creatures as described here by Ezekiel are unique in the Hebrew Bible. The noun *hayyah* always denotes wild quadrupeds, in contrast to domestic animals,[33] and nothing we know about the biblical *hayyot* prepares us for Ezekiel's hybrid creatures. It is obvious that for the author himself, these creatures were so unusual that he did not coin a neologism but simply called them *hayyot*, living creatures. It is tempting to identify them with the cherubs (*keruvim*), winged hybrid creatures, indigenous to many ancient Near Eastern cultures, that found their way into the Bible, all the more so as the book of Ezekiel itself (ch. 10) provides this identification. What the cherubs have in common with Ezekiel's depiction of the *hayyot* is that they are winged – in Solomon's Temple their wings cover the ark in the Holy of Holies (1 Kings 6:23–28) – and that they seem to carry God's throne (God is said in the Bible to be "enthroned on the cherubs").[34] But their shape, which plays such an important role in Ezekiel, is not communicated more concretely. Ezekiel clearly does *not* want to identify his *hayyot* straightaway with the cherubs in the Temple, probably for the very reason that they are not bound to the Temple! Nor does he identify his creatures with the seraphs seen by Isaiah (6:2), which likewise stand in attendance at the divine throne and have three sets of wings: with one set they fly, with another they cover their legs (like the creatures in Ezekiel), and with the third set they cover their faces (in order not to look at God).

If we broaden our perspective and include the Mesopotamian iconography – of which Ezekiel naturally was aware – we come to the same conclusion: the ancient Near East is full of composite zoomorphic and anthropomorphic creatures (most notable among them the winged quadrupeds with human faces) that might have inspired Ezekiel, but none of them resembles Ezekiel's *hayyot*.[35] On the other hand, there are examples of four-winged gods and goddesses or genii in human shape that support the heaven with their hands or wings and

---

[32] Following the reading of the Septuagint.
[33] See, e. g., Gen. 1:28, 7:14.21, 8:19, 37:20; Lev. 26:6; Isa. 35:9; Ps. 104:25.
[34] Isa. 37:16; Ps. 80:2, 99:1; 1 Sam. 4:4; 2 Sam. 6:2; 2 Kings 19:15. On the cherubs' function in Ezekiel, see below.
[35] See the useful summary of the evidence in Greenberg, *Ezekiel 1–20*, pp. 55 f.

that Othmar Keel regards as the closest parallel to Ezekiel's quadrupeds.[36] And finally, a few examples of four-faced deities have come to light, but all with the same faces.[37] None of them bears four different faces. So the conclusion is unavoidable that, despite the obvious absorption of certain elements from the local culture (composite creatures, four wings, four faces), Ezekiel's creatures are unique and must be seen as his own creation.[38]

The second stage of the vision is a detailed description of the "wheels" accompanying the four creatures[39]:

> (15) As I looked at the creatures I saw one wheel (*ofan*) on the ground alongside each of the four-faced creatures.[40] (16) As for the appearance (*mar'eh*) of the wheels and their design, they were like (*ke-'ein*) chrysolite (*tarshish*),[41] and all four had the same shape (*demut*); their appearance (*mar'ehem*) and their design (*ma'asehem*) was as if one wheel were inside the [other] wheel. (17) When those went, these went on their four sides, without turning around when they went. (18) As for their rims (*gabbehem*), they were tall and frightening;[42] for the brows (*gabbotam*) of the four of them were inlaid all around with eyes.[43] (19) When the creatures went, the wheels went beside them; when the creatures rose off the ground, the wheels rose too. (20) Wherever the spirit would go, they went – wherever the spirit would go[44] – and the wheels rose alongside them, for the spirit of the creature was in the wheels: (21) when these went, those went, and when these stood still, those stood still; and when these rose off the ground, the wheels rose alongside them, for the spirit of the creature[45] was in the wheels.

The four creatures are each accompanied by four wheels, and the creatures with their wheels move in perfect harmony. This whole passage emphasizes the unity and harmony of the creatures and their wheels, which always move in the same

---

[36] Othmar Keel, *Jahwe-Visionen und Siegelkunst: Eine neue Deutung der Majestäts-schilderungen in Jes 6, Ez 1 und 10 und Sach 4* (Stuttgart: Katholisches Bibelwerk, 1977), p. 207.

[37] Greenberg, *Ezekiel 1–20*, pp. 55 f.

[38] This is also Greenberg's conclusion (*Ezekiel 1–20*, p. 58): "The specific combinations, such as the four distinct faces, and the ensemble remain unprecedented for us – and for the prophet"; see also Block, *Ezekiel*, p. 98.

[39] The caesura is marked by the repeated *wa'ereh* in v. 15 (see v. 4).

[40] I follow here the Septuagint. The Hebrew text applies the four faces to the wheels, hence: "with its [the wheel's] four faces," which strongly indicates a later transference of the motif of the four faces from the *hayyot* to the wheels. This identification is clearly made in 10:14.

[41] "Chrysolite" is the Septuagint's translation of *tarshish* in Ex. 28:20; here (in Ezek. 1:16) it transliterates *tharsis*, and in 10:9 and 28:13 it translates *anthrax* (a stone of dark red color). According to Greenberg, *Ezekiel 1–20*, p. 47, chrysolite is a bright yellow stone; Wevers, *Ezekiel*, p. 47, on the other hand, declares that it is a dark green stone, "whereas a yellow colour is expected." Block, *Ezekiel*, p. 99, translates "beryl" and suggests that it "is probably to be equated with Spanish gold topaz."

[42] Lit. "they had height and they had dread."

[43] The rims of the wheels are like eyebrows because they are covered with eyes.

[44] This seems to be a gloss.

[45] The Septuagint and the Vulgate have *pneuma zōēs* and *spiritus vitae*, respectively, which could also be translated as "spirit of life."

direction, both on and above the ground. The strange image of one wheel inside the other (v. 16) does not explain the technical structure of the wheels but rather seems to express the idea that the four wheels, although located at four different sides of the square formed by the four creatures, always move in the same direction. The wheels do not move freely and independently but are steered by a power emanating from the creatures: it is the "spirit" of the creatures that commands the wheels (and the unity of the creatures is again emphasized by the singular "creature" in vv. 20 and 21).

There can be no doubt that it is the function of the wheels to evoke the image of a chariot; any observer or reader will have thought immediately of one of the throne-chariots so characteristic of the ancient Near East.[46] But if we look at the parallels, we reach the same conclusion as with the *hayyot*: Ezekiel has clearly adopted and combined images that were familiar to him, but the end product is not identical with any single one of these images. For, strictly speaking, his creatures and wheels do not constitute a chariot. The wheels and the creatures are not joined together; it is solely the *spirit* that coordinates the movements of the creatures and the wheels. The same is true for the only biblical parallel adduced by most commentators, the lavers in the Temple, which had four bronze wheels and were decorated with cherubs, lions, and oxen (1 Kings 7:23–39). But although the lavers were mobile and carried something (water), they obviously were not a throne.

The apparition with the creatures and wheels does not approach Ezekiel; it is not something that moves toward him so that he can have a closer look. Rather, the open heavens grant him a look at something that takes place in heaven: the movement of the *hayyot* with their wheels (and what is on top of them; see below). The text gives the impression of a rather incoherent and chaotic movement back and forth in all possible directions. There can be no doubt, however, that the number four (four creatures, four wheels) is no coincidence but refers to the four corners of the world.[47] Hence, it is likely that the chariot-throne moves more concretely back and forth to all four corners of the world and that Ezekiel sees this celestial movement, which is normally hidden from human view (because it takes place above our visible world). The purpose of this movement is not explicitly mentioned but is hinted at by the frightening eyes on the rims of the wheels. The strange chariot-throne with its (yet to be revealed) master cruises heaven in all directions to keep a watchful eye on everything that happens above and below, and it is this that Ezekiel, the newly appointed prophet, becomes a witness of.

Now (the third stage) the vision moves to the area above the heads of the creatures:

---

[46] Some examples in Greenberg, *Ezekiel 1–20*, p. 57.
[47] Greenberg, *Ezekiel 1–20*, p. 57.

(22) There was a shape (*demut*) over the heads of the creature,[48] an expanse (*raqia'*) that looked like (*ke-'ein*) dreadful ice (*ha-qerah ha-nora*),[49] stretched over their heads above. (23) Below the expanse their wings were extended[50] one toward the other; each had two [wings] giving cover[51] to his body. (24) I heard the sound of their wings as they went like the sound of the deep sea (*mayim rabbim*),[52] like the voice[53] of the Almighty (*shaddai*), a sound of tumult (*hamullah*) like the sound of an army (*mahaneh*); when they stood still, they let their wings drop. (25) There was a sound from above the expanse that was over their heads; when they stood still, they let their wings drop.[54]

The first thing Ezekiel notices is the "expanse," for which the technical term *raqia'* is used – a clear allusion to the "firmament" of the Creation narrative (Gen. 1:6 ff.), which divides the upper from the lower waters, that is, heaven from earth.[55] It is nowhere described in more detail in the Bible (only Dan. 12:3 knows that it is "shining," and according to Job 37:18 the heavens are beaten out and firm like a "mirror of cast metal"), and Ezekiel's image of cold (gleaming?) ice is unique. Then the gaze of the prophet goes back to the creatures below the expanse: we have heard already that two of their wings are spread out and touch the wings of their companions and that an additional set of wings covers their bodies, but v. 23 makes it seem as if the outspread wings carry – or at least support – the expanse above them. One has to conclude, therefore, that the expanse above their heads, which is supported by their wings, moves with the creatures and their wheels.

Finally, a new element is introduced. The vision is accompanied by an audition because Ezekiel now hears something. First, he hears the sound that arises from the beating of the creatures' wings; it is compared to the sound of mighty waters (a cosmic-mythical element), the sound of an army, and the voice of the Almighty. The voice of the Almighty in particular is conspicuous: not only because God is (suddenly) mentioned at all, in addition to natural phenomena, but also because of the use of the word "Almighty" (*shaddai*) for God. The precise meaning of this archaic epithet for God is unknown, but its full form, *el shaddai*, is used as the divine name mainly by the patriarchs in the Priestly Code.[56] It is quite clear, therefore, that Ezekiel has deliberately taken up this archaic name of

---

[48] Again the singular *hayah*.

[49] JPS translation: "with an awe-inspiring gleam as of crystal." *Qerah* in biblical Hebrew is "ice," but the Septuagint translates "crystal."

[50] Lit. "straight toward."

[51] "Each had two [wings] giving cover" is repeated twice in the Hebrew text, one phrase clearly being a gloss.

[52] Lit. "many waters," that is, mighty waters (JPS translation).

[53] The Hebrew word *qol* means both "sound" and "voice."

[54] This repetition is missing in the Septuagint.

[55] Block, *Ezekiel*, p. 101, following examples of ancient Near Eastern art, prefers the translation "platform," but I do not think that the allusion to the firmament should be ignored.

[56] Gen. 17:1, 28:3, 35:11, 43:14, 48:3; Ex. 6:3, which explicitly states that God appeared to Abraham, Isaac, and Jacob as "El Shaddai"; Ez. 10:5.

God from the time of the patriarchs. The God with whose voice the sound of the wings is compared is the God of the antediluvian patriarchs.

The sound of the creatures' wings can only be heard when they move around; as soon as they stop, however, the prophet hears another, still faint sound from above the expanse. Since we do not yet know what is located above the expanse, we can only guess – and Ezekiel does not immediately satisfy our curiosity. But this sound clearly alludes to what is to come: God's speech to Ezekiel. Then follows the climax of the vision (stage four):

> (26) Above the expanse that was over their heads was the shape (*demut*) of a throne (*kisse*) with the appearance (*ke-mar'eh*) of sapphire-stone;[57] and above, on the shape (*demut*) of the throne was a figure (*demut*)[58] with the appearance (*ke-mar'eh*) of a human being (*adam*). (27) From the appearance (*mar'eh*) of his loins upward I saw the like of (*ke-'ein*) *hashmal*, having something with the appearance (*mar'eh*) of fire surrounding it; and from the appearance (*mar'eh*) of his loins downward I saw something with the appearance (*mar'eh*) of fire (*esh*); and he was surrounded by a radiance (*nogah*). (28) Like the appearance (*ke-mar'eh*) of the bow that is in the cloud on a rainy day, such was the appearance (*mar'eh*) of the surrounding radiance (*nogah*). That was the appearance (*mar'eh*) of the figure (*demut*) of the Glory of YHWH (*kevod-YHWH*). When I saw it, I fell on my face. Then I heard the voice of someone speaking.

Now, with the prophet's vision having reached its climax, the circumspect and roundabout language increases almost unbearably. Everything that he sees does not just become visible but has the shape (*demut*) and the appearance (*mar'eh*) of something or looks like something (*ke-'ein*). The first thing that takes shape is a throne (therefore, the text confirms here that the creatures with their wheels indeed carry a throne, which is located on the expanse above their heads). However, it is not just any throne but a throne with the appearance of sapphire-stone. This again is very important information, since the sapphire immediately recalls Ex. 24:10, where it is said that Moses, Aaron, Nadab, Abihu, and the seventy elders of Israel "saw the God of Israel: under his feet there was something like (*ke-ma'aseh*) a sapphire-brick (*livnat ha-sappir*), like the very sky for purity." This notoriously difficult verse cannot be explained here in all its implications; in our context it is essential that we have a vision of God here and that God rests his feet on something that looks like a brick of sapphire (in fact, Ex. 24:10 is the only verse in the Hebrew Bible, except for Ezekiel, that connects a vision of God in heaven with a sapphire stone).[59] The only difference seems to be that in

---

[57] Block, *Ezekiel*, p. 102, with n. 89, translates "lapis lazuli" and cautions: "Hebrew *sappîr* ... should not be confused with modern sapphire (blue corundum), since this stone was scarcely known in ancient times."

[58] I translate *demut* here with "figure" because it is the form of a human being.

[59] Ezkiel's "sapphire-stone" (*even-sappir*) seems to be a deliberate reference to and correction of the enigmatic "sapphire-brick" (*livnat ha-sappir*) in Exodus. This is not to say that Ezekiel had the text of the Torah available, but he may well have been aware of the tradition reflected in Ex. 24.

Exodus the sapphire is the foundation on which God's throne stands, whereas in Ezekiel the throne itself is made of sapphire. Moreover, God on his throne is evidently located in heaven, above Mount Sinai. So we have here in Ezekiel again an allusion to the time of the patriarchs, before the erection of the Tabernacle (let alone the Temple) and before the giving of the Torah. God sits enthroned in heaven, not in the Temple, and the prophet(s) can see him in a vision.

What does God look like? Ezekiel is here particularly circumspect: he sees a figure that appeared to him like a human being – but a human being it was: the word *adam* is unambiguous. In fact, Ezekiel is the only biblical author who uses this word in connection with God. To be sure, the Bible takes it for granted that God is of human form.[60] The creation story tells us that, when God created "man" (*adam*), he created "him" in the "image" (*tzelem*) and "likeness/shape" (*demut*) of God, using the same word (*demut*) as Ezekiel, which fluctuates between "likeness," "shape," and "figure" (Gen. 1:26 f.). Hence, if "man" is created in the "likeness" of God, it is only fair to conclude that God looks like "man" (*adam*),[61] and this is precisely what Ezekiel does. But it is a conclusion that nobody had the courage to state expressly hitherto. Ezekiel's fellow prophets clearly perceived a human figure when they saw God, but none of them elaborates on this. Amos, for example, sees God standing on a wall, holding a plumb line in his hands (Amos 7:7); similarly, he sees God standing by an altar (Amos 9:1), obviously in the Temple. Hence, he must be of human shape – but this can be inferred by implication only and is not the main message that Amos wishes to convey. The same holds true for Jeremiah, whose mouth is touched by God's hand (Jer. 1:9): the message is not that God is of human shape and has a hand but that God puts his words into Jeremiah's mouth and that he is appointed prophet through this gesture. Closer to Ezekiel's vision is that of his predecessor, Isaiah, who describes God as sitting on a "high and lofty throne" with the skirts of his robe filling the Temple (Isa. 6:1). If God has a robe, it is again fair to assume that he is of human shape, but this insight is certainly not at the center of Isaiah's vision.[62]

Apart from Ezekiel, the only biblical texts that show some interest in the physical shape of God are Exodus, chapter 33, and Daniel, chapter 7. Daniel, Ezekiel's much later fellow prophet, has a dream and sees a vision while lying on his bed – a far cry from Ezekiel's dramatically opening heavens. Among other things, he sees that thrones are set in place and that the "Ancient of Days" (*'atiq yomin*) takes a seat (Dan. 7:9). That this "Ancient of Days" is physically

---

[60] Despite passages such as Deut. 4:15 (contradicted by Num. 12:8) and Isa. 40:18, 25, and despite the so-called aniconic tradition of the Jewish religion.

[61] The matter is further complicated by the fact that Gen. 1:27 goes on to state that God created "man" not just in his own image, but also both male and female. The far-reaching implications of this bold statement come to the surface only much later, in the Kabbalah.

[62] Like Isaiah, Micah sees God "seated upon his throne, with all the host of heaven standing in attendance to the right and to the left of him" (1 Kings 22:19), but there is even not an allusion to God's physical shape.

an old man becomes clear when he is further described as having hair the color of pure lamb's wool. The text does not explicitly state who the old man on his throne is, but there can be no doubt that he is God: his throne is blazing fire and has wheels, just like Ezekiel's throne, and hosts of angels serve him. So God does indeed look like a human being, although it is never expressly stated that he looks like a man. Interestingly enough, however, the enigmatic figure that pays him a courtesy visit is described as someone "like a human being/man" (*ke-bar enash*: the Aramaic equivalent of *ke-ben adam*); hence, according to Daniel, God himself and his mysterious visitor – who here starts his career as the "Son of Man" – are of human shape.

And there is Ezekiel's most distinguished predecessor, Moses, whose encounter with God in Ex. 33 is the climax of several earlier attempts. At first, God "appears" to him in a "blazing fire" out of a thornbush, and when the curious Moses wishes to have a closer look at why the burning bush is not consumed, God's voice calls out from the bush and tells him to come no closer, and then reveals himself as the God of Abraham, Isaac, and Jacob. Immediately, Moses "hid his face, for he was afraid to look at God" (Ex. 3:2–6). The clear message is that God can be heard but not seen. The second encounter is on Mount Sinai (Ex., chs. 19 f.) where God descends (*yarad*) in a "thick cloud" (*'av he-'anan, 'anan kaved, 'arafel*) and in "fire" to meet Moses there and talk to him. Both the cloud and the fire are, of course, strongly reminiscent of the beginning of Ezekiel's vision. More dramatically than in Ezekiel, however, God's appearance here is also accompanied by "thunder," "lightning," "a very loud blast of the horn," and "smoke." The people can see all these visible signs of God's coming down to Mount Sinai and, most important, they can hear God and Moses talking to each other (19:9); but they don't want God to speak to them directly (20:16). Moses, on the other hand, obviously hears God, but the text says nothing about him seeing God. God calls Moses to the top of the mountain (19:20) and Moses follows his command, but that's it. The closest the text comes to describing the physical encounter between God and Moses is the laconic statement toward the end (20:18) that "Moses approached the thick cloud (*nigash el ha-'arafel*) where God was (*asher-sham ha-'elohim*)" – he approaches the cloud in which God is hidden, but he does not enter it and therefore does not see him. Moreover, the final explanation (20:19) that God was speaking "from the very heaven" (*min ha-shamayim*) may indicate that the "thick cloud" did not actually alight on Mount Sinai but hovered above it. Hence, the circumstances of Moses's and Ezekiel's vision are quite similar (in fact, it appears as if Ezekiel's vision is shaped, at least in part, according to the theophany on Mount Sinai), but with the major difference that Ezekiel takes the next step and sees as well as describes the figure that is surrounded by the cloud.

Finally, the third major and most detailed encounter between God and Moses is described in Ex. 33. The setting this time is the "Tabernacle" or "Tent" (*ohel mo'ed*) in the wilderness. Whenever Moses visits the Tent, a pillar of cloud descends to guard the entrance of the Tent while God speaks with him in the Tent (Ex. 33:9). Although God would *speak* to Moses "face to face (*panim el panim*), as one man (*ish*) *speaks* to another" (v. 11), the text makes it absolutely clear that Moses does not actually see God; the emphasis is unambiguously on the auditory and not on the visionary communication. When he bids God, "Show me your Glory (*kevodekha*)," God gives a complicated response, leaving no doubt that Moses cannot see him.

God first promises him that he will make his "beauty" (*tuv*)[63] pass before him; in other words, he himself in all his *kavod* and *tuv* will actually pass before him. This is followed by the pledge that he will proclaim before him the name "Lord" (presumably to assure him that the figure that passes before him is indeed God), as well as the grace that he will grant him and the compassion he will show him. In other words, God's passing before Moses is an act of benevolence. However, as God immediately adds, Moses should not mistake this divine performance for actually seeing him: "But you cannot see my face, for man (*adam*) may not see me and live" (v. 20). God then tells Moses that there is a place close to him (*maqom 'itti*), namely, a rock, on which Moses should station himself. When his Glory (*kavod*) passes by, he will put Moses in a cleft of the rock: "And I will shield you with my hand until I have passed by. Then I will take my hand away and you will see my back (*ahori*), but my face (*panai*) must not be seen!" (vv. 22 f.).

This is the closest to God Moses can get. Hidden and shielded in a cleft of a rock, he "sees" God pass by – but in fact he does not see very much, because at the precise moment of passing God shields him with his hand (which can only mean that he covers the opening of the cleft with his hand); only after he has passed by the cleft does he allow Moses to see the "back" of his shape. From this it can be concluded that God is indeed of human shape, because he has not only a "face" and "hands" but also a "back" (a bluntly anthropomorphic statement of the Hebrew Bible that would later trouble a great many exegetes). But this conclusion is communicated only in passing, as it were. That God is of human shape can be inferred from the story, yet this is not its main message. Rather, the real message is clearly that God cannot be seen and that a human being who sees God must die. Hence, like the other major stories about Moses's encounter with God, this most elaborated narrative reinforces what we have been told time and again: that Moses, like any other human being, could not see God – although he desperately wanted to.[64] This result, in turn, makes Ezekiel's undertaking all

---

[63] The noun *tuv* most likely means here the "beauty" and the "glory" of God, and not (literally) his "goodness" (JPS translation); hence, it would seem to be synonymous with *kavod*.

[64] A remake of Moses's encounter with God in Ex. 33 is Elijah's encounter on Mount Horeb: Elijah stands in a cave on Mount Horeb and God passes by, not in the "great and mighty wind," not in the "earthquake," not in the "fire," but in the "soft murmuring sound" (*qol demamah*

the more striking. His vision of God in human shape – as vague and veiled as it remains – and seated on his throne reads like a deliberate counter-narrative to Moses's aborted vision. Ezekiel is the new Moses, who has seen more of God than Moses and any of his predecessors.

The details that Ezekiel communicates about the human-like figure bear little resemblance to an ordinary man. We learn that the figure has "loins," but these loins are mainly introduced in order to distinguish between the appearance of the upper and the lower parts of the figure: whereas the upper part looks like *hashmal* surrounded by fire, the lower part looks like plain fire. This is immediately reminiscent of the beginning of the vision (v. 4), in which the *hashmal* appears out of the fire. Now the vision becomes clearer: the division between the upper and the lower parts of the figure obviously indicates two different degrees of brightness. The *hashmal* of the upper part seems to be of a brighter and stronger brightness than the plain fire of the lower part. It is possible that the less intense brightness of the lower part of the divine body is caused by a robe that covers it.[65] In any case, the entire figure is enclosed in a radiance (*nogah*) that was mentioned at the beginning as well (v. 4). The overwhelming impression of this human-like figure is that of radiating fire: God's body is of human shape, but its essence is fire.

Then, quite unexpectedly, the radiance emanating from the divine figure is compared to "the bow that is in the cloud on a rainy day," the rainbow. The significance of this comparison has gone unnoticed by most modern commentators.[66] It is no doubt a deliberate allusion to Gen. 9:12 f., where God sets his bow in the clouds as a sign of the covenant between him and his people.[67] The rainbow in Genesis was the visible sign of the covenant between God and humankind following the deluge, and now, after the anticipated destruction of the Temple, the priest Ezekiel refers back to this priestly tradition. This is yet another intentional recourse to the pre-Temple, patriarchal period: just as the rainbow after the catastrophe of the deluge sets the seal on a new period of salvation, so too the rainbow after the catastrophe of the destruction of the Temple inaugurates a new period of hope for the people of Israel. Ezekiel's vision of God in human shape, radiating

---

daqqah). When Elijah hears the "soft murmuring sound" he covers his face, stands in the entrance of the cave and hears the voice of God addressing him (1 Kings 19:11 ff.). Like Moses, Elijah cannot see God but hears only his voice; unlike Moses, he knows this and covers his face. See Frank Moore Cross, *Canaanite Myth and Hebrew Epic: Essays in the History of the Religion of Israel* (Cambridge, MA: Harvard University Press, 1973), p. 166.

[65] Suggested by Fohrer, *Ezechiel*, p. 14.

[66] An exception is Ernst Vogt, *Untersuchungen zum Buch Ezechiel* (Rome: Biblical Institute Press, 1981), p. 11. Martha Himmelfarb, *Ascent to Heaven in Jewish and Christian Apocalypses* (New York: Oxford University Press, 1993), pp. 19 f., suggests that the rainbow might be understood as part of a depiction of the figure on the throne in priestly terms.

[67] The phrasing is very similar: *et qashti natati be-'anan* (Gen.) versus *ha-qeshet asher yihyeh ve-'anan* (Ezek.).

in bright colors like a rainbow, claims that ultimately nothing is lost. Not only does the reassuring rainbow once more appear in the clouds of heaven, but this time God makes himself visible, encased in the rainbow's radiance.

The concluding sentence – "That was the appearance of the figure of the Glory (*kavod*) of YHWH" – reaffirms that Ezekiel has indeed seen God. The term *kavod* is frequent in the Hebrew Bible and is also used for the visible manifestation of God, in particular in the Tabernacle[68] and in the Temple.[69] In most cases the *kavod* is said to be hidden in a cloud, and nowhere is mention made of its physical appearance; only Ezek. 1,[70] and indeed Ex. 33, revealing itself more and more as a precursor and model of Ezek. 1, identify the *kavod* with a human-like figure. But whereas Moses is desperate to get a closer look at the actual shape of God's figure and is denied his request, Ezekiel, who made no such requests, is granted his unexpected vision of God. The appropriate response to this overwhelming experience can only be that the prophet throw himself down before the *kavod* of his God.

In what follows, the vision turns into an audition. What already announced itself in v. 25 now comes true: the figure seated on the throne above the heads of the four creatures speaks to Ezekiel (Ezek. 1:28–3:15). God reveals to him that he appoints him prophet and sends him to his rebellious people, who will, however, be stubborn and refuse to listen to him. So as to prepare Ezekiel for his mission, God makes him eat a scroll on which is written everything that God has ordered to be conveyed to the people of Israel (the scroll is put into Ezekiel's mouth by a "hand that was sent forth toward me," another indication of the anthropomorphic shape of the divine figure). Twice, at the beginning and end of the audition, God impresses upon his newly appointed prophet that he must speak to the people with the full authority of his prophetical mission, whether they listen to him or not: "Thus said the Lord YHWH" (2:4, 3:11). Then God disappears (3:12–15):

> A wind[71] lifted me and I heard behind me a great roaring noise – "Blessed be the Glory of YHWH from its place (*mimqomo*)" – (13) the noise of the creatures' wings beating against one another, and the noise of the wheels alongside them, a great roaring noise. (14) A wind lifted me and took me, and I went, bitter, my spirit raging, overpowered by the hand of YHWH.[72] (15) I came to the exiles at Tel Aviv, who were living by the Chebar canal and, where they were living, there I sat seven days, desolate among them.

---

[68] Ex. 40:34 f.; Lev. 9:23; Num. 14:10, 16:19.

[69] 1 Kings 8:11; 2 Chron. 7:1.

[70] In Ezek. 3:23 Ezekiel stands in a valley before the Glory of God, "like the Glory I had seen at the Chebar canal," and in 8:4 the glory appears again, "like the vision that I had seen in the valley"; in chapter 10, the remake of chapter 1, the "radiance" (*nogah*) of the Glory is mentioned again.

[71] Or "spirit" (*ruah*).

[72] Lit. "with the hand of YHWH strong upon me."

God's and Ezekiel's departure coincide, or, more precisely, God terminates the vision by raising Ezekiel up so as to bring him back to the community of exiles, and, lifted up by a wind to heaven, Ezekiel hears behind him the noise of the creatures and their wheels, indicating the departure of God. He does not actually see God disappear; he simply hears the noise of his departing chariot. Ironically, Ezekiel is lifted up to heaven when the vision is finished, not during the vision. This once again underscores the distance that is kept between God and Ezekiel during the vision: when God appears to him in the open heaven, the prophet remains on earth and is not elevated to heaven. He can see God, but he is not invited to get physically close to him.

The phrase "Blessed be the Glory of YHWH from its place (*mimqomo*)" is an exegetical crux. In the present Hebrew text it appears as a doxology, most likely from the four creatures, "a salute to the departing Majesty."[73] The main philological problem of this doxology is the awkward *mimqomo*, literally – as translated above – "from its [the Glory's] place." The suggestion, first made by scholars of the nineteenth century,[74] that *barukh* ("blessed") is corrupt and should be corrected to *berum* ("I heard behind me a great roaring noise, when the Glory of YHWH *rose* from its place") makes for a much smoother reading but is clearly the *lectio facilior* and hence not very likely. The Targum translates the phrase as "Blessed be the Glory of the Lord from the place of the house of his Shekhinah,"[75] thus "solving" the problem by reading into it what it definitely does not want to say: that the Glory of the Lord is praised in the Temple (which is the standard opinion). However, the opposite seems to be the true meaning of the phrase, namely, that God's Glory is blessed wherever it is, even if it is *not* in the Temple. The Temple no longer exists, but God's Glory can nevertheless be seen and praised. I therefore agree with what was apparently first suggested by Martin Buber,[76] namely, that God can be praised here and now (in exile) in the same manner as he was once praised from Zion (which is now destroyed). The once fixed place (for God's presence and the appropriate praise) in the Temple has given way to the open space in heaven.

The vision leaves Ezekiel with two feelings. He is "overpowered" by the hand of God, a reference to the ecstatic experience mentioned first in v. 3; and he is "bitter," spending seven distressful days among his fellow exiles, until God addresses him again and reminds him of his mission (3:16 ff.). The bitterness may

---

[73] Greenberg, *Ezekiel 1–20*, p. 70.

[74] Ferdinand Hitzig, *Der Prophet Ezechiel* (Leipzig: Weidmann, 1874); Samuel David Luzzatto, *Erläuterungen über einen Theil der Propheten und Hagiographen* (Lemberg: A.I. Menkes, 1876, in Hebrew); and see Greenberg, *Ezekiel 1–20*, p. 70; Block, *Ezekiel*, p. 132, with n. 1, pp. 134 f.

[75] TJ Ezek. 3:12.

[76] Martin Buber, "Zu Jecheskel 3:12," *MGWJ* 78 (1934), pp. 471–474. I do not see any necessity, however, to put this insight into the mouth of Ezekiel himself; it makes sense, too, if it is uttered by the four creatures and heard by Ezekiel.

well be a reflection of God's bitterness toward his people and of Ezekiel's own feelings with regard to the task imposed on him by God.[77] In any case, he returns to the community of exiles and abides there in silence without immediately revealing his new status.

To conclude and to summarize what has been observed so far: what then is the purpose of the vision and the message it wishes to convey? To begin with, as I have already emphasized, like many other prophetical visions it is a "call vision": through the vision God appoints Ezekiel his chosen prophet. Since there often exists a tension or even contradiction between the call and the expectations of the people or the ruling class, the vision serves as the divine approval of the prophet's views, which oppose those of the majority of the people. This is explicitly the case with Moses on Mount Sinai, when God promises him, "I will come to you in a thick cloud, in order that the people may hear when I speak with you and *so trust you ever after*" (Ex. 19:9). Likewise, when God starts speaking to Ezekiel after the vision in chapter 1, he admonishes him again and again to repeat his words to them, "whether they listen or not, for they are rebellious" (Ezek. 2:7); he even prepares him for the possibility that they "will refuse to listen to you, for they refuse to listen to me" (3:7). According to Moshe Greenberg, this divine confirmation of Ezekiel's prophetical task is the gist of the vision: "Distressed by his people's fate, convinced of impending doom, Ezekiel was cast out by his community, which clung to the hopeful oracles of the prophets promising the exiles a speedy restoration to their homeland. ... By way of response, and in accord with traditional imagery, the heavens opened and the Majesty of God appeared, vindicating the nonconformist and proving that right and divine favor were with him, not with the many."[78]

Within the narrative strategy of the book this is certainly one of the vision's more important aspects, but I do not think that such a minimalist reading does justice to its complexity. I therefore agree with the widespread view that it is the aim of the vision to confirm that neither God nor his revelation is bound to the land of Israel: God does reveal himself to his chosen prophet outside the land of Israel, in unclean foreign land.[79] But it is much more than that. The archaic imagery used in the description of the chariot and God residing above the *raqia'* points to a worldview before the erection of the Tabernacle in the wilderness and the building of the Temple in Jerusalem. The God who appears to Ezekiel is the God of the patriarchs, the God of the cosmos, who is not (yet) confined to the

---

[77] Pace Greenberg, *Ezekiel 1–20*, p. 71, I do not see this as an alternative; Block, *Ezekiel*, p. 137, emphasizes "the divine imposition on his [Ezekiel's] life and the implications of Yahweh's commission for him."

[78] Greenberg, *Ezekiel 1–20*, p. 80.

[79] Fohrer, *Ezechiel*, pp. 14–16; Vogt, *Untersuchungen zum Buch Ezechiel*, pp. 12, 25; Walther Zimmerli, *Ezekiel 1: A Commentary on the Book of the Prophet Ezekiel, Chapters 1–24* (Philadelphia: Fortress Press, 1979), p. 140.

boundaries of the Temple. To be sure, the Jerusalem Temple is not yet destroyed when Ezekiel sees his vision of God as observer and ruler of the entire cosmos (in 592 BCE), but it will be destroyed soon (in 586 BCE), and it is one of the major tasks of the newly appointed prophet to announce the destruction of the Temple.[80] The vision anticipates what will happen soon, and its message is therefore not only that God reveals himself even outside the land of Israel but that God reveals himself outside the Temple. God does not need the Temple to reveal himself after the destruction of the Temple, just as he did not need the Temple in the dim and distant past of the patriarchs. The cosmos is his Temple.

This is not to say that the Temple is superfluous according to Ezekiel. On the contrary, his book climaxes in announcing the construction of the new Temple (chs. 40–48). But this new Temple is the eschatological Temple, the Temple at the end of time, when Israel will live in peace and happiness again. The same Glory (*kavod*) of God that he saw in his vision at the Chebar canal will enter the newly built Temple (Ezek. 43:3); God will take his place in the Temple again. In the meantime we must resort to the pre-Temple period of the patriarchs, to the God who inhabits the entire cosmos – and who can be seen in the vault of heaven. This, I maintain, is the meaning of the enigmatic phrase in Ezek. 11:16, where God assures the exiles: "Thus said the Lord YHWH: Though I have removed them far among the nations and though I have scattered them among the countries, I have become to them a small sanctuary (*miqdash me'at*) in the countries into which they have come."[81] God himself, when he manifests himself in the open heavens, has become a "small sanctuary" to the people of Israel during their exile, during that time when the Temple is destroyed. God is no longer bound to the land of Israel, as the inhabitants of Jerusalem claim (v. 15), and to the Temple in Jerusalem; wherever he is, the Temple is with him. To be sure, the Temple will be rebuilt, and God will then return to his Temple, but for the time being he is his own Temple – a "small sanctuary," a substitute.[82] But what better substitute could there be for the Temple than God himself?[83]

---

[80] In fact, as Martha Himmelfarb has pointed out (*Ascent to Heaven*, p. 12), God has abandoned the Temple for a chariot even before the destruction of the Temple.

[81] I interpret "I have become to them a small sanctuary" as the main clause of the sentence and don't regard the sentence as incomplete with the resolution in the next verses ("Though I have removed them ... I will gather you from the peoples ...") as Greenberg, *Ezekiel 1–20*, p. 190, suggests. The Hebrew syntax does not necessitate such a translation, which is actually meant to downplay the importance of the "small sanctuary."

[82] Block, *Ezekiel*, p. 350, emphasizes the ambiguity of *me'at*: "It could be interpreted adjectivally, viz., 'a little sanctuary' ... However, the expression may also be [understood] adverbially, either temporally, 'for a little while,' hinting at the limited duration of the exile, or qualitatively, 'to a limited extent.'" The adverbial interpretation may solve the problem of why God is called a *small* sanctuary. The adjectival reading doesn't make much sense, since one would God expect to be a greater one than the physical Temple.

[83] The JPS translation, in its usual tendency to smooth out any roughness and flavor of the original Hebrew, translates *miqdash* as "sanctity" ("I have become to them a diminished sanc-

Finally, how does the vision with audition affect Ezekiel the new prophet? Here, as we have seen, the text is very restrained. Ezekiel appears as the passive "victim" of the hand of God, which is strongly imposed on him (vv. 1:3 and 3:14). It is clear that the main reason for this procedure is to single him out as God's chosen prophet, a "favor" to which he responds only reluctantly and unwillingly (v. 14). But it must remain an open question as to whether God's hand upon him also transforms his state of mind and induces some kind of ecstatic experience, as I have considered above. The emphasis is on the overpowering violence of the experience, not so much on the seer's spiritual, let alone physical, transformation. In this regard Ezekiel remains still far from the process of spiritual and physical transformation as depicted in the later apocalypses, but one can see how he paves the way for such more elaborate descriptions.

---

tity"), as if the Hebrew were *qedushah*. This is a perfect example of replacing one evil with another, because the idea of God as a "diminished sanctity" is much worse than the notion of God as the substitute for the Jerusalem Temple.

Chapter 2

Enoch and His Circle

Ascent to Heaven

When the heavens opened for the prophet Ezekiel, he had a vision of God seated on his chariot, which assured him that God was still there, in heaven, despite the imminent destruction of the Temple, God's chosen place on earth. This was consolation enough for the prophet; he made no attempt to get closer to God and enter heaven. In fact, nowhere in the Hebrew Bible is the gap between heaven and earth bridged in such a way that a human being leaves his place on earth and explores heaven. This experience is left to the postbiblical apocalyptic literature, in particular to the so-called ascent apocalypses that originated in the circle gathered around the patriarch Enoch.

The Book of the Watchers (1 Enoch 1–36)

Enoch is the biblical hero to whom the first ascent to heaven is attributed. The Bible does not tell us much about him, just that he was one of the descendants of Adam's third son Seth, who was born after the murder of Cain: Enoch was the son of Jared and the father of Methuselah and died at the age of 365 years, considerably younger than his ancestors and his son Methuselah or his grandson Lamech, the father of Noah (Gen. 5). This deviation in age is coupled with a strange deviation in the description of his "short" life. Whereas the pattern in the case of all his ancestors and descendants is "When so and so had lived such and such many years, he begot so and so; after the birth of so and so he lived for such and such (more) years and begot sons and daughters; all the days of so and so came to such and such many years; then he died," in the case of Enoch (Gen. 5:21–24) the text reads:

> When Enoch had lived sixty-five years, he begot Methuselah. After the birth of Methuselah, Enoch walked with God (*wa-yithalekh Hanokh et-ha-'elohim*) for (another) 300 years and begot sons and daughters. All the days of Enoch came to 365 years. Enoch walked with God (*wa-yithalekh Hanokh et-ha-'elohim*); then he was no more (*we-'enennu*), for God had taken him away (*ki-laqah oto elohim*).

The major differences are, first, that Enoch did not just "live" for a certain amount of years but "walked with God," and second, that he did not simply "die" but "was no more," because God "had taken him away," presumably while walking with him.

These few enigmatic sentences in the Hebrew Bible became the springboard for much speculation in the postbiblical Jewish and (later) Christian literature.[1] If the Bible emphasizes twice that Enoch walked with God, we must conclude that he was not only the privileged favorite of God among his fellow patriarchs (because he lived an exceptionally ethical life) – and this may well have been the reason why God took him away so early – but also that he was physically, in the literal sense of the word, walking with God. Since, after the expulsion from paradise, God no longer walks with human beings on earth, Enoch's walking with God could only have taken place in heaven. Hence, Enoch must have ascended to heaven to visit God, and at the relatively young age (in comparison to his fellow patriarchs) of 365 years he did not return but stayed with God in heaven.

This is what we can deduce from the short biblical narrative of Enoch's extraordinary life. The first text to expound and expand on the biblical *Vorlage* is the "Book of the Watchers" (1 En. 1–36), one of the earliest originally independent works constituting the so-called Ethiopic book of Enoch. It dates from the late third or the first quarter of the second century BCE[2] and is itself a composite text with five discrete units (1 En. 1–5, 6–11, 12–16, 17–19, and 20–36).[3] Whereas the first unit (1–5) serves as an introduction, the second – and probably oldest – unit (6–11) establishes a major theme of the Book of the Watchers, namely, the story of the fallen angels, which originates from the narrative in Gen. 6:1–4. From the Bible we only learn that the "Sons of God" (*benei ha-'elohim*), usually understood as angels, saw how beautiful the daughters of men were on earth and that they took wives from among them. Their offspring are called Nefilim (the Hebrew root *nafal* means "fall," hence the "fallen" angels) and are identified as the "heroes (*gibborim*) of old, the men of renown (*anshei ha-shem*)." God apparently disapproves of this miscegenation and reduces the life span of humanity to 120 years.

This brief and by no means unambiguous biblical text is developed into a much broader narrative in the Book of the Watchers (1 En. 6–11). Here the

---

[1] On this, see recently Philip S. Alexander, "The Enochic Literature and the Bible: Intertextuality and Its Implications," in Edward D. Herbert and Emanuel Tov, eds., *The Bible as Book: The Hebrew Bible and the Judaean Desert Discoveries* (London: British Library and Oak Knoll Press, 2002), pp. 57–69.

[2] See James C. VanderKam, *Enoch and the Growth of an Apocalyptic Tradition* (Washington, DC: Catholic Biblical Association of America, 1984), p. 114 ("a paleographically determined *terminus ad quem* of ca. 200 or slightly later is reasonably certain, but there is no firm evidence that would allow one to specify a *terminus a quo*. It is possible and indeed likely that the BW is a third-century composition; it is almost certain that it is pre-Maccabean"); Himmelfarb, *Ascent to Heaven*, pp. 5, 10.

[3] I follow here the useful summary in chapter 1 of Annette Yoshiko Reed, *Fallen Angels and the History of Judaism and Christianity: The Reception of Enochic Literature* (New York: Cambridge University Press, 2005).

"Sons of God" are a whole gang of angels who take an oath not only to seduce the daughters of men but also to teach them all kinds of hidden wisdom (among other things the art of warfare and cosmetics); the children they beget, the Nefilim from Genesis, here called "great giants," turn against the people and animals of earth and devour them greedily and relentlessly. These horrible events and the pleading of the people on earth do not go unnoticed by the remaining angels in heaven. They bring the case before God, who condemns the fallen angels and their offspring to everlasting damnation. Only Noah will be saved from the imminent judgment (the deluge).

In this first account of what happened with the fallen angels Enoch plays no role; he is not even mentioned. This is hardly the case in the second account, the unit 1 En. 12–16.[4] Here Enoch is the hero and serves as mediator between the angels in heaven and the fallen angels on earth (both are called "Watchers" now). The very beginning of the unit addresses the problem of Enoch's whereabouts, which remain so mysterious in the Bible and are only hinted at. The Book of the Watchers knows precisely where he is: "And before these things Enoch was taken up, and none of the children of men knew where he had been taken up, or where he was or what had happened to him. But his dealings were with the watchers, with the holy ones, in his days" (12:1–2).[5] Since Enoch lived before all the dreadful things related in the preceding unit (Noah was his great-grandson), he was indeed taken up into heaven. It was only his earthly life that accounted for his 365 years; after this he continued his life in heaven among the angels. Now the Watchers that remained in heaven ask Enoch to announce the divine judgment to the Watchers who have abandoned heaven (ch. 12). He duly follows this request and descends to that place on earth where the Watchers are gathered, Mount Hermon. When they hear what their fate is to be they beg Enoch to bring their petition for forgiveness to God. Reading the memorandum of their requests, he falls asleep, and in his dreams has a vision that makes clear there won't be any forgiveness for the fallen Watchers (ch. 13).

The following chapter (14) presents Enoch's vision of God in heaven. It opens with a solemn introduction that reaffirms that Enoch saw all this in a vision when he was asleep, and then it summarizes the verdict: although he wrote down the petition of the fallen Watchers, the vision he is about to communicate revealed to him that their petition will not be granted in eternity; they will never be able

---

[4] For a literary analysis of the narrative in this section, see Carol A. Newsom, "The Development of *1 Enoch* 6–19: Cosmology and Judgment," *CBQ* 42 (1980), pp. 310–329; George W. E. Nickelsburg, *1 Enoch 1: A Commentary on the Book of 1 Enoch, Chapters 1–36, 81–108* (Minneapolis, MN: Fortress Press, 2001), pp. 229 ff.

[5] Translation according to *The Book of Enoch or 1 Enoch: A New English Edition*, with commentary and textual notes by Matthew Black, in consultation with James C. Vanderkam (Leiden: Brill, 1985). Italics indicate an emended or problematic text (p. XII). See also Nickelsburg, *1 Enoch 1.*

to ascend to heaven again but will remain imprisoned inside the earth forever (14:5). And then follows the vision itself:

> (8) And it was shown to me thus in a vision: Behold! clouds were calling me in my vision, and dark clouds were crying out to me; fireballs and lightnings were hastening me on and driving me, and winds, in my vision, were bearing me aloft, and they raised me upwards and carried and brought me into the heavens.

It has long been observed that Enoch's vision is to a large degree informed by Ezekiel.[6] The clouds and lightnings are immediately reminiscent of Ezekiel's "large cloud and flashing fire"; the "dark clouds" are literally "mist" or "fog" (*homichlai*, in the Greek translation)[7] and may well refer to the "thick cloud" or "mist" in Ex. 19 f. But whereas the cloud and flashing fire in Ezekiel 1 descend from above toward the prophet-seer, who remains on earth, the clouds and fireballs in 1 Enoch draw him upward and carry him from earth to heaven. This dramatically staged movement from low to high comes as a surprise in the wider context of the Book of the Watchers, since Enoch had just come down from heaven in order to meet the fallen Watchers on earth, and he actually needs no vision to see God, because his true place is in heaven anyhow. But it makes sense in contrast to Ezekiel's vision and clearly wishes to emphasize that Enoch, the original human being, moves freely between earth and heaven, whereas the Watchers, the original spiritual beings, are explicitly forbidden to ascend to heaven again and thus remain earthbound. What Enoch concretely sees in heaven is related in several stages (again not unlike Ezekiel):

> (9) And I went in till I drew near to a wall, built of hailstones, with tongues of fire surrounding it on all sides; and it began to terrify me. (10) And I entered into the tongues of fire and drew near to a large house built of hailstones; and the walls of the house were like tesselated paving stones, all of snow, and its floor was of snow. (11) Its upper storeys were, as if it were, fireballs and lightnings, and in the midst of them (were) fiery Cherubim, *celestial watchers*.[8] (12) And a flaming fire was around *all* its walls, and its doors were ablaze with fire. (13) And I entered into that house, and it was hot as fire and cold as snow; and there were no delights in it;[9] horror overwhelmed me, and trembling took hold of me. (14) And shaking and trembling, I fell on my face.

The first thing Enoch espies in heaven is a huge wall that, as becomes immediately clear, shields and apparently surrounds a large house. Thus, what he approaches is an architectural structure similar to buildings on earth. Different

---

[6] See Himmelfarb, *Ascent to Heaven*, pp. 10 ff.

[7] Black, *1 Enoch*, p. 146.

[8] Another possibility: "and their heaven [was like] water"; see Michael A. Knibb, in consultation with Edward Ullendorf, *The Ethiopic Book of Enoch: A New Edition in the Light of the Aramaic Dead Sea Fragments*, vol. 2: *Introduction, Translation and Commentary* (Oxford: Clarendon Press, 1978), p. 98; Nickelsburg, *1 Enoch 1*, p. 257; Black, *1 Enoch*, p. 147, suggests that the text is corrupt and proposes to read *'irei shemaya*.

[9] Nickelsburg, *1 Enoch 1*, p. 257: "no delight of life was in it."

from any building familiar to a human being, however, is its wall built of hail-stones and surrounded by fire (the "tongues of fire" seem to literally "lick" at the hailstones without consuming them). This strange image of opposing natural forces coexisting with each other is repeated in the house behind the wall. Its walls are built of hailstones or snow and are surrounded by "flaming fire" (v. 12). Moreover, the upper stories of the house are completely of fire; hence, the fiery upper part of the building rests on snow – again without consuming it, because otherwise the house would collapse (what it obviously does not do).

The hailstones or snow[10] are reminiscent of Ezekiel's "dreadful ice" (*ha-qe-rah ha-nora*) of which the "expanse" above the heads of the creatures consisted (Ezek. 1:22) – although a different word is used (in Hebrew "hailstones" are *avnei barad*) – but there is no miraculous coexistence of ice and fire in Ezekiel (unless one wishes to see a similar image in the fire emanating from the creatures below the expanse of ice and from the figure seated on the throne above it). In any case, the dramatic juxtaposition of ice and fire in the building structure of the surrounding wall and the house itself is of major importance in Enoch's vision. Accordingly, the house that Enoch enters is simultaneously hot and cold (v. 13). I know of no other passage, certainly not in the Hebrew Bible, wherein a similar architectural structure consisting of opposite elements is described.[11] The only parallel that comes to mind is the much later rabbinic tradition (in the name of R. Shim'on b. Yohai),[12] which marvels at the fact that the firmament (which consists of water) and the stars (which consist of fire) "live together and do not hurt each other";[13] another rabbi[14] adds that even the angels consist of half water and half fire and do not hurt each other[15] (this is, of course, an almost ironical reversal of the traditional view that the angels are created of fire).[16]

Another reference to Ezekiel is, most likely, the cherubs (v. 11). The author of the Book of the Watchers knew, of course, the identification of the four creatures in Ezek. 1 with the cherubs in Ezek. 10, and he may well have preferred the more common name *keruvim* instead of the unique and mysterious *hayyot*. Also, the connection of the cherubs with water in some manuscripts may hint

---

[10] Knibb, *The Ethiopic Book of Enoch*, p. 98 (on 14:10), points out that in Ethiopic, the same word is used for "hail" and "snow."

[11] The Bible does know the phenomenon, however, of something that is burning but still not consumed by the fire: Moses's burning bush in the desert (Ex. 3:2).

[12] A Tanna of the third-generation Usha period, after the Bar Kokhba war.

[13] The biblical proof-text for this is Job 25:2: "he imposes peace in his heights."

[14] R. Abun/Bun = R. Abin I, the fourth-generation Palestinian Amora (early fourth century).

[15] y Rosh ha-Shanah 2:5/2 (Peter Schäfer and Hans-Jürgen Becker, eds., *Synopse zum Talmud Yerushalmi*, vol. II/5–12: *Ordnung Mo'ed: Traktate Sheqalim, Sukka, Rosh ha-Shana, Besa, Ta'anit, Megilla, Hagiga und Mo'ed Qatan* [Tübingen: Mohr Siebeck, 2001], p. 194) and parallels; see Peter Schäfer, *Rivalität zwischen Engeln und Menschen: Untersuchungen zur rabbinischen Engelvorstellung* (Berlin: Walter de Gruyter, 1975), p. 51, n. 64.

[16] Schäfer, *Rivalität*, ibid.

at the original function of the expanse above the head of the four creatures: the "firmament" that divides the waters above and below (Gen. 1:7).

When he enters the terrifying building that rises in front of him, Enoch's only appropriate reaction is fear and horror. This is repeated twice: already terrified by the surrounding wall of hailstones with its tongues of fire, his horror is intensified after he enters the hot-cold house with "no delights in it"; now he is overwhelmed by horror and falls on his face. This reaction is in stark contrast to Ezekiel: to be sure, the prophet prostrates at the end of his vision (Ezek. 1:28), but there is no mention of any fear of this vision. Ezekiel was "overpowered by the hand of God" and left the place of his vision in bitterness (Ezek. 3:14), but these feelings have nothing to do with what he has seen: he does not fear God. Enoch, in contrast to Ezekiel, trembles at the mere sight of the terrifying building – not yet knowing what it is or what it accommodates – in anticipation of more horrible things to come.[17] The next step reveals the secret of the house:

> And I saw in a vision, (15) and behold! another house greater than that one and its door was completely opened opposite me; and it [the second house] was all constructed of tongues of fire. (16) And in every respect it so excelled in glory and honour and grandeur that I am unable to describe to you its glory and grandeur. (17) And its floor was of fire, and its upper chambers were lightnings and fireballs, and its roof was blazing fire. (18) And I beheld and saw therein a lofty throne; and its appearance was like the crystals of ice and the wheels thereof were like the shining sun, and (I saw) *watchers, Cherubim*.[18] (19) And from underneath the throne came forth streams of blazing fire, and I was unable to look on it.

Standing in the house he has entered, Enoch sees another even greater house; since he has not yet left the first house, the second house must be located within the first house (the apparent contradiction of a second greater house within the first house does not seem to bother our author). This time, Enoch does not enter the second house (at least not immediately); he just looks through its open door and describes the interior of the second house from his position in the first one. The major distinction between the second and the first house is not only that it is larger[19] but also that it consists completely of fire (instead of ice and fire): the walls, floor, upper chambers and roof are all various manifestations of fire. As such, it is clearly more magnificent than the first house (v. 16).

---

[17] This has also been emphasized by Himmelfarb, *Ascent to Heaven*, p. 16. But I would not go as far as to argue that the Book of the Watchers "emphasizes the glory of God's heavenly temple by making it, rather than the vision of God himself, the cause of Enoch's fear." Enoch is afraid not only of the building in which God dwells (as he will realize soon) but also, of course, of God himself (1 En. 14:24).

[18] Nickelsburg, *1 Enoch 1*, p. 257, proposes "and its <guardians> were cherubim."

[19] This is Knibb's translation, *The Ethiopic Book of Enoch*, p. 98.

But whereas the second house is made completely of fire, the throne Enoch sees therein looks like "crystals of ice,"[20] thus suggesting a remnant of the fire-versus-ice motif so characteristic of the first house.[21] This does not refer to Ezekiel, because the throne in Ezek. 1 is explicitly said to resemble sapphire (v. 26); the expanse on which the throne rests looks like ice, not the throne.[22] The same is true for the wheels: whereas the somewhat inexplicable fact of the throne having wheels (in contrast to Ezekiel, Enoch's throne does not move but stands firmly fixed in the second house) is no doubt taken from Ezekiel, Ezekiel's wheels look like chrysolite (*tarshish*) – apparently a bright yellow stone – and not like the shining sun.[23] In contrast, mention of the cherubs clearly alludes to Ezekiel's identification of the four creatures with the cherubs.

The throne in the second building leaves no doubt that the architectural structure Enoch sees is a palace in heaven, the palace of the King of Kings – God. It consists of an outer wall (surrounding and protecting the inner buildings?), a first building, and, apparently inside this first building, a second building that serves as God's throne room. Scholars have long observed that this three-part structure resembles the structure of Solomon's Temple as described in 1 Kings 6:3, 5: the *hekhal* (sanctuary), the *devir* (inner sanctuary) or *qodesh ha-qodashim* (Holy of Holies), in which was located the ark covered by the cherubs, and an outside "wall" (*qir*), which surrounded both *hekhal* and *devir*. Accordingly, the first house in Enoch's vision would correspond to the *hekhal*, and the second house together with God's throne would correspond to the *devir*.[24] Whatever the precise details of the correspondence between the earthly Temple and Enoch's heavenly structure – one should not forget that, quite unlike the *hekhal* and *devir* in the earthly Temple, the two houses in heaven are nested within each other[25] – it is very likely that the architectural structure in heaven is modeled after the First Temple on earth: God's heavenly residence is no mere palace but more concretely a temple, similar to the Temple in which he resides on earth.

---

[20] The translation is not entirely clear: Knibb, *The Ethiopic Book of Enoch*, p. 99, and Nickelsburg, *1 Enoch 1*, p. 257, have just "ice," whereas E. Isaac, "1 (Ethiopic Apocalypse of) Enoch," in *OTP*, vol. 1, p. 21, has "crystal." Milik (in Józef T. Milik, ed., with the collaboration of Matthew Black, *The Books of Enoch: Aramaic Fragments of Qumrân Cave 4* [Oxford: Clarendon Press, 1976], p. 199) reconstructs the Aramaic *zekhukhei* – "crystal-glass."

[21] Nickelsburg, *1 Enoch 1*, p. 264, posits that "the point of comparison is not cold and heat, but brilliance."

[22] Black's remark (*1 Enoch*, p. 149) is therefore misleading.

[23] Pace Black, *1 Enoch*, p. 149, it is not the throne in Ezekiel that is surrounded by fire but the figure seated on the throne.

[24] Himmelfarb, *Ascent to Heaven*, p. 14.

[25] Also, the *ulam* (explicitly mentioned in 1 Kings 6:3), which served as vestibule to the two inner chambers of the Temple, is missing in Enoch's structure – unless one accepts Himmelfarb's suggestion (following the Greek translation; see also Milik, *The Books of Enoch*, p. 195, who translates 1 En. 14:9 "And I entered it until I drew near to the walls *of a building* built with hail-stones") that the "wall" is in reality a building, namely, the missing *ulam* (Himmelfarb, *Ascent to Heaven*, p. 14).

Finally, Enoch sees blazing fire streaming forth from beneath the throne. This graphic detail again has no counterpart in Ezekiel. It is reminiscent, however, of the throne vision in Daniel 7, which displays some striking parallels with our Enoch text: "His [God's] throne was flames of fire; its wheels were blazing fire. A river of fire streamed and came forth from before him/it"[26] (Dan. 7:9 f.). Here we have the throne (albeit not of ice but of fire), the wheels (of fire, which come closer to the sun in Enoch than the chrysolite in Ezekiel), and the river issuing forth from beneath the throne (completely lacking in Ezekiel). But if the imagery of Enoch's vision is, as this parallel suggests, drawn from both Ezekiel and Daniel, we have a chronological problem: the book of Daniel was composed around 165 BCE, during the peak of Hellenization under Antiochus IV Epiphanes (175–163 BCE), hence considerably later than the last quarter of the third century or the first quarter of the second century BCE, the date most scholars assign to the Book of the Watchers. So, either the dating of the Book of the Watchers is incorrect and must be moved closer to the book of Daniel (which is not very likely), or Daniel's vision cannot have influenced Enoch. One obvious solution to this dilemma is to turn the tables and argue that Enoch's vision (in the Aramaic original of the Book of the Watchers or in its literary archetype)[27] influenced Daniel, not the other way around.[28] In any case, the rivers of fire streaming from beneath the throne clearly require the attribution of some kind of interdependent relationship between not only Ezekiel and the Book of the Watchers but also between the Book of the Watchers and Daniel.

Now comes the climax of Enoch's vision:

(20) And the Glory of the Great One[29] sat thereon, and his raiment was brighter than the sun,[30] and whiter than any snow. (21) And no angel was able to enter this house, or to look on his face, by reason of its splendour and glory; and no flesh was able to look at him. (22) A blazing fire encircled him, and a great fire stood in front of him, so that none who surrounded him could draw near to him; ten thousand times ten thousand stood before him. He had no need of counsel; in his every word was a deed. (23) And *the watchers and holy ones*[31] who draw near to him turn not away from him, by night or by day, nor do they depart from him. (24) As for me, till then I had been prostrate on my face, trembling, and the Lord called me with his own mouth and said to me: "Come hither, Enoch, and hear my word." And there came to me one of the holy angels and he raised me up[32] and brought me to the door, and I bowed my face low.

---

[26] The Aramaic *qodamohi* could refer to either God or the throne.

[27] Himmelfarb, *Ascent to Heaven*, p. 17, suspects that the fiery streams originate from ancient traditions of the divine council. I myself am less convinced of this divine council motif in the Book of the Watchers (see below).

[28] Black, *1 Enoch*, pp. 151 f. The other possibility, of course, is a common source; see below, n. 38.

[29] Nickelsburg, *1 Enoch 1*, p. 257: "the Great Glory."

[30] Nickelsburg, ibid., emends the text: "his raiment was like the appearance of the sun."

[31] Nickelsburg, ibid.: "and the holy ones of the watchers."

[32] Nickelsburg, ibid., p. 267, adds: "and stood me (on my feet)."

What Enoch finally sees in the second house is God himself, seated on his throne; the "Glory of the Great One," of course, is the *kevod YHWH* of Ezekiel.[33] Strictly speaking, however, Enoch does not see much of God: the narrative moves immediately from the Glory of the Great One seated on the throne to his garment;[34] otherwise the text only communicates that God is surrounded by blazing fire (v. 22), not unlike Ezekiel's figure on the throne (Ezek. 1:27). The description of God's garment is again reminiscent of Daniel: "As I looked, thrones were set in place, and the Ancient of Days took his seat. His raiment was like white snow, and the hair of his head was like pure wool" (Dan. 7:9). In Ezekiel there is no mention of any particular garment belonging to the figure sitting on the throne (unless one wants to argue that Ezek. 1:27 hints at some kind of robe covering the lower part of God's body), but Enoch and Daniel once again concur that God's garment is shining like white snow (Enoch intensifies the imagery: brighter than the sun and whiter than snow).[35] Martha Himmelfarb has made a convincing case for the whiteness of God's robe being influenced by the plain linen (*bad*) garments worn by the high priest in the earthly Temple as he entered the Holy of Holies (Lev. 16:4). This clearly adds to the Temple imagery and the priestly flavor of the whole scene, which Himmelfarb duly emphasizes – although, strictly speaking, one would expect *Enoch* to be the counterpart of the earthly high priest and accordingly garbed in white clothes, not God.[36]

Whereas Ezekiel was quite elaborate in his description of the human-like figure seated on the chariot, Enoch must content himself with the divine garment; he tells us nothing of God's appearance, and he certainly does not tell us that God resembles a human being (the only hint given of God's human shape is the fact that he wears a robe). To the contrary, he explicitly states that no angel and no flesh was able to look at him – very much in contrast to Ezekiel and yet closer again to the biblical Moses. Moreover, Enoch emphasizes that the angels could not even enter the house in which God's throne was located, though he goes on to say that "ten thousand times ten thousand stood before him" (v. 22). The latter is again similar to the vision of Daniel, who notes – immediately after seeing the river of fire streaming forth from God or the throne – that "thousands upon thousands served him; myriads upon myriads attended him" (Dan. 7:10). The following verse in 1 Enoch (v. 23) makes clear that the angels indeed stand in close attendance to him, that is, in his throne chamber, and not, for example, in the first house in which Enoch is standing and peering through the open door at the inner house. The text displays, therefore, a conspicuous tension between the

---

[33] In the Septuagint *doxa kyriou*. On the phrase "Glory of the Great One" and its Greek equivalents, see Black, *1 Enoch*, pp. 149 f., and Nickelsburg, *1 Enoch 1*, p. 264.

[34] This has also been noticed by Himmelfarb, *Ascent to Heaven*, pp. 16 ff.

[35] This strikingly close parallel makes the problem of the interdependence between 1 Enoch and Daniel all the more critical.

[36] Himmelfarb, *Ascent to Heaven*, ibid.

unambiguous statement that neither human beings nor even angels can enter the inner house and the fact that some angels – actually, quite a large number – do enter it and stand close to God, separated from him only by the fire that surrounds him.[37] Yet there is no ambiguity as to whether or not the angels can see God: there is no hint that any of the angels ever actually looks at him.

Nor is the text very explicit about the precise function of the angels, except for the fact that they surround him but cannot draw near to him because of the blazing fire that "encircles" him (v. 22), and that they never leave him (v. 23). There is no word of the heavenly liturgy, which we would expect in such a setting, and no word of any concrete mission for the angels. On the contrary, it is stated quite unambiguously in the middle of the angels' description that God has "no need of counsel," for "in his every word was a deed" (v. 22). This is odd enough, because it seems to be directed at the angels and to imply that God has no need of the angels, neither for his counsel nor for his actions. The angels in the inner Sanctuary of the heavenly Temple are reduced to mere decoration; at best they shield him (but from what?). The firm rejection of the angels' function as divine counselors is all the more conspicuous if we take into consideration the parallel in Daniel, which – immediately after mentioning the thousands and myriads that serve God – says that "the court took seat and the books were opened" (Dan. 7:10). Here the angels clearly belong to the divine council that takes place in heaven.[38] This idea of the angels as the counselors to God follows a well-established biblical tradition: the prophet Micah's vision of God seated on his throne and surrounded by the host of heaven, for example, depicts a heavenly council at which one of the counselors volunteers to lead the King of Israel to his ruin (1 Kings 22:19–23). Similarly, Satan in the book of Job proposes in the heavenly council to tempt Job and gets God's approval for this experiment (Job 1:6–12, 2:1–6).[39] Hence, in ostentatiously depriving the angels of their traditional role as counselors and messengers, the Book of the Watchers is making a statement against the angels. The heavenly scene that Enoch observes is not God's council with his angels, the result of which is a task handed over to one of the angels or a group of angels;[40] rather, the man Enoch, instead of the angels,

---

[37] This tension has been noticed also by Maxwell J. Davidson, *Angels at Qumran: A Comparative Study of 1 Enoch 1–36, 72–108 and Sectarian Writings from Qumran* (Sheffield, UK: JSOT Press, 1992), p. 58.

[38] Again, it is important to consider the relationship between Daniel and the Book of the Watchers. In this particular case it looks very much as though the Book of the Watchers *answers* Daniel or its *Vorlage* – but if Daniel was here the *Vorlage* for the Book of the Watchers, we get into chronological trouble, since the Book of the Watchers is supposed to be older than Daniel (see above). Therefore, we must assume a common source for both the Book of the Watchers and Daniel or indeed move the Book of the Watchers closer to Daniel, that is, to the second quarter of the second century BCE. Again, the former is much more likely than the latter.

[39] In Isa. 6 (the heavenly throne room) the angels are not depicted as counselors.

[40] Pace Himmelfarb, *Ascent to Heaven*, pp. 13 f.

will become God's messenger and deliver God's judgment to the Watchers on earth (I return to this later).

Enoch's reaction to the grandiose scene that he observes from his place in the first house, peering through the open door of the second house, is again fear and trembling: he is still prostrate on his face, the appropriate position he took up from the moment he entered the outer house (vv. 14, 24). But now God calls him "with his own mouth" and asks him to come closer. What precisely this coming closer means is unequivocally stated in v. 25: one of the angels approaches him – obviously coming from the inner house – stands him on his feet and brings him to the door of the throne chamber. There is no reason to assume that Enoch enters the inner house. He apparently stands now in the entrance door to the throne chamber and listens to God – and the text is at pains to make clear that Enoch listens and does not look: he bows his face down, in order to listen intently to the word of God and not look at him.

The emphasis placed on God's speaking to Enoch "with his own mouth"[41] directs the listener's and reader's attention away from the vision to the following audition (this again is similar to Ezekiel, although Ezekiel saw much more than Enoch). God now begins his long speech – introduced by "Fear not, Enoch, righteous man and scribe of righteousness. Come hither and hearken to my voice" (15:1) – in which he explains to him what to tell the Watchers, who have chosen him to intercede on their behalf. Since the Watchers have defiled themselves with the daughters of men and begotten giants for sons, who are responsible for all the evil on earth, they and their offspring are condemned, and there will be no peace for them forever (16:4). Hence, what in the preceding unit (1 En. 6–11) was the task of the angels, who remained in heaven,[42] is now bestowed on Enoch. Enoch, a human being but elevated among the angels, becomes the mediator between the (fallen) angels and God. To fulfill this task, he must be brought up into heaven and enter the "sanctuary" (*hekhal*) of the heavenly Temple so as to look through the door of the "Holy of Holies" (*qodesh ha-qodashim*), God's throne chamber, and be instructed by the words of God.[43]

With this the narrative of Enoch's vision is completed. The following two units of the Book of the Watchers (1 En. 17–19, and 20–36) recount Enoch's two tours above the surface of the earth and do not return to his vision in heaven. So what, then, is the purpose of the vision? The answer can only be that it is

---

[41] The phrase is reminiscent of what God says to Aaron and Miriam at the entrance to the Tabernacle in the wilderness when he clarifies what Moses' mission is (and what distinguishes him from other human beings): "Not so with my servant Moses; … with him I speak mouth to mouth (*peh el peh*), plainly and not in riddles, and he beholds the likeness of the Lord (*temunat YHWH*, lit. 'the image of the Lord')" (Num. 12:7). As we know from Ex. 33:20, Moses could not see God's face, just some kind of vague "image."

[42] More specifically, Sariel, Raphael, Gabriel, and Michael.

[43] According to Himmelfarb, *Ascent to Heaven*, p. 25, the author combines in Enoch the "three roles of prophet, priest, and scribe."

definitely not an end in itself but firmly embedded in the narrative of the fallen Watchers. Like Ezekiel, to whom God reveals himself on his chariot in the open heavens so as to entrust him with the mission for his fellow-exiles, Enoch ascends to the heavenly Temple so that he might be entrusted with the mission for the fallen angels.[44] I agree therefore with Martha Himmelfarb that there is no point in extracting the vision from the narrative.[45] For what would remain of the vision's purpose if we separated the vision as depicted in the Book of the Watchers from the surrounding narrative? Even if we tried to imagine an earlier version or an *Urtext* of the vision without the narrative provided by the Book of the Watchers, we cannot ignore the fact that the vision culminates in an audition and that the audition inextricably links the vision with the destiny of the Watchers (like Ezekiel's vision, which culminates in an audition about the future destiny of the people of Israel).

In other words, the purpose of both Ezekiel's and Enoch's vision is directed toward the community at large, the community of Israel, not toward the individual; as the subject of the vision, the individual here plays no significant role. Although "overpowered by the hand of the Lord" and probably in an ecstatic mental state, Ezekiel has no particularly personal reaction to what is happening to him: he falls on his face, which is the standard biblical reaction to divine revelations. Enoch is somewhat more preoccupied with his horror and fear, but his reaction, too, climaxes in a prostration. And neither of them gets very close to God. In Ezekiel's case God approaches him and hovers above him on his chariot in the open heavens. Enoch ascends to heaven but only attains to the open door of the heavenly Holy of Holies. Ezekiel sees God, but only vaguely, as a human figure veiled in various manifestations of fire. Enoch sees God's raiment behind a veil of fire. For neither of them is seeing God the purpose of their journey.

Nor is it the individual experience of the visionary. The attempt of some modern scholars to uncover behind the narratives of these early visions the ecstatic experiences of their authors simply misses the point. A prominent example of this trend is Christopher Rowland in his book *The Open Heaven*,[46] whose alleged proof of such ecstatic experiences does not add up to much. The description of the first house as simultaneously hot and cold and inducing the feeling of horror and trembling in Enoch (1 En. 14:13) is explained by Rowland as the "physical result" of Enoch's experience (and standing in for "Enoch," of course, is the anonymous writer who expresses here his "mystical" feelings); Enoch is no longer able to distinguish whether *he* is hot or cold: "one of the symptoms of shock, induced by great fear, is a feeling of cold, which can in certain instances

---

[44] See also Davidson, *Angels at Qumran*, p. 57: "The function of the divine throne in the narrative … is to underscore the authority and reliability of the message the seer is to convey."

[45] Himmelfarb, *Ascent to Heaven*, pp. 103 f.

[46] Christopher Rowland, *The Open Heaven: A Study of Apocalyptic in Judaism and Early Christianity* (London: SPCK, 1982).

manifest itself in the form of a cold sweat. Such symptoms, induced by the fear of what was to come as the seer went further into the heavenly world, may well account for this comment."[47] This pseudopsychological explanation of Enoch's bodily symptoms unfortunately ignores the fact that the text does not describe the reaction of Enoch's body but simply the condition of the house: the *house* is hot and cold because it is composed of hailstones or snow and fire, and there is no reason to assume that this condition of the house is passed on to Enoch's body.

It is true, as Rowland suspects, that the vision in 1 En. 14 does not fit well with chapter 12, according to which Enoch had already been taken up to heaven and was living with the angels. This clearly points to a tension created by the attempt to include Enoch in the story of the Watchers as recounted in 1 En. 6–11. The biblical *Vorlage* compels the conclusion that Enoch did not in fact die but was taken up to heaven and did not return to earth, whereas here he needs to be brought back to earth in order to be able to ascend to heaven to receive his instructions from God. In other words, the story of Enoch's ascent as embedded in the narrative of the Watchers presupposes the existence of an ascent account template, as it were. Since Enoch's ascent is the first such account known to us, we have no access to an earlier story that may have served as a model for Enoch's ascent in the Book of the Watchers. It would be naïve, however, to conclude from this that behind the narrative as we have it in the Book of the Watchers lies the original story of "a man" – presumably, as Rowland insinuates, the author – who personally experienced his ascent to heaven and incorporated it into Enoch's ascent account. Even if Enoch's vision "has been integrated into its present context,"[48] there is no exegetic path leading back to a version – and experience – of a vision independent of the context provided by the Book of the Watchers. Nor is there any basis for reconstructing postexilic "prophetic circles," which laid a claim to the validity of their visionary experience and served as the breeding ground whence the apocalyptic movement grew.[49]

It seems appropriate to conclude this section about the first ascent apocalypse with a few words about the function of the Temple in it. As we have seen, the Temple plays an important role in Ezekiel's vision: defiled by its present occupants, inaccessible to the exiled part of the people, and soon to be destroyed, the earthly Temple can no longer be the proper place for God's Glory. God appears to Ezekiel on earth in his fiery chariot as the God of the universe, transcending the Temple walls, and reveals to him the dimensions and the appearance of the future eschatological Temple. As such, the vision and its message are doubtless a critique of the present Temple on earth.

---

[47] Ibid., p. 232.

[48] Ibid., p. 241.

[49] Ibid., p. 246. See also Himmelfarb's critique of this concept (*Ascent to Heaven*, pp. 110 ff.).

About 400 years after Ezekiel's vision the author of the Book of the Watchers has his hero Enoch ascend to the heavenly Temple. Now the heavens are open not only to show the seer God's chariot tirelessly cruising the celestial realm and observing everything that happens in heaven and on earth, but to lead Enoch to the Temple in heaven and to the divine throne in its Holy of Holies. To be sure, the earthly Temple has been rebuilt – if the dating of the Book of the Watchers to the last quarter of the third century or the first quarter of the second century (hence around 200 BCE) is correct, we are in the heyday of the Second Temple – but it is clearly not Ezekiel's eschatological Temple; rather, it is only a poor copy of the First Temple with the ark and the cherubs, God's visible throne on earth, missing. Although there is a Temple on earth, with its priests and its high priest, the author of the Book of the Watchers nevertheless puts all his energy and creativity into describing the heavenly Temple as the complete and perfect counterpart to the earthly Temple. So the Book of the Watchers must be read as a continuation and updating of Ezekiel's critique of the present Temple under different historical circumstances. It does not postpone the true and perfect Temple to the eschatological future but rather moves it into heaven, where it can be visited and observed, and compared with the deficient earthly Temple.

I would even like to go a step further and posit that Enoch's heavenly Temple can be understood as a devastating critique of the Temple in Jerusalem. It has been argued that the fallen Watchers correspond to the earthly priests and that the charge that the Watchers defiled themselves with human women echoes polemics against the priests of the Second Temple.[50] According to this interpretation, the fallen Watchers are "the counterparts of the polluted priests" on earth;[51] therefore – continuing the argument – the remaining Watchers in heaven are the true priests: the true Temple service has been moved from earth to heaven because of the defilement of the Jerusalem Temple. Moreover, since the goal of Enoch's ascent to the heavenly Temple is to approach God on his throne in the Holy of Holies, his vision could even imply the most pitiless critique, namly, that God in fact can no longer be found in the Temple on earth: the Holy of Holies in the earthly Temple is indeed empty; the missing Ark signals that God is gone, that he has withdrawn himself to his Temple in heaven.

This interpretation is at odds with that of Martha Himmelfarb, who diagnoses only "a milder condemnation of the Jerusalem priesthood in the Book of the watchers" and who wants to place the book in an intermediate stage between Ezekiel and the Qumran literature.[52] It is true that a milder attitude toward the

---

[50] David Suter, "Fallen Angel, Fallen Priest: The Problem of Family Purity in 1 Enoch 6–16," *HUCA* 50 (1979), pp. 115–135; George W.E. Nickelsburg, "Enoch, Levi, and Peter: Recipients of Revelation in Upper Galilee," *JBL* 100 (1981), pp. 575–600; idem, *1 Enoch 1*, pp. 230 f.; Himmelfarb, *Ascent to Heaven*, pp. 21 ff.

[51] Himmelfarb, *Ascent to Heaven*, p. 22.

[52] Ibid.

priests in Jerusalem fits in well with the praise of the high priest sung by the author of the book of Sirach at the beginning of the second century BCE (this is one of Himmelfarb's arguments), and one could add that the sharp and irreconcilable critique that I draw much better suits the period of aggressive Hellenization after 175 BCE. I do not wish to enter here into the problem of dating the Book of the Watchers; however, it may be sufficient to point out that it would be highly contestable to presuppose one and the same attitude toward the priests around 200 BCE. Also, the fact that some Watchers remain in heaven does not inevitably lead to the conclusion that "not all earthly priests are bad," as Himmelfarb suggests.[53] In her version, the fallen Watchers on earth represent the bad priests, and the remaining Watchers in heaven represent the good priests *on earth*. This seems to overstretch the imagery of the Watchers and the two Temples. The fallen Watchers are not defiled priests of the heavenly Temple;[54] rather, they become defiled when they descend to earth. They are originally pure spirits that lusted after the daughters of men and will be condemned forever. Accordingly, when the priests of the Second Temple polluted themselves, they defiled the earthly Temple forever. The Temple in heaven, which Enoch is allowed to see, has become the substitute for the Temple on earth.[55]

The Testament of Levi

The Testament of Levi takes up and intensifies this critique of the Second Temple and its priests. The book is an ascent apocalypse that now belongs to the so-called Testaments of the Twelve Patriarchs, a Christian collection of texts that depends on Jewish sources. The dependency on a Jewish *Vorlage* varies from testament to testament (and is disputed),[56] but in the case of the Testament of Levi there can be no doubt that the present Greek Testament draws on an Aramaic *Vorlage* (which is, however, only partially preserved).[57] This Aramaic Levi

---

[53] Ibid. See now Himmelfarb, "Temple and Priests in the Book of the Watchers, the Animal Apocalypse, and the Apocalypse of Weeks," in Gabriele Boccaccini and John J. Collins, eds., *The Early Enoch Literature* (Leiden: Brill, 2007), pp. 219–235, esp. p. 228.

[54] Himmelfarb, ibid.

[55] This is not to say that I am arguing here and elsewhere that any text talking about the heavenly Temple must ipso facto be against the earthly Temple in Jerusalem and regard it as corrupt. I am aware of the fact that the idea of a heavenly Temple matching an earthly Temple goes back to ancient Near Eastern mythology and that originally it was presumably intended to *validate* the earthly sanctuary (as Philip Alexander reminded me in a private communication). But this does not mean that the idea of a heavenly Temple ipso facto excludes any critique of the earthly sanctuary.

[56] For a brief summary of the relevant scholarship, see Himmelfarb, *Ascent to Heaven*, p. 30.

[57] In fragments from Qumran and one fragment from the Cairo Genizah. See Michael E. Stone, "Aramaic Levi in Its Contexts," *JSQ* 9 (2002), pp. 307–326.

document is dated before the middle of the second century BCE and is attributed to the same circles whence the Book of the Watchers originated. The Greek Testament of Levi is much later, but since the two visions in the Testament of Levi that concern us are attested to in the Aramaic fragments (although, unfortunately, the remaining fragments are too scanty to be of any use for reconstructing the original Aramaic text), it is justifiable to discuss it here, immediately after the Book of the Watchers.

The book recounts the life of Levi, son of Jacob, and begins with the story of vengeance against Shechem, the son of Hamor. According to the Hebrew Bible, Shechem had defiled Dinah, the sister of Jacob's sons; as a consequence, Levi and his brother Simeon took cruel revenge on all the Shechemites (Gen. 34). This cautionary tale against fornication and sexual relations with gentiles becomes the leitmotif of the Testament of Levi: Levi, the hero of the biblical story, is chosen to be the progenitor of all priests and to denounce and condemn the kind of moral corruption of which the future priests will be guilty.

When, after the incident with his sister Dinah, lamenting the sinfulness of the human race, Levi falls asleep, he sees the heavens open (2:6). An angel invites him to ascend, and Levi apparently enters the first three of altogether seven (?) heavens.[58] Standing in the third heaven (?), the angel proclaims that he "shall stand near the Lord," become "his priest," and "shall tell forth his mysteries to men" (2:10). He then briefly explains the contents of the seven (?) heavens and tells him that[59]

> (3:4) in the uppermost heaven of all dwells the Great Glory in the Holy of Holies superior to all holiness. (5) There with him[60] are the archangels, who serve and offer propitiatory sacrifices to the Lord in behalf of all the sins of ignorance of the righteous ones. (6) They present to the Lord a sweet savor,[61] a reasonable and bloodless offering.[62]

The "Great Glory" (*hē doxa hē megalē*) refers back to Ezekiel's *kevod YHWH*,[63] and the precise location of God in the "Holy of Holies" (*qodesh ha-qodashim*) makes it unambiguously clear that he dwells in his heavenly Temple (as in the

---

[58] On the development of the seven heavens schema, see Peter Schäfer, "In Heaven as It Is in Hell: The Cosmology of *Seder Rabbah di-Bereshit*," in Ra'anan S. Boustan and Annette Yoshiko Reed, eds., *Heavenly Realms and Earthly Realities in Late Antique Religions* (Cambridge: Cambridge University Press, 2004), pp. 233–274.

[59] The translation follows H. C. Kee, "Testaments of the Twelve Patriarchs," in *OTP*, vol. 1, pp. 788 ff., and H. W. Hollander and M. de Jonge, *The Testaments of the Twelve Patriarchs: A Commentary* (Leiden: Brill, 1985), pp. 130 ff.

[60] Hollander and de Jonge explain this as another (the sixth) heaven: "In the (heaven) next to it [the highest heaven]. ..."

[61] Kee: "pleasing odor"; Hollander and de Jonge: "pleasant odour."

[62] This is Hollander and de Jonge's translation; Kee has "a rational and bloodless oblation."

[63] The Greek (Septuagint) translation *doxa kyriou* seems to reflect the original phrase; see above.

Book of the Watchers). He is surrounded by (arch)angels who offer expiatory sacrifices on behalf of the righteous. This latter information is new; the angels surrounding God in the Book of the Watchers do not do anything. Here their sacrifices are identified as sacrifices for the righteous only, and they are described as "a sweet savor" and as "reasonable and bloodless."

This juxtaposition of "sweet savor" and "bloodless" has given rise to some discussion among scholars. It has been observed that the "sweet savor" in Greek (*osmē euōdias*) is the Septuagint's standard translation for the Hebrew *reah nihoah*, a "soothing odor" (for example, Gen. 8:21: "The Lord smelled the soothing odor");[64] this is the odor of the burnt offering on the altar, which rises to heaven and soothes God and induces merciful feelings when he smells it. Since the *reah nihoah,* as delicate and fragrant as it might be when it arrives in heaven, presupposes the bloody slaughtering and subsequent burning of an animal, it does not fit in well with "bloodless," as posited in our text. Therefore, some scholars have seen in the angels' "bloodless offering" a certain Christian influence that polemicizes against the bloody sacrifice of the Jews on earth.[65] Against this, Martha Himmelfarb has suggested we read the juxtaposition of the "sweet savor" with the "bloodless offering" as a "further statement of the differences between heavenly and earthly sacrifice": true, the earthly sacrifice is a bloody and cruel matter, but what arrives in heaven is just "the most ethereal product of the sacrifices performed on earth."[66]

I do not think that this separation of the *reah nihoah* in heaven from the bloody sacrifice on earth really works, and so propose a more literal reading of the text: in the heavenly Temple, the angels perform a sacrifice that is radically different from the sacrifice in the earthly Temple. In contrast to the sacrifice on earth, it is bloodless and *therefore* gives off a sweet odor; its odor is truly sweet *because* it is bloodless. Hence, instead of diagnosing a Christian polemic I would argue that we are confronted here again with Jewish polemic against the Second Temple and its service as performed by the Jerusalem priests. The Testament of Levi stands in one line of tradition with the Book of the Watchers and Ezekiel – which, after all, is a very biblical tradition. That this critique of the Jerusalem Temple will live on in Christianity – with its own specific emphases – does not speak against such an interpretation.

Having described to Levi the heavens with their contents, the angel proclaims the divine judgment upon all "sons of men" and the priestly office that will be

---

[64] The JPS translation again smoothes the Hebrew text (and follows the Septuagint) when it translates "The Lord smelled the pleasing odor."

[65] Hollander and de Jonge, *The Testaments of the Twelve Patriarchs*, p. 138.

[66] Himmelfarb, *Ascent to Heaven*, p. 35; eadem, "Earthly Sacrifice and Heavenly Incense: The Law of the Priesthood in *Aramaic Levi* and *Jubilees*," in Boustan and Reed, *Heavenly Realms and Earthly Realities*, pp. 103–122 (esp. p. 121).

given to Levi forever (with clearly eschatological overtones). Then follows Levi's vision of God in the uppermost heaven:

> (5:1) At this moment the angel opened for me the gates of heaven and I saw the holy Temple and the Most High (*ton hypsiston*) upon a throne of glory (*epi thronou doxēs*).[67]
> (2) And he said to me, "Levi, to you I have given the blessings of the priesthood, until I shall come and dwell in the midst of Israel."

This vision is remarkably modest in comparison with Enoch's vision in the Book of the Watchers and Ezekiel's vision at the Chebar canal. As is to be expected, God's place in heaven is identified as a Temple, and it goes without saying that he sits on a throne.[68] But nothing about hosts of angels surrounding him, no fire, no overpowering heavenly scene that elicits in the seer the feelings of horror and fear and to which the appropriate reaction can only be trembling and shaking and falling on one's face. Instead, God tells Levi quite matter-of-factly that he is going to bestow on him the priesthood until one day he himself returns to Israel, obviously to the eschatological Temple. That's all. Immediately after, the angel leads Levi back to earth and instructs him to take action against Shechem. Whether or not the author/editor of the Greek Testament of Levi is to be blamed for this toned-down vision of God (and we might hope for a more elevated version in the Aramaic Levi),[69] Levi's vision is a far cry from what Enoch and Ezekiel have seen. But still, all three visions considered so far coincide in one important aspect: in all of them it is not the vision of God that is the primary goal (and certainly not the visionary's elevated state of mind) but the message conveyed by God during the vision. And in all three cases this message is concerned with the future of the people of Israel, in particular the future of its Temple (and priests). In this latter respect the Testament of Levi is definitely the most radical one, denouncing outright the class of priests that is holding office at the time of its author.

The second vision (ch. 8) describes Levi's investiture and consecration as priest. He is invested with "the robe of priesthood, the crown of righteousness, the breastplate of understanding, the garment of truth, the plate of faith, the turban of (giving) a sign, and the ephod of prophecy" (8:2) and anointed with holy oil (8:4). The locale of this investiture is not mentioned, but it doubtless takes place in heaven again. Nor is there any hint at God's presence. The investiture and consecration is carried out by seven angels, and nothing points to the fact that Levi actually sees God or that God is in any way involved in this scene. The

---

[67] The Greek according to Marinus de Jonge, ed., in cooperation with H. W. Hollander, H. J. de Jonge, and Th. Korteweg, *The Testaments of the Twelve Patriarchs: A Critical Edition of the Greek Text* (Leiden: Brill, 1978), p. 29.

[68] The phrase "throne of glory" (*thronos doxēs*) is strikingly similar to the *kisse ha-kavod* in the Hekhalot literature. But see already Jer. 14:21, 17:12 (*kisse kavod*; Septuagint: *thronos doxēs*) and 1 En. 9:4.

[69] Himmelfarb, *Ascent to Heaven*, p. 32.

angels confirm that from now on the priesthood is given to Levi and all his posterity (8:3) and define the exceptional position of the priests in Israel: "To you and your posterity will be everything desired in Israel, and you shall eat everything attractive to behold, and your posterity will share among themselves the Lord's table. From among them will be priests, judges, and scribes, and by their word the sanctuary will be controlled" (8:16 f.).

Unfortunately, the priesthood in Israel did not live up to the promise of this grandiose beginning, and the reminder of the book is concerned with a history of its gradual decline. Already Levi's grandfather Isaac admonishes him to be "on guard against the spirit of promiscuity,[70] for it is constantly active and through your descendants it is about to defile the sanctuary" (9:9);[71] in particular, he warns him not to take a wife who is "from the race of alien nations" (9:10)[72] – a clear reminiscence of the fate of the Shechemites. In a dramatic speech Levi summarizes what harm his descendants will do to the priesthood; interestingly enough, he maintains that he knows this "from the writings of Enoch" (14:1), drawing a striking parallel between the corruption of the fallen Watchers and the Jerusalemite priests of his time:

> (14:5) You plunder the Lord's offerings; from his share you steal choice parts, contemptuously eating them with whores. (6) You teach the Lord's commands out of greed for gain; married women you profane;[73] you have intercourse with whores and adulteresses. You take gentile women for your wives[74] and your sexual relations will become like Sodom and Gomorrah. (7) You will be inflated with pride over your priesthood, exalting yourselves not merely by human standards but contrary to the commands of God. (8) With contempt and laughter you will deride the sacred things.

The priesthood on earth will be corrupt until finally, at the end of time, God will "raise up a new priest" (18:2), the eschatological priest, whose priesthood will endure forever (18:8). He will inaugurate a period of everlasting peace that will culminate in the restoration of the primordial paradise (18:10). For him, the "heavens will be opened" again, and from the heavenly Temple "sanctification will come upon him (18:6). As I have already noted,[75] this is a remarkable reversal of Ezekiel's open heaven and the subsequent ascent tradition of the Enoch circles. The movement from below to above is reversed again into a movement from above to below: from his place in heaven, obviously the heavenly Temple, God confirms his appointed redeemer, who stays on earth. But the relationship between God and the eschatological priest remains conspicuously vague. No word about the concrete circumstances of the redeemer's appearance: who he

---

[70] De Jonge: "spirit of impurity."
[71] De Jonge: "the holy things."
[72] De Jonge: "of a race of strangers or Gentiles."
[73] De Jonge adds: "defile virgins of Jerusalem."
[74] De Jonge adds: "purifying them with an unlawful purification."
[75] See above, chapter 1, p. 36.

is, where he comes from, and what his relationship is to God. No ascent and no descent, either of God or of the redeemer, and no vision. In stark contrast to the consecration of the first priest Levi, the last priest remains completely impersonal and colorless.

Similitudes of Enoch (1 Enoch 37–71)

Another book that belongs to the Enoch cycle and is firmly embedded in the traditions provided by the Book of the Watchers as well as by Daniel is the so-called Similitudes or Parables of Enoch (1 En. 37–71). It is no doubt of Jewish origin and dated by most scholars to the late first century BCE or even the turn of the era.[76] Presenting a hodgepodge of many earlier traditions, one of its major characteristics is the concern for the figure of the messianic redeemer, called here – drawing on Daniel 7 – the "Son of Man" and the "Chosen" or "Elect One."[77] Enoch is again the human being who ascends to heaven and to whom the heavenly secrets are revealed.

But there is not much left in the Similitudes of the ascent account so graphically described in the Book of the Watchers. We are only told that "at that time clouds and a storm-wind snatched me up from the face of the earth and set me down at the ends of heaven" (1 En. 39:3), a faint echo of the Book of the Watchers' dramatic story (14:8 ff.). Also, there is no mention of the heavenly Temple, let alone of any vision of God (at least not immediately). The Similitudes' concern is with the fate of the righteous after death and Enoch's desire to belong to them. He first sees the dwellings of the righteous with the angels and the "holy ones," among them apparently also the place of the "Elect One" (39:6): "There I desired to dwell and my soul longed for that abode; there had my lot been assigned before" (39:8). Hence, it becomes clear from the very beginning that Enoch's elevation to heaven means his association with the angels; the text does not (yet) state explicitly that he has been transformed into an angel, but it comes close to such an idea. In a response, Enoch bursts out into praising the Lord's name and is deemed worthy of hearing the angels' praise. This alternating praise concludes with Enoch's reaction: "And my countenance was changed until I was unable to look" (39:14). The fear and horror that overwhelmed Enoch at sight of the heavenly Temple (1 En. 14:13 f.) and of God seated on his throne (14:24)

---

[76] George W. E. Nickelsburg, *Jewish Literature between the Bible and the Mishnah* (Philadelphia: Fortress Press, 1981), pp. 221–223; John J. Collins, *The Apocalyptic Imagination: An Introduction to Jewish Apocalyptic Literature*, 2nd ed. (Grand Rapids, MI / Cambridge: William B. Eerdmans, 1998), p. 178, suggests now the early or mid-first century CE.

[77] Apparently derived from the "Servant of the Lord," whom God has "chosen" (*behartikha*) and whom he calls "my chosen one" (*behiri*): Isa. 41:8 f.; 42:1.

in the Book of the Watchers is here prompted by mere sight of the angels who praise God (although he has in fact become one himself).

The long and convoluted chapters that follow alternate between descriptions of the angels, their dwelling places in heaven, the prayers of the righteous, revelations of the secrets of heaven, and the role of the Elect One, who sits on his own throne of glory and whose major task is to execute the divine judgment. To be sure, the actual vision of God does occur, but it is buried under a huge amount of quite chaotic and confusing information and is related rather in passing. The first such vision appears in chapter 46, which suddenly opens:

> (46:1) And there I saw One who had a head of days,
> And his head was white like wool,
> And with him was another, whose countenance had the appearance of a man,
> And his face was full of graciousness, like one of the angels.

There can be no doubt that this vision is modeled along the lines of Daniel 7: the "One who had a head of days"[78] is the "Ancient of Days" in Dan. 7:9; that "his head was white like wool" appropriates Daniel's "and the hair of his head was like pure wool" (ibid.). And, of course, the "another" one who is with him and has the appearance of a man is the "Son of a Man" (*bar enash*), who comes with the clouds of heaven and to whom the Ancient of Days gives "dominion, glory, and kingship" (Dan. 7:13 f.).[79] Closely following Daniel and elaborating on his short description of what transpires in heaven between the "Ancient of Days" and the "Son of Man,"[80] Enoch's vision has as its hero this "Son of Man" – not God, and certainly not Enoch. The purpose of the vision, therefore, is to convey to Enoch the message that history has come to an end: the Son of Man will judge the wicked and vindicate the righteous, who are registered in the "books of the living" (46:4–47:4).[81] For the author of the Similitudes, this elevated "Son of Man" is definitely an angelic figure, not a human being.[82]

The second vision of God is recounted in chapter 60, which solemnly begins:

> (60:1) In the year five hundred, in the seventh month, on the fourteenth (day) of the month in the life of Enoch. ... I saw how a mighty quaking made the heaven of heav-

---

[78] On this translation from Ethiopian, see Black, *1 Enoch*, pp. 192 f.

[79] Interestingly enough, the precise information that this "another" has "the appearance of a man" recalls Ezekiel's "figure with the appearance of a human being (*ke-mar'eh adam*)" (Ezek. 1:26) rather than Daniel's *ke-bar enash*.

[80] Black, *1 Enoch*, p. 192, correctly observes that this Similitudes passage reads like a midrash on Daniel.

[81] 1 En. 47:3 again "quotes" Dan. 7:10: God sits on his throne of glory, the "books of the living" are opened before him, and the angels are his council (note that the angels' counsel was suppressed in the Book of the Watchers; see above, p. 62).

[82] Hence, one of the earliest interpretations of Dan. 7 solves the problem of the identity of the "Son of Man," which in no uncertain terms has occupied scores of scholars. On this problem, see John J. Collins, *Daniel: A Commentary on the Book of Daniel* (Minneapolis, MN: Fortress Press, 1993), pp. 310 ff., 318.

ens to quake, and the host of the Most High, and the angels, thousands upon thousand and myriads upon myriads, were disquieted with a great disquiet. (2) And the Chief of Days sat on the throne of his glory, and the angels and the righteous ones stood around him. (3) And a great trembling seized me, and fear took hold of me, and my loins gave way, and dissolved were my reins, and I fell upon my face.

The scene that so terribly frightens Enoch would appear to be a judgment scene, probably the last judgment. Confirming this is the fact that the righteous are present (as angels!). Enoch is overwhelmed and responds with all the routine signs of trembling, fear, and prostration, but this seems to be less his reaction to the vision of God than to the sight of the punishment that God has in store for the wicked. Moreover, it is highly doubtful that this vision originally belonged to the Enoch cycle: the 500 years by far exceed Enoch's life span of 365 years and would seem to have a greater affinity to his great-grandson Noah, who was 500 years old when he begat Shem, Ham, and Japhet (Gen. 5:32). It has been suggested, therefore, that the vision belongs to a "Noah apocalypse," which was interpolated into the Similitudes.[83]

Finally, the most grandiose vision of God in heaven is reserved for the very last chapter of the Similitudes (ch. 71):[84]

> (71:1) And it came to pass after this that my spirit was translated,
> And I ascended into the heavens:
> And I saw the sons of the holy angels.
> They were treading on flames of fire:
> Their garments were white ...
> And the light of their countenances (shone) like snow.
> (2) And I saw two streams of fire,
> And the light of that fire shone like hyacinth,
> And I fell on my face before the Lord of spirits.

Enoch ascends to heaven and is struck first by sight of the angels – who are the heavenly Watchers known from the Book of the Watchers.[85] Their white garments and the snowlike brightness of their faces are again inspired by Daniel 7,[86] but the imagery of God's garment and hair in Daniel is transferred to the angels: Enoch is apparently more interested in the angels than in God. Accordingly, he prostrates – to be sure, before God, but he has not yet seen God, and

---

[83] See Black, *1 Enoch*, p. 225.

[84] Whatever the precise relationship between chapter 71 and the bulk of the Similitudes is (some scholars regard chapter 71 as a later addition), it seems to me that the links between the surprising revelation at the end and the main part of the book are too close that one can sever chapter 71 from the rest of the book.

[85] Black, *1 Enoch*, pp. 246, 251.

[86] The "two streams of fire" may well refer to the "river of fire" in Dan. 7:10, although the two in number are odd. Equally strange is the hyacinth color of these two streams of fire. Black, *1 Enoch*, p. 251, derives it from the blue color of the sapphire in Ezek. 28:13, but much more likely is the throne of God in Ezek. 1:26, which has the appearance of sapphire.

the text only half-heartedly, or routinely, veils the fact that in reality, Enoch pays his respect to the angels!

After the archangel Michael has shown Enoch all the secrets of the heavens (71:3 f.), he is elevated to the "heaven of heavens," presumably the highest heaven:

> (5) And he [Michael] translated my spirit, and I, Enoch, was in the heaven of
>   heavens,
> And I saw there, in the midst of those luminaries, *a house as it were* built of
>   hailstones,
> And among those hailstones tongues of fire of the *living creatures*.
> (6) And my spirit saw the girdle which was encircling the house with fire;
> On its four sides were streams filled with the fire of the *living creatures*,
> And they girt that house.

Having arrived at the uppermost heaven Enoch sees the house known from the Book of the Watchers; it is built half of ice and half of fire, clearly the first house according to the Book of the Watchers' topography (the *hekhal* of the heavenly Temple). If Black is correct in his assumption that behind the allegedly "un-Semitic" Ethiopic expression "living fire" lie the "living creatures" of Ezekiel,[87] it would have been more appropriate for our author to have embellished his Book of the Watchers *Vorlage* with a greater number of elements from Ezekiel. This jibes with the Similitudes author's obvious fondness for the angels, because subsequent to the living creatures he mentions the seraphim, cherubim, and ophannim (who guard the divine throne), countless angels according to Dan. 7:10, and the four archangels Michael, Raphael, Gabriel, and Phanuel. The text explicitly says that all these angels "go in and out of that house" (71:8): this, together with the following statement that they come from this house and approach Enoch, inclines me to suspect that meant now is the second house from the Book of the Watchers, the Holy of Holies with God's throne:

> (9) And Michael, and Gabriel, Raphael and Phanuel,
> And many holy angels without number,
> Came forth from that house.
> (10) And with them the Chief of Days,
> His head was white and pure as wool,
> And his raiment indescribable.
> (11) And I fell on my face,
> And my whole body became weak from fear,[88]
> And my spirit was transformed;
> And I cried with a loud voice,
> With the spirit of power,
> And blessed and glorified and extolled.

---

[87] Black, *1 Enoch 1*, pp. 246, 251.

[88] E. Isaac, "1 (Ethiopic Apocalypse of) Enoch," in *OTP* 1, p. 50, has "my whole body mollified."

Now the scene changes from what we know from the author's *Vorlage* in the Book of the Watchers: Enoch does not prostrate himself, trembling and shaking at the sight of what he sees, from the open door, in the Holy of Holies of the heavenly Temple; rather, the four archangels, accompanied by countless angels, and God himself approach him, presumably walking to him from the throne chamber in the Holy of Holies to the Sanctuary in which he waits. In looking at the spectacle of this divine procession moving toward him, Enoch falls on his face in horror and fear. Hence, what we encounter here is a kind of reversal of the *Vorlage*, the procession of God and his angels approaching him apparently intending to *honor* the visionary, and his reaction is not only fear but also a feeling of power and of being blessed and extolled.[89] Enoch responds by praising God and finally learns the reason for this extraordinary activity:

(12) And these blessings which went forth out of my mouth were well pleasing before the Chief of Days. (13) And the Chief of Days came with Michael and Gabriel, Raphael and Phanuel, and thousands and myriads of angels without number. (14) And that angel (Michael) came to me and greeted me with his voice and said to me:

"You are the Son of Man who is born for righteousness,
And righteousness abides upon you,
And the righteousness of the Chief of Days forsakes you not."

The climax and ultimate message of Enoch's vision is the discovery that Enoch himself is the Son of Man, the Chosen and Elect One, the epitome of righteousness – in other words, Israel's redeemer/Messiah. This explains his desire to see the dwelling place of the (deceased) righteous, who have since become angels, and to live among them. Enoch, the human being who ascended to heaven, could not remain human but was transformed into an angel. So Israel's redeemer *was* indeed human, but in order to become the redeemer he needed to become an angel. We learn little of how and when this transformation takes place. It obviously occurs when the divine procession approaches him (v. 11), but the text does not elaborate on this. Enoch trembles in anticipation of what is going to happen to him, but the main act of transformation seems to be its announcement by the archangel Michael (v. 14). In any case, with this confirmation of Enoch as the Son of Man the period of everlasting peace dawns:

(15) And he (Michael) said to me:
"He proclaims to you peace in the name of the world to come;
For from hence has proceeded peace since the creation of the world,
And so shall it be to you for ever and for ever and ever.

[89] If Black's translation is correct; E. Isaac's translation, "1 (Ethiopic Apocalypse of) Enoch," p. 50, conveys a much more traditional image: "Then I cried with a great voice by the spirit of power, blessing, glorifying, and extolling."

2 Enoch

The ascent of the seer Enoch to heaven and his transformation into an angel is also the major theme in the so-called Second Book of Enoch (2 Enoch). The book's literary history is more complex – and frustratingly more inextricable – than is the case with most of the Jewish apocalypses pertinent to our subject. For here we are confronted with an unusually wide gap (even for this kind of literature) between the oldest fourteenth-century CE manuscript in Old Slavonic[90] and the original (Greek) work's provenance, presumably from first-century CE Egyptian Judaism.[91]

As with all the texts discussed so far, the affinity to the Book of the Watchers is evident. The major difference between 1 Enoch and 2 Enoch is that the latter makes use of the by then conventional schema of seven heavens (instead of one heaven); the longer of the two preserved recensions even outbids the seven with ten heavens.[92] The text begins with the very moment at which Enoch has reached his biblical age of 365 years (Gen. 5:23); hence, it is obvious that its purpose is to explain the enigma of what happened to Enoch when he "was no more," as intimated in the Bible (Gen. 5:24):[93]

> (1:1) And at that time Enoch said, When 365 years were complete for me, (2) in the first month, on the assigned day of the first month, I was in my house alone, (3) weeping and grieving with my eyes. When I had lain down on my bed, I fell asleep. (4) And two huge men appeared to me, the like of which I had never seen on earth.
>
> (5) Their faces were like the shining sun;
> their eyes were like burning lamps;
> from his mouth[94] (something) like fire was coming forth;
> their clothing was various singing;[95]

---

[90] For greater detail, see F. I. Andersen, "2 (Slavonic Apocalypse of) Enoch," in *OTP*, vol. 1, pp. 91 ff.; André Vaillant, *Le livre des secrets d'Hénoch* (Paris: Institut d'Études Slaves, 1952), pp. III ff., XIII ff.; and Andrei A. Orlov, "God's Face in the Enochic Tradition," in DeConick, *Paradise Now*, p. 181, with n. 6.

[91] Martha Himmelfarb has made a strong case for a Jewish author from first-century Alexandria, before the destruction of the Second Temple (*Ascent to Heaven*, pp. 38, 43, 85 f.). Andersen is much more cautious but sees some resemblance to Philo's Therapeutae ("2 [Slavonic Apocalypse of] Enoch," p. 96), which coincides with Himmelfarb's observation of certain similarities between 2 Enoch and Philo.

[92] On this, see Schäfer, "In Heaven as It Is in Hell," pp. 253 ff.

[93] If not otherwise indicated, all quotations are from Andersen's translation of the shorter version; the division of the text into chapters also follows Andersen.

[94] Longer version: "from their mouths."

[95] Andersen, "2 (Slavonic Apocalypse of) Enoch," pp. 106 f., n. m, here regards the text as "incorrigibly corrupt," but the poetic personification of attire and objects of the heavenly equipment is common in both the Qumran and the Hekhalot literature.

their arms were like wings of gold[96] –
at the head of my bed.[97]

And they called me by my name. (6) I got up from my sleep, and the men were standing with me in actuality. (7) Then I hurried and stood up and bowed down to them; and the appearance of my face was glittering because of fear.[98]

Here the story begins on earth, and the angels descend to earth to inform Enoch what will happen to him (at first in his dream, and then in reality). So, unlike the vision in the Book of the Watchers (in which Enoch is immediately lifted up to heaven), Enoch's first encounter with the heavenly world occurs on earth (and, as in the Similitudes, initially with angels and not immediately with God). Moreover, again as in the Similitudes, the appearance of these angels is described in images that were originally reserved for God: brightness of their faces, and snowlike whiteness – this time not of their garments but of their hands. And already it is the sight of these angels that frightens him to death: when they waken him from his sleep and he realizes they are real, he displays all the expected signs of fear usually reserved for God and prostrates. The angels calm him and explain that they are emissaries of God and that Enoch will ascend with them to heaven (1:8). No doubt, the role of the angels becomes ever more important. Now they descend to earth, proclaim to the seer his imminent ascent to heaven, and escort him during his journey through the various heavens.

This journey is described in tiresome detail. The angels take him to every single heaven of the seven heavens and show him what each contains (for example, the punishment of the fallen Watchers in the second, paradise and hell in the third, the mournful Watchers in the fifth, and the seven archangels in the sixth heaven). Finally, he arrives at the seventh heaven:[99]

(20:1) And those men lifted me up from there, and they carried me up to the 7th heaven. And I saw there an exceptionally great light, and all the fiery armies of the great archangels, and the incorporeal forces and the dominions and the origins and the authorities, the cherubim and the seraphim and the many-eyed thrones; (and) 5 regiments and the shining *otanim*[100] stations. And I was terrified, and I trembled with a great fear. (2) And those men picked me up and led me into their midst. And they said to me, "Be brave, Enoch! Don't be frightened!" (3) And they showed (me) the Lord, from a distance, sitting on his exceedingly high throne.

---

[96] The longer version has the more meaningful: "their wings were more glistering than gold; their hands were whiter than snow."
[97] Longer version: "And they stood at the head of my bed."
[98] Longer version: "and I was terrified; and the appearance of my face was changed because of fear."
[99] I quote now the longer version.
[100] In almost all the Slavonic manuscripts corrupt for *ofannim*; see Andersen, "2 (Slavonic Apocalypse of) Enoch," pp. 134f., n. b.

At first Enoch is frightened again by the sight of the heavenly hosts in all their manifestations and ranks known to us from the Hebrew Bible and the subsequent literature (note the "many-eyed thrones," which obviously are transformations of the eyes on the rims of the wheels in Ezek. 1:18, or the *otanim = ofannim*, which are the wheels of the divine chariot in Ezekiel and later became a class of angels all their own). The angels calm him and show him God seated on his throne, but still from a distance. In the longer recension this is the distance between the seventh heaven, where Enoch is located, and the tenth heaven, where God resides (explicitly called *'Aravot*);[101] in the shorter recension all this takes place in the seventh heaven.

Enoch sees, still from a distance, the ever-present angels surrounding the divine throne and hears the cherubim and seraphim singing the *trishagion* of Isa. 6:3 (ch. 21). The angels serving as his guide now tell him they must leave and, terrified, Enoch prostrates again: "And the men went away from me, and from then on I did not see them anymore. But I, I remained alone at the edge of the seventh heaven. And I became terrified; and I fell on my face, and I said in myself, 'Woe to me! What has happened to me?'" (21:2). This second prostration (following the first one when he recognizes the angels sent to him on earth) is in response to the departure of the angels guiding him through the seven heavens. Hence, Enoch prostrates twice before the angels, not (yet) before God, a fact that undoubtedly highlights the importance of the angels in 2 Enoch.[102] Now God sends the archangel Gabriel to bring him before God, but Enoch, in some odd delaying tactics, asks for the return of the angels who had just left him. Interestingly enough, and again underscoring the prominence of the angels in 2 Enoch, Enoch addresses Gabriel as follows: "Woe to me, *my Lord!*" (21:4) – that is, by the title generally reserved for God.[103] Gabriel ignores Enoch's delaying tactics and carries him up "like a leaf carried up by the wind. He moved me along and put me down in front of the face of the Lord" (21:5). Enoch has arrived at his destination in the seventh heaven (shorter recension) or the tenth heaven (longer recension):

(22:1) And on the 10th heaven, Aravoth, I saw the view of the face of the Lord, like iron made burning hot in a fire and brought out, and it emits sparks and is incandes-

---

[101] The word *'aravot* is biblical and used for a desert or steppe, but a phrase like "He [God] who rides *'aravot*" (Ps. 68:5) is usually explained as God riding on the clouds of heaven. In the Hekhalot literature *'aravot* becomes the *terminus technicus* for the uppermost (seventh) heaven, the full name of which is *'arevot raqia'*, namely, the (seventh) heaven, which is called *'aravot*; see Schäfer, "In Heaven as It Is in Hell," p. 272.

[102] To be sure, "the intensity of Enoch's fear at being left without his guides serves to emphasize the magnitude of what takes place next" (namely the vision of God himself), as Himmelfarb, *Ascent to Heaven*, p. 40, argues, but it is more than just this: it also serves to emphasize the significance of the angels.

[103] As has also been noticed by Andersen, "2 (Slavonic Apocalypse of) Enoch," p. 136, n. h.

cent. Thus even I saw the face of the Lord. But the face of the Lord is not to be talked about, it is so very marvellous and supremely awesome and supremely frightening. (2) And who am I to give an account of the incomprehensible being of the Lord, and of his face, so extremely strange and indescribable? And how many are his commands, and his multiple voice, and the Lord's throne, supremely great and not made by hands, and the choir stalls all around him, the cherubim and the seraphim armies, and their never-silent singing. (3) Who can give an account of his beautiful appearance, never changing and indescribable, and his great glory? (4) And I fell down flat and did obeisance to the Lord.

The vision's climax – the description of God sitting on his throne – has finally been attained. It begins with Enoch seeing not just God but, most concretely, God's face. This is a deliberate departure from – or rather a well-considered objection to – the biblical principle, "But you cannot see my face (*et-panai*), for man (*adam*) may not see me and live" (Ex. 33:20). True, the author of our apocalypse argues, Moses could not see God's face, but in contrast to Moses, the antediluvian hero Enoch could see God's face. So, according to our vision, the biblical statement needs to be qualified: the man Moses may not see God and live; however, the man Enoch, who will soon be transformed into an angel, may indeed see God and live. Enoch, therefore, is greater than Moses.[104]

Yet we do not learn much about the physical shape of God's face, only that it looks like white-hot iron – quite a prosaic image for the brightness of God's face. We know, since Ezekiel, that fire imagery is the most common metaphor used to describe the figure of God, but to compare God's face with a fiery piece of iron is not particularly imaginative. The image of ironworks is intensified yet more by the sparks that the iron emits; one can hardly avoid the mental picture of heated iron struck by an ironworker to give it shape – not the most flattering image for God's face. The short recension, to be sure, contains nothing of this. It contents itself with telling us, almost laconically, that Enoch "saw the Lord" and that his face was "strong and very glorious" (22:1).[105]

Immediately after this bizarre climax comes the anticlimax. It is not that Enoch is incapable of grasping just *what* he saw but that he was deemed *worthy* of seeing God's face. In other words, immediately after reporting the fact

---

[104] Orlov, "God's Face," p. 187, draws the opposite conclusion. He reads Ex. 33 in the light of 2 Enoch and suggests that in fact, "the Exodus account implicitly asserts that Moses could see the divine form." It is one thing to argue (following Moshe Weinfeld) that "the warning about the danger of seeing the Deity usually affirms the possibility of such an experience" – a proposition that certainly makes sense – and another thing to conclude therefrom an affinity between Ex. 33 and 2 Enoch on the basis of some Mesopotamian parallels. The message of Ex. 33 is that "man" cannot see God's face, possible earlier layers of this text and implicit polemics notwithstanding, and the message of 2 Enoch is that Enoch may see God's face.

[105] Andersen, "2 (Slavonic Apocalypse of) Enoch," pp. 136 f., n. c, points out that the Slavonic manuscripts betray "the embarrassment of scribes over this attempt to describe the appearance of the Lord." He believes that the comparison of God's face with hot iron is original and was heavily censored in the short manuscripts.

of Enoch's seeing God's face, the author of our apocalypse begins reflecting on this marvel. He starts by "humbly" pointing out that "even" he, Enoch, saw the face of the Lord, certainly knowing quite well that Enoch is the first (and only?) human being ever to be granted this privilege. And then he caps it all by stating there is no way of communicating what he saw because in fact the face is indescribable. He soon resorts to enumerating the traditional inventory of the seventh heaven (for example, the divine throne, the incessantly singing cherubim and seraphim, the choir stalls – the latter, however, seeming to owe their appearance here to the structure of a medieval monastery rather than to that of a heavenly throne chamber), and finally decides to react to the vision of God with the customary prostration. But God is not yet finished with him:

> (22:5) And the Lord, with his own mouth, said to me, "Be brave, Enoch! Stand up, and stand in front of my face forever." (6) And Michael, the Lord's archistratig,[106] lifted me up and brought me in front of the face of the Lord. And the Lord said to his servants, sounding them out, "Let Enoch join in and stand in front of my face forever!" (7) And the Lord's glorious ones did obeisance and said, "Let Enoch yield in accordance with your word, O Lord!"

That God speaks to Enoch "with his own mouth" is an obvious reference to the Book of the Watchers (1 En. 14:24), where God calls Enoch "with his own mouth" from the heavenly Holy of Holies, and there it is also an angel (although not Michael) who brings him to the door that leads to the divine throne chamber. But whereas in the Book of the Watchers Enoch does not enter the throne chamber, here he is ushered directly before God's face, in immediate physical proximity to God. Moreover, quite unlike in the Book of the Watchers, which stresses that God "had no need of counsel" (14:22), our author has God consult his heavenly assembly, asking and at the same time commanding the angels to let Enoch join their ranks and stand before God forever. This no doubt is the message of Enoch's vision of God: that he is chosen to become one of the angels.[107] The strange "conversation" between God and his angels – the question that is actually a command, and the angels' vaguely reluctant obedience – is reminiscent of the rabbinic interpretation of Gen. 1:26, which understands the biblical verse as God's question to the angels ("Shall we make man in our image, after our

---

[106] A Slavonic military title not translated by Andersen; it is obviously derived from Greek *archistrategos*, "commander in chief."

[107] But I do not think that Enoch's angelification is the direct result of his vision, as Andrew Chester has suggested (*Messiah and Exaltation: Jewish Messianic and Visionary Traditions and New Testament Christology* [Tübingen: Mohr Siebeck, 2007], p. 67), nor do I believe that God's invitation to Enoch to stand before his face "forever" should be taken too literally (ibid.); after all, Enoch must return to earth and will resume his heavenly existence only later. Chester, in his monumental book, has collected anew all kinds of the evidence from Second Temple literature related to the transformation of human beings, with a view to the question of an evolving Christology. Extremely useful as his survey is, my approach differs in that it is interested in the full context of the phenomenon and not in isolated quotations.

likeness?").[108] Whereas according to the rabbinic literature most angels object to God's request and argue against man's creation,[109] here the angels immediately obey and accept Enoch as one of them.[110] What yet remains is his physical transformation into an angel:

> (22:8) And the Lord said to Michael, "Go, and extract Enoch from his earthly clothing. And anoint him with my delightful oil, and put him into the clothes of my glory." (9) And so Michael did, just as the Lord had said to him. He anointed me and he clothed me. And the appearance of that oil is greater than the greatest light, and its ointment is like sweet dew, and its fragrance myrrh; and it is like the rays of the glittering sun. (10) And I looked at myself, and I had become like one of the glorious ones, and there was no observable difference.

The closest parallel to Enoch's transformation is Levi's consecration as priest.[111] But even if Enoch's anointing and clothing suggests that he is consecrated a priest as well,[112] the priestly connotation here is much less prominent than in the Testament of Levi. Like Levi, who is first clothed and then anointed, Enoch receives his new clothes before his anointment.[113] However, whereas Levi is clothed in the full regalia of the high priest, Enoch's clothes play no significant role; they are "just" the clothes of God's glory (and not necessarily of the priesthood). Moreover, whereas in the Testament of Levi the anointment is mentioned only in passing, here it has become the most important element of the transformation and is described in highly elevated prose: not only is the ointment like sweet dew (a comparison not found in the Bible) and its fragrance myrrh (this is biblical, the myrrh being one of the spices in the sacred anointing oil for the consecration of the Tabernacle and Aaron and his sons),[114] the oil also shines as brightly as the sun. Here the oil seems to invest Enoch with a quality usually reserved for the appearance of God and the angels; through the holy oil and the appropriate clothes he becomes one of the "glorious ones" – or, more precisely, he is physically transformed into one of the highest angels, which serve in the uppermost (seventh or tenth) heaven.

That the oil has a particularly transformative effect in particular on Enoch's face and makes it "incandescent," like God's face (22:1), is confirmed later

---

[108] Because of the plural *na'aseh*, commonly translated as "Let us make man," but the rabbis had a problem with this divine plural and interpreted it as a question directed at the angels.

[109] Schäfer, *Rivalität*, pp. 75 ff.

[110] Some of the Slavonic manuscripts still disclose the rabbinic opposition of the angels to the creation of man; see Andersen, "2 (Slavonic Apocalypse of) Enoch," p. 138, n. l, who was unaware of this background. Also, in the much later (and "rabbinized") 3 Enoch, the angels need some divine "persuasion" to accept God's command; see below, pp. 319 ff.

[111] See above, p. 70.

[112] Himmelfarb, *Ascent to Heaven*, p. 40.

[113] Himmelfarb, ibid., observes that the sequence in both the Testament of Levi and 2 Enoch of (1) clothing and (2) anointing is in striking contrast to the biblical instructions for the consecration of Aaron as high priest (Ex. 29).

[114] Ex. 30:22–29.

in the apocalypse when God commands Enoch to descend to earth once more and impart knowledge to his sons and grandchildren. God entrusts an angel to physically chill his face, for "if your face had not been chilled here [in heaven], no human being would be able to look at your face" (37:2). Enoch is no longer human, at least in the fullest sense of the word, and accordingly requires no food. During his stay on earth, when his son Methuselah prepares him food, Enoch explains to him: "Listen child! Since the time when the Lord anointed me with the ointment of his glory, food has not come into me, and earthly pleasure my soul does not remember; nor do I desire anything earthly" (56:2).

Hence, in order to attain the closest possible proximity to God, Enoch needs to be transformed into an angel of highest rank. It is the sacred oil in particular that has the desired effect; the clothes of God's glory, in which he is dressed following the anointment, complete the transformation. The oil causes his face to shine like the faces of the angels, which in turn shine like the face of God. That there is a full physical transformation and that Enoch not only *looks* like the angels is confirmed by the almost surprised final statement: "and there was no observable difference." Enoch *is* an angel, in the full sense of the word. But still the text remains conspicuously vague with regard to the question of how this transformation affects his body. To be sure, he ascended into heaven with his body, but it is not entirely clear whether or not he keeps it.[115] If we take literally his being stripped of his earthly clothes and subsequently being invested with new heavenly garb, one might assume that he remains in his body and just receives new clothes. But the old and new "clothes" may well be referring to two completely different states of existence, one human with a human body and the other angelic with no human body. However, since Enoch must return to earth for a period of thirty days in order to teach his sons (chs. 36 ff.), he apparently keeps his body or else returns to his body for a limited time. Nevertheless, even during this new earthly existence, he no longer needs food, as we have just seen. It would seem, therefore, that the text here is not fully consistent or that the different manuscript traditions reflect different attitudes or at least a certain ambiguity with regard to the question of Enoch's bodily transformation. Obviously, 2 Enoch is in the process of a complete bodily transformation of its hero; but it may not yet have fully grasped the consequences and implications of such an idea. One thing, however, remains clear: as close as Enoch comes to God, he does not become like God, let alone enter into some kind of union with him. Enoch and God remain distinct, as distinct as God and his angels.

---

[115] See the discussion in Andersen, "2 (Slavonic Apocalypse of) Enoch," pp. 138 f. (n. l–q). Philip Alexander is convinced that the Enoch of 2 Enoch definitely ascended bodily to heaven; see his "From Son of Adam to Second God: Transformations of the Biblical Enoch," in Michael E. Stone and Theodore A. Bergren, eds., *Biblical Figures Outside the Bible* (Harrisville, PA: Trinity Press International, 1998), p. 104.

To sum up, Enoch in the Book of the Watchers is the first human being to experience fully a heavenly ascent. Remarkably, it is not Elijah, the other biblical figure who was mysteriously taken up into heaven (2 Kings 2:11), who has been chosen for this task but the antediluvian hero Enoch. With this ascent he attains to the entrance of the Holy of Holies of the heavenly Temple, where God resides on his lofty throne. Yet the goal of his ascent is not a vision of God – in fact, Enoch does not see all that much of God (less than Ezekiel) and must content himself with the divine garment – but, as in Ezekiel, an audition: God has chosen him as his divine messenger to convey his judgment to the fallen Watchers – and, on a higher level, to convey to the community of Israel his critique of the earthly Temple. Enoch as an individual plays no particular role. He acts as God's tool – nothing more, nothing less. Accordingly, the author of the book is not concerned about Enoch's individual experience and state of mind; any attempt to read the vision as an account of Enoch's or even the author's (or circle of authors') ecstatic experience is misguided and imposes categories on the text that are alien to it.

The same is true for the (much less vivid) vision of Levi in the Testament of Levi: the primary goal of the narrative is not a description of the vision, let alone of the visionary's mental state, but the future of the people of Israel, more precisely of the Temple and its priests. Ultimately, Israel will be redeemed by an eschatological priest whose priesthood will endure forever.

In the Similitudes, certain new elements are added. First, the importance of the angels increases: they are invested with insignia (garments, brightness, fire) that are typically reserved for God. Second, the importance of the visionary increases: instead of standing (or rather falling down) horrified at the entrance of the Holy of Holies and surreptitiously peeking at God on his throne, God and his angels set out to move toward him and greet him as the Son of Man, that is, as Israel's redeemer. To reach this stage, Enoch needs to be physically transformed into an angel. The Similitudes are still rather vague about this process, but a first step in this direction is taken.

Both these characteristics are reinforced in 2 Enoch. There, Enoch even prostrates before the angels until he finally attains to God in the seventh (or tenth) heaven; and he is fully and quite graphically transformed into an angel with "no observable difference." Yet, to be sure, he becomes an angel and as such remains entirely within the framework and nomenclature of the Hebrew Bible: in order to approach God as closely as he does, he cannot and must not remain a human being; although, strictly speaking, his transformation is achieved through his new clothes and the oil with which he is anointed – there is no unambiguous mention of his *bodily* transformation[116] (unless one chooses to understand the

---

[116] Which becomes so important in 3 Enoch; see below, p. 320.

removal of his "earthly clothing" as signifying the transformation of his body as well). In any case, his transformation has nothing to do with an attempt to express some kind of physical union with God.

Chapter 3

Enoch's Companions

From the Community to the Individual

One of the major motivating forces behind the visions of Ezekiel and the earlier circle around the antediluvian hero Enoch is anxiety about the future destiny of the Temple as the center of Israel. Expecting the immediate destruction of the earthly Temple, Ezekiel sees God on his chariot-throne roaming through the cosmos and, in response, designs the model of the future Temple; the Book of the Watchers has Enoch ascend to heaven and observe the true and perfect Temple service in heaven; and the Testament of Levi uses Levi's investiture and consecration as priest in heaven as a way of denouncing the corrupt priests on earth. This Temple-critical motif recedes in the Similitudes and 2 Enoch, but still, in both apocalypses heaven is modeled after the Temple, and concern for the fate of Israel remains dominant. Moreover, both apocalypses include an additional element that was alien to the earlier works: the transformation of the visionary into an angel. The Similitudes retell Enoch's ascent in the Book of the Watchers in order to transform him into an angel and identify him with Israel's ultimate redeemer; 2 Enoch likewise transforms Enoch into an angel of the highest rank to reveal to him the future history and all the marvels of heaven. It is only through the emphasis placed on the motif of the ascending hero's righteousness – in the Similitudes, in particular, Enoch is presented as the paragon of righteousness – that we can guess at the emerging concern for the destiny of the individual who undertakes the heavenly journey.

The apocalypses discussed in this chapter continue along the route established by their predecessors, Ezekiel and the Enoch circle, but with a growing emphasis on the individualistic element. My survey includes the Apocalypse of Abraham, the Ascension of Isaiah, the Apocalypse of Zephaniah, and the Apocalypse of John, all of which originated around the end of the first or the beginning of the second century CE.

Apocalypse of Abraham

The Apocalypse of Abraham still follows the older Temple-critical tradition and shows no sign of any shift toward the individual (it also lacks the explicit physical transformation so prominent in the Similitudes and 2 Enoch, as well as in some of the other apocalypses to be discussed). Like 2 Enoch, the Apocalypse of Abraham is preserved in an Old Slavonic translation only, the manuscripts dating from the fourteenth to the seventeenth centuries. Its original language is Hebrew and it was probably composed in Palestine sometime after 70 CE, because the destruction of the Temple is mentioned (ch. 27).[1] Despite some Christian interpolation (ch. 29), the Jewish provenance of the work seems very likely.[2]

The apocalypse begins with Abraham living as a boy in his father Terah's house in Ur in Mesopotamia. The Hebrew Bible does not tell us much about this early period in Abraham's (or rather Abram's) life, only that he had two brothers, one of whom died during the lifetime of Terah while still in Ur; that Abram and his remaining brother took wives; and that Abram's wife Sarai was barren (Gen. 11:26–29). Following this rather meager information we learn that Terah, together with his son Abram, his daughter-in-law Sarai, and his grandson Lot (the son of the deceased son), left Ur for the land of Canaan. The postbiblical Jewish tradition, however, knows much more about Abraham's childhood in Ur. The Apocalypse of Abraham[3] recounts the long story of Abraham's encounter with his father Terah's idols, his gradual discovery of the vanity of idolatry, and his desperate search for the one true God. After a dramatic prayer to this still unknown God, he hears the "voice of the Mighty One" coming down from heaven and identifying himself as the "God, the Creator" whom Abraham seeks (8:1–3). He orders Abraham to leave his father's house because it will soon be burned down.

The "voice" continues to speak to Abraham (ch. 9), and what it says is modeled on Gen. 15, the so-called covenant between the pieces. In fact, the entire narrative in the Apocalypse of Abraham is a graphic dramatization of the enigmatic phrase that opens Gen. 15: "the *word* of the Lord came to Abram in a vision (*ba-mahazeh*)," with its apparent tension between the spoken word and the seen vision, in other words, between an audition and a vision. In the Bible, Abram hears God speaking to him but does not see him; this audition, however, is accompanied by certain visual elements (the stars in heaven, the smoking oven, the flaming torch passing between the pieces). Likewise, in the Apocalypse of Abraham the seer only hears God, who nevertheless promises him that he "will see great things, which you have not seen" (9:6; see also v. 9).[4] The vi-

---

[1] Ryszard Rubinkiewicz, "Apocalypse of Abraham," in *OTP*, vol. 1, pp. 681 ff.

[2] A. Pennington, "The Apocalypse of Abraham," in H. F. D. Sparks, *The Apocryphal Old Testament* (Oxford: Clarendon Press, 1984), p. 365.

[3] For parallels in the rabbinic and related literature see Louis Ginzberg, *Legends of the Jews*, vol. 1, (Philadelphia: Jewish Publication Society, 1909, repr. 1947), pp. 209 ff.; G. H. Box with J. I. Landsman, *The Apocalypse of Abraham* (London: SPCK, 1919), Appendix 1, pp. 88–94.

[4] If not indicated otherwise, all quotations are from Rubinkiewicz, "Apocalypse of Abraham," in *OTP*, vol. 1, pp. 689 ff.

sion, which is only intimated in Genesis, finally materializes in the Apocalypse of Abraham.

The first and most startling step in this materialization is the sudden appearance of the angel Iaoel. After Abraham has responded to the voice of God with the appropriate prostration (10:2: "And my spirit was amazed, and my soul fled from me. And I became like a stone, and fell face down upon the earth, for there was no longer strength in me to stand up on the earth"), he hears God commanding the angel Iaoel to "consecrate"[5] Abraham and to "strengthen him against his trembling" (10:3). Iaoel does as commanded, strengthens Abraham, and tells him that he will accompany him to the highest heaven to meet God (10:8 f.). This is routine. But what goes far beyond the usual pattern of the angel(s) coming down to earth and leading the seer up through the seven heavens is the identity of the angel Iaoel. First of all, Iaoel's name is explicitly identified as the "same name,"[6] that is, the same name as God's name (10:3) – which is certainly correct, because "Iao" is the Greek equivalent of the Hebrew Tetragrammaton YHWH[7] and the ending "-el" (literally "God") the customary theophoric ending of many Hebrew names; hence, the name of God is represented twice in the angel's name Iaoel. This close relationship between God and his angel Iaoel, as indicated by the angel's name, is further emphasized by the fact that God commands Iaoel to "consecrate" Abraham "through the mediation of my ineffable name" (10:3): Iaoel bears God's name, and it is this name that empowers him. Finally, and most important, Iaoel is from the very beginning of his encounter with Abraham described as someone who appears to him "in the likeness of a man" (10:4). This, of course, is a direct allusion to the figure "in the likeness of a man" (*ke-mar'eh adam*) sitting on the throne above the expanse above the heads of the four creatures in Ezekiel's vision (Ezek. 1:26). God's angel Iaoel, who bears his name, in fact looks like God![8] This surprising aspect climaxes in the following more precise description of the angel:

> (11:1) And I stood up and saw him [Iaoel] who had taken my right hand and set me on my feet. (2) The appearance of his body was like sapphire, and the aspect of his face was like chrysolite, and the hair of his head like snow. (3) And a *kidaris*[9] (was) on his

---

[5] Pennington, "Apocalypse of Abraham," p. 376, translates "sanctify."

[6] Only in Rubinkiewicz's translation.

[7] See Peter Schäfer, *Judeophobia: Attitudes toward the Jews in the Ancient World* (Cambridge, MA: Harvard University Press, 1997), p. 52, with n. 128 (p. 232).

[8] The text may also allude to the *ke-var-enash* ("like a human being" in Dan. 7:13, traditionally "misunderstood" as "like a Son of a Man"), but the continuation makes clear that it has Ezekiel in mind rather than Daniel.

[9] Pennington, "Apocalypse of Abraham," p. 377, translates: "and *there was* a linen band about his head." Rubinkiewicz, "Apocalypse of Abraham," p. 694, n. b, refers to the Septuagint's use of the Greek *kidaris* for "headdress" (Ex. 28:39, 39:28), "turban" (Zech. 3:5), and "cap" (Ezek. 44:18).

head, its look that of a rainbow, and the clothing of his garments (was) purple; and a golden staff[10] (was) in his right hand.

Iaoel's sapphire-like body no doubt references the throne on which God is seated in Ezekiel (1:26): "Above the expanse that was over their heads was the shape (*demut*) of a throne with the appearance (*ke-mar'eh*) of sapphire-stone," which, as we have seen, recalls the "sapphire-brick" in Ex. 24:10 under God's feet in heaven.[11] The appearance of his face like chrysolite is reminiscent of the wheels of Ezekiel's chariot (1:16), which were like chrysolite (*tarshish*), and the snowlike color of the angel's hair refers to God's hair in Dan. 7:9. Iaoel's clothes combine priestly and royal elements: the headdress resembles Aaron's turban, and the staff may well refer to Aaron's rod in the story of the confrontation with the pharaoh (Ex. 7:9, 19 f.; 8:1, 12), as has been suggested by Himmelfarb.[12] The purple color of his garments, however, would seem to allude to royal rather than priestly attire, and the staff may as well be a scepter. Hence, I do not wish to overstress the priestly connotations. The rainbow, again, may indeed be part of the scene's priestly connotations,[13] but we should not forget that the "bow in the clouds" was also used to describe the fiery radiance surrounding God on his throne in Ezekiel (1:28). The rainbow, therefore, is also associated with God, and it is hardly accidental that in Genesis it seals the covenant with Noah (Gen. 9:12), the renewed covenant with Adam's offspring, survivor of the deluge.

Following the biblical *Vorlage* of Gen. 15, Abraham must now prepare a sacrifice for God. The prescribed sacrificial animals are those listed in Gen. 15:9 (Apocalypse of Abraham 9:5 and 12:6), but, in contrast to its *Vorlage*, the apocalypse knows the precise location where the sacrifice takes place: it is Mount Horeb (= Sinai), which Abraham and the angel reach after a journey of forty days. Hence, Abraham is identified with Moses, and his sacrifice and subsequent ascent to heaven reenacts (or rather prefigures) Moses's ascent to Mount Sinai. As prescribed in the Bible, Abraham slaughters the animals and cuts them into halves, with the exception of the birds (Gen. 15:10; Apocalypse of Abraham 12:8). Whereas the Bible gives no reason for the different treatment of the birds, our apocalypse comes up with a quite surprising rationale: their wings will be used for Abraham's and the angel's impending ascent to heaven. More concretely, they are not part of the sacrifice to God but are to be given to the angel as tools in their ascent: "The turtledove and the pigeon you will give to me [Iaoel], for I will ascend on the wings of the birds to show you (what) is in the heavens, on the earth and in the sea, in the abyss, and in the lower depths, in

---

[10] Rubinkiewicz, ibid., n. c, also suggests "scepter."

[11] Pennington, "Apocalypse of Abraham," p. 377, n. 1, mentions two manuscripts that have only his feet being like sapphire.

[12] Himmelfarb, *Ascent to Heaven*, p. 62.

[13] Ibid.

the garden of Eden and in its rivers, in the fullness of the universe" (Apocalypse of Abraham 12:10).

The brief biblical note that "birds of prey came down upon the carcasses, and Abraham drove them away" (Gen. 15:11) is expanded into a longer narrative about Azazel's attempt to intervene and Abraham's success in fending him off (ch. 13 f.); this might allude to the story of the fallen Watchers. Then the biblical "smoking oven" and "flaming torch" passing between the pieces (Gen. 15:17) are transformed respectively into a "smoke like that of a furnace" and angels, who take the divided pieces and ascend with them from the top of the smoking furnace to heaven (Apocalypse of Abraham 15:1) – obviously so as to bring them before God. Now, instead of the brief declaration of the covenant in the Bible (Gen. 15:18–21), comes finally the description of Abraham's ascent to heaven:

> (15:2) And the angel took me with his right hand and set me on the right wing of the pigeon and he himself sat on the left wing of the turtledove, (both of) which were as if neither slaughtered nor divided.[14] (3) And he carried me up to the edge of the fiery flames. (4) And we ascended as if (carried) by many winds to the heaven that is fixed on the expanses. (5) And I saw on the air to whose height we had ascended a strong light which can not be described. (6) And behold, in this light *I saw* a burning fire of people – many people, males all of them.[15] (7) They all were changing in aspect and shape, running and changing form and prostrating themselves and crying aloud words[16] I did not know.

Having arrived at the heaven's apex, the first thing Abraham sees is a bright light, and in the midst of this light the heavenly host. Since Ezekiel, the fiery composition of this heavenly arsenal is routine; what is conspicuous, however, is the ever-changing form of the angels: Abraham arrives at a scene that seems to describe the heavenly *liturgy* of the angels, a grandiose choreography of angels changing, running, prostrating, and singing on the stage of heaven. Although he does not understand their praise, he sees its visualization in the angelic choreography. The appropriate response, again, is fear (but note that this fear responds to the vision of the angels, not of God!):

> (16:1) And I said to the angel, "Why is it you now brought me here? For now I can no longer see, because I am weakened and my spirit is departing from me." (2) And he said to me, "Remain with me, do not fear. (3) He whom you will see coming directly toward us in a great sound of sanctification[17] is the Eternal One who has loved you. (4) You will not look at him himself.[18] But let your spirit not weaken,[19] for I am with you, strengthening you."

---

[14] Some manuscripts omit "as if."
[15] The translation of v. 6 follows Pennington rather than Rubinkiewicz.
[16] Pennington, "Apocalypse of Abraham," p. 380, has "in a language."
[17] Pennington, ibid.: "with a great and holy voice."
[18] Pennington, ibid., n. 4: "But himself you will not see."
[19] Some manuscripts add "because of the shouting."

It is the praise of the angels that frightens Abraham, not the vision of God. To the contrary, the text makes it abundantly clear that Abraham does not in fact see God: "But himself you will not see." This unambiguous statement immediately recalls God's instruction to Moses: "but my face must not be seen" (Ex. 33:23). Abraham in heaven is indeed like Moses in the wilderness; he cannot and must not see God (a definite statement that is highly unusual in the apocalypses we have encountered thus far). The climax of the vision confirms this interpretation:

> (17:1) And while he was still speaking, behold the fire coming toward us round about, and a voice was in the fire like a voice of many waters, like a voice of the sea in its uproar. (2) And the angel knelt down with me and worshiped. (3) And I wanted to fall face down on the earth. And the place of highness on which we were standing now stopped on high, now rolled down low.[20] (4) And he said, "Only worship, Abraham, and recite the song which I taught you." (5) Since there was no ground to which I could fall prostrate, I only bowed down, and I recited the song which he had taught me. (6) And he said, "Recite without ceasing."

The vision does not go beyond the all-encompassing fire; God is not seen but only heard – the vision turns into an audition. What God says does not yet matter, but his voice is terribly frightening – "like a voice of many waters" is a direct quotation from Ezek. 1:24, where the creatures' wings sound "like the voice of many waters," a description that is immediately followed by "like the voice of Shaddai," namely God – and demands not only prostration but also joining in with the praise of the angels. Ceaseless singing would seem an odd response to what the visionary sees and hears; however, it is the only way to survive the terrifying experience and not to be devoured, literally and physically, by God's fire, which surrounds Abraham and the angel. Abraham and Iaoel indeed sing a long song of praise (17:8–21), to which ultimately the fire and the voice in the midst of the fire respond. A right and proper song causes the fire to soar up to ever higher heights: "And as I was still reciting the song, the tongues of fire on the expanse rose up higher. And I heard a voice like the roaring of the sea, and it did not cease from the plenitude of the fire" (18:1 f.). Abraham/Iaoel and the blazing fire with the roaring voice engage in an antiphonal chant between God and his creature.

The text fails to state explicitly that Abraham is transformed into an angel, but it is likely that his joint song with Iaoel means precisely this, that he indeed had to become an angel in order to participate in the heavenly liturgy. Moreover, his and Iaoel's song seems to mark the peak of the angelic liturgy, because it is only after they have finished their song that the divine fire with the voice from its midst reacts to the heavenly praise. One might even go a step further and sug-

---

[20] Pennington, "Apocalypse of Abraham," p. 380: "And I would have fallen prostrate on the ground; but the place on the height, where we were standing, at one moment lifted itself up *and* at the next sank back *again*."

gest that it is only after the human-angelic Abraham, God's beloved, has lent his voice to and enriched the angels' praise that the heavenly song attains the peak to which God's voice in the fire responds with such delight.

It is obvious, and has been noticed by Scholem and others, that some of the distinctive characteristics of the Apocalypse of Abraham are amazingly close to those of the Hekhalot literature. Scholem refers, among other things, to God's voice from the fire "like a voice of many waters, like a voice of the sea in its uproar" (17:1), which resembles the song of praise sung by God's throne to God the King, in Hekhalot Rabbati ("like the voice of the waters,[21] like the roar of the rushing streams, like the waves of Tarshish when the south wind sets them in uproar"),[22] or to Iaoel's function in the Apocalypse of Abraham, which indeed resembles the role that the angel Metatron plays in many texts of the Hekhalot literature.[23] It seems to me, however, that the closest parallel between the Apocalypse of Abraham and the Hekhalot literature consists in the importance that is attached to the participation of the visionary in the heavenly liturgy – the transformation that the visionary undergoes through this participation and, most important, the visible divine reaction to the heavenly liturgy as augmented by the active participation of the seer/initiate.[24] I have called this event *unio liturgica*, the liturgical communion of the Merkavah mystic, as Israel's emissary, with God.[25] Although the Apocalypse of Abraham does not go as far as the Hekhalot literature, the similarity between both texts cannot be overlooked.[26]

The fire blazing up as a result of the song intoned by Abraham and Iaoel reveals the immediate surroundings of God, but still not God himself (emphasizing yet again that God cannot be seen): the throne of fire, the "many-eyed ones," the four creatures, and the chariot with its wheels of fire, all "full of eyes" (ch. 18). This description is heavily influenced by Ezekiel and strongly emphasizes the fiery appearance of the heavenly entourage and their song "like the voice of a single man" (18:14).[27] Now, finally, God speaks to Abraham from the fire and shows him, who is looking down from the seventh heaven to earth, the future of humankind in general and of his descendants in particular. The Temple, or rather the desecration of the Temple by idolatry, plays a major role in this revelation

---

[21] "Waters" only in one manuscript; the other manuscripts have "oceans."

[22] Peter Schäfer, ed., *Synopse zur Hekhalot-Literatur* (Tübingen: J.C.B. Mohr [Paul Siebeck], 1981), § 162.

[23] Scholem, *Major Trends*, pp. 52, 58 f. See below, pp. 294 ff.; 318 ff.

[24] See Peter Schäfer, *The Hidden and Manifest God: Some Major Themes in Early Jewish Mysticism* (Albany: State University of New York Press, 1992), p. 18.

[25] Ibid., p. 165.

[26] Himmelfarb suggests (*Ascent to Heaven*, p. 64) that "the Apocalypse of Abraham treats the song sung by the visionary as part of the means of achieving ascent." This does indeed become important in the Hekhalot literature, but I do not think it plays a role here.

[27] Completely new, however, is the information that the four creatures threaten each other and that it is Iaoel's task to pacify them by teaching them the "song of peace" (18:11). This strange aspect requires further clarification.

of the future history. It is the irony of human history – this is the message of the revelation – that Abraham's descendants will sink into the same idolatry as that practiced by Abraham's father, Terah: "I saw there the likeness of the idol of jealousy, like a carpenter's figure such as my father used to make, and its body was of glittering copper, and before it a man, and he was worshiping it. And (there was) an altar opposite it and boys being slaughtered on it in the face of the idol" (25:1 f.). The only appropriate response to this decline of the Temple is its destruction:

> (27:1) And I looked and I saw, and behold the picture swayed. And from its left side a crowd of heathens ran out and they captured the men, women, and children who were on its right side. (2) And some they slaughtered and others they kept with them. (3) Behold, I saw (them) running to them for four generations,[28] and they burned the Temple with fire, and they plundered the holy things that were in it.

This refers to the destruction of the First Temple, which in reality, however, is the destruction of the Second Temple. The apocalypse concludes with the traditional repertoire: the last judgment, the final tribulations, and the salvation of the righteous, including the coming of the "Chosen One."[29] The ultimate message that Abraham's vision in heaven seeks to convey is that after Abraham abolished idolatry, the Temple was intended as the proper place of worship for Abraham's descendants, the chosen people of Israel. Yet unfortunately, idolatry was not eradicated forever; it gradually returned and gained victory over Israel. Therefore, the Temple, like Terah's house, had to be destroyed by God, and the people of Israel placed under foreign domination. But this desolate situation will not last forever – such is the very traditional (and weak) comfort that the author of the Apocalypse of Abraham has to offer.

Ascension of Isaiah

The Ascension of Isaiah marks a definite shift from the destiny of the community to that of the (righteous) individual – to what happens to the individual after his death. The work consists of two clearly distinguishable parts (which may originally have been independent): an account of Isaiah's martyrdom (chs. 1–5) and of the prophet's ascent to heaven (chs. 6–11). The former is regarded as a Jewish text; the latter no doubt is of Christian origin and is believed to belong to the early second century CE.[30] It is only the ascent account (Vision of Isaiah)

---

[28] "For four generations" is Pennington's translation ("Apocalypse of Abraham," p. 387).

[29] Interwoven into this scenario is the appearance of a figure, worshiped by the pagans as well as by some of Abraham's descendants, who is clearly inspired by Jesus (ch. 29:1–13). This part has to be regarded as a Christian interpolation.

[30] See J. M. T. Barton, "The Ascension of Isaiah," in Sparks, *The Apocryphal Old Testament* (Oxford: Clarendon Press; New York: Oxford University Press, 1984), pp. 780 f.

that concerns us here. Although its Christian origin is beyond dispute, it is likely that it depends on a Jewish source[31] (as we will see, its similarity to the Hekhalot literature is particularly striking). The original language was Greek, but the full text is preserved solely in Ethiopic.

The setting of Isaiah's ascent account is a prophetic session at which Isaiah – in the presence of a group of prophets, the Princes of Israel, the eunuchs, and the King's counselors – prophesies before King Hezekiah. During this session, all those assembled suddenly "heard a door opened and the voice of the Holy Spirit" (6:8).[32] They immediately recognize this as a divine revelation and respond by prostrating themselves and worshiping God. The door that opened – only for Isaiah – and that is explained as a "door into an unknown world" (v. 9) is apparently the door to heaven, or, as we soon learn, to all seven heavens. For the first time the seer's response to what is happening to him is described in greater detail (6:13–16):

> And while he [Isaiah] was speaking in the Holy Spirit in the hearing of all, he *suddenly*[33] became silent, and his spirit was caught up into heaven, and he no longer saw the men who were standing in front of him. But his eyes were open although his lips were silent, and the spirit of his body was taken up from him. And only his breath remained in him, for he was in a vision.

From this it becomes clear that Isaiah remains physically on earth, within the assembly of the prophets and the other notables, and that it is only his *spirit* that is taken up into heaven, not his body. He is obviously in a trancelike state with his eyes wide open; but instead of perceiving his immediate surroundings he is caught in the vision "of the world that is hidden from man" (v. 15). Throughout the duration of the vision he utters not a word, and his body looks "like a corpse" (v. 17). Only when the vision is terminated does he give an account of it to King Hezekiah and the group of prophets. The other notables and the people are not allowed to hear his account, with two important exceptions: Samnas the scribe

---

[31] See Martha Himmelfarb, *Tours of Hell: An Apocalyptic Form in Jewish and Christian Literature* (Philadelphia: Fortress Press, 1985), pp. 136 f., 156, n. 56; eadem, *Ascent to Heaven*, pp. 55, 135, n. 30. But see Robert Hall, "Isaiah's Ascent to See the Beloved: An Ancient Jewish Source for the *Ascension of Isaiah*?" *JBL* 113 (1994), pp. 463–484, who convincingly argues for the vision of Isaiah's unity and maintains that in fact, nothing in the text speaks in favor of a clear-cut *Quellenscheidung* between "Jewish" and "Christian" sources. He adds a methodologically very apt caveat against using the labels "Jewish," "Christian," or "gnostic" with regard to the vision: "Initial soundings suggest that the Vision of Isaiah is very much at home in the worlds of Jewish apocalypticism, of early Christianity, and of early gnosticism. ... Perhaps the group behind the Vision has not yet had to define itself over against other groups. They may have never had to decide whether they are Jewish or Christian" (ibid., p. 470).

[32] All quotations from the Ascension of Isaiah follow the translation of R. H. Charles, revised by J. M. T. Barton, "The Ascension of Isaiah," pp. 775–812.

[33] Italics in Spark's edition "indicate that the word or words so printed are not actually found in the text being translated, but they have been added to improve the sense" (*The Apocryphal Old Testament*, p. XXII).

and Joachim son of Asaph, the secretary of state, remain present, "for they were men who did what is right and were approved by the Spirit" (v. 17). Their function presumably was to record and testify to his account.

This description of the council of prophets and the circumstances of Isaiah's visionary experience – with his bodily presence on earth while his spirit had left him to visit the seven heavens – is surprisingly similar to the so-called havurah account in the Hekhalot literature.[34] There, R. Ishmael assembles all the famous rabbis, who are arranged according to their rank: an inner circle sits, surrounded by an outer circle of colleagues who stand, and in the middle of the inner circle sits R. Nehunya b. Haqanah, who explains matters of the Merkavah, "ascent and descent,[35] how one ascends, and who ascends; how one descends, and who descends" (§ 203). What Nehunya b. Haqanah explains is the ascent of the mystic through the seven heavenly "palaces" to the throne of glory. The means by which he achieves his vision are not communicated, but from the later description of the rabbis' attempt to recall him from the vision of the Merkavah (§§ 225 ff.) it becomes clear that he remains seated in the midst of the rabbis throughout his vision. Like Isaiah among his fellow prophets, Nehunya b. Haqanah remains physically present among his fellow rabbis, and it is apparently only his "spirit" that is in the heavenly realm and sees its secrets. To bring him back, the rabbis put a rag on his knees that has been in contact with a minuscule amount of female impurity (some even question whether there is any tangible impurity at all). This is sufficient to release him from his vision of the Merkavah without doing him any harm (a heavier dose of impurity would have killed him immediately).

Successfully released, he then relates to his fellow rabbis a certain difficult aspect of the heavenly journey (§ 228) that goes beyond the scope of our present investigation. But in this context it is important to note that his relating of this detail presupposes the presence of scribes who record the mystic's account of his heavenly journey. The scribal character of the early apocalypses is well known – already in the Book of the Watchers, Enoch receives the honorary title "scribe of righteousness" (1 En. 12:4 and 15:1) – but it is only here and in the Ascension of Isaiah that we encounter scribes whose official task it is to record what they hear from the visionary. As is the case in the Ascension of Isaiah (v. 17: "for they were men who did what is right and were approved by the Spirit"), Hekhalot Rabbati, too, sets great store in competent scribes (§ 228) because the angels at the entrance to the sixth palace are determined to kill the unfit scribes (unlike in the Ascension of Isaiah, the scribes seem to accompany the seer during his heavenly journey).

---

[34] Schäfer, *Synopse zur Hekhalot-Literatur*, §§ 202 ff. (Hekhalot Rabbati); see below, pp. 270 ff.

[35] The text follows the characteristic reverse terminology and uses "descent" for "ascent" and vice versa; see below, p. 247.

Isaiah does not need to be brought back from his trance by means of some so-phisticated device; he is suddenly back and relates what he has seen. Accompa-nied by an angelic guide from the seventh heaven he is taken up through all the seven heavens in a highly formalized procedure. In each of the first five heavens he sees a throne in the middle of the heaven with an angel seated on the throne, and groups of angels to the right and the left of the throne who all sing praises together. It becomes clear from the very first heaven that the angels on the right of the throne are always greater than the angels on the left[36] and that the angel seated on the throne is the greatest of all (with a gradual increase of glory in each heaven).[37] Already in the second heaven Isaiah falls prostrate and attempts to worship the angel on the throne, but his angelic guide explains to him that he must worship only the figure he will be seeing in the seventh heaven. In the third heaven Isaiah notices that the gradual increase of glory in each heaven is mirrored in his own physical transformation: the higher he gets, the brighter be-comes his face (7:25).

The sixth and seventh heavens are different not only in their glory and the sublimity of the angelic praise, but "from the sixth heaven and above it there are no more *angels* on the left, nor is there a throne set in the middle" (8:7). More-over, the angel guiding Isaiah makes it clear that he is not his Lord (as Isaiah believes) but his companion (8:5). Obviously, Isaiah has come very close to the angels, although his final transformation will take place in the seventh heaven. All the angels in the sixth heaven "looked the same and their praises were equal. And I was allowed to sing praises with them too, and also the angel who was accompanying me, and our praises were like theirs" (8:16 f.). In joining the *unio liturgica* with the angels in the sixth heaven, Isaiah is regarded as one of them. They all together praise "the Father of all," "his Beloved, the Christ," and "the Holy Spirit" – that is, the Holy Trinity (v. 18). Overwhelmed by what he sees, Isaiah begs his angelic guide that he might stay in heaven and not be forced to return to his body, but the angel explains to him that his time has not yet come and that he must return to his physical existence on earth. It is here for the first time that we learn that the seer is "troubled": unlike in the earlier ascent apoca-lypses, he is not afraid of what he sees but rather troubled by the idea that he won't be allowed to stay in heaven and enjoy its marvels. Only after his death, he is told, will he receive the garment, throne, and crown that are stored up for the righteous in the seventh heaven.

---

[36] Cf. in the Hekhalot literature the guardian angels at the entrances of the seven palaces, where the angel at the right side of the gate is always greater than the angel at the left side: Schäfer, *Synopse zur Hekhalot-Literatur*, §§ 206 ff., 219 ff., 230, 233 (Hekhalot Rabbati); below, p. 275.

[37] There is, of course, no angel sitting in each of the seven palaces of the Hekhalot literature, but cf. the enigmatic passage in Hekhalot Rabbati (*Synopse zur Hekhalot-Literatur*, § 206), where it is said of God that he sits in seven palaces, "a chamber within a chamber."

Finally, about to enter the seventh heaven, Isaiah hears a voice – his guide explains to him that this is the voice of the angel presiding over the praises in the sixth heaven – that wants to prevent him from entering because he "lives among aliens" (9:2) – in other words, because he is human, and because human beings are not allowed to enter the seventh heaven. This is the well-known motif of the angelic jealousy of human beings; in the classical rabbinic literature it manifests itself as the angels' opposition to the gift of the Torah to Israel,[38] and in the Hekhalot literature it is aimed, as in the Ascension of Isaiah, against the ascent of the mystic to the seventh palace. In Hekhalot Zutarti and in Merkavah Rabbah, when R. Aqiva approaches the curtain in front of the divine throne in the seventh palace, he is rejected by a group of "destructive angels" who want to kill him, but the angels in turn are reproached by the voice of God, who tells them: "Leave the old man alone for he is worthy to gaze at my Glory."[39] Likewise, in the Ascension of Isaiah the trembling seer hears another voice – his guide explains to him that this is the voice of Jesus Christ – which says: "The holy Isaiah is permitted to come up here, for here is his garment" (9:2).

Yet Isaiah will receive his heavenly garment[40] only temporarily, because he must return to his body. For, as we now learn, the seventh heaven is distinguished by a sophisticated hierarchy of angels, deceased righteous, and the Father with his beloved Son (and, less important, the Holy Spirit). In this hierarchy the deceased righteous are simultaneously like the angels and superior to them. Stripped of their "garments of flesh" and clothed in the "garments of the world above" they are like the angels (9:9), yet whereas the angels see God but cannot actually look at him (9:37), the deceased righteous "gaze intently upon the Glory" of their Maker (9:38). Isaiah's place in this heavenly hierarchy is among the angels of the seventh heaven. His transformation attains its peak; he becomes "like an angel" (9:30) and joins in with the praise of the angels *and* the righteous, but "**my**[41] glory was not transformed so that I looked like them [the righteous]" (9:33). He is not yet one of the deceased righteous because he will resume his bodily existence.

Isaiah, in his angelic state, reaches the highest stage a human being can ever achieve. Like the angels, he sees "One standing, whose glory surpassed that of all the others, and his glory was great and wonderful" (9:27), as well as "another glorious One like him" (9:33) – obviously the Father and his beloved Son. But, like the angels, he sees God only vaguely: "And the eyes of my spirit were open,

---

[38] See Schäfer, *Rivalität*, pp. 111 ff.

[39] Schäfer, *Synopse zur Hekhalot-Literatur*, § 346 (Hekhalot Zutarti) and § 673 (Merkavah Rabbah); see also b Hagigah 15b, where this passage is quoted.

[40] As the angel had promised him in the sixth heaven (8:14).

[41] Bold characters in Sparks's edition indicate "that the word or words so printed are a conjectural emendation" (*The Apocryphal Old Testament*, p. XXII). The Ethiopic text has "his glory" (Barton, in ibid., p. 805, n. 39).

and I saw the Great Glory; but I could not then look upon *him*, nor could the angel who was with me, nor any of the angels I had seen worshipping my Lord" (9:37).[42] The privilege of "gazing intently upon the Glory" (9:38) is reserved for the righteous alone. Here again we encounter a version of the familiar motif of the rivalry between angels and human beings and the ultimate superiority of human beings to the angels. In the classical rabbinic literature Israel is superior to the angels because the Torah is given only to them, not to the angels,[43] and in the Hekhalot literature the mystic, who has ascended to the seventh palace, is not hurt by the destructive force of the divine countenance – quite in contrast to the angels, who cannot observe God's beauty without perishing.[44]

In what follows, Isaiah's ascent to the seventh heaven with his "vision" of God is counterbalanced by Christ's descent to the earth and the Netherworld. Structurally speaking, the two narratives are in perfect symmetry: whereas Isaiah during his ascent was progressively transformed into an angel of the highest rank (namely, of the seventh heaven), Christ during his descent is gradually transformed into a human being. He first becomes like one of the angels of the first five heavens (remember the difference between the first five heavens and the sixth and seventh heaven) so that they recognize him as one of their own and not as the Lord (ch. 10).[45] Then he becomes a human being born from the Virgin Mary and, after the people of Israel had crucified him, he descends to the angels of the She'ol. Finally, after three days, he travels upward through all the heavens again without transforming himself into the respective angels so that they immediately recognize him as their Lord and praise him. Isaiah's account achieves its climax with Christ's return to the seventh heaven and his enthronement to the right of the Father:

> (11:32) And I saw how he ascended into the seventh heaven and all the righteous and all the angels praised him; and then I saw him sit down on the right hand of the Great Glory, whose glory I told you I was not able to look upon. (33) And I saw also the angel of the Holy Spirit sitting on the left hand. (34) And this angel said to me, Isaiah, son of Amoz, I set you free; for you have seen what no mortal has *ever* seen *before*. (35) Yet you must return to your garments *of the flesh* until your days are completed. Then will you come up here.

The message of this ascent apocalypse is clear: the chosen human being, in this case Isaiah, can anticipate with his ascent to heaven the destiny that awaits the

---

[42] See also 10:2, which confirms that Isaiah could not "look upon" the glory of the "Glorious One."

[43] Schäfer, *Rivalität*, pp. 111 ff., 228 ff.

[44] See *Synopse zur Hekhalot-Literatur*, §§ 159 ff., 169 (Hekhalot Rabbati); see also §§ 183 f., 189 (Hekhalot Rabbati). On both passages, see Schäfer, *Hidden and Manifest God*, pp. 17 f., 47–49, and below, pp. 259, 265 f.

[45] Interestingly enough, and again reminiscent of the Hekhalot literature, at his descent from the third to the first heaven and to the vault of heaven the angels demand a password from him to let him through.

righteous after their death. These righteous, once they have arrived at their place in the seventh heaven – stripped of their garment of flesh and clothed in the garment of heaven – are superior even to the angels because they gaze intently on the Glory of God. The human hero, who is privileged to ascend to the seventh heaven before his death, must be transformed into an angel of the highest rank in order to attain this goal. He does not, however, achieve the state of the righteous, neither in his spiritual transformation nor in the quality of his vision of God, for this highest state of existence is reserved for the righteous dead. The Ascension of Isaiah, therefore, is solely concerned with the destiny of the individual. The righteous individual, it promises, will be granted life after death, a purely spiritual existence superior to that of the angels. Its essence is the continuous praise of God (in this regard there is no difference between the righteous and the angels) and the ability to see God face to face (here the righteous and the angels differ). Yet the distance between God and the righteous remains, as there is no indication of any union of the righteous with God.

Apocalypse of Zephaniah

The Apocalypse of Zephaniah is a fragmentary work whose beginning and end are missing; even the identity of its hero, the biblical prophet Zephaniah, remains uncertain.[46] Zephaniah is mentioned only once, in a Sahidic Coptic manuscript; some scholars, therefore, regard this text as the only surviving fragment of the Apocalypse of Zephaniah and the bulk of the work as an independent anonymous apocalypse.[47] This major part is preserved in a single manuscript written in the Akhmimic Coptic dialect, but it is generally assumed that this version is a translation from a Greek original. The apocalypse is definitely Jewish (with some possible Christian adaptations) and most likely of Egyptian provenance; it is dated before the end of the first century CE[48] or to the second century CE.[49]

Unlike the Ascension of Isaiah, in which the seer anticipates his postmortem existence during an ascent to heaven, after which he must return to his body, the Apocalypse of Zephaniah describes the actual ascent of a dead soul after his

---

[46] See O. S. Wintermute, "Apocalypse of Zephaniah," in *OTP*, vol. 1, p. 499; Himmelfarb, *Ascent to Heaven*, pp. 51 f.

[47] In his translation, K. H. Kuhn distinguishes between the Apocalypse of Zephaniah and an anonymous apocalypse; Kuhn, "The Apocalypse of Zephaniah and an Anonymous Apocalypse," in Sparks, *The Apocryphal Old Testament*, pp. 919 ff.

[48] Himmelfarb, *Ascent to Heaven*, p. 51 (on the basis of the single heaven scheme).

[49] Wintermute, "Apocalypse of Zephaniah," p. 500 (on the basis of a quotation by Clement of Alexandria); his speculations about a pro-Edomite tradition in 3:2, which may point to a date before 70 CE, are groundless: if the simple mention of Mount Seir indicates an early pro-Edomite tradition, many Midrashim must be regarded as early and pro-Edomite.

death; this has been convincingly argued by Martha Himmelfarb[50] against the customary view that locates the apocalypse in the tradition of apocalyptic writing "that is concerned with demonstrating God's justice and mercy by permitting a seer to witness scenes of post-mortem judgment and places of blessing prepared for the righteous."[51] The seer indeed witnesses scenes of postmortem judgment and places of blessing, but it is above all his own judgment and ultimate justification that stand at the center of the narrative. As such, the Apocalypse of Zephaniah marks a decisive step toward the concern about the destiny of the individual (despite its apparently traditional ending with God's final judgment on heaven and earth).

The fragmentary Sahidic text, which seems to belong to the beginning of the apocalypse, sets the tone by having the guiding angel tell the seer that he will "triumph over the accuser" and "come up from Hades" (B:4)[52] – this is precisely what the bulk of the apocalypse in the Akhmimic dialect is going to expound. The journey begins with a view from above the seer's city, presumably Jerusalem, at the place for the souls of the righteous and the sinners; where precisely this place is, is not communicated (ch. 2). The second stage of the journey takes place at Mount Seir, where the seer learns that two different groups of angels record the deeds of the righteous and sinners in the appropriate books (ch. 3). At the next (unspecified) place, "Zephaniah" sees ugly angels ("the servants of all creation"), who bring up the souls of "ungodly men" to the place of their eternal punishment; the angel confirms to him that they are not permitted to touch him because he is "pure" (ch. 4). The subsequent stop is within a "beautiful city" with bronze gates, presumably the heavenly Jerusalem, in which the angel accompanying the seer transforms himself (ch. 5). Withdrawing from this "beautiful city" (whose bronze gates hurl fire against him), the seer finds himself in Hades and confronted with two angels, both of whom he mistakes for God and attempts to worship (ch. 6). The first angel is described as follows:

> (6:8) His hair was spread out like the lionesses'. His teeth were outside his mouth like a bear. His hair was spread out like women's. His body was like the serpent's when he wished to swallow me. (9) And when I saw him, I was afraid of him so that all of my parts of my body were loosened and I fell upon my face.

Realizing that this apparition is not God, he prays to God to save him – and sees another angel, whom he again mistakes for God:

> (6:11) Then I arose and stood, and I saw a great angel standing before me with his face shining like the rays of the sun in its glory since his face is like that which is perfected in its glory. (12) And he was girded as if a golden girdle were upon his breast. (13) His

---

[50] Himmelfarb, *Ascent to Heaven*, p. 52.

[51] Wintermute, "Apocalypse of Zephaniah," p. 505.

[52] All translations as well as the chapter and verse divisions of the apocalypse follow Wintermute, "Apocalypse of Zephaniah," pp. 508 ff.

feet were like bronze which is melted in a fire. (13) And when I saw him, I rejoiced, for I thought that the Lord Almighty had come to visit me. (14) I fell upon my face, and I worshiped him. (15) He said to me, "Take heed. Don't worship me. I am not the Lord Almighty, but I am the great angel, Eremiel, who is over the abyss and Hades, the one in which all of the souls are imprisoned from the end of the Flood, which came upon the earth, until this day."

The angel explains to him that he is now in Hades and that the first terrifying angel he encountered there was the accuser, "who accuses men in the presence of the Lord" (6:17). Eremiel is well-known already from the Book of the Watchers, where he is called Remiel and, as one of the seven archangels, is "set over those who rise (from the dead)" (20:8). He appears as Jeremiel in 4 Ezra (4:36) and as Ramael in 2 Baruch, where he is "set over true visions" (55:3; see also 63:6). But his description here goes far beyond anything communicated in the parallels. His face shining like the sun is an attribute reserved not only for the highest angels but for God himself. As an angelic attribute we encountered it in 2 Enoch, where the faces of the two angels that come to take Enoch up to heaven are "like the shining sun" (2 En. 1:5) and where the oil with which he is anointed is "like the rays of the glittering sun" (22:9). Yet in the Book of the Watchers it is the wheels of the divine throne in the "inner house" that are "like the shining sun" (1 En. 14:18), and even the raiment of God himself sitting on his throne is "brighter than the sun" (14:20). In particular, Eremiel's feet looking like bronze melted in fire are reminiscent of the description of God's body "from his loins downward" that appears to Ezekiel as fire surrounded by a radiance (Ezek. 1:27). The angel, indeed, comes very close to God, and it is not surprising that "Zephaniah" attempts to worship him (much less surprising than the ugly first angel, the accuser, he sees in Hades). In fact, Eremiel's appearance is the closest "Zephaniah" gets to God: there is no vision of God in the remaining text of the apocalypse (and it is not very likely that the missing end contained such a vision).

It is also in Hades that "Zephaniah" sees the books in which his bad and good deeds are recorded. He learns that his good deeds outweigh his sins and that he therefore has triumphed over the accuser (ch. 7). Set on a boat, he embarks on the final part of his trip to the place of the righteous souls:

> (8:1) ... [53] They helped me and set me on that boat. (2) Thousands of thousands and myriads of myriads of angels gave praise before me. (3) I, myself, put on an angelic garment. I saw all of those angels praying. (4) I, myself, prayed together with them, I knew their language, which they spoke with me.

This is the usual procedure for the hero approaching the final stage of his heavenly journey: the garment he dons symbolizes his transformation into an angel,

---

[53] Two pages are missing here in the Coptic text. Wintermute ("Apocalypse of Zephaniah," pp. 513 f.) is certainly right in assuming that discussed in the missing pages is the content of the second book that "should have recorded the good deeds of the seer."

since it is only in the angelic state that he can enter the highest heaven. As in the other ascent apocalypses, he immediately chimes in with the heavenly praise of the angels and, as the necessary prerequisite, understands their language. In "Zephaniah's" case, however, this is not a heavenly journey anticipating the final destiny of the visionary; rather, it is a journey with no return – the last journey of the righteous soul to his place in heaven. A trumpet announces his triumph and his arrival at the place destined for the righteous:

> (9:1) Then a great angel came forth having a golden trumpet in his hand, and he blew it three times over my head, saying, "Be courageous! O one who has triumphed, Prevail! O one who has prevailed. For you have triumphed over the accuser, and you have escaped from the abyss and Hades. (2) You will now cross over the crossing place. For your name is written in the Book of Living."

This scene is reminiscent of the ascent of the successful Merkavah mystic, who finally reaches the throne of glory in the seventh "palace": having proved himself a worthy adept and having survived all the dangers of his ascent, the angels support him when he enters the seventh palace and give him strength. And then a "horn sounds" from above the highest heaven and announces his entry into the seventh palace before the divine throne.[54]

But there seems to be a distinct hierarchy in the Apocalypse of Zephaniah's heaven. Unlike in the Ascension of Isaiah, where Isaiah joins the ranks of the highest angels (and where the decisive hierarchical difference remains between the angels and the righteous), here not all righteous souls achieve the rank of the highest angels. For the text continues, "I wanted to embrace him [the great angel with the golden trumpet], (but) was unable to embrace the great angel because his glory is great" (9:3). "Zephaniah's" soul seems not to be the great angel's equal. This becomes even clearer when the angel runs to all the righteous assembled in heaven and awaiting "Zephaniah's" arrival (Abraham, Isaac, Jacob, Enoch, Elijah, and David) and addresses them "as friend to friend speaking with one another" (9:5). The great heroes of the past – obviously our deceased soul's role models – are apparently the great angel's equal, something that seems to be denied the more simple soul of our seer.

The received text concludes with a second blowing of the trumpet that opens the heaven and once more shows "Zephaniah" the fiery sea in Hades that swallows up all the sinners (ch. 11). At another sounding of the trumpet, blown daily by the great angel, all the righteous – led by Abraham, Isaac, and Jacob – intercede on behalf of the tormented sinners and pray to God (ch. 11). A final sounding of the golden trumpet will announce the coming wrath of God – the last judgment (ch. 12). Here the text of the apocalypse breaks off, with four further pages missing.

---

[54] Schäfer, *Synopse zur Hekhalot-Literatur*, § 250 (Hekhalot Rabbati).

Apocalypse of John

The Apocalypse of John or the Book of Revelation, the last ascent apocalypse to be discussed here, is no doubt of Christian origin: it belongs to the canon of the New Testament and centers on the "Lamb," that is, the Son of Man and Messiah Jesus Christ.[55] Its author reveals his identity as "John,"[56] but it remains uncertain who precisely this "John" is (although ancient authorities such as Papias[57] and Justin[58] are convinced that our John is none other than the apostle John, the son of Zebedee).[59] This John received his revelation on the island of Patmos in the Aegean Sea,[60] about fifty-five miles southwest of Ephesus, from where he writes seven letters to seven Christian communities in Asia Minor.[61] The emerging Christian Church in the Roman province of Asia clearly supplies the apocalypse with its local color. It seems likely that the apocalypse was written toward the end of the reign of the emperor Domitian (81–96 CE).[62] But despite its unmistakable Christian origin, the book draws on the rich treasure trove of traditional Jewish material. This fact, which holds particularly true for the vision in chapters 4 and 5, justifies the inclusion of the apocalypse in this chapter.

After an introductory vision in which John sees "one like the Son of Man" (*homoion hyion anthrōpou*),[63] easily recognizable as Jesus, who instructs him to write the seven letters to the seven "churches," the seer receives a second vision (chs. 4 and 5):[64]

---

[55] Latterly, John W. Marshall wants to read the Apocalypse of John as a thoroughly *Jewish* text; see his *Parables of War: Reading John's Jewish Apocalypse* (Waterloo, ON: Wilfrid Laurier University Press, 2001). Laudable as the attempt may be to break up once more the all too static categories of "Judaism" and "Christianity," I am not convinced that John's apocalypse can be adequately described as a Merkavah text and that it *therefore* belongs to the realm of Judaism (ibid., p. 207).

[56] Rev. 1:1, 4, 9; 22:8.

[57] Irenaeus, Adv. haer. V, 33:4 (Alexander Roberts and James Donaldson, eds., *The Ante-Nicene Fathers: Translations of the Writings of the Fathers down to A. D. 325*, vol. 1: *The Apostolic Fathers – Justin Martyr – Irenaeus,* rev. A. Cleveland Coxe [New York: Charles Scribner's Sons, 1925], p. 563).

[58] Dialogue with Trypho 81:4 (Robertson and Donaldson, *The Ante-Nicene Fathers*, vol. 1, p. 240).

[59] Mt. 10:2; Mk. 3:17; Lk. 6:14.

[60] Rev. 1:9.

[61] Rev., chs. 2 and 3.

[62] As already suggested by Irenaeus, Adv. haer. V, 30:3, end (Roberts and Donaldson, *The Ante-Nicene Fathers*, vol. 1, p. 560). John Marshall posits that Revelation reflects the turmoil of the "long year" 69 CE and should be dated around 70 CE; see his *Parables of War*, pp. 88 ff., and idem, "Who's on the Throne? Revelation in the Long Year," in Boustan and Reed, *Heavenly Realms and Earthly Realities*, pp. 123–141.

[63] Rev. 1:13. The figure combines attributes of the "Son of Man" and the "Ancient of Days" in Daniel (Dan. 7:9) and of the "figure with the appearance of a human being" in Ezekiel (1:26 f.).

[64] The translation follows the RSV and the NRSV (with some adaptations).

(4:1) After this I looked, and behold, in heaven a door stood open! And that first voice, which I had heard speaking to me like a trumpet, said: "Come up here (*anaba hōde*), and I will show you what must take place after this." (2) At once I was in the spirit (*en pneumati*), and behold, a throne was set in heaven, with one seated on the throne! (3) And the one seated there looks like jasper and carnelian (*homoios horasei lithō iaspidi kai sardiō*), and around the throne is a rainbow that looks like an emerald (*homoios horasei smaragdinō*). (4) Around the throne are twenty-four thrones, and seated on the thrones are twenty-four elders (*presbyterous*), dressed in white robes, with golden crowns on their heads. (5) Coming from the throne are flashes of lightning (*astrapai*), and voices (*phōnai*) and peals of thunder (*brontai*), and in front of the throne burn seven torches of fire, which are the seven spirits of God; (6) and in front of the throne there is something like a sea of glass (*hōs thalassa hyalinē*), like crystal (*homoia krystallō*).

Like most of its predecessors, this vision is the seer's or prophet's *inaugural* vision, heavily indebted to Ezekiel. Unlike Ezekiel, however, but like most of his successors, the seer does not remain on earth (peering through the open heavens);[65] rather, he is explicitly asked to "come up," that is, to ascend to heaven. The invitation to ascend comes from a "voice" that the seer immediately identifies as belonging to the Son of Man (= Jesus), who appeared to him in the first vision.[66] Quite conspicuously, there is no angel who accompanies the seer on his journey to the highest heaven and who explains to him what he sees (the familiar *angelus interpres*),[67] nor are there marvels to be admired in the heavens (in fact, there is no mention of various heavens at all, and there is not much of a journey either): the seer is immediately lifted up to (the highest?) heaven, replete with its throne chamber and someone sitting on the throne. The ascent is reduced to the enigmatic phrase "I was in the spirit,"[68] which refers either to a peculiar (ecstatic) state of mind (alluding to Ezek. 2:2: "a spirit [*ruah*] entered into me") or to the wind or spirit (*ruah*) that carries Ezekiel away after his vision (Ezek. 3:14) and lifts him up and brings him to Jerusalem (Ezek. 8:3, 11:1).

The voice of the Son of Man/Jesus Christ promises the seer that he will reveal the future to him and thereby anticipates the Lamb's breaking of the mysterious scroll's seals after the vision (ch. 6). In most of the classical ascent apocalypses, the revelation of the future is reserved for God himself; hence, in attributing such an important revelation to the Son of Man/Jesus Christ, the author of our apocalypse hints (at the very beginning of the vision, even before the seer gets a chance to gaze on the enthroned figure) at the very peculiar state of the Son of Man/Jesus Christ – a state that goes far beyond what we might expect from an *angelus interpres* or any "ordinary" angelic being. As we will soon come to understand, the Son of Man/Jesus Christ is much more than just an angel.

---

[65] See Ezek. 1:1; 2 Bar. 22:1; Acts 7:56; 10:11; see above, chapter 1, p. 36.

[66] Rev. 1:10, 12 ff.

[67] But see Rev. 19:9 f.

[68] See on this phrase the commentary by R. H. Charles, *A Critical and Exegetical Commentary on the Revelation of John*, vol. 1 (Edinburgh: T. & T. Clark, 1920, repr. 1975), pp. 109 ff.

But first comes the vision of the figure on the throne – quite a casual vision, or, to be more precise, not much of a vision at all. To be sure, this figure is God in all his glory, but our author makes no attempt to describe it in any detail: no human shape as in Ezekiel, and not even a description of his clothes or the hair on his head as in Daniel and the apocalypses following Daniel's lead;[69] not by coincidence, the author has heaped all these attributes, which in Dan. 7 and Ezek. 1 are reserved for God, on his Son of Man,[70] indicating that the dividing lines between God and the Son of Man are indeed blurred. As to God's appearance, he confines himself to two precious stones (jasper and carnelian), to which he adds the emerald-like rainbow that surrounds the throne.[71] It is not entirely clear which precious stones are concealed behind these stones – the names of gems are notoriously difficult to identify[72] – but the message is obvious: God's features cannot be described. What the seer does perceive is a brilliant radiance, such as is emitted by the most beautiful and precious gems. With this message the author follows the tradition inaugurated by Ezekiel (Ezek. 1:26–28: the throne appears like sapphire, and the figure on the throne resembles *hashmal* and fire, surrounded by a radiance comparable to that of a rainbow) and continued by Ezekiel's successors: God's raiment is "white as snow" in Daniel (7:9) and "brighter than the sun, whiter than any snow" in 1 Enoch (14:20),[73] whereas his face in 2 Enoch is "like iron made burning hot in a fire and brought out, and it emits sparks and is incandescent" (22:1).[74]

Yet our author may have had more in mind than simply wanting to emphasize that God shines like precious stones. Some commentators have pointed to the fact that the three stones mentioned in our vision also appear among the stones

---

[69] Also toward the end of his vision, John sees just "a great white throne and the one who sat on it" (Rev. 20:11), nothing more specific. Only when the eschaton has come – with the new Jerusalem descending from heaven, the water of life flowing from the throne of God and of the Lamb, and the tree of life – then "his servants will worship him" and "they will see his face" (Rev. 22:3 f.): this is clearly the eschatological scenario of the resurrected righteous, who are finally found worthy of seeing God face to face.

[70] Rev. 1:13–16: long robe, white hair, feet like burnished bronze, voice like the sound of many waters.

[71] Charles, *Commentary*, p. 113: "the writer avoids anthropomorphic details. No form is visible"; ibid., p. 115: "Thus anthropomorphic details are avoided still more than in Ezekiel."

[72] See the commentaries, especially Isbon T. Beckwith, *The Apocalypse of John: Studies in Introduction with a Critical and Exegetical Commentary* (New York: Macmillan, 1919 [repr. 1967, Baker Book House, Grand Rapids, MI]), p. 497; Charles, *Commentary*, pp. 114 f.

[73] Where the author explicitly adds that no angel and no flesh could see his face "because of its splendor and glory" (14:21).

[74] As we have seen above, in the Apocalypse of Abraham it is the angel Iaoel who looks like sapphire and chrysolite (11:2), whereas God is not seen but just heard; and in the Apocalypse of Zephaniah it is said of the angel Eremiel that his face shines "like the rays of the sun" and that his feet were "like bronze which is melted in a fire" (6:11, 13). The two God-like angels are described in terms that are usually reserved for God.

on the breastplate of the high priest as described in Ex. 28:17–21.[75] The breast-plate consists of four rows of stones with three stones in each row, making for a total of twelve stones. The first and the last of these twelve stones (the first stone of the first row and the last stone of the fourth row) are the stones that in Hebrew are called *odem* (generally translated as "carnelian") and *yashfeh* (generally translated as "jasper").[76] Hence, the stones symbolizing the brilliant splendor of God assume a prominent place on the high priest's breastplate.[77] This can hardly be a coincidence. Since the twelve stones on the breastplate correspond to the "names of the sons of Israel," that is, to the twelve tribes (Ex. 28:21), the stones symbolizing God's splendor refer to – or rather literally reflect – the twelve tribes of Israel.[78] The message, then, would be that God's glory is not self-sufficient, just brilliant and beautiful to behold; quite to the contrary, it has a function, for it correlates with his people – Israel.[79]

This interpretation is corroborated by what follows (v. 4): the twenty-four elders sitting on thrones arranged in a circle around God's throne. Scholars are divided as to the identity of these twenty-four elders,[80] but the most likely ex-planation is that they refer to the representatives of the people of Israel – two leaders of each of the twelve tribes, or twelve leaders of the tribes and twelve kings[81] – or even the leaders of the twelve tribes (representing the "old Israel") and the twelve apostles (representing the "new Israel").[82] Whatever the precise

---

[75] See, e. g., J. Massyngberde Ford, *Revelation: Introduction, Translation, and Commentary*, The Anchor Bible (New York: Doubleday, 1975), p. 71.

[76] In the Septuagint, of the three stones mentioned in Revelation *sardion* ("carnelian") is in-deed the first stone of the first row, but *iaspis* is the third stone of the second row on the breast-plate (and *smaragdos* the third stone of the first row).

[77] The "emerald" of the rainbow is *bareqet* in Hebrew, the third stone of the first row.

[78] The jasper and the sea of glass looking like crystal return in chapter 21: the new Jerusa-lem, coming down from heaven as the "bride, the wife of the Lamb" (21:9), has "a radiance like a very rare jewel, like jasper, clear as crystal" (21:11). Moreover, this Jerusalem has twelve gates on which are inscribed the names of the twelve tribes (21:12).

[79] Interestingly enough, the precious stones on the high priest's breastplate reappear in Ezek. 28:13, where it is said of a mysterious mythic figure (the primordial "man"?) that it was covered with three rows of precious stones (three stones each row). The stones are identical with the first, fourth, and second row in Ex. 28 (the third row is left out), with the third stone of the first and second rows switched. In Ezekiel, carnelian and jasper are the first stone of the first row and the third stone of the second row respectively, whereas the emerald appears as the third stone of the third row, that is, the last stone. If the author of Revelation wants to refer to Ezekiel rather than to Exodus, his stones may well correlate with the Son of Man rather than with the people of Israel. Or with both, with the Son of Man as the "mediator" between God and his people?

[80] See Charles, *Commentary*, pp. 128 ff., and the useful summary in Ford, *Revelation*, pp. 72 f.

[81] According to Ford (*Revelation*, p. 80), Jesus Sirach, in his praise of the ancestors (chs. 44–49), counts twenty-four "fathers" of Israel, but one needs quite some imagination to arrive at precisely the number twenty-four.

[82] The latter suggested by Ignaz Rohr, *Der Hebräerbrief und die Geheime Offenbarung des Heiligen Johannes*, 4th ed. (Bonn: Peter Hanstein, 1932), p. 91; see also the note on v. 4 in the NRSV. This interpretation is corroborated by the fact that the heavenly Jerusalem, in addition

meaning of the stones and the elders might be, there can be hardly any doubt that our seer observes, at the very beginning of his vision, a close relationship between God and the heavenly representatives of his people on earth, a relationship furthermore that will soon find its expression in liturgical activity. And as we will see, this relationship with its liturgical interaction becomes one of the major characteristics of Merkavah mysticism.[83]

Then the description returns to the divine throne, with imagery again heavily influenced by Ezekiel (1:13) and the theophany on Mount Sinai (Ex. 19:16 ff.; Deut. 4:11 f.). Particularly noteworthy is the "sea of glass" in front of the throne that looks like crystal (v. 6). This strange image may well have been derived from Ezekiel's "expanse (*raqia'*) that looked like dreadful ice (*ha-qerah ha-nora*)," with *qerah* translated as "crystal" in the Septuagint (Ezek. 1:22), and from Enoch's first house with its floor of snow (1 En. 14:10).[84] One of the most mysterious features of the Hekhalot literature is the pavement in the sixth heaven that consists of marble stones whose splendor the unworthy mystic mistakes for water.[85] We certainly cannot rule out the possibility that the Hekhalot literature continues precisely this tradition of the frozen ice/crystal as inaugurated by Ezekiel and developed further by apocalypses, such as the Book of the Watchers in 1 Enoch and the Book of Revelation.

The heavenly throne room is filled not only with the twenty-four elders; another prominent place is taken by those creatures we would expect, following the example of Ezekiel, to be mentioned first: the four *hayyot* that in Ezekiel carry the expanse on which stands the divine throne. Here they do not carry the throne; they just stand on either side of the throne, but presumably closer to the throne than the twenty-four elders:

> And around the throne, on each side of the throne,[86] are four living creatures (*tessara zōa*), full of eyes in front and behind: (7) the first living creature like a lion, the second living creature like an ox, the third living creature with a face like a man (*anthrōpos*), and the fourth living creature like a flying eagle. (8) And the four living creatures, each of them with six wings, are full of eyes all around and inside. Day and night without ceasing they sing:

> "Holy, holy, holy,
> The Lord God the Almighty,
> Who was and is and is to come."

---

to the names of the twelve tribes on the city gate, has the names of the "twelve apostles of the Lamb" inscribed on its twelve foundations (21:14). According to Lk. 22:30, Jesus promises his disciples that they will sit on thrones and judge the twelve tribes of Israel.

[83] See below, pp. 263, 274, 279, 280 f., 328 f.

[84] The second house has a floor of fire, but the divine throne located in the second house looks like "crystals of ice" (1 En. 14:18). Charles, *Commentary*, pp. 117 f., suggests that the "sea of glass" just refers to the waters above the firmament of Gen. 1:7.

[85] See below, chapter 8, pp. 298 f.

[86] On the strange *en mesō ... kai kyklō*, see Ford, *Revelation*, p. 74.

(9) And whenever the living creatures give glory and honor and thanks to the one who is seated on the throne, who lives forever and ever, (10) the twenty-four elders fall down before the one who is seated on the throne and worship the one who lives forever and ever; they cast their crowns before the throne, singing:

> "You are worthy, our Lord and God,
> to receive glory and honor and power,
> for you created all things,
> and by your will they existed and were created."

The creatures' features are taken from Ezekiel: four in number (Ezek. 1:5), with four different faces (Ezek. 1:6, 10: although in Ezekiel each one of the creatures has four faces, whereas here each creature represents just one different being) and full of eyes (Ezek. 1:18: the rims of the wheels accompanying the creatures). Only the six wings of the creatures are obviously influenced by Isaiah and not by Ezekiel: the four creatures in Ezekiel each have four wings, whereas Isaiah's seraphim are furnished with six wings (Isa. 6:2). This harmonizes well with the song of the creatures as inspired by the Qedushah of Isaiah (Isa. 6:3), supplemented by a formula that emphasizes God's eternity, and also reminiscent of Isaiah (Isa. 41:4, 44:6, 48:12).[87] The heavenly liturgy, initiated by the four creatures, clearly imitates an antiphonal chant, with the twenty-four elders responding and praising God as the creator of all things.

This is the first part of the vision, culminating in the praise of God uttered by the four living creatures and the twenty-four elders. The second part (ch. 5), although equally dependent on Ezekiel and, above all, on Daniel, ventures into new territory. It begins with our visionary seeing God holding a scroll in his right hand, "written on the inside and on the back" (5:1), and an angel (Gabriel?) asking, "Who is worthy to open the scroll and break its seals?" (5:2). When it turns out that no one is able to open the scroll, John weeps bitterly; but one of the elders comforts him: "Do not weep! See, the Lion of the tribe of Judah, the Root of David, has conquered, so that he can open the scroll and its seven seals" (5:5). The scroll, of course, refers to Ezekiel, where the prophet, after his vision, sees God's hand stretched out to him, holding a scroll that is spread out before the visionary and has "writing on the front and on the back" (Ezek. 2:9 f.). But quite in contrast to our apocalypse, Ezekiel sees what is written on the scroll (Ezek. 2:10: "and written on it were words of lamentation and mourning and woe") and is even asked to eat it (Ezek. 3:1) in order to remember its contents and convey its message to the people of Israel. So, in fact, the Apocalypse of John turns Ezekiel (and the later ascent apocalypses) upside down: the prophet-seer loses his importance and recedes into the background. Not only is he *not* transformed into an angel, he even forfeits his mission. His place between God and the people of Israel is taken by another mediator, the Lion of Judah and Root

---

[87] See also Rev. 1:8, 21:6, 22:13.

of David, the Messiah. The title "Lion of Judah" is taken from Gen. 49:9 ("Judah is a lion's whelp"), a verse that, with its continuation 49:10 ("the scepter shall not depart from Judah"), has acquired a messianic connotation. This connotation is made even more explicit in the epithet "Root of David," which refers to Isa. 11:1, 10, the classical designation of the Messiah from the house of David. Since this Messiah is introduced as someone who "has conquered" (*enikēsen*), it is made immediately clear that he has already accomplished his task as the savior of his people: because he has done precisely what was expected of him, he is able to open the scroll.

Then the Messiah appears, in the form of a Lamb (*arnion*), "standing as if it had been slaughtered (*hōs esphagmenon*)" (5:6), that is, displaying marks of being slaughtered. This can only mean that the Lamb, although it was slaughtered and hence had died, presents itself alive – an obvious reference to Jesus's death and resurrection: the Lamb is Jesus, after his death, Passion, and resurrection, or, to put it differently, it is the Messiah after he has accomplished the task of redemption.[88] This enables him to take the sealed scroll from God's hand (5:7). But instead of opening it immediately (this happens only in the next chapter), the Lamb first receives the praise and worship of the four living creatures and the twenty-four elders. They fall down before the Lamb, holding harps and bowls of incense (the classical objects of worship), and "sing a new song" (*ōdēn kainēn*):

> (5:9) "You are worthy to take the scroll and to open its seals,
> for you were slaughtered and by your blood you ransomed for God
> (men) from every tribe and language and people and nation;
> (10) you have made them a kingdom and priests to our God,
> and they will reign on earth."

After the four living creatures and the twenty-four elders had first praised God in their antiphonal chant, they now combine efforts to praise the Lamb with "a new song." In opening their songs with the same words ("you are worthy" – to receive glory and honor and to open the scroll), they hint at a very close relationship between God and the Lamb. And in labeling their song as "new," the author makes clear that a new era was inaugurated with the appearance of the Lamb, an era that goes beyond "solely" praising God on his throne. Just as the Son of Man receives from God dominion and everlasting kingship (Dan. 7:14) – and, therefore, kingship and dominion being given to the people of Israel on earth (Dan. 7:27) – so too does the Lamb (the new Son of Man), through his sacrifice, confer kingdom and priesthood on all the peoples on earth.[89]

---

[88] Taking up elements of the Suffering Servant in Isa. 53:4–7, the Passover Lamb (Ex. 12), and John 1:29, 36.

[89] The priesthood seems to be inspired by Ex. 19:6: "you shall be for me a priestly kingdom and a holy nation."

This new era becomes even more apparent with the next developments. The song of the living creatures and the elders is followed by another song, uttered by "myriads of angels":

> (5:12) "Worthy is the Lamb that was slaughtered
> to receive power and wealth and wisdom and might
> and honor and glory and blessing!"

Again praised as "worthy," the slaughtered Lamb now receives not only the same epithets as God in 4:11 (glory, honor, and power), it gets four more (wealth, wisdom, might, and blessing). The angels' praise of the Lamb surpasses, in a certain sense, the elders' praise of God (although, to be sure, only God is exalted as creator). Hence, it comes as little surprise that, after two songs addressed to God and two songs addressed to the Lamb, the vision concludes with a final song addressed to both God and the Lamb:

> (5:13) Then I heard every creature in heaven and on earth and under the earth and in the sea, and all that is in them, singing:

> > "To the one seated on the throne and to the Lamb,
> > be blessing and honor and glory and might
> > forever and ever!"

> (14) And the four living creatures said: "Amen!" And the elders fell down and worshiped.

The whole universe completes the heavenly liturgy, conjoining God and the Lamb as addressees of their song and objects of their worship.[90] No doubt, the Son of Man/Lamb has been elevated to a position that equals God. He is more than just a prophet or a seer; he assumes the position of a second power in heaven.

With this final step, the author of the Book of Revelation forsakes the realm of what has been offered to him by the rich tradition starting with Ezekiel and Daniel and climaxing with the ascent apocalypses. Or, better put, he has employed the treasure trove of this tradition to his own purpose, weaving a new fabric that is admirable and beautiful in its texture, while at the same time extending the confines of the received material. For the first time ever within the genre of the apocalyptic literature, he promulgates a dual divinity, or, as modern scholars would have it, a binitarian theology.[91] With this conclusion, I do not wish to make a definite statement on the issue of whether or not he places himself outside the received *Jewish* tradition, as I believe that such a question is irrelevant here. Suffice it to say that the author of this apocalypse has boldly developed, out of the received tradition, something that, if not inherent in this tradition, could certainly not have been formulated without it.

---

[90] See also Charles, *Commentary*, p. 151.
[91] For the term see below, chapter 8, p. 323.

To sum up, all four apocalypses reviewed in this chapter are strikingly reticent about the seer's vision of God. In the Apocalypses of Abraham and of Zephaniah, God remains unseen (although God's voice is heard in the Apocalypse of Abraham); in the Ascension of Isaiah the visionary is permitted only a brief and inchoate glimpse of God (quite in contrast to the deceased righteous, who gaze intently upon God); and in the Apocalypse of John the vision is reduced to the brilliant brightness emitted by precious stones. Instead, both the Apocalypse of Abraham and the Apocalypse of Zephaniah emphasize the God-like stature of the highest angels (Iaoel and Eremiel), whereas the Apocalypse of John goes a decisive step further and elevates the heavenly Son of Man/Messiah to a divine figure. The Ascension of Isaiah, on the other hand, decreases the power of the angels by subordinating them to the deceased righteous: the righteous after their death are superior to the angels.

As to the physical condition of the visionary, according to both the Ascension of Isaiah and the Apocalypse of Zephaniah the visionary and the dead soul undergo a progressive transformation into an angel because it is only in an angelic state that the visionary and the dead soul can approach the highest heaven or God (against this traditional background it is all the more conspicuous that the deceased righteous in the Ascension of Isaiah achieve a state that is higher than that of the angels). Hence, although the traditional apocalyptic arsenal – with its final judgment and the ultimate salvation of the people of Israel – is kept (to a varying degree), the Ascension of Isaiah and the Apocalypse of Zephaniah in particular mark a decisive shift toward concern about the destiny of the individual. Moreover, it is definitely the individual *soul* that is at stake; nothing indicates that the deceased righteous remain in their body (on the contrary, Isaiah laments the fact that he must return to his body before he can set out on his final journey to heaven).[92] Finally, in the Ascension of Isaiah we get a rare insight into the procedure by which the heavenly ascent is attained: the visionary is in a trance-like mental state that allows his spirit to undertake the journey while his body remains on earth. I have suggested that this procedure comes remarkably close to R. Nehunya b. Haqanah's vision of the Merkavah in Hekhalot Rabbati.

Despite its close proximity to the other ascent apocalypses, the Apocalypse of John has retained none of these features. The figure of the prophet-seer recedes completely into the background. His task is assumed by the Lamb, Jesus Christ, who is the only one able to open the seals of the book and usher in the eschaton, and who will ultimately take his seat, together with God, on a throne in the new Jerusalem. Here a crucial step has been taken toward a new, binitarian theology.

---

[92] The dead sinners in the Apocalypse of Zephaniah, however, remain in their body (10:12 f.).

Chapter 4

Qumran

Communion with the Angels

After his decisive victory over the Seleucid army, and supported by the emerging superpower of Rome, in 153 BCE the Maccabee Jonathan, son of Judas, assumed the office of high priest in Jerusalem. This dramatic step, confirmed thirteen years later under his brother and successor Simon by the Jerusalem Great Assembly, was an important turning point in the history of the Maccabean movement. Having set out not only to battle the oppression of the foreign rulers but also to fight against their Jewish accomplices – chief among them the priestly nobility – and in particular against what they called the usurpation of the high priesthood by candidates not belonging to the appropriate lineage of the Zadokite family, the Maccabees had achieved their goal of depriving the Seleucids and the illegal high priests dependent on them of power. Yet this achievement went far beyond the original objectives of the movement. Emerging from the lower ranks of the priesthood, the Maccabean family hardly had any more entitlement to the office of high priest than the "usurpers" that they had so bitterly opposed.

It was precisely at this turning point that the Maccabees began experiencing opposition to their rule, particularly to their presumptuous step of laying claim to the office of high priest. The fight they had undertaken against the "usurpers" was turned against themselves, for they could easily be accused of doing the same: usurping an office to which they were no more entitled than their illegitimate predecessors. Most scholars regard this as the birth of the movement of the "pious," about to enter history as the Qumran sect. This movement was founded by a leader whose name is unknown but who is mentioned in the Qumran sources as the "Teacher of Righteousness." Since his opponent is called the "Wicked Priest," it is generally assumed that he is to be identified with the incumbent Maccabean high priest, most likely Jonathan. The Pesher Habakkuk, the Qumran exposition of the biblical book Habakkuk, explains the verse "Because of the blood of the city and the violence done to the land" (cf. Hab. 2:17) as: "'the city' is Jerusalem in which the Wicked Priest committed abominable deeds and defiled the Temple of God."[1] The defilement of the Jerusalem Tem-

---

[1] 1QpHab XII:7 f. All translations from the Qumran texts follow, with some variations, Florentino García Martínez and Eibert J. C. Tigchelaar, eds., *The Dead Sea Scrolls: Study Edi-*

ple by the Wicked Priest and his supporters was the immediate reason why the Teacher of Righteousness and his group left Jerusalem, withdrew into the desert, and founded the community of the true and eternal covenant at Qumran.

The Qumran community was in every respect the counterimage to the despised Jerusalem community led by the high priest. In contrast to the official cultic calendar in Jerusalem, a lunar calendar, the Teacher of Righteousness introduced a solar calendar of 364 days.[2] The members of the community regarded themselves as living in the decisive last period before the end of history. They alone were the chosen ones, the holy remnant of Israel that could expect to be saved at the time of judgment; all the others, in particular their fellow Jews in Jerusalem, were wicked and ungodly, destined for damnation. In an elated apocalyptic mood they called themselves the "Sons of Light" and their opponents the "Sons of Darkness." The Sons of Light, they predicted, would fight a final battle against the Sons of Darkness, from which the Sons of Light would emerge triumphant to live in eternal bliss on a renewed and transformed earth. Two Messiahs, a Davidic "Messiah from Israel" and a priestly "Messiah from Aaron," would lead the community into the decisive battle.[3]

A Community of Priests

The most conspicuous characteristic of the Qumran community was its priestly orientation. Not only was the Messiah from Aaron superior to the Messiah from Israel, the whole structure of the community was shaped according to a pro-

---

tion, 2 vols. (Leiden: Brill, 1997–1998); I also consulted the translation by Geza Vermes, *The Dead Sea Scrolls in English*, 3rd ed. (Sheffield, UK: JSOT Press, 1987).

[2] It is by no means clear, however, whether the solar calendar was actually observed at Qumran or whether it was an ideal calendar. As Philip Alexander reminds me (private communication), it would have taken only thirty years for the solar calendar to be one month out of sync with the movement of the sun, and for the observance of the agricultural festivals to be in trouble. Another theory maintains that the solar calendar was, in fact, the original calendar of the Temple in Jerusalem that was replaced by the lunar calendar by the Hasmonean high priests; see Annie Jaubert, "Le calendrier des Jubilés et de la secte de Qumrân: Ses origines bibliques," *VT* 3 (1953), pp. 250–264; eadem, "The Calendar of Qumran and the Passion Narrative in John," in Raymond E. Brown and James H. Charlesworth, eds., *John and Qumran* (London: Geoffrey Chapman, 1972), pp. 62–76; James C. VanderKam, "The Origin, Character and History of the 364 Day Calendar: A Reassessment of Jaubert's Hypotheses," *CBQ* 41 (1979), pp. 390–411. On Rachel Elior's far-reaching conclusions based on this theory, see her *Three Temples*, pp. 84 ff., and the critique by Sacha Stern ("Rachel Elior on Ancient Jewish Calendars: A Critique," *Aleph* 5 [2005], pp. 287–292; Elior's response: "Ancient Jewish Calendars: A Response," *Aleph* 5 [2005], pp. 293–302) and Himmelfarb, "Merkavah Mysticism since Scholem," pp. 25 ff.

[3] The literature about the Messianic expectation of the Qumran community is vast; see the useful overview in John J. Collins, *The Scepter and the Star: The Messiahs of the Dead Sea Scrolls and Other Ancient Literature* (New York: Doubleday, 1995), in particular chapter 4, "The Messiahs of Aaron and Israel," pp. 74 ff.

found priestly ideal, clearly intended as a substitute for the despised priesthood of the Jerusalem Temple. The members of the community could no longer offer any sacrifices but instead propagated prayer and worship within the community as (temporary) compensation for the sacrificial rites in the Temple (not unlike some of the prophets):[4]

> (IX, 3) When these exist in Israel in accordance with all these rules in order to establish the spirit of holiness according to eternal truth, (4) in order to atone for the guilt of iniquity and for the unfaithfulness of sin, that they may obtain loving kindness for the land, without the flesh of burnt offerings and without the fats of sacrifice. And the heave offering (5) of the lips in compliance with the decree will be like the pleasant fragrance of righteousness, and perfection of behavior will be acceptable like a freewill offering.

Like the priests in the Temple, they practiced daily immersion as the appropriate purification from ritual impurity. Accordingly, it was the priests who presided over the daily meals of the community, which, like the offerings in the Temple, were prepared in cultic purity. Josephus gives a graphic account of these proceedings:[5]

> They [the ordinary members of the community] are then dismissed by their superiors to the various crafts in which they are severally proficient and are strenuously employed until the fifth hour, when they again assemble in one place and, after girding their loins with linen cloths, bathe their bodies in cold water. After this purification, they assemble in a private apartment which none of the uninitiated is permitted to enter; pure now themselves, they repair to the refectory, as to some sacred shrine. When they have taken their seats in silence, the baker serves out the loaves to them in order, and the cook sets before each one plate with a single course. Before meat the priest says a grace, and none may partake until after the prayer. When breakfast is ended, he pronounces a further grace; thus at the beginning and at the close they do homage to God as the bountiful giver of life. Then laying aside their raiment, as holy vestments, they again betake themselves to their labours until the evening. On their return they sup in like manner, and any guests who may have arrived sit down with them.

It appears that at least some members of the Qumran community practiced celibacy, whereas others were married; this is what scholars conclude from the conflicting tendencies presented by the Community Rule (1QS), on the one hand, which – presumably intended for the leaders of the community – presupposes celibacy, and the Damascus Rule (CD), on the other, which – probably addressing a wider audience of members – takes marriage for granted.[6] If this view is correct, the members practicing celibacy did so not because of any ascetic ideal

---

[4] 1QS IX, 3–5.
[5] Bellum, 2:129–132; see also 1QS VI, 4–6.
[6] The former being the more radical group that developed out of the latter. But see Eyal Regev, *Sectarianism in Qumran: A Cross-Cultural Perspective* (Berlin: Walter de Gruyter, 2007), pp. 321 ff.

but most likely because they were following again the example of the Temple priests, who were forbidden sexual intercourse during the time of their service in the Temple unless they had taken the proper bath of immersion before sunset so as to be pure for the next day's sacrifices. The same may be true for the ideal of poverty and the shared property practiced by the members of the sect and imposed on all its new initiates (1QS VI, 19, 22): it is the priestly paragon of law (*torah*), justice (*mishpat*), and purity (*tohorah*) that governs the rules for admission of the adept into the community (1QS VI, 22) – which culminate in the adept handing over his property to the full control of the Bursar of the Congregation – rather than some romantic notion of an ascetic life (inspired, as some scholars would have it, by Christian monasticism).

Thus, it comes as little surprise that the Qumran community claims the concept of the Temple for itself – or, more precisely, that it transfers the concept of the Temple from the physical building in Jerusalem with its priests and its offerings to the Qumran community with its priestly leaders as the spiritual and true Temple. The community as such, with its worship and prayers, is the "House of Holiness" and the "Holy of Holies":[7]

> (VIII, 4) When these things exist in Israel, (5) the Council of the Community shall be founded on truth, to be an everlasting plantation, a House of Holiness (*bet qodesh*) for Israel and the foundation of the Holy of Holies (*sod qodesh qodashim*)[8] (6) for Aaron, true witnesses for the judgment and chosen by the will (of God) to atone for the land and to render (7) the wicked their retribution. This [the community] is the tested rampart, the precious corner-stone, (8) whose foundations shall neither shake nor tremble from their place (cf. Isa. 28:16). (It will be) a dwelling of the Holy of Holies (*ma'on qodesh qodashim*)[9] (9) for Aaron with eternal knowledge of the covenant of justice and in order to offer a pleasant fragrance; and it will be a house of perfection and truth (*bet tamim we-emet*) in Israel (10) that they may establish a covenant in compliance with the everlasting decrees. And these will be accepted in order to atone for the land and to determine the judgment of wickedness, and there will be no (more) iniquity.

Here the Qumran community with its hierarchically organized structure represents the true Temple, consisting of *qodesh* (obviously the *hekhal* – "Sanctuary," in the biblical terminology) and *qodesh (ha-) qodashim* (the Holy of Holies). Whereas the former is accessible to all of Israel – meaning, of course, the ordinary members of the community – the latter remains reserved for the priests: they are, literally, the Holy of Holies of the Qumran community. The same distinction seems to hold true for 1QS IX, 5 f.: "At that time, the men of the community (*anshei ha-yahad*) shall set apart a House of Holiness (*bet qodesh*) for

---

[7] 1QS VIII, 4–10.

[8] Vermes's "an Assembly of Supreme Holiness" smoothens the translation but glosses over the allusion to the "Holy of Holies" in the Temple.

[9] Both García Martínez and Tigchelaar and Vermes have a "most holy dwelling," glossing over the allusion to the "Holy of Holies" in the Temple.

Aaron in order to be united as a Holy of Holies (*qodesh qodashim*), and a House of the Community (*bet yahad*) for Israel, those who walk in perfection."[10] Again, the House of the Community is for the ordinary members, whereas the priests are the community (*yahad*) of the Holy of Holies, the innermost part of the Temple where God resides.

It is only against this background of the community's priestly orientation and its identification with the Temple that the concept of the sect's communion with the angels can be fully understood. The wholly integrated members of the sect with the priests at their head lived a life in absolute cultic purity and were therefore worthy of communicating with the angels. More precisely, the Qumran sect was convinced that the angels were united with its members and were spiritually present in the community. In other words, we encounter here the exact reverse of the ascent apocalypses. It is not some chosen hero who ascends to heaven and is transformed into an angel in order to approach the divine throne but rather the angels that descend to earth into the community of the chosen and elect of Israel so as to unite with them. The fact that the earthly Temple is polluted does not result in a hero's ascent to heaven to see the true heavenly Temple; instead, the priests of the heavenly Temple unite with the true priests of the true earthly Temple to assist them in their fight against the forces of darkness and to jointly usher in the period of salvation and eternal bliss on earth. Two major if overlapping concepts of the sect's communion with the angels can be distinguished, as detailed in the next two sections.[11]

Communion with the Angels in the Holy War

The eschatological holy war, which the Qumran community expects to begin soon, is not only a battle of the Sons of Light against the Sons of Darkness

---

[10] Vermes's translation unfortunately obfuscates the meaning of the text: "the men of the Community shall set apart a House of Holiness in order that it may be united to the most holy things and a House of Community for Israel."

[11] For the relevant literature, see especially Heinz-Wolfgang Kuhn, *Enderwartung und gegenwärtiges Heil* (Göttingen: Vandenhoeck and Ruprecht, 1966), pp. 66–93; Peter von der Osten-Sacken, *Gott und Belial. Traditionsgeschichtliche Untersuchungen zum Dualismus in den Texten aus Qumran* (Göttingen: Vandenhoeck and Ruprecht, 1969), pp. 222–232; Georg Klinzing, *Die Umdeutung des Kultus in der Qumrangemeinde und im Neuen Testament* (Göttingen: Vandenhoeck and Ruprecht, 1971), pp. 125 ff.; Schäfer, *Rivalität*, pp. 33–40; Hermann Lichtenberger, *Studien zum Menschenbild in Texten der Qumrangemeinde* (Göttingen: Vandenhoeck and Ruprecht, 1980), pp. 224–227; Michael Mach, *Entwicklungsstadien des jüdischen Engelglaubens in vorrabbinischer Zeit* (Tübingen: J.C.B. Mohr [Paul Siebeck], 1992), pp. 209 ff. I am following here my own distinction between military and liturgical communion, with the purity of the camp resulting from the military communion, since I find Mach's distinction between military, priestly-liturgical, and present (*präsentisch*) communion rather confusing (pp. 209 f.). All of these communions are "present" in the sense that the presence of the angels is experienced as immediate.

but also a battle between the heavenly Prince Michael, backed by his angelic host, and Belial, the Prince of Darkness, who is backed by his angels. Michael is known from the biblical book of Daniel as the angel of the people of Israel (Dan. 12:1) who, together with the angel Gabriel, fights first against the angelic Prince of Persia and then against the Prince of Greece (Dan. 10:20 f.); each nation, therefore, has an angel who represents his nation in heaven. Whereas in Daniel the battle between the angels of the various nations and their hosts takes place in heaven and is mirrored in the earthly battle of the Maccabees against the Seleucid oppressors (with their Jewish supporters) – in fact, the battle on earth "replays" what has been decided already in the celestial battle – in Qumran the angels physically join forces with the human army on earth and lead it to victory.

The major Qumran text that describes the eschatological battle is the so-called War Scroll (1QM, 4QM), which is preserved in a number of versions and may have achieved its final form in the last decades of the first century BCE or at the beginning of the first century CE.[12] As in Daniel, the final battle is waged against the Jewish opponents of the Qumran community in Jerusalem, as well as against the foreign oppressor. At this point in history the latter are no longer the Greeks but the Romans, who in the Qumran documents are denoted by the symbolic name "Kittim" – a name that is mentioned several times in the Hebrew Bible but is applied to the Romans for the first time in Daniel (Dan. 11:30).[13] These Kittim figure most prominently in the War Scroll (1QM I, 9–12):

> (I, 9) On the day on which the Kittim fall, there shall be battle, and savage destruction before the God (10) of Israel, for this will be the day determined by him since ancient times for the war of extermination against the sons of darkness (*benei hoshekh*). On this (day), the assembly of gods (*'adat elim*) and the community of men (*qehillat anashim*) shall confront each other for great destruction. (11) The sons of light (*benei or*) and the lot of darkness (*goral hoshekh*) shall battle together for God's might, amid the roar of a huge multitude and the shout of gods and men (*teru'at elim wa-'anashim*), on the day of the calamity. It will be a time of (12) suffering fo[r al]l the people redeemed by God. Of all their sufferings, none will be like this, from its sudden beginning until its end in eternal redemption.

The two camps that fight the decisive and ultimate battle are the "Kittim" with the "sons" or "company of darkness," on the one hand, and the "assembly of gods" with the "community of men" and the "sons of light" on the other. The

---

[12] Vermes, *Dead Sea Scrolls*, p. 104. Jean Duhaime suggests a *terminus a quo* around 164 BCE and a *terminus ad quem* around the middle of the first century BCE; see his *The War Texts: 1QM and Related Manuscripts* (London: T. & T. Clark International, 2004), pp. 97 f.

[13] This verse most likely refers to the collapse of Antiochus's IV campaign against Egypt in 168 BCE, when the Romans forced him to end his war and vacate Egypt once and for all, although the possibility cannot be excluded that the term "Kittim" in some Qumran documents or in certain early layers of the Qumran documents was used to designate the Seleucids rather than the Romans.

Kittim are definitely the Romans, and the "sons/company of darkness" presumably are the Jewish rivals of the Qumran sect with their angelic supporters. As to their opponents, it is obvious that the "assembly of gods" refers to the angelic supporters of the Qumran community: the Hebrew *elim* (literally "gods") designates angels – as already in the Hebrew Bible, where originally Canaanite gods have been demoted to mere angels in order to be integrated into the Jewish concept of the one and only God. The "community of men," of course, is the Qumran community, and the "sons of light" refers to both the members of the sect and their angelic supporters. Hence, we encounter here a perfectly balanced structure: two camps standing in opposition to one another, each consisting of humans and angels who fight a merciless battle. That this battle is ultimately fought between human and divine forces on both sides is graphically demonstrated by the battle shouts of "gods and men": humans and their angelic comrades in arms spur each other on to supreme military performances. There can be no doubt, finally, that all this is taking place on earth, not in heaven; and there can likewise be no doubt as to the ultimate triumph of the superior camp – the Qumran sect with its angels.

This antagonism is expressed in similar terms in a number of texts in the War Scroll. When it is said (1QM XV, 14), for example, that the "[w]arrior gods (*gibborei elim*) gird themselves for battle," the text refers again to the angels as participants in the decisive conflict; but when it goes on to say "and the formation[s of] the h[o]ly ones (*sidrei qedoshim*) [pre]pare [themselves] for the day of [revenge]," it is unclear whether the angels are still meant or their human companions, for the term *qedoshim* can refer to both angels and humans (in the sense of "holy community" or "holy people").[14] Some texts make clear that it is not just humans and angels that fight each other but that even God himself is present during the final battle (1QM XII, 7–9):[15]

> (XII, 7) For you, God, are awe[some] in the glory of your kingdom, and the congregation of your holy ones (*'adat qedoshekhah*) is among us for everlasting assistance. We will [treat] kings with contempt, with jeers (8) and mockery the heroes, for the Lord is holy and the King of Glory (*melekh ha-kavod*) is with us together with the Holy Ones (*qedoshim*). [Our] he[roes and] the army of his angels are enlisted with us. (9) The Hero of war (*gibbor ha-milhamah*) is with our congregation; the host of his spirits (*tzeva'ruhaw*) is with our steps. Our horsemen are [like] clouds and fogs of dew that cover the earth.

Here the "Holy Ones" are clearly the angels, as are the "army of his angels" and the "host of his spirits." They fight together with the "horsemen" of the earthly community – and God, the "King of Glory," is in their midst to lead them to victory.

---

[14] The Aramaic equivalent to *qedoshim* in Daniel is *qaddishin* or *qaddishei 'elyonin* (cf. Dan. 7:22, 27); there it refers to the human community, not to the angels.

[15] Cf. the parallel in 1QM XIX, 1 f.

The detailed description of the weapons and military tactics employed in this battle plays an important role in the War Scroll; scholars have argued that both are inspired by the art of war practiced by the Roman legion rather than by the Greek phalanx.[16] Particularly instructive is the graphic depiction of the "towers" surrounded on three sides by "shields" and equipped with "spears," advancing from the formation of soldiers (1QM IX, 10 ff.). These are obviously the fortified towers used in the Roman battle order, but what is unique in this battle order as envisaged by the Qumran sect is the continuation (1QM IX, 14–16): "And on all the shields of the towers (15) they shall write: on the first, *Michael*, [on the second, *Gabriel*, on the third,] *Sariel*, and on the forth, *Raphael*. (16) *Michael* and *Gabriel* on [the right, and *Sariel* and *Raphael* on the left]." Instead of the emblems borne by the Roman soldiers, the holy warriors at Qumran carry no pictorial images but solely the names of the four archangels who head the angelic host fighting with them: Michael, Gabriel, Sariel, and Raphael. These angels – except for Sariel, who is replaced by Phanuel – are immediately reminiscent of the four archangels Michael, Gabriel, Raphael, and Phanuel in the Similitudes who accompany God when he approaches Enoch from his throne in the heavenly Holy of Holies (1 En. 71:9 f.).[17] The archangels (whatever their number, mostly four or seven) are the immediate entourage of God; they surround him and accompany him when he leaves his throne. Hence, the fact that their names are inscribed on the shields of the towers used in the final battle not only means that they are present (this is taken for granted), it also indicates that God himself is present in the battle order of the Qumran warriors.

One of the major theological doctrines of the Qumran sect is that everything is preordained or predestined by God. This holds true as well for membership in the community of the elect, of those who will be rescued in the final battle. In fact, from the very beginning, the Qumran warriors are registered in the heavenly book of life (1QM XII, 1–5):

(XII, 1) For there is a multitude of the holy ones (*qedoshim*) in heaven and hosts of the angels (*tziv'ot mal'akhim*) is in your holy dwelling (*zevul qodshekha*) to [praise] your [truth]. And the chosen ones of the holy people (*behirei 'am qodesh*) (2) you have established for yourself among t[hem.] The book of the names of all their armies (*tzeva'am*) is with you in your holy abode (*bi-me'on qodshekha*), and the num[ber of the ju]st is in your glorious dwelling-place (*bi-zevul kevodkha*). (3) The favors of your blessings and the covenant of your peace you engraved for them with the chisel of life, in order to rule [over them] during all times eternal, (4) to muster the arm[ies] of your [ch]osen ones (*tziv'ot behirekha*) according to their thousands and their myriads, together with your holy ones (*qedoshekha*) [and with] your angels (*mal'akhekha*), to have the upper hand (5) in battle [and destroy] the rebels of the earth in the lawsuit of your judgments, so that [they may] triu[mph] together with the chosen ones of heaven (*behirei shamayim*).

---

[16] See Vermes, *The Dead Sea Scrolls*, p. 104; Duhaime, *The War Texts*, pp. 83 ff.

[17] In the Book of the Watchers it is Michael, Sariel, Raphael, and Gabriel who "looked down from the Sanctuary in heaven" (1 En. 9:1).

Here, the "holy ones" in vv. 1 and 4 are identical with the "host of the angels";
they are angels and not humans. They do what they are supposed to do: they
reside in heaven and praise God. The "chosen ones of the holy people," on the
other hand, are the members of the Qumran community; they are listed with God
and his angels in the book of life, and it is registration in this heavenly record
that qualifies them for the final battle together with the angels (v. 4) and for the
expected triumph over their enemies (v. 5). Only one's predestined registration
in the book of life determines who in the end belongs to those elect few who
will survive the battle. One may even go a step further and argue that heavenly
registration not only guarantees participation in the final battle but in a way depicts or anticipates the participation of the members of the Qumran community
in the heavenly praise of the angels. True, the "holy ones" who praise God are
the angels and not the members of the Qumran community; but still, just as the
"chosen ones of the holy people" are chosen to fight with the angels, in a similar
way they are also present among the angels when they commence their heavenly praise. This passage, therefore, seems to indicate that military communion
with the angels cannot be separated from liturgical communion. The human and
angelic elect are closely bonded, both in their military action and in their praise
of God.

Because of the presence of the angels among the holy warriors, it is also imperative that only men fit for the battle be admitted to the ranks of warriors and
that there be absolute bodily and cultic purity in their camp. Here again priestly
and military ideas merge (1QM VII, 3–7):[18]

> (7:3) And no young man, small boy[19] or woman at all shall enter their camps when
> they leave (4) Jerusalem to go to war, until they return. And no lame (*pisseah*), or blind
> (*'iwwer*), or paralyzed (*higger*) person nor any man afflicted with an indelible blemish
> on his flesh, nor any man smitten with an impurity (5) of his flesh, none of these shall
> go out to war with them. They shall all be volunteers for war, perfect in spirit and in
> body (*temimei ruach u-vasar*) and ready for the day of vengeance. And every (6) man
> who has not cleansed himself of his "spring" (*lo'yihyeh tahor mimqoro*) on the day of
> the battle shall not go down with them, for the holy angels (*mal'akhei qodesh*) are to-

---

[18] See also the parallel 1QSa (1Q28a) II, 3–10, which contains the statutes of the messianic
community:
> (3) And no man, smitten with any of the impurities (4) of man, shall enter the assembly of
> these; and no man smitten with any of these should be (5) established in his office amongst
> the congregation: everyone who is smitten in his flesh, or paralyzed in his feet or (6) in his
> hands, or lame, or blind, or deaf, or dumb, or smitten in his flesh with a blemish (7) visible
> to the eyes, or the tottering old man unable to keep upright in the midst of the assembly; (8)
> these shall not en[ter] to take their place [a]mong the congregation of the men of renown, for
> the angels (9) of holiness (*mal'akhei qodesh*) are [with] their [congre]gation.

[19] García Martínez and Tigchelaar have only "young boy" (Vermes has just "boy"), but the
text distinguishes between *na'ar* ("young man") and *za'atut* ("small boy, kid"). But, of course,
it is also possible to read *za'atut* as an adjective: *na'ar za'atut*, "small boy."

gether with their armies (*'im tziv'otam yahad*). And there shall be a space (7) between all their camps for the place serving as a latrine[20] of about two thousand cubits, so that no immodest nakedness will be seen in the surroundings of all their camps.

This text describes the military camp of the eschatological community before the holy warriors leave Jerusalem for the final battle. It is an all-male camp (or rather, as we learn from v. 7, there are several camps) filled with warriors who are "perfect in spirit and body." Excluded from the camp are (1) boys, who are not yet adults, and women, and (2) adult men who have some kind of bodily blemish or who are impure for some other unspecified reason. The bodily blemish is specified as lame, blind, and crippled or some other *lasting* bodily affliction. An additional impurity is given in v. 6, where the impurity of the "spring" refers to a nocturnal emission (*ba'al qeri* in the later rabbinical terminology). Finally, we learn (v. 7) that a certain distance must be kept between the camps and the place serving as latrine.

Scholars have referred to several biblical texts as the background against which these instructions must be seen and interpreted. First, there is the obvious parallel of Deut. 23:10–15, which describes the camp of the Israelites, who are setting off on a military expedition. It is concerned with the impurity caused by a nocturnal emission (a person rendered unclean by a nocturnal emission must leave the camp and is allowed to reenter it only after he has taken a bath of immersion) and the impurity caused by human excrement (an area outside the camp is designated for bodily relief, and the excrement must be covered with earth). Therefore, Deut. 23:10–15 and 1QM VII, 3–7 tally with regard to the setting (military camp) and instructions concerning nocturnal emissions and the latrine. Moreover, there is remarkable congruence as to the reasons given for these instructions: according to 1QM it is the presence of the "holy angels" in the camp, and according to Deuteronomy it is because "the Lord, your God, moves about in your camp to protect you and to deliver your enemies to you" (Deut. 23:15). As we have seen, the presence of the angels in the Qumran camp includes, or rather is the prerequisite for, the presence of God; hence the requirement of absolute purity.

A second biblical text adduced by some scholars is Num. 5:1–4, which refers to the camp of the Israelites in the wilderness (not necessarily connected with military action). Here, instructions are given to remove from the camp any person, male or female, who is afflicted with leprosy or defiled by a corpse; the reason again is God's presence in the camp: "put them outside the camp so that they do not defile the camp of those in whose midst I dwell" (5:3). Leprosy and corpse impurity are not mentioned in 1QM, but both may be included in the "indelible bodily blemish" and the unspecified impurity (1QM VII, 4).

---

[20] Lit. "for the place of the hand."

The third biblical text, which is neglected by many scholars but seems to me highly pertinent to our passage from the War Scroll, is Lev. 21:17–21. It contains God's instructions to Moses regarding the priesthood of Aaron and his descendants: "(17) Speak to Aaron and say: No man of your offspring throughout the ages who has a defect shall be qualified to offer the food of his God. (18) No one at all who has a defect shall be qualified: no man who is blind (*'iwwer*), or lame (*pisseah*), or mutilated (*harum*) or has a limb too long (*sarua'*);[21] (19) no man who has a broken leg or a broken arm; (20) or who is a hunchback, or a dwarf, or who has a growth in his eye, or who has a boil-scar, or scurvy, or crushed testes." This list of bodily afflictions is more detailed than the one in 1QM, but it is striking that the first two afflictions listed ("blind" and "lame") are identical with those specified in 1QM ("lame" and "blind"); only the third affliction in 1QM (*higger*) is missing in the Bible, but it is not impossible that the difficult *sarua'* in Leviticus would include someone who limps or is paralyzed. In any case, it is evident that only the passage in Leviticus specifies the "blemish on the flesh" mentioned so prominently in 1QM. Hence it appears that the instructions regarding the military camp of the Qumran warriors are informed by a patchwork of at least three biblical texts (the nocturnal emission and the place for the latrine stemming from Deuteronomy, the bodily defect from Leviticus, and the impurity from Numbers), with Leviticus 21:17–21 giving 1QM a distinctly priestly flavor.

Liturgical Communion with the Angels

The liturgical or cultic communion of the Qumran sectarians with the angels, only hinted at in the texts referring to the eschatological battle, finds full expression in the hymns of the community and in the rules governing its daily life. The so-called Hodayot or Thanksgiving Hymns (1QH) are a collection of hymns in which the members of the sect praise God for having saved them from the lot of the wicked and having gifted them with special knowledge of the divine mysteries. Some of the hymns seem not to refer to all the community's members but to an individual, probably the Teacher of Righteousness himself, the founder of the sect. The various hymns hardly belong to the same time but originated at different times and under different circumstances. The entire collection may have reached its final stage during the last century BCE.[22]

The hymns share with the texts discussed so far the firm conviction that the members of the community are purified and free from sin, and that it is this ex-

---

[21] For *harum o sarua'* the JPS translation suggests the alternative: "has a limb too short or too long."

[22] Vermes, *The Dead Sea Scrolls*, p. 165.

traordinary purity that allies them with the angels. Hence, when the Qumran sectarians perform their privileged task of praising God, they can be certain that they join in with the celestial praise of the angels (1QHª XI, 19–23):[23]

> (19) I thank you, Lord,
> for you have saved my soul from the Pit (*shahat*),
> and from the Netherworld of Abaddon (*she'ol avaddon*)
> (20) have lifted me up to an eternal height,
> so that I can walk on limitless plain.
> And I know there is hope for someone
> (21) you formed from dust
> for an eternal community (*sod 'olam*).
> The depraved spirit you have purified from great offence
> so that he can stand with (22) the host of the holy ones (*tzeva' qedoshim*),
> and can enter in communion (*la-vo be-yahad*)
> with the congregation of the sons of heaven (*'adat benei shamayim*).
> You have cast for man an eternal destiny (*goral 'olam*)
> with the spirits (23) of knowledge (*ruhot da'at*),
> so that he might praise your name in a common rejoicing (*be-yahad rinnah*)
> and tell your marvels before all your works.

Here the sectarians speak in full awareness of the fact that they, as members of the community, are already saved from the Pit and the Netherworld of Abaddon. In other words, they experience salvation in their own lifetime, by virtue of their membership in the sect; they know that they are saved and will not descend to the Netherworld. This is a clear example of immediately realized eschatology, an eschatological concept that experiences salvation in the here and now.[24] To be sure, the sectarians continue to expect the full realization of salvation in the future (in the very near future, indeed), but they already know that, whatever happens, they will be part of this salvation. There is a certain tension between immediate eschatology (the firm conviction that one *is* already saved) and traditional eschatology (which expects salvation in the future), and it goes without saying that this tension can be the more easily tolerated the closer the current situation is to the expected ultimate decision and becomes all the more unbear-

---

[23] Cf. the parallel 1QHª XIX, 10–14. The text division does not follow Sukenik's *editio princeps* but 1QHª in García Martínez and Tigchelaar, *The Dead Sea Scrolls*, vol. 1, pp. 147 ff.

[24] On this concept, see David E. Aune, *The Cultic Setting of Realized Eschatology in Early Christianity* (Leiden: Brill, 1972); John J. Collins, *Apocalypticism in the Dead Sea Scrolls* (London: Routledge, 1997), pp. 115–129; Hermann Lichtenberger, "Auferstehung in den Qumranfunden," in Friedrich Avemarie and Hermann Lichtenberger, eds., *Auferstehung – Resurrection: The Fourth Durham-Tübingen Research Symposion: Resurrection, Transfiguration and Exaltation in Old Testament, Ancient Judaism and Early Christianity* (Tübingen: Mohr Siebeck, 2001), pp. 79–91. To be sure, the assurance of salvation does not work automatically: sinfulness remains a constant threat to the members of the community, some of whom even get expelled temporarily or permanently.

able the greater the gap that exists between the imperfect present and the full realization of salvation in the future.

Whereas the War Scroll puts the emphasis on future salvation (although expected very soon), the Thanksgiving Scroll is imbued with the certainty that salvation has already taken place or, to be more precise, that the decisive prerequisite for salvation – to be chosen by God – has been fulfilled: the members of the community *are* redeemed from the Netherworld and raised up to "eternal height" *because* they belong to the "eternal community" of the Qumran sectarians. They *are* free of sin and *therefore* able to stand with the "holy ones." The full Hebrew expression for "stand" is *le-hityatztzev be-ma'amad 'im*, literally "to take a stand/to station oneself in a position/the (same) standing place with": the one who prays is physically standing in the very same place with the angels. Since the original place of the angels is in heaven, we may conclude that the members of the community envisage themselves standing with the angels in heaven when singing the hymn (although the possibility cannot be ruled out that the opposite movement has taken place: that the angels have descended to earth to join the humans in their worship). This is reinforced through the statement that they enter into a *yahad* (literally "union/communion") with the "sons of heaven" and that this presence of humans among the "spirits of knowledge" (again the angels) is an "eternal destiny," that is, it will be experienced by the chosen sectarians forever. The use of the word *yahad* together with the preposition *'im* ("with") is typical of the Qumran concept of the communion of angels and humans.[25] The same is true for the word *goral,* which appears frequently in texts mentioning this communion;[26] moreover, it is not unlikely that the idea of an everlasting destiny for humans together with the angels again has priestly connotations.[27]

The hymn climaxes in the last two lines, which specify the purpose of the heavenly communion of humans and angels: they praise God's name *be-yahad rinnah,* literally "in a joint/united rejoicing." This phrase alludes to Job 38:7: "When the morning stars (*kokhvei boqer*) rejoice together (*be-ron-yahad*),[28] then all the sons of God (*benei elohim*) shout for joy." In the biblical context both the "morning stars" and the "sons of God" are, of course, angels, and the verse describes the heavenly praise of the angelic hosts. In contrast to the Bible, in the Thanksgiving Scroll those who are united in rejoicing are angels and humans, and the only parallel that similarly applies Job 38:7 not just to angels but to both

---

[25] See Kuhn, *Enderwartung,* pp. 66 ff.; von der Osten-Sacken, *Gott und Belial,* pp. 223 ff.; Schäfer, *Rivalität,* p. 38, with nn. 24–26.

[26] Schäfer, *Rivalität,* p. 38, n. 27.

[27] See Kuhn, *Enderwartung,* p. 72, with reference to Ps. 16:5 f., 73:26, and 142:6.

[28] Lit. "at the joint/united rejoicing of the morning stars."

angels and humans is a large midrash complex in the rabbinic literature.[29] There the "morning stars" are identified with Israel,[30] and only the "sons of God" remain angels. This specification is not particularly exciting (it is typical of the rabbinic literature); what is provocative, however, is the conclusion drawn from it, namely, that the angels ("sons of God") must withhold their praise until Israel (the "morning stars") have finished apportioning theirs! This interpretation reads a temporal sequence into the Job verse: the "sons of God" may shout for joy only *after* the "morning stars" have rejoiced together. The angels must rein in their praise of God because it is inferior to the praise of Israel. Hence, whereas the Thanksgiving Scroll uses Job 38:7 to underline the liturgical communion of angels and humans in heaven, elevating humans to one and the same level with the angels, rabbinic Judaism uses the very same verse to elevate the humans (Israel) above even the angels, in a sphere that is commonly regarded as the prerogative of the angels: divine praise.

Liturgical communion with the angels entails not only participation in the heavenly praise; it also means that the Qumran community shares with the angels its singular knowledge of God. The angels are the "spirits of knowledge" (1QH^a XI, 22 f.), the "mediators of knowledge" (1QH^a XXIII, 6) or just "those who know" (1QH^a XIX, 14); the privileged elect, who belong to their community, have no further need of a mediator because they share their knowledge (1QH^a XIV, 12 f.):

> (12) All the nations may know your truth.
> and all the people your glory.
> For you have brought [your truth and] your [glo]ry
> (13) to all the men of your council,
> and in a common lot (*goral yahad*)
> with the angels of the face (*'im mal'akhei panim*),
> without a mediator (*melitz benayim*) for [your] h[oly ones] [...].

Here we have the same combination of *goral* and *yahad* that we observed previously and that is so characteristic of the Qumranic idea of a shared human and angelic destiny. The angels are specified as the "angels of the face," a phrase that has a distinctive history. The singular "angel of his face/countenance" (*mal'akh panaw*) appears only once in the Hebrew Bible, in Isa. 63:9, a verse that was already causing difficulties for the early interpreters.[31] It figures most

---

[29] See, e. g., Bereshit Rabbah 65:21; Sifre Deuteronomy § 306 (ed. Finkelstein, p. 343), and parallels; cf. Schäfer, *Rivalität*, pp. 170 ff.

[30] Because of Dan. 12:3, where it is said that "those who lead the many to righteousness [Israel] will be like the stars forever and ever."

[31] The Hebrew can be read in two ways. First, it can be translated as "(63:8) So he was their Deliverer. (9) In all their [Israel's] troubles he [God: following the *Qere* reading *lo* instead of the *Ketiv* reading *lo* '] was troubled, and the angel of his face (*mal'akh panaw*) delivered them. In his love and pity he redeemed them." Taken literally, this translation creates a tension between v. 8 (where the subject is God) and v. 9, which presupposes that not God himself but his angel

prominently, however, in Jubilees, a book that according to the standard view was composed around 150 BCE[32] and was found in a number of fragments in the Qumran library.[33] There, the revelation to Moses on Mount Sinai is delegated to the "angel of countenance," and the boundaries between God and his angel are blurred.[34] Our 1QH^a text, however, which uses the plural "angels of the face," apparently follows the more traditional concept of God surrounded by (mostly) four prominent angels ("archangels") that we also encountered in the War Scroll (the four angels inscribed on the shields of the fortified towers used in the decisive battle). It goes back to the Book of the Watchers (1 En. 9:1) and to the Similitudes (1 En. 40:9; 71:8 ff.), where the angels are termed "four presences" (*panim* = *prosōpa*), who stood "on the four sides of the Lord of spirits" and "uttered praises before the Lord of glory" (1 En. 40:2 f.). In reassuring the members of the Qumran community that they share a "common lot" with the four "angels of face/countenance," the Thanksgiving Scroll elevates them not just to the angelic host but to the level of the four highest angels surrounding God. By implication this means that the sectarians come as close to God as possible.

Moreover, the four angels and the human sectarians communicate directly with each other; they need no mediator between them. It seems as if angels and humans are not only physically together on the same geographic plane but become almost ontologically identical because they understand each other immediately. This is an extremely bold step if we consider the biblical concept of the prophets – and Moses in particular – as mediating between Israel and God, or the ascent apocalypses with the premortem ascent to heaven of a chosen hero. The members of the Qumran community no longer need a Moses who mediates between them and God and transmits the divine revelation; they are like the angels, not only very close to God but enjoying direct access to angelic knowledge of him. Nor do they need to undergo the complicated procedure of physical transformation into an angel. As a priestly community on earth they *are* angels, privileged to share the angels' liturgy as well as their knowledge.

---

redeemed Israel because God shared their troubles to such an extent that he was caught up, so to speak, together with Israel in their troubles. (The JPS translation again smoothes this interpretation by adding "himself" after "he": "In His love and pity he Himself redeemed them." But the "he" relates equally well – or even better – to the "angel of his face.") In order to avoid this problematic interpretation, the Septuagint reads: "(63:8) So he was their Deliverer (9) in all their troubles. No (using the *Ketiv* reading *lo'* instead of the *Qere* reading *lo*) messenger (reading *tzir* instead of *tzar*) or angel, his own face (separating between *mal'akh* and *panaw*) delivered them. ..." Here there is no real problem – God alone is Israel's redeemer – but the polemical tone ("no messenger or angel") and the awkward Hebrew ("his face delivered them") make it apparent that this translation is a secondary interpretation directed against the more literal first one.

[32] Martha Himmelfarb (private communication) prefers to place it in the 130s or even a little later.

[33] 1Q17–18; 2Q19–20; 3Q5; 4Q176a+b; 4Q216–224; 4Q482; 11Q12.

[34] See Schäfer, *Rivalität*, pp. 13–15.

The Community Rule (1QS) – probably composed around 100 BCE and re-garded as one of the oldest documents of the sect – expresses the same idea of the Qumran sect as the community of the (few) elect who share the knowledge reserved for angels. 1QS deals with the statutes of the community – initiation into the sect, its internal hierarchical structure, its discipline – and seems to have served as a kind of manual for its leaders; in addition, it includes liturgical cer-emonies, a model sermon, reflections on moral issues, and, at the end, a liturgical hymnlike piece in which a person (the community's master?) praises God and reflects on his destiny and duties. To this hymnic piece belongs the following quotation (1QS XI, 5–8):

> (XI, 5) From the fount of his righteousness (*meqor tzidqato*)
> is my justification,
> and from his marvelous mysteries (*razei pela'aw*)
> is the light in my heart.
> My eyes have gazed (*hibitu*)
> on what always is,
> (6) on wisdom that has been hidden from humankind (*tushiyyah
>   asher nisterah me-'enosh*),
> on knowledge (*de'ah*) and prudent understanding (*mezimat 'ormah*)
> (hidden) from the sons of men;
> on a fount of righteousness (*meqor tzedaqah*)
> and a well of strength (*miqweh gevurah*),
> on a spring (7) of glory (*ma'ayan kavod*)
> (hidden) from the assembly of flesh (*sod basar*).
> To those whom God has chosen (*la-'asher bahar*)
> he has given them as an everlasting possession,
> and has given them an inheritance
> in the lot (8) of the holy ones (*goral qedoshim*).
> He has joined (*hibber*) their assembly (*sod*)
> to the sons of heaven ('*im benei shamayim*)
> in order (to form) a council of the community ('*atzat yahad*),
> and a foundation of the building of holiness (*sod mavnit qodesh*)
> to be an everlasting plantation (*le-matta'at 'olam*) throughout all (9) future
>   ages.

The first part of this hymn contains a number of key terms that are characteristic of the knowledge granted the Qumran community in general and its master in particular: God's *tzedaqah* ("righteousness" or "justice") is the source of every-thing – of their "judgment" or "justification" and of their knowledge ("light in my heart"). The goal and content of their peculiar knowledge are described in terms – "marvelous mysteries" (*razei pela'aw*), "wisdom" (*tushiyyah*), "knowl-edge" (*de'ah*), and "prudent understanding" (*mezimat 'ormah*) – that are strik-ingly similar to those used in the Hekhalot literature and that there refer to the full knowledge of the Torah obtained by the Merkavah mystic.[35] It is very likely that the same association is evoked here, too: the Qumran sectarians have access to the direct and full knowledge of God that is revealed in the Torah. This is confirmed by the phrase "my eyes have gazed (*hibitu*)," which apparently does not refer to some kind of vision (in the sense of the ascent apocalypses) but to the mysteries of the Torah as already described in the Bible (Ps. 119:18): "Open my eyes that I may gaze (*abitah*) on the wonders/mysteries of your Torah (*nifla'ot mi-toratekha*)."

As obtained by the sectarians, God's knowledge issues in "righteousness/justice" (*tzedaqah*), "power/strength" (*gevurah*), and "glory" (*kavod*). These are theologically loaded terms; to be sure, none of them is reserved for God alone, but it is striking that *gevurah* and *kavod* in particular become terms – already in the Hebrew Bible, and increasingly in postbiblical texts – synonymous with God. Hence it would seem that the members of the community, when portrayed as drinking from the fount of divine righteousness, strength, and glory, are imagined as coming very close to and even participating in the divine realm.

However, the text makes it very clear that this wonderful destiny is not granted to ordinary humans ("sons of men," "assembly of flesh"); rather, it is reserved for the "chosen ones," who belong to the community of the elect. It is granted them forever and consists in the communion ("[common] lot") with the angels, who are again called "holy ones" and "sons of heaven." Angels and humans together form a joint community, which is specified as a "foundation of the building of holiness" (*sod mavnit qodesh*) and an "everlasting plantation" (*matta 'at 'olam*). Both phrases are reminiscent of 1QS VIII, 5, a passage that also speaks of an "everlasting plantation" and calls the council of the community a "house of holiness (*bet qodesh*) for Israel" and a "foundation of the Holy of Holies (*sod qodesh qodashim*) for Aaron."[36] As we have observed, the latter refers to the community as the true Temple, allocating the front part of the Temple (the Sanctuary) to the ordinary members and the back part (the Holy of Holies) to the priests. The word used here in 1QS (*mavnit*) is derived from *mivneh*, a *hapax legomenon* in Ezek. 40:2 that refers to Ezekiel's eschatological Jerusalem with the Temple at its center. Hence the everlasting communion of angels and humans, guaranteeing a perpetual flow of divine knowledge, is again envisaged in priestly terms.

The priestly connotation is even more evident in the final text to be discussed here, a passage that belongs to the Rule of Blessings (1QSb). The surviving fragments of this Rule apparently belonged to a collection that was attached to the Community Rule (1QS) and the War Scroll (1QM). The Rule is no doubt

---

[35] See, e. g., Schäfer, *Synopse zur Hekhalot-Literatur*, § 14 (3 Enoch) or § 623 (Adjuration of the Prince of the Countenance).

[36] On the Qumranic use of "plantation" and "building," see Johann Maier, *Die Texte vom Toten Meer*, vol. 2 (Munich: Ernst Reinhardt Verlag, 1960), pp. 89–91, 93 f.

eschatologically oriented and contains the blessings bestowed (1) on the members of the community, (2) on the high priest (obviously the priestly Messiah of Aaron), (3) on the priests, and (4) on the Prince of the Congregation (the Davidic Messiah of Israel). The blessings are intended for the messianic age, and it is not clear whether they served any practical purpose; on the other hand, it is hard to imagine that they were composed and preserved simply for future use (even though this future was expected to transpire relatively soon), and it may well be that they were actually recited in the community "during the course of some liturgy anticipating and symbolizing the coming of the Messianic era."[37] In the part containing the blessing bestowed on the priests we read the following (1QSb [1Q28b] IV, 22–28):

(22) [For] he has chosen you (*bahar bekhah*) [...] (23) to raise above the heads of the holy ones (*la-set be-rosh qedoshim*) and with you to [...] of your hand (24) the men of the council of god (*'atzat el*), and not by the hand of the prince (*sar*) of [...] one to his fellow. May you be (25) like an angel of the face (*ke-mal'akh panim*) in the abode of holiness (*ma'on qodesh*) for the glory of the God of the Hos[ts.[38] ... You shall] be around, serving in the Temple of the (26) kingdom (*hekhal malkhut*), casting the lot (*mappil goral*) with the angels of the face (*mal'akhei panim*) and (in) common council (*'atzat yahad*) [with the holy ones] for eternal time and for all the perpetual periods. For (27) [all] his [ju]dgments [are truth]. And may he make you hol[y] among his people, like a luminary [...] for the world in knowledge (*da'at*), and to enlighten the face of the Many! (28) [... And may he make you] a diadem of the Holy of Holies (*qodesh qodashim*), because [you shall be made ho]lly for him and you shall glorify his name and his holy things (*qodashaw*).

The priests (addressed in the singular) are the chosen of the chosen ones, the vanguard of the community of the elect (the "holy ones" in v. 23, above whose heads they rise, seem to be the members of the community and not the angels). They are "like the angel of the face," which is reminiscent of 1QH[a] XIV, 13,[39] where all members of the community are said to "share a common lot with the angels of the face." Here they "cast the lot with the angels of the face," which probably indicates that they collaborate with the angels on passing the sentence at the final judgment. The priests and the angels enter into a close bond; they are identical. They serve together in the heavenly Temple, called "abode of holiness" (*ma'on qodesh*)[40] and "Temple of the kingdom" (*hekhal malkhut*);[41] or rather, the priests of the Qumran community represent the Holy of Holies of the

---

[37] Vermes, *Dead Sea Scrolls*, p. 235.
[38] See also 1QSb III, 25 f., where the priests are blessed from God's "holy Abode" (*ma'on qodsho*) and called a "glorious ornament (*mikhlol hadar*) in the midst of the holy ones."
[39] See above, p. 125.
[40] The term *ma'on qodshekha* is biblical (see, e. g., Deut. 26:15) and refers in most cases to God's heavenly abode.
[41] The term *hekhal malkhut* is not biblical; only *hekhal melekh*, which, however, refers to the palace of an earthly king, not to God's Temple (see 2 Kings 20:18; Ps. 45:16; Dan. 1:4).

earthly Temple (v. 28) and as such intermingle with the angels in heaven. Earthly and heavenly Temple overlap or even become the same, because priests and angels likewise overlap or become the same.[42] To be sure, the priests are only the leaders of the community, and what is here said of the priests refers elsewhere to all full members of the community (see above); the privileged position of the priests only reinforces the priestly character of the Qumran community as a whole. Finally, the aspect of divine knowledge is again emphasized, for armed with their knowledge the priests enlighten "the Many," presumably the members of the community.

The Songs of the Sabbath Sacrifice

The so-called Songs of the Sabbath Sacrifice (*shirot 'olat ha-shabbat*) are a cycle of thirteen songs altogether, discovered in a number of manuscripts in caves 4 and 11 at Qumran and at Masada; they were first made public in a lecture by John Strugnell,[43] and the *editio princeps* was provided by Carol Newsom.[44] Whether they originated within the Qumran community and are sectarian documents in the strict sense of the word or whether they were produced outside the community and are to be regarded as extra- or even presectarian is a matter of debate.[45] There can be no doubt, however, that they played a vital role in the literary and historical context of the Qumran community; this can be inferred from the sheer quantity of fragments found in Qumran and the many parallels between the songs and other Qumranic texts[46] (the discovery of a fragment at Masada should not be taken as decisive proof of nonsectarian authorship).[47]

---

[42] See also 1QSb III, 5 f., a very fragmentary text, where the messianic high priest is addressed and mentioned together "with the holy angels" (*mal'akhei qodesh*).

[43] John Strugnell, "The Angelic Liturgy at Qumran–4Q Serek Šīrōt 'Olat Haššabbāt," in *Congress Volume: Oxford 1959* (Leiden: Brill, 1960), pp. 318–345.

[44] Carol Newsom, *Songs of the Sabbath Sacrifice: A Critical Edition* (Atlanta, GA: Scholars Press, 1985).

[45] In her *editio princeps* Newsom concluded her deliberations on the provenance of the songs with the cautious working hypothesis "that the scroll of the Sabbath Shirot is a product of the Qumran community" (*Songs of the Sabbath Sacrifice*, p. 4). Since then, however, she has changed her mind and regards as the "most plausible explanation" that the songs originated "outside of and probably prior to the emergence of the Qumran community" but nevertheless "became an important text in the community": Carol Newsom, "'Sectually Explicit' Literature from Qumran," in William H. Propp, Baruch Halpern, and David N. Freedman, eds., *The Hebrew Bible and Its Interpreters* (Winona Lake, IN: Eisenbrauns, 1990), p. 184.

[46] See the useful list of thematic and formal features that the songs share with sectarian material in Ra'anan S. Boustan (Abusch), "Angels in the Architecture: Temple Art and the Poetics of Praise in the *Songs of the Sabbath Sacrifice*," in Boustan and Reed, *Heavenly Realms and Earthly Realities*, p. 198, n. 11.

[47] Vermes (*The Dead Sea Scrolls*, p. 221) suggests that either "some Essenes joined the revolutionaries and took with them some of their manuscripts, or that the rebels occupied

The thirteen songs were apparently composed for performance during the first thirteen Sabbaths of the year according to the solar calendar of the Qumran community.[48] The surviving openings of the songs connect them with a holocaust offering made on these Sabbaths (as described in Num. 28:9 f. and Ezek. 46:4 f.), but there is no evidence whatsoever that the sectarians ever offered sacrifices; it has been suggested, therefore, that the songs were part of a liturgical performance intended to serve as replacement for the cultic Sabbath sacrifices offered in the polluted Jerusalem Temple.[49] On closer inspection, however, it is difficult to determine the precise liturgical function of the songs within the framework of the community. For even a cursory reading of the songs immediately reveals that we are not here dealing with liturgical texts in the conventional sense of the word: the songs describe the angelic worship for each of the thirteen Sabbaths, but they remain conspicuously silent with regard to the actual words of praise intoned by the angels; instead, they invite the angels to praise God, and then describe the order and manner of the liturgical activities performed by the angels in heaven.[50] As such, scholars assign the songs to the genre of "liturgical invitation" rather than to the category of texts that record the contents of actual praises.[51]

The first song calls on the angels to praise God (*hallelu*) and sets the tone for the whole cycle with its distinct terminology. From the very outset the angels are given the striking designation of *elohim* or *elim* – literally "gods" – and in a

---

the Qumran area after its evacuation by the Community and subsequently transferred Essene manuscripts to their final place of resistance"; Christopher Morray-Jones rightly observes that "if discovery outside Qumran were held to be proof of non-sectarian authorship the unambiguously sectarian *Damascus Rule* would likewise be excluded": Christopher Morray-Jones, "The Temple Within: The Embodied Divine Image and Its Worship in the Dead Sea Scrolls and Other Early Jewish and Christian Sources," *SBL.SPS* 37 (1998), p. 410.

[48] Newsom, *Songs of the Sabbath Sacrifice*, p. 19.

[49] Cf. A. S. van der Woude, "Fragmente einer Rolle der Lieder für das Sabbatopfer aus Höhle XI von Qumran (11QŠirŠabb)," in Wilhelmus C. Delsman et al., eds., *Von Kanaan bis Kerala: Festschrift J. P. M. van der Ploeg* (Kevelaer: Butzon und Bercker; Neukirchen-Vluyn: Neukirchener Verlag, 1982), p. 332; Johann Maier, "Zu Kult und Liturgie der Qumrangemeinde," *RdQ* 14 (1989/90), p. 572; idem, "*Shire ʿOlat hash-Shabbat*. Some Observations on Their Calendric Implications and on Their Style," in Julio Trebolle Barrera and Luis Vegas Montaner, eds., *The Madrid Qumran Congress*, vol. 2 (Leiden: Brill; Madrid: Editorial Complutense, 1992), pp. 552 f.

[50] Therefore, it is too simplistic an approach in my view to declare that the songs are "liturgy" and meant to be "performed," and to conclude from this that "the performance is clearly intended to induce an altered state of consciousness – a mystical *experience*" (Philip Alexander, private communication). Even if the songs are a liturgical performance, I don't see how a performance necessarily leads to an altered state of consciousness in the sense of a mystical experience.

[51] Bilhah Nitzan, *Qumran Prayer and Religious Poetry* (Leiden: Brill, 1994), pp. 183–189, 195–200; Raʿanan Boustan (Abusch), "Sevenfold Hymns in the *Songs of the Sabbath Sacrifice* and the Hekhalot Literature: Formalism, Hierarchy and the Limits of Human Participation," in James Davila, ed., *The Dead Sea Scrolls as Background to Postbiblical Judaism and Early Christianity: Papers from an International Conference at St. Andrews in 2001* (Leiden: Brill, 2003), p. 225.

remarkable intensification: "the gods of all the holiest of the holy ones" (*elohei kol qedoshei qedoshim*),[52] the latter phrase, of course, alluding to the "Holy of Holies" (*qodesh ha-qodashim*) of the Temple, and therefore the text explicitly states: "[He es]tablished them [for] himself as the ho[liest of the holy ones in the ho]ly of holies" (l. 10). As such, they are also called the "ministers of the face (*mesharetei panim*) in the inner sanctuary of his glory" (*devir kevodo*)[53] – *devir* being the equivalent of "Holy of Holies" (*qodesh ha-qodashim*) according to the structure of Solomon's Temple as described in 1 Kings 6:5 – or, in a terminology unique to Qumran, the "priests of the inner sanctum" (*kohanei qorev*).[54] Addressed here – and throughout most of the cycle – are only the angels in their capacity as priests of the heavenly Temple. Human beings play an inferior role (if they play a role at all); we learn merely in passing that the angels "appease his will for all who repent of sin" (l. 16).

The only song that explicitly raises the question of the status of human beings in relation to the angels is Song II. After having stated that the angels are "glorified in all the camps of the gods (*mahanei elohim*) and are fearsome (*nora'im*) to the human councils (*le-mosadei anashim*),"[55] the author asks, "But [...] how shall we be considered [among] them? And how shall our priesthood [be considered] in their dwellings? And [our] ho[liness ...] their holiness? [What] is the offering of our tongues [compared] with the knowledge of the g[ods ...]?"[56] Not only are human beings inferior to the angels, the human priesthood (and accordingly human knowledge), too, is nothing compared to the angelic priesthood in heaven. Since this critique is obviously directed at the members of the Qumran community and not at the despised Jerusalem priesthood, it seems as if the firm conviction of a close communion of angels and human beings is somewhat muted in the songs. If the songs reflect such a communion, the human side of this communion acts much more modestly than in some of the texts discussed above; our author is keenly aware of the fact that the human sectarians are not really angels and that they owe everything that they embody and achieve to the angels.

Songs III–V are almost completely destroyed, but most of Songs VI–VIII is preserved; in fact, these three songs occupy a pivotal position within the whole cycle. Carol Newsom has argued that Song VII constitutes the climax of the cycle,[57] whereas Christopher Morray-Jones opts for Song VII as the "prelimi-

---

[52] 4Q400 1 i, l. 2: I follow the edition and translation (with modifications) by Carol Newsom, in Esther Eshel, Hanan Eshel, Carol Newsom, Bilhah Nitzan, Eileen Schuller, and Ada Yardeni, eds., *Qumran Cave 4*, vol. 6: *Poetical and Liturgical Texts*, part 1 (Oxford: Clarendon Press, 1998), pp. 173–401; see also García Martínez and Tigchelaar, *The Dead Sea Scrolls*, pp. 807 ff.

[53] Ibid., l. 4.

[54] Ibid., l. 17 and 19.

[55] 4Q400 2, l. 2, and 4Q401 14 i, l. 8.

[56] Ibid., l. 5–7.

[57] Newsom, *Songs of the Sabbath Sacrifice*, pp.13–15.

nary crescendo" and Song XII as the "true climax of the liturgical cycle as a whole."[58] Whatever the structure and function of the cycle may be, there can be no doubt that Songs VII and XII are crucial within the composition of the cycle. "Sandwiched in a climactic position"[59] between Song VI (which describes the praises of the seven chief angelic princes) and Song VIII (describing the praises of the corresponding seven secondary princes), Song VII not only calls on the angels to perform their praise but introduces the active participation of the animate architecture of the heavenly Temple for the first time into the cycle. This phenomenon, which Ra'anan Boustan (Abusch) called the "increasing angelification of temple architecture," is new and most prominent in the Songs of the Sabbath Sacrifice.[60]

Song VII begins with the typical invitations to the angels to praise God; they are again called "gods" (*elohim, elim*), with phrases blurring the divisions between them and God: the "exalted ones among all the gods of knowledge (*elei da'at*),"[61] the "holy ones of the gods (*qedushei elohim*),"[62] "gods of the gods of exaltation (*elohim me-'elei rum*),"[63] "wondrous gods (*elohei pele*),"[64] and so forth. Accordingly, God is "[God (*el*) of gods (*elim*)] to all the chiefs of exaltation (*rashei meromim*) and king of king[s] to all the eternal councils."[65] But then the song suddenly switches from the angels to architectural elements of the heavenly Temple. "With these [the angels]," the text continues, "let all the f[oundations of the hol]y of holies (*yesodei qodesh qodashim*) praise, the uplifting pillars (*'amudei masa*) of the most exalted abode (*zevul rum rumim*), and all the corners of its structure (*pinot mavnito*)."[66] Now the foundations of the Holy of Holies of the heavenly Temple, together with its pillars and the corners of its structure, join in with the praise of God; the architectural structures of the Temple are animated and become living and praising creatures, like the angels.[67] But then the song switches to the angels once more:

[58] Morray–Jones, "The Temple Within," p. 417. Boustan ("Sevenfold Hymns," pp. 226f.) modifies this by arguing that the middle Songs VI–VIII function as a "microcosm of the larger whole."
[59] James R. Davila, *Liturgical Works* (Grand Rapids, MI / Cambridge: William B. Eerdmans, 2000), p. 84.
[60] Boustan, "Sevenfold Hymns," p. 227.
[61] 4Q403 1 i, l. 30f.
[62] Ibid., l. 31.
[63] Ibid., l. 33.
[64] Ibid., l. 36.
[65] Ibid., l. 34.
[66] Ibid., l. 41. Davila (*Liturgical Works*, p. 123) fails to recognize the syntax of the Hebrew and translates: "With these let all the fo[undations of] the most [hol]y (place) psalm the load-bearing pillars of the most exalted abode and all the corners of its construction." According to this interpretation it is not the foundations, the pillars, and the corners (of the heavenly Temple) that praise God but the foundations that praise the pillars and corners!
[67] As Philip Alexander aptly remarks (private communication): "I think the most obvious explanation of the singing architecture of the celestial temple is that it is meant to convey the

Sin[g praise] to Go[d who is aw]esome in power, [all you spirits of knowledge and light
(*ruhei da'at we-'or*)] in order to [exa]lt together the most pure firmament (*raqia' tohar
tehorim*) of [his] holy sanctuary (*miqdash qodsho*). [And praise hi]m, O spirits of Go[d]
(*ruhei elohim*), in order to pr[aise for ever and e]ver the firmament of the upper[m]ost
heaven (*raqia' rosh meromim*), all [its] b[eams] (*qorotaw*) and its walls (*qirotaw*), a[l]l
its [for]m (*mavnito*), the work of [its] struc[ture] (*tavnito*).[68]

Now the angels return as the subject of the praise, but the object is no longer
God alone but also the firmament of the heavenly Temple with its beams and
walls. Hence, the animate architecture of the heavenly Temple not only joins in
with the angelic praise, it also becomes its object; the text wavers between the
angels praising God, the architectural elements of the Temple participating in
this praise, and the structure of the heavenly Temple as the object of the praise.
The "most pure firmament" alludes, of course, to the "very heavens in purity"
(*'etzem ha-shamayim la-tohar*) in Ex. 24:10 and to the firmament of "dreadful
ice" in Ezek. 1:22 that carries God's throne.[69] Here the firmament carries the
heavenly Temple, which doubtless accommodates the divine throne. This becomes clear from the beginning of the second column of 4Q403, where God's
"footstool" (*hadom raglaw*) is explicitly mentioned.[70] It is the Glory of God
seated on his throne in the heavenly Holy of Holies or *devir* that is the climax
of the seventh song.

The language of this second part of the song is deeply imbued with Ezekiel's imagery. Not only is God's Glory (*kavod*) addressed (4Q403 1 ii, l. 4; cf.
Ezek. 1:28), but the activity of the angels comes very close to the function of
the creatures (*hayyot*) as described in Ezekiel. Compare the song's "from between them gods (*elohim*) run (*yarutzu*) like the appearance of coals of [fire …]
(*mar'eh gahalei esh*) moving round about (*mithalekh saviv*)"[71] with Ezek. 1:13:
"the shape of the creatures (*hayyot*), their appearance (*mar'ehem*), was like coals
of fire (*gahalei esh*)," a firelike appearance that "was moving to and fro (*mithale-
khet*) among the creatures."[72] Also, whereas in Ezekiel the seer hears (*eshma'*)
the sound of the creatures' wings, in Song VII "the sound of blessing is glorious
in the hearing (*mishma'*) of the gods (*elohim*)."[73] Unlike in Ezekiel, however, the

---

idea that it is a living temple, made up, in fact, of angels, just as the community on earth is a
living temple – a *miqdash adam*."

[68]   4Q403 1 i, l. 41–44.

[69]   Moreover, the text probably plays with *raqia'* and *meqareh* ("set the beams") as in the
later rabbinic interpretation of Ps. 104:3 ("He who sets the beams [*meqareh*] of his lofts ['*ali-
yyotaw*] in the waters"); see Bereshit Rabbah 1:3 and parallels; Schäfer, *Rivalität*, pp. 52 f.

[70]   4Q403 1 ii, l. 2.

[71]   Ibid., l. 6.

[72]   The *yarutzu* in 4Q403 is mirrored in Ezek. 1:14: "and the creatures darted to and fro
(*ratzo wa-shov*)."

[73]   4Q403 1 ii, l. 12. Interestingly enough, the copyist originally wrote *nishma'*, which he
deleted and corrected to *nikhbad* ("is glorious").

"decorations of the inner shrine" (*mahashavei*[74] *devir*) participate in the praise of the angels "with wondrous psalms,"[75] and finally the "chariots" (*merkavot*, plural) join in together with the cherubim and ofannim.[76]

The participation of the animate Temple architecture in the angelic praise appears for the first time in the Songs of the Sabbath Sacrifice, but it is hardly unique to them. The closest parallel is, not by accident, the Hekhalot literature. Like the angels and the architectural elements in the songs, in the Hekhalot literature God's throne (called *kisse ha-kavod*, "throne of Glory") is often personified and called upon to praise God.[77] The following highly poetical invitation, addressed to the throne by the angels who carry the divine throne (obviously the *hayyot*), is repeated several times in Hekhalot Rabbati and other texts of the Hekhalot literature:[78]

> Rejoice, rejoice, supernal dwelling!
> Shout, shout for joy, precious vessel!
> Made marvelously and a marvel!
> Gladden, gladden the king who sits upon you!

The throne speaks directly to God and invites him to sit down upon him,[79] and even its hymn is disclosed in Hekhalot Rabbati:[80]

> Like the voice of the seas,
> like the roaring of the rivers,
> like the waves of Tarshish,
> which the south wind drives forward,
> like the voice of the hymn of the throne of glory,
> which calls to mind and extols
> the magnificent king
> [with] loud voice and extremely great roaring.
> Voices rush away from him,
> from the throne of glory,

---

[74] The word is derived from "to imagine designs" (*lahshov mahashavot*) in Ex. 31:4.

[75] 4Q403 1 ii, l. 13.

[76] Mention of the ofannim is another indication of Ezekiel's influence (the juxtaposition of cherubim and ofannim clearly goes back to the identification of the *hayyot* and their "wheels" with the cherubim in Ezek. 10). The "chariot" (*merkavah*) in the technical sense of the word does not appear yet in Ezekiel, who instead uses "throne" (*kisse*) – cf. Ezek. 1:26 – but the two words are soon to be identified (first in 1 Chron. 28:18; cf. also Sir. 49:8).

[77] The throne in the Hekhalot literature, however, is not the object of the angelic praise (at most indirectly).

[78] *Synopse zur Hekhalot-Literatur*, §§ 94, 154, 634, 687, cf. also § 686. The translation follows Schäfer, *Hidden and Manifest God*, pp. 13 f. This parallel has been noticed by Newsom in Eshel et al., *Qumran Cave 4*, vol. 6, p. 277, but strangely enough has been missed by Davila, *Liturgical Works*, whose commentary on the songs abounds with (often unwarranted) parallels from the Hekhalot literature.

[79] *Synopse zur Hekhalot-Literatur*, § 99.

[80] Ibid., § 162; cf. also § 251.

to help him,
to strengthen him,
when he calls to mind and praises
the mighty of Jacob,
as is written: "Holy, holy, holy." (Isa. 6:3)

The following songs (IX–XI) are again badly preserved. What remains of Song IX refers to the "vestibules of their entryways" (*ulamei mevo'ehem*) or the "vestibules where the King enters" (*ulamei mevo'ei melekh*),[81] clearly alluding to the "vestibule" (*ulam*) of Solomon's Temple,[82] which led into the Sanctuary (*hekhal*), which in turn led to the Holy of Holies or inner Sanctuary (*qodesh ha-qodashim* or *devir*). These vestibules, as well as the "glorious shrines" (*devirim*),[83] are engraved with figures of "living gods" (*elohim hayyim*), that is, with images of angels.[84] This idea of the Temple as decorated with images is apparently inspired by Ezek. 41, where the walls of the "vestibule" (*ulam*) and the "sanctuary" (*hekhal*) as well as the doors leading to the sanctuary and to the Holy of Holies (*qodesh [ha-qodashim]*) were carved with engravings of cherubs and palm trees (Ezek. 41:18, 25).[85] Hence, the angels (paradoxically called *elohim hayyim*) turn into decorations of the heavenly Temple and, in order to become part of the praise of the Temple's architecture, are "reanimated" again.

This description is continued in what remains of Songs X and XI. Song X mentions "rivers of fire" (*naharei 'or*)[86] and the "curtain of the inner shrine of the King" (*parokhet devir ha-melekh*),[87] obviously referring to the curtain in front of the Holy of Holies with cherubim worked into it.[88] Song XI returns to the animate celestial architecture with "figures of gods" (*elohim*),[89] the "floor of the wondrous inner shrines" (*midras devirei pele*),[90] "images of living gods" (*tzurot elohim hayyim*),[91] "[fi]gures of the shapes of gods, engraved round about their [gl]orious brickwork" (*tzurot elohim mehuqqaqei saviv le-livnei kevodam*),[92] and so on – all taking part in the heavenly praise of God, but a praise that culminates in a "sound of quiet stillness" (*qol demamat sheqet*).[93] The latter is clearly again inspired by Ezekiel (see below), as is the movement of God's chariots (plural),

---

[81] 4Q405 14–15 i, l. 4 f.
[82] 1 Kings 6:3; 1 Chron. 28:11; Ezek. 40:48.
[83] Multiplication of the structures of the heavenly Temple is typical of the songs.
[84] 4Q405 14–15 i, l. 5–7.
[85] This concept in turn goes back to the description of Solomon's Temple in 1 Kings 6:29–35 (here calyxes are added to the cherubim and palms).
[86] 4Q405 15 ii–16, l. 2 (alluding to the *nehar di-nur* in Dan. 7:10).
[87] Ibid., l. 3 and 5.
[88] Ex. 26:31–33; Ex. 36:35; Lev. 16:2: the Tabernacle; 2 Chron. 3:14: Solomon's Temple.
[89] 4Q405 19, l. 2.
[90] Ibid., l. 2 f.
[91] Ibid., l. 4
[92] Ibid., l. 5 f.
[93] Ibid., l. 7.

described at the very end of the song: "as they move (*be-lekhtema*) [they do not turn aside (*lo yissabu*) to any … they go straight (*yishru*) to …]."[94]

Then follows Song XII, presumably the ultimate climax of the cycle. The first part of it describes the service of the cherubs in the celestial Temple, closely modeled along the lines of Ezek. 1 (and also 10):[95]

> (7) In the tabern[acle (*mishkan*) of God of] knowledge the [Cheru]bim fall before him; and they bl[es]s. When they rise, a sound of divine stillness (*qol demamat elohim*)
>
> (8) [is heard]; and there is a tumult of jubilation (*hamon rinnah*) at the lifting up of their wings, a sound of divine [stillnes]s. The image of the chariot throne (*tavnit kisse merkavah*) do they bless (which is) above the expanse (*raqia'*) of the Cherubim.
>
> (9) [And the splend]or of the expanse of light (*hod raqia' ha-'or*) do they sing (which is) beneath the seat of his glory (*moshav kevodo*). And when the wheels move (*be-lekhet ha-ofannim*), the holy angels return. They go out from between
>
> (10) its glorious [h]ubs ([*ga*]*lgalei kevodo*). Like the appearance of fire (*ke-mar'eh esh*) (are) the spirits of the holy of holies (*ruhot qodesh qodashim*) round about (*saviv*), the appearance of streams of fire (*mar'eh shevulei esh*) like *hashmal* (*bi-demut hashmal*). And there is a [ra]diant substance (*ma'aseh [n]ogah*),
>
> (11) gloriously multi-coloured (*be-ruqmat kavod*), wondrously hued, brightly blended (*memulah toha[r]*),[96] the spirits of living gods which move (*mithalekhim*) continuously with the glory of [the] wondrous chariots.
>
> (12) And there is a still sound of blessing (*qol demamat berekh*) in the tumult of their movement (*be-hamon lekhtam*) and holy praise[97] as they return on their paths. When they rise, they rise wondrously; and when they settle,
>
> (13) they [stand] still. The sound of glad rejoicing falls silent (*qol gilot rinnah hishqit*), and there is a stillne[ss] of divine blessing (*demama[t] berekh elohim*) in all the camps of the gods; [and] the sound of prais[es …]
>
> (14) […] from between their divisions on [their] side[s … and] all their mustered troops rejoice, each o[n]e in [his] stat[ion.

This whole passage reads like an interpretation of Ezekiel, taking up many of his key terms. The "expanse/firmament (*raqia'*) of the Cherubs" (l. 8) is apparently the "expanse" stretched over the heads of the creatures (*hayyot*) in Ezek. 1:22 ff., who are identified with the cherubs in Ezek. 10; and the "image of the chariot throne above the expanse" (ibid.) no doubt recalls the "shape (*demut*) of a throne" above the expanse above the heads of the *hayyot* (Ezek. 1:26). Likewise,

---

[94] 4Q405 20 ii-21–22, l. 5. Cf. Ezek. 1:9, 12, 17 (for the movement of the *hayyot*) and Ezek. 1:7, 23 (for their straight legs).

[95] Ibid., l. 7–14.

[96] Lit. "purely salted"; the phrase seems to be derived from Ex. 30:35, where the incense for the Sanctuary is described as "salted (probably meaning refined), pure, and holy." Lev. 2:13 mentions the "salt of the covenant of your God" (*melah berit elohekha*), and Num. 18:19 calls the covenant between God and his priests an "everlasting covenant of salt" (*berit melah 'olam*).

[97] Following Newsom's emendation of *hallel qodesh* instead of *hallelu qodesh* ("they praise [with] holiness" or "they praise the holy one"?).

the constantly moving wheels (*ofannim*) originate in Ezekiel's wheels, which move alongside each of the four creatures (Ezek. 1:15); the shift from *ofannim* (l. 9) to *galgalim* (l. 10) goes back to the identification of both in Ezek. 10:2 and 6. The angels going out from between the wheels (l. 9 f.) would seem to refer to Ezek. 1:20, where it is said that the "spirit (*ruah*) of the creature(s) was in the wheels" (note that the angels are explicitly called "spirits" in l. 10). So the angels not only prostrate before God and praise him (l. 7) together with the "expanse/firmament of light" (l. 9), they constantly move in and out of the wheels of God's throne. What is most striking, however, and quite unlike Ezekiel's vision: these angelic spirits are described in a way that in Ezek. 1:27 is reserved for the human-like figure seated on the throne, that is, for God himself. Whereas Ezekiel sees the "appearance of a human being" (God), who from his loins upward looks like *hashmal* surrounded with fire and from his loins downward looks like fire surrounded by radiance (*nogah*), the song assigns precisely these terms – the appearance of fire like *hashmal* and a radiant substance (*ma'aseh nogah*) – to the angelic spirits.[98] It is now the angels who appear as a miraculous fiery substance – and the description of this substance is further developed in terms of iridescent colors (l. 11) – no longer God. In other words, what Ezekiel encounters as a vision of God has been transferred to the angels in Song XII. The angels move to center-stage; God's physical appearance recedes into the background and is hardly mentioned at all. That which remains important is only his praise, not the vision of his shape.

The praise of God as described in the song bears also the distinct traits of Ezekiel's language. In Ezek. 1:24 f. the seer hears the sound of the creatures' wings as they move – obviously a very noisy sound, as it is specified as the "sound of the deep sea," a sound "like the voice of the Almighty," and "a sound of tumult like the sound of an army"; but when they stand still and let their wings drop, the sound produced by their wings obviously ceases. The reason for this is clear: only when their noisy sound (= praise) stops can another, still faint "sound from above the expanse" be heard, the sound that announces the voice of God speaking to the seer (Ez. 1:25, 28). In Song XII, the cherubs likewise generate a sound of praise when they lift up their wings and move (l. 7 f., 12 f.). However, the sound they produce is paradoxically termed a "sound of divine stillness" (*qol demamat elohim*)[99] or a "still sound of blessing" (*qol demamat berekh*).[100] This phrase, which seems to be derived from 1 Kings 19:12 (the voice of God that Elijah hears is a *qol demamah daqah*, "a still faint sound"), contrasts with the noisy sound in Ezek. 1:24 and 3:12 f., where the blessing of the creatures at their departure is explicitly described as "a great roaring noise" brought about

---

[98] Only the "streams of fire" are not mentioned in Ezekiel, but they are merely an embellishment of the "fire" that is prominent enough in Ezekiel.

[99] 4Q405 20 ii-21–22, l. 7 f.

[100] Ibid., l. 12; cf. also l. 13: "a stillness of divine blessing" (*demamat berekh elohim*).

by their wings and their wheels. Hence, although the lifting up of the creatures' wings produces a "tumult of jubilation," it is nevertheless a "sound of divine stillness" (l. 8); accordingly, the "still sound of blessing" emerges "in the tumult of their movement" (l. 12). What can be meant by this paradox of the creatures' noisy-still sound, which stands in such palpable contradiction to Ezekiel? It seems that the author of Song XII is proposing another new interpretation of Ezek. 1: not only is there no vision of God in his description of the service in the celestial Temple, there is also no divine voice heard in response to the angelic praise (let alone a seer being addressed). Whereas in Ezekiel, the creatures fall silent to allow God's voice to be heard (and then begin their noisy praise again after God has finished speaking to the prophet), in Song XII it is their own sound of blessing that is "still."[101] The creatures and all the other angels praise God continuously, even with a "still sound of blessing," but their God is neither seen nor heard.

The second part of Song XII introduces another task of the angels. In a badly preserved passage that is difficult to understand, it first addresses the angels as the "gods of his whole offering" (*elohei kelilo*),[102] a phrase that foreshadows the topic of the last song, the angelic high priests in charge of the celestial sacrifice. But before this subject is developed in more detail, the song turns to the divine mission of the angels:[103]

(8) Whenever the gods of knowledge (*elei da'at*) enter by the portals of glory, and whenever the holy angels (*mal'akhei qodesh*) go out to their dominion,

(9) the portals of entrance and the gates of exit make known the glory of the King, blessing and praising all the spirits of

(10) God (*ruhot elohim*) at (their) going out and at (their) coming in by the ga[t]es of holiness. There is none among them who omits a law (*hoq*); and never against the commands

(11) of the King (*imrei melekh*) do they set themselves. They do not run from the way or tarry away from his territory. They are not too exalted for His missions (*mish-luhotaw*);

(12) nor are [they] too lowly.

---

[101] Only l. 13 seems to imply that the creatures' "stillness of divine blessing" is not a paradoxical but a real stillness (because the "sound of glad rejoicing falls silent"), but l. 14 continues with some praise of the "mustered troops," apparently another group of angels. Hence, as Newsom has observed (*Qumran Cave 4*, vol. 6, p. 354), "the silence of the creatures of the chariot allows the praises of the angelic camps to be heard." The silence of one group of angels makes room for the praise of another group, but not for the voice of God.

[102] 4Q405 23 i, l. 5. The meaning of *kalil* is unclear: the obvious rendering with "crown" makes little sense here; Newsom (*Qumran Cave 4*, vol. 6, p. 358) suggests that we "construe *kalil* as the nominalised adjective, 'whole, entire', which is used as a synonym for *'olah*," hence for "holocaust offering." But instead of referring to the "whole-offering," *kalil* may be used elliptically for *kelil tekhelet*, as in Ex. 28:31 and 39:22, and may also allude to the "robe of the Ephod all of blue (= of pure blue)." The *elohei kelilo* would then be the gods/angels who wear the "all-blue" Ephod.

[103] 4Q405 23 i, l. 1–14.

The purpose of the angels' mission is not directly communicated; the song again focuses on their behavior: they go in and out of the heavenly sanctuary, and in doing so they are always faithful to the mission entrusted to them by God. But from what follows it becomes clear that the angels are sent down to God's creatures on earth, their human counterparts, in order to carry out his judgment: "He will n[o]t show compassion in the dominion of the fury of his annihila[ting wra]th; (but) he will not judge those who are made repentant by his glorious anger."[104] This refers back to Song I, where it is said of the angels that they "appease his will for all who repent of sin" (l. 16) – the only other passage in the songs that addresses the question of repentance (and hence of human beings). The angels are portrayed in their traditional role as God's messengers and as mediators between him and human beings on earth.[105]

From what remains of the badly damaged Song XIII it can be inferred that this last song of the cycle deals with the celestial sacrifices and the angelic priests. It mentions the "sacrifices of the holy ones" (*zivhei qedoshim*), the "odor of their offerings" (*reah minhotam*), and the "odor of their libations" (*reah niskhehem*)[106] – terms that are taken from the animal sacrifices in the Hebrew Bible: *zevah* is the technical term for animal sacrifices, *reah minhotam* alludes to the *reah nihoah* ("soothing odor" of Gen. 8:21, for example), and *nesekh* ("libation") usually accompanied the whole burnt offering (holocaust offering). Unfortunately, the precise circumstances under which these sacrifices were performed are not preserved, but there can be no doubt that they are offered by the angels. In another part of the song (preserved in another fragment),[107] the angelic priests with their priestly/high priestly garments are described as follows: they wear "ephods"[108] and are clothed in garments of "mingled colors (*ruqmah*), like woven work (*ma'aseh oreg*), engraved with figures of splendor."[109] The Ephod is one of the robes of Aaron and his sons (Ex. 28:4 ff.) and the "woven work" in the Hebrew Bible refers to the "robe for the Ephod" (Ex. 28:32; 39:22) and the "tunics of fine linen" (Ex. 39:27), also worn by Aaron and his sons.[110] No doubt, therefore, that the angels who offer the celestials sacrifices are modeled on the priests (or more precisely on the high priests) in the earthly sanctuary.[111]

---

[104] Ibid., l. 12.

[105] The supposition entertained by Davila (*Liturgical Works*, p. 157) that the text deals with *angelic* repentance is mistaken and ignores the context (l. 10 f.).

[106] 11Q17 ix, l. 4 f. (edition and translation in García Martínez and Tigchelaar, *The Dead Sea Scrolls*, vol. 2, p. 1219; see also the translation in Davila, *Liturgical Works*, p. 158).

[107] 4Q405 23 ii (Newsom, pp. 361 ff.).

[108] Ibid., l. 5.

[109] Ibid., l. 7.

[110] In the Bible they are blue, whereas the angelic garments are multicolored.

[111] I fail to see how the reference to Ezek. 1:28 in 4Q405 23 ii, l. 9, proves that the community's high priest in Song XIII is identified with the Glory of God in Ezekiel, as Fletcher-Louis claims (*All the Glory of Adam*, pp. 374 ff., 392).

Moreover, and most strikingly, the "woven work" of the angelic garments is repeated in l. 10 and is paired there with the phrase *memulah tohar*: "And all their designs are brightly blended (*memulah tohar*), an artistry like woven work (*ma'aseh oreg*)." The phrase *memulah tohar* (which literally means "purely salted" and is another technical term related to the incense in the sanctuary and the priestly covenant with God),[112] together with the term *ruqmah* ("mingled colors"), was used, as we recall, in describing the angels who move in and out of the wheels of the divine chariot.[113] Hence, it seems highly likely that the very same angels who serve the divine chariot (and are sent out as God's messengers) also hold office as the priests/high priests who offer the sacrifices in the celestial Temple.

This, of course, goes far beyond Ezekiel and any other possible biblical *Vorlage*. But the Greek Testament of Levi mentions "propitiatory sacrifices" offered by the archangels in the "uppermost heaven" in which the "Great Glory" dwells (3:4–6);[114] and the Babylonian Talmud, which provides us with the classical list of the seven heavens, describes the fourth heaven (*zevul*) as the one "in which [the heavenly] Jerusalem and the Temple and the altar are built, and Michael, the great Prince, stands and offers up thereon an offering, for it is said: 'I have now built for you a house of habitation (*bet zevul*), a place where you may dwell forever' (1 Kings 8:13)."[115] The biblical proof-text makes clear that the heavenly Sanctuary corresponds to the earthly Temple, but the very fact that the "great Prince" Michael (who is also Israel's guardian angel)[116] officiates as the celestial high priest may be taken as indicating a critical stance vis-à-vis the earthly worship[117] – or at least as an attempt to transfer the sacrifice in the earthly Temple (which no longer exists) to the celestial Sanctuary. The critique is obvious in the parallel in Seder Rabbah di-Bereshit, where Michael, the "great Prince," holds office as high priest, "clothed with high-priestly garments," and presents a "pure offering of fire" (followed by the same biblical proof-text, 1 Kings 8:13).[118]

We do not know the purpose of the celestial sacrifices offered by the angelic priests/high priests, but within the context of the Qumran community, which preserves and recites the songs, these sacrifices only make sense as substitutes

---

[112] See above, n. 96.

[113] 4Q405 22, l. 10f. This has been noted by Newsom (*Qumran Cave 4*, vol. 6, p. 364), but she confuses the description of the angels with the description of the Glory of God: it is not the Glory of God that is described in 4Q405 22 but the appearance of the angels (as she remarks correctly on p. 353). The point is that the text describes the angels very much along the lines of God's Glory itself in Ezekiel, and specifically that the angels serve almost as God's substitute (see above).

[114] See above, p. 68.

[115] b Hagigah 12b.

[116] Cf. Dan. 10:13, 21; 12:1.

[117] Not the sacrifice as such, but the way it was performed.

[118] Seder Rabbah di-Bereshit, in *Synopse zur Hekhalot-Literatur*, § 772; for an analysis of the text and the parallels, see Schäfer, "In Heaven as It Is in Hell," pp. 233–274.

for the sacrifices in the polluted earthly Temple. Although the Jerusalem Temple still exists, the sacrifices offered there are tainted with a blemish; the sole true sacrifices are now carried out by the angelic priests in the celestial Temple.[119] Like the sacrifices offered by Michael in b Hagigah and in Seder Rabbah di-Bereshit, the angelic sacrifices in the songs are offered, therefore, on Israel's behalf, for the benefit of the people of Israel, or rather on behalf of those who regard themselves as the true remnant of the people of Israel, the members of the Qumran community. Hence it is somewhat rash to conclude that Songs VII[120] or XII serve as the dramatic peak or crescendo of the cycle, while Song XIII functions as a kind of dénouement.[121] Whereas both Song VII and Song XII no doubt form a climax of the cycle (for whatever reason), we should not neglect Song XIII – which, after all, concludes the cycle – with its emphasis on the angelic priests/high priests as offering the celestial sacrifice for the benefit of the community on earth.[122]

The question of the cycle's structure and inner dynamic is closely connected with the function it served within the Qumran community. In her first comprehensive edition of the Songs, Carol Newsom set the tone for what has since become a remarkable and influential trend in Qumran scholarship and in the modern attempt to establish a historical context for the early mystical system known as Merkavahh mysticism.[123] The purpose of the cycle, she argues,

---

[119] I am aware, as both Martha Himmelfarb and Philip Alexander remind me, that the idea of a celestial Temple and a celestial cult does not automatically imply a critique of the earthly Temple and the earthly cult. But the fact remains that, for the Qumran community, the earthly cult is polluted. I therefore don't think that the celestial cult is just a bloodless and hence spiritualized form of the (ongoing) bloody earthly cult; rather, it substitutes the (forever) blemished earthly sacrifice with the pure celestial sacrifice.

[120] This has been argued by Newsom, *Songs of the Sabbath Sacrifice*, pp. 13–17.

[121] As Boustan (Abusch) summarizes the view presented by Morray-Jones, "The Temple Within," pp. 417–420. Morray-Jones does argue there (p. 417) for Song VII as the "preliminary crescendo" and Song XII as the "true climax of the liturgical circle as a whole," but I cannot find his assessment of Song XIII as the dénouement. He simply neglects Song XIII.

[122] In fact, Devorah Dimant has suggested that the cycle reaches its climax in Song XIII; cf. her "The Apocalyptic Interpretation of Ezekiel at Qumran," in Ithamar Gruenwald, Shaul Shaked, and Guy Stroumsa, eds., *Messiah and Christos: Studies in the Jewish Origins of Christianity Presented to David Flusser on the Occasion of His Seventy-Fifth Birthday* (Tübingen: J. C. B. Mohr [Paul Siebeck], 1992), p. 41, n. 40.

[123] The culmination of this tendency can be found in Elior, *The Three Temples*, pp. 232 ff.; Alexander, *The Mystical Texts*; but see already Lawrence H. Schiffman, "*Merkavah* Speculation at Qumran: The 4Q*Serekh 'Olat ha-Shabbat*," in Jehuda Reinharz and Daniel M. Swetschinski, eds., with the collaboration of Kalman P. Bland, *Mystics, Philosophers, and Politicians: Essays in Jewish Intellectual History in Honor of Alexander Altmann* (Durham, NC: Duke University Press, 1982), pp. 15–47; Joseph M. Baumgarten, "The Qumran Sabbath Shirot and Rabbinic Merkabah Traditions," *RdQ* 13 (1988), pp. 199–213; James R. Davila, "The Dead Sea Scrolls and Merkavah Mysticism," in Timothy H. Lim, ed., *The Dead Sea Scrolls in Their Historical Context* (Edinburgh: T.&T. Clark, 2000), pp. 249–264. For a thorough critique of Elior, see Himmelfarb, "Merkavah Mysticism since Scholem."

is better described as the praxis of something like a *communal mysticism*. During the course of this thirteen week cycle, the community which recites the compositions is led through a lengthy preparation. The mysteries of the angelic priesthood are recounted, a *hypnotic celebration* of the sabbatical number seven produces an anticipatory climax at the center of the work,[124] and the community is then *gradually led* through the spiritually animate heavenly temple until the worshippers *experience the holiness of the merkabah* and of the Sabbath sacrifice as it is conducted by the high priests of the angels."[125]

Here we have the key terms that present the liturgy of the songs as the original source of Merkavah mysticism and that would determine much of the subsequent discussion: we are dealing here with mysticism, more concretely with the mysticism of a community (not just of an individual), which puts itself in a hypnotic state and, being led through the celestial Temple, experiences the divine throne.[126] The whole purpose of this "communal mysticism" is experiencing the "holiness" of the Merkavah and of the Sabbath sacrifice. The most elaborate development of this approach has been offered by Christopher Morray-Jones in his article "The Temple Within," in which he quotes Newsom – precisely the passage quoted above – and then spins out her theory in the following manner (ignoring, however, her inclusion of the Sabbath sacrifice in the "experience" of the mystic):

> The songs, then, enabled the community to gain access to the heavenly temple and to join with the angelic hierarchy in its worship before the throne. By performing the liturgical cycle, the worshippers undertake a "ritual journey," which involves an "ascent" through the seven *debirim* (songs 1–7), followed by a detailed tour of the celestial temple, moving inwards towards the center, where the Glory manifests upon the throne. It may also be admissible to think of this as a process of "ritual construction." The performance of this liturgical cycle, presumably combined with intensive visualisation of the images described, will have had the effect of "building" the celestial temple in the personal and collective imagination of the participants. The imperative formulae of the early hymns indicates (sic) that they are calling on the angels to participate with them in this ritual "temple-building" project. The process of construction culminates in song 11, performed at or immediately before the renewal of the community's covenant at the feast of *Shabu'ot*. On the two sabbaths following this act of rededication, in songs 12 and 13, the divine Glory is called upon to indwell the temple that has been constructed by the now reconsecrated community, and to receive the sacrifices offered there. As observed above, it is the descent of the Divine Glory in the Holy of Holies, described in song 12, that forms the true climax of the cycle. The sacred structure within which this manifestation occurs has been constructed by means of this extended ritual perfor-

---

[124] That is, Song VII.

[125] Newsom, *Songs of the Sabbath Sacrifice*, p. 19 (my emphasis); on p. 59 she speaks of a "quasi-mystical liturgy."

[126] Cf. the useful summary of the research literature by Elisabeth Hamacher, "Die Sabbatopferlieder im Streit um Ursprung und Anfänge der jüdischen Mystik," *JSJ* 27 (1996), pp. 119–154 (pp. 123–125); see also Boustan, "Sevenfold Hymns," p. 221; idem, "Angels in the Architecture," pp. 195 f.

mance. The worship of the holy community and its celestial, angelic counterpart is, so to speak, the substance of which the temple is composed."[127]

This is a remarkable interpretation of the cycle, reflecting a certain understanding of Merkavah mysticism that is taken for granted. Like the yored merkavah – the Merkavah mystic who "descends" through the seven heavens or palaces (*hekhalot*) to the divine throne (*merkavah*) – the Qumran sectarians on earth ascend through the seven Holy of Holies (*devirim*) to God's Glory seated on his throne. This heavenly journey is an inward journey, occurring solely in the imagination of the worshippers. Moreover, in undertaking their imagined ascent, the sectarians construct the celestial temple as a "spiritual temple" within their own inner self. The ascent culminates in a kind of "adjuration" (a term typical of the Hekhalot literature but not used here by Morray-Jones) of the divine Glory, which descends to its imagined throne in the imagined celestial Holy of Holies.

This retelling of the cycle in light of later Merkavah mysticism is highly problematic.[128] First, the angels play a conspicuously minor role, with the sectarians acting as the central figures; they take the initiative and ask the angels to participate in their "temple-building project." True, it is the community on earth that calls on the angels in the songs, but to praise God and not to build a spiritual Temple! And this request, together with the likely supposition that the members of the community recite the songs in their service, is the only link that connects the earthly community with the angels in heaven. That the sectarians call upon the angels to participate "with them" in their ritual (whatever this might entail), as Morray-Jones maintains, is simply not borne out by the text. The *angels* perform a ritual, not the humans, and the humans participate in this celestial ritual by reading it during their worship. Morray-Jones improperly confuses the textual level (the heavenly ritual) and the performative level (the enacting of the text in the worship of the sectarians). As we have seen, humans – let alone the sectarians – are almost nonexistent in the songs; there are no traces of the idea of a liturgical communion of angels and humans that is so dominant in the unquestionably Qumranic texts discussed above. In assigning a major role to the humans in this dramatic performance, Morray-Jones turns the intention of the songs upside down.

Second, there is nothing in the songs to suggest that they are meant to evoke the idea of a heavenly journey or an *ascent* of the community through the seven "*devirim*" to the throne of God. The first seven songs do not depict seven successive "*hekhalot*," nor do Songs VIII–XI describe a "detailed tour of the celestial temple" that reaches its climax in the vision of the Merkavah in Song XII. As

---

[127] Morray-Jones, "The Temple Within," p. 420.
[128] Johann Maier and others have warned against establishing an immediate dependence between the songs and the Hekhalot corpus; cf. Johann Maier, "Zu Kult und Liturgie der Qumrangemeinde," p. 572; Carol A. Newsom, "Merkabah Exegesis in the Qumran Sabbath Shirot," *JJS* 38 (1987), p. 29; Hamacher, "Die Sabbatopferlieder," pp. 132 ff.

we have seen, Song XII is not at all concerned with the vision of the Merkavah but with the angels attending the Merkavah. Nor is Song XII concerned with the vision of God: the Glory of God and its manifestation plays only a minor role in the songs (if it plays a role at all). In this regard the songs fall far behind Ezekiel's and Enoch's visions; the angels – their praise, their appearance, and their task – are now the heroes of our author's imagination. God recedes into the background, or, to put it differently, he is overshadowed by his angels.[129]

Moreover, an interpretation that is obsessed with the Qumran community's heavenly journey and focused on the vision of the Merkavah as the climax of the cycle completely ignores the function of the celestial sacrifice within the songs – which is no accident, because the sacrifice performed by the angels in heaven plays no role at all in the Hekhalot literature (except for the few passages in Seder Rabbah di-Bereshit mentioned above, which can hardly lay claim to belonging to the core of Merkavah mysticism). This is further proof that the Hekhalot literature should not be used as a tool to trim anything and everything in the songs in accordance with its ideal. Rather than downplay or completely ignore the status of the celestial sacrifice because of its insignificance in the Hekhalot literature, we must acknowledge that it forms the climax of the cycle, and hence conclude that the Hekhalot literature cannot serve as the appropriate standard for our interpretation of the songs.[130] The celestial worship as described in the songs begins with the abundant praise of the angels and culminates in the sacrifice performed by the angelic high priests. This is what the community on earth urgently calls upon the angels to do: to praise God and offer the celestial sacrifice. Whereas the members of the community can participate, to some degree, in the angelic praise by reciting the songs in their worship, they can no longer offer the expiatory sacrifice. The sacrifice on earth has become corrupt, and it is only the angels in heaven who are still able to perform this ritual so crucial to the existence and well-being of the earthly community (until it becomes

---

[129] Philip Alexander, too, believes that the songs recount the ascent of the mystic through the various heavens and that the alleged description of the Merkavah in Song XII forms the climax of the cycle. Therefore, he finds it puzzling that the cycle does not conclude with Song XII but adds Song XIII. Hence he entertains the possibility that Song XIII does not serve as a coda to the cycle but is in fact its climax. Although he correctly points out that the song deals with the heavenly offerings and the celestial high priests, he is nevertheless convinced that Song XIII "could signify the transformation of the mystic: he dons the celestial priestly robes, and serves in the temple, and it is this enrobement that marks the climax of the experience" (*The Mystical Texts*, p. 50). I find it difficult to locate "the mystic" in Song XIII, even if we limit this mystical experience to the "priestly prayer-leader" of the congregation.

[130] Davila's commentary in his *Liturgical Works* is a good example of this misguided tendency in recent scholarship. He explains the songs through the treasure trove of Hekhalot literature, as if the latter were a document contemporary with the songs. There can be no doubt that the Hekhalot literature *continues* certain ideas that have their origin in the songs (and that later manifestations of an idea can sometimes help us understand its earlier form), but to project the Hekhalot literature back into the songs means to turn the evidence on its head.

fully united with the angels). In this sense the sacrifice in heaven has *replaced* the sacrifice on earth, since there is no hope for the restitution of the proper sacrifice in the Jerusalem Temple. Or, to put it differently: as far as the sacrifice is concerned, the angels in heaven have replaced the humans on earth; there is not much left in the songs of the communion of angels and humans. Hence the urgency and gravity with which the sectarians call upon the angels to perform their duty.

The Self-Glorification Hymn

The last Qumranic text to be discussed is a hymn known as the Self-Glorification Hymn, composed by an unknown author. It was originally thought to be part of the War Scroll,[131] has since been identified as belonging to the Hodayot (because one fragment of the Hodayot collection was recognized as a witness to the hymn),[132] and is now treated as an independent composition, of which two recensions have survived.[133] So far, the fragments 4Q471[b] (fragments 1–2),[134] 4Q491[c] (fragments 1–2),[135] 4Q427 (fragment 7, col. I and fragment 12),[136] and 1QH[a], col. XXVI, have been classified as part of the Self-Glorification Hymn and dated to the late Hasmonean and (early) Herodian periods.[137] The text of the hymn can be divided in two parts: one in which the author boasts of his being lifted up among the angels, and a second part in which he calls on the angels (and humans?) to praise God. As to the first part, I follow Eshel's publication of 4Q491[c] (fragment 1), but include the parallel fragments where these add important aspects:[138]

> (3) He established his truth of old, and the secrets of his devising (*razei 'ormato*) throughout all [generations
> (4) [ ] and the council of the humble (*'atzat evyonim*) for an everlasting congregation.
> (5) [for]ever a mighty throne (*kisse 'oz*) in the congregation of the gods (*elim*). None of the ancient kings shall sit in it, and their nobles shall not [

---

[131] M. Baillet, *Qumrân Grotte 4.3 (4Q482–4Q520)*, DJD 7 (Oxford: Clarendon Press, 1982), pp. 26–30.

[132] Martin G. Abegg, "4Q471: A Case of Mistaken Identity?" in J. C. Reeves and J. Kampen, eds., *Pursuing the Text: Studies in Honor of B. Z. Wacholder on the Occasion of His Seventieth Birthday* (Sheffield, UK: Sheffield Academic Press, 1994), pp. 137 f.

[133] Esther Eshel, "4Q471B: A Self-Glorification Hymn," *RdQ* 17/65–68 (1996), pp. 189 ff.

[134] Also designated 4QM[g].

[135] Also known as 4Q491, fragment 11, col. I, and as 4QM[a].

[136] Also known as 4QH[a].

[137] See Eshel, "4Q471B," p. 177.

[138] Ibid., pp. 184 f.

(6) [ ] shall not be like my glory (*kevodi*), and none shall be exalted save me, nor shall come against me. For I have taken my seat in a/the[139] [throne] in the heavens (*ki ani yashavti be* (...) *be-shamayim*) and none

(7) [ ] I shall be reckoned with the gods (*ani 'im elim ethashev*), and my dwelling place is in the holy congregation (*u-mekhoni be-'adat qodesh*). I do not desire as would a man of flesh [ ] everything precious to me is in the glory of

(8) [the gods in the] holy [dwelli]ng place (*bi-me'on ha-qodesh*). Who has been despised on my account? And who can be compared with me in my glory (*u-mi bi-khvodi yiddameh li*)? Who [

(9) [ ] who be[ars all] griefs as I do? And who [suff]ers evil like me? [ ] and (any) teaching (*horayah*) will not be equal to [my teaching]

(10) [ ] Who will stop me from speaking and who shall measure the flow of my speech, and who shall be my equal, and be like (me) in my judgment?

(11) [ ] For I shall be reckoned with the gods (*elim*), and my glory (*kevodi*) with [that of] the King's sons (*benei ha-melekh*).

The author of this hymn extols himself as someone who has taken his seat – a "mighty throne" (l. 5) – among the angels. The angels are again called *elim* ("gods") as in the Songs of the Sabbath Sacrifice discussed above; the location of the angels as well as of this particular throne is no doubt in heaven (l. 6, 8). The elevated status of the speaker is further emphasized by the fact that he boasts of being superior to the "ancient kings" and "their nobles": none of them shall be worthy of sitting on this throne among the angels of heaven. With the "ancient kings" he is certainly alluding to the kings of Israel and Judah, more precisely to the dynasty of the house of David. Since by the time this hymn was composed the Davidic dynasty had acquired messianic qualities,[140] the author is not only criticizing the traditional image of those kings from the house of David as the natural leaders of the Jewish people; he also, at least implicitly, disregards any expectation of the restoration of the Davidic dynasty with its messianic implications. Our author's glory (*kavod*) and exaltation are unique, most notably in comparison with the ancient kings, and for precisely this reason it is not unlikely that he claims for himself messianic qualities.

Two of the parallel fragments of our hymn carry the superior angelic status of the author even further. There the speaker explicitly asks, "Who is like me among the angels?" (*mi kamoni ba-'elim*),[141] a rhetorical question by which he apparently means, Who else is like me among the angels? Is there anybody else as elevated as me among the angels? (And the answer, of course, is no.) But the question is ambiguous because it obviously imitates the biblical phrase (Ex. 15:11) "Who is like you, O Lord, among the gods/angels?" (*mi kamokha*

---

[139] I don't see any basis for Eshel's "his" in the Hebrew text.

[140] See the summary in Peter Schäfer, "Diversity and Interaction: Messiahs in Early Judaism," in: Peter Schäfer and Mark R. Cohen, eds., *Toward the Millennium: Messianic Expectations from the Bible to Waco* (Leiden: Brill, 1998), pp. 15–35.

[141] 4Q471[b], fragments 1–2, l. 5; 4Q427 (4QH[a]), fragment 7, col. I, l. 8.

ba-'elim YHWH),[142] and this question definitely means, Is there anybody among the gods/angels who is like you, God, who can be compared with you? (Again the answer is no.) One could, therefore, go a step further and argue that our author is playing with this double meaning: not only is there no one as elevated as he is among the angels, but in his elevated status he is even superior to the angels and (almost) becomes God's equal. All that can be said, however, is that he plays with this double meaning – and hence with theological fire. Soon after his bold question he steps back and repositions himself "modestly" among the angels: "I am the friend of the King (*yedid ha-melekh*), a companion of the ho[ly ones] (*rea' la-qedoshim*)."[143] That he is "reckoned with the gods/angels" and with the "sons of the King" – just one among many, and not necessarily superior to any – is the recurrent leitmotif of the hymn.[144]

There are several other attributes that the speaker uses to characterize himself: he is an unequalled teacher,[145] whose speech cannot be interrupted,[146] and he is a judge.[147] These are common enough attributes, fitting to his elevated status. But what about him bearing "all grievances" (*kol tza'arim*) and suffering "evil" (*ra'*), and what about the strange phrase *mi la-vuz nehshav bi*, which Eshel translates as "Who has been attributed to me, to be despised?"[148] or, "Who has been despised on my account?"[149] Unfortunately, she does not explain in her commentary how she understands the phrase in the present context. Obviously, someone is seen as despised because of our speaker, that is, because he belongs to him. Does this mean that the speaker himself is despised? Probably. That the speaker bears all grievances, suffers evil, and is despised is inappropriate to the angelic status of which he himself boasts, or rather, it is inappropriate to the image commonly associated with such a status. But the attributes evoked here are reminiscent of the Suffering Servant in Isaiah, particularly Isa. 53:3 f., where the Suffering Servant is described as "despised" (*nivzeh*), a "man of suffering" and "bearing our sickness." Hence, it seems that the author has modeled himself along the lines of Isa. 53: he is the despised Suffering Servant who bears all (our) grieves and suffers evil, but is nevertheless (or because of this?) elevated among the angels and seated on a throne that even the Israelite kings cannot claim for themselves.

---

[142] As has been correctly observed by Eshel, "4Q471B," p. 180.

[143] 4Q471[b], fragments 1–2, l. 6 f.; 4Q427 (4QH[a]), fragment 7, col. I, l. 10.

[144] 4Q491[c], fragment 1, l. 7, 11; 4Q471[b], fragments 1–2, l. 8; 4Q427 (4QH[a]), fragment 7, col. I, l. 11 f.

[145] 4Q491[c], fragment 1, l. 9; 4Q471[b], fragments 1–2, l. 3 f.

[146] 4Q491[c], fragment 1, l. 10; 4Q471[b], fragments 1–2, l. 5 f.; 4Q427 (4QH[a]), fragment 7, col. I, l. 9.

[147] 4Q491[c], fragment 1, l. 10; 4Q471[b], fragments 1–2, l. 6; 4Q427 (4QH[a]), fragment 7, col. I, l. 10.

[148] 4Q471[b], fragments 1–2, l. 7; 4Q427 (4QH[a]), fragment 7, col. I, l. 10 f.

[149] 4Q491[c], fragment 1, l. 8.

Although he is attacked by others (some envious opponents?), he has his follow-ers and has taken his seat in heaven among the sons of the divine King.

In its second part the hymn moves, with no apparent caesura,[150] to the in-vitation to praise God: "Sing, O beloved ones (*yedidim*), sing of the King of [glory]."[151] The epithet "beloved ones" (*yedidim*) would seem to indicate that the addressees are the angels (note that the author called himself a *yadid* of the King in the companionship of the holy ones), and the location where the praise takes place would seem to be the heaven ("in the assembly of God"[152] and "in the holy dwelling").[153] This is certainly correct, but only half the truth. On closer inspection it becomes clear that not only are the angels being addressed but also human beings, most likely the members of the Qumran community. Phrases like "extol together (*romemu yahad*) among the eternal hosts"[154] and "in the united assembly" (*be-yahad qahal*)[155] leave no doubt that the author now includes his fellow sectarians in his hymn and that he is again taking up the technical lan-guage of the communion of angels and humans in their joint praise of God. The speaker, who is elevated among the angels, now calls upon his followers on earth to join in with the praise initiated by him and his fellow angels. In other words, what has been left out (or has receded into the background) in the Songs of the Sabbath Sacrifice – the communion of angels and humans – returns forcefully in the Self-Glorification Hymn.[156]

Who, then, is this speaker? To begin with, he is certainly a human being and not an angel.[157] This is indicated by the phrase, "I do not desire as would a man of flesh,"[158] which makes little sense in the mouth of an angel, as it is highly im-probable that an angel should boast of being elevated among the angels. More feasible is another suggestion that takes into account the resemblance between the Hodayot and our text (and the possibility that our hymn was appended, at a certain stage in its transmission, to the Hodayot).[159] In his attempt to refute Baillet's identification of the speaker with the archangel Michael, Morton Smith considered the Teacher of Righteousness a better candidate[160] but in the end left

---

[150] Only 4Q491^c, fragment 1, leaves one line (l. 12) empty before starting the praise.

[151] 4Q427 (4QH^a), fragment 7, col. I, l. 13; 1QH^a, col. XXVI, l. 9.

[152] 4Q427 (4QH^a), fragment 7, col. I, l. 14; 1QH^a, col. XXVI, l. 10.

[153] Ibid.

[154] 4Q427 (4QH^a), fragment 7, col. I, l. 15; 1QH^a, col. XXVI, l. 11.

[155] 4Q427 (4QH^a), fragment 7, col. I, l. 18; 1QH^a, col. XXVI, l. 14.

[156] This is a phenomenological description only and not meant to impose a chronological sequence on the texts.

[157] As has been suggested by M. Baillet, who published the first fragment and identified the speaker with the archangel Michael: *Qumrân Grotte 4.3 (4Q482–4Q520)*, pp. 29–35.

[158] 4Q491^c, fragment 1, l. 7.

[159] Eshel, "4Q471B," pp. 191–194.

[160] Morton Smith, "Ascent to the Heavens and Deification in 4QM^a," in Lawrence H. Schiff-man, ed., *Archaeology and History in the Dead Sea Scrolls: The New York University Confer-ence in Memory of Yigael Yadin* (Sheffield, UK: JSOT Press, 1990), pp. 181–188 (p. 187); idem,

the question open and concluded, "Nevertheless, it is probably better to suppose that the Dead Sea group or groups produced more than one preposterous poet with an exaggerated notion of his own sanctity."[161] The emphasis placed on the speaker's teaching in the Self-Glorification Hymn is indeed striking,[162] and it is most likely, therefore, that the author was a leading figure of the community. There are, however, problems with such a straightforward identification of our speaker with the Teacher of Righteousness:[163] the bold tone of the hymn and its speaker's claim to be the only one to have been seated on the throne in heaven among the angels goes far beyond what the author of the Hodayot asserts for himself. Moreover, the hymn displays some messianic characteristics that are completely lacking in the Hodayot: in its second part, the actual praise, it alludes to "tents of salvation" (*oholei yeshu'ah*)[164] and, in one fragment, even mentions the establishment of the "horn of his Mess[iah]" (*qeren mesh[iho]*).[165]

Taking the messianic implications seriously, it makes sense to argue that the speaker of the Self-Glorification Hymn is an eschatological figure,[166] or more precisely, some kind of Teacher of Righteousness *redivivus*: the founder of the sect who was imagined by his later followers as elevated into heaven and expected to return at the end of time as the priestly Messiah in order to lead the members of the community in the final battle. In his "angelified" status he would have anticipated what the earthly community fantasized regarding the communion with the angels, namely, the physical transformation into divine beings, the *elim*, who surround God and praise him forever.[167] This is not a "deification," as

---

"Two Ascended to Heaven: Jesus and the Author of 4Q491," in James H. Charlesworth, ed., *Jesus and the Dead Sea Scrolls* (New York: Doubleday, 1992), p. 297.

[161] Smith, "Two Ascended to Heaven," p. 298. Similarly, John J. Collins ("A Throne in the Heavens: Apotheosis in Pre-Christian Judaism," in John J. Collins and Michael Fishbane, eds., *Death, Ecstasy, and Other Worldly Journeys* [Albany: State University of New York Press, 1995], p. 55) proposes that "the author of this hymn may have been, not the Teacher, but a teacher in the late first century B.C.E."

[162] 4Q491c, fragment 1, l. 9f.; 4Q471b, fragments 1–2, l. 3f.; 4Q427 (4QHa), fragment 7, col. I, l. 9.

[163] Emphasized also by Smith, "Two Ascended to Heaven," p. 298; Collins, "A Throne in the Heavens," p. 55 (Collins's argument, following Smith, about the alleged Edomite = Herod is based on a misreading of the text; see Eshel, "4Q471B," p. 195, n. 68).

[164] 4Q427 (4QHa), fragment 7, col. I, l. 14.

[165] 4Q491c, fragment 1, l. 15.

[166] This has been suggested already by Eshel, "4Q471B," p. 202, following Collins, *The Scepter and the Star*, p. 148. Rejecting any messianic connection, Martin G. Abegg nevertheless entertains the possibility that it was not the historical Teacher of Righteousness who made the claim to have ascended to heaven and taken his place among the angels, but rather that such a claim was made "*on behalf* of the Teacher of Righteousness" by the author(s) of the hymn; see Martin G. Abegg, "Who Ascended to Heaven? 4Q491, 4Q427, and the Teacher of Righteousness," in C.A. Evans and P.W. Flint, eds., *Eschatology, Messianism, and the Dead Sea Scrolls* (Grand Rapids, MI: William B. Eerdmans, 1997), p. 72.

[167] Alexander (*The Mystical Texts*, pp. 90f.) wants to read the Songs of the Sabbath Sacrifice and the Self-Glorification Hymn together as the expression of one and the same mystical experi-

some scholars have it,[168] and one need not resort to Jesus[169] or Paul[170] to assert the importance of such a concept. Suffice it to note that it is very much along the lines of ascent apocalypses like the Aramaic Levi document/Testament of Levi or 2 Enoch with the physical transformation of their heroes into angels. Although the speaker of the Self-Glorification Hymn comes very close to God, closer probably than in any of the texts we have discussed so far, the distance between him and God is kept. Moreover, there is nothing in the hymn that seems to be interested in a vision of God, let alone in a description of his appearance.

Summary

The Qumran community conceives itself as a community of priests that represents the true and spiritual Temple, since the physical Temple in Jerusalem is considered to be polluted and malfunctioning. In their capacity as priests who live in absolute cultic purity, the members of the community regard themselves as united with the angels. This concept of the communion of humans and angels is a major theme in the writings of a community that should not, however, be lumped together but takes on different forms in the various writings associated with the sect:

In the War Scroll, which visualizes the eschatological battle between the forces of light and darkness, humans and angels are united in their decisive holy war *on earth*. The angels descend to earth in order to be present in the military camp of the holy warriors and to lead them to the final victory. A different view is expressed in the concept of the liturgical communion with the angels – another major strand in the Qumran literature and represented primarily by the Hodayot. There, the Qumran sectarians, when performing their privileged task of praising God, join in with the praise of the angels in heaven. Although the possibility cannot be excluded that they envisage the angels being present among them during their worship, it is more likely that they regard themselves as standing together with the angels and intermingling with them *in heaven*. As such, they are like the angels or even become angels. Unlike the ascent apocalypses, however, the

---

ence – not just of the chosen hero but of the Qumran community as a whole. He even entertains the possibility: "One could imagine the Self-Glorification functioning as a sort of introit to the Sabbath Songs, to establish the Maskil's credentials to lead the liturgy, or possibly as coming after Song 13, if that described his investiture as a celestial high priest" (ibid., p. 91, n. 8).

[168] Smith, "Two Ascended to Heaven," p. 298; Collins, "A Throne in the Heavens," p. 55.

[169] Smith, ibid., p. 299; Collins, ibid. Israel Knohl wants to identify the speaker of the hymn not just with a Qumranic Messiah but more concretely with the direct forerunner of Jesus, who influenced Jesus and Christian messianism; see Israel Knohl, *The Messiah before Jesus: The Suffering Servant of the Dead Sea Scrolls* (Berkeley and Los Angeles: University of California Press, 2000), pp. 42 ff.

[170] Abegg, "Who Ascended to Heaven?" p. 73.

Qumran literature is not concerned with the process of the physical transformation from human beings into angels.

The unknown author of the Self-Glorification Hymn, probably the Teacher of Righteousness *redivivus*, imagines himself to be elevated among the angels *in heaven*. He boasts of being seated on a celestial throne and superior to the Israelite kings, not to mention ordinary mortals. But the actual praise communicated in the hymn includes the human sectarians on earth in the angelic praise and uses again the technical language of the communion of angels and humans. In certain respects the speaker of the hymn represents the members of the earthly community in heaven and shares with them his elevated status during their joint worship.

In contrast to both the Hodayot and the Self-Glorification Hymn, in the Songs of the Sabbath Sacrifice, humans, including the human members of the Qumran sect, recede into the background. It is only the angels who are addressed in the songs; humans play an inferior role and are not placed on the same level with the angels. The angels are the priests/high priests in the celestial Temple and offer the sacrifice in heaven because the sacrifice on earth has become polluted. The only likely connection between angels and humans in the Songs of the Sabbath Sacrifice is the (not unlikely) supposition that the Qumran sectarians, through the performative act of reading the songs during their worship, unite with the angels in heaven. Yet we should not forget that the songs do not record the contents of the angels' actual praises but rather invite them to perform their liturgical and sacrificial activities. It may well be that the gist of the songs consists of this intense and almost desperate request directed at the angels to do what is required of them.

In all Qumranic texts there is no emphasis whatsoever on the vision of God and a description of his appearance. To be sure, the presence of the angels in the military camp in the War Scroll signals the presence of God, but the latter is conspicuously muted, as if God has hidden himself behind his angels. The same is true for the Hodayot, where the liturgical communion of angels and humans means that the humans share the angels' *knowledge* of God; the visual aspect is completely neglected. Similarly, in the Self-Glorification Hymn, the speaker is obsessed with his communion with the angels and makes no attempt to approach God. This dearth of any interest in a vision of God is most striking in the Songs of the Sabbath Sacrifice. There, the angels are the center of attraction and seem to have replaced God. What Ezekiel saw of God's shape, albeit vaguely and veiled, is now transferred to the angels; and the divine voice he heard is replaced by the angels' silence.

It is plainly misguided to attempt to discover in the Songs of the Sabbath Sacrifice the earliest version of the heavenly journey as described in the Hekhalot literature, and therefore the hidden source of what is later called Merkavah mysticism. Neither can the Songs be read as an account of an ascent through the seven heavens, nor do they culminate in a vision of God on his throne of glory. The songs' focus on the sacrifice offered by the angels in the celestial Temple (as a substitute for the sacrifice in the Jerusalem Temple) is very different from the message conveyed by the Hekhalot texts. Whereas the possibility cannot be ruled out that some of the ideas and motifs expressed in the songs are taken up in the Hekhalot literature, it is pointless to try and establish a literary and historical connection between the songs and Hekhalot literature,[171] and equally pointless to define "mysticism" as the common denominator between the "movements" behind both groups of texts. In particular, it is highly problematic to establish the priests as the link between the allegedly Qumranic and the Merkavah mystical strands of Jewish mysticism. Indeed, the texts from Qumran are deeply imbued with priestly ideology, starkly contrasting with the claims of the reigning priests in the Jerusalem Temple, but it would be more than bold to argue that the authors of the Hekhalot literature are the direct heirs of the Qumran priestly community.

There is nothing in the Qumranic texts that would allow the reader to read into them the notion of *unio mystica*, or mystical union with God, a category so cherished by historians of religion (especially those with a Christian background). Some of the texts suggest the idea of a *unio angelica*, or "angelification" of humans, similar to what we encounter in the ascent apocalypses. Others, probably the majority, advocate a *unio liturgica*, or liturgical (comm)union with the angels in heaven, similar to what occurs in the Hekhalot literature. However, quite in contrast to Merkavah mysticism, this is largely (with the sole exception of the Self-Glorification Hymn) an experience accomplished by the earthly community as a whole and not by an individual that acts as the emissary and mediator of the community on earth.

---

[171] A first survey of certain key-words and related concepts in the Qumranic and Hekhalot literatures (such as *shamayim* and *parokhet*) yields the unequivocal result that no lexicographic and conceptual link can be established between the two corpora of text. See now the illuminating article by Noam Mizrachi, *"Sh'elat ha-ziqqah ben shirot 'olat ha-shabbat le-sifrut ha-hekhalot: hebetei lashon we-signon,"* *Megillot* 7 (2008), pp. 263–298.

Chapter 5

Philo

The Ascent of the Soul

With Philo of Alexandria (ca. 20 BCE–ca. 50 CE), the great Jewish philosopher of late antiquity, we enter a completely different realm. Philo was born into one of the noblest Jewish families in Egyptian Alexandria, but otherwise we know little of his personal life. He must have exercised considerable political influence, since in 40 CE he headed the delegation of the Jewish community of Alexandria to the Roman emperor Gaius Caligula, a mission he described in his famous *Legatio ad Gaium*. His brother Alexander Lysimachus was a high official (Alabarch) in the fiscal administration in Egypt, and his nephew Tiberius Julius Alexander made a career in the Roman military and civil service, as procurator of Judaea and prefect of Egypt. Philo Judaeus, as he is also called, left behind a rich and voluminous output in Greek – whether or not he knew Hebrew is a matter of dispute – thus betraying his profound knowledge of and rigorous training in classical Greek literature, philosophy, and rhetoric. He did not present, however, a philosophical doctrine in any systematic way but developed his philosophical ideas through extensive allegorical exegeses of the Bible, which he used in its Greek translation.

As a philosopher, Philo was clearly no original thinker but was deeply imbued with the ideas of Plato and later varieties of his philosophy; as such, he was a congenial representative of the philosophical mainstream of his time, combining Middle Platonism (that variety of Platonism somewhere between the Old Academy and Neoplatonism),[1] Middle Stoicism, and Neopythagoreanism, even giving us a foretaste of what later became known as Neoplatonism.[2] In his unique

---

[1] On Philo's Middle Platonism, see, e.g., John Dillon, *The Middle Platonists. A Study of Platonism 80 B.C. to A.D. 220* (London: Duckworth, 1977 [rev. ed. with a new afterword, 1996, Cornell University Press, Ithaca, NY, pp. 139–183]); Robert M. Berchman, *From Philo to Origin: Middle Platonism in Transition* (Chico, CA: Scholars Press, 1984), pp. 23–53; David Winston, "Philo and the Contemplative Life," in Arthur Green, ed., *Jewish Spirituality*, vol. 1: *From the Bible throughout the Middle Ages* (New York: Crossroad, 1987), pp. 198–231; David T. Runia, "Redrawing the Map of Early Middle Platonism: Some Comments on the Philonic Evidence," in André Caquot, Mireille Hadas-Lebel, and Jean Riaud, eds., *Hellenica et Judaica: Hommage à Valentin Nikiprowetzky* (Leuven: Peeters, 1986), pp. 85–104.

[2] Maren R. Niehoff, who was kind enough to read the chapter on Philo, draws my attention to her recent article, in which she argues that Philo may have played a more active role in

combination of philosophical speculation and biblical exegesis he has often been portrayed as the "legatee of both Jewish and Greek culture,"[3] the mediator between "Athens" and "Jerusalem"[4] who concocted a grandiose synthesis of two fundamentally opposed cultural traditions. Whatever the usefulness of such stereotypes, we can be sure of one thing: "Jerusalem" rejected his synthesis. There is virtually no trace of Philo in the vast corpus of rabbinic literature.[5] His writings were completely forgotten in the subsequent Jewish tradition until the second half of the sixteenth century, when Azariah de' Rossi read them in a Latin translation and utilized them in his *Me'or 'Einayim*.[6] It was left to the Christian variety of "Jerusalem" to rescue Philo from oblivion – to such an extent and with such success that he was absorbed into Christianity and was regarded as one of the Church Fathers.[7] The latter might have been flattered by this company: they were well informed about Philo's philosophical ancestry, and the Latin Church Father Jerome quotes a proverb, allegedly famous among the Greeks, that "either Plato philonizes or Philo platonizes."[8]

Philo's Concept of God

Philo's God is absolutely transcendent: we know *that* God exists – in labeling him, Philo uses the Platonic term *to on* ("that which exists")[9] or, in singling out

---

promoting Plato's work than has often been acknowleged; see her "Did the *Timaeus* Create a Textual Community?" *GRBS* 47 (2007), pp. 170 ff.

[3] Samuel Sandmel, *Philo of Alexandria: An Introduction* (Oxford: Oxford University Press, 1979), p. 4.

[4] David Winston, *Logos and Mystical Theology in Philo of Alexandria* (Cincinnati, OH: Hebrew Union College Press, 1985), p. 58.

[5] Maren Niehoff (private communication) reminds me that some caution is advisable here: although the rabbinic sources never quote Philo explicitly, "it still remains to be investigated whether the rabbis may have been familiar with him through Christian writers (e. g., Origen's library in Caesarea, where Jews worked for him, possibly even on the copying of Philo's texts)."

[6] As Momigliano succinctly put it: "The Jews forgot Philo even before they forgot Greek. Philo was rediscovered for the Jews in a Latin translation by the Italian Jew Azariah de' Rossi" (Arnaldo D. Momigliano, "Greek Culture and the Jews," in M. I. Finley, ed., *The Legacy of Greece: A New Appraisal* [Oxford: Clarendon Press, 1981], p. 343); see also Ralph Marcus, "A Sixteenth Century Hebrew Critique of Philo," *HUCA* 21 (1948), pp. 29–71. De' Rossi's quotations from Philo (whom he calls Yedidyah the Alexandrian) can now be easily retrieved through the index in Joanna Weinberg, ed., *The Light of the Eyes: Azariah de' Rossi*, trans. from the Hebrew with an introduction and annotations (New Haven, CT: Yale University Press, 2001).

[7] Winston, *Logos and Mystical Theology*, p. 10, gives some stunning examples of this adaptation; and see now David T. Runia, *Philo and the Church Fathers: A Collection of Papers* (Leiden: Brill, 1995).

[8] De Viris Illustribus, 11: "*Ē Platōn philōnizei ē Philōn platōnizei*, id est '*Aut Plato Philonem sequitur, aut Platonem Philo*'" (Kōnstantinos Siamakēs, *Hierōnymou De viris illustribus* [Thessalonica: Kentro Byzantinōn Ereunōn, 1992], pp. 182 f.).

[9] See, e. g., Conf., 95, 97; Post., 28; Abr., 80.

one of God's major characteristics, *ho agenētos* (the "Uncreated One") – but we will never know *what* he is, his essence.[10] Such is Philo's axiomatic premise:

> Doubtless hard to unriddle and hard to apprehend is the Father and Ruler of all (*ho patēr kai hēgemōn tōn sympantōn*), but that is no reason why we should shrink from searching for Him. But in such searching two principal questions arise which demand the consideration of the genuine philosopher. One is whether the Deity exists (*ei esti to theion*), a question necessitated by those who practise atheism, the worst form of wickedness, the other is what [the deity] is in essence (*ti esti kata tēn ousian*). Now to answer the first question does not need much labour, but the second is not only difficult but perhaps impossible to solve.[11]

The question of God's existence is promptly answered with reference to the created world: just as a statue presupposes a sculptor, a painting a painter, or a well-ordered city good rulers, "so then he who comes to the truly Great City, this world ... must he not naturally or rather necessarily gain the conception of the Maker and Father and Ruler also?"[12] Any sensible human being must conclude from the well-ordered structure of our visible world that it was planned and created by a rational being standing outside of and superior to it; this is taken for granted: "In this way we have gained the conception of the existence of God."[13] The second question, however, of God's essence is much more difficult to address. Philo casts his answer in the form of a lengthy meditation on Ex. 33:17–23, the famous passage in which Moses expresses his desire to see God. Moses, a true philosopher in Philo's terms, has learned his lesson and knows that "this universe has been my teacher, to bring me to the knowledge that you [God] are and do subsist. As your son, it has told me of his Father, as your work of its contriver."[14] But Moses wants to know more. When he addresses his bold request to God, "Reveal yourself to me!" – this is Philo's version of the biblical "Oh, let me behold your Glory!" (Ex. 33:18) – he really means, "But what you are in your essence I desire to understand."[15] God answers that this is impossible for any created being, but Moses insists and wants to see "at least the Glory that surrounds you, and by your Glory I understand the powers (*tas dynameis*) that

---

[10] On the transcendence of God in Philo, see John M. Dillon and Wilhelm H. Wuellner, eds., *The Transcendence of God in Philo: Some Possible Sources.* Protocol of the Sixteenth Colloquy, 20 April 1975, Center for Hermeneutical Studies in Hellenistic and Modern Culture (Berkeley, CA: The Center, 1975); Gerhard Sellin, "Gotteserkenntnis und Gotteserfahrung bei Philo von Alexandrien," in Joachim Gnilka et al., eds., *Monotheismus und Christologie: Zur Gottesfrage im hellenistischen Judentum und im Urchristentum* (Freiburg: Herder, 1992), pp. 17–40.

[11] Spec. Leg., I, 32; cf. also Mut. Nom., 11 ff.; Praem., 40. All translations of Philo's works follow, if not indicated differently, the Greek-English text in the Loeb Classical Library edition (with some modifications).

[12] Spec. Leg., I, 34.

[13] Ibid., 35.

[14] Ibid., 41.

[15] Ibid.

keep guard around you."[16] With the "Glory" surrounding God, Philo is referring quite literally to God's Glory (*kavod*) in the biblical text, but Moses's explanation of "Glory" as God's "powers" (*dynameis*) transfers the biblical language to the realm of Platonic/Philonic philosophy. The "powers" are the facets of the unknowable, unattainable, transcendent God; as such, in their essence, they are unknowable as well, but they nevertheless embody and enable the transition from the transcendent *to on* (through many stages) down to our visible world. They are the divine activities that lead to the world of ideas and ultimately to the created world perceptible to our senses:

> The powers (*dynameis*) which you seek to know are discerned not by sight but by mind ... But while in their essence they are beyond your apprehension, they nevertheless present to your sight a sort of impress and copy of their active working. You men have for your use seals which when brought into contact with wax or similar material stamp on them any number of impressions while they themselves are not docked in any part thereby but remain as they were. Such you must conceive My powers to be, supplying quality and shape to things which lack either and yet changing or lessening nothing of their eternal nature. Some among you call them not inaptly "forms" or "ideas" (*ideas*), since they bring form to everything that is, giving order to the disordered, limit to the unlimited, bounds to the unbounded, shape to the shapeless, and in general changing the worse to something better. Do not, then, hope to be ever able to apprehend Me or any of My powers in Our essence (*kata tēn ousian*). But I readily and with right goodwill will admit you to a share of what is attainable. That means that I bid you come and contemplate the universe and its contents, a spectacle apprehended not by the eye of the body but by the unsleeping eyes of the mind.[17]

God's "powers" as facets of a multifaceted God are the "instruments" by which he puts his imprint on something that is not described in detail but would seem to be some kind of raw material (the disordered, unlimited, unbounded, and shapeless) that receives form through them. In doing so these powers create a "copy of their active working" – that is, of themselves – much as a stamp produces a copy of itself on impressionable material. No doubt, Philo is openly alluding here to the archetypical intelligible world of Platonic "ideas" (*ideai*). In "creating" the intelligible world, these powers lose nothing of their "eternal nature" (their substance and power) but simply give form to something new, something that is nevertheless identical with them. (Philo goes to great lengths here in identifying the divine powers with the Platonic ideas,[18] or, to put it differently, in arguing that the intelligible world is simultaneously a copy of the divine powers and identi-

---

[16] Ibid., 45.

[17] Ibid., 46–49.

[18] This is one of the extremely rare cases in which Philo identifies the "powers" with Plato's "ideas." Maren Niehoff cautions against too strong a formulation here: "I am not sure whether Philo identifies the Divine powers with the Platonic ideas or rather whether he is consciously borrowing language from Plato, which he knows to be widely familiar" (private communication).

cal with these powers.) It goes without saying that the powers and the universe created by them can be contemplated only by the mind, not by the senses.

That universe of eternal and unchangeable ideas which is created by the divine powers (and at the same time identical with them) is in Philo's terminology the *kosmos noētos*, the "world/universe discernible by the (human) mind/intellect." Its younger brother – quite literally "younger brother," because Philo also uses the metaphorical language of God's two sons, one elder and one younger[19] – is the *kosmos aisthētos*, the "world/universe perceived by (our) senses" – our temporal, changeable, and visible earthly world. Just as the divine powers and the intelligible world are related to each other in the way that "archetype" and "imprint" or "copy" are related, so too must the visible world (God's younger son) be regarded as a "copy" of the intelligible world (the elder son).

In the quoted passage from *De Specialibus Legibus*, Philo is not very explicit about those powers that (or rather *who*, since they are often personified) set God's creative act in motion. There can be no doubt, however, that two powers stand out and play a superior role, namely, Logos and Wisdom. In another parable using the image of the great city as a metaphor for the world, Philo identifies the Logos as the divine power responsible for the origin of the intelligible world:

> The conception we have concerning God must be similar to this, namely that when he had decided to found the great cosmic city, he first conceived its outlines. Out of these he composed the intelligible cosmos (*kosmos noētos*), which served him as a model when he composed the sense-perceptible cosmos (*kosmos aisthētos*) as well. Just as the city that was marked out beforehand within the mind of the architect had no location outside, but had been engraved in the soul of the craftsman as by a seal, in the same way the cosmos composed of the ideas (*ho ek tōn ideōn kosmos*) would have no other place than the divine Logos (*ton theion logon*) who gives these (ideas) their ordered disposition.[20]

The Platonic pattern of this passage is unmistakable. God, the eternal architect, conceives in his mind the world of ideas, which is the intelligible world (*kosmos noētos*) and which in turn serves as the pattern of the sense-perceptible world (*kosmos aisthētos*). Just as the architect first mentally designs the city to be built before carrying out his plan, so too does God first mentally conceive of the world of ideas before creating the world. Moreover, we learn precisely what – or rather *who* – among the divine powers is the active power in God's mind contemplating the intelligible world: it is the divine Logos, the creative

---

[19]   Quod Deus, 31 f.; Conf., 146 f.

[20]   Op. Mund., 19 f. (the translation follows *Philo of Alexandria: On the Creation of the Cosmos According to Moses*, transl. with an introduction and commentary by David T. Runia [Leiden: Brill, 2001], pp. 50 f.); see also Mos., II, 127. In Spec. Leg. I, 81, he calls the Logos the "image of God" (*logos d' estin eikōn theou*); according to Som., I, 75, the Logos contains "all His [God's] fullness – namely light."

power within God. Philo even goes so far as to identify the intelligible world of ideas with the Logos (similar to his identification of the unspecified powers with the intelligible world):

> If you would wish to use a formulation that has been stripped down to essentials, you might say that the intelligible kosmos (*ton noēton kosmon*) is nothing else than the Logos of God (*theou logon*) as he is actually engaged in making the cosmos.[21]

That Philo uses the Logos as the creative power within God has philosophical as well as theological reasons. Philosophically, Philo adopts the Stoic concept of Logos as the chief power immanent in the world. Theologically, the concept of Logos is not particularly prominent in the Bible, since the Septuagint translates the frequent biblical "word of God" (*devar YHWH*) mostly as *rhēma Kyriou* and not as *logos Kyriou*.[22] However, in Psalm 119, which identifies God's word with the Torah, the Hebrew *devarkha* ("your [God's] word") is rendered in the Septuagint by *logos sou* (or, in the plural, *logoi*).[23] It may well be that Philo deliberately alludes to this translation, all the more so as the identification of Logos with Torah certainly suited his purpose – the Torah as the "active agent" of God in the world (and note the identification of Torah with Wisdom in Jesus Sirach[24] and in the rabbinic Midrash).[25] Moreover, whereas the Greek rendering of the creation narrative in Genesis does not use the word *logos* (although the act of creation is produced by speech: "And God *said* …"),[26] the noncanonical Wisdom of Solomon explicitly attributes creation to God's Word (and Wisdom): "O God of my fathers and Lord of mercy, who has made all things by your Word (*en logō sou*), and through your Wisdom (*tē sophia sou*) has equipped man."[27] It is more than likely that Philo knew the postbiblical Wisdom literature, in particular the Wisdom of Solomon, and was influenced by it.[28]

The obvious identification of Logos and Wisdom in the Wisdom of Solomon is a case in point. Wisdom (Greek *sophia*) plays a prominent role in Philo as well and is yet another power among the divine powers that acts as an agent of creation. Whereas the Logos, as we have seen, is responsible for the intelligible world, Wisdom would seem to be responsible for the world perceived by the senses:

---

[21] Op. Mund., 24 (transl. Runia, *Philo of Alexandria: On the Creation of the Cosmos*, p. 51); cf. also Fug., 12.

[22] Pace Winston, *Logos and Mystical Theology*, p. 15, who states categorically and with no reference: "But the special suitability of the Logos for Philo's exposition of God's creative aspect lies in the fact that it could readily be assimilated to the 'word of God' in Scripture, which had been rendered in the Septuagint by the term *logos*."

[23] LXX Ps. 118:9, 16, 17, 25, 28, 42, 57, 67, 74, 81, 101, 114, 139, 147, 160, 169.

[24] Sir. 24:23; on this, see Schäfer, *Mirror of His Beauty*, pp. 29 ff.

[25] Bereshit Rabbah 1:1.

[26] The Hebrew *wayyomer* is translated with *eipen*.

[27] Sap. Sal. 9:1.

[28] See Schäfer, *Mirror of His Beauty*, p. 39.

Now "father and mother" is a phrase that can bear different meanings. For instance, we should rightly say and without further question that the architect (*dēmiourgos*) who made this universe[29] was at the same time father of what was thus born, while its mother was the knowledge (*epistēmē*) possessed by its Maker. With this knowledge God had union, though not as human beings have it, and begat created being. And knowledge, having received the divine seed and when her travail was consummated, bore the only beloved son who is apprehended by the senses (*aisthētos*), the world which we see (*ton kosmon*). Thus in the pages of one of the inspired company [the author of the biblical book of Proverbs], Wisdom (*sophia*) is represented as speaking of herself after this manner: "God obtained me first of all his works and founded me before the ages" (Prov. 8:22).[30]

This passage describes the origins of the visible world, the *kosmos aisthētos*: it emerges out of the union between God (the divine architect) and his knowledge (*epistēmē*), which is also called Wisdom (*sophia*). Their offspring is not the only son of the divine "couple" but the only son "who is apprehended by the senses," since there is, as we have seen, another older son: the intelligible world (*kosmos noētos*). Hence, Logos and Wisdom are the two chief powers in God responsible for the two worlds – the world of ideas and its image, our visible world. Philo combines here the biblical Wisdom concept and the postbiblical/philosophical idea of the Logos in order to explain the effect of the creative powers within God. Philo's metaphorical language should not mislead us, however. That Logos is responsible for the "older son" and Wisdom for the "younger son" does not mean that Wisdom is inferior to Logos. On the contrary, ontologically both Logos and Wisdom are identical (as in the Wisdom of Solomon); they are used only to differentiate between different aspects of God and his creative activity.[31]

Through his powers of Logos and Wisdom, God intervenes in our human world. We cannot know his essence, but we are able to experience the activity of Logos and Wisdom in our visible world. Since the visible world is the copy of the invisible world of ideas, we can approach this higher world – and hence God – with the part of us closely related to it: our mind. In other words, the movement from above, from God to his created world, has its complement in a reverse movement from below – from us to God. In order to understand this better, we need to examine more closely Philo's concept of body and soul.

Body and Soul, Senses and Mind

The distinction between body and soul is alien to Biblical Judaism; the Hebrew words *nefesh* and *neshamah* (sometimes translated as "soul") mean "breath (of

---

[29] Lit. "the All."
[30] Ebr., 30 f.
[31] For more on this aspect, see Schäfer, *Mirror of His Beauty*, pp. 44 f.

life)" and do not presuppose any notion of the soul as an entity independent of the body. It was only under the influence of Greek philosophy during the Hellenistic period that there entered into Jewish thought the idea of an immortal soul as distinct from the body and as the true essence of human beings (bestowed on the body at birth and taken away after death). Although traces of this concept can be found as early as the second century BCE (a prominent example is Dan. 12:2 f., which seems to express the belief in a spiritual resurrection, some kind of starlike existence of the righteous after death), it was left to Philo, following his model Plato, to introduce into Judaism a fully developed concept of body and soul as two distinct and even hostile entities. To be sure, Philo was not only a good Platonist but also a good Jew, and therefore he could not ignore the biblical view and simply discard the body. On the contrary, he was fully aware of the practical needs of the body; it has even been concluded from his language and his fondness for athletic metaphors that he himself "must have been a passionate devotee of athletics."[32]

Philosophically, however, he was less patient with the body. The body, he argues, is "wicked and a plotter against the soul ... even a corpse and a dead thing."[33] Only after the death of the body will the soul be liberated from its "tomb" and enjoy its proper life. Quoting Heraclitus' saying that, "We live their death, and are dead to their life,"[34] he concludes:

> He [Heraclitus] means that now, when we are living, the soul is dead and has been entombed in the body as in a sepulchre; whereas, should we die, the soul lives forthwith its own proper life, and is released from the body, the baneful corpse to which it was tied.[35]

In one of his characteristically metaphorical interpretations of the Bible, Philo identifies Er (the patriarch Judah's first-born son) with the body, because "Er" means "leathern bulk" (deriving "Er" from Hebrew *'or*, "skin" and "leather"). When the Bible says, "But Er, Judah's first-born, was displeasing to the Lord,[36] and the Lord killed him" (Gen. 38:7), we must take this as a metaphor for the wicked body that ultimately perishes and liberates the soul. In this regard, he concludes, there is a difference between the approach of the athlete and the philosopher to their respective bodies:

> For the athlete refers everything to the well-being of the body, and, lover of the body that he is, would sacrifice the soul itself on its behalf; but the philosopher being enamored of the noble thing that lives in himself, cares for the soul, and pays no regard

---

[32] Winston, *Logos and Mystical Theology*, p. 12.

[33] Leg. All., III, 69.

[34] Hippolytus, Refutatio Omnium Haeresium, IX, 10:6: *athanatoi thnētoi, thnētoi athanatoi, zōntes ton ekeinōn thanaton, ton de ekeinōn bion tethneōtes* ("Mortals are immortals and immortals are mortals, the one living the other's death and dying the other's life").

[35] Leg. All., I, 108.

[36] Lit. "wicked/evil (*ra'*) in the eyes of the Lord."

to that which is really a corpse, the body, concerned only that the best part of him, his soul, may not be hurt by an evil thing, a very corpse, tied to it.[37]

Accordingly, it is our "fleshly nature" that is the source of "ignorance" (*agnoia*) and "stupidity" (*amathia*). Only the

> souls that are free from flesh and body (*asarkoi kai asōmatoi*) spend their days in the theater of the universe and with a joy that none can hinder see and hear things divine, which they have desired with love insatiable. But those which bear the burden of the flesh, oppressed by the grievous load, cannot look up to the heavens as they revolve, but with necks bowed downwards are constrained to stand rooted to the ground like four-footed beasts.[38]

The latter are ordinary human beings who "have abandoned themselves to the unstable things of chance, none of which has anything to do with our noblest part, the soul or mind (*psychēn ē noun*), but all are related to that dead thing which was our birth-fellow, the body." The former are the "souls of those who have given themselves to genuine philosophy, who from first to last study to die to the life in the body,[39] that a higher existence immortal and incorporeal, in the presence of Him who is Himself immortal and uncreated, may be their portion."[40]

The means by which the true philosopher – during his lifetime, when his soul is still entombed in his body – attains a foretaste of his released soul's life after death is the mind (*nous, dianoia*), or more precisely the higher mind (to be distinguished from the lower mind, which responds to sensory perception). As we have seen in the quotation above, Philo uses "soul" and "mind" almost synonymously, but "soul" seems to be the more comprehensive term, whereas "mind" is the specifically rational part of the soul that is responsible for the ability to reason.[41] With their mind, human beings can rise above the world of sense perception and participate in the intelligible world of ideas; it is their mind or intellect that connects them with the world above, created and dominated by the divine Logos: "Every man, in respect of his mind (*dianoia*), is allied to the divine Logos (*logō theiō*), having come into being as an imprint (*ekmageion*) or fragment (*apospasma*) or effulgence (*apaugasma*) of that blessed nature."[42] It is certainly no accident that Philo uses here the rare term *apaugasma* ("effulgence" or "radiance"), which in the Wisdom of Solomon is reserved for God's Wisdom, "the effulgence (*apaugasma*) that streams from everlasting light, the flawless mirror of the active power of God, and the image of his goodness" (Sap. Sal. 7:26). Just as Wisdom/Logos is the reflection of the transcendent God, so

---

[37] Leg. All., III, 72.
[38] Gig., 30 f.
[39] This is an allusion to Plato, Phaedo, 67e.
[40] Gig., 14.
[41] Sandmel, *Philo of Alexandria*, p. 100.
[42] Op. Mund., 146.

too is the human mind a reflection of Wisdom/Logos. God, the divine Logos, and our Logos (mind) are closely related:

> One is the archetypical Logos above us, the other the copy (*mimēma*) of it which we possess [our mind]. Moses calls the first the "image of God" (*eikona theou*), the second the impress of that image (*tēs eikonos ekmageion*). For God, he says, made man not "the image of God" but "after the image" (Gen. 1:27).[43] And thus the mind (*nous*) in each of us, which in the true and full sense is the "man," is an expression at third hand from the Maker, while between them is the Logos which serves as paradigm of our reason, but itself is the copy/representation (*apeikonisma*) of God.[44]

Now, how in fact does the human mind connect itself with the divine Logos or Wisdom? It is the prerogative and task of the philosopher, the "lover of wisdom," to direct his mind to the invisible, immaterial, and eternal world above. Yet there is a huge difference, Philo argues, between the wisdom of the philosophers, or traditional knowledge, which can be taught and learned, and divine Wisdom, which cannot be acquired solely by education but is bestowed upon the adept:[45]

> No doubt it is profitable ... to feed the mind on ancient and time-honored thoughts, to trace the venerable tradition of noble deeds, which historians and all the family of poets have handed down to the memory of their own and future generations. But when, unforeseen and unhoped for, the sudden beam of self-inspired Wisdom (*automathous sophias*) has shone upon us, when that Wisdom has opened the closed eye of the soul and made us spectators rather than hearers of knowledge, and substituted in our minds (*dianoia*) sight (*opsin*), the swiftest of senses, for the lower sense of hearing, then it is idle any longer to exercise the ear with words.[46]

Here, traditional wisdom is confronted with divine Wisdom. Traditional wisdom is that which is handed down by historians and poets (and philosophers, one might add), the "cultural memory" of all previous generations, whereas divine Wisdom is unrelated to our past human history; it cannot be taught and learned but shines upon us in a sudden beam. As such, it is *automathēs* (subsequently also *autodidaktos*), "self-inspired" or "self-taught," that is, it is its own source and obtained by the adept automatically or intuitively. The faculty of the soul or mind that receives it is silent sight (one is tempted to say vision), in contrast to verbose hearing. To be sure, Philo continues, we should not disregard traditional knowledge, but in repeating this plea over and over again, he fosters precisely such a disregard, because ultimately divine Wisdom sweeps away traditional knowledge:

---

[43] Translating the Hebrew *be-tzalmo* literally.
[44] Her., 230 f. Cf. also Op. Mund., 69.
[45] For a more thorough analysis, see Schäfer, *Mirror of His Beauty*, pp. 50 ff.
[46] Sac., 78.

We must not indeed reject any learning that has grown grey through time, nay, we should make it our aim to read the writings of the sages and listen to proverbs and old-world stories from the lips of those who know antiquity, and ever seek for knowledge about the men and deeds of old. Yet when God causes the young shoots of self-inspired Wisdom (*autodidaktou sophias*) to spring up within the soul (*en psychē*), the knowledge that comes from teaching must straightaway be abolished and swept off. Ay, even of itself it will subside and ebb away. God's scholar, God's pupil, God's disciple ... cannot any more suffer the guidance of men.[47]

Although the knowledge stored in the writings of our sages will not and must not be neglected,[48] it is nothing compared to the divine Wisdom that emerges within the human soul and of which God himself is the source. It "springs up" in the soul in a sudden act of recognition, without any toil or labor,[49] and it sweeps away the "old" wisdom of human knowledge. The chosen "seer" is now directly guided by God and does no longer needs the guidance of men. His reward will be "a treasure of perfect happiness" (*thesauron eudaimonias teleias*)[50] and the "knowledge and understanding of God" (*gnōsis ... kai epistēmē theou*).[51] To be sure, and to reiterate, this goal can only be reached by forfeiting bodily pleasure and by following the workings of the mind, the cognitive part of the soul, which allows divine Wisdom to overwhelm us with its (her) work:

> In the same way the pleasures of the body descend upon us in gathered force like a cataract deluging and obliterating one after the other all the things of the mind; and then, after no long interval, Wisdom with strong and vehement counterblast both slackens the impetus of pleasures and mitigates in general all the appetites and ambitions which the bodily senses kindle in us.[52]

The Soul's Vision of God

Who, then, are the privileged ones granted the gift of divinely inspired knowledge of God? And what does this gift entail, what is its effect on the human soul?[53] As to be expected, first in line among the privileged are the prophets.

---

[47] Ibid.

[48] Traditional learning is symbolized in the Bible by Hagar, Sarah's handmaid, whereas divine Wisdom is symbolized by Sarah, the mistress, herself. Union with Hagar produces Ishmael, "the lower branches of school lore," but union with Sarah produces Isaac, a child of "higher birth" (Cong., 14).

[49] Quod Deus, 92.

[50] Ibid.

[51] Ibid., 143.

[52] Som., II, 13.

[53] On Philo's "mysticism," see in particular David Winston, "Was Philo a Mystic?" in Joseph Dan and Frank Talmage, eds., *Studies in Jewish Mysticism: Proceedings of Regional Conferences Held at the University of California, Los Angeles and McGill University in April, 1978* (Cambridge, MA: Association for Jewish Studies, 1982), pp. 15–39. Cf. also the illuminat-

They are the "spokesmen" of God, the truly "God-inspired" and "possessed."[54] Interpreting Gen. 15:12 in the Septuagint version ("About sunset an ecstasy [*ekstasis*] fell upon Abraham and lo a great dark terror [*phobos skoteinos megas*] falls upon him"), Philo explains how divine inspiration takes place within the prophet's soul. The "sun," he says, is a metaphor for our mind (*nous*): like the sun, which shines during the day, the mind, when active, "pours as it were a noonday beam into the whole soul"; this is the "ordinary" state of mind, which is self-contained, not possessed. This changes, however, when the sun/mind sets:

> But when it [the sun/mind] comes to its setting, naturally ecstasy (*ekstasis*) and divine possession (*entheos katokōchē*) and inspired frenzy (*mania*)[55] fall upon us. For when the light of God shines, the human light sets; when the divine light sets, the human dawns and rises. This is what regularly befalls the fellowship of the prophets. The mind (*nous*) is evicted at the arrival of the divine Spirit (*kata tēn tou theiou pneumatos aphixin*), but when that departs the mind returns to its tenancy. Mortal and immortal may not share the same home. And therefore the setting of reason (*tou logismou*) and the darkness (*skotos*) which surrounds it produce ecstasy (*ekstasin*) and inspired frenzy (*theophorēton manian*).[56]

This is a particularly telling passage. Not only do we learn that the light of God sparks ecstasy, divine possession, and inspired frenzy within the human soul – Philo underscores this repeatedly (and I return to it later) – but, more important in this context, he stresses that the divine light is incompatible with human light, the mind. When the divine light (identified with the Holy Spirit) shines upon the prophet, the mind recedes, or rather, as he so drastically puts it, is removed or banished from its house, the human body (*exoikizetai*). Hence the human mind is not elevated to the divine light and dissolved into it, but is replaced by something completely and essentially different. The "great dark terror" that Abraham experienced when the divinely inspired ecstasy fell upon him is the darkness left by the "setting of reason," the human Logos. On the other hand, however, it is precisely this darkness that is the precondition for the dawn of the divine light – ecstasy and frenzy.

The paragon of prophecy, of course, is Moses. In his case, Philo's language sometimes becomes exceedingly hymnic and theologically daring. To be sure, as we have seen, Moses's request to see God's Glory was rejected by making clear to him that he could never see God's essence but still might be allowed to catch a glimpse of God through his "powers." The following passage is in keeping with this cautious attitude. There, Philo praises Moses's mind as a "mind more per-

---

ing and richly documented article by Maren R. Niehoff, "What Is in a Name? Philo's Mystical Philosophy of Language," *JSQ* 2 (1995), pp. 220–252.

[54] *Her.*, 259.

[55] The Greek *mania* means both "madness" and "inspired frenzy." Below, Philo uses the full phrase *theophorēton manian* to make sure he is not talking just about "madness."

[56] *Her.*, 264–265.

fect and more thoroughly cleansed, which has undergone initiation into the great mysteries (*nous ta megala mystēria myētheis*), a mind which gains its knowledge of the First Cause (*to aition*) not from created things ... but lifting its eyes above and beyond creation obtains a clear reflection[57] (*emphasin enargē*) of the Uncreated One (*tou agenētou*)."[58] Moses's mind is elevated above the created world and approaches the hidden essence of the First Cause through his "reflection," the world of ideas (chiefly Logos and Wisdom). Yet Philo goes much further in his commentary on Exodus 24:2:

> Why does He say, "Moses alone shall come near to God, and they [Aaron, Nadab and Abihu, and the seventy elders of Israel] shall not come near, and the people shall not go up with them" (Ex. 24:2)?

> O most excellent and God-worthy ordinance, that the prophetic mind (*ton prophētikon noun*) alone should approach God and that those in second place should go up, making a path to heaven, while those in third place and the turbulent characters of the people should neither go up above nor go up with them but those worthy of beholding should be beholders of the blessed path above. But that "(Moses) alone shall go up" is said most naturally. For when the prophetic mind becomes divinely inspired and filled with God (*enthousia kai theophoreitai*), it becomes like the monad, not being at all mixed with any of those things associated with duality. But he who is resolved into the nature of unity, is said to come near to God in a kind of family relation, for having given up and left behind all mortal kinds, he is changed into the divine, so that such men become kin to God and truly divine.[59]

Here, a clear distinction is made between Moses, the only true prophet who comes near to God, his entourage (Aaron, Nadab and Abihu, and the seventy elders of Israel), who are allowed to climb the mountain togther with Moses but are not permitted to come close to God, and the people who must stay at the foot of the mountain. It is only the prophet's mind that, in approaching God, is possessed by divine inspiration. So far, the text fits well with what we already know about Moses. But that he, during this process, loses his "duality" and becomes "like the monad," that he is "resolved into the nature of unity" and "changed into the divine" – these qualifications are quite unique. Unfortunately, the *Quaestiones* are preserved only in Armenian translation, and it is difficult to reconstruct the original Greek text behind the translation. In this particular case the closest parallel is in *De Vita Mosis*, which apparently employs some of the key terms used in our passage:

> Afterwards the time came when he [Moses] had to make his pilgrimage from earth to heaven, and leave this mortal life for immortality, summoned thither by the Father who resolved his twofold nature (*auton dyada onta*) of soul and body into a single unity (*eis*

---

[57] The translation by Colson and Whitaker (*Philo*, vol. 1, p. 369) has, somewhat inaccurately, "vision."

[58] Leg. All., III, 100 f.

[59] Q. E., II, 29.

monados anestoicheiou), transforming his whole being into mind, pure as the sunlight (*eis noun hēlioeidestaton*).[60]

From this passage it becomes clear that the divinely inspired prophetic mind of Moses leaves behind the duality of body and soul and is transformed into a single entity, a monad, that is characterized as pure mind. What *De Vita Mosis* describes is precisely the stage at which the soul liberates itself from its bodily prison and returns to its ideal and always longed-for state. That is to say, it captures the very moment at which Moses crosses the border from mortality to immortality. To be sure, he still prophesies, namely his very last blessings over the tribes (Deut. 33), but this prophecy is uttered at the threshold of immortality, immediately before his death, and hence just prior to his transformation into a monad.

In employing this vocabulary for Moses's ascent to Mount Sinai and his "coming near to God," the *Quaestiones in Exodum* take an enormous and bold step. They transfer Moses's transformation from duality to unity – from body and soul to pure soul – from the realm of immortality to the realm of mortality: Moses attained this stage, which is usually reserved for the time after death, during his lifetime! He came as close as possible to God, because when God asked him to come near to him, he was still a human being with body and soul (and he would return to this human stage following this unique experience).

Moreover, the *Quaestiones* go further than *De Vita Mosis* in describing what precisely this transformation entails. Whereas the phrase that Moses is "resolved into the nature of unity" can be understood, with *De Vita Mosis*, as his transformation from the duality of body and soul to the unity of pure soul – and hence not as a unity/unification with God – further along the *Quaestiones* stress that Moses enters into a "kind of family relation" with God and, being "changed into the divine," thus becomes "truly divine." Here, of course, it would be imperative to know the original Greek text (which we do not). The only other passage where Philo speaks of the "divinization" of the "holy soul" through its ascent to a region above the heavens – that is, to God – is in his commentary on Ex. 24:12 ("Come up to Me to the mountain and be there"), hence within the same pericope.[61] The translator from the Armenian remarks that the Armenian word for becoming divinized "usually renders *theousthai*, a word that seems not to occur elsewhere in Philo" and proposes *theophoreisthai* as the Greek *Vorlage*.[62] But although this word is commonly used by Philo to signify being possessed or inspired by God (in Q. E., II, 29, Marcus translates it with "filled with God"), it

---

[60] Mos., II, 288.

[61] Q. E., II, 40.

[62] *Philo*, Supplement II, *Questions and Answers on Exodus*, trans. from the ancient Armenian version of the original Greek by Ralph Marcus (Cambridge, MA: Harvard University Press; London: William Heinemann, 1961), p. 82, n. n. Maren Niehoff informs me (private communication) that the Armenian word in question is *astwardzanam* and means "to make oneself God, to become God, to unite or join someone to God, to resemble God."

does not necessarily take on the strong meaning of becoming divinized in the sense of becoming united with the divine. Altogether, therefore, although he goes very far in the exceptional case of Moses, Philo seems reluctant to overstate his case.[63] We cannot preclude the possibility that the Armenian translator retains responsibility for the particular tone of our two passages in the *Quaestiones*, with their emphasis on Moses's "deification."[64]

Ultimately, however, it is not only Moses's soul that can ascend to the heights of the divine during its lifetime but *any* human soul if it follows the proper procedure. Any mind (*nous*), "which has been perfectly cleansed and purified, and which renounces all things pertaining to creation, is acquainted with One alone (*hen monon*) and knows the Uncreated (*to agenēton*), to Whom it has drawn nigh, by Whom also it has been taken to Himself."[65] That purified soul that has left behind the created world is drawn close to God, the Uncreated One. When Hannah says, "I will pour out my soul before the Lord" (1 Sam. 1:15), according to Philo this refers to the desire of the human soul to obtain a vision of God:

> What else was meant by the words, "I will pour out my soul before the Lord" but "I will consecrate it all to him, I will loosen all the chains that bound it tight, which the empty aims and desires of mortal life had fastened upon it; I will send it abroad, extend and diffuse it, so that it shall touch the bounds of the All (*tōn tou pantos hapsasthai peratōn*), and hasten to that most glorious and loveliest of visions (*thean*) – the vision of the Uncreated (*tou agenētou*)"?[66]

This is one of the rare cases in which Philo does not employ the philosophical pattern of the soul's transformation into pure soul and its being "overpowered" by the divine mind but resorts to the traditional (biblical and postbiblical) language of the vision of God. He does not explain what this vision entails, but there can be no doubt that for him it is precisely this: the transformation of the soul, and not the vision of God's shape in terms of the biblical and apocalyptic narratives.

In a number of passages Philo describes in greater detail what this ascent of the soul/mind involves. The mind of the sage (who is the perfect man) is in a kind of liminal state, "midway between mortal and immortal kind," on the borderline between the created and the uncreated. When it directs itself to God, it is driven by its own desire as much as by God's overwhelming force:

---

[63] The only passage in which Philo uses the word *henōsis* ("union") is in Post., 12, where he explains the biblical command to "cleave" to God (Deut. 30:20): "He [Moses] bids them to 'cleave to Him,' bringing out by the use of this word how constant and continuous and unbroken is the concord (*harmonia*) and union (*henōsis*) that comes through making God our own."

[64] Niehoff, "What Is in a Name?" pp. 240 f., n. 59, is convinced that the first passage in the *Quaestiones* "even implies *unio mystica*," but she also underlines the fact that "this passage is highly exceptional."

[65] Plant., 64.

[66] Ebr., 152.

When the mind is mastered by the love of the divine (*erōtos theiou*), when it strains its powers to reach the inmost shrine, when it puts forth every effort and ardor on its forward march, under the divine impelling force (*theophoroumenos*)[67] it forgets all else, forgets itself, and fixes its thoughts and memories on Him alone whose attendant and servant it is, to whom it dedicates not a palpable offering, but incense, the incense of consecrated virtues. But when the inspiration (*to enthousiōdes*) is stayed, and the strong yearning abates, it hastens back from the divine and becomes a man.[68]

In other words, the divinely inspired mind is no longer a human mind but in some kind of intermediate stage between the human and the divine,[69] completely overwhelmed by the inspiration granted from above. As we have seen, Philo distinguishes between divine Wisdom and the ordinary wisdom of the philosophers: whereas the latter can be taught and learned, the former is bestowed upon the adept as a divine gift and therefore called *automathēs* or *autodidaktos*, "self-inspired" or "self-taught." The truly wise man, Philo argues, is a man

> who learns directly from no teacher but himself (*automathēs kai autodidaktos*); for he does not by searchings and practisings and toilings gain improvement, but as soon as he comes into existence he finds Wisdom (*sophian*) placed ready to his hand, shed from heaven above, and of this he drinks undiluted draughts, and sits feasting, and ceases not to be drunken with the sober drunkenness which right reason brings. This is he whom Holy Writ calls "Isaac," whom the soul did not conceive at one time and gave birth to at another, for it says "she conceived and gave birth" (Gen. 21:2) as though timelessly. For he that was thus born was not a man, but a most pure thought (*noēma katharōtaton*), beautiful not by practice but by nature. And for this reason she that gave birth to it is said "to have forsaken the ways of women" (Gen. 18:11), those human ways of custom and mere reasoning. For the nature of the self-taught (*to automathes genos*) is new and higher than our reasoning (*logou*), and indeed divine (*theion*), arising by no human will or purpose but by a God-inspired ecstasy (*entheō mania*).[70]

Much as human beings can (and must) aspire to receiving the "pure thought" of divine Wisdom, it cannot be absorbed by a mere act of the human will but is given by God as the gift of inspired/possessed frenzy.[71] Like the prophets and Moses, any true "lover of learning"[72] can attain this ecstatic state of mind. Like Abraham, who was asked by God to leave his native land and his father's house

---

[67] Literally: "possessed/inspired by God," that is, the same word as discussed above.

[68] Som., II, 232 f.

[69] This is exemplified by the high priest: when the high priest "enters into the Holy of Holies," as Philo explains Lev. 16:17, "he will not be a man until he comes out" (Som., II, 231). Needless to say, Philo's exegesis runs quite contrary to the biblical text, which only says that nobody *shall be with* the high priest in the Tabernacle until he reemerges. In Som., II, 185, the high priest is called a "father of holy Logoi" (*patēr logōn hierōn*) and hence identified with the divine Logos; on this, see Sellin, "Gotteserkenntnis," p. 30.

[70] Fug., 166–168.

[71] "Self-taught" therefore does not mean, in the literal sense of the word, that one can teach this kind of higher Wisdom oneself but rather that it comes "automatically" from "above," without any previous education.

[72] Her., 63.

(Gen. 12:1), the soul is asked to leave the prison of its body and arrive at the new "land" of divine inspiration:

> Therefore, my soul, if you feel any yearning to inherit the good thing of God (*tōn theiōn agathōn*) leave not only your land, that is the body, your kinsfolk, that is the senses, your father's house (Gen. 12:1), that is speech, but be a fugitive from yourself also and issue forth from yourself (*ekstēthi seautēs*). Like persons possessed and Corybants (*hoi katechomenoi kai korybantiōntes*), be filled with inspired frenzy (*bakcheutheisa kai theophorētheisa*),[73] even as the prophets are inspired. For it is the mind which is under the divine afflatus (*theophorētheisa*), and no longer in its own keeping, but is stirred to its depths and maddened by heavenward yearning, drawn by the truly existent (*hypo tou ontōs ontos*) and pulled upward thereto, with truth to lead the way and remove all obstacles before its feet, that its path may be smooth to tread – such is the mind, which has this inheritance.[74]

The soul that is lifted up to the divine realm leaves not only its body but itself; filled with divine frenzy, it is no longer itself but becomes something different. Philo fails to tell us what precisely this difference is, yet it is clear that it is a completely new state of mind. The only comparison he draws is with the Corybants, who are "inspired with Bacchic frenzy and possessed by a god." The "Bacchic frenzy" refers to the Bacchanalia, the Dionysian mysteries and orgies that were particularly popular in the first centuries CE and must have been well-known to Philo's readers. The Corybants are the cultic dancers of Kybele, the fertility goddess of Asia Minor,[75] mentioned also by Plato.[76] So it is a state of ecstasy and rapture in which the mind is caught up, similar to the rapture of the initiate in the ancient mystery cults. Philo leaves no doubt, however, that this rapture is effected by the truly existent God (*to on*), who draws the soul close to himself.

The following passage describes in greater detail the soul's journey through the various stations of the heavenly realm – through the atmosphere, the ether, the planets and fixed stars – always "following that love of wisdom which guides its steps." Finally leaving the world of senses behind, it arrives at the intelligible world:

> Then, after being carried around in the dances of the planets and fixed stars in accordance with the laws of perfect music, and following the guidance of its love of wisdom, it peers beyond the whole of sense-perceptible reality (*pasan tēn aisthētēn ousian*) and desires to attain the intelligible realm (*tēs noētēs*). And when the intellect has observed in that realm the models and forms (*ta paradeigmata kai tas ideas*) of the sense-percep-

---

[73] Lit. "be inspired with Bacchic frenzy and be possessed by a god."

[74] Her., 69f.

[75] Konrat Ziegler and Walther Sontheimer., eds., *Der Kleine Pauly: Lexikon der Antike*, vol. 3 (Munich: Deutscher Taschenbuch Verlag, 1979), p. 379, s.v. "Kureten"; James Miller, *Measures of Wisdom: The Cosmic Dance in Classical and Christian Antiquity* (Toronto: University of Toronto Press, 1986), pp. 56–80.

[76] Euthydemus 277d–e. See also Phaedrus, 244 ff., where Plato speaks of ecstasy and *mania* as important elements of philosophy.

tible things which it had seen here, objects of overwhelming beauty, it then, possessed by a sober drunkenness,[77] becomes enthused like the Corybants (*hoi korybantiōntes*). Filled with another longing and a higher form of desire, which has propelled it to the utmost vault of the intelligibiles,[78] it thinks it is heading towards the Great King himself (*ton megan basilea*). But as it strains to see (him), pure and unmixed beams of concentrated light pour forth like a torrent, so that the eye of the mind, overwhelmed by the brightness, suffers from vertigo.[79]

This is the climax of Philo's description of the soul's destiny, which leaves the sense-perceptible world (*kosmos aisthētos*) behind and arrives at the intelligible world (*kosmos noētos*), the world of ideas created by the divine Logos. Having reached that stage it is filled with the "sober drunkenness" or "intoxication" of Corybantic frenzy and divine possession – and here Philo takes great care to make clear that the Corybantic frenzy is nothing in comparison to the state of mind and longing that characterizes the true adept. For now the initiate is faced with another and much more arduous border to cross, namely, that border between the intelligible world and the hidden God, to whom he assigns here not the philosophical appellation *to on* but the biblical appellation King. The soul "thinks it is heading towards the Great King," Philo says, obviously with careful consideration. For now the soul has reached the "utmost vault of the intelligibiles," that is, the very end of the intelligible world perceptible to the mind, a borderline that cannot be crossed. The soul's longing to finally see God will not be fulfilled: the beams of light that stream forth from the hidden essence of God blind its eyes. At the climax of his description of the soul's journey, Philo again resorts to the metaphor of light. The soul is overpowered by a stream of divine light that dazzles its "eyes," so that ultimately it sees – nothing.[80] What

---

[77] Other translations: "intoxication."

[78] Lit. "the things discernible [by the intellect]."

[79] Op. Mund., 70 f. (transl. Runia, *Philo of Alexandria: On the Creation of the Cosmos*, p. 64).

[80] This important aspect has also been emphasized by Niehoff, "What Is in a Name?," pp. 238 f.: "Ultimately, the human soul cannot behold God, because the intensity of His light is said to be too strong and thus dazzling. ... If at all existent, it [the light emanating from the soul that corresponds to and is activated by the divine light] seems to be far too weak to take any active part *vis-à-vis* the onslaught of the Divine rays. ... In fact, man's soul can therefore not really be said to be congenial to the Divine rays." In this context, Niehoff points out – and rightly so – that Philo's description of Abraham's and Jacob's vision remains "relatively pale" (ibid., p. 240). With regard to Abraham, Philo states: "That is why we are told not that the Sage saw God, but that God was seen by him. For it were impossible that anyone should by himself apprehend the truly Existent (*to pros alētheian on*), did not He reveal and manifest Himself" (Abr., 80). Similarly, concerning Jacob he makes clear: "The Father and Saviour perceiving the sincerity of his [Jacob's] yearning in pity gave power to the penetration of his eyesight and did not grudge to grant him the vision of Himself in so far as it was possible for mortal and created nature to contain it. Yet the vision only showed that He is, not what He is. For this which is better than the good, more venerable than the monad, purer than the unit, cannot be discerned by anyone else; to God alone is it permitted to apprehend God" (Praem., 39 f.).

remains to be communicated is that the divine befalls the soul, transforming it into something different and leaving it blind and helpless.

In contrast to this very last stage of the soul's journey and transformation – which ends in silence and can at most be described as a state of "immutable tranquility"[81] and happiness[82] – Philo is more outspoken on the immediately preceding stage, when the soul attains to the intelligible world of the divine Logos:

> But it is the special mark of those who serve the Existent (*to on*), that theirs are not the tasks of cupbearers or bakers or cooks, or any other tasks of the earth earthy …, but in their thoughts ascend to the heavenly heights, setting before them Moses, the nature beloved of God, to lead them on the way. For then they shall behold the place (*ton men topon … theasontai*) which in fact is the Logos (*hos dē logos esti*),[83] where stands God the never changing, never swerving, and also what lies under his feet like "the work of a brick of sapphire, like the form of the firmament of the heaven" (Ex. 24:10), even the world of our senses, which he indicates in his mystery. For it well befits those who have entered into comradeship with knowledge to desire to see the Existent (*to on*) if they may, but, if they cannot, to see at any rate his image (*tēn goun eikona autou*), the most holy Logos (*ton hierōtaton logon*), and after the Logos its most perfect work at all that our senses know, even this world.[84]

This is Philo's interpretation of the notorious, and notoriously difficult, biblical verse Ex. 24:10 (in the Septuagint version): "And they [Moses, Aaron, Nadab and Abihu, and the seventy elders] saw the place where the God of Israel stood; and under his feet was as it were the work of a brick of sapphire, like the form of the firmament of the heaven in its purity." The "place where the God of Israel stands," he explains, is in fact the Logos, together with Wisdom the most potent of God's potencies. And what lies "under his feet" – the "work of a brick of sapphire" – is the world of our senses, the *kosmos aisthētos*. So Moses and his entourage did not see God; they saw instead his "image," the Logos, and everyone who wants to become their equal can see and will see the Logos (and through the Logos its creation, our world). The utmost that can be "seen" by our soul is the world of ideas, created by and identical with the Logos; beyond it reigns silence.

---

[81] Gig., 49: "true stability and immutable tranquility is that which we experience at the side of God, who Himself stands always immutable."

[82] Abr., 58: "But he to whom it is given not only to apprehend by means of knowledge all else that nature has to show, but also to see the Father and Maker of all (*ton patera kai poiētēn tōn sympantōn horan*), may rest assured that he is advanced to the crowning point of happiness (*ep' akron eudaimonias*); for nothing is higher than God, and who so has stretched the eyesight of the soul to reach Him should pray that he may there abide and stand firm."

[83] Following the emendation of the editors and translators of *hos dēlos esti*; see F. H. Colson and G. H. Whitaker, eds., *Philo, with an English Translation*, vol. 4 (London: William Heinemann; Cambridge, MA: Harvard University Press, 1958), p. 60, n. 2.

[84] Conf., 95–97.

Finally, it is Philo's own experience as a philosophic writer that he describes in terms of divine "possession," similar to the experience of the prophets, Moses, and the human soul:

> I feel no shame in recording my own experience, a thing I know from its having happened to me a thousand times. On some occasions, after making up my mind to follow the usual course of writing on philosophical tenets, and knowing definitely the substance of what I was to set down, I have found my understanding incapable of giving birth to a single idea, and have given it up without accomplishing anything. ... On other occasions, I have approached my work empty and suddenly became full, the ideas falling in a shower from above and being sown invisibly, so that under the influence of the divine possession I have been filled with Corybantic frenzy (*hypo katochēs entheou korybantian*) and been unconscious of anything, place, persons present, myself, words spoken, lines written. For I obtained language, ideas, an enjoyment of light, keenest vision (*opsin*), pellucid distinctness of objects, such as might be received through the eyes as the result of clearest showing.[85]

Philosophical writing is also a divine gift, and the true philosopher is divinely inspired and possessed like the true prophet.[86] The "higher thought ... comes from a voice in my own soul, which oftentimes is god-possessed and divines where it does not know."[87] When the Bible says that "God cast a trance (*ekstasin*) upon Adam, and he went to sleep" (Gen. 2:21), this teaches us that the ecstasy of mind – the "fitting thought" – cannot be obtained but is given by God alone.[88] Appropriate thinking and successful writing depend on inspiration and intuition – the prophet has become a philosopher.

In sum, Philo arrives at a completely new answer to the perennial question of how God approaches his created world and how human beings in turn approach God. Through his divine powers, notably Logos and Wisdom, God reaches down into our universe, and through the most supreme of our faculties, the higher mind, we ourselves can ascend to him. Human beings are composed of body and soul, with the soul locked up in the prison of its body. On the death of the body the soul is freed to return to its place of origin, the divine world, but even during our lifetime we can ignore our bodily bonds and release our soul into those higher spheres above the material world. The prophets are prime examples of human beings who successfully undertook this journey, chief among them being Moses – but in principle, everybody who is willing to resist the temptations of the body can follow their lead.

The topmost region attainable by the human soul is the intelligible world of ideas created by and identical with the divine Logos. Since the Logos (together

---

[85] Mig., 34 f.

[86] On Philo's concept of inspiration, see Helmut Burkhardt, "Inspiration der Schrift durch weisheitliche Personalinspiration," *ThZ* 47 (1991), pp. 214–225.

[87] Cher., 27.

[88] Leg. All., II, 31 f.; cf. also II, 85.

with Wisdom) is the image of the hidden God, he reflects the truly Existent and Uncreated; but the essence of the transcendent God behind his reflection in the world of ideas is unknowable and unattainable. No human soul will ever achieve this realm.

The prophets, Moses (the true philosopher), and not least Philo – their souls are lifted up in a state of ecstasy and rapture that Philo calls "divine possession" and "inspired frenzy" and that he compares with the mystery cults of his time, more precisely with the Corybants and Bacchants. This state of mind is characterized, first, by the fact that it occurs suddenly and unexpectedly, automatically and intuitively, without the adept's active participation (except for the necessary preparation); in other words, it is a gift from God and cannot be acquired. Second, the soul/mind filled with divine frenzy is not itself any more. Having reached the "utmost vault of the intelligibiles," the soul leaves itself and is transformed into something different (thus distinguishing, Philo claims, his adept from initiates of the mystery cults). It is difficult to determine what precisely that "different" is, yet it seems as if the soul does not remain a human soul in the strict sense of the word but is replaced by some divine essence; following the example of Moses, this state may be called the monad of pure soul, bordering on divinization. However, once the divine frenzy is over the soul returns to its prison, the human body.

What Philo describes here goes far beyond the biblical and postbiblical concept of God revealing himself to the chosen seer and of the human hero ascending to heaven and obtaining a vision of God. To be sure, Philo sometimes uses the traditional language of vision and ascent, but whereas the seer in the ascent apocalypses no doubt ascended in his body *and* soul, Philo splits the unity of body and soul and is only concerned with the fate of the soul as the better half of human existence. Moreover, whereas the ancient seer approached the figure of God seated on his throne in the uppermost heaven, Philo's soul becomes transformed into a divine essence and obtains a state that is completely different from its entombed condition in the human body.

Chapter 6

The Rabbis I

Approaching God through Exegesis

The imposition of direct Roman rule in the early first century CE sealed the end of the political autonomy of the Jewish people, and the destruction of the Temple in 70 CE terminated the institution of the sacrifice, which had dominated Jewish religious life for centuries. Out of this a power vacuum arose: the kingship was deeply compromised through Herod and his successors, as were the nobility and the office of the high priest, and the priests lost most of their raison d'être. Slowly, and certainly not without resistance, a new group emerged laying claim to both the religious and political leadership of the Jews under Roman supremacy – the rabbis, self-appointed heroes of what would become one of the most fruitful and momentous periods of Jewish history. During the first five centuries of the Christian era, from about 100 until about 600 CE, these rabbis, with their two centers in Palestine and in Babylonia, created an enormous literary corpus (from the Mishnah and its companion, the Tosefta, to the Midrashim and the Talmud in its twofold form of the Yerushalmi and the Bavli) that would define the religious and cultural life of the Jews for centuries to come, up until the modern period.

A mere glimpse at the literary output of the rabbis makes it immediately clear they were not concerned with physically storming the heavens in order to get a closer look at God. Theirs was not a world of ascents to heaven, so graphically described in the ascent apocalypses. Nor did they envision themselves in liturgical communion with the angels, the ideal of the Qumran community; on the contrary, they did everything they could to play down the role of the angels, and they made no secret of their conviction that human beings are actually superior to the angels.[1] Nor did they aspire, with Philo, to abandon their body and have their soul reunited with its divine origin. To be sure, they were equally determined to get closer to their God, but their "vision" of approaching God was bound to study and learning, the toilsome study of the Holy Scripture, not to ascent and rapture. They perceived the reality of their entire existence – from trivial day-to-day tasks to religious experiences – through the lens of their careful and inexhaust-

---

[1] See Schäfer, *Rivalität*, pp. 228 ff.

ible exegeses of the Hebrew Bible. For them, reading the Bible properly meant understanding their life better and exploring their relationship with God.

Reading the Bible the rabbis knew, of course, that the great prophets claimed to have had visions of God, and they were certainly aware that individual heroes of the past were taken up by God into the heavens. Whereas with regard to Elijah, the Bible makes fairly clear that he ascended to heaven in a "fiery chariot (*rekhev esh*) with fiery horses" (2 Kings 2:11), it is much vaguer, as we have seen, with regard to Enoch (Gen. 5:24), and hence left room for the rabbis to deliberate on his fate. Moreover, nothing prevents us from assuming that they were quite aware of the literature that had evolved around Enoch and his circle or other figures of the past. Yet they opted to not promote or even to denigrate these traditions, for whatever reason, focusing instead on the exegesis of the received biblical texts. However, since they believed in the unity and integrity of the biblical corpus as a whole (according to the tripartite canon that obtained its final form during the second century CE), they could not ignore the fact that their Bible contained some highly troubling pieces that gave rise to even more troubling speculations. It will come as no surprise, then, that Ezekiel's vision of the divine chariot on the river Chebar (Ezek. 1 and 10) belongs to those sections regarded as problematic by the rabbis. Since the rabbis' concern was not so much private preoccupation with the Bible as its public reading and explanation, it was primarily within the context of reading and expounding the Torah in the synagogue service that biblical texts such as Ezek. 1/10 were discussed. I begin my survey of the relevant rabbinic texts with the Mishnah and the Tosefta, the nucleus around which almost all subsequent discussions revolved.[2]

Reading and Expounding the Torah

In tractate Megillah, the Mishnah determines the synagogue functions (reading the Torah portion, translating the Torah portion into Aramaic, reciting the Shema,[3]

---

[2] All the relevant rabbinic passages have been thoroughly analyzed by David J. Halperin, first in his excellent dissertation, published as *The Merkabah in Rabbinic Literature* (New Haven, CT: American Oriental Society, 1980), and later, in a much broader – and sometimes idiosyncratic – context, in *The Faces of the Chariot: Early Jewish Responses to Ezekiel's Vision* (Tübingen: J. C. B. Mohr [Paul Siebeck], 1988). Many of Halperin's analyses and findings, in particular in *The Merkabah in Rabbinic Literature*, are still valid today, and I gratefully acknowledge my debt to his pioneering work. Unlike Halperin, though, I am not trying to reconstruct the supposedly "original" versions of the relevant passages and put them into an "original" *Sitz im Leben*; rather, I attempt to follow their literary development in the Mishnah/ Tosefta and later on in the Yerushalmi and the Bavli. Yet in so doing I indeed wish to establish a historical framework within which the literary evidence should be read.

[3] The Hebrew is *pores et/ 'al ha-shema '*: for the meaning of this phrase, see Marcus Jastrow, *A Dictionary of the Targumim, the Talmud Babli and Yerushalmi, and the Midrashic Litera-*

passing before the ark)[4] of a minor, a man in tattered clothes, and the blind. With regard to the last category, the blind, it says anonymously: "A blind man (is allowed to) recite the Shema and (to) translate (the Torah portion into Aramaic)"[5] – obviously because both reciting the Shema and translating the Bible text into Aramaic are performed orally, whereas the Torah must be *read* from the written scroll (which is impossible for a blind person). To this anonymous Mishnah, R. Yehudah responds: "One who has never seen (the) lights (*me'orot*)[6] in his life (*miyyamaw*) may not recite the Shema"[7] – presumably because the first benediction before the Shema praises God as the creator of light (*yotzer or*), and the poor man, blind from birth, has never seen these lights. The Tosefta continues this dialogue between the anonymous Mishnah and R. Yehudah by adding: "They said to him [R. Yehudah]: Many expounded the Merkavah (*dareshu ba-merkavah*) and never saw it in their life."[8]

No doubt, the anonymous Tosefta respondent to R. Yehudah (b. Ilai, a student of R. Aqiva, hence from the middle of the second century CE) wants to support the anonymous first Mishnah: just as many people expounded the Merkavah without having ever actually seen it (and nobody objected to this practice), a blind person may recite the blessing before the Shema without ever having seen the light. Hence it is obvious that the halakhic ruling follows the anonymous Mishnah and allows the blind man to recite the Shema in public (note that his capacity in translating the Torah portion is not questioned). This is clear enough, but what about the *contents* of the Tosefta's objection: "Many expounded the Merkavah and never saw it"? First of all, it deviates from the Mishnah context because it does not deal with *reading* and *translating* the Torah or *reciting* the Shema but with *expounding* or *interpreting* something. The Hebrew phrase *darash be-* refers to the *public exposition* of the Torah portion read in the synagogue,[9] that is, the midrash or sermon following the Torah reading in the synagogue service; therefore, *dareshu ba-merkavah* means: many expounded publicly the Bible passage that is captured by the keyword "Merkavah." The connecting link between the Mishnah and the Tosefta is the *public* practice of reciting the Shema and expounding the Merkavah.

---

ture, 2 vols. (New York: Pardes, 1950), vol. 2, p. 1232, s. v. "*paras*"; Halperin, *The Merkabah in Rabbinic Literature*, p. 173, n. 118.

[4] Hebrew: *'over lifne ha-tevah*: see Jastrow, *Dictionary*, vol. 2, p. 1643, s. v. "*tevah*."

[5] m Megillah 4:6.

[6] The heavenly lights from Gen. 1:14–17.

[7] m Megillah 4:6.

[8] t Megillah 3 (4):28: "in their life" (*miyyemehem*) in Ms. Erfurt; Ms. Vienna has *me-'olam* ("ever").

[9] Wilhelm Bacher, *Die exegetische Terminologie der jüdischen Traditionsliteratur*, part 1: *Die bibelexegetische Terminologie der Tannaiten* (Leipzig: Hinrichs'sche Buchhandlung, 1899 [repr. 1965, Olms, Hildesheim]), p. 27.

What is it, then, that the Tosefta here refers to under the heading "Merkavah"? Since it is by definition a passage from the Hebrew Bible, it can only be the chapter with Ezekiel's vision in the biblical book of Ezekiel (Ezek. 1 and 10).[10] Although the technical term *merkavah* for the divine chariot observed by Ezekiel is not used in the book of Ezekiel (but *kisse*, "throne"),[11] there can be no doubt that it is precisely Ezekiel's vision of the divine chariot that the rabbis summarized under the heading "Merkavah." So what the Tosefta reveals here in passing (because its subject is not the Merkavah at all) is the fact, first of all, that the Merkavah – that is, Ezek. 1/10 – was often expounded in the synagogue, and second, that expounding the Merkavah does not necessarily presuppose actually seeing it: *Ezekiel* in his time saw the Merkavah, and now the *rabbis* expound the biblical text reporting this visionary experience. In other words, the rabbinic enterprise evidently reflects a second, derivative, if not third stage of the affair – from Ezekiel's experience to the biblical text to the rabbinic exposition of the text. The rabbis are solely, and quite consciously, occupied with textual exegeses, not with visionary experiences. It makes no sense, therefore, to see in our Tosefta remark an echo of some mystical practice on the part of the rabbis. As has already been pointed out by Halperin, the Tosefta unambiguously speaks of the many who *expounded* the "Merkavah" and not of the many who attempted to *see* the "Merkavah."[12]

Finally, it needs to be emphasized that the Tosefta refers to "many." This casual remark can only mean that the custom of expounding the Merkavah was widespread and uncontested. At least according to this particular Tosefta passage (we will soon see that the matter was not so plain and simple), nobody had any problem with publicly interpreting Ezek. 1 (10); otherwise the Tosefta editor would not have used it in the discussion with R. Yehudah. Therefore, our Tosefta passage runs counter to the notion, expressed elsewhere, that the exegesis of Ezek. 1 (as well as of other biblical texts, most prominently of Gen. 1) was a matter of esotericism, that is, an esoteric discipline reserved for a small elite of initiates.[13] Nothing supports such a theory; on the contrary, our Tosefta is clear evidence that at least at a certain stage in the history of rabbinic Judaism, the rabbis felt perfectly comfortable with exposing their audience to an interpretation of Ezek. 1.

Unfortunately, this by no means settles the issue of public exposition of the Merkavah. As always with rabbinic literature, things are not that easy and

---

[10] Ezekiel 1 became the Haftarah (reading from the prophets) for the Shavu'ot service; for details, see Halperin, *The Merkabah in Rabbinic Literature*, pp. 55 ff.

[11] It appears in the noncanonical book Jesus Sirach as the content of Ezekiel's vision (Sir. 49:8, Hebrew original). The rabbis were so well acquainted with Jesus Sirach that they often quote it as if they regarded it as canonical.

[12] Halperin, *The Merkabah in Rabbinic Literature*, p. 173; idem, *The Faces of the Chariot*, p. 12.

[13] See below, pp. 180 ff.

straightforward. At the very end of its tractate Megillah, the Mishnah provides a detailed list of problematic biblical passages and it rules that some of them are to be read and translated (that is, publicly read in the synagogue and, after being read in Hebrew, translated into Aramaic), while others are to be read but not translated, and, the most restricted category, still others are not to be read and not to be translated. The list follows the sequence of the questionable texts in the Hebrew Bible:[14]

  – the story of Reuben (Gen. 35:22): read but not translated;
  – the story of Tamar (Gen. 38): read and translated;
  – the first story of the (Golden) Calf (Ex. 32:1–20): read and translated;
  – the second story (of the Calf) (Ex. 32:21–25, 35): read but not translated;
  – the blessing of the priests (Num. 6:24–26), the story of David (2 Sam. 11–12) and Amnon (2 Sam. 13): not[15] read and not translated.

After this carefully arranged list the Mishnah adds, in a clearly different style:

> The Merkavah is not to be used as Haftarah.
> R. Yehudah permits.
> R. Eliezer says: "Declare to Jerusalem" (Ezek. 16:2) is not to be used as
>   Haftarah.[16]

From this it is obvious that the Mishnah editor ruled against using Ezek. 1 and Ezek. 16:2 as a Haftarah, that is, against including the Ezekiel texts in the prophetic portions to be publicly read in the synagogue. This decision plainly contradicts the aforementioned anonymous dictum in the Tosefta (Megillah 3 [4]:28) that "many expounded the Merkavah." The editor acknowledges, however, that there was opposition to this ruling ("R. Yehudah permits").

That the public reading (and expounding) of Ezek. 1 must indeed have been controversial becomes apparent when we look at the Tosefta parallel dealing with the problematic biblical passages.[17] Not only is the Tosefta list much more detailed (it includes, among other things, Gen. 1, so conspicuously left out in the Mishnah) and more systematically arranged (it orders the passages according to the categories "read and translated," "read and not translated," and "not read and not translated"), with regard to Ezek. 1 it declares precisely the opposite of the Mishnah. At the very end of the category "read and translated" it simply states: "The Merkavah is read to the public";[18] that is, according to the Tosefta, Ezek. 1

---

[14] m Megillah 4:10. On this famous passage, see Philip S. Alexander, "The Rabbinic Lists of Forbidden Targumim," *JJS* 27 (1976), pp. 177–191; Halperin, *The Merkabah in Rabbinic Literature*, pp. 39 ff.

[15] For the variant readings in the Mishnah manuscripts see Halperin, *The Merkabah in Rabbinic Literature*, p. 40, n. 80.

[16] m Megillah 4:10.

[17] t Megillah 3 (4):31–38; a very close parallel is the Baraitha in b Megillah 25a–b.

[18] t Megillah 3 (4):34.

is perfectly legitimate as a Haftarah. In other words, our Tosefta editor is consistent with his previous remark that "many expounded the Merkavah."

In terms of our context, it is hardly necessary to undertake a close comparison of the parallel versions of our list in the Mishnah, the Tosefta, and the Baraitha in the Bavli. (To make things even more complicated, the Baraitha in the Bavli, which is overall very similar to the Tosefta, completely excludes the Merkavah.) Halperin, who has meticulously compared the three versions,[19] suggests a certain development from an older version preserved in the Bavli Baraitha (no mention of the Merkavah, hence no doubts whatsoever as to the suitability of Ezek. 1 for public reading) through an intermediate stage in the Tosefta (the suitability was questioned and had to be explicitly affirmed) to a final stage in the Mishnah (public reading of Ezek. 1 is categorically forbidden). I feel very uncomfortable with any such interpretation that imposes on the rabbinic sources a linear historical development from A through B to C,[20] and I am quite content with the observation that the public reading and exposition of Ezek. 1 was a contested area about which the rabbis patently disagreed. What can be said about our sources, though, is that the more lenient attitude toward the use of Ezek. 1 is reserved for the Tosefta, whereas the Mishnah seems to follow – or rather attempts to enforce – a stricter position. In other words, we possess clear and undeniable evidence that some rabbis had no qualms about reading and interpreting Ezek. 1 (and related texts), whereas others, who ultimately carried the day, saw in the public use of Ezek. 1 a potential danger that needed to be addressed.[21] But the dissent was about how to deal with certain passages from the Bible in a *public synagogue setting* (reading and expounding), nothing more and nothing less, and there is no indication in our texts of a discussion as to whether or not such passages could or should be used as recipes for mystical experiences.

The restricted and cautious approach to the Merkavah in the Mishnah finds its affirmation in yet another Mishnah dictum that has become the cornerstone of all subsequent rabbinic discussions of the Merkavah, the famous Mishnah in Hagigah 2:1:

> Forbidden sexual relations may not be expounded (*en doreshin ba-'arayot*)[22] by/to[23] three,
> nor the work of creation (*ma'aseh bereshit*) by/to two,

---

[19] Halperin, *The Merkabah in Rabbinic Literature*, pp. 39–63.

[20] Halperin, ibid., p. 51, has his own reservations.

[21] This deliberately sober and careful statement should not be identified with Halperin's imaginative picture of the Merkavah as being happily expounded at first, during the feast of Shavu'ot, to huge crowds of people in the synagogue and then being suppressed by the grim editors of the Mishnah (*The Faces of the Chariot*, pp. 11–37).

[22] Lit. "One does not expound *'arayot*."

[23] Here and in the following two cases all Mishnah manuscripts have the preposition *be-* ("by"); only Ms. Cambridge reads *le-* ("to"); see Halperin, *The Merkabah in Rabbinic Literature*, p. 11, n. 3.

nor the Merkavah by/to an individual, unless he is wise [a scholar] and understands[24] on his own.

Anyone who gazes at (*mistakkel be-*)[25] four things, it would be merciful to/ fitting for him[26] if he had not come into the world:
what is above (*lema'lan*) and what below (*lemattan*),
what is before (*lefanim*) and what after (*le'ahor*).

Anyone who has no concern for the honor of his creator (*kevod qono*), it would be merciful to/fitting for him if he had not come into the world.

This Mishnah is fraught with difficulties, and almost every word has received heaps of interpretations.[27] I won't go into all the details here but will focus on those aspects essential to our present context. Let me first state some assumptions that I accept, following previous scholarship, without further discussion:

The three components of this Mishnah were originally independent units that were spliced together by an editor for reasons not entirely clear. The key word that gave rise to their inclusion in Mishnah Hagigah is *'arayot*, because the previous Mishnah (Hagigah 1:8) concludes with Halakhot regarding forbidden sexual relations. Although this insight fails to further our understanding of the contents of Hagigah 2:1, it does explain why Hagigah 2:1 begins with *'arayot*.

The three topics mentioned in the first unit all refer to biblical passages: "forbidden sexual relations" to Lev. 18 and 20, the "work of creation" to Gen. 1 (and 2), and "Merkavah" to Ezek. 1 (and 10). Hence what is at stake here is clearly some exegetical activity, the exposition of these problematic biblical passages (as is made clear by the technical term *doresh be-*, which we already encountered in the Tosefta). The second and the third units most likely deal with the question of creation alone: "what is above and what below" would seem to refer to above and below the earth, that is, heaven and the Netherworld, hence to cosmology; and "what is before and what after" apparently alludes to the temporal dimension of creation – what is or rather was before the zero hour of creation, and what will be after creation comes to an end (eschatology). The third unit either concludes both the first and the second unit (woe betide those who do not heed the restrictions of the Mishnah) or just the second unit. The language ("anyone who," "it would be merciful to/fitting for him if he had not come into the world") and the

---

[24] So Mss. Cambridge and Munich; Mss. Parma and Kaufmann have "and has understood."

[25] Or "who contemplates"; see Halperin, *The Merkabah in Rabbinic Literature*, pp. 12 f., n. 10.

[26] The manuscripts vary between *ratui lo* and *ra'ui lo*; see ibid., p. 12, n. 7.

[27] Most usefully summarized by Halperin, ibid., pp. 19 ff., and *The Faces of the Chariot*, pp. 23 ff.

explicit mention of the "honor of the creator" make the latter possibility more
likely,[28] but I do not whish to rule out the first one (see below).

But what precisely is the exegetical activity that the Mishnah has in mind?
If we follow the better attested *doreshin be-* version, it restricts the number of
those engaged in such an activity from (not) three to (not) two to (not) one,
hence, in an increasingly stricter order, from forbidden sexual relations to creation to finally the Merkavah: forbidden sexual relations may not be expounded
by three – *but by two*; the work of creation may not be expounded by two – *but
by one*; and the Merkavah may not be even expounded by one – *unless he is
wise and understands on his own*. This reading is made explicit in the Tosefta
parallel to our Mishnah:

> Forbidden sexual relations may not be expounded by three – *but they may be
> expounded by two*;
> nor the work of creation by two – *but it may be expounded by an individual*;
> nor the Merkavah by an individual – *unless he is wise, understanding on his
> own*.[29]

Whereas the *doreshin be-* version leaves open the setting in which the exposition of the three Bible passages takes place – it is primarily concerned with the
number of people engaged in such an activity (two, one, nobody – unless ...) –
the *doreshin le-* version obviously has a teacher-student relationship in mind:
forbidden sexual relations may not be expounded (by a teacher) to three (students) – *but to two*; the work of creation may not be expounded (by a teacher) to
two – *but to one*; and the Merkavah may not be expounded (by a teacher) even to
one – *unless the student is wise and understands on his own*. However, I would
not lay too much emphasis on the difference between the two versions,[30] since
the *doreshin be-* version can also be easily understood as referring to a teacher-
student setting: X may not be expounded – under the instruction of a teacher – by
three students but by two, Y not by two students but by one, Z not even by one
student, unless he is wise and does not really need the teacher's instruction.[31]

If this interpretation is correct, our Mishnah in Hagigah shifts the focus from
a synagogue setting (Megillah) to a teacher-student scenario. This is not to say
that the latter excludes the synagogue, but the emphasis now is not so much on
reading and interpreting these biblical passages in the context of synagogue worship as within the framework of rabbis teaching their students. Now, the point

---

[28] Bereshit Rabbah 1:5 also speaks of the honor of God in relationship to the creation of
the world.

[29] t Hagigah 2:1 (my emphases).

[30] Halperin, in my view, overinterprets this difference, claiming that the *doreshin be-* version ultimately aims at prohibiting *private* study of the Merkavah (*The Merkabah in Rabbinic
Literature*, p. 35).

[31] This is precisely the way in which the subsequent rabbinic tradition understands the
Tosefta.

is not whether or not such passages may be publicly read and expounded in the synagogue; rather, our Mishnah is concerned with restricting knowledge of these biblical texts to a limited circle of particularly qualified students. In other words, Mishnah Hagigah turns the subjects of forbidden sexual relationships, creation, and the Merkavah into an esoteric discipline, open only to a chosen elite of very few.[32] This is clearly a trend that was followed in the later rabbinic traditions evolving around our Mishnah. It needs to be reemphasized, however, that this esoteric discipline remains concerned with the proper exegesis of problematic biblical texts and not with some kind of ecstatic experience.

It has long been observed by scholars that the Mishnah's attempt to restrict access to certain biblical passages reflects an anxiety about such texts that was more widespread and not limited to Jewish circles. The Church Father Origen of Caesarea (ca. 185–253 CE) in his commentary on the Song of Songs provides us with a list of problematic texts that contains two of the three passages mentioned in our Mishnah:

> It is said that the custom of the Jews is that no one who has not reached full maturity is permitted to hold this book [Son of Songs] in his hands. And not only this, but although their teachers and sages (*doctores et sapientes*) are wont to teach all the scriptures (*omnes scripturas*) as well as [the texts] that they call *deuterōseis* to the young boys, they defer to the last (*ad ultimum*) the following four [texts]: the beginning of Genesis, where the creation of the world is described; the beginnings of the prophet Ezekiel, where (the story) of the Cherubim is told (*in quibus de Cherubin refertur*); the end (of the same book) which contains (the description of) the building of the (future) Temple; and this book of the Song of Songs.[33]

---

[32] I do not concern myself here with the Mishnah's rationale for attaching the particular numbers to particular subjects (forbidden sexual relations: three, creation: two, Merkavah: one), but I agree with Halperin's conclusion that the starting point of our Mishnah is the Merkavah (with one) and that the Mishnah editor attached to the two other subjects the numbers two and three in the order that he believed to be commensurate with the issue's importance; see Halperin, *The Merkabah in Rabbinic Literature*, p. 36.

[33] Origen, "Commentarium in Cant. Canticorum Prologus," in *Patrologia Graeca*, ed. Migne, vol. XIII (Paris, 1857), cols. 63 f.; Latin text with French translation: Origène, *Commentaire sur le Cantique des Cantiques*, vol. 1: *Texte de la Version Latine de Rufin*, introduction, traduction et notes par Luc Brésard et Henri Crouzel, avec la collaboration de Marcel Borret (Paris: Cerf, 1991), pp. 84–87; English translation: *Origen: The Song of Songs. Commentary and Homilies* (Westminster, MD: Newman Press; London: Longmans, Green and Co, 1957), p. 23. This information is confirmed by Jerome, in *Patrologia Latina*, ed. Migne, vol. XXV (Paris 1845), col. 17C. My translation of Origen follows, with some deviations, that of Scholem in his *Jewish Gnosticism*, p. 38. I disagree with both the French and the English translation, which interpret the syntax of the Latin sentence differently ("while at the same time the four that they call *deuterōseis* ... should be reserved for study till the last"), understanding *deuterōseis* as part of the Scripture and not of the Oral Torah (see the following note). On this passage, see also Nicholas R. M. de Lange, *Origen and the Jews: Studies in Jewish-Christian Relations in Third-Century Palestine* (Cambridge: Cambridge University Press, 1976), p. 60.

Origen conveys here, in passing, some important information about the Jewish curriculum of his time, that is, in the first half of the third century, and most likely from firsthand experience in Caesarea (in 231 CE he moved permanently to Caesarea, one of the major Jewish centers in Palestine): young Jewish boys are instructed in "all the scriptures" (obviously all the books of the Hebrew Bible) as well as in the *deuterōseis* (presumably all the Jewish traditions outside of the Hebrew Bible, collectively assembled under the heading *deuterōsis* – lit. "of second rank").[34] But Origen also points out that certain biblical texts are excluded from this standard curriculum or, more precisely, are deferred "to the last," that is, to an age at which the students have reached full maturity:[35] Gen. 1, Ezek. 1 (10), Ezek. 40–48, and the book of the Song of Songs in its entirety. If Origen indeed had some reliable information about the Jews of his time, why then are Ezek. 40–48 and the Song of Songs not included in our Mishnah list? Here we can only speculate. With regard to the Song of Songs, the most likely explanation is that by interpreting this book as an allegory of love between God and his people of Israel, the rabbis were taking the necessary precaution of making it less dangerous for their audience – but that the unguided exegesis of the book could nevertheless yield some unwarranted results.[36] As far as Ezek. 40–48 is concerned, it is apparent that these chapters, which deal with the rebuilding of the eschatological Temple, "could have been linked to apocalyptic speculations,"[37] and we know only too well that the rabbis were not particularly prone to such speculations. But other, potentially even more dangerous passages leading to apocalyptic speculations (such as Daniel) are also not included in the Mishnah list. Hence, whereas Origen clearly reflects some rabbinic reservations and misgivings about the exegesis of certain biblical passages, the reason for these misgivings could have varied.

This leads us finally to the question: What, then, is the danger that the rabbis saw in an unguided or misguided exegesis of the biblical passages that deal with forbidden sexual relations, creation of the world, and the Merkavah? I am less concerned with the first subject, forbidden sexual relations, because I believe it was added to the list for the purpose of integrating it in Mishnah Hagigah.[38] The crucial subjects are the creation and the Merkavah – also covered by Origen. If we take seriously the Mishnah's own explanation in the third of its three units, we do then have an explanation as to why the rabbis were troubled by the pos-

---

[34] The singular *deuterōsis* refers to the Mishnah (as second in rank to the Bible), whereas the plural *deuterōseis* seems to refer to the corpus of the oral Jewish tradition as a whole.

[35] Origen does not bother to tell us what age this is, but Jerome is more precise on this point: the thirtiest year is the *perfecta aetas* of human beings, and "from the thirtiest [year] on the priests begin to serve in the Temple" (Jerome, Commentaria in Ezechielem 1:1, in *Patrologia Latina*, ed. Migne, vol. XXV [Paris 1845], col. 17C).

[36] Scholem, *Jewish Gnosticism*, p. 38.

[37] Scholem, ibid.

[38] See above, p. 181.

sible outcome of an exegesis at least of Genesis, but probably also of Ezek. 1 (if we understand the third unit as concluding both the first and the second units of the Mishnah). At stake here is God's honor, and this indeed is the common denominator in the rabbis' anxiety about Gen. 1 and Ezek. 1: those who do not follow the Mishnah's restrictions may impugn God's honor, that is, in the case of Gen. 1, by not strictly limiting themselves to the *creation* – as described in the Bible – but by extending their undesirable curiosity to encompass the entire cosmic sphere (beyond the created world) and to the time before the beginning of creation and after the end of the world. And in the case of Ezek. 1? Quite literally, in expounding Ezek. 1, one "looks" at what is "above," namely at God's throne in the heaven above the created world, and this is deemed a dangerous enterprise, because such unrestrained curiosity could damage God's glory. (I am deliberately playing here with the double meaning of the Hebrew word *kavod*, connoting both "honor" and "glory.")

This, I believe, is what Mishnah Hagigah is primarily concerned about – that improper, unbridled exegesis of Gen 1 and Ezek. 1 may infringe on God's privacy, so to speak, God's own sovereign realm, spatially and temporally, and that such an exegesis might bring one too close to God, in any event, too close to accommodate the rabbis' sense of decency. Obsessed as they were with the exegesis of the Holy Scripture, the rabbis were only too aware of the dangers of their obsession, and thus erected another fence around the Torah – not the proverbial halakhic fence but a theological fence that made clear to their students: just so far and no farther, at least for most of you fellows!

The Cycle of Seven Stories

Immediately following its repetition of the first Mishnah unit, the Tosefta presents a cycle of seven additional units,[39] not preserved in the Mishnah, that are obviously meant to illustrate the mishnaic principle of *en doreshin*, set up in m/t Hagigah 2:1. These stories appear also in both the Yerushalmi and the Bavli (except for two that are missing in the Bavli), although in quite a different order and with remarkable alterations. I will first analyze each of these seven units separately, comparing the versions in all three documents, since it would be naïve to assume that the earliest version should be preserved in the Tosefta and the latest in the Bavli, with the Yerushalmi in the middle. Rather, I do believe (with Halperin) that the cycle of stories following the Mishnah's restriction was not composed by the editor of the Tosefta but that there existed a version of an earlier collection on which the editors of the Tosefta as well as of the Yerushalmi

---

[39] Halperin, *The Merkabah in Rabbinic Literature*, pp. 65 ff., calls them the "mystical collection," without ever making clear what precisely he means by "mystical."

and the Bavli drew as a common source.[40] Having said this, however, we must
be aware that reconstructing such presumed earlier versions and the stages of
their development is a most delicate enterprise and a tightrope walk between
sheer guesswork and sound assumptions. Although there can be no doubt that
versions of stories appearing in later documents may contain earlier elements
than the same story in an earlier document has cared to preserve, to prove this
postulate remains a difficult task – and it certainly does not mean that we have
carte blanche to read freely and without restraint later elements into earlier versions. Moreover, I am aware that any such selective procedure that looks at our
seven stories as isolated and self-contained units (following the sequence of the
Tosefta) fails to do justice to the overall structure in which they appear in the
Yerushalmi and the Bavli. In chapter 7 I address this important aspect, which has
been largely ignored by previous scholarship.

1. Yohanan b. Zakkai and Eleazar b. Arakh: Teacher and Student

The first unit – introduced as a *ma'aseh*, that is, a case story that, according to
the Mishnah's taxonomy, is supposed to underline and illustrate the preceding
halakhic ruling – provides us with the teacher-student setting that is presumably
presupposed in the Mishnah (the Tosefta clearly understands the Mishnah this
way):[41]

> There is a case story regarding (*ma'aseh be-*) Rabban Yohanan b. Zakkai, who was
> mounted on the ass, and R. Eleazar b. Arakh was serving as ass-driver after him.
> He [Eleazar b. Arakh] said to him [Yohanan b. Zakkai]: Rabbi, teach me (*sheneh li*)[42]
> one chapter of the work of the Merkavah (*ma'aseh merkavah*).
> He [Yohanan b. Zakkai] said to him [Eleazar b. Arakh]: Did I not say to you from the
> beginning: The Merkavah may not be taught (*en shonin ba-merkavah*)[43] to an individ-
> ual, unless he is wise [a scholar], understanding on his own?
> He [Eleazar b. Arakh] said to him [Yohanan b. Zakkai]: Very well then,[44] I will lecture
> (*artzeh*) before you![45]
> He [Yohanan b. Zakkai] said to him [Eleazar b. Arakh]: Speak.[46]
> R. Eleazar b. Arakh commenced and expounded the work of the Merkavah (*patah ...
> we-darash be-ma'aseh merkavah*).

---

[40] Ibid., p. 104.

[41] t Hagigah 2:1. I follow the Vienna manuscript and refer to the Erfurt manuscript where
necessary.

[42] Ms. Erfurt: "expound to me" (*derosh li*).

[43] Ms. Erfurt: "the Merkavah may not be expounded" (*en doreshin ba-merkavah*).

[44] That is what the Hebrew *me-'attah* here means: If there is such a restriction, I will demonstrate that I am one of those who understand on their own.

[45] Ms. Erfurt: "Give me permission, and I will lecture before you."

[46] This and the following sentence are missing in Ms. Erfurt.

Rabban Yohanan b. Zakkai descended from the ass and wrapped himself[47] in his cloak,[48] and the two of them sat upon a stone under the olive tree, and he [Eleazar b. Arakh] lectured (*hirtzah*) before him.

He [Yohanan b. Zakkai] arose, kissed him [Eleazar b. Arakh] on his head and said: Blessed be the Lord, the God of Israel, who gave a son to Abraham, our father, who knows to understand (*lehavin*) and to expound (*lidrosh*) the glory (*kavod*) of our Father in heaven. There are those who expound (*doresh*) properly but do not practice (*meqayyem*), those who practice properly but do not expound properly, yet Eleazar b. Arakh expounds properly and practices properly. Happy are you, Abraham our father, that Eleazar b. Arakh has gone forth from your loins, who knows to understand and to expound to the glory (*likhevod*)[49] of our Father in heaven.

Rabban Yohanan b. Zakkai is well known as one of the heroes of rabbinic Judaism, most notably because of his major role in reorganizing Judaism after the destruction of the Second Temple. He had gathered around him a circle of five famous students, among them Eleazar b. Arakh, his favorite disciple,[50] and this story clearly underlines the prominent position enjoyed by Eleazar b. Arakh. The subject no doubt is the exegesis of Ezek. 1 – in using the phrase "the work of the Merkavah" (instead of just "Merkavah"), the Tosefta editor presumably adapts to the similar phrase "the work of creation," and in using the word "teach" (*shanah*) instead of "expound" (*darash*), the scribe of the Vienna manuscript emphasizes the teacher-student setting. The student demands from his teacher instruction in the exegesis of Ezek. 1, and the rabbi duly answers with the Mishnah's prohibition of expounding the Merkavah. The student prodigy boldly applies the Mishnah's loophole ("unless he is a scholar of his own") to himself and declares that despite the rabbi's and the Mishnah's warning, he will nevertheless proceed with his own exegesis. Yohanan b. Zakkai complies with his student's wish, and they both sit down under a tree, the rabbi wrapped in his cloak. When the student is finished, the pleased teacher gives him a solemn blessing and happily declares that his student is indeed one of those who understand on their own because he is among the very few who know to expound and practice the Scripture properly. In particular, he is a true descendant of Abraham because he knows how to expound Ezek. 1, that is, without infringing on the glory and honor of God.

The teacher's verbose blessing at the end cannot belie the fact that the story is completely silent regarding the content of the student's exegesis. We, the readers, are taught the lesson that the exposition of the Merkavah is indeed a most exclusive and mysterious enterprise – precisely as the Mishnah wishes us to believe. Hence, within the Tosefta framework, the story clearly sets out to underline the Mishnah's ruling about the exegesis of Ezek. 1. Yet nothing guarantees that the

---

[47] Ms. Erfurt: "they wrapped themselves."

[48] Lit. "prayer-shawl."

[49] Ms. Erfurt: "the glory" (*bikhevod*).

[50] m Avot 2:8 f.: R. Eliezer b. Hyrkanus, R. Yehoshua b. Hananyah, R. Yose ha-Kohen (the priest), R. Shim'on b. Netan'el, and R. Eleazar b. Arakh.

Tosefta version of the story is the "original" version, in other words, that some earlier (and fuller) version was not used and edited by the Tosefta editor in order to adapt it to the strict ruling of the Mishnah. In fact, we do have a fuller version of our story preserved in both the Yerushalmi and the Bavli, along with some remarkable details left out in the Tosefta. There is no way to prove whether or not this fuller version also reflects an earlier stage of the story's development, but there is reason to believe that at least the first addition may have belonged to a more "original" rendering. It relates to the section of the story in which Eleazar b. Arakh begins his exposition of the Merkavah. The Tosefta version is unclear or even garbled because, when Yohanan b. Zakkai gives him permission to speak, it states that Eleazar began expounding the Merkavah and that then, somehow unmotivated, Yohanan descended from his ass. Both the Yerushalmi and the Bavli are much more coherent:

> When R. Eleazar b. Arakh opened his discourse concerning the work of the Merkavah, Rabban Yohanan b. Zakkai descended from the ass. He said [to Eleazar b. Arakh]: It is not fitting that I should hear the glory of my creator (*kevod qoni*), while I am mounted on the ass.
> They went and sat down under a tree. And fire descended from heaven and surrounded them. And the ministering angels were jumping (*meqappetzin*) before them, like a wedding party rejoicing before the bridegroom. One angel answered from the midst of the fire and said: In accordance with your words, Eleazar b. Arakh, so is the work of the Merkavah. Immediately all the trees opened their mouths and uttered song: Then all the trees of the forest shall shout with joy (Ps. 96:12).[51]

We do not get here either any information about the content of Eleazar's exposition of the Merkavah, but we do hear more about what happens if someone does it properly: fire surrounds him, the angels jump up and down before him, one angel approves of the successful exegesis, and then all the trees (that is, the surrounding nature) burst into applause.[52] Only after this heavenly approval of his student's efforts does the rabbi himself approve of the exegesis.

It has long been observed that some of the miraculous circumstances accompanying Eleazar's successful exposition of the Merkavah are reminiscent of the revelation of the Torah on Mount Sinai as described in the Bible.[53] According to Ex. 19:18 f., God descended upon Mount Sinai in fire, and when Moses spoke to him, "God answered him with a voice," or, according to Deut. 5:4, God spoke with the people of Israel "face to face … on the mountain, out of the fire." In our

---

[51] y Hagigah 2:1/9 f., fol. 77a (Ms. Leiden). The Bavli (Hagigah 14b) is even smoother: after Yohanan b. Zakkai gives his permission to Eleazar b. Arakh to speak, he immediately descends from his ass, and the student asks him, why did you do this? and only thereafter does the student begin his exegesis.

[52] The Bavli, in its typical sober attitude, wants to know precisely what song the trees did utter; the answer: Ps. 148:7, 9, 14.

[53] See the summary in Halperin, *The Merkabah in Rabbinic Literature*, pp. 128 ff.

story it is not God who answers from the midst of the fire but an angel – yet this is clearly as close to a divine appearance (theophany) as our rabbinic authors dare go (and we should not forget that in the Bible the "angel of God" often stands for God himself). So what happens in our Yerushalmi and Bavli versions of the story is that R. Eleazar's successful exposition of the Merkavah causes fire to descend from heaven and with it a group of angels, among them one (special?) angel who responds from the midst of the fire and approves of the student's exegesis. I do not think it necessary, as Halperin proposes,[54] to reconstruct here a reenactment of the revelation on Mount Sinai during the Shavu'ot festival in the synagogue (positing, with not much evidence, the exposition of the Merkavah as a Shavu'ot Haftarah); rather, we are dealing with a tradition that associates elements of the "original" revelation of the Torah on Mount Sinai with *any* successful interpretation of the Torah (in the widest sense of the word): when the rabbis do their job properly, that is, expound the Torah correctly, God responds with a reenactment of the revelation on Mount Sinai – he returns, through his fire and angels, to the earth and confirms the rabbinic exposition.

That the exegesis of Ezek. 1 is but one example of such a "correct" and divinely approved rabbinic interpretation of the Torah (although an outstanding one) becomes clear from the passages in which the successful "stringing together" of biblical verses from the three parts of the Hebrew Bible (the Torah, the Prophets, and the Writings) is accompanied by heavenly fire. In a collection of stories about the arch-heretic Elisha b. Avuyah (Aher), the Yerushalmi relates that at the celebration of Elisha's circumcision, R. Eliezer and R. Yehoshua, two other students of Yohanan b. Zakkai, were among the many guests. While the other guests were busy with dancing, the two rabbis occupied themselves "with the words of the Torah: from the Torah to the Prophets, and from the prophets to the Writings, and fire came down from heaven and surrounded them." When the frightened host fears for his house, they calm him:

> God forbid, we were just sitting and stringing together[55] the words of the Torah: from the Torah to the Prophets, and from the Prophets to the Writings, and the words (of the Bible) rejoiced as on the day when they were given from Sinai, and the fire was licking them [the words of the Bible] as it was licking them (when they descended) from Sinai.[56]

A very similar interpretation is provided as an exegesis of Cant. 1:10: "Your cheeks are comely with ornaments, your neck with strings of jewels (*haruzim*)": "When they [some rabbis] were stringing together (*horezim*) from the words of the Torah to the Prophets and from the Prophets to the Writings, the fire flashed

---

[54] Halperin, *The Faces of the Chariot*, pp. 16 ff.
[55] *Hozerin* ("turning to"), most likely to be corrected to *horezin* ("stringing together") as suggested by Bacher, *Exegetische Terminologie*, vol. 1, p. 65.
[56] y Hagigah 2:1/20 f., fol. 77b.

around them and the words rejoiced as on the day when they were given from Sinai."[57] Hence, proper exegesis complements and completes the revelation of the Written Torah on Mount Sinai: since the rabbis are the standard-bearers and guardians of the Oral Torah, their exegesis brings about the same phenomena as did the revelation of the Written Torah – fire (and angels) as signs of God's approval. Or, to put it differently, adequate exegesis – connecting the three parts of the Hebrew Bible and, in particular, explaining such dangerous passages as Gen. 1 and Ezek. 1 (10) – brings heaven close to earth again, if not God back down. This is our rabbis' version of the ascent to heaven.[58] They do not attempt to go up to the heavenly realm; rather, they communicate with their creator through the exposition of Scripture – they achieve communion with God through exegesis.[59]

Both the Yerushalmi and Bavli present us with yet another addition to the Tosefta version of the story about Yohanan b. Zakkai and his student Eleazar b. Arakh. It is attached to the very end of the story, after Yohanan's blessing. I quote first the Yerushalmi version:

> When R. Joseph ha-Kohen and R. Shim'on b. Netan'el heard (this), they also initiated discourse concerning the work of the Merkavah (*patehu be-ma'aseh ha-merkavah*). They said it was a summer day,[60] and the earth shook (*ra'ashah ha-aretz*) and the rainbow (*ha-qeshet*) was seen in the cloud. And a heavenly voice (*bat qol*) went forth and said to them: The place is ready for you, and the dining couch[61] is spread out for you. You and your students are invited into the third class (*kat shelishit*).[62]

---

[57] Shir ha-Shirim Rabbah 1:53 (on Cant. 1:10).

[58] See also Arnold Goldberg, "Der Vortrag des Ma'ase Merkawa: Eine Vermutung zur frühen Merkawamystik," in idem, *Mystik und Theologie des rabbinischen Judentums: Gesammelte Studien I*, ed. Margarete Schlüter and Peter Schäfer (Tübingen: Mohr Siebeck, 1997), p. 15: "Von einer Himmelsreise, wie sie Jordej-Merkawa praktizierten, ist hier noch nichts zu erkennen, auch nicht von einer Entrückung in den Himmel, wie bei den Apokalyptikern."

[59] Interestingly enough, the story in Shir ha-Shirim Rabbah continues as follows (parallel in Wayyiqra Rabbah 16:4):
Once as Ben Azzai sat and expounded, the fire (played) round him. They went and told R. Akiva: Rabbi, Ben Azzai sits and expounds, and the fire is flashing round him. He [Aqiva] went to him and said to him: I hear that as you were expounding, the fire flashed round you. He replied: That is so. He [Aqiva] said to him: Were you perhaps occupied with the chambers of the Merkavah (*hadrei merkavah*)? No, he replied, I was only sitting and stringing together (*horez*) the words of the Torah – from the Torah to the Prophets and from the Prophets to the Writings, and the words rejoiced as when they were given from Sinai, and they were sweet as at their original utterance.
Here we find, put into the mouth of R. Aqiva, a move toward the "chambers of the Merkavah," that is, to what is technically called Merkavah mysticism.

[60] Lit. "a day in the Tammuz season," that is, a particularly hot and cloudless day.

[61] *Teriqlin*, from Greek *triklinon* = Latin *triclinium*, the dining room with couches for dining or the dining couch as *pars pro toto* for the dining room.

[62] The Hebrew *kat* means "class," "section," or "company."

This accords with the opinion of him who says: A plenitude (*sova'*) of joys with your face (Ps. 16:11) – seven (*sheva'*) classes (*kittot*) of righteous (are there) in the messianic future (*le-'atid la-vo'*).[63]

R. Joseph ha-Kohen and R. Shim'on b. Netan'el are among the five favorite students of Rabban Yohanan b. Zakkai, and this is clearly the reason why this presumably originally independent story was added here. The framework of the mishnaic restriction regarding the exposition of the Merkavah either has disappeared or was never there to begin with, depending on whether one wants to read this story as a post- or premishnaic composition. Again, the listener/reader is not deemed worthy of learning any of the content of the two rabbis' Merkavah exegesis, but we are given some important new details: the setting (a hot summer day) and the heavenly voice. As to the former, our story makes the point that despite it being the peak of the hot summer season – when no clouds and certainly no rain are expected in Palestine – a rainbow miraculously appeared in the clouds, no doubt after some heavy rain. The most likely explanation for this detail is that it alludes to Ezek. 1:28, the very end of Ezekiel's vision: "Like the appearance of the (rain)bow (*ha-qeshet*) that is in the cloud on a rainy day, such was the appearance of the surrounding radiance (*nogah*). That was the appearance of the figure (*demut*) of the Glory of YHWH (*kevod-YHWH*)." Also, the shaking of the earth that, together with the rainbow, accompanies the apparently successful exposition of the two students may have well been taken from the imagery of Ezekiel's vision: the sound (*qol*) of the wings of the four creatures that Ezekiel hears (1:24) is later described, when he departs from his vision on the river Chebar, as a "great roaring noise" (*qol ra'ash gadol*) (3:12 f.).[64]

The same is true, I presume, of the heavenly voice (*bat qol*) that the two students hear. Halperin glosses over the Yerushalmi version and prefers the Bavli version (see below), but it is only too obvious that the Yerushalmi here reflects the divine voice that Ezekiel hears when the four creatures stand still and let their wings drop: "There was a sound (*qol*) from above the expanse that was over their heads; when they stood still, they let their wings drop" (Ezek. 1:25). Yet it is certainly not a vision or audition that is taking place in the Yerushalmi – the divine voice that Ezekiel encounters on the Chebar canal has been transformed into the *bat qol*, that notorious rabbinic substitute for genuine prophecy.[65] The shaking of the earth, the rainbow, and the *bat qol* approve of the rabbis' successful *exposition* of Ezek. 1; they are not elements of a successful *reenactment* of

---

[63] y Hagigah 2:1/12, fol. 77a.
[64] With Halperin (*The Merkabah in Rabbinic Literature*, p. 128), I prefer this explanation to connecting the shaking of the earth to the revelation on Mount Sinai (although both may be implied).
[65] See Peter Kuhn, *Offenbarungsstimmen im antiken Judentum: Untersuchungen zur Bat Qol und verwandten Phänomenen* (Tübingen: J.C.B. Mohr [Paul Siebeck], 1989).

Ezekiel's Merkavah experience (or, to put it differently, the exegesis of Ezek. 1 *is* the rabbinic reenactment of Ezekiel's experience).

This interpretation is confirmed by what the *bat qol* assures the two rabbis of: a secured place in the heavenly dining hall, no doubt meaning a secured place in paradise after their death. That the righteous will enjoy a heavenly banquet is a standard rabbinic promise, but what precisely does the Yerushalmi have in mind when it has the *bat qol* assign the happy rabbis to a place in the third class of the righteous? The explanation added by the Yerushalmi editor refers to another midrash, which is preserved in a number of rabbinic texts.[66] The version in Wayyikra Rabbah reads: "Another explanation (on): A plenitude (*sova'*) of joys with your face (Ps. 16:11) – do not read s*ova'* ("plenitude") but *sheva'* ("seven"): these are the seven classes (*kittot*) of righteous who in the (messianic) future will be permitted to receive the face of the Shekhinah."[67] It is evident that the Yerushalmi editor, who added the midrash on Ps. 16:11, was referring to this or a similar tradition. However, this does not yet explain the very specific allocation to the *third* class of righteous that our rabbis enjoy. This is made explicit in another midrash, which seems to be quite early:

> Seven classes (*kittot*) of righteous are one on top of the other in paradise (*gan 'eden*):
> The first: Surely the righteous shall praise your name; they shall sit upright (in front of) your face (Ps. 140:14);[68]
> the second: Happy is (the man) you choose and bring close so that he dwells in your courts (Ps. 65:5);
> the third: Happy are those who dwell in your house (Ps. 84:5);
> the fourth: Oh Lord, who may sojourn in your tent? (Ps. 15:1);
> the fifth: Who may dwell on your holy mountain? (ibid.);
> the sixth: Who may ascend (*ya'aleh*) to the mountain of the Lord? (Ps. 24:3);
> the seventh: Who may stand in his holy place? (ibid.).[69]

---

[66] Sifre Deuteronomy 10 (Louis Finkelstein, ed., *Siphre ad Deuteronomium* [Berlin: Jüdischer Kulturbund, 1939], p. 18), and see also ibid., 47 (p. 105); Wayyiqra Rabbah 30:2 (Mordecai Margulies, ed., *Midrash Wayyiqra Rabba*, 5 vols. [Jerusalem, 1953–1958], pp. 692 f.); David Hoffmann, ed., *Midrash Tanna'im* (Berlin: H. Itzkowski, 1908–1909), p. 6; Pesiqta de-Rav Kahana 27:2 (Bernard Mandelbaum, ed., *Pesikta de Rav Kahana*, 2 vols. [New York: Jewish Theological Seminary of America, 1962], p. 405); Midrash Tehillim 11:6.

[67] The version in Pesiqta de-Rav Kahana is almost identical.

[68] This is the literal reading of the Psalm verse normally understood as "the upright shall sit in your presence." The parallel version in Midrash Tehillim adds a second, very similar, Psalm verse (Ps. 11:7).

[69] Sifre Deuteronomy, 10 (ed. Finkelstein, p. 18); Midrash Tannaim (ed. Hoffmann, p. 6); Midrash Tehillim 11:6. Goldberg tries to play down the relevance of the version in the early (tannaitic) Midrash Sifre Deuteronomy (he does not mention Midrash Tannaim) with the strange argument that it "stands so oddly in the text that one is inclined to regard it as a late addition" (Arnold Goldberg, "Rabban Yohanans Traum: Der Sinai in der frühen Merkavamystik," in idem, *Mystik und Theologie des rabbinischen Judentums*, vol. 1, p. 23, n. 36). Instead he prefers the version in the much later Midrash Tehillim.

Apparently the classes of righteous in paradise are arranged in descending order: from the first class – closest to God's presence, directly before his face – to the seventh, which is at the lowest end of the heavenly hierarchy (standing on the rather vague "his holy place").[70] From this it becomes clear that the third class is pretty high up, still in God's "house" (in all likelihood his heavenly Temple).[71] However, the parallel version in Midrash Tehillim offers quite a different order, namely, Ps. 140:14 and 11:7 for the first class, Ps. 84:5 for the second, Ps. 24:3 for the third, Ps. 65:5 for the fourth, Ps. 15:1 for the fifth, Ps. 15:1 for the sixth, and Ps. 24:3 for the seventh. Hence, this version connects the third class with the ascent to the mountain, presumably Mount Sinai. For no sound reason, Goldberg prefers the sequence in the indisputably late Midrash Tehillim[72] and regards this as proof that the experience of our two rabbis is connected with Mount Sinai, thus allowing him to reconstruct some early type of Merkavah mysticism associated with a vision of God on Mount Sinai.[73] I see no reason for any such speculation nourished by a remarkable and highly creative combination of various midrashim. The story in the Yerushalmi remains completely within the realm of biblical exegesis (Ezek. 1) and the divine promise that successful rabbis will be rewarded with eternal life in paradise.[74]

Now let us have a brief look at the Bavli version of the story concerning the two students of Yohanan b. Zakkai who followed the example of their colleague, Eleazar b. Arakh. In the Bavli it is R. Yehoshua (instead of R. Shim'on b. Netan'el) and R. Yose ha-Kohen, but their experience is very similar to the one described in the Yerushalmi (with some deviations of no significance to our context). But instead of the Yerushalmi's immediate confirmation by the heavenly voice, the Bavli has R. Yose go to Yohanan b. Zakkai and seek his confirmation, adopting the pattern of the Tosefta story. And this is what he gets:

He [Yohanan b. Zakkai] said: Happy are you,[75] and happy is she who bore you! Happy are my eyes, which have seen thus!
Further, I and you[76] in my dream were reclining (*mesubbin*) on Mount Sinai, and a heavenly voice (*bat qol*) was given forth upon us from the heavens (exclaiming): As-

---

[70] The number seven, of course, is analogous to the standard number of seven heavens (see Schäfer, "In Heaven as It Is in Hell," pp. 233–274), but our midrash conspicuously avoids any reference to the seven-heaven tradition.

[71] The "courts" reserved for the second class are then the inner courts of the Temple. The parallel in Midrash Tannaim exchanges "courts" and "house."

[72] But Goldberg feels uneasy about this and finds the sixth class more appropriate for those who ascend to the mountain ("Rabban Yohanans Traum," p. 23, n. 36).

[73] Ibid., pp. 24 ff.

[74] Even if there is some kind of Sinai connection in our story, it does not go beyond the obvious fact that the rabbis' exegesis (the Oral Torah) complements the revelation on Mount Sinai (the Written Torah). There is absolutely no visionary component in the Yerushalmi story (which is why Goldberg also prefers the Bavli version; see below).

[75] Plural, that is, R. Yose and R. Yehoshua.

[76] Again plural.

cend hither, ascend hither (*'alu le-khan*)! Large dining rooms (*teriqlin*) and large dining couches (*matza'ot*) are prepared[77] for you! You and your disciples and your disciples' disciples are invited into the third class (*kat shelishit*).[78]

Here, the confirmation by the *bat qol* – following the confirmation by the teacher and which, oddly enough, also includes the teacher, not just his students – is transposed to a dream of the teacher (presumably some time ago) that took place on Mount Sinai. This setting is unique and strange enough, but even stranger is the fact that the heavenly voice asks the teacher and his two students to ascend – obviously from Mount Sinai to the dining rooms in heaven (where they will join, as in the Yerushalmi, the third class of the righteous). In other words, the three rabbis, who are already "reclining" – that is, dining on Mount Sinai (the Hebrew word *mesubbin* no doubt means to recline for dining in company, precisely what happens on the dining couch in the dining room) – are invited to the banquet of the righteous in heaven. This makes little sense and clearly indicates a secondary stage in the development of the story.

If this interpretation is correct, the conclusion cannot be avoided that the Sinai connection in our story is altogether secondary, that is, that the Bavli editor has tried to combine the Merkavah exegesis of Yohanan b. Zakkai's students with the revelation on Mount Sinai.[79] Whatever the reason for this (certainly not because there was an early connection between the Merkavah exegesis and Mount Sinai), in artificially distinguishing between a banquet on Mount Sinai and in heaven and in having the *bat qol* explicitly inviting the three rabbis to *ascend* to heaven, the Bavli editor introduces a new element into our story. Still, even in its current version, the Bavli story may just refer to the postmortem ascent of the rabbis to their place in heaven, but the very dramatic "ascent hither" of the *bat qol* (which goes far beyond the simple function of confirmation in the Yerushalmi version) makes it seem as if the Bavli wants to allude to a *present* experience, possible during the rabbis' lifetime. Hence, what may be happening in the Bavli is the slow and still rudimentary infiltration of a tradition that identifies the Merkavah *exegesis* with an *ascent* to the Merkavah.

---

[77] Lit. "spread."

[78] b Hagigah 14b.

[79] It is remarkable that none of the scholars who are so intent on preferring the Bavli over the Yerushalmi version have noticed the strange doubling of the banquets in the Bavli. Goldberg's major arguments for his preference for the Bavli version are (1) he cannot find a plausible reason why the Bavli would have invented a dream and (2) the dream contains intrinsic characteristics of a real dream ("Rabban Yohanans Traum," p. 23), and Halperin resorts to the claim that the Bavli story resembles the pre-Christian account of Levi's ascent to heaven in the Testament of Levi 2:5 f. (*The Merkabah in Rabbinic Literature*, pp. 130 f.). Goldberg's arguments are nothing but vague impressions, and Halperin's claim is weakened by the fact that he relies on a few isolated literary similarities and completely ignores the detail that there is no heavenly banquet in the Testament of Levi; moreover, his translation of *mesubbin* as "sitting" (instead of "reclining") blurs a decisive difference between the Bavli and the Testament of Levi.

2. Chain of Transmission

The second unit in the Tosefta is very brief. It simply states:

> R. Yose b. R. Yehudah says: R. Yehoshua lectured (*hirtzah*) before Rabban Yohanan b. Zakkai; R. Aqiva lectured before R. Yehoshua; Hananyah b. Hakinai lectured before R. Aqiva.[80]

R. Yose b. Yehudah is a contemporary of R. Yehudah ha-Nasi, the editor of the Mishnah. According to him, a certain exegetical tradition was established through a chain of transmission that started with Yohanan b. Zakkai: Yehoshua, Yohanan b. Zakkai's student, presented it first to his teacher (who apparently approved of it), then it was repeated by Aqiva (and approved by Yehoshua), and again repeated by Hananyah b. Hakinai (and approved by Aqiva). The content of the lecture is not revealed, but there can be no doubt that the editor of the Tosefta understood it as referring to the exposition of the Merkavah.[81] This becomes clear from the context in which he puts this unit: it immediately follows Eleazar b. Arakh's successful exposition and seems to argue that, in addition to Eleazar b. Arakh, Yehoshua, another cherished student of Yohanan b. Zakkai, also carried out the daunting task.[82]

It is not surprising, then, that the three students singled out here are all well connected with the Merkavah. Aqiva shows up again in the immediately succeeding unit, and Hananyah b. Hakinai, one of Aqiva's students,[83] is mentioned among the Ten Martyrs (whose story is incorporated in the Hekhalot literature)[84] as well as among the members of the famous havurah (circle of initiated scholars) in Hekhalot Rabbati.[85] Furthermore, in a Genizah fragment that has received little attention we find the conspicuous phrase: "R. Eliezer expounds the Merkavah (*doresh ba-merkavah*), R. Aqiva explores the Merkavah from one end to the other (*mefallesh ba-merkav[ah]*), and [Hananyah b.] Hakinai speaks about the Merkavah (*mesapper ba-merkavah*)."[86] There is no way to date the text in which this phrase appears,[87] but it is remarkable that we have here Aqiva and Hananyah b. Hakinai joined in some Merkavah business (whatever this is, most

---

[80] t Hagigah 2:2.

[81] I do not think, despite Halperin's rather convoluted efforts (*Merkabah in Rabbinic Literature*, pp. 84–86), that we can reconstruct an earlier version of this unit which had nothing to do with the Merkavah.

[82] This is corroborated by the fact that in both Eleazar b. Arakh's and Yehoshua's cases the verb *lehartzot*, "lecture," is used. Note also that in the Bavli addition to the Eleazar b. Arakh story it is indeed R. Yehoshua who is one of the other two students of Yohanan b. Zakkai, whose exegesis is approved by their teacher.

[83] t Berakhot 4:18.

[84] Schäfer, *Synopse zur Hekhalot-Literatur*, § 109.

[85] Ibid., § 203.

[86] T.-S. K 21.95.A, fol. 1b, l. 10f., in Peter Schäfer, ed., *Geniza-Fragmente zur Hekhalot-Literatur* (Tübingen: J. C. B. Mohr [Paul Siebeck], 1984), p. 175.

[87] The fragment belongs to the early period of Genizah documents (before the middle of

likely again some exegetical activity).[88] No doubt, therefore, that this second unit wishes to establish a chain of transmission of the successful and approved Merkavah exposition.

Why this chain ends with Hananyah b. Hakinai remains an open question, but the Yerushalmi editor encountered the same problem. He concludes his otherwise almost identical version with the sentence: "From then on, their knowledge is not pure"[89] – in other words, there were no more students worthy of the task. The Bavli editor combines this with yet another problem. He asks: Why is Eleazar b. Arakh excluded from this chain? After all, he was the most important student to expound the Merkavah before Yohanan b. Zakkai.[90] His answer is typical of the Bavli: the chain of tradition mentions only those students who lectured before their teacher and subsequently became the teacher for another student who lectured before them (which is not the case with Eleazar b. Arakh). But why then Hananyah b. Hakinai, whose student is also not mentioned? Answer: he must indeed have had a student, but his name is not recorded because this unknown student did not have a student himself. This logical stretch reveals once more that the Bavli is more interested in an exercise of logical consistency than in the essence of the students' activity.

3. Four Entered a Garden

This third unit in the Tosefta is the most famous and most thoroughly discussed of all the rabbinic texts related to the Merkavah:

> Four entered a garden (*nikhnesu le-fardes*): Ben Azzai, Ben Zoma, Aher, and R. Aqiva.
> One looked (*hetziz*) and died; one looked and suffered harm (*nifga'*); one looked and cut down the shoots (*qitztzetz ba-neti'ot*); and one ascended (*'alah*) safely and descended (*yarad*) safely (*be-shalom*).[91]
> Ben Azzai looked and died. Concerning him, Scripture says: Precious in the eyes of the Lord is the death of his pious (Ps. 116:15).
> Ben Zoma looked and suffered harm. Concerning him, Scripture says: If you have found honey, eat only enough for you (lest you have eaten too much of it and vomit it out) (Prov. 25:16).
> Aher[92] looked and cut down the shoots. Concerning him, Scripture says: Let not your mouth lead your flesh into sin (and say not before the angel that it was an error;

---

the eleventh century: see *Geniza-Fragmente zur Hekhalot-Literatur*, p. 171), but this date, of course, says nothing about the date of the tradition as such.

[88] And if we correct "Eliezer" to "Eleazar," we have yet another one of the usual suspects (Eleazar b. Arakh).

[89] y Hagigah 2:1/14, fol. 77b.

[90] b Hagigah 14b.

[91] This sentence is missing in Ms. Erfurt.

[92] Ms. Vienna: "Elisha."

why should God become angry at your voice and destroy the work of your hands?)
(Eccl. 5:5).

R. Aqiva entered (*nikhnas*) safely and went out (*yatza*) safely.[93] Concerning him, Scripture says: Draw me after you, let us run, etc. (the king has brought me into his chambers) (Cant. 1:4).[94]

This brief unit is the showpiece for all those scholars who wish to see the origins of what would come to be labeled "Merkavah mysticism" as being at the very core of rabbinic Judaism. It is repeated in a variety of versions in the Hekhalot literature,[95] and most scholars argue – following the lead of Gershom Scholem in his famous article, "The Four Who Entered Paradise and Paul's Ascension to Paradise"[96] – that our story presents the earliest version of a mystical ascent to the Merkavah in heaven.[97] I have dealt with this unit elsewhere[98] and will here reflect on what, in my view, are the most important elements (without going into all the details), and on what still holds up (and does not hold up) in my earlier interpretation.

A still valid starting point is the remarkable fluctuation in terminology with regard to what the four rabbis did:[99] according to the introductory sentence, which serves as a kind of heading, the rabbis entered/went into a garden,[100] but when it comes to R. Aqiva, the text cannot make up its mind whether he "entered" and "went out"[101] or "ascended" and "descended."[102] Since the "enter" and "go out" terminology fits the object "garden" best (that's what one does with a garden: one goes in and out; one does not ascend and descend) and since the heading in all the rabbinic versions of our story preserves this terminology (even in the Bavli), I contend that this is the original reading of our unit. Since there can be no doubt, however, that the terminology of ascending and descending to the

---

[93] Ms. Vienna: "ascended (*'alah*) safely and descended (*yarad*) safely."

[94] t Hagigah 2:3 f.

[95] See the details in my article, below n. 98, and see below, pp. 286 f.

[96] Scholem, *Jewish Gnosticism*, pp. 14–19; see idem, *Major Trends*, pp. 52 f.

[97] See the summary of previous scholarship in Halperin, *The Merkabah in Rabbinic Literature*, pp. 88 f., and in my article (next note, *Hekhalot Studien*, pp. 239 f., n. 35).

[98] Peter Schäfer, "New Testament and Hekhalot Literature: The Journey into Heaven in Paul and Merkavah Mysticism," *JJS* 35 (1984), pp. 19–35 = id., *Hekhalot-Studien* (Tübingen: J. C. B. Mohr [Paul Siebeck], 1988), pp. 234–249.

[99] In the Tosefta as well as in the parallel versions in the Yerushalmi (Hagigah 2:1/15 and 2:1/18, fol. 77b) and in the Bavli (Hagigah 14b, 15a, 15b).

[100] The same in all three versions.

[101] Tosefta Ms. Erfurt and y Hagigah.

[102] Tosefta Ms. Vienna and b Hagigah. In the sentence immediately after the heading, which does not list the names of the rabbis, the last rabbi (of course, Aqiva) "ascended" and "descended" in the Tosefta (only in Ms. Vienna), but "entered" and "went out" in the Yerushalmi (this sentence is left out in the Bavli). Hence it is noteworthy that the Yerushalmi does not use the "ascend"/"descend" terminology at all.

Merkavah is one of the major hallmarks of Hekhalot literature,[103] we must perforce conclude that the ascend/descend layer of our story reflects the intrusion of the ascent and descent tradition as described in this literature.[104]

So originally the four rabbis entered a garden, looked at something, and only one of them, Aqiva, managed to get in and out safely. Much ink has been spilled over the meaning of "garden" (*pardes*) and "looking at" (*hetzitz*). The proponents of a "mystical" reading wish to understand *pardes* as "paradise" (located in one of the heavens) and *hetzitz* as looking at the Merkavah.[105] But even in the Hekhalot literature *pardes* is nowhere combined with an ascent/descent (except in the Hekhalot parallel of our story), and nowhere in rabbinic literature is *hetzitz* linked with the Merkavah (note that even our *pardes* story fails to mention the Merkavah); it simply means "to look closely."[106] Moreover, only very few passages in the Hekhalot literature combine *hetzitz* with an object that relates to the Merkavah: God's robe,[107] his beauty,[108] and the vision of the Merkavah.[109]

What, then, is the "original" meaning of our story? I am still convinced that Urbach's interpretation of our text as an allegory – using the literary form of a parable, with an "image" (*mashal*) and its "application" (*nimshal*) – is the most likely one.[110] The heading and the immediately succeeding sentence describing what the four rabbis did constitute the *mashal*, and the biblical proof-texts present the application or interpretation. This means that the *mashal* is to be understood metaphorically and that the metaphors "garden," "looked," "died," "suffered harm," "cut down the shoots," and "entered/went out" are explained in the *nimshal* through the respective biblical verses. Unfortunately, "garden" has no equivalent in the *nimshal* explanations, so we can only hope to understand it through the interpretation of the other metaphors.

---

[103] See the monograph by Annelies Kuyt, *The "Descent" to the Chariot: Towards a Description of the Terminology, Place, Function, and Nature of the Yeridah in Hekhalot Literature* (Tübingen: J. C. B. Mohr [Paul Siebeck], 1995.

[104] Interestingly enough, the Hekhalot literature in most cases uses a reverse terminology, namely *yarad* (lit. "descend") for the ascent and *'alah* (lit. "ascend") for the descent; see below, p. 247. Since this would not make any sense in our story, the original Hekhalot terminology had to be adapted to the garden image.

[105] See the details in Halperin, *The Merkabah in Rabbinic Literature*, and Schäfer, *Hekhalot-Studien*, passim.

[106] See the references in Schäfer, *Hekhalot-Studien*, p. 241, n. 50.

[107] Schäfer, *Synopse zur Hekhalot-Literatur*, § 102.

[108] Ibid., § 159 (§ 173 in *Hekhalot-Studien*, p. 241, n. 46, is a misprint) and the Genizah fragment T.-S. K 21.95.C, fol. 2a, l. 25 (*Geniza-Fragmente zur Hekhalot-Literatur*, p. 103).

[109] *Synopse zur Hekhalot-Literatur*, § 225.

[110] Ephraim E. Urbach, "The Traditions about Merkabah Mysticism in the Tannaitic Period," in Ephraim E. Urbach, R. J. Zwi Werblowsky, and Chaim Wirszubski, eds., *Studies in Mysticism and Religion Presented to Gershom G. Scholem on His Seventieth Birthday* (Jerusalem: Magnes Press, 1967), pp. 13–17 (in Hebrew). He is followed by Halperin, *The Merkabah in Rabbinic Literature*, p. 89.

In looking more closely at those Bible verses that are supposed to interpret the allegory, we immediately notice they indeed aim at explaining what happened to the four rabbis – that is, the consequences of their looking. In the case of Ben Azzai, the verse tells us that he died the "death of the pious"; in other words, God took him away because he regarded him as one of his righteous pious. His death, therefore, was by no means a punishment for what he did in the "garden"; on the contrary, I would posit that God took him to heaven because he liked him so much and approved of what he did. If we read this in light of the previous two units, we may even go a step further and assume that God approved of his exposition of the Scripture. In the case of Ben Zoma the Bible verse clearly hints at some bad result of his looking: he could not get enough of whatever it was he did, so he got an upset stomach and was punished by "vomiting it out." Again, what precisely it was that he did remains open, but it becomes evident that he was punished. As for Elisha b. Avuyah/Aher, the proverbial heretic, he definitely did something bad, whatever the cutting down of the shoots means:[111] the Bible verse makes it very clear that he had led someone into sin and that he should not pretend that his bad behavior was an error.[112] And finally, with regard to Aqiva, I am still convinced that the Bible verse puts the emphasis on explaining his safe exit (*draw me* after you, let us *run*), but I do not want to exclude the possibility that the second half of the verse alludes to his entrance. If this is the case, the emphasis would seem to be here on the king, in the sense that the king (God) has brought me (Aqiva) here (into the garden) and hence has approved of my entering the garden.

But there still remain the "chambers," explicitly mentioned in the proof-text Cant. 1:4 – are they the desired clue to the meaning of "garden"? Many scholars have pointed out that the image of the chambers is reminiscent of the chambers of the Merkavah in the Hekhalot literature. Although the full expression "chambers of the Merkavah" does not appear in the Hekhalot literature,[113] there can be no doubt that "chambers" (*hadarim*) frequently refer to the heavenly palaces so characteristic of Merkavah mysticism.[114] Is this finally what our unit is all about – the rabbis' entrance into/ascent to the heavenly chambers, the seventh of which contains the Merkavah, as the earliest rabbinic version of an ecstatic heavenly journey? I am not persuaded because, for one thing, in such a case

---

[111] The Yerushalmi explains that he prevented the young Torah students from learning the Torah (y Hagigah 2:1/15 f., fol. 77b).

[112] Obviously understood by the editor of our story as referring to his heresy.

[113] Only in the phrase "the mystery of the chambers of the *hekhal* of the Merkavah" (*Synopse zur Hekhalot-Literatur*, § 556).

[114] See the many references in Peter Schäfer, ed., *Konkordanz zur Hekhalot-Literatur*, vol. 1 (Tübingen: J. C. B. Mohr [Paul Siebeck], 1986), p. 242: in phrases such as "the chambers of the *hekhal* of ..." (followed by an object, e. g., *'arevot raqia'* [that is, the seventh heaven], *raqia' 'elyon* [the highest heaven], *ge'awah* [pride, majesty], etc.) or, very often, "the chambers of the chambers" (*hadrei hadarim*).

the editor would then have done quite a poor job, hiding his main intention in
a part of a Bible verse that is not even quoted, and for another thing, because
the more explicit ascend-descend terminology, as we have seen, is clearly secondary. Instead, I suggest taking a closer look at the *rabbinic* use of the word
heder. In addition to the commonplace meaning of "room, chamber, private
room, bedroom," it can take on a more specific connotation.[115] In halakhic terminology, *heder* signifies the innermost part of the female genitals, that is, the
uterus, followed by the *'aliyyah* (lit. "attic" = the vagina) and the *prozdor* (lit.
"vestibule" = the vulva).[116] In the figurative sense, the plural *hadarim* denotes
the "secrets, mysteries" of something,[117] as, for example, in an interpretation of
our verse Cant. 1:4:

> Whence was Elihu, the son of Berakh'el, the Buzite, to know[118] and to reveal to Israel
> the secrets (*hadrei*, lit. "the chambers") of Behemoth and Leviathan, and whence was
> Ezekiel to know and to reveal to them the secrets (*hadrei*) of the Merkavah? Rather,
> this is what is written (that is, they both knew these secrets from what is written in the
> Bible): the King has brought me into his chambers (Cant. 1:4).[119]

The secrets of Behemoth and Leviathan are explained in Job 40:15–24 and 41:1–
34 respectively (although, strictly speaking, in the book of Job it is not Elihu who
reveals these secrets to Job but God himself), and the secrets of the Merkavah are
disclosed in Ezek. 1. What this midrash argues, then, is that it was God himself
who revealed to Elihu and to Ezekiel the mysteries of Behemoth/Leviathan and
of the Merkavah, and who allowed them to reveal these secrets to Israel. The
revelation of such mysteries and the divine approbation are not bound up with an
ascent to heaven (even Ezekiel did not undertake a heavenly journey); this is not
the point here. The point is the secrecy, an esoteric knowledge of certain "innermost" mysteries that God nevertheless made public to a few, very special adepts.
Hence, applied to our four rabbis, this means that God invited them to "look at"
and to understand some very special mysteries and that the four responded quite
differently. One (Ben Azzai) was so perfect in his understanding that God took
him away, one suffered physical and presumably also mental harm (Ben Zoma),
one did harm to others (Aher), and only one (Aqiva) managed to absorb what he
"saw" and understood, without doing any harm to himself or others.

---

[115] See Jastrow, *Dictionary*, vol. 1, p. 427, s.v. *"heder"*; Jacob Levy, *Wörterbuch über die
Talmudim und Midraschim*, 2nd ed. (Berlin: B. Harz, 1924 [repr. 1963, Wissenschaftliche Buchgesellschaft, Darmstadt], vol. 2, p. 17, s.v. *"heder."*

[116] m Niddah 2:5; b Niddah 17b.

[117] Accordingly, *be-hadrei hadarim* ("in the chambers of the chambers") means "in strictest
secrecy"; see b Betzah 9a.

[118] Lit. "to come."

[119] Shir ha-Shirim Rabbah 1:28 (on Cant. 1:4). One could argue that this is a rather late midrash, but the Hekhalot literature is hardly earlier.

If the original meaning of *hadarim* – as the word is used also in the proof-text of our story – is indeed "secrets" and "mysteries," nothing compels us to connect it inevitably and automatically with the mysteries of the Merkavah. The rabbis may have been initiated in God's garden,[120] that is, by God himself, into any kind of mystery (after all, Behemoth and Leviathan have absolutely no connection with the Merkavah). If there was ever an original version of our story, independent of its present context, there is no way to prove any such "original" mystery – although I am confident that it must have had something to do with mysteries hidden in the *text* of the Bible.[121] However, in its present context in the Tosefta (with its parallels in the Yerushalmi and the Bavli), the mystery revealed to the rabbis was either the mystery of creation (Genesis) or of the Merkavah (Ezekiel), since this is the knowledge that the Mishnah limits and that the editor sets out to illustrate with his cycle of stories.[122]

What I want to argue, then, is that the rabbis were initiated by God into the innermost mysteries of the Torah. I leave open whether the "garden" is used as a metaphor for these mysteries (Aher's cutting the shoots could indicate this: he cuts the tender shoots of Torah exegesis?) or just as the metaphorical place where God reveals his secrets, reserved only for the very few, of which at least two were a complete failure. This, I posit, is the message of the story of the four who entered the garden. The editor of the story in all the relevant rabbinic collections most likely understood it as referring to the *exegesis* of the *Merkavah*, that is, of Ezek. 1 (10) and not of Gen. 1 – although there is no definite proof of this.[123] What is clear, however, is that he did not understand it as a *vision* of the Merkavah (either as the result of the proper exegetical procedure[124] or as the result of an ecstatic ascent to heaven).[125]

I conclude this unit with a brief look at the version in the Bavli, since the Bavli presents the only notable deviation from the otherwise very similar versions in the three major documents. Immediately following the heading with the four rabbis' names[126] it states:

---

[120] Although the text does not explicitly say they entered *God's* garden; but if we take Cant. 1:4 seriously, it cannot have been just any garden. Also, one of the following units refers to the "garden of the king."

[121] I modify here my previous suggestion (in *Hekhalot-Studien*, p. 242) that the four rabbis are four different types of Torah teachers, but I still maintain that the story has to do with the exegesis of certain passages of the Hebrew Bible.

[122] The mystery of forbidden sexual relations is very unlikely, since it is completely ignored in all the units relating to the Mishnah prohibition.

[123] Only the Bavli makes the connection with the Merkavah explicit; see below.

[124] This is Urbach's take on the story; see his "Traditions," p. 13.

[125] Halperin, with his undifferentiated use of the term, nevertheless insists on calling it "mysticism" (*The Merkabah in Rabbinic Literature*, p. 91).

[126] The heading is introduced by the formula "our masters taught," establishing the story as an early tradition (Baraitha).

R. Aqiva said to them: when you arrive at[127] the stones of pure marble (*avnei shayish tahor*), do not say "water, water," for it is said: No one who utters lies shall be established before my eyes (Ps. 101:7).[128]

This element of the story makes no sense in its present context. It says neither to whom Aqiva is talking (presumably, however, to his three colleagues)[129] nor where they are; nor does it bother to explain the meaning of the stones of pure marble or why the rabbis should not say "water, water." From the biblical proof-text it becomes clear that somehow saying "water, water" must be a lie and that God – who is the subject of the Psalm verse – does not wish to see such a liar. Since the verse Ps. 101:7 begins, "No one who practices deceit shall stay within my house," we may assume that the Bavli editor understands the verse as referring to the heavenly Temple.

It has long been observed that we have a much fuller version of this brief Bavli story (I call it the "water episode") in the Hekhalot literature. More precisely, we have two major incarnations of it, one connecting it with the *pardes* narrative and one independent of it. I have analyzed the various Hekhalot versions elsewhere and have suggested, I still believe convincingly, that the combination of the *pardes* narrative with the water episode is redactional (hence secondary) and that the original *Sitz im Leben* of the water episode is the testing of the adept, who undertakes a heavenly ascent.[130] It reads as follows:

The sixth *hekhal* looks as though hundreds of thousands and myriads of waves of the sea are poured over him [the adept], although there is not a single drop of water in it, but (this impression is given) by the (flicker of) the air (caused by) the radiance of the marble stones with which the *hekhal* is paved and the radiance (of which) is more terrible than water. And do not the servants [angels] stand before him [the adept]? If he (now) says: "Those waters, what is the meaning of them?", they immediately run after him to stone him, and they say to him: "(You) fool, now you shall not see with your eyes! Are you of the seed of those who kissed the (golden) calf? You are unworthy to see the king in his beauty!"[131]

Although we still do not know the precise meaning of the experience of the radiant marble stones that look like water but have nothing to do with water, the story makes perfect sense as a test for the adept who approaches the sixth chamber or

---

[127] Or probably "come across" (*maggi'in etzel*).

[128] b Hagigah 14b. The Bavli leaves out the following sentence ("One looked and died, etc.").

[129] Some manuscripts add "to the sages" or "to his disciples" (see Halperin, *The Merkabah in Rabbinic Literature*, p. 75, n. 27).

[130] *Hekhalot-Studien*, pp. 243–246, and see below, p. 286, n. 165.

[131] *Synopse zur Hekhalot-Literatur*, § 408. Immediately thereafter, a heavenly voice approves of the angels' verdict, and then follows a warning to behave properly at the entrance to the sixth *hekhal* (ibid., § 409) and subsequently (as a dictum of Aqiva) the example of Ben Azzai is added, who was unable to heed this advice and was therefore cruelly killed by the angels (§ 410).

heaven (that is, the last one before the seventh in which God's throne is located). No doubt, then, that this is what Aqiva refers to in the Bavli: when you, my dear friends and colleagues, who have undertaken the dangerous heavenly journey, arrive at the sixth chamber/heaven (*hekhal*) and see these radiant marble stones, do not mistake them for water! They only look like water, but they are the marble stones with which the sixth *hekhal* is paved. If you cannot refrain from exclaiming "water, water" – presumably because you are so frightened by the view of the radiant stones – you are a "liar," that is, you do not belong where you are and you will be forbidden from seeing God on his throne in the seventh *hekhal*.

So, obviously, what happens here in the Bavli is again the infiltration into the rabbinic literature – and into the later stages of the rabbinic literature at that – of material that is part and parcel of Merkavah mysticism. We cannot know whether the Bavli editor introduces this material in an abbreviated version (because his readers knew very well what he was talking about) or in a truncated form (because he no longer understood its true context), although I prefer the former alternative. In any case, I find it most likely that the Bavli editor *imported* the water episode from its original context within the Hekhalot literature and not vice versa, the Hekhalot version of the water episode attempting to interpret the Bavli version.[132] Such a literary development from a cryptic (to say the least) if not meaningless rendering to a full-blown story does not make much sense. The reason, however, why he added his version of the water episode is clear enough: he wanted to turn the *pardes* narrative into an ascent account to ensure that the reader would understand the entrance of the four rabbis into the "garden" as an ascent to the Merkavah in heaven. Ironically, he did not even bother to change the heading from "entered" to "ascended," and he also did not care how ill-suited his newly added water episode was to the continuation of the *pardes* narrative.[133]

4. Parable of the King's Garden

The experience of the four rabbis is followed by two parables, the first of which takes up the *pardes* motif and makes sure we are talking about the *pardes* of the king, that is, God:[134]

---

[132] As suggested by Halperin, *The Merkabah in Rabbinic Literature*, p. 88.

[133] In the next chapter (ch. 7) I discuss the larger structure of the Bavli's sugiah and how it affects the meaning of its respective units.

[134] This sequence is preserved in Ms. Vienna; Ms. Erfurt places the Ben Zoma story (unit six) immediately after unit three:

Ms. Erfurt: 1–2–3–6–4–5–7

Ms. Vienna: 1–2–3–4–5–6–7

I regard the sequence in Ms. Vienna as more plausible because it continues the garden motif and the motif of looking (*lehatzitz*).

> They provided a parable: to what may the matter be likened? To a king's garden (*pardes*), with an upper chamber/story (*'aliyyah*) built upon it. What is one to do (*mah 'alaw 'al adam*)? Just to look (*lehatzitz*) – only let him not feast his eyes upon it (*yaziz*[135] *'enaw mimenno*)![136]

This brief unit is missing in the Bavli and has a parallel only in the Yerushalmi.[137] There, it concludes: "just to look, but not to touch." Again, the standard explanation is that the parable refers to the heavenly *hekhalot* and that it wants to convey the message: just look at the divinity – that is, in the Hekhalot terminology, at "the king in his beauty" – but do not feast your eyes on what you see. The rabbinic proof text usually provided for this interpretation is a midrash about Nadab and Abihu, who were destined to die because they had feasted their eyes on the Shekhinah on Mount Sinai.[138] Such a connection is possible, but nevertheless odd: why should one be allowed to look at God but not to feast on what one sees? Let us therefore try to understand the parable without immediately seizing on a Merkavah mystical context.

The parable offers only a *mashal*, not the customary *nimshal* (interpretation, application). What we have is a garden with some kind of structure in it, apparently a building with an upper story (probably also a tower), from which one looks down into the garden. We are not told who is standing on the tower, but it is clearly a human being; if the structure is a tower, it could even be a watchtower and the human being a guard watching over the king's garden. In any case, the person standing on the structure is called upon to look but not feast his eyes on what he sees. The verb used for "look" is the same as in the preceding (third) unit: *lehatzitz*, literally "to look out," "to peep," or "to peer" (to look closely).[139] And the phrase *la-zun et ha-'enayim min* literally means "to feed the eye, to derive pleasure from a sight" (mostly from an illicit sight).[140] But the sight in our parable cannot be illicit because the person on the upper story of the building in the garden has been explicitly allowed to look: his task is to look intently, but not to derive pleasure from what he sees.

These are the basics of our parable, but we still do not know who it is that stands on that upper story in the garden with an unimpeded view of it. The easiest explanation would be that the garden is an orchard and the person in the building a guard watching over the crop. The message then would be: just keep an eye out, that's your job, but do not enjoy the beauty of the garden! Such a sober

---

[135] Correcting, with Ms. London, *yaziz* to *yazun*.

[136] t Hagigah 2:6.

[137] y Hagigah 2:1/42, fol. 77c. I do not follow Halperin (*The Merkabah in Rabbinic Literature*, p. 92) in his preference for the Yerushalmi over the Tosefta version.

[138] Wayyiqra Rabbah 20:10 (ed. Margulies, p. 466) and parallels; see Goldberg, "Rabban Yohanans Traum," pp. 25 ff.

[139] Jastrow, *Dictionary*, vol. 2, p. 1269, s. v. "*tzutz*."

[140] Ibid., vol. 1, p. 387, s. v. "*zun*."

interpretation cannot be ruled out, but I doubt that this is the ultimate message of our parable (it is certainly not the message that the Tosefta and Yerushalmi editors had in mind). It does not seem likely that the person on that upper story was put there on a regular basis (as a guard); rather, he seems to have quite unexpectedly gained access to the mysterious garden and now marvels at what he sees. This also helps better to explain the tension between his looking and the warning not to feast his eyes on what he sees: he is allowed to look – not *called upon* to look – but is warned not to derive pleasure from the marvels he sees.

It is this tension that is at the core of our parable. The rabbinic parallels using the phrase *la-zun et ha-'enayim* (apart from the midrash about Nadab and Abihu's eyes feasting on the view of the Shekhinah) refer to the Holy of Holies (when the craftsmen in the Temple had to do repairs in the Holy of Holies – which they were not allowed to see – they were lowered into it in boxes from the upper story above the Holy of Holies, so that they could do their job but "might not feast their eyes upon the Holy of Holies")[141] and to sexual matters (a person who happens to see some nakedness/obscenity [*devar 'erwah*] and does not feast his eyes on it is worthy of receiving the face of the Shekhinah).[142] In both cases someone sees something that *normally* one is not supposed to see (only the high priest enters the Holy of Holies and sees it; one does not gaze at nakedness) but that one sometimes cannot avoid seeing (the craftsmen in the Temple have to do their repairs, even in the Holy of Holies; one does encounter naked people). Accordingly, our anonymous visitor in the king's garden sees there something that under normal circumstances human beings are not supposed to see. Like the craftsmen in the Temple and the involuntary voyeur, if he happens to be in the garden he may look, but in no way may he feast his eyes on what he sees.

This is as far as the larger rabbinic context brings us, but unfortunately, we still do not know what our visitor sees. Since I do not think we can simply infer the object of his seeing from one of these rabbinic parallels (the Shekhinah, the Temple, nakedness), or, to put it differently, since all of these objects are equally possible, we are confined to our context in the Tosefta (Yerushalmi). Since the context of the units analyzed so far is the *exegesis* of certain biblical passages, I find it most plausible to assume that this is likewise what is at stake here: one who sees the marvels of Scripture, in particular of those passages not accessible to everyone, may look at them, that is, understand them – but he must not feast his eyes on them and excel in them. Any exaggeration in his exposition, any boasting about it – probably also anything that goes beyond sober and modest understanding (such as practice?) – is absolutely forbidden. Whether our Tosefta/Yerushalmi editor had in mind all three passages restricted in the

---

[141] m Middot 4:5; b Pesahim 26a; see also y Bikkurim 2:1/3, fol. 64c.
[142] Wayyiqra Rabbah 23:13 (ed. Margulies, p. 548); see also b Shabbat 64a–b.

Mishnah (forbidden sexual relations, Genesis, Ezekiel) or just the Merkavah remains an open question. Much speaks in favor of the Merkavah, although it is conspicuous that the Yerushalmi editor has wrenched the parable from its Tosefta context and placed it in the middle of his Genesis exegesis, clearly reading it as part of the "work of creation."[143]

5. Parable of the Middle Course

It is only in the Tosefta that the second parable is directly attached to the first one; the Yerushalmi has placed it on top of its discussion of the Mishnah's Merkavah restriction (even before the Yohanan b. Zakkai-Eleazar b. Arakh unit),[144] and the Bavli leaves it out altogether:[145]

> They provided another parable:[146] to what may the matter be likened? To a public road (*istrata*)[147] running between two roads, one of fire and one of snow. If he turns to this side, he is burned by the fire, and if he turns to that side, he is burned by the snow. What is one to do (*mah 'alaw 'al adam*)?[148] Walk in the middle, and he should not turn to either side.[149]

As seen in the identical phrase "What is one to do?" this parable is modeled along the lines of the first parable.[150] The metaphor, however, is quite different: someone is walking on a major public road that runs between two (smaller) roads, one of burning fire and the other of ice-cold (that is, also "burning") snow. He is advised to steer a safe middle course so that he may not be consumed by either the fire or the snow. This image does not make any sense in real terms, and Halperin is probably right in suggesting that the original image was that of a single path running between fire and snow on each side, on which was superimposed the tradition of two paths, one leading to paradise and the other to hell. Moreover, the "public road" may well have penetrated into our parable from the Ben Zoma narrative (next unit) that takes place on an *istrata*.[151]

---

[143] See below, p. 222.

[144] y Hagigah 2:1/8, fol. 77a.

[145] t Hagigah 2:6.

[146] Ms. Vienna; Ms. Erfurt reads: "Another explanation: they provided a parable. ..."

[147] *Istrata* (a loanword from Latin *strata*, transcribed in Hebrew in various forms) is a major public road, presumably paved; see Jastrow, *Dictionary*, vol. 1, p. 91, s.v. "*istrata*"; Michael Sokoloff, *Dictionary of Jewish Palestinian Aramaic of the Byzantine Period* (Ramat-Gan: Bar Ilan University Press, 1990), p. 52, s.v. "*istrat*." Jacob Neusner, *The Tosefta Translated from the Hebrew: Second Division Moed* (*The Order of Appointed Times*) (New York: Ktav, 1981), p. 313, suggests the strange translation "platoon."

[148] This reading (in Ms. Vienna) is preferable to the reading in Ms. Erfurt (*ma'alin 'al adam*).

[149] Lit. "to this [side[or to that [side]."

[150] The Yerushalmi version, reading *mah ya'aseh* ("what should he do") instead of *mah 'alaw 'al adam*, ignores this connection.

[151] Halperin, *The Merkabah in Rabbinic Literature*, p. 95.

The parable as such does not give any clue as to its subject (the *nimshal*): what is the "matter" that it sets forth to explain? In my view, the only plausible answer to this question can be that it is the exegesis of the Torah. This is definitely the way the Yerushalmi editor understands the parable, because he opens the unit with the unambiguous sentence: "This Torah (*ha-torah ha-zu*) resembles two paths, one of fire and one of snow." Of course, this does not prove that the Yerushalmi editor's explanation was the original one, but another persuasive alternative hardly exists. Supporting this interpretation is a midrash in the Mekhilta[152] that uses similar imagery:

> Because the Lord descended upon it in fire (Ex. 19:18). This tells (us) that the Torah is fire, was given from fire, and is compared to fire. As it is the way of fire, if one (*adam*) comes (too) close to it, he gets burned, and if he keeps (too) far away from it, he gets cold (*tzonen*) – (hence) one should only warm oneself by its light.[153]

That the Torah is of fire is standard rabbinic theology.[154] But remarkable about this midrash is the fact that it uses the metaphor of choosing a middle course between getting too close (burned) and drifting too far afield (cold): one should avoid getting too close to the Torah while also avoiding the opposite – one should just warm oneself by its "light." This or a similar midrash, referring to the exegesis of the entire Torah, may have been the *Vorlage* of our Tosefta/Yerushalmi editor. Yet it is almost certain that the Tosefta editor did not have the entire Torah in mind when he added this parable to his stories illustrating the Mishnah's restrictions; rather, he clearly understood the parable as another example of the caveat against the improper preoccupation with certain dangerous biblical passages, most likely again Ezek. 1.

6. Ben Zoma and Creation

There is a case story regarding (*ma'aseh be-*) R. Yehoshua, who was walking on a public road (*istrata*),[155] and Ben Zoma was coming toward him. When he [Yehoshua] reached him [Ben Zoma], he [Ben Zoma] did not greet him.
He [Yehoshua] said to him [Ben Zoma]: "Whence and whither, Ben Zoma?"
He [Ben Zoma] said to him [Yehoshua]: "I was looking at[156] the work of creation (*ma'aseh bereshit*), and there is not even a handbreadth between the upper waters and the lower waters. As it is said: The Spirit of God was hovering (*merahefet*) over the

---

[152] Suggested by Halperin, ibid., pp. 96 f.
[153] Mekhilta de-Rabbi Ishmael, ba-hodesh Yitro, 4 (ed. Horovitz-Rabin, p. 215; ed. Lauterbach, pp. 220 f.).
[154] See, e. g., y Sheqalim 6:1/26, fol. 49d; Sota 8:3/22, fol. 22d (the Torah written with black fire on white fire, "fire mixed with fire, hewn out of fire, and given from fire").
[155] Now Neusner, *The Tosefta Translated from the Hebrew*, p. 313, translates the same word *istrata* as "piazza."
[156] Ms. Vienna: *tzofeh hayiti*; Ms. Erfurt: *mistakkel hayiti*.

face of the waters (Gen. 1:2). And it says: As an eagle stirs up its nest, etc.[157] [over its young it hovers (*yerahef*)] (Deut. 32:11). Just as an eagle flies over its nest, touching and not touching, so there is not even a handbreadth between the upper waters and the lower waters."

When he heard this,[158] R. Yehoshua said to his disciples: "Ben Zoma is already outside (*miba-hutz*)."

Only a few days passed before Ben Zoma departed (*nistalleq*) [from this world].[159]

The heroes of this strange anecdote are Ben Zoma, whom we know from the *pardes* story (unit 3) and R. Yehoshua, who is part of the chain of the (Merkavah) transmission (unit 2). The setting on a public road is obviously the reason why Tosefta Ms. Vienna combined this and the preceding unit, whereas Ms. Erfurt has the Ben Zoma anecdote immediately follow the *pardes* story (certainly another option). The Yerushalmi, the Bavli, and in addition the Midrash Bereshit Rabbah transmit very similar versions of the encounter between the two rabbis.[160]

There is no need for us to analyze this unit in full detail[161] because, for our purpose, the major and striking result is the fact that it evidently deals with the "work of creation" – that is what it explicitly says and what its transmission in Bereshit Rabbah presupposes. Ben Zoma, when R. Yehoshua meets him on a road, is "looking at" the work of creation, that is, he is contemplating the biblical text of Gen. 1. However Ben Zoma discovered that the upper and lower waters – which were separated by the firmament on the second day – still remain very close to each other (less than a handbreadth), he seems to have reached this conclusion through a comparison of Gen 1:2 and Deut. 32:11: using the key word *lerahef* ("hovering over"), he applies the hovering of the eagle over its nest (almost touching it) to the hovering of the Spirit of God over the waters of Gen. 1:2. Unfortunately, this is poor exegesis because the waters of Gen. 1:2, over which the Spirit of God hovers, are the waters of the first day of creation, *before* their separation into upper and lower waters (as described in Gen. 1:7). The Bavli, with its typically sober mind, points to this discrepancy, and it may well be that this unsuccessful exegesis of Gen. 1 is the reason why R. Yehoshua predicts Ben Zoma's death.[162] The death of the poor rabbi may seem a rather

---

[157] "Etc." only in Ms. Vienna.

[158] Lit. "at this hour," only in Ms. Erfurt.

[159] t Hagigah 2:5. The Yerushalmi (see next note) has "passed away" (*niftar*).

[160] y Hagigah 2:1/13, fol. 77a/b; b Hagigah 15a (locates the encounter on the Temple Mount); Bereshit Rabbah 2:4 (has instead of "whence and whither" the strange phrase "whence the feet").

[161] See the succinct summary in Halperin, *The Merkabah in Rabbinic Literature*, pp. 96–99.

[162] Not to mention the fact that in the *pardes* story it is not Ben Zoma but Ben Azzai who dies the death (of the righteous). But maybe our story wishes merely to illustrate the fact that Ben Zoma "suffered harm" and that his subsequent death is just the natural result of suffering harm.

harsh punishment for an erroneous exegesis, but still this could well be its message: Do not mess around with the work of creation. If you become involved in it, be extremely careful, because your life is at stake.

In any case, there can be no doubt that the plain meaning of the text is the exposition of the work of creation, and I see no reason to connect it with an ascent to the Merkavah (in the sense that Ben Zoma was physically on earth but mentally in heaven). The story does not speak about the Merkavah; rather, the editor added here the encounter between Ben Zoma and R. Yehoshua because he understood it as an illustration of the Mishnah's warning against the exegesis of Gen. 1.

7. Creation

The last unit of our cycle of midrashim, intended to explain the limitations of biblical exegeses, again deals with the creation (Gen. 1). It is preserved in the Tosefta as well as in the Yerushalmi and the Bavli.[163] Since the text in the Tosefta is corrupt, with various distortions in both the Vienna and the Erfurt manuscripts,[164] I translate here the Yerushalmi version:[165]

> R. Yonah in the name of R. Ba: It is written: For ask now concerning the first days, which were before you (Deut. 4:32a).
> One might think (*yakhol*):[166] Before the work of creation. [No, because] Scripture says (*talmud lomar*): From the day that God created man upon the earth (Deut. 4:32b).
> One might think: From the sixth day and onward. [No, because] Scripture says: [For ask now concerning] the first [days, which were before you] (Deut. 4:32a). …
> One might think: [One is entitled] to know what is above the heavens and what is below the abyss. [No, because] Scripture says: From one end of the heavens to the other end of the heavens (Deut. 4:32c).[167]

This unit has nothing to do with the Merkavah; rather, it illustrates the Mishnah's prohibition against dealing with cosmological matters. This is also made clear in the Tosefta's opening phrase, which quotes the Mishnah sentence: "Anyone who gazes at four things, it would be merciful to/fitting for him if he had not

---

[163] t Hagigah 2:7; y Hagigah 2:1/33 f., fol. 77c; b Hagigah 11b.

[164] See the detailed analysis in Halperin, *The Merkabah in Rabbinic Literature*, pp. 100–103. Pace Halperin, I believe, however, that the initial cause of the confusion is the ambiguous phrase in m Hagigah 2:1: "what is above and what below, what is before and what after." Whereas the first part of this mishnah clearly refers to a spatial category, the second part can be understood as either spatial or temporal.

[165] The Bavli version is close to the Yerushalmi.

[166] Lit. "it could be."

[167] There follows, solely in the Yerushalmi, a brief sentence stating: "But, before the world was created, you expound and your heart agrees. From the time when the world was created, you go and your voice goes from one end of the world to the other." This statement plainly contradicts the first clause, and I regard it as the addition of an editor who wants to tone down – by distinguishing between private and public study of Genesis – the strict message: Do not tamper with the time before creation!

come into the world: what is above and what below, what is before and what after."[168] Accordingly, both the Yerushalmi and the Bavli incorporate the unit into the larger context of their exegesis of the "work of creation" and not of the "work of the Merkavah."

Our midrash illustrates the Mishnah prohibition with an exegesis of Deut. 4:32, using the classical exegetic terminology of "one might think" (*yakhol*) and "Scripture says" (*talmud lomar*): the *yakhol* clause introduces a hypothetical understanding of a biblical verse that is refuted by another biblical verse (in our case, parts of the same verse that illuminate each other).[169] It is developed here in three steps:

1. If you think that "ask now concerning the first days, *which were before you*" (Deut. 4:32a) refers to the time before the beginning of the creation, you are plain wrong, because the Bible continues with Deut. 4:32b, which limits your inquiry to the time from which you (man) were (was) created, that is, the sixth day.

2. If, however, you conclude from this that you may *only* inquire into the time after man's creation (that is, after the sixth day), you are wrong again, because Deut. 4:32a clearly says: ask concerning the days which were *before you*, that is, from day one of creation to day six.[170]

3. If you finally believe that you may inquire into the *realm above* heaven and *below* the abyss (the Netherworld), you are wrong once more, because Deut. 4:32c limits your curiosity to the visible cosmos.[171]

Hence our last unit defines the temporal and spatial dimensions of the created world: the time before God commenced his creation is off limits, as is the realm of heaven (most likely the seven heavens, according to rabbinic cosmology) and of the Netherworld.[172] In restricting human thirst for knowledge to the visible world, our author may even implicitly wish to launch an attack against those who are (too) eager to explore the Merkavah.

Summary

We started our journey to the rabbinic Merkavah with the Mishnah and Tosefta texts, which deal with the public exposition of Ezek. 1 in a synagogue setting. Whereas the Tosefta proudly declares that "many expounded the Merkavah"

---

[168] m Hagigah 2:1; t Hagigah 2:7.

[169] Bacher, *Exegetische Terminologie*, vol. 1, p. 72.

[170] The Bavli version makes this clearer: "One might think: one might *not* inquire concerning the six days of creation."

[171] Since the heaven in rabbinic cosmology was understood as a vault covering the earth (perceived as a disc), the verse means: the earth and the realm between earth and heaven.

[172] On rabbinic cosmology, see Schäfer, "In Heaven as It Is in Hell."

(t Megillah 3[4]:28) and that Ezek. 1 was indeed read to the public (t Megillah 3 [4]:34), the Mishnah denies any such custom and flatly declares that Ezek. 1 must not be used as Haftarah (m Megillah 4:10). Whatever the reason for such contradictory opinions – apparently the Tosefta is more lenient and the Mishnah stricter in its approach to the Merkavah – both of them talk about the public presentation and exegesis of the biblical text of Ezek. 1 and *not* about some kind of mystical experience (whatever that might entail).

Then we encountered the Mishnah's famous restriction concerning certain biblical topics (m Hagigah 2:1), which is at the center of all the subsequent rabbinic preoccupation with the Merkavah. It shifts the emphasis from the public realm of the synagogue to a more private teacher-student setting and presents the three subjects of forbidden sexual relations (Lev. 18/20), creation (Gen. 1), and the Merkavah (Ezek. 1) as an esoteric discipline reserved for an elite of only a select few. I suggest that the emphasis is on the creation and the Merkavah, and that both subjects are understood as exegetical exercises, not as ecstatic experiences aiming at an ascent to the Merkavah: the exegesis of Gen. 1 and Ezek. 1 is dangerous in that it threatens to infringe on God's privacy, a realm that the rabbis were fiercely protective of. The rabbis of the Mishnah apparently shrank away from physically getting too close to God.

The seven units, attached to the Mishnah in the Tosefta (and scattered over the Yerushalmi and the Bavli in different contexts), all attempt to illustrate the Mishnah's restriction, although, in some earlier or "original" version they may have had a life of their own. The first unit, Eleazar b. Arakh's successful exposition of the Merkavah in front of his teacher Yohanan b. Zakkai, seeks to underscore the Mishnah's restriction: there are only a select few students who fulfill the Mishnah's requirement of autonomous understanding, but they do exist, and Eleazer b. Arakh is among them. The parallel versions of this story in the Yerushalmi and the Bavli, with fire coming down from heaven and the angel approving the student's exposition, may reflect an (earlier?) stage at which any successful exegesis of difficult passages in the Torah was perceived as an reenactment of the revelation on Mount Sinai (the Oral Torah of the rabbis complementing the Written Torah given by God to Moses). When the rabbis do their job properly, God comes down to earth again. However, just as Moses did not see God on Mount Sinai face to face, so too do the rabbis not see God (but unlike Moses, they do not even *want* to see God). They communicate with God through exegesis – this is the closest they dare to approach God. Within the context of the Merkavah, the successful exegesis of Ezek. 1 is the reenactment of Ezekiel's vision: approaching God through exegesis, certainly not through a heavenly journey. Finally, the addendum in the Yerushalmi and Bavli versions promises the blessed student a secure place in heaven after death. Only in the Bavli, with its explicit invitation to ascend, do we discover clear traces of an intrusion of the Merkavah mystical ascent tradition: a move from an exegetical exercise, exciting as it may be, to the new experience of an ascent to heaven during one's own lifetime.

The second unit establishes a chain of transmission from Yohanan b. Zakkai to Hananyah b. Hakinai (a student of R. Aqiva). It is only from the context of this unit that we can infer, and quite safely so, that the subject of this transmission refers to the successful Merkavah exegesis. Why this chain is so short, we do not know. One can only suspect that the editor of this unit was very pessimistic about the future of the Merkavah's proper study.

The story of the four rabbis who entered the garden (unit 3) also focuses on the experience of exegesis. The subject of such exegeses may originally have been certain hidden mysteries in the Torah's text, in a still undefined sense, that are not accessible to everyone. However, in its present context, the story is no doubt preoccupied with the exegesis of the Merkavah, that is, of Ezek. 1. I posit that in its original form this unit had nothing to do with a vision of the Merkavah, although I admit that it reveals clear signs (in some manuscripts) of editorial interventions in the text attempting to adapt it to the ascent tradition in the technical (Merkavah mystical) sense of the word. Yet I also maintain that these interventions reflect a later stage of development under the influence of what is called Merkavah mysticism. This influence becomes apparent in the Bavli's import of the water test into the *pardes* story.

The same is true for the two parables of the king's garden and of the public road (units 4 and 5). The observer in the king's garden gazes at those marvels of the Scripture that are not accessible to everyone: he may look at them and understand them, but he may not go too far in this enterprise (whatever this entails – in his exposition or his personal experience thereof). Similarly, the one who walks on the road of Torah exegesis should steer a safe middle course lest he be burned by its extremes. Again, within the present context, at stake here is the exegesis of the Merkavah in particular.

Finally, the two last units, Ben Zoma's strange experience and the exegesis of Deut. 4:32, openly set out to illustrate the Mishnah's limitation with regard to the exegesis of the "work of creation." Ben Zoma is deeply absorbed in this project – with devastating results for his own life – and the midrash on Deut. 4:32 defines the temporal and spatial dimensions of the world created by God and made accessible to his creatures. Everything that is outside these carefully demarcated parameters, in particular God's own intrinsically "private" realm, is off limits. Very few rabbis are capable of entering the dangerous minefield of Gen. 1 exegesis – and even fewer survive this curiosity of theirs unharmed.

This, I posit, is the overall message of the stories illustrating and illuminating the Mishnah's harsh restriction: do not meddle with the two most difficult and dangerous parts of the Bible, the "work of creation" (Gen. 1) and the "work of the Merkavah" (Ezek. 1). They are both so sensitive and delicate, as they affect the "glory of the creator" – a matter not to be trifled with. If you cannot restrain yourself from entering them, be aware that you put your life at risk and that very few of your colleagues have succeeded in this daunting task. All of the seven units were originally concerned with the *exegesis* of these passages as an *esoteric* discipline. Unlike their predecessors, who penned the ascent apocalypses, the rabbis seek their God through exegesis, and not through a heavenly journey. They do not set out to see God; they content themselves with the excitement of discovering him in his Torah. There can be no doubt, however, that some of the stories, most notably in the Bavli versions, betray the influence of the Merkavah mystical ascent experience.

Chapter 7

The Rabbis II

The Merkavah in Context

We have looked at certain passages, mainly in the Mishnah and the Tosefta (with their respective parallels in the Yerushalmi and the Bavli), that deal with the rabbinic treatment of the Merkavah, that is, the rabbinic exposition of the first chapter of Ezekiel. These selected passages revolve around the public reading and translation of Ezek. 1 in the synagogue service, as well as the Mishnah's quite straightforward prohibition of teaching the Merkavah to a student. The Mishnah's prohibition triggered a number of (presumably originally independent) stories that are collected in the Tosefta and scattered, in a different order, throughout the Yerushalmi and the Bavli. Having analyzed the stories in the Tosefta collection separately, I will now focus on the structure in which they are presented in the Yerushalmi and the Bavli.

Yerushalmi

The Yerushalmi[1] opens the discourse on the anonymous Mishnah (prohibition or rather restriction of the exposition of forbidden sexual relations/work of creation/Merkavah) with an attempt to identify the author(s) of its three sections and hence the valid halakhic practice. As to the Mishnah's ruling on forbidden sexual relations, following an early Amoraic tradition (R. Ba in the name of Rav Yehudah) it determines R. Aqiva to be the author and proponent, who, however, encounters disagreement from the side of his opponent R. Ishmael, according to whom one *does* teach the prohibitions of Lev. 18. In order to decide between the two perennial antagonists, the common practice (*'uvda*) is invoked, and, since R. Ammi[2] is known to have publicly taught biblical prohibitions with regard to homosexual intercourse, it is decided that the valid Halakhah is according to R. Ishmael and not according to R. Aqiva.

---

[1] y Hagigah 2:1/1–2:1/33, fol. 77a–c. On this section, see Halperin, *The Merkabah in Rabbinic Literature*, pp. 27–29, 69–74, 141–152; see also the excellent German translation by Gerd A. Wewers, *Hagiga: Festopfer* (Tübingen: J. C. B. Mohr [Paul Siebeck], 1983), pp. 32 ff.

[2] A Palestinian Amora in Tiberias of the third generation of Palestinian Amoraim.

The same is true for the Mishnah's second ruling on the work of creation. Again, R. Aqiva is identified as the author and proponent of this mishnah, R. Ishmael disagrees, and the quest for common practice yields the fact that R. Yehudah b. Pazzi[3] did indeed publicly expound matters of creation; hence it is determined that the Halakhah is according to R. Ishmael. After providing an example of Yehudah b. Pazzi's exegesis – he proves with a series of biblical verses, culminating in Amos 4:13 and Ps. 148:8, that the physical world "hangs" on nothing more substantial than the wind and the storm, which in turn "hang" like some kind of amulet on God's arm – the Yerushalmi editor finally arrives at the third ruling on the Merkavah. Here he declares that the Mishnah is not just according to R. Aqiva; rather, this ruling reflects the universal opinion "in order that one may know to be concerned about the honor of his creator" (obviously taking up the phrase from the last sentence of m Hagigah 2:1). Yet again, in what follows, Aqiva and the universal opinion meet with opposition corroborated by common practice (see below).

Hence the Yerushalmi editor's tendency becomes clear from the outset: he is apparently more lenient than the Mishnah. The practice, which in the end determines the valid Halakhah, contradicts the Mishnah's = Aqiva's overly strict ruling. The details concerning forbidden sexual relations may indeed be publicly taught, the process of creation may be explained, and, despite universal opinion, even the Merkavah may be discussed between teacher and student (under certain provisions). The fact that R. Aqiva, of all rabbis, is identified as the author of the stricter mishnah reveals a sense of consistency (if not humor) on the part of our Yerushalmi editor, since it is Aqiva who, according to units 2 and 3 of the story cycle in the Tosefta, the Yerushalmi, and the Bavli, acts as the prime example of someone who satisfies the rigorous condition of a scholar who understands on his own and is in no need of explicit instruction by his teacher.

The opponent of the Mishnah's strict ruling regarding the Merkavah is not R. Ishmael but Rav, the famous Babylonian Amora of the first half of the third century who studied in Palestine with R. Yehudah ha-Nasi. His response to the Yerushalmi's statement that the Mishnah's ruling on the Merkavah is not according to Aqiva but to "universal opinion" is textually difficult and much discussed in scholarly literature.[4] The *editio princeps* of the Yerushalmi (Venice 1523 f.) reads:

> Did not Rav say (against this): No one is permitted to say anything in his master's presence (*ke-neged rabbo*), unless he has seen or served (*ella im ken ra'ah o shimmesh*). How does he do it? In the beginning, his master opens for him the openings of the verses (*rashei pesuqim*), and agrees (*u-maskim*).[5]

---

[3] Palestinian Amora of the fourth generation, in Lydda.

[4] See Halperin, *The Merkabah in Rabbinic Literature*, pp. 141 ff.; Wewers, *Hagiga*, p. 35, with nn. 13 and 14.

[5] y Hagigah 2:1/7, fol. 77a.

Much of this enigmatic statement remains unclear. First, what does it mean that the student of the Merkavah needs to have "seen" or "served"? If we take it as a reference to the vision of the Merkavah, "seen" of course would mean that the student is required to have seen the Merkavah first before he can begin expounding it in the presence of his master. But this explanation does not fit the context because "seen" is closely linked to "served," and even the most ardent proponent of the ecstatic experience of the Merkavah in rabbinic Judaism has not come up with the suggestion to interpret "seen" and "served" here as "unless he has seen the Merkavah or served it." The verb *shimmesh* clearly refers to the student-teacher relationship and means something like "unless the student has duly and appropriately served his teacher" (which Eleazar b. Arakh does so efficiently in the first story of the Tosefta cycle); hence, "seen" makes little sense in our present (Merkavah) context.

Equally problematic is the second part of the statement, the actual description of how student and teacher proceed with regard to their exposition of the Merkavah. To be sure, the teacher is required to make accessible to the student the *rashei pesuqim*, presumably the rudiments of the biblical text – but how do we explain the continuation "and agrees"? Who agrees, the student or the master? That the student agrees with the master makes no sense; judging from the structure of the dictum, it is much more likely that after the master has made the rudiments accessible to the student, the *student* fills in the rest (that is, supplies a full exposition of the Merkavah) and that finally the *master* approves of and agrees with the student's performance (either explicitly or silently).[6] Alternatively, one might suggest – following some parallels – that it is the student who, after having heard his master's version of the rudiments, expounds the Merkavah and agrees with the received tradition/Halakhah.[7] This explanation follows the pattern in a dialogue between R. Tarfon and R. Aqiva. In a difficult halakhic matter,[8] Aqiva opposes Tarfon's Halakhah, and Tarfon is furious (because he relies on a custom that he has witnessed, whereas Aqiva merely reaches an exegetical conclusion), but Aqiva convinces him that he (Aqiva) is right. Struck by Aqiva's exegetic ingenuity, Tarfon exclaims:

> By God, you have not invented it! Happy are you, Abraham our father, that Aqiva has gone forth from your loins. Tarfon saw (*ra'ah*) [a certain custom] but forgot. Aqiva expounds by himself (*doresh me-'atzmo*) and agrees with the Halakhah (*u-maskim le-halakhah*).[9]

---

[6] See the commentaries Penei Moshe and Qorban ha-'Edah, ad loc.

[7] Wewers, *Hagiga*, p. 35, n. 14; Bacher, *Exegetische Terminologie*, vol. 1, p. 132.

[8] As to whether Num. 10:8 ("The sons of Aaron, the priests, shall blow the trumpets") refers only to unblemished priests or also to priests with a blemish (*ba'alei mum*), Tarfon includes the blemished priests whereas Aqiva reserves the blowing of the trumpets for unblemished priests alone.

[9] Sifre Numbers, § 75 (ed. Horovitz, p. 70). In the parallels y Megillah 1:12/9 (fol. 72b), y

This is a remarkable parallel to our enigmatic Yerushalmi passage.[10] Not only does it provide us with a subject and an object of our difficult *maskim* (the subject is definitely the student, and the object is the received Halakhah); it also explains the incomprehensible "unless he has seen (*ra'ah*)" in our Yerushalmi passage. In the Tarfon-Aqiva dialogue the conflict is about a custom that one rabbi (Tarfon) actually saw practiced (which usually takes halakhic priority) versus a mere exegetical procedure exercised by another rabbi (Aqiva), and Aqiva does not argue that the custom is wrong but rather that Tarfon's memory is erroneous (and hence his own exegetical conclusion is correct). Accordingly, in our Yerushalmi passage the phrase "unless he has seen or served" means: the student is only permitted to say something in his master's presence if he has actually *seen* a certain custom or if he has *served* his master long enough to be able to develop his own argument, building on what he has learned from the master. The second sentence then explains how they proceed (if the condition of having served applies): the master summarizes the rudiments of the halakhic problem in question, the student fills in the details and, if successful, agrees with the Halakhah.

Seen in this larger context, there can be no doubt that the subject matter of our Yerushalmi introduction to the following Merkavah stories is concerned with the proper *exegesis* of the Merkavah, that is, of Ezek. 1, and not with some kind of ecstatic experience. It is certainly no coincidence that Aqiva, deriving the correct Halakhah from exegesis, receives the same blessing as Eleazar b. Arakh after his successful exposition of the Merkavah in the first unit of the Tosefta's Merkavah cycle: "Happy are you, Abraham our father, that Eleazar b. Arakh has gone forth from your loins."[11] Proper exegesis, of whatever halakhic or aggadic subject, deserves the appropriate blessing by one's colleague or teacher.

This interpretation is finally corroborated by the fact that our introductory passage in the Yerushalmi originally had nothing to do with the Merkavah. The only complete manuscript of the Yerushalmi (Ms. Leiden, finished in 1289 CE), serving as the basis for the *editio princeps*, provides us with a very different version of Rav's statement:

> Did not Rav say (against this): No one is permitted to say anything concerning the affliction of leprosy (*be-nega' tzara'at*), unless he has seen or served.

Yoma 1:1/37 (fol. 38d), y Horayot 3:3/37 (fol. 47d), and cf. also b Zevahim 13a, the object is "and agrees with the traditional legal decision (*shemu'ah*)."

[10] Noticed by Wewers, expanding on Bacher (see above, n. 7), and not sufficiently recognized by Halperin, *Merkabah in Rabbinic Literature*, pp. 143 ff. Wewer's ingenuity in translating and explaining the Yerushalmi cannot be praised enough (nor his untimely death sufficiently lamented). Certainly, his translation contains mistakes (he would have been the last person not to agree with this judgment), but still, his translation is superior to any other translation into a modern language.

[11] See above, p. 187.

The second corrector of the Leiden manuscript corrected *be-nega' tzara'at* to *ke-neged rabbo* ("in his master's presence"), changing the meaning of the sentence completely.[12] I take the "affliction of leprosy" reading as the original one – without going into much detail (mainly because it is the *lectio difficilior* and because *ke-neged rabbo* is a strange phrase for "in his master's presence": one would expect *bifnei* or *lifnei rabbo*)[13] – meaning: a student may only deal with the Halakhah regarding leprosy if he has actually "seen"[14] evidence of skin disorders or if he has attended a teacher. The reading "in his master's presence" is but a secondary attempt on the part of a medieval scribe to adapt Rav's dictum about leprosy to the subject of the Merkavah. Hence, originally Rav's statement is just another example of how master and student cooperate successfully with regard to difficult exegetical matters. With a few strokes of the pen, the scribe changed the original meaning completely.

But if this is indeed the case, why did the Yerushalmi editor include Rav's dictum in his introduction to the following cycle of Merkavah stories in the first place? Although the content clearly does not fit, the structure does: both the mishnah in Hagigah 2:1 and Rav's dictum begin with a negation (*en*, "one does not X") and continue with an affirmation (*ella im ken*, "unless Y"), hence both determine under which circumstances a student is permitted to expound the Merkavah or to discuss the affliction of leprosy. This formal affinity may have prompted the Yerushalmi editor to refer to Rav's dictum. Yet if this reference is meant to be more than just an empty association – and there is every reason to believe that the editor had a purpose in quoting it – then its meaning must be gauged by its immediate context. This context, as I have shown above, is a series of three dicta, all supplied to prove that the mishnah attributed to R. Aqiva is not to be regarded as a valid Halakhah: (1) contrary to Aqiva, one does expound the prohibitions regarding forbidden sexual relations, (2) contrary to Aqiva, one does expound the work of creation, and now (3) contrary to universal opinion (including Aqiva), a student who has seen the evidence or who has served his teacher does expound the affliction of leprosy – or, indeed, expounds the Merkavah. In other words, the Yerushalmi editor uses Rav's dictum in order to argue against m Hagigah 2:1: whereas the Mishnah declares that only a scholar who understands on his own may expound the Merkavah, our Yerushalmi editor adapts Rav's dictum to the Merkavah and interprets it in the sense that a student may raise the subject in his master's presence if he has seen the proper evidence (presumably one who has been eyewitness to a respective custom, probably in the synagogue) or has served his teacher and received the appropriate instruction. As in the first two cases, this is quite the opposite of what the Mishnah de-

---

[12] See the documentation of the correction in y Hagigah 2:1/7.

[13] See the thorough discussion in Halperin, *The Merkabah in Rabbinic Literature*, pp. 143 ff.

[14] In this context the "seen" makes perfect sense.

crees.[15] Now the student does not need to understand on his own; he just needs the proper education. The medieval scribe, who changed the wording of Rav's dictum, made the Yerushalmi editor's implicit intention explicit.

The final passage in the Yerushalmi's introductory section (before the Yerushalmi turns to the cycle of stories illustrating the Mishnah's prohibition) provides the first example of a student expounding the Merkavah – unfortunately an unsuccessful one:[16]

> R. Hiyya said in the name of R. Yohanan: Rabbi had a distinguished student (*talmid watiq*), and he expounded (*darash*) a chapter of the work of the Merkavah (*ma'aseh merkavah*), but Rabbi did not agree (*we-lo hiskimah da'ato shel rabbi*),[17] and he [the student] was smitten with leprosy.[18]

This brief story artfully takes up elements from the preceding dictum by Rav: the student – no doubt one who has properly served his rabbi and learned from him (a *talmid watiq* is a faithful and distinguished student) – expounds a chapter of the Merkavah[19] (obviously of Ezekiel), but his master outright disagrees.[20] This disapproval has fatal consequences: the poor student is immediately smitten with leprosy, a direct reference to Rav's original dictum about leprosy. What is more important (and quite conspicuous) is the fact that Rabbi is singled out as someone in whose presence a student expounds the Merkavah. "Rabbi," of course, is R. Yehudah ha-Nasi, editor of the Mishnah, but hitherto we have not encountered him as a teacher concerned with the exposition of the Merkavah. On the contrary, in the Tosefta cycle of Merkavah stories the usual suspects are Yohanan b. Zakkai with his favored pupil, Eleazar b. Arakh, as the prime example of a successful student (unit 1), Yohanan b. Zakkai, R. Yehoshua, R. Aqiva, and Hananyah b. Hakinai (unit 2), Ben Azzai, Ben Zoma, Aher, and R. Aqiva (unit 3), and Ben Zoma (unit 6). Moreover, and most remarkable, it is the Yerushalmi that concludes the chain of Merkavah transmission in unit 2 with the sentence, "From then on, their knowledge is not pure,"[21] explicitly stating that the chain breaks off with Hananyah b. Hakinai, a student of Aqiva. Hence, the example of Rabbi's anonymous student plainly contradicts the tradition regarding the chain of transmission – unless one wishes to read it as proof that the chain did indeed break off with Hananyah b. Hakinai and that no other effort was ever successful. But I would not leap to such a seemingly logical conclusion. To begin with, there

---

[15] Pace Halperin, *The Merkabah in Rabbinic Literature*, p. 145: "I suggest that the compiler included section A [Rav's dictum] because it underlined the perceived message of M. Hag. 2:1."

[16] y Hagigah 2:1/8, fol. 77a.

[17] Lit. "and Rabbi's opinion did not agree (with him)."

[18] Lit. "boils."

[19] Note that here the full phrase *ma'aseh merkavah* is used, unlike m Hagigah 2:1, which refers only to *merkavah*.

[20] Hence, here it is definitely the master who is the subject of *hiskim*.

[21] y Hagigah 2:1/14, fol. 77b; see above, p. 196.

is no editorial connection in the Yerushalmi between the story about Rabbi's student and the chain of Merkavah transmission;[22] moreover, and more important, the story about Rabbi's student is clearly meant to illustrate the preceding dictum by Rav (a student who has served his master properly may expound the Merkavah). Therefore, despite his status as a "distinguished student," Rabbi's student was unsuccessful because he did not fulfill this requirement – unfortunately, he was not distinguished enough, and failed.

If this interpretation is correct, it follows that the Yerushalmi editor seeks to emphasize that even R. Yehudah ha-Nasi, of all rabbis, instructed some of his students in the exposition of the Merkavah – the same R. Yehudah who declares in his Mishnah that only a student who is wise and understands on his own may deal properly with the Merkavah! That a certain student perchance failed hardly proves the opposite; on the contrary, it underlines the fact that, according to the Yerushalmi, the Mishnah editor and some of his students were engaged in the exposition of the Merkavah. This is again a dramatic deviation from the Mishnah's prohibition/restriction and clear evidence of the Yerushalmi's more lenient approach to the subject of Merkavah exegesis.

After this introductory section the Yerushalmi proceeds with presenting the cycle of Merkavah/creation stories in the following order: unit 5 (the parable of the middle course on the road), unit 1 (Yohanan b. Zakkai and Eleazar b. Arakh, with the long addition about Joseph ha-Kohen and Shim'on b. Netan'el), unit 6 (Ben Zoma and creation), unit 2 (the chain of transmission), unit 3 [a] (the *pardes* story: up to Aher), unit 3 [b] (the Aqiva part of the *pardes* story), unit 7 (creation), and finally unit 4 (parable of the king's garden). In choosing the parable of the road as his first story and introducing it with "This Torah (*ha-torah ha-zu*) resembles two paths," the Yerushalmi editor makes clear that he is dealing with multiple Torah passages and does not wish to limit the story cycle to the subject of the Merkavah, or, to put it differently, that he does not subsume under the Mishnah's Merkavah lemma only those stories related to the Merkavah in the strictest sense of the word (although, as we have seen, he does try to adapt some of them to the Merkavah subject). Of all the cycle's stories the parable of the road is the most open-ended one that can, however, be easily accommodated to the topic of the Merkavah.

With unit 1 following unit 5 and elaborating extensively on the students' exposition of the Merkavah, the Yerushalmi editor nevertheless emphasizes his particular interest in the Merkavah exegesis. However, when it continues with unit 6 about Ben Zoma's fatal destiny, the Yerushalmi apparently moves on to the subject of creation, because it wishes to make clear that it regards the subject of creation as equally important. This sequence is markedly different from the Tosefta, which keeps the Merkavah and the creation stories together. Again, in introducing the following unit 2 with "Three lectured their Torah (*hirtzu toratan*) before their master" – instead of just "R. X lectured before R. Y," as in the Tosefta – the Yerushalmi may wish to be deliberately ambiguous with regard to the subject of the students' lecture (although, to be sure, in its present context, the Yerushalmi editor wants the subject to be understood as the Merkavah). Moving to unit 3, the Yerushalmi returns once more to the Merkavah, but it splits the story of the four rabbis who entered *pardes*: having reached the arch-heretic Aher, it interrupts the unit with a first bunch of Aher stories. (Who is Aher, and what did he do?)[23] Then it concludes unit 3 with Aqiva and adds another, much larger section of stories related to Aher (R. Meir, Aher's student; Aher's circumcision; again R. Meir and Aher; why did Aher become apostate; Aher's death; R. Meir's reaction; Aher's daughters).[24] Clearly, our Yerushalmi editor is much more interested in Aher's destiny than in elucidating the *pardes* story. Moreover, his collection of Aher stories sheds no light whatsoever on what happened to the four rabbis in the *pardes* – this remains as enigmatic as ever.

After this long digression the Yerushalmi turns to the subject of creation again; hence it would seem that the editor, within the overall structure of his explanation of the Mishnah lemma, opens with the Torah in the broadest sense of the term and then alternates between the two topics of the Merkavah and creation. Quantitatively, his treatment of the creation takes up considerably more space than his treatment of the Merkavah.[25] The material that he collects here is to a large extent parallel to the collection of midrashim in Bereshit Rabbah.[26] He begins with a quotation from the noncanonical book Ben Sira that aptly underlines the Mishnah's warning against gazing at what is above and below, before and after: "Why do you want to know what is hidden from you; why do you investigate that which is deeper than the Netherworld? Reflect upon what you have been given permission, for what is hidden is not your concern."[27] Then some

---

[23] y Hagigah 2:1/15 end – 2:1/17, fol. 77b.

[24] y Hagigah 2:1/18, fol. 77b – 2:1/29, fol. 77c.

[25] It is worth emphasizing that the subject of creation is largely treated under the Mishnah lemma of the Merkavah; the material that the editor collects under the (proper) Mishnah lemma of the work of creation is extremely meager.

[26] On this, see Hans-Jürgen Becker, *Die großen rabbinischen Sammelwerke Palästinas: Zur literarischen Genese von Talmud Yerushalmi und Midrasch Bereshit Rabba* (Tübingen: Mohr Siebeck, 1999), pp. 16–60.

[27] y Hagigah 2:1/30, fol. 77c. This is a version of Ben Sira 3:21 f., with some remarkable deviations from the Hebrew text of Ben Sira known to us; see Moshe Z. Segal, ed., *Sefer ben Sira ha-shalem*, (Jerusalem: Bialik Institute, 1958), ad loc. Most conspicuous is "why do you investigate that which is deeper than the Netherworld" in the Yerushalmi versus "what is hidden from you do not investigate" in Ben Sira. As Becker has suggested (*Die großen rabbinischen Sammelwerke*, p. 20), it may well be an attempt to adapt the Ben Sira quotation to the Mishnah's "what is above and what below."

midrashim follow that warn against dealing with the work of creation because it infringes on the glory of the creator – a direct allusion to the Mishnah's contempt for someone who has no concern for the honor/glory of his creator. Added finally is unit 7, which defines those temporal and spatial dimensions of the created world accessible to human curiosity.

But this is not yet the end of the Yerushalmi's explanation of the Mishnah's lemma on the Merkavah. After unit 7, more midrashim are added that deal with the creation (again parallel to the material in Bereshit Rabbah: the letters through which the world was created;[28] the famous parable about the palace of the king that is built on a site of sewers, dunghills, and garbage;[29] the much debated question as to whether heaven or earth was created first),[30] and between them our Yerushalmi editor has sandwiched unit 4 (the parable of the king's garden). As I have noted above, this context is clear proof that the Yerushalmi interprets the parable as part of the exegesis of Genesis and most definitely not of the Merkavah.

Altogether, our Yerushalmi editor has provided us with a remarkable recast of the story cycle illuminating m Hagigah 2:1. He furnishes it with an introduction that displays a much more lenient attitude toward teaching the Merkavah than the Mishnah itself. Moreover, he arranges the stories in an order – and places them in a context – that leaves no doubt that he is concerned with the exegesis of problematic Bible passages, that he puts even more weight on exposition of the work of creation than on exposition of the work of the Merkavah, and that he is equally (if not more) interested in details left out in the original stories (for example, the tragic fate of Aher). The strict ruling of the Mishnah is softened, but there is no indication whatsoever of a move beyond the realm of exegesis and toward a visionary experience of the Merkavah.

Bavli

The Bavli's discussion of the three components of m Hagigah 2:1 is much more comprehensive and complex than any of its parallels; it extends from fol. 11b to fol. 16a in tractate Hagigah. Clearly, the Bavli editor has made an effort to collect most of the relevant material – in particular about creation and the Merkavah – under the appropriate Mishnah lemma. After a brief discussion of the textual problem caused by the variant reading in the Mishnah regarding the preposition *be-* versus *le-*, which refers to all three components,[31] and followed

[28] Bereshit Rabbah 1:10.
[29] Bereshit Rabbah 1:5.
[30] Bereshit Rabbah 1:15.
[31] b Hagigah 11b.

by its (rather brief) comment on forbidden sexual relationships,[32] the Bavli turns to the work of creation.[33] I have dealt with this sugiah elsewhere[34] and so will summarize here only a few of the more important points.

The Talmud begins, interestingly enough, with the midrash on Deut. 4:32 concerning the boundaries of any acceptable inquiry into cosmogony (the creation of the cosmos) and cosmology (the makeup and structure of the cosmos), that is, unit 7 in the Tosefta cycle – making clear by this that some of the material subsumed in the Tosefta under the lemma "Merkavah" indeed belongs to the work of creation (or, to put it differently, that the work of creation and the work of the Merkavah overlap). After a brief digression on the size of the first man, the Talmud proceeds with a description of the ten things that were created on the first day and of ten divine attributes through which the world was created. The discussion of the creation of heaven and earth (which came first?) moves to the famous midrash about the world hanging as an amulet on God's arm, transmitted in the Yerushalmi in the name of R. Yehudah b. Pazzi.[35] The Bavli, however, instead of being interested in cosmological details, stresses the fact that the pillars or the pillar on which the world rests are the twelve tribes or the proverbial righteous, regarded as the "foundation of the world" (Prov. 10:35). Hence, the Bavli is less concerned with cosmology than with ethics: the world is sustained through the proper behavior of Israel, in particular the efforts of the righteous, and ultimately the world's physical makeup is irrelevant.

The same is true for the Bavli's lengthy discourse about the seven heavens. To be sure, it gives some cosmological information, but the relevant traditions are interrupted by or rather supplemented with material about the study of the Torah and proper ethical behavior. Most revealing is the Bavli's inventory of the seventh heaven, 'Aravot. For the Bavli, this highest heaven is primarily a storehouse of good things that are beneficial to Israel (such as righteousness, justice, and justness, the treasures of life, peace, and blessing, the souls of the righteous and the souls that will be born in the future, and finally the dew with which God will revive the dead). Again, the emphasis is on the relationship between God and Israel, not on cosmology, let alone on what Ezekiel's first chapter is all about: the vision of God seated on his throne in the uppermost heaven above the heads and wings of the four creatures. The Bavli editor is obviously aware of this shortcoming (from the point of view of those interested in the seventh heaven as God's

---

[32] Ibid.

[33] b Hagigah 11b–13a.

[34] Peter Schäfer, "From Cosmology to Theology: The Rabbinic Appropriation of Apocalyptic Cosmology," in Rachel Elior and Peter Schäfer, eds., *Creation and Re-Creation in Jewish Thought: Festschrift in Honor of Joseph Dan on the Occasion of His Seventieth Birthday* (Tübingen: Mohr Siebeck, 2005), pp. 39–58.

[35] See above, p. 215.

dwelling place), for he continues almost reluctantly, as if he has been suddenly reminded of something that he would have preferred to ignore:

> There (too) are the Ofannim and the Seraphim and the holy creatures and the minister-ing angels and the throne of glory, (and) the King, the living God, high and exalted, dwells above them in 'Aravot, as it is written: Extol him who rides upon 'Aravot,[36] Yah is his name (Ps. 68:5).[37]

This is indeed the inventory that someone – having Ezekiel, the ascent apoca-lypses, and not least the Hekhalot literature in mind – might expect. More pre-cisely, as I have shown, the Bavli's language is deeply imbued here with the lan-guage of the apocalyptic and, in particular, the Hekhalot literature.[38] Yet in fact the Bavli unabashedly betrays the very goal of this literature. For it continues to explain that the God residing in the seventh heaven is hidden behind an impen-etrable thicket of darkness; in other words, that God, despite our knowledge of the inventory of the seventh heaven, cannot be attained to or seen. This cosmo-logical anticlimax is further underscored by the last unit of the Bavli's sugiah about the creation: a midrash presented as a Baraitha and ironically put into the mouth of Yohanan b. Zakkai, the hero of the Tosefta's Merkavah cycle, which serves as the editor's bridge between the creation and the Merkavah lemmas.[39] This midrash is a devastating critique of King Nebuchadnezzar's (the rabbis' arch-villain) attempt to ascend to heaven (Isa. 14:14). Instead of reaching the goal of his hubris, the midrash informs us, Nebuchadnezzar will be hurled down into the She'ol, the innermost part of the Netherworld (Isa. 14:15).

I interpret not only this midrash but much of the Bavli's exposition of the work of creation as a polemic against the ascent apocalypses and Merkavah mysticism in the technical sense of the word – the attempt to actually ascend to heaven and to see God on his throne. This polemic sets out to make clear that the "science of the cosmos," which may lead to such an attempt, is dangerous because it ignores or forgets what really matters: God's love for Israel and Israel's proper response. God cannot and must not be visited and seen. Anybody who embarks on a heav-enly journey misses the true purpose of Israel's destiny in the world.

Now comes the Bavli's final step, the discourse about the Mishnah's Merkavah lemma. It begins with a first unit, attributed to four Palestinian Amoraim of the third generation, three of whom had emigrated from Babylonia to Palestine. The first (R. Hiyya) qualifies the Mishnah lemma "nor (may) the Merkavah (be expounded) to an individual (unless he is wise and understand on his own)"[40]

---

[36] Lit. "upon the clouds" or "upon the heavens."
[37] b Hagigah 12b.
[38] Schäfer, "From Cosmology to Theology," pp. 55 f.
[39] b Hagigah 13a.
[40] Although the Bavli quotes the Mishnah version "nor the Merkavah *by* an individual," its very first explanation of *be-* as meaning *le-* (see above) and the following discussion make clear that it is in fact using the version "nor the Merkavah *to* an individual."

by allowing that the "rudiments" (*rashei peraqim*)[41] may be transmitted to him – obviously meaning that someone who does not understand on his own may be taught the rudiments of the Merkavah. This coincides with the Yerushalmi's equally more lenient attitude.[42] The second Amora (R. Zera) seems to qualify R. Hiyya's qualification by limiting the transmission of the rudiments to the head of a (rabbinic) court (*av bet din*) and to someone "whose heart is anxious with him."[43] We know the head of the court from m Hagigah 2:2, of all places – the mishnah immediately following our mishnah Hagigah 2:1 – where the famous "pairs" (*zugot*) of m Avot 1:4 ff. are identified as patriarchs (*nesi'im*) and heads of the court (*avot bet din*), respectively. R. Zera presumably wants to cast the patriarchs and the heads of the court in a teacher-student relationship: the patriarchs are the teachers who transmit the rudiments of the Merkavah to the heads of the court. This, of course, is pure fiction, an exercise in scholastic ingenuity, inspired solely by the fact that the patriarchs and the heads of the court appear in the mishnah following the mishnah dealing with the Merkavah.[44] R. Zera does not seem to have much real interest in the transmission of the Merkavah – if his contribution to the subject is not outright irony. The two final statements of this first section by R. Ammi and R. Assi[45] broaden the subject of the Merkavah and restrict the transmission of the "secrets of the Torah" (R. Ammi) or the "words of the Torah" (R. Assi) to a rabbinic elite[46] and to Jews (as opposed to Gentiles), respectively. These two dicta underline the fact that the "Merkavah" is regarded as a subsection of Torah exegesis.

After this introductory section the Bavli presents two examples of studying and teaching the "work of the Merkavah."[47] The first reads as follows:

> R. Yohanan said to R. Eleazar: "Come, I will teach you the work of the Merkavah (*ma'aseh merkavah*)." He [R. Eleazar] answered him: "I am not old enough."
> When he was old enough, R. Yohanan died.
> R. Assi said to him [R. Eleazar]: "Come, I will teach you the work of the Merkavah." He answered him: "If I had been worthy, I would have learned from R. Yohanan, your teacher."

With its dramatis personae Yohanan, Eleazar, and Assi, this strange story is purportedly set in the historical context of the school of Tiberias, obviously referring to R. Yohanan (b. Nappaha) as the head of the school and R. Eleazar (b. Pedat),

---

[41] Lit. "beginnings of chapters."
[42] See above, pp. 215 ff.
[43] The latter is an anonymous tradition qualifying the former explanation even further to a head of the court whose heart is anxious with him.
[44] Already the identification of the patriarchs and the heads of the court with the "pairs" is a gross historical anachronism.
[45] "R. Assi" only in the manuscripts; the printed editions have "R. Ammi."
[46] Quoting the verse Isa. 3:3, which is interpreted (in b Hagigah 14a) as referring to specifically qualified rabbis.
[47] b Hagigah 13a.

who succeeded him as head, and R. Assi as his students. Yet this touch of historical reality becomes highly suspicious when we notice that it is clearly modeled along the lines of the Yohanan (b. Zakkai) and Eleazar (b. Arakh) story in the Tosefta cycle.[48] Contrary to the Yohanan b. Zakkai-Eleazar b. Arakh model, however, now it is not the student who asks his teacher for permission to expound the Merkavah in front of him but the teacher who politely asks the student whether he will graciously accept instruction in the Merkavah. And the student modestly rejects the offer – only to learn that, when he feels old enough for the subject, his teacher has died. When his fellow student Assi (who apparently has learned the Merkavah from Yohanan) suggests filling in for their beloved teacher, Eleazar rejects the offer again, because he would have preferred to have been taught by their teacher and not a fellow student.

No doubt, this new incarnation of the Yohanan b. Zakkai-Eleazar b. Arakh story takes for granted that Merkavah exegesis can be taught and is being taught. Unlike the former, however, it presupposes that the student has reached a certain age so as to be mature enough for the secrets and perils of the Merkavah.[49] Remarkably, it is not the teacher who sets the age for the study of the Merkavah but the student. The irony cannot be overlooked here, since the poor student, in all his modesty, in the end misses the opportune moment and comes away empty-handed. Hence, the message is that if you want to study the Merkavah, do not miss out on the right moment because, if you exaggerate your modesty, you may lose everything.

The second story addresses the same problem:

Rav Joseph had studied the work of the Merkavah; the elders of Pumbeditha had studied the work of creation. They [the elders] said to him [Rav Joseph]: "Let the master teach us the work of the Merkavah. He said to them: Teach me (first) the work of creation."

After they had taught him (the work of creation), they said to him: "(Now) let the master (finally) teach us the work of the Merkavah." He said to them: "I have learned concerning it[50] [the work of the Merkavah]: Honey and milk under your tongue (Cant. 4:11) – matters that are sweeter than honey and milk shall (remain) under your tongue." ...

They said to him: "We have learned concerning it[51] [the work of the Merkavah] up to: He said to me: Son of man (Ezek. 2:1)." He said to them: "This is indeed the work of the Merkavah!"

---

[48] Halperin (*The Merkabah in Rabbinic Literature*, p. 162) struggles with the alternative of whether it is a piece of fiction (composed to stress that the work of the Merkavah is esoteric) or based on actual events. He cannot make up his mind (although he notices the similarity with the Yohanan b. Zakkai-Eleazar b. Arakh story) but does not want to rule out the latter.

[49] It does not tell us what this age is, but presumably it presupposes the traditional age of forty years.

[50] Lit. "them."

[51] Same.

Now the setting moves to Babylonia: the school of Pumbeditha and Rav Joseph, a Babylonian Amora of the third generation (d. 333 CE). Rav Joseph is portrayed as an expert in the exegetic discipline of the Merkavah, whereas his colleagues at Pumbeditha are experts in the exegetic discipline dealing with creation. Again, both subjects are taken for granted as academic disciplines (apparently both R. Joseph and the "elders" have reached the appropriate age), and again the irony of the story is obvious: the elders' desire to be taught properly the work of the Merkavah turns out to be futile because Rav Joseph, although the elders fulfilled the condition mutually agreed upon, ultimately retracts his promise to teach them and resorts to the alleged secrecy of the subject. But, unlike R. Eleazar in the first story, they do not miss their moment. When Rav Joseph backs down, they proudly declare: we nevertheless did it – we did not wait until you were ready but did it on our own, and we did the full first chapter of Ezekiel. Hence, all that remains to Rav Joseph is to confirm that Ezek. 1 is indeed what is called the work of the Merkavah. The elders do not find it necessary to present their exposition to Rav Joseph and to get his approval, and Rav Joseph does not ask for it or even indicate that they need it. Both Rav Joseph and the elders take for granted that the elders can expound the Merkavah and that they do not really need his instruction.

From here the Bavli's discourse moves on to the question of what precisely the Ezekiel text consists of, that is, the subject of the Merkavah. The elders of Pumbeditha had defined it as the complete first chapter of Ezekiel, but the Bavli's editor objects and asks:

> How far does the work of the Merkavah extend?
> Rabbi says: "Up to the last 'I saw' (*wa'ere*) (Ezek. 1:27)."
> R. Yitzhaq says: "Up to *hashmal* (ibid.)."[52]

In order to answer his question about the definition of the exegetical subject of the Merkavah, the Bavli editor provides two conflicting answers, one by Rabbi (apparently R. Yehudah ha-Nasi, editor of the Mishnah) and one by R. Yitzhaq (presumably R. Yitzhaq Nappaha, another student of R. Yohanan at Tiberias). Rabbi is more narrow in his definition in that he restricts the study of the Merkavah to the passage extending from Ezek. 1:4 (the first "I saw") to Ezek. 1:26 (the second "I saw" is the first word of Ezek. 1:27), whereas R. Yitzhaq includes the phrase immediately following the second "I saw": "I saw the like of *hashmal* (*ke-'en hashmal*)." That is, both disagree about whether the second "I saw" marks the end of the Merkavah text in the sense that the biblical Merkavah includes everything *before* "I saw" or everything *up to* "I saw," including its immediate object "the like of *hashmal*." This is not some vainglorious battle about nothing. Although both agree that the subject of the Merkavah does

---

[52] b Hagigah 13a.

not include the description of the figure on the throne, that is, of God's Glory (Ezek. 1:27 and 28),[53] R. Yitzhaq's slightly broader definition ventures into just this dangerous territory: whatever *hashmal* means, it is closely connected with the appearance of the figure sitting on the throne, a subject that Rabbi's more restrictive approach seeks to avoid.[54]

The Bavli editor is not satisfied with R. Yitzhaq's broader definition of the Merkavah, including *hashmal*, and asks, "Is it really so that we expound *hashmal*"? He answers this question with two almost identical stories, one in Aramaic and one in Hebrew (a Baraitha).[55] The Aramaic version simply states, "Behold, a certain child expounded *hashmal* (*derash be-hashmal*), and fire came forth[56] and devoured him,"[57] from which the Bavli editor concludes: "A child is different because it has not (yet) reached his time." This conclusion follows the line of reasoning of the preceding stories: for the Bavli, study of the Merkavah is definitely permissible but requires a certain age. The poor child was burned because it did not fulfill this requirement. Finally, the child's experience reminds the Bavli editor of another story,[58] according to which attempts were made to conceal[59] the book of Ezekiel, obviously because of its danger.[60] Yet a certain Hananyah b. Hisqiyah, an early Tanna of the first generation, saved the book from falling into oblivion through his exegesis (which presumably solved the alleged contradictions with the rest of the Torah).[61] Hence, again the message is that the book of Ezekiel – in particular its first chapter about the Merkavah – is certainly not for everybody. But a rabbinic scholar of the right (mature) age may well deal with it, including the dangerous *hashmal* of Ezek. 1:27.

---

[53] As Halperin, *The Merkabah in Rabbinic Literature*, p. 157, has correctly pointed out.

[54] It is certainly no coincidence that Rabbi, of all rabbis, is presented as the author of the more restrictive approach. And it is also no accident that the Bavli's editor tries to harmonize the two conflicting statements, supporting the broader definition: "Up to 'I saw' we teach; from there on we transmit the rudiments (*rashei peraqim*). Some say: Up to 'I saw' we transmit the rudiments; from there on, if he is a scholar understanding on his own, yes, and if not, no."

[55] b Hagigah 13a.

[56] In most manuscripts: "from *hashmal*"; see the details in Halperin, *The Merkabah in Rabbinic Literature*, p. 155.

[57] According to the version of the Hebrew Baraitha, the child read the book of Ezekiel, understood *hashmal*, and was burned.

[58] Again in two versions, this time both in Hebrew.

[59] The technical term for this procedure is *lignoz*: to put in a Genizah, a storehouse of books that were deemed unfit for further use.

[60] The first version goes yet a step further and argues: "because its words contradicted the words of the Torah."

[61] According to the second version, this goal was achieved by a certain R. Yehoshua b. Gamala (only in the manuscripts: the printed editions have the same Hananyah b. Hisqiyah; see Halperin, *The Merkabah in Rabbinic Literature*, p. 156 with n. 29), the high priest Yehoshua b. Gamla of the last years of the Second Temple, turned into a rabbi. His argument is: "If this one [the poor child] is a scholar, all are scholars," meaning, that a child (who is not a scholar) was burned does not mean that the book of Ezekiel is off limits for (real) scholars.

Immediately after its impressive caveat, the Bavli, apparently unmoved by its graphic description of the attendant dangers, sets about practicing this maxim. It begins a long sequence of exegeses, starting with Ezekiel's *hashmal* and then venturing into other verses of Ezekiel and even into Daniel and Isaiah. So once again, the Bavli editor could not make clearer his point that he is concerned with exegeses, not with experience of any sort. Remarkably, he first asks what *hashmal* means – precisely the insight that put such a tragic end to the life of the poor child (he had better read the Bavli). The Bavli's sober answer states: *hashmal* is the fire that the four creatures utter, and its following exegeses are meant to demonstrate precisely this – that *hashmal* is connected with the creatures and not, God forbid, with God.[62] With this, the Bavli plainly contradicts the biblical text because it completely ignores Ezek. 1:27 f. (but follows its own principle that the Merkavah exegesis covers Ezek. 1:4–26, moving the dangerous *hashmal* in 1:27 to this section – a clever move, indeed). All the Bavli's Ezekiel exegeses in this sugiah stick to its self-imposed limitation of the Merkavah chapter: they proceed from the *hashmal* in 1:27 to 1:14, 1:4, 1:15, 1:10, 10:14 (the contradiction between 1:10 and 10:14), and finally to 1:6 (the contradiction between Ezek. 1:6 and Isa. 6:2).

Having resolved the contradiction between Ezek. 1:6 and Isa. 6:2, the Bavli moves to another set of contradictions, this time between the book of Daniel and some other biblical verses. So, although the discussion of contradictions between biblical verses seems to be the formal catalyst for turning now to Daniel, there can be no doubt that the Bavli editor, who has assembled these exegeses, regarded the book of Daniel (or more precisely its chapter 7) as yet another problematic biblical text, the study of which should be restricted. He begins with Dan. 7:10 and, having discussed the verse's alleged contradiction with Job 25:3, focuses on the "stream of fire" (*nehar di-nur*) of 7:10.[63] The stream or streams of fire are a well-known motif, particularly in the apocalyptic and Hekhalot literature, but they appear also in the rabbinic literature proper. They make their debut in chapter 14 of the Book of the Watchers of 1 Enoch ("And from underneath the throne came forth streams of blazing fire") and are there, as well as in Daniel, closely connected to the divine throne (that is, part of the heavenly makeup).[64] Only in later texts are they placed in a different context, namely, that of the punishment of the wicked (for example, 2 En. 10:2[65] and Testament of Isaac 5:21–25).[66] The Hekhalot literature, interestingly enough, mainly adopts the earlier apocalyptic tradition, describing the rivers of fire as part of the heav-

---

[62] b Hagigah 13b.
[63] b Hagigah 13b–14a.
[64] See also the Similitudes (1 En. 71:2, 6), which depend on this earlier tradition.
[65] "River of fire in the singular" (as in Daniel).
[66] Also singular.

enly inventory.[67] However, in having the angels – who make an error in reciting their hymns – punished in the river of fire,[68] it seems to adopt elements of the later strand.

Conspicuously, the Bavli follows this later tradition: asking first, where the stream of fire comes from (answer: "from the sweat of the creatures"),[69] it devotes much more effort to discussing where it goes – namely, on the head of the wicked in Gehinnom. No doubt, the Bavli is more interested in the river of fire as a tool of punishment (that is, in the fate of the wicked and the righteous as part of the ethical makeup of humankind) than it is in satisfying our curiosity as to the heavenly inventory. To be sure, the sugiah continues with a dictum by Shemuel (a Babylonian Amora of the first generation), who informs us that the ministering angels are indeed created from the stream of fire,[70] but the Bavli editor counters this idea with another dictum by R. Shemuel b. Nahmani in the name of R. Yohanan (b. Nappaha) – of all rabbis (see above) – who holds: No, this is nonsense, we have no need of this fancy stuff. God creates with the words he utters, not with fire, and accordingly, the angels are created "from every utterance that goes forth from the mouth of the Holy One, blessed be He."[71]

The next two contradictions to be solved are between Dan. 7:9 (the description of God as an old man) and Cant. 5:11 (the description of God as a young lover) and between two sections of Dan. 7:9 itself (the beginning of the verse says that "thrones [pl.] were set in place and an Ancient One took his seat," whereas later on the same verse states: "His throne [sing.] was flames of fire"). Of all rabbis, it is R. Aqiva who is quoted as solving the latter contradiction by arguing that Dan. 7:9 is indeed referring to two different thrones, one for God (the throne of fiery flames) and one for David (the throne for the Ancient One). This explanation, of course, contradicts the plain meaning of the biblical text, according to which the Ancient One is God, who takes his seat on one of the thrones in heaven (the other thrones are for the heavenly court) and whose throne is later described as consisting of fiery flames. That Aqiva imports David into the heavenly scenery of Dan. 7 can have no other reason than to deemphasize its mythical or mystical impact: David, the beloved poet-king of Israel and future Messiah, occupies a throne in heaven, together with God! In other words, Israel is present there as well, represented by David, and there is no need, indeed, to ascend to heaven and to have a look at what is going on there. No wonder that another rabbi (Yose the Galilean) immediately objects and accuses Aqiva of profaning the Shekhinah.

---

[67] See *Konkordanz zur Hekhalot-Literatur*, vol. 2, s. v. "nahar²."

[68] *Synopse zur Hekhalot-Literatur*, § 67; in ibid., § 58, the angels are punished by the fire that goes out from the little finger of God.

[69] This explanation might again be an attempt to remove it from the divine throne, that is, from immediate proximity to God.

[70] b Hagigah 14a.

[71] Ibid.

Instead, R. Yose proposes that one throne is meant for the divine attribute of justice and the other one for the attribute of loving kindness, and the Bavli editor maintains that Aqiva accepted this interpretation. Yet another rabbi (Eleazar b. Azarya) still disagrees – apparently, because two separate thrones for two divine attributes may hint at some kind of duality in the Godhead. In harsh words he demands that Aqiva leave the Aggada and that he would do better turning his attention to difficult halakhic problems, his real specialty: one throne, Eleazar b. Azarya concludes, is God's throne proper and the other one serves as his footrest (proof-text Isa. 66:1). Again, the irony of this passage cannot be overlooked. R. Aqiva, precisely the rabbi who is said to have entered the *pardes* of the exegesis of Ezek. 1 (if not, in this context, of the heavenly realm) and to have been the only one who left it unharmed – it is this Aqiva who is rebuked for his aggadic exegesis and is told to stick to his last, that is, Halakhah.

The quotation of Isa. 66:1 triggers yet another set of biblical exegeses, this time of Isa. 3:1–7. It is unclear why these Isaiah exegeses are added here to the exegeses of Ezekiel and Daniel, since they have nothing to do with the heavenly realm. The verses Isa. 3:1–5 are interpreted as curses against Israel, that is, as referring to the subversion of the social order during king Sennacherib's attack on Judah and his siege of Jerusalem in 701 BCE. Presumably, these passages are regarded as devastating and hence not suitable for public discourse, and it seems to be this latter qualification that prompted the Bavli editor to combine them with the expositions of Ezekiel and Daniel.[72] Hence, the composition of the sugiah strongly emphasizes the fact that the Bavli's main concern is about biblical exegeses and not about experiences of whatever kind.

Having discussed Jerusalem's destruction, the Bavli finally, and for no apparent reason, turns to the cycle of stories attached to the Merkavah and the work of creation.[73] It begins with unit 1 (Yohanan b. Zakkai and Eleazar b. Arakh, with the long addition about R. Yehoshua and R. Yose ha-Kohen),[74] followed by units 2 (chain of transmission), 3 (the four rabbis who entered *pardes*, with Aqiva's Hekhalot dictum about the marble stones, but without the proof-texts for Aher and Aqiva, yet with an addition about Ben Zoma), 6 (Ben Zoma's exposition of Genesis), 3 [a] (Aher in the *pardes* story, with an addition about Metatron), 3 [b] (Aqiva in the *pardes* story, with another addition), and finally unit 7 (Genesis); units 4 (the royal garden) and 5 (the parable of the road) are missing in the Bavli. Hence, like the Tosefta and unlike the Yerushalmi, the Bavli keeps the first three (Merkavah) units together; however, like the Yerushalmi, it splits the *pardes* story into distinct sections and adds additional material, particularly about Aher.

---

[72] Pace Halperin, *Merkabah in Rabbinic Literature*, p. 17, who suggests that the trigger is the phrase *navon lahash* (lit. "understanding a whisper") in Isa. 3:3.

[73] b Hagigah, fol. 14b–16a.

[74] Discussed above, chapter 6, pp. 193 f.

The first addition to the *pardes* story, Aqiva's dictum about the stones of pure marble, was discussed above.[75] Looking at it from the perspective of the sugiah's overall structure, it becomes even more obvious how out of context and incomprehensible it is without full knowledge of those parallels in the Hekhalot literature. As has been observed above, by adding Aqiva's dictum to the *pardes* story, the Bavli editor gives it a completely new meaning. Having said this, however, I should like to qualify this statement and add that, within the sugiah's full context, the impact of the new "Merkavah mystical" interpretation of the *pardes* story carries much less weight. The Bavli does not dwell on it; rather, it seems as if the editor simply wanted to throw in this tradition so as to give the *pardes* story a particular twist and to make sure that it would be understood in this way. But this new interpretation remains completely isolated; it has no immediate continuation. On the contrary, the next addition about Ben Zoma is even counterproductive to such a reading. The Bavli editor, who knows nothing of any Merkavah experience on the part of Ben Zoma (although he does know the material about Ben Zoma's exposition of Genesis), comes up with the following addition:

> They asked Ben Zoma: "Is it permitted to castrate a dog?" He answered: "[Any animal that has its testicles bruised or crushed or torn or cut, you shall not offer to the Lord;] such you shall not do within your land (Lev. 22:24) – (this means), to no (animal) that is in your land shall you do this."

> Ben Zoma was (further) asked: "May a high priest marry a virgin that has become pregnant? Do we (in such a case) take into consideration Shemuel's statement, for Shemuel said: I can have repeated sexual intercourse without (causing) bleeding; or is perhaps the case of Shemuel rare?" He answered: "The case of Shemuel is indeed rare; therefore, we must consider (the possibility) that she may have conceived in a bath." But behold, hasn't Shemuel said: An emission of semen that does not shoot forth like an arrow cannot impregnate? – In the first instance [in the bath], it had also shot forth like an arrow.[76]

The first halakhic question addressed to Ben Zoma is quite straightforward: Is it permitted to castrate dogs, although castration is explicitly forbidden only in the case of animals that are offered as sacrifices (and dogs are not offered)? Ben Zoma concludes from a literal reading of Lev. 22:24 that castration of all animals that live in the land of Israel, regardless of whether or not they are offered as sacrifices, is forbidden.

The second question deals with the bizarre problem of whether a pregnant woman who is about to be married to a high priest (who, according to the Torah, may marry only a virgin)[77] may claim that she is still a virgin, despite her preg-

---

[75] Chapter 6, pp. 202 f.

[76] b Hagigah 14b–15a.

[77] Lev. 21:13.

nancy. Ben Zoma is asked whether Shemuel's[78] statement applies here, according to which it is possible to have sexual intercourse without physically deflowering the virgin, or whether such a case is exceptional and therefore cannot be taken into account halakhically. He rules that Shemuel's case is indeed exceptional and cannot be taken into account, but that the possibility still does exist of the pregnant virgin having conceived in the bathtub. Finally, an objection (also put into the mouth of Shemuel), namely, that only an emission of semen that has shot forth like an arrow can make a women pregnant (and hence that the bathtub explanation does not apply to the pregnant virgin), is fended off: the virgin was sitting in a bathtub into which a man had shot his semen. Conclusion: a virgin may have become pregnant without sexual intercourse, and may be married by a high priest.

As such, these two halakhic questions are perfectly reasonable, although slightly odd (the problem of the castrated dog may have had some practical implications, but the problem of the pregnant virgin and the high priest was certainly outdated),[79] and Ben Zoma's answers are not only reasonable but seem to have been accepted by the Bavli. What makes them peculiar and almost funny is the present context – namely, immediately following the story of the four rabbis in the *pardes* and the biblical proof text illustrating why Ben Zoma suffered harm: "If you have found honey, eat only enough for you, lest you have eaten too much of it and vomit it out" (Prov. 25:16). Although they do not help elucidating what happened to him in the *pardes*, they nevertheless could be read as belonging to this context: "They asked Ben Zoma," that is, some people there (his fellows? the angels?), in the *pardes*, asked Ben Zoma. If we take this context seriously, the down-to-earth halakhic questions and Ben Zoma's answers can only be understood as an antidote to a Merkavah mystical reading of the *pardes* story, almost a parody of Aqiva's mysterious warning: "When you arrive at the stones of pure marble, do not say 'water, water.'" Hence, I want to posit that the Bavli editor not only was not particularly interested in what happened to Ben Zoma in the *pardes*; he even wished to portray him as someone who was knowledgeable in difficult halakhic matters and who was undeserving of any harm.

A similar conclusion can be drawn from the Bavli's version of unit 6 (Ben Zoma's Genesis exegesis).[80] Of all the parallel versions of this story in the Tosefta, the Yerushalmi, and the Bavli,[81] it is only the Bavli that omits the pointed conclusion that, as a consequence of his exegesis, poor Ben Zoma died. Moreover,

---

[78] Mar Shemuel, the Babylonian Amora of the first generation and head of the academy of Nehardea.

[79] That is, irrelevant after the destruction of the Second Temple. Some scholars even considered the (in my view highly unlikely) possibility that the pregnant virgin is meant to be a parody of the Virgin Mary; see Johann Maier, *Jüdische Auseinandersetzung mit dem Christentum in der Antike* (Darmstadt: Wissenschaftliche Buchgesellschaft, 1982), p. 230, n. 263.

[80] b Hagigah 15a.

[81] And, in addition, Bereshit Rabbah 2:4.

after having indicated that the verse Gen. 1:2 (the Spirit of God hovering over the waters) does not fit as a proof-text for the separation of the waters – because the separation occurred on the second day, whereas Gen. 1:2 refers to the first day – the Bavli ostentatiously continues the discussion of the distance between the upper and lower waters, unmoved by R. Yehoshua's verdict and Ben Zoma's fate. Whereas Ben Zoma had defined the distance as "not even a handbreadth" (in the Tosefta and the Yerushalmi versions) or "only three fingers' breadth" (in the Bavli version), the Bavli adds a number of opinions that reduce the space between the waters to the absolute minimum: as a hair's breadth, as between the boards of a gangway, as between two cloaks spread one over the other, or as between two cups placed one in the other. So in fact, the Bavli sees nothing improper in Ben Zoma's exposition of the work of creation (and no reason for him to be punished) but feels stimulated to continue and improve it.

Ben Zoma is followed in the *pardes* story by Aher, that is, the arch-heretic Elisha b. Avuyah. Accordingly, after quoting the proof-text for Elisha-Aher (Eccl. 5:5: "Let not your mouth lead your flesh into sin"), the Bavli continues by adding some new material about Aher (unit 3 [a]):[82]

> Why this?[83] He [Aher] saw that permission had been given to Metatron to sit[84] and write down the merits of Israel. He [Aher] said: "It is taught as a tradition that above (*le-ma'lah*) there is no standing[85] and no sitting, no jealousy[86] and no rivalry, no back and no weariness. Perhaps, God forbid, there are two powers (*reshuyyot*) [in heaven]!?"
> [Thereupon] they led Metatron forth and flogged him with sixty fiery lashes. They said to him: "Why, when you saw him [Aher], did you not rise before him?" Permission was [then] given to him [Metatron] to erase the merits of Aher.
> A heavenly voice went forth and said: "Return, backsliding children (Jer. 3:14, 22) – except for Aher." [Thereupon] he [Aher] said: "Since I have been driven forth from that world [the future world], I will go forth and enjoy this world." So Aher fell into bad ways (*tarbut ra'ah*).[87]

This story sets out to explain why Aher became a heretic. In explicitly attributing to him a vision of Metatron, the highest angel in heaven, it makes clear that it wants to read the *pardes* story as a heavenly journey in which the rabbis, including Aher, attained their goal. Similar to the passage with Aqiva's warning regarding the marble stones in heaven, but much more explicit, it transfers the *pardes* story from an exercise in exegesis to the experience of a heavenly ascent. Because of the unexpected sight of a *sitting* angel – angels are supposed

---

[82] The association that triggered off the addition of this tradition may have been the continuation of the verse Eccl. 5:5: "and say not before the *angel* that it was an error."

[83] Most manuscripts have the better version, "What did he see?" See Halperin, *The Merkabah in Rabbinic Literature*, p. 167 with n. 84.

[84] Most manuscripts add "one hour a day"; see Halperin, ibid., with n. 85.

[85] "No standing" with most manuscripts; Halperin, ibid., p. 168 with n. 87.

[86] "No jealousy" (*qin'ah*) with most manuscripts; Halperin, ibid., with n. 88.

[87] b Hagigah 15a.

to have no knee joints and therefore cannot sit; moreover, there is no competition among the angels in heaven; the angels do not turn their backs to each other (because they have faces in all directions and do not need to turn around); and they certainly do not suffer from physical weariness – Aher concludes that there must be two divine powers in heaven, not just the one and sole God. Although it results from a misunderstanding, this sin causes Aher's eternal and irrevocable damnation, pronounced by a voice from heaven (*bat qol*).

So far so good. We now understand why Aher is punished forever – he mistook Metatron for God, and this was regarded as a cardinal sin. But what goes against the grain of the story in its present context is the fact that not only is Aher punished but, even more conspicuously, so is Metatron. Immediately after Aher's ill-advised conclusion about two powers in heaven, it is Metatron who is first punished (because he did not rise before Aher and thereby neglected to make clear that he isn't God, sitting on his throne, but just an angel, standing around like any other angel), and only thereafter does Aher receive the punishment he deserves. Metatron's humiliation comes quite unexpectedly in the present context (the *pardes* story with Aher's ascent to heaven), and I would like to suggest once more that it can only be understood as a counterpoint to the gist of the ascent tradition, arguing: it may well be that Aher, together with his fellow rabbis, went up to heaven and saw things that are normally hidden from human view. But make no mistake – not only was Aher punished for his rash and incorrect conclusion, and not only did he *not* see God but an angel (albeit the highest angel in heaven), but this highest angel, the "Lesser YHWH" according to 3 Enoch, was also punished because he failed to prevent Aher from mistaking him for God. So in fact, despite its coloring of the *pardes* story in terms of an ascent account, the Bavli betrays its own transformation of the *pardes* story by simultaneously toning it down, making its impact less powerful, and telling its reader: what is such an ascent actually worth if one does not in fact see God, if one makes a (quite understandable) mistake, is nevertheless punished forever, and even causes the highest angel in heaven to be punished as well.

Not surprisingly, just as in Aqiva's warning of the marble stones, our story too has a parallel in the Hekhalot literature, where it is transmitted in two different macroforms[88] and in two different versions: one within the macroform called Merkavah Rabbah[89] and the other in the macroform called 3 Enoch.[90] Whereas in the former it is part of the *pardes* story and most likely influenced by our Bavli Hagigah tradition,[91] in the latter it is independent of the *pardes* story but follows the tradition of Enoch's elevation from a human being to the highest angel in

---

[88] On this term, see below, pp. 243 ff.
[89] *Synopse zur Hekhalot-Literatur*, § 672.
[90] Ibid., § 20.
[91] Only in the (late) Ms. New York 8128; see Peter Schäfer, ed., *Übersetzung der Hekhalot-Literatur*, vol. 4: §§ 598–985 (Tübingen: J. C. B. Mohr [Paul Siebeck], 1991), pp. 72–75.

heaven – his transformation into Metatron, the "Lesser YHWH,"[92] almost on a par with God.[93] He sits on a throne, similar to God's, at the entrance of the seventh heaven, judging all the angels in heaven and assigning to them their respective angelic rank.[94] And then the story suddenly incorporates the Elisha b. Avuyah/Aher tradition and continues:

> But when Aher came to behold the vision of the Merkavah (*bitzfiyyat ha-merkavah*) and set eyes upon me [Metatron], he was afraid and trembled before me. His soul was alarmed to the point of leaving him because of his fear, dread, and terror of me, when he saw me seated upon a throne like a king, with ministering angels standing beside me as servants and all the princes of kingdoms crowned with crowns surrounding me. At that hour he opened his mouth and said: "There are indeed two powers (*reshuyyot*) in heaven!"
>
> Immediately a heavenly voice came out from the presence of the Shekhinah and said: "Return, backsliding children (Jer. 3:14, 22) – except for Aher."
>
> Then Anafiel YWY,[95] the honored, glorified, beloved, wonderful, terrible, and dreadful Prince, came at the command of the Holy One, blessed be He, struck me [Metatron] with sixty fiery lashes and made me stand on my feet.[96]

Here, Aher's misperception of Metatron's role in heaven forms the climax of Metatron's elevation to the "Lesser YHWH" – or rather, to be more precise, the anticlimax, for it causes, as in the Bavli, Metatron's punishment. However, the story flows more smoothly in 3 Enoch than in the Bavli, since in the 3 Enoch version it is, consequentially, first Aher who gets his punishment (immediately after he "recognizes" two powers in heaven) and then Metatron. We even learn who executes it: Anafiel, another high angel, and at the command of God himself. Howsoever the relationship between the two versions can be defined,[97] it is highly conspicuous that ultimately, in emphasizing Metatron's punishment, both tone down the impact of the experience of the Merkavah (versus the Merkavah as an exegetic discipline).[98]

The Aher-Metatron encounter (explaining why Aher became a heretic) is followed by a series of stories about Aher's fate after his apostasy.[99] They cluster

---

[92] *Synopse zur Hekhalot-Literatur*, § 15.

[93] See below, chapter 8, p. 320.

[94] *Synopse zur Hekhalot-Literatur*, § 20.

[95] A variant of the tetragrammaton YHWH.

[96] *Synopse zur Hekhalot-Literatur*, § 20; see also below, chapter 8, p. 322. I follow (with variations) the translation by Philip Alexander, "3 (Hebrew Apocalypse of) Enoch," in *OTP*, vol. 1, p. 268.

[97] See on this Philip Alexander, "3 Enoch and the Talmud," *JSJ* 18 (1987), pp. 40–68; Christopher R.A. Morray-Jones, "Hekhalot Literature and Talmudic Tradition: Alexander's Three Test Cases," *JSJ* 22 (1991), pp. 1–39.

[98] On the possible Babylonian origin of 3 Enoch, see Peter Schäfer and Klaus Herrmann, eds., *Übersetzung der Hekhalot-Literatur*, vol. 1: *§§ 1–80* (Tübingen: J.C.B. Mohr [Paul Siebeck], 1995), pp. L–LV.

[99] b Hagigah 15a–b.

around Aher and his faithful student R. Meir, as well as around the rabbis' reaction to this extraordinary student-teacher relationship, even after the teacher's apostasy. Meir remains faithful to Aher beyond both their deaths and takes care, against his fellow rabbis' advice, that Aher is punished in Gehinnom and ultimately forgiven. After Aher's death, when his impoverished daughter approaches Rabbi (Yehudah ha-Nasi) for sustenance and Rabbi at first wants to rebuff her, fire comes down from heaven and envelops his bench – apparently threatening to burn him (an ironical inversion of the fire that surrounds R. Yohanan and R. Eleazar b. Arakh during the latter's successful exposition of the Merkavah). A few passages are added, explaining why R. Meir could study with Aher even after his apostasy, and finally God himself is conjured (in a revelation of Elijah): how did he react to Meir's loyalty to his teacher Aher:

> Rabbah bar Shela[100] (once) met Elijah.
> He [Rabbah bar Shela] said to him [Elijah]: "What is the Holy One, blessed be He, doing?" (Elijah answered:) "He [God] utters traditions in the name of all the rabbis, but in the name of R. Meir he does not utter (any)."
> (Rabbah bar Shela) asked him: "Why?"
> (Elijah:) "Because he learned traditions from the mouth of Aher."[101]

When the rabbi insists that the essence of Aher's teaching was not compromised because of his sin ("R. Meir found a pomegranate; he ate [the fruit] within it, and the peel he threw away"), even God gives in. Elijah informs him that now, at this very moment – after the rabbi has intervened on Meir's behalf – God utters a tradition in the name of R. Meir! In other words, the rabbis plead with God to forgive Aher and Meir, and God conforms to their plea. Hence the overall message of the story cycle (following Aher's heavenly ascent) is that Aher did sin and did become a heretic, but that ultimately it was less his than the angel Metatron's fault. An ascent to heaven is ill-advised – not so much because of the human adept's inadequacies (to be sure, they are bad enough and certainly play a role) but because of the deficiency of the heavenly host, in particular of the angel whom God has elevated to the rank of a lesser God. Heaven is a dangerous and unsafe territory, and human beings had better avoid it and stay with their fellow rabbis on earth. Their task is to expound the Torah in the earthly academies and not to ascend to heaven.

After a couple of more Aher-Meir stories, the Bavli's sugiah finally turns to Aqiva's experience. In quoting the *pardes* story as "R. Aqiva went up (*'alah*) safely and went down (*yarad*) safely" (followed by the quotation from Cant. 1:4), it makes immediately clear (as was the case with Aher) that it seeks to understand the event as a heavenly ascent. This is further emphasized by the continuation: "And R. Aqiva, too, the ministering angels wanted to push away,

---

[100] A Babylonian Amora of the late third to early fourth century.
[101] b Hagigah 15b.

(but) the Holy One, blessed be He, said to them: Leave this old man (alone), for he is worthy to avail himself of my glory (*le-hishtammesh bikhvodi*)."[102] Not surprisingly, this passage again has an almost verbatim parallel in the Hekhalot literature, this time in Hekhalot Zutarti[103] as well as in Merkavah Rabbah.[104] In both macroforms it follows, as in the Bavli, Aqiva's successful ascent and descent according to the *pardes* story, culminating in the quotation of Cant. 1:4. Here is the Hekhalot Zutarti version:

> R. Aqiva said: At that hour when I ascended to the height [of heaven], I put one sign more on the entrances of the *raqia'* than (on) the entrance to my house.[105] And when I arrived at the curtain (*pargod*), the angels of destruction came forth to destroy me, (but) the Holy One, blessed be He, said to them: Leave this old man (alone), for he is worthy to behold my glory (*le-histakkel bikhvodi*)."[106]

According to this version, Aqiva himself explains (presumably to his fellow rabbis after his safe return from the Merkavah) how he managed to escape the *pardes* unharmed: he was clever enough, during his ascent, to put markers at the entrances of the (seven) palaces or heavens in order to find his way back. But when he finally arrived at the curtain that veils the divine throne, the angels in heaven were not pleased to see him and tried to kill him. He only managed to escape the fury of the angels because God told them not to harm him. Only this second part about the angels and God's intervention on Aqiva's behalf is mentioned in the Bavli – with the remarkable difference that the Hekhalot Zutarti/ Merkavah Rabbah version[107] uses the phrase typical of the ascent accounts in the Hekhalot literature, "to behold my glory," whereas the Bavli version uses the phrase "to avail himself of my glory," which is characteristic of the Hekhalot literature's magical-theurgical strand. To be sure, the relationship between both versions needs further clarification, but I find it hard to imagine that the shorter Bavli version served as the basis for the more elaborate Hekhalot version; rather, it seems reasonable to assume that some kind of Hekhalot version is being quoted in an abbreviated form in the Bavli.

Whatever the relationship may be, much more telling is the way in which the Bavli and the Hekhalot literature continue after God's intervention. Whereas Hekhalot Zutarti proceeds with more passages related to Aqiva's Merkavah ex-

---

[102] Ibid.

[103] *Synopse zur Hekhalot-Literatur*, § 346. A remarkable parallel is preserved in the Genizah fragment T.-S. K 21.95.B, the only Genizah fragment containing passages from Hekhalot Zutarti; see Peter Schäfer, *Geniza-Fragmente zur Hekhalot-Literatur* (Tübingen: J.C.B. Mohr [Paul Siebeck], 1984), p. 88 (fol. 2a, l. 11–15).

[104] Ibid., § 673, immediately following the passage about Aher and Metatron, § 672.

[105] Ms. New York (§ 673): "more signs on the entrances of the *raqia'* than on the entrances to my house."

[106] As part of Hekhalot Zutarti (§ 346) only in Ms. Munich 22; in Mss. Oxford 1531 and New York 8128 the paragraph follows the *pardes* story in Merkavah Rabbah.

[107] Also in the Genizah fragment: *Geniza-Fragmente zur Hekhalot-Literatur*, p. 88, l. 14.

perience (Merkavah Rabbah breaks off the Aqiva passages in the middle of the following paragraph but nevertheless continues with Hekhalot material), the Bavli's narrative takes a very different turn. In asking, "What did he expound (*mai derash*),"[108] it provides a number of Bible verses, all of which prove that Aqiva, unlike Aher, knew how to distinguish between God and his angels:

– He came (*atah*) from the myriads of holy ones (Deut. 33:2): He is a sign (*ot*) among his myriad – meaning that God is distinguished among his holy angels;
– Preeminent (*dagul*) among the myriad (Cant. 5:10): He is an outstanding example (*dugmah*) among his myriad – meaning that he distinguishes himself from his angels;
– The Lord of hosts is his name (Isa. 48:2): He is the Lord among his host – meaning that he is recognizable as the Lord of his angels;
– [There was a great and strong wind …,] but the Lord was not in the wind; after the wind – an earthquake, but the Lord was not in the earthquake. After the earthquake – fire, but the Lord was not in the fire. And after the fire – a soft sound of stillness,[109] and behold, the Lord passed by (1 Kings 19:11 f.)[110] – meaning that God could be distinguished from all these natural phenomena and that Aqiva knew precisely where he was and where not.

Hence, what is important for the Bavli is how Aqiva reached his conclusion about who and where God was, which prevented him from falling into the same trap as Aher, that is, mistaking an angel for God. And, most conspicuously, his was not a visionary experience (such as poor Aher's: angels do not sit, so someone who sits in heaven must be God) but the result of an *exegetical procedure*. In other words, the Bavli is not interested in Aqiva's experience but in the proper exegesis of biblical verses. This again is an anticlimax to any attempt at a mystical ascent to heaven. When Aqiva has finally reached the goal of his desire, after God has allowed him to enter the innermost chamber of his divine presence, the Bavli editor's only concern is the biblical verses and the correct exegesis allowing Aqiva to escape Aher's fate. Or, to put it differently, *because* Aqiva was such an excellent interpreter of the Bible, God allowed him into his presence: the rabbi, who does his job properly, is the true Merkavah "mystic" (*yored la-merkavah*). Merkavah exegesis turned into an ascent to the Merkavah and again turned into exegesis – this is the message of the Bavli.

That the Bavli's main concern is with exegetical distinctions rather than with visionary experiences becomes clear also from the next segment of the sugiah. Having discussed the difference between God and his angels (correctly per-

---
[108] b Hagigah 16a.
[109] Lit. "the sound of delicate/soft stillness," usually translated as "a soft murmuring sound" or "a still, small voice" (JPS), or "a sound of sheer silence" (NRSV).
[110] "And behold, the Lord passed by" appears in the Hebrew Bible at the beginning of this list of natural phenomena (v. 11), not at the end (v. 12).

ceived in, or rather concluded from, biblical verses by Aqiva), the sugiah moves on to explain the difference between angels and demons and between angels and human beings. Obviously, this clarification has nothing to do with the experience of an ascent to heaven.

Then, finally, the Bavli's Merkavah sugiah comes to an end: it concludes with unit 7 about the Mishnah lemma, "Anyone who gazes at four things" and "Anyone who has no concern for the honor of his creator," referring to matters of creation. Having dealt extensively with the topic of creation in its sugiah about the work of creation, the Bavli is here rather brief – and again conspicuously down to earth. It first states, rather dryly, that this restriction makes sense with regard to what is above and below as well as to what is after (that is, in the world to come after the end of days), "but as regards what was before – what happened, happened (*mah de-hawah hawah*)!"[111] In using the famous phrase *mai de-hawah hawah*[112] the Bavli editor expresses his disregard for historical events and developments: what happened, happened, and we are not really interested in the history of something, not even in the prehistory of the time before creation. Yet he feels compelled to add – in the names of R. Yohanan and R. Eleazar (one wonders again whether he refers to Yohanan b. Nappaha and Eleazar b. Pedat or to Yohanan b. Zakkai and Eleazar b. Arakh)[113] – the risky parable about the palace of the king built on dunghills, which does deal with precreational matters.[114]

Similarly toned down is the remaining material about the glory of the creator. As to the question, why is it that "anyone who has no concern for the honor of his creator, it would be merciful to/fitting for him if he had not come into the world," the Bavli gives two answers. The first answer indicates someone who looks at the rainbow – an explicit reference to Ezek. 1:28 (the vision of God). But the impact of this reference becomes much less significant with another explanation that states: "Anyone who looks at three things, his eyes become dim: at the rainbow, at the Prince (*nasi*),[115] and at the priests." Here, the rainbow with its association with the vision of God is coupled with the Prince and the priests, two considerably less dangerous and esoteric matters. Moreover, much more emphasis is placed on the second answer: "This refers to someone who commits a transgression in secret," that is, someone who sins secretly and who lets the

---

[111] b Hagigah 16a.

[112] On this phrase, see recently Isaiah Gafni, "Rabbinic Historiography and Representations of the Past," in Charlotte E. Fonrobert and Martin S. Jaffee, eds., *The Cambridge Companion to the Talmud and Rabbinic Literature* (Cambridge: Cambridge University Press, 2007), pp. 295–312. Gafni emphasizes (p. 299) that the phrase appears primarily "in the reflections of later redactors ... [the] *stammma'im* (as Halivni would call them)."

[113] See above, pp. 186 ff., 225 f.

[114] See above, p. 222.

[115] Either a secular ruler or the rabbinic patriarch. The Bible verse quoted as proof text (Num. 27:20) refers to Joshua son of Nun, Moses's successor as the leader of the people, but the patriarch cannot be ruled out.

evil inclination (*yetzer ha-ra*ʻ) prevail upon him. Hence, the Bavli editor moves from the vision of the Merkavah to ethical questions, because this is what really matters for him and what occupies him until the end of the sugiah.

To sum up, the broader view of how the Bavli editor structures both his sugyot on the work of creation and on the Merkavah yields a striking result that significantly qualifies the conclusions drawn from our analysis in chapter 6 of the Tosefta cycle's stories as discrete units of their own. The sugiah about the work of creation concludes with Nebuchadnezzar's vain attempt to ascend to the heavens, and in my view this forms a fitting bridge to the sugiah about the Merkavah. Two abortive attempts to study the Merkavah underline the Bavli's conviction that the Merkavah is an exegetical discipline, but nevertheless a dangerous one restricted to scholars of a certain age. In limiting the subject of the Merkavah to Ezek. 1:4–26, the editor makes clear that he wants to exclude from the exegetical exercise the description of the figure of God seated on his throne (Ezek. 1:26 f.). This applies also to the enigmatic word *hashmal* in 1:27, which is part of God's appearance (two unlucky "children" expounding *hashmal* were burned by fire), but the Bavli, not particularly moved by the poor children's fate, continues with an exegesis of precisely the word *hashmal*. Exegeses of various Ezekiel verses follow, all emphasizing the Bavli's view of the Merkavah as an exegetical discipline.

After long exegeses of Dan. 7 and Isa. 3:1–7 the sugiah finally approaches the Tosefta's story cycle (units 1–7, omitting units 4 and 5). True, the Bavli adds new material to some stories – to units 1 (R. Yehoshua and R. Yose ha-Kohen) and, in particular, 3 (Aqiva's warning of the heavenly marble stones; Aher and Metatron; Aqiva's rescue from the angels' attack) – that gives them a peculiar "Merkavah mystical" tinge, as opposed to just referring to the exegesis of Ezek. 1. But in most cases the editor immediately counters the impact of this new meaning by qualifying it and playing it down: Ben Zoma was more of an expert on the burning question of whether a dog may be castrated or whether a high priest may marry a pregnant virgin rather than on the Merkavah; and the problem of the distance between the upper and the lower waters, raised by him (with disastrous consequences), is indeed a problem worthy of discussion. Aher's conclusion, on the occasion of his vision of Metatron, that there are two powers in heaven, which led to his apostasy, was not actually his fault. To be sure, he deserved to be punished – but ultimately he was saved, thanks to his faithful student R. Meir, and the one who really deserved punishment was Metatron, the lesser God, himself. As to Aqiva, what spared him Aher's mishap is the fact that he knew his job as a rabbi well enough to conclude from the correct Bible verses that, and how, God is distinguished from his angels.

In three cases – Aqiva's warning of the marble stones, Aher and Metatron, the angels of destruction that threatened Aqiva – the new material in the Bavli has direct parallels in the Hekhalot literature. The Bavli editor clearly knew of such material from other sources, and it seems as if he tried (or felt compelled?) to incorporate it, to flavor his exposition of the Merkavah with a sprinkling of Merkavah "mysticism" in the technical sense of the word. Yet apparently he made every effort to neutralize this – in his view – even more dangerous and rather unwelcome stuff by adapting it to his rabbinic mindset, in other words, by thoroughly rabbinizing it.[116]

---

[116] The only case in which the editor did not succeed with this approach – or more precisely, did not even attempt it – is Aqiva's brief dictum about the danger of the marble stones: this passage gives the impression that the editor has just thrown it in, without making an attempt to further qualify it.

Chapter 8

The Merkavah Mystics

This last chapter of my investigation is devoted to Merkavah mysticism proper, that unique and enigmatic movement regarded by most scholars as the first fully developed manifestation of Jewish mysticism. Revolving around God's divine chariot (*merkavah*) and focusing on the ascent of the mystic through the seven heavens and heavenly palaces, as well as on magic adjurations, Merkavah mysticism is considered to be the climax of a long process of mystical thought that was initiated by Ezekiel. The literature in which this movement was preserved is called Hekhalot literature, a term that alludes, not by coincidence, to the architecture of the earthly Temple (where *hekhal* refers to the entrance hall to the Holy of Holies).

The individual undertaking the ascent is assigned the technical term *yored (la-) merkavah*, that is, one who "descends to the Merkavah."[1] For the sake of convenience I use the terms "mystic" and "Merkavah mystic," as well as "adept" and "initiate" – without making, at this point, any attempt to define mysticism. As to the literature, I employ the various texts' traditional terms but once more tender my frequently expressed caveat, namely, that we are dealing here with an extremely unstable literature that only in its later stages congealed into more or less fixed "works" with rather fancy (and varying) titles assigned to them; therefore, I avoid the term "work" and instead use the terms "macroforms" and "microforms."[2] With regard to the sequence of the major macroforms, I follow the order Hekhalot Rabbati, Hekhalot Zutarti, Ma'aseh Merkavah, Merkavah Rabbah, and 3 Enoch. In my view, this order also constitutes the most likely internal chronology of the Hekhalot texts.[3] In this survey, however, I confine

---

[1] As regards this (reversed) terminology – one would expect the mystic to "ascend" and not "descend" to the Merkavah; see below, p. 247, n. 23.

[2] For greater detail, see Peter Schäfer, *Hekhalot-Studien* (Tübingen: Mohr Siebeck, 1988), pp. 199 ff.; idem, *The Hidden and Manifest God*, p. 6 with n. 14. For an excellent survey of the current research on Hekhalot literature and Merkavah mysticism in general, see the introduction in Ra'anan S. Boustan (Abusch), *From Martyr to Mystic: Rabbinic Martyrology and the Making of Merkavah Mysticism* (Tübingen: Mohr Siebeck, 2005), pp. 1 ff., and the updated summary in idem, "The Study of Heikhalot Literature: Between Mystical Experience and Textual Artifact," *CBR* 6 (2007), pp. 130–160. Very useful for a broader readership is Michael D. Swartz, "Mystical Texts," in Shmuel Safrai Z"L, Zeev Safrai, Joshua Schwartz, and Peter J. Tomson, eds., *The Literature of the Sages*, part 2 (Assen: Royal Van Gorcum and Fortress, 2006), pp. 393–420.

[3] See Schäfer, *The Hidden and Manifest God*, pp. 7 f.

myself to the macroforms Hekhalot Rabbati, Hekhalot Zutarti, Shi'ur Qomah,[4] and 3 Enoch.[5]

Hekhalot Rabbati

The macroform conventionally captured under the heading Hekhalot Rabbati ("The Greater Palaces") is far from being a carefully composed and thoroughly edited literary work. True, later scribes and editors of the respective manuscripts took great pains to organize the text into chapters and subunits, but these quite artificial attempts barely disguise the fact that we are dealing with highly disparate and often even fragmentary pieces (microforms) that have been joined together more or less successfully. Any effort to unravel the mysteries of this "work" must take its unique literary makeup into consideration, if one wants to avoid the danger of rashly and unduly harmonizing what appear to be distinct and sometimes even conflicting layers of tradition.

In the manuscripts published in the *Synopse*, the macroform Hekhalot Rabbati is sandwiched between the macroforms 3 Enoch and Hekhalot Zutarti. Its precise extent is far from being a given, since the available manuscripts[6] vary greatly with regard to the microforms constituting the overarching macroform Hekhalot Rabbati.[7] A relatively stable range of the microforms constituting the macroform seems to be, in terms of the *Synopse* paragraphs, the units §§ 81–276 or §§ 81–306, respectively.[8] The former unit concludes the ascent accounts of §§ 198–267 with some hymns of praise; the latter regards the Sar ha-Torah narrative (§§ 282–306) as part of Hekhalot Rabbati. The microforms Pereq R.

---

[4] Whether or not Shi'ur Qomah should be treated as an independent macroform is open to question; it is preserved, as a larger and coherent unit, in Merkavah Rabbah and, independently, in Ms. Munich 40 (see below, p. 307). In presenting it separately I do not want to make a claim with regard to its literary status.

[5] On Ma'aseh Merkavah and Merkavah Rabbah, see the summaries in Schäfer, *The Hidden and Manifest God*, pp. 77 ff. and 97 ff.; on Ma'aseh Merkavah, see Naomi Janowitz, *The Poetics of Ascent: Theories of Language in a Rabbinic Ascent Text* (Albany: State University of New York Press, 1989), and Michael D. Swartz, *Mystical Prayer in Ancient Judaism: An Analysis of Ma'aseh Merkavah* (Tübingen: Mohr Siebeck, 1992).

[6] I am referring here to all the preserved manuscripts, not just the manuscripts in the *Synopse zur Hekhalot-Literatur*.

[7] See Peter Schäfer, "Handschriften zur Hekhalot-Literatur," in idem, *Hekhalot-Studien*, pp. 154–233 (originally in *FJB* 11 [1983], pp. 113–193); idem, *Übersetzung der Hekhalot-Literatur*, vol. 2: *§§ 81–334*, pp. XIV–XXXVI; James R. Davila, "Prolegomena to a Critical Edition of Hekhalot Rabbati," *JJS* 45 (1994), pp. 208–226; and the very useful summary in Boustan (Abusch), *From Martyr to Mystic*, pp. 36–49.

[8] See Schäfer, "Zum Problem der redaktionellen Identität von *Hekhalot Rabbati*," in idem, *Hekhalot-Studien*, pp. 63–74, and the charts in *Synopse zur Hekhalot-Literatur*, pp. XXIV–XXV; *Übersetzung der Hekhalot-Literatur*, vol. 2, p. XXVI; and Boustan, *From Martyr to Mystic*, pp. 41 f.

Nehunya b. Haqanah (§§ 307–314), Metatron's ascent (§§ 315–317), the Great Seal/Awful Crown (§§ 318–321), and hymns and prayers (§§ 322–334) are only loosely connected with Hekhalot Rabbati.

I refrain from dating the macroform Hekhalot Rabbati, but I see no reason to retract my earlier conclusion that much of the Hekhalot literature, Hekhalot Rabbati included, is a late rabbinic or even postrabbinic phenomenon (sixth century and later) – notwithstanding the possibility, of course, that some of the material collected and edited in this literature may well be earlier (third to sixth centuries).[9] Moreover, I continue to posit that the predilection of most scholars for a Palestinian origin of the Hekhalot *literature* is unwarranted (and certainly not supported by the mention of Caesarea and the valley of Kidron in Hekhalot Rabbati)[10] and that at least the formative *shaping* of Hekhalot Rabbati (and other Hekhalot texts) in Babylonia must be seriously considered[11] (with additional redactional layers in Ashkenaz).[12]

1. The Gedullah Hymns

Let us now look at the major microforms contained in Hekhalot Rabbati, with particular emphasis on the overall editorial strategy of their inclusion in the macroform and the message they are intended to convey (as independent microforms and as part of the macroform Hekhalot Rabbati). The first microform is the so-called Gedullah hymns (§§ 81–93), which praise the superiority of the Merkavah mystic. They open the macroform Hekhalot Rabbati with the enigmatic question, put into the mouth of R. Ishmael and repeated several times in subsequent sections: "Which are the hymns recited by one who wishes to behold the vision of the Merkavah (*le-histakkel bitzfiyyat merkavah*), to descend (*lered*) in peace and to ascend (*la-'alot*) in peace?"[13] This opening sentence confronts the reader with a number of important and highly charged presuppositions that are not explained but obviously taken for granted:

1. There is such a thing as "the vision of the Merkavah," which, moreover, appears to be an eminently desirable goal. The Hebrew employed here (*tzefiyyat*

---

[9] Schäfer, *Hekhalot-Studien*, p. 293; idem, *The Hidden and Manifest God*, p. 159; idem, *Übersetzung der Hekhalot-Literatur*, vol. 2, pp. XX–XXV; Boustan, *From Martyr to Mystic*, pp. 288, 292; idem, "The Emergence of Pseudonymous Attribution in Heikhalot Literature: Empirical Evidence from the Jewish 'Magical' Corpora," *JSQ* 13 (2006), pp. 1–21.

[10] See, e.g., Scholem, *Jewish Gnosticism*, p. 32.

[11] See *Übersetzung der Hekhalot-Literatur*, vol. 2, p. XXIV.

[12] On the Ashkenazi redaction of Hekhalot manuscripts, see Israel M. Ta-Shma, "The Library of the Ashkenazi Sages in the Eleventh and Twelfth Centuries," *QS* 60 (1985), pp. 298–309; Klaus Herrmann, "Re-Written Mystical Texts: The Transmission of the Hekhalot Literature in the Middle Ages," *BJRL* 75 (1993), pp. 97–116.

[13] *Synopse zur Hekhalot-Literatur*, § 81. I follow, unless otherwise stated, Ms. Oxford 1531 and use the English translation prepared by Aubrey Pomerance and Ra'anan Boustan (Abusch).

[*ha-*] *merkavah*) is unusual and seems unique to the Hekhalot literature: "to be-hold the vision of the Merkavah" is introduced as a well-established practice re-quiring no further explanation. A similar phrase occurs in the very first paragraph of 3 Enoch, where R. Ishmael says: "When I ascended (*'aliti*) to the height to behold in my vision the Merkavah (*le-histakkel bitzfiyyati ba-merkavah*),"[14] and, later, when the arch-heretic Elisha b. Avuyah (Aher) ascends to heaven and mis-takes Metatron for God: "When Aher came to behold the vision of the Merkavah (*le-histakkel bitzfiyyat ha-merkavah*) and set his eyes upon me [Metatron]."[15] In addition to "beholding" the vision of the Merkavah, one may also "gaze" (*le-hatzitz*)[16] or "closely look" (*le-tzapot*)[17] at it. Therefore, it comes as no surprise that "the vision of the Merkavah" is presented as a subject that can be taught, again according to R. Ishmael: "Thus do they teach (*kakh hayu shonin*) about the vision of the Merkavah."[18] Any adept wishing to bind himself to the Prince of the Torah, concludes the Sar ha-Torah narrative at the end of (the larger) macro-form Hekhalot Rabbati, needs to follow certain ascetic practices and, if success-ful, should be able to "go out to all the measures of the Torah he wishes, be it to Scripture, be it to Mishnah, be it to Talmud, be it[19] to the vision of the Merkavah (*tzefiyyat* [*ha-*] *merkavah*)."[20] No doubt, in all these texts, with a clear focus on Hekhalot Rabbati, the vision of the Merkavah is a discipline that one practices and that one can study.

2. In order to achieve the desired goal, the vision of the Merkavah, one is sup-posed to recite certain hymns: all the manuscripts in the *Synopse* use the verb *amar* (lit. "say") together with the noun *shirot* ("hymns"), indicating that these hymns are not sung but rather recited. From this we may conclude that the hymns are not just any kind of songs but, more precisely, are poetical-liturgical pieces. We are not told, however, what these hymns contain, at least not immediately, since the text continues with the praise of the Merkavah mystic (the Gedullah hymns proper).[21] Moreover, although the hymns seem to be a necessary tool for the vision of the Merkavah, it remains unclear whether they are a *vehicle* for achieving this goal (that is, whether the very recitation of the hymns induces the vision) or whether they just *accompany* the visionary on his journey. Yet, since

---

[14] Ibid., § 1 (Ms. Vatican 228).

[15] Ibid., § 20.

[16] R. Nehunya b. Haqanah (*Synopse zur Hekhalot-Literatur*, § 225).

[17] Using the same root for the verb as for the noun (*tzipiti bitzfiyyat ha-merkavah*) and clearly a later phrase (*Synopse zur Hekhalot-Literatur*, §§ 403 and 579).

[18] *Synopse zur Hekhalot-Literatur*, § 93.

[19] Ms. Vatican 228 adds "even": "be it even to the vision of the Merkavah."

[20] *Synopse zur Hekhalot-Literatur*, § 303: the manuscripts vary with regard to the definite article before *merkavah* and the inclusion of "Talmud."

[21] Unless one wants to argue that the Gedullah hymns are meant to be the hymns that the adept recites, but I do not think this is likely.

they enable the mystic to undertake his journey "in peace" (that is, safely), they are clearly essential for the successful accomplishment of his adventure.

3. Contemplation of the Merkavah vision entails some mysterious "descent" and "ascent," the precise meaning of which the author/editor does not bother to explain, or rather again takes for granted. In other words, the usage of *yarad* and *'alah* here is clearly that of a coined phrase that required no further explanation. It immediately evokes the *pardes* story in the Tosefta (Hagigah 2:1, Ms. Vienna), according to which only R. Aqiva "ascended (*'alah*) safely and descended (*yarad*) safely." I have argued above[22] that originally the verbs "enter" (*nikhnas*) and "go out" (*yatza*) were used here (as preserved in Ms. Erfurt) and that later editors of the *pardes* story adopted the technical vocabulary of "ascend" and "descend" in order to convert the story into a Merkavah mystical experience. What is striking, however, is the fact that the Tosefta adaptation presents the verbs "ascend" and "descend" in what seems to be the logical order (one first ascends somewhere, presumably to heaven, and then descends back home again), whereas Hekhalot Rabbati introduces the (in)famous inverted word order (one first descends and then ascends), for which a satisfactory explanation has not yet been found.[23]

4. Instead of communicating to the reader the contents of the hymns and explaining how precisely one "descends" and "ascends" safely, the opening sentence continues with the solemn praise of the Merkavah mystic, using the enigmatic phrase *gedullah mi-kullam*, which presumably means something like "The greatest thing of all is that. ..."[24] The following units present a catalogue of all the qualities by which the Merkavah mystic is distinguished from and regarded as superior to his fellows, and the very first one (§ 81) focuses on his accomplishment as the one who "descends" to the Merkavah (*yored la-merkavah*):

The greatest thing of all is (that they) are bound to him (*le-hizzaqeq lo*),
lead him (*le-hakhniso*)
and bring him (*lehavi'o*)[25] into the palace chambers (*hadrei hekhal*) of *'arevot
raqia'*

---

[22] Chapter 6, pp. 197 f.

[23] See Schäfer, *The Hidden and Manifest God*, pp. 2 f., n. 4; Kuyt, *The "Descent" to the Chariot;* Elliot Wolfson, "*Yeridah la-Merkavah*: Typology of Ecstasy and Enthronement in Ancient Jewish Mysticism," in *Mystics of the Book: Themes, Topics, and Typologies*, ed. R. A. Herrera (New York: P. Lang, 1993), pp. 13–44; idem, *Speculum*, pp. 82–85; Boustan, *From Martyr to Mystic*, p. 11, n. 24; Schäfer, "In Heaven as It Is in Hell," pp. 273 f.

[24] *Gedullah* seems to be a noun here, meaning "greatness." The awkward combination of the feminine *gedullah* with the masculine *mi-kullam* is difficult to harmonize, but the most likely explanation is that the "greatness" of the Merkavah mystic that distinguishes him "from all the others" consists of what follows. "From all the others" may well refer to both "all the other people" and "all the other abilities of the Merkavah mystic" enumerated in what follows. See Schäfer, *Übersetzung der Hekhalot-Literatur*, vol. 2, pp. 1 f., n. 6.

[25] According to all the other manuscripts *u-lehavi'o*, instead of the incomplete *u-lehavi* here in Ms. Oxford.

and place him (*le-ha'amido*) to the right of the throne of his [God's] glory
    (*kisse kevodo*),
and sometimes he stands opposite T'TzŠ, the Lord, the God of Israel,
in order to see everything that they do before the throne of his glory
and to know everything that will occur in the world in future.

"They" are obviously the angels, who bind themselves to him, the Merkavah
mystic, granting his every wish and desire.[26] Here, his (unspoken) desire is to
be brought up to the palace chambers of *'arevot raqia'*, which is, as we learn
from other Hekhalot sources, the seventh heaven called 'Aravot. The terminology employed here is informed by the imagery of both the Temple (*hekhal* as
the entrance hall to the Holy of Holies in Solomon's and Ezekiel's Temple)[27]
and the cosmos (*'aravot* as the clouds of heaven on which God rides).[28] Hence,
the mystic ascends to the heavenly Temple, located in the seventh heaven, that
accommodates the "throne of glory" (another term characteristic of the Hekhalot
literature),[29] that is, the throne on which God resides. There can be no doubt,
therefore, that the object of the Merkavah mystic's desire is God[30] seated on
his throne in the heavenly Temple, or, to put it differently, the "vision of the
Merkavah" that the mystic beholds according to the opening unit of Hekhalot
Rabbati is indeed the vision of God seated on his throne. In other words, we are
definitely dealing here with a true visionary experience and not with a mere exegetical exercise.

Our first Gedullah hymn in §§ 81 f. reveals certain details beyond the sheer
fact that the mystic ascends to the heavenly Temple. At first, it tells us that he is
placed "to the right of the throne of glory" without explaining what precisely this
means. We know from the Bible that the prophet Micah saw "the Lord seated
upon his throne, and all the host of heaven standing (*'omed*) in attendance to
his right and to his left" (1 Kings 22:19), using the same root *'amad* as does our
hymn in Hekhalot Rabbati. So it seems that the Merkavah mystic joins the rank
of the angels when he attains his desired goal. That he is put, moreover, at the
right side of the throne is clearly an indication of his special and superior status.
The right side of God is no doubt the more important one: it is his right hand
and his mighty arm, with which God swears (Isa. 62:8), and it is again with his
right hand that God offers, according to rabbinic tradition, the Torah to his people (Deut. 33:2).[31] When Bathsheba, King Solomon's mother, wishes to speak
to him, he receives her in his throne chamber, seated on his throne, and has a

---

[26] *Zaqaq* in the Nif'al has a magical connotation; see Schäfer, *Hekhalot-Studien*, p. 259.

[27] 1 Kings 6:2, 7:50 = 2 Chron. 4:22 and more often; Ezek. 8:16, 41 passim.

[28] Ps. 68:5.

[29] See Schäfer, *Konkordanz zur Hekhalot-Literatur*, vol. 1, pp. 353 ff., s. v. *kisse*.

[30] The strange name employed for God here is peculiar to the Hekhalot literature; see also
Synopse zur Hekhalot-Literatur, §§ 92 and 591.

[31] Among the many examples, see Mekhilta de-Rabbi Ishmael, wa-yehi beshallah 5 (ed.
Horovitz-Rabin, p. 107); Mekhilta de-Rabbi Shim'on b. Yohai, Ex. 14:22 (ed. Epstein-Mela-

throne prepared on his right for her to sit on (1 Kings 2:19). The same is true for David, who is offered a seat at the right hand of God: "The Lord said to my lord [David]: Sit at my right hand, while I make your enemies your footstool" (Ps. 110:1). This latter verse seems to have been the *Vorlage*[32] for Jesus's prediction to the members of the Sanhedrin: "From now on you will see the Son of Man seated at the right hand of the Power (*ek dexiōn tēs dynameōs*) and coming on the clouds of heaven" (Mt. 26:64).[33]

But to be seated at God's right side is not enough for the Merkavah mystic. Sometimes, Hekhalot Rabbati continues, he is placed opposite God on his throne – obviously so as not to be just a participant in the heavenly liturgy, like one of the angels, but to become an observer of what is happening around the throne of glory: presumably in direct eye contact with God, he not only observes what the angels do before the throne (that is, how they perform their liturgy) but from this privileged position he also learns what will happen to the world (that is, to the people of Israel on earth) in the future. If we read the following paragraph (§ 82) as the continuation of this sentence – which makes a great deal of sense in my view[34] – it explicates precisely what the mystic sees of the future:

> (Namely) whom they humiliate, whom they exalt,
> whom they weaken, whom they strengthen,
> whom they impoverish, whom they enrich,
> whom they kill, whom they let live,
> from whom they take an inheritance, to whom they give an inheritance,
> to whom they bequeath Torah, to whom they give wisdom.

"They," of course, again refers to the angels, and accordingly, in addition to observing the heavenly liturgy, the Merkavah mystic gains knowledge of the future history as carried out by the angels. The text does not explicitly state how this knowledge is obtained, but it apparently depends on the mystic's privileged position vis-à-vis God. We may assume, therefore, that his knowledge follows directly from his vision of God. Moreover, since it is the angels who execute God's will on earth, it is possible that during their heavenly liturgy the angels "perform" what will soon become "history," and that the mystic, through his direct contact with God, is enabled to "read" the angels' performance before the throne of glory. Most important, however, is the fact that it is *history* that is revealed to the mystic – more concretely, the history of the people of Israel, culminating in the revelation of the Torah. No doubt, Hekhalot Rabbati adopts

---

med, p. 64); Wayyiqra Rabbah 4:1 (ed. Margulies, vol. 1, pp. 79f.); Pesiqta Rabbati 31 (ed. Friedmann, p. 144b); b Berakhot 62a.

[32] Together with Dan. 7:13.

[33] See also Mk. 14:62; Lk. 22:69.

[34] Despite the remark *seleq (hilkheta)* in most of the manuscripts, which is clearly a later addition. Hence, I follow the suggestion made in *Übersetzung der Hekhalot-Literatur*, vol. 2, p. 3, n. 6.

here a feature with which we are well acquainted from apocalyptic literature, yet with a peculiar twist: the goal of history, as briefly summarized in § 82, is the revelation of the Torah.[35]

All the subsequent Gedullah hymns emphasize the chosen position of the Merkavah mystic among his fellow Jews, that is, within his community on earth. In other words, the purpose of his vision is not an end in itself, nor does it aim at his personal gratification. To be sure, the hymns take great pains to emphasize that the mystic's chosen position is anything but self-evident; on the contrary, it is quite precarious and needs to be reinforced by God and his angels. Whoever raises his hand against him will be severely punished by the heavenly court (§ 85): "great, evil, and severe blows will fall upon him from heaven" (§ 85) such as plagues, leprosy, and rash, tumors, foul bruises and wounds, out of which moist boils seep (§ 84). This is the complete arsenal of deadly illnesses associated in the Bible in particular with leprosy. Clearly, the position of the mystic in his community and the validity of his message are rigorously contested. Some of his fellow Jews insult, despise, and slander him – that is, they do not accept his claim to be the chosen one of God – but they will immediately be punished by the angels and destroyed (§ 91). So it is only through the intervention of God and his angels that the exceptional position of the Merkavah mystic within his community can be achieved and asserted.

What, then, is the mystic's message that he delivers on earth, after his return from heaven and empowered by his vision of the Merkavah? The first mention of his extraordinary qualities (the second Gedullah hymn in § 83) points out that he "sees (*tzofeh*) and recognizes all the deeds (*ma'aseh*) of human beings, even (those) that they do in the chambers of chambers (*hadrei hadarim*), whether they are good or corrupt deeds." This sentence is striking because it uses the very same terminology otherwise reserved for the mystic's vision of the Merkavah: *tzofeh* versus *tzefiyyat ha-merkavah* (the vision of the Merkavah), *ma'aseh* versus *ma'aseh merkavah* (the work of the Merkavah), and in particular *heder* (chamber), which is very often employed for the heavenly chambers of the Merkavah, even in the combination *hadrei hadarim* ("the chambers of the chambers").[36] Hence, our mystic applies his visionary power in a kind of reversed vision. Having returned from the "work" of the Merkavah, he now sees the hidden "deeds" of his fellow Jews. Unfortunately, the hidden deeds he sees are all "corrupt" deeds; none of those listed are actually "fine" as promised in the

---

[35] Another possible reading of § 82, of course, is to relate this part of the hymn not to the people of Israel in general but to the Merkavah mystic in particular: the mystic learns what will happen *to him* in the future, when he returns to earth; he will be the one to whom *real* knowledge of the Torah will be revealed. This interpretation fits well with the overall tenor of the hymns – the unabashed praise of the Merkavah mystic. But even then the fact remains that the most important aspect of future history is true knowledge of the Torah.

[36] See Schäfer, *Konkordanz zur Hekhalot-Literatur*, vol. 1, p. 242, s.v. "*heder*."

introductory sentence. The list of corrupt deeds presented in the hymn is pretty common: it singles out robbery, adultery, murder, intercourse with a menstruating woman, and slander,[37] most of which are part of the Ten Commandments (murder, adultery, robbery, and bearing false witness against one's neighbor)[38] and constitute the core of the seven Noachide Laws (adultery, bloodshed, and robbery).[39] What is remarkable here is not so much *what* he sees but rather *that* he sees all these hidden deeds, and, moreover – as the hymn continues – identifies the culprits. He knows precisely who did what and, although the text does not say so explicitly, it is very unlikely that he keeps this knowledge to himself. And even if he does, the sinners against the Ten Commandments and the Noachide Laws (which even gentiles are expected to observe) must have been prepared – and frightened to death – that their secret sins could be brought to light any time. This explains the fury directed at him by his fellow Jews and the need for divine protection.

Another hymn praising the qualities of the Merkavah mystic is even more revealing. I quote it verbatim (§ 86):

> The greatest thing of all is the fact
> that all the creatures will be before him
> like silver before the silversmith, who perceives
> which silver has been refined,
> which silver is impure,
> and which silver is pure.
> He even sees (*tzofeh*) into the families,
> how many bastards there are in the family,
> how many sons sired during menstruation,
> how many with crushed testicles,
> how many with mutilated penis,
> how many slaves,
> and how many sons from uncircumcised (fathers).

According to this hymn, the Merkavah mystic is the ultimate judge who separates, like the silversmith, the pure from the impure, the qualified from the unqualified. What is at stake is nothing less than the halakhic purity of the families of his fellow Jews – more precisely, who among his fellows cannot claim to be a Jew in the full (halakhic) sense of the word.[40] This is a devastating critique of the

---

[37] The following "The greatest thing of all is that he recognizes all those knowledgeable in magic" seems to be a later addition because it breaks the formal pattern of the hymn. But note that sorcery is also listed, together with committing adultery and swearing falsely, in Mal. 3:5 (see below).

[38] Ex. 20:13 ("slander" in Hekhalot Rabbati could cover "false witness against your neighbor" in the Bible).

[39] b Sanhedrin 56a: the other laws are to follow established social laws and to refrain from blasphemy, idolatry, and eating flesh cut from a living animal.

[40] Those with crushed testicles, with their penis cut off, and the bastards (*mamzerim*) are

social makeup of the mystic's community because it presupposes that his purg-
ing act is sorely needed: there is much impure silver in his community, he claims,
that needs to be refined, that is, to be eliminated from the community – a very
bold claim that the mystic arrogates to himself here, and one that becomes even
bolder if we notice the connection with the "messenger of the Lord" in the biblical book Malachi, who clearly serves as the background for our hymn. There
the messenger – who is identical with the angel of the covenant[41] and with the
prophet Elijah[42] as the precursor of the Messiah[43] – is announced who prepares
the final day of judgment (Mal. 3:2–5, JPS):

> (2) But who can endure the day of his [the messenger-angel's] coming, and who can
> hold out when he appears? For he is like a smelter's fire and like the fuller's lye. (3) He
> shall act like a smelter and purger of silver; and he shall purify the descendants of Levi
> and refine them like gold and silver, so that they shall present offerings in righteous-
> ness. ... (5) But [first] I will step forward and contend against you, and I will act as a
> relentless accuser against those who have no fear of Me: Who practice sorcery, who
> commit adultery, who swear falsely, who cheat laborers of their hire, and who subvert
> [the cause of] the widow, orphan, and stranger, said the Lord of Hosts.

In assuming the role of the messenger-angel Elijah, the Merkavah mystic becomes the precursor of the Messiah and purifies the community of Israel on
earth. To be sure, the messenger's act of purification in Malachi is directed primarily at the descendants of Levi, that is, the priests, but we may assume that in
our hymns in Hekhalot Rabbati the community of Israel has adopted the function
of the priests: there is no Temple and there are no longer any priests on earth;
Israel as a whole represents the community of priests needing to be purified, before the final day of judgment, by the chosen one who has been appointed (in
the heavenly Temple by God himself) as divine messenger and precursor of the
Messiah. Ultimately, then, the vision that the *yored merkavah* receives in heaven
is what one might call community-oriented:[44] it prepares him for his mission on
earth, no more and no less. Any kind of personal encounter between the mystic
and God, any description of God seated on his throne, is conspicuously absent.
The goal of the vision is the destiny of Israel, not the physical appearance of
God – let alone a union between the mystic and his master.

The last Gedullah hymn concludes with a bleak warning against a Merkavah
mystic, who has achieved his goal, standing before God on his throne and

---

explicitly mentioned in Deut. 23:2–3 as the ones who shall not be admitted into the congregation of the Lord (followed by the no less detested Ammonites and Moabites).

   [41] Mal. 3:1.

   [42] Mal. 3:23.

   [43] References in Schäfer, *The Hidden and Manifest God*, p. 43, n. 137.

   [44] It is true, as Martha Himmelfarb reminds me (private communication), that these paragraphs in the Gedullah hymns are heavily flavored with magic, but I don't think that the mystic
uses the knowledge and power he attains to his own advantage. What is at stake is not the fate
of the individual but of the community.

contemplating (*hoshesh*) [45] the Merkavah – but then "leaves him" (apparently God). [46] The following paragraph (§ 93) explains what this means: contemplation of the Merkavah must not be interrupted unless the mystic encounters, during his contemplation, a king, a high priest, or the complete Sanhedrin with the patriarch (*nasi*) in its midst. This provision clearly alludes to the mishnaic restriction according to which the Shema prayer may only be interrupted under certain conditions, namely, if one needs to greet or return the greeting of a higher-ranking person. [47]

What is remarkable here is not only the fact that contemplating the Merkavah is compared with praying the Shema but that contemplation of the Merkavah is accordingly located on earth and not in heaven. For it makes little sense to imagine the Merkavah mystic encountering the king, high priest, and Sanhedrin in heaven. Hence, need we conclude that the mystic is visualized here as someone who remains with his body on earth, whereas (only) his mind/soul [48] has ascended to heaven? This fits well with the famous story about R. Nehunya b. Haqanah's release from the Merkavah, in which his colleagues put a branch of myrtle soaked in pure balsam on his knees to bring him back from his "vision of the Merkavah" [49] – if his colleagues can put something on his knees, R. Nehunya b. Haqanah must still be physically present among them during his contemplation of the Merkavah. Since the provision regarding contemplation of the Merkavah in § 93 is introduced by the phrase, "Thus do they teach about the vision of the Merkavah (*bitzfiyyat ha-merkavah*)," which refers back to the opening phrase in § 81 (*le-histakkel bitzfiyyat [ha-]merkavah*), one might be inclined to argue that the vision of the Merkavah as perceived in the Gedullah hymns (at the programmatic beginning of Hekhalot Rabbati) is indeed meant to be a mental rather than a bodily experience and is presented here as a discipline that certain chosen individuals practice on earth, with their mind/soul in heaven, for the benefit of the earthly community. This is certainly a possibility, but still, we shouldn't overemphasize the problem of the mystic's physical presence on earth. The comparison of contemplating the Merkavah with praying the Shema inevitably leads to the question of whether or not this act may be interrupted – despite the fact that praying the Shema is located on earth, whereas contemplating the Merkavah nevertheless may well take place in heaven. The Hekhalot literature does not always follow our logic.

---

[45] This here is the meaning of *hashash*, as in the following section § 93, and not as rendered in the German translation (*Übersetzung der Hekhalot-Literatur*, vol. 2, p. 9): "who fears the Merkavah."

[46] *Synopse zur Hekhalot-Literatur*, § 92.

[47] m Berakhot 2:1.

[48] The texts do not distinguish between body and soul/mind; but if the body remains on earth, something of the individual's persona must ascend to heaven.

[49] *Synopse zur Hekhalot-Literatur*, §§ 225 ff.; see below, pp. 276 f.

2. The Qedushah Hymns

The Gedullah hymns are followed by the Qedushah hymns, a series of songs
that climax in the solemn quotation of Isa. 6:3 "Holy, holy, holy is the Lord of
Hosts" – the so-called Qedushah or Trishagion (§§ 94–106).[50] They are connected to the first paragraph (§ 81) with an opening phrase whose precise meaning unfortunately remains cryptic.[51] Whether it refers to hymns different from
those mentioned in § 81 (which seems to me unlikely) or to hymns at a different stage of the descent to the Merkavah, or just to the proper recitation of the
hymns, [52] there can be little doubt that they apply to the Merkavah mystic and
hence are hymns to be recited by the mystic. What they contain, however, are
highly poetic descriptions of the Qedushah, that is, the heavenly throne ritual,
as performed by the angelic hosts; again, the mystic is nowhere explicitly mentioned in these hymns.

The hymns begin with the praise uttered daily by the "princes" (*sarim*) who
serve God and his throne. The throne plays almost as important a role as God,
since he – the throne – is personified and addressed as someone who not only
carries God but is in constant dialogue with his Lord (§ 94). The rejoicing and
recitation emanating from the mouth of the angelic hosts materializes in moun-
tains of fire (§ 95). One high angel in particular is singled out as someone who
is in awe and horrified because he is called daily to serve the (divine) might and
literally dragged on his knees to the throne of glory (§ 96). We are not told who
this angel is, but he may well be Metatron[53] or the soon to appear Angel of the
Countenance (that is, of the divine presence). The divine voice from Ezek. 1:25
explains to him that those who drag him to the throne – presumably his fellow
angels – are right to do so (§ 97). Then God is described as seated in the chambers of his palace of exaltation, stillness, terror and fear, holiness, and purity
(ibid.), followed by a description of the throne, who[54] does not rest his feet on
the ground of the highest heaven "but rather is like a bird who hovers and rises
beneath him [God]" (§ 98). Even the angels who carry the throne of glory do
not rest their feet on the ground of heaven but hover like birds, and three times
daily the throne asks God (here the name ZHRRY'L is used) to sit down on him
(§ 99).

---

[50] See Alexander Altman, "Qedushah Hymns in the Early Heikhalot Literature," *Melilah* 2
(1946), pp. 1–24 (in Hebrew).

[51] *Synopse zur Hekhalot-Literatur*, § 81: "which are the hymns"; ibid., § 94: "what is the
difference [from] the hymns/what is the explanation/what is the [proper] recitation of the
hymns."

[52] See the discussion of the various possibilities in *Übersetzung der Hekhalot-Literatur*,
vol. 2, pp. 10 f., n. 2.

[53] On Metatron, see below, pp. 294 ff, 318 ff.

[54] I purposely employ the pronoun "who" here, because the throne is clearly envisioned as
a person.

The heavenly liturgy culminates in a description of God himself[55] as he approaches on the highest heaven – or rather, not a description of God but of the horror experienced by those present and kept at bay by the fire emanating from the mouth of the keruvim (=cherubim), ofannim, and holy creatures when they utter the Qedushah (strikingly, the text finds it necessary to emphasize that this is precisely the time when Israel pronounces the Qedushah in its synagogues on earth). They are terrified, faint, and fall backward (§ 101), very much like the seer in the earlier apocalypses who approaches God. The horror is intensified by the vision of the gown worn by God (again ZHRRY'L) when he comes to sit down on his throne, because it is covered with various manifestations of the divine name, the Tetragrammaton (§ 102).[56]

The text is remarkably ambiguous about the witnesses of God's appearance and his taking a seat on the throne of glory. It refers vaguely to "all those who are in the height (of heaven)" (§ 101), and one is inclined to read this as an allusion to all kinds of angels (exclusive of the keruvim, ofannim, and holy creatures, who carry the throne and exude fire when pronouncing the Qedushah). But this is too simplistic a reading, not only because Israel's Qedushah is mentioned as well, but even more so because the text explicitly continues that no creature can see the divine gown, "not the eyes (of a human being) of flesh and blood, and not the eyes of his [God's] attendants," and that the "man" who beholds the gown will be burned (§ 102).[57] Hence, it is obviously the angels *and* human beings who are imagined as observers of God's appearance in the highest heaven. Paradoxically, *both* are declared incapable of beholding God's gown (let alone himself), although the disastrous consequences are more gravely emphasized for human beings than for the angels. This impression is reinforced by the following Qedushah hymn (§§ 103 f.), which drastically pictures the consequences for the one who listens to the song of the keruvim, the ofannim, and the holy creatures (the bearers of the throne of glory): he becomes insane, he is seized by spasms and dies immediately, his body is shattered, his ribs are torn out, he is dissolved in blood, his heart is stabbed, and his gall will become like water – all allusions to human beings and not to angels. So it seems, in fact, that it is more the mystic's approach to and vision of God that is at stake here than that of the angels. Ultimately, then, the Qedushah hymns describe what the Merkavah mystic sees in heaven and the dangers that await him there. The last paragraph concluding

---

[55] God is clearly the subject here and not the Angel of the Countenance, who is previously mentioned as a major player in the heavenly performance.

[56] Further down in the paragraph the frightening vision is that of the "eyes" of the gown, presumably the eyes on the gown that consist of divine names. In §§ 246 f. the mystic is frightened by the eyes of the holy creatures.

[57] I do not see what this paragraph should have to do with the transformation of the mystic, as Morray-Jones claims; see Christopher R.A. Morray-Jones, "Transformational Mysticism in the Apocalyptic-Merkabah Tradition," *JJS* 43 (1992), p. 25, following Scholem, *Jewish Gnosticism*, p. 60.

the Qedushah hymns (§ 106) clearly wishes to convey this message: it maintains that R. Aqiva heard all these hymns during his descent to the Merkavah and that he learned them – hardly for the sake of heaven but rather so as to remember and, most likely, pass them on to his worthy colleagues.

3. The Ten Martyrs Narrative

The next unit (microform), inserted into the macroform Hekhalot Rabbati by its editor, is the famous story of the Ten Martyrs in its Merkavah mystical form (§§ 107–121). As Ra'anan Boustan, following Gottfried Reeg,[58] has pointed out, it is a very peculiar version of the post-talmudic "Story of the Ten Martyrs" (*Ma'aseh asarah harugei malkhut*), in fact a complete inversion of traditional Jewish martyrology: the rabbinical martyr, who suffers and sacrifices himself for the benefit of the community of Israel, is superseded by the rabbinical mystic, who is miraculously vindicated by God's intervention without suffering and sacrifice.[59]

After the Merkavah mystic has been proven, in the Gedullah hymns, to be superior to his fellow Jews – that is, as Boustan has put it, to the "enemy-within" – the Ten Martyrs Narrative in Hekhalot Rabbati comes to prove his superiority to the outside enemy, the Roman Empire. In a highly ironical story, the horrible fate meant for the ten sages of Israel – namely to be executed by the Roman government as punishment for the sin of the sons of Jacob who sold their brother Joseph to the Midianites – is inverted and inflicted on the Roman emperor Lupinus:[60] one of the ten would-be martyrs, R. Hananyah b. Teradyon, takes the place of the emperor Lupinus, whereas Lupinus takes the place of the rabbi, and the rabbi-emperor (Hananyah) has the emperor-rabbi (Lupinus) executed in his stead – exactly ten times, because Lupinus impersonates not only Hananyah b. Teradyon but all ten sages.

This remarkable story is fitted into Hekhalot Rabbati by means of a descent to the Merkavah: one of the rabbis, R. Nehunya b. Haqanah (the rabbi whom we will encounter later as the one who is "called back" by his fellow rabbis from his vision of the Merkavah), learns of the decree issued against the ten rabbis and leads R. Ishmael, the narrator of the story and his fellow rabbi, down to the Merkavah. Not only is the terminology employed here unusual enough (the typical *yarad*, "to descend," is used in the causative Hif'il: he [Ishmael] was caused by someone else [Nehunya b. Haqanah] to descend to the Merkavah), R. Ish-

---

[58] Gottfried Reeg, ed., *Die Geschichte von den Zehn Märtyrern* (Tübingen: J.C.B. Mohr [Paul Siebeck], 1985).

[59] Boustan, *From Martyr to Mystic*, pp. 30 ff. (the literary relationship between the narrative in Hekhalot Rabbati and "The Story of the Ten Martyrs"), pp. 199 ff. (genre inversion and identity reversal).

[60] A fictitious name.

mael does not see the divine throne and the happenings around it (as one would expect); rather, he encounters Suriyah, the Prince of the Countenance, asks him what this is all about, and receives a proper explanation from him. Thereafter, when he returns from heaven, the text quite stereotypically remarks that he reports to his fellow rabbis what he has witnessed before the throne of glory, although in fact, he has heard only Suriyah's explanation and has himself seen nothing. So the connection of the Ten Martyrs Narrative with Hekhalot Rabbati is quite superficial and clearly very late. It takes a descent to the Merkavah for granted but modifies it to adapt it to its inverted version of the story of the Ten Martyrs. The underlying message is that the Merkavah mystic is not only master over his fellow Jews but also – as the martyr-turned-savior – master over the greatest enemy of the Jewish people, the Roman Empire. Moreover, and most important, the story tells us that the Merkavah mystic is not just any Jew but that he belongs to the rabbinical elite. We ought to have gathered this already from the very beginning of Hekhalot Rabbati, which is put into the mouth of no less a rabbi than R. Ishmael, but now we know for sure: R. Ishmael is one of the ten rabbinical heroes who are miraculously saved from martyrdom and instead become saviors of the Jewish people.

4. The Apocalypses

The quasi-messianic qualities of the Merkavah mystic (Gedullah hymns), the dangers that the chosen mystic is exposed to and ultimately overcomes (Qedushah hymns), and the martyr-turned-savior role that he assumes (Ten Martyrs Narrative) all leave scant room for the traditional rabbinic concept of the Messiah and messianic expectations. It should come as no surprise, therefore, that the Hekhalot literature remains conspicuously silent about the Messiah: the mystic has rendered him superfluous. This is a remarkable claim, and it should also come as no surprise that certain editors of Hekhalot manuscripts were not particularly happy with such a message and found it necessary to add more traditional Messiah-oriented material. This is precisely what happened in the New York manuscript:[61] its editor added three units that in form and content more closely resemble the classical apocalypses than what we can expect from Merkavah mystical texts. Since these three apocalypses appear only in Ms. New York (written around the end of the fifteenth or the beginning of the sixteenth century),[62] which is prone to additions from the viewpoint of the Hasidei

---

[61] Ms. New York 8128 in the *Synopse zur Hekhalot-Literatur*; see the details there, pp. X–XIV.

[62] With the exception of the first one, the David apocalypse, which is also preserved in Ms. Budapest, an Italian manuscript from the fifteenth century.

Ashkenaz,[63] and since all of them are also transmitted independently,[64] it is safe
to assume that their insertion into Hekhalot Rabbati was indeed the work of an
editor who wished to counterbalance the too radical message – for his taste – of
the macroform.

The first one, the David apocalypse (§§ 122–126), comes as a revelation of
Sasangi'el, the Prince of the Countenance, to R. Ishmael. It is replete with the
traditional language of the classical apocalypses (heavenly treasure houses, different classes of angels, audition, vision, the visionary falling backward) and dis-
guises itself only superficially and awkwardly as a Merkavah mystical ascent.[65]
After a rather enigmatic prediction of the destruction of the Temple (§ 123), it
culminates in a vision of King David appearing at the head of a procession of all
the Davidic kings and taking his place of honor on a throne opposite the throne
of God (§§ 125 f.). David utters "hymns and praises that no ear has ever heard"
(§ 126) – except, of course, R. Ishmael's – and that culminate in the praise of
God's kingship. No doubt that David is imagined here as the Davidic Messiah,
of whose privileged position in heaven (and speedy appearance on earth?) the
visionary is reassured.

The second apocalypse (§§ 130–138),[66] published separately under the title
"Aggadat R. Ishmael" by Even-Shemuel,[67] presents a peculiar mix of calcula-
tions of the end and the rabbinic emphasis on repentance as the prerequisite for
redemption. And finally, the last apocalypse (§§ 140–145)[68] is the most blatantly
messianic.[69] Metatron, the Prince of the Countenance, reveals to R. Ishmael the
messianic end: the final battle of the nations against Israel and the public appearance of the Messiah (released from his prison), who resuscitates those killed in
action and proves himself to be the leader of the world to whom all the nations
surrender. A very active Messiah indeed compared with the role granted him in
most apocalyptic as well as rabbinic texts, where at least the resuscitation of the
dead is left to God alone.[70]

---

[63] See Klaus Herrmann and Claudia Rohrbacher-Sticker, "Magische Traditionen der New
Yorker Hekhalot-Handschrift JTS 8128 im Kontext ihrer Gesamtredaktion," *FJB* 17 (1989),
pp. 101–149.

[64] See the references in *Synopse zur Hekhalot-Literatur*, p. XI.

[65] *Synopse zur Hekhalot-Literatur*, § 123: "at the hour when I descended from before him
(*yaradeti mi-lefanaw*)."

[66] The following § 139 recapitulates § 120.

[67] Yehudah Even-Shemuel, *Midreshe Ge'ullah*, 2nd ed. (Jerusalem: Mosad Bialik, 1953–
1954), pp. 148–152.

[68] The following §§ 146–151 are only loosely connected traditions about cosmology, repentance, Metatron's ascent, and texts that are also known from the Bavli (Hagigah 13a, Berakhot 7a).

[69] Published separately under the title "Messiah Aggada" by Even-Shemuel, *Midreshe
Ge'ullah*, pp. 326–327.

[70] Although, to be sure, here too it is ultimately God who does the job, since the Messiah
prays to God before the dead are resurrected. But still, the Messiah's role seems to receive
greater emphasis than usual.

5. Qedushah Hymns and Hymns of Praise

With the beginning of § 152 most of the other manuscripts of Hekhalot Rabbati join in again. The paragraphs 152–197 are a loosely edited collection of units that focus on hymns of praise and protocols of the heavenly liturgy, many of these hymns concluding once more with the Trishagion of Isa. 6:3 and thus proving to be Qedushah hymns that refer back to the Qedushah hymns of §§ 94–106.

Like the earlier Qedushah hymns, the hymns to be discussed here deal mainly with the bearers of the divine throne (according to the taxonomy of Hekhalot Rabbati the keruvim, ofannim, and holy creatures), God, the exalted King sitting on his throne in the highest palace, and the throne as the subject and even object of praise.[71] In addition to the bearers of the throne, however, some higher angels are singled out (§ 156) who are in direct dialogue with God (§ 157) and are praised as those who "abolish the decree" and "remind (God?) of his (?) love (for Israel?),"[72] possibly a reference to the Ten Martyrs Narrative and the apocalypses. Then, quite unexpectedly, a passage follows (§ 159) praising God's countenance, a new subject in Hekhalot Rabbati. The beauty of God's countenance is so overwhelming that it has a destructive effect on the observer:

> Who looks at him [God],
> will immediately be torn;
> and who gazes at his beauty,
> will immediately be poured out like a jug.

This obviously refers back to § 104, but whereas § 104 remained vague about the addressees of this caveat (yet most likely having human beings in particular in mind), the continuation of our text makes it unequivocally clear that now it is the angels who are unable to bear God's beauty:

> Those who serve him today,
> will no longer serve him tomorrow,
> and those who serve him tomorrow,
> will no longer serve him.
> For their strength becomes weak
> and their faces grow dark,
> their hearts go astray,
> and their eyes become darkened,
> due to the embellishment
> of the splendor of the beauty of their king,
> as it is said: Holy, holy, holy (Isa. 6:3).

---

[71] Quite literally, §§ 94, 95, and 81 are quoted or alluded to in §§ 154 and 155. One major difference between these hymns and the Qedushah hymns of §§ 94–106 is the use of the term Shekhinah for God here.

[72] *Synopse zur Hekhalot-Literatur*, § 158.

So the angels (God's servants, who surround him and carry his throne) are unable to see his beauty – that is, unless they perish. But what about human beings, what about the Merkavah mystic? The text now turns to them, after once again describing the heavenly choreography of the bearers of the throne and praising them as true servants of their God (§ 160). From the liturgy of the keruvim, ofannim, and holy creatures emanate, literally, rivers of praise, but this praise of the bearers of the throne is supplemented – or more precisely, chronologically coordinated – with the Qedushah of Israel on earth. Here, slowly but unmistakably, the earthly community of Israel sneaks in; the Qedushah is no longer the heavenly Qedushah of the angels alone but the Qedushah of the angels and of Israel. To be sure, the people of Israel were also mentioned in the Qedushah hymns of §§ 94–106,[73] but now they are much more prominent and even more important than the angels. The Qedushah uttered by the throne of glory (§ 162) praises God as the "mighty of Jacob/Israel," and this praise leads to two passages (§§ 163 and 164) that are hitherto unheard of in Hekhalot Rabbati. Now, for the very first time, the Merkavah mystic is directly and bluntly addressed:

> Blessed unto heaven and earth are they who descend to the Merkavah,
> when you tell and make known to my sons
> what I do during the morning prayer, during the Minha and the evening
>   prayer,
> every day and at every hour,
> when Israel says before me "holy."
> Teach them and tell them:
> Raise your eyes to the heaven (*raqia'*) opposite your house of prayer
> at the hour when you say before me "holy."
> For I have no joy in my entire eternal house, which I created,
> except[74] at that hour,
> in which your eyes are raised to my eyes
> and my eyes are raised to your eyes,
> (namely) at the hour in which you say before me "holy."

The scenario described here is that of the Merkavah mystic in heaven, directly addressed by God and instructed as to what message he is to convey to the community of Israel on his return to earth. God wants the mystic to tell the earthly community what he does during Israel's daily prayers in their synagogues and what the mystic obviously witnesses, but, using highly dramatic delaying tactics, he does not immediately reveal what the mystic sees and what he wants him to convey to Israel; rather, he first instructs the mystic to tell the earthly community to raise their eyes to the *raqia'* – that is, to the highest heaven, God's abode – at precisely the time when they utter the Qedushah. This is unusual

---

[73] Ibid., § 101.

[74] "Except" (*ella*) according to Mss. New York 8128 and Munich 22. All the other manuscripts in the *Synopse zur Hekhalot-Literatur* leave *ella* out and distort the meaning of the sentence.

enough, because it is assumed that somehow they are expected to gaze heavenward during their prayer, presumably outside the synagogue (of course, one could argue that Israel may well see the *raqia'* within their synagogues, but the text explicitly says "opposite – *ke-neged* – your house of prayer").[75] But then God continues, even more conspicuously, that he in fact couldn't care less about Israel's synagogue service (with the synagogue suddenly called "eternal house, which I [God] created," clearly comparing or rather equating the synagogue with the Temple) except at that precise and very precious moment when Israel, during the Qedushah, looks directly into God's eyes and God looks directly into Israel's eyes.

The climax – what God does during Israel's Qedushah as observed by the mystic – comes in the following section (§ 164):

> Bear witness to them[76] of what testimony you see in me
> regarding what I do to the countenance of Jacob, your father,[77]
> which is engraved unto me upon the throne of my glory.
> For at the hour when you say before me "holy,"
> I bend down over it,
> caress, kiss and embrace it,
> and my hands (lie) upon his[78] arms,
> three times, when you say before me "holy,"
> as it is said: Holy, holy, holy (Isa. 6:3).

That the image or, more precisely, the countenance/visage of Jacob is engraved on God's throne in heaven is a well-known rabbinic tradition, attested to in a large number of Palestinian as well as Babylonian sources[79] and discussed by several scholars.[80] What is completely new, however, and unique to Hekhalot Rabbati is God's dramatic expression of love to Jacob. In a gesture that can hardly be overestimated in its erotic intimacy, he embraces and kisses the image of Jacob's countenance on his throne. Elliot Wolfson has observed that several

---

[75] I do not think that *ke-neged* here means "facing your house of prayer," a possibility we considered in *Übersetzung der Hekhalot-Literatur*, vol. 2, p. 96, n. 8.

[76] Following Mss. Vatican 228 and Budapest 238.

[77] Following Mss. New York 8128, Munich 40, Munich 22, Dropsie 436, and Budapest 238.

[78] Following Mss. Vatican 228 and Munich 22; the other manuscripts read "my arms," which does not make much sense. However, "his arms" is also not easy to understand, because it is the countenance of Jacob that is engraved on the throne, not Jacob's entire body. Wolfson, *Speculum*, p. 101, n. 129, translates "its arms," which he understands as referring to the throne.

[79] See, e.g., Fragment-Targum and Targum Pseudo Jonathan Gen. 28:12; Bereshit Rabbah 68:12; 82:2; b Hullin 91b.

[80] See most recently and comprehensively Elliot R. Wolfson, "The Image of Jacob Engraved upon the Throne: Further Reflection on the Esoteric Doctrine of the German Pietists," in idem, *Along the Path: Studies in Kabbalistic Myth, Symbolism, and Hermeneutics* (Albany: State University of New York Press, 1995), pp. 1–62; idem, *Speculum*, pp. 101 f. (with the most important references on p. 101, n. 127).

of the pronouns and suffixes employed in the text are feminine, as opposed to the masculine forms one would expect with *qelaster panim* ("countenance/visage") as the subject.[81] This can easily be explained, however, as referring to the fact that the heavenly Jacob, engraved on God's throne, is obviously visualized as the celestial representative of Israel on earth, the (feminine) *kenesset Israel* – without here venturing into the contested territory of God's sexuality and an alleged sacred union in male-female or male-male – that is, homoerotic – terms.[82] When Israel utters the Qedushah on earth, this would seem to be the message of our paragraph, God displays his overwhelming love to the image of Jacob, Israel's counterpart in heaven, which is physically closer to him than anything else. Presumably, the image is engraved on the armrests of his throne and therefore is easily touched by God when he sits down on the throne. And this is no doubt the message that God wishes the Merkavah mystic to convey to his community on earth: God is there, up in heaven; I have seen him, and he still loves us more than anything else. When we, in our synagogues, sing the Qedushah, he not only listens to us, he embraces and kisses us through the image of our father Jacob/ Israel, who is engraved on his throne in perpetual memory of God's unceasing love for us.[83]

The subject of God's preference for Israel over the angels – including his beloved holy creatures, the bearers of his throne – becomes an ever more prominent feature in subsequent sections of our microform. The holy creatures utter the secret name of God by which heaven and earth were created (§§ 165 f., 168), and their praise leads to a brief and rather fragmentary Shi'ur Qomah piece (§ 167: the distance between the throne and the figure seated on the throne, the measurement of the figure's eyes and arms, concluding with the classical quotation from Cant. 5:9–16).[84] Then the text returns to the Merkavah mystic, threatening him with severe punishment if he does not convey to the earthly community what he has heard and seen in heaven (§ 169):

> A heavenly decree (of punishment shall befall) you,
> you who descend to the Merkavah,
> if you do not report and say what you have heard,
> and if you do not testify what you have seen upon the countenance:
> countenance of elevation and might,
> of pride and eminence,
> which exalts itself,
> which raises itself,
> which rages (and) shows itself great.

---

[81] Wolfson, *Speculum*, p. 101, nn. 125, 126, 128.

[82] Wolfson, "Image of Jacob," pp. 26 ff.; idem, *Speculum*, p. 102.

[83] For an intriguing attempt to locate this passage in the cultural context of the early, pre-Iconoclast Byzantine period, see Rachel Neis, "Embracing Icons: The Face of Jacob on the Throne of God," *Images* 1 (2007), pp. 36–54.

[84] Only in Ms. Budapest 238.

The countenance shows itself mighty and great
three times daily in the heights,
and no human being knows and recognizes it,
as it is said:
Holy, holy, holy (Isa. 6:3).

This passage clearly refers back to § 159, which also praises and describes God's countenance – a countenance that cannot be perceived by the angels. Here, on the contrary, the Merkavah mystic is called on to communicate his vision to the people of Israel on earth: to be sure, no human being can perceive God's countenance, as the text emphasizes at the end, but nevertheless, the Merkavah mystic not only *does* see and perceive it, he is explicitly instructed not to keep it to himself but to reveal it to the earthly community. Unfortunately, the text fails to tell us what it is the mystic sees on God's countenance; but I have argued that it is most likely the reflection of the heavenly liturgy on God's face – God's response, so to speak, to the liturgical event taking place in heaven as expressed on his face.[85] I would even go a step further and add, in light of § 163, that God responds not only to the heavenly liturgy performed by the angels but also to the liturgy of Israel performed in their synagogues on earth. As we have learned from § 163, the heavenly liturgy is incomplete without Israel's participation (or rather, does not really count without Israel's Qedushah); therefore, God's face reacts to the full force of the combined heavenly and earthly Qedushah, and it is the Merkavah mystic's task to communicate this reaction – God's majesty and might nourished, as it were, by angelic and human praise – to his fellow Jews on earth.

The following sections (§§ 170 ff.) again praise the bearers of the divine throne (the ofannim, keruvim, and above all the holy creatures) – but also do not miss the opportunity to emphasize that God is particularly pleased with Israel's prayer and with the ascent of the Merkavah mystic to his throne (presumably because he will report all this to the earthly community). Paragraph 173 makes God's preference for Israel over the holy creatures once more explicit:

Every day when the dawn approaches,
the adorned king sits and blesses the (Holy) Creatures (*hayyot*):
To you, Creatures, do I speak,
before you, Creatures, do I make myself heard,
Creatures, Creatures,
who carry[86] the throne of my[87] glory,
wholeheartedly and gladly.

---

[85] Schäfer, *The Hidden and Manifest God*, p. 18.
[86] Following all the other manuscripts (with the exception of Munich 22), instead of the corrupt reading in Ms. Oxford 1531.
[87] According to most of the other manuscripts, instead of "his" in Ms. Oxford 1531.

> Blessed is the hour (in which) I created[88] you;
> exalted is the constellation under which I formed you.
> The light of that day shall light up,
> (that day on which) you came to mind in my heart,
> for you are (the) precious vessel
> that I have prepared and completed on that (very day).[89]
> Do silence for me[90] the voice of my creatures[91] that I created,
> so that I can hear and hearken to the prayer of my sons.

At first sight there is nothing new about this passage. It contains the usual and well-known favor that God bestows on his beloved holy creatures.[92] The setting is just before dawn, presumably immediately before the morning prayer. What is completely unexpected, however, is the sudden turn that God's speech takes at the end: despite all the hard work that the holy creatures devote to their Master (in carrying his throne), when the time for the morning prayer has come he wants them to keep all the heavenly creatures[93] silent, and themselves to remain silent, because he wants to listen first to the prayer of Israel, which is about to rise up to heaven from the earthly synagogues. If there could be any doubt that the "creatures" meant to be silenced are the heavenly creatures, two manuscripts (New York 8128 and Vatican 228) add a paragraph (§ 174) that makes God's message crystal clear: "Do silence for me the voice of the creatures that I created, (namely) every individual angel and every individual Seraph, every individual Holy Creature and every individual Ofan that I created until I can hear and hearken to the beginning of all the hymns and praises and prayers and the pleasant chant of Israel's songs." There is no doubt that when it comes to the morning prayer, God wishes to concentrate on Israel, and not on the heavenly host. The text does not tell us what happens to the angels' prayer, but we may

---

[88] So with the other manuscripts, instead of the double "formed" in Ms. Oxford 1531.

[89] Unlike the German translation (*Übersetzung der Hekhalot-Literatur*, vol. 2, p. 112), I apply the difficult *bo* not to *keli* ("vessel") but to *yom* ("day").

[90] Mss. Oxford 1531, New York 8128, Munich 40, and Dropsie 436 actually have here a subordinate clause, introduced by *ki* – "for": "for you should silence for me …," which does not fit in well with the preceding passage. I follow, therefore, Mss. Munich 22, Vatican 228, and Budapest 238 which leave out the *ki*.

[91] "Creatures" here not in the technical sense of the holy creatures but of all the heavenly creatures, including the holy creatures.

[92] What is unique, however, is that the holy creatures are called God's "precious vessel" (*keli hemdah*). This term is used in the Bible in a neutral way (see Jer. 25:34; Hos. 13:15; Nah. 2:10; 2 Chron. 32:27), but serves in the rabbinic literature as a term for the Torah (see m Avot 3:14). In the Hekhalot literature the term is assigned to the throne of glory (see, e. g., *Synopse zur Hekhalot-Literatur*, §§ 94, 154, 634, 686, 687, and Schäfer, *The Hidden and Manifest God*, pp. 13, with n. 7, 97, 118 f.). Presumably, the holy creatures become the precious vessel because they carry God's throne, but what is remarkable is the shift in emphasis from the Torah in the classical rabbinic literature to God's throne in the Hekhalot literature.

[93] This is what "creatures" can only mean in this context, as opposed to "my sons."

presume – as is made explicit in the following paragraphs[94] – that the angels are allowed to join in with Israel's prayer after Israel gets started (and after God has had a chance to listen to their voice alone).

Only when the angels in heaven have heard Israel's prayer on earth are they able to join in with their Qedushah from above (§ 179). However, since it is the (regular) angels' task to go down to earth for certain errands on behalf of God, they need to purify themselves when they return to heaven (§ 181 f.). After their purification they join the holy creatures and the other angels serving the divine throne, but they are not allowed to see the image of God seated on the throne (§ 183). The same is even true for the holy creatures: "they cover their faces[95] with lightning, and the Holy One, blessed be He, uncovers his face" (§ 184). There is nothing peculiar about this restriction: we know by now that even the angels that are closest to God (the bearers of his throne) do not really see him, quite in contrast to the Merkavah mystic. This message is reinforced by § 189, the first paragraph that is once more shared by all the major manuscripts:

> Each and every day when the Minha prayer approaches,
> (the) adorned king sits and extols the (Holy) Creatures (*hayyot*).
> Even before the speech from his mouth is completed,
> the Holy Creatures come forth from beneath the throne of glory,
> from their mouths the fullness of rejoicing,
> with their wings the fullness of exaltation;
> their hands playing (instruments)
> and their feet dancing.
> They go around and surround their king,
> one from his right and another one from his left,
> one from in front of him and another one from behind him.
> They embrace and kiss him
> and uncover their countenance;
> they[96] uncover, but the king of glory covers his countenance.
> And the *'arevot raqia'*[97] bursts open like a sieve[98]
> because of the glorious king,
> of the radiance,
> of the beauty,
> of the form,
> of the desire,

---

[94] *Synopse zur Hekhalot-Literatur*, §§ 178 ff. The paragraphs 178–188 seem to be an originally independent unit that was incorporated into Seder Rabbah di-Bereshit (Ms. Oxford 1531) and Hekhalot Rabbati (only in Mss. New York 8128 and Vatican 228); cf. Schäfer, *Hekhalot-Studien*, pp. 267 ff.

[95] So with Ms. Munich 22 (§ 534) instead of the less meaningful "his face" in Ms. New York 8128. Ms. Oxford 1531 leaves this sentence out.

[96] According to all the other manuscripts *hen*, instead of the corrupt *hu* here in Ms. Oxford 1531.

[97] That is the topmost heaven, 'Aravot.

[98] "Like a sieve" in Mss. New York 8128, Munich 40, Vatican 228, and Budapest 238.

of the compassion,
of the longing (for the) brilliance of the tiara,
in which their countenance appears,
as it is said: Holy, holy, holy (Isa. 6:3).

Whereas during the Qedushah of the morning prayer the angels and the holy creatures cover their faces and God uncovers his face (§§ 183 f.), we now learn that during the afternoon prayer's Qedushah just the opposite takes place: the holy creatures uncover their faces and God covers his face. Obviously, God does not want his face to be seen by the angels or even by the holy creatures that he explicitly extols over and over again. But apart from this message, the scene described in this paragraph gets an almost unprecedented sexual tinge: the holy creatures court God as a bridegroom courts his bride. The climax of their courtship is to embrace and kiss God and to uncover their faces – clearly in the expectation that God will respond by likewise uncovering his face and embracing and kissing them. This is sexual enough, and I think there is little need to go to the extremes of a Halperin or Wolfson, with their vaginamorphic and phallomorphic interpretations.[99] But God rejects his beloved holy creatures, whose radiant faces and desire are so forceful that they break open the highest heaven; he rebuffs them, and, in covering his face, withdraws from them. Their exuberant longing and desire do not meet with the hoped-for response.

There is only one passage in Hekhalot Rabbati (and actually in the entire Hekhalot literature) that uses similar language and imagery, and that is the passage discussed above describing what God does to the face of Jacob, engraved on his throne, when Israel utters the Qedushah on earth (§ 164): he "caresses, kisses, and embraces it." But whereas in § 164 it is God who kisses and embraces Jacob, Israel's counterpart in heaven, here it is the four holy creatures that surround God from all four sides, "embrace and kiss him," and, in so doing, eagerly uncover their faces. Hence, when God refuses to respond to their advances by covering his face, he does not just reject the courtship of the holy creatures because they are not supposed to see his face; rather, he rejects their courtship because he favors Israel over the holy creatures. This, I believe, is the true message of our paragraph, and not the sexual implications (that, to be sure, are undoubtedly present, but have been overemphasized by Halperin and Wolfson) or God's attempt to establish peace in heaven by allaying the angels' envy of their human rivals, as has been suggested by Goldberg.[100] As to the latter suggestion, just the

---

[99] David Halperin, "A Sexual Image in Hekhalot Rabbati and Its Implications," in Joseph Dan, ed., *Early Jewish Mysticism: Proceedings of the First International Conference on the History of Jewish Mysticism* (Jerusalem: Hebrew University of Jerusalem, 1987), pp. 117 ff.; Wolfson, *Speculum*, pp. 103–105.
[100] Arnold Goldberg, "Einige Bemerkungen zu den Quellen und den redaktionellen Einheiten der Grossen Hekhalot," in idem, *Mystik und Theologie des rabbinischen Judentums*, vol. 1, pp. 49–77.

opposite is true: God does not allay the angels' envy but in almost brutal fashion exposes their unwanted affection. Despite his fondness for the holy creatures in particular, when it comes to Israel, God makes it unmistakably clear once more that his real love is for Israel and Israel alone.

The following paragraph (§ 190) supports this interpretation in quite an ironical way. Although the addressees of this again highly poetical section are not explicitly mentioned, it is almost certain that the angels, including the holy creatures, are being invoked. They are addressed as those who abolish the divine decree against Israel, who remind God of his love for his people when he is angry with them:[101]

> They throw down their crowns
> and loosen their loins
> and beat their heads
> and fall upon their faces and say:
> Loosen, loosen, former of creation,
> forgive, forgive, noble one of Jacob,
> pardon, pardon, holy one of Israel,
> for you are a powerful one of the kings. ...
> Why do you feel hostility against the seed of Abraham?
> Why do you feel jealousy against the seed of Isaac?
> Why do you feel rivalry against the seed of Jacob?

After this powerful intervention of the angels on behalf of Israel, there immediately follows the divine approbation:[102]

> Blessed are you who intercede for my sons.
> Be praised, (you) who extol the fathers.

Ironic here is, first, the fact that the angels of all people ask God to restrain himself from hostility, jealousy, and rivalry toward Israel. Normally (that is, in the classical midrash as well as in the Sar ha-Torah piece of Hekhalot Rabbati) it is the angels who feel jealousy and rivalry toward Israel and whom God outmaneuvers in his undisguised love for his people.[103] Second, and more important, it is ironic that the angels and the holy creatures, whose fervent courtship God has only lately brusquely rejected in favor of Israel, now act as selfless mediators between God and his people – just as if nothing had ever happened between them and their God. In other words, in the present context, they are the most unlikely of mediators between God and Israel – but this, I posit, is precisely the punch line of our section in Hekhalot Rabbati. The angels, including the holy creatures, are indeed loved by God, yet there is no one in the entire universe that God loves

---

[101] *Synopse zur Hekhalot-Literatur*, §§ 190 f.

[102] Ibid., § 192.

[103] Classical midrash: Schäfer, *Rivalität*; Sar ha-Torah: *Synopse zur Hekhalot-Literatur*, §§ 281–306.

more than Israel. Despite the fact that nobody can see God, neither angels nor human beings, when Israel utters the Qedushah in their daily prayers, both God and Israel look each other directly in the eyes (§ 163), and the Merkavah mystic observes God kissing and caressing Jacob's face (§ 164) – in order to report this vision to his fellow Jews upon his return to earth. Ultimately, even the angels have to acknowledge Israel's superiority, and, one might add, this ultimate acknowledgment is the main reason why God loves them. Hence, it is only logical that God, toward the end of this large microform, is called the Lord, the *God of Israel* (§ 195) and that the section, harking back to § 188, concludes with the Trishagion (uttered by three classes of angels) and the response from Ezek. 3:12 (uttered by the ofannim and the holy creatures).[104]

6. The Ascent Accounts

Sections 198–268 contain what has been called the havurah account, actually a number of loosely conjoined accounts describing the particular circumstances of the Merkavah mystic's ascent(s) to heaven. The main protagonists are R. Ishmael b. Elisha (the well-known hero of Hekhalot literature) along with his teacher, R. Nehunya b. Haqanah, as well as the enigmatic "company" (*havurah*) of those who are instructed in the mysteries of the ascent. The first paragraph of our section (§ 198) explicitly connects it, through R. Nehunya b. Haqanah, with the Narrative of the Ten Martyrs (§§ 107–121). This connection is clearly superficial and made by an editor who took the persecution of Israel's famous rabbis as a pretext for Nehunya b. Haqanah's attempt to reveal the "mystery of the world," that is, initiation into the mysteries of the *yoredei merkavah*. More precisely, the text now explains the specifics of *what* the Merkavah mystic sees during his ascent, of *who* is worthy of undertaking it, and of *how* he carries out the ascent.[105]

As to the *what*, we learn that it is the goal of the mystic's ascent "to behold the king and his throne (*le-histakkel be-melekh we-kiss'o*), his majesty (*hadaro*), and his beauty (*yofyo*)," which refers back to the very beginning of Hekhalot Rabbati (§ 81) but gives more details: to behold the vision of the Merkavah (§ 81) means now to see God, in all his majesty and beauty, seated on his throne. Moreover, it includes not only seeing the holy creatures, the keruvim, and the ofannim (hardly unexpected after what we have heard in the meantime about the bearers of the throne) but also the "awesome *hashmal*" (known from Ezekiel) and the rivers of fire (known from Daniel) that surround the throne with their flames and smoke

---

[104] *Synopse zur Hekhalot-Literatur*, § 197, only in Ms. New York 8128.

[105] These specifics are all subsumed under the heading *middah* (lit. "measure, measurement"), which clearly means here something along the lines of "nature, character/characteristic, quality/qualification," or even "condition." See *Synopse zur Hekhalot-Literatur*, §§ 198, 199, 201, 234.

covering all the chambers of the palace of the highest heaven. Not least, we learn that God is accompanied by a high angel who is called Suriyah and bears the epithet "Prince of the [divine] Countenance" (*sar ha-panim*).

This is quite a program for the mystic – but *who* now is worthy of the exercise? First we are told that the Merkavah mystic is like someone (a man, a human being [*adam*]) "who has a ladder in his house upon which he ascends and descends, and there is no creature that can hinder him."[106] In other words, ascending and descending seems to be rather effortless, like going up and down a ladder in one's house. This ladder is described in more detail in § 201, where it is said that "one end of it rests upon the earth and the other end rests against the right foot of the throne of glory." Hence, the ladder in the mystic's house leads him directly to the throne of glory in the highest heaven. The second condition increases this impression of an easy job awaiting the Merkavah mystic – anybody, the text continues, is entitled to undertake the ascent[107]

who is innocent and free from
idolatry,
incest,
bloodshed,
slander,
false oaths,
desecration of the (divine) name,
impudence,
and senseless hostility,
and who observes all the positive and negative commandments.

Since God himself and his servant, the Prince of the Countenance, despise these bad qualities (§ 200),[108] someone who is not free of any of them is not entitled to undertake the heavenly journey. One would expect that the requirement of being unsullied by these negative qualities should be relatively easy to fulfill, all the more so as four of them (idolatry, incest, bloodshed, and desecration of the divine name) are part of the seven Noachide Laws, the minimal ethical demands expected of all people, also and especially of non-Jews.[109] But the requirements

---

[106] Ibid., § 199, following Mss. Munich 22, Vatican 228, and Budapest 238.

[107] Ibid.

[108] They are counted as eight in *Synopse zur Hekhalot-Literatur*, §§ 200 and 201, the last condition ("who observes all the positive and negative commandments") obviously serving as a summary of all the good requisites.

[109] Idolatry, incest, and bloodshed are the three Noachide Laws often mentioned in representation of all seven; cf. Max Kadushin, "Introduction to Rabbinic Ethics," in Menahem Haran, ed., *Yehezkel Kaufmann Jubilee Volume: Studies in Bible and Jewish Religion Dedicated to Yehezkel Kaufmann on the Occasion of His Seventieth Birthday* (Jerusalem: Magnes, 1960), p. 96. On their use in the Hekhalot literature, see Nick A. van Uchelen, "Ethical Terminology in Heykhalot-Texts," in Jan W. van Henten et al., eds., *Tradition and Re-interpretation in Jewish and Early Christian Literature: Essays in Honour of Jürgen C. H. Lebram* (Leiden: Brill, 1986), pp. 253 ff.

turn out to be not at all easy, and R. Ishmael, desperate in his fear that no human being will be able to meet them, asks R. Nehunya b. Haqanah for help, that is, to be more specific about who can undertake the journey and what precisely is required of him. Nehunya b. Haqanah follows his request and asks him to convene the members of the havurah, that distinguished society of fellows dealing with the mysteries of the Torah: they are the chosen ones to whom he will reveal all the mysteries of the cosmos and, most important, the "path of the ladder" that leads to the seventh heaven (§ 201). Apparently, this path is more complicated than it at first seemed.

R. Ishmael convenes the havurah, which is anachronistically called the greater and the lesser Sanhedrin and is located "at the third large entrance that is in the house of the Lord" – clearly referring to the Temple. Moreover, R. Ishmael is portrayed as sitting "upon a bench of pure marble that Elisha, my father, gave me from my mother's property that she had transferred to him in her dowry" (§ 202). This is a remarkable pseudohistorical setting, the main elements of which are the location in the Temple, the bench of pure marble, and the explicit genealogy of R. Ishmael. The allusion to the Temple serves as a hint that the mystic's ascent to the seventh heaven is nothing less than an ascent to the heavenly Temple: R. Ishmael sits on a bench at the entrance to the Temple gate to receive instruction, together with the rabbinic fellowship, from R. Nehunya b. Haqanah; accordingly, the (successful) mystic will be able to enter the seventh heaven, which is the heavenly Temple. And indeed, in § 233 we learn that the angel Dumiel sits at the entrance to the sixth palace on a "bench of pure stone" and invites the worthy mystic to sit down next to him. The mystic who has successfully made it to this point will be immediately escorted into the seventh palace. And finally, the explicit mention of R. Ishmael's genealogy reinforces the link with the Temple: according to the Tosefta, R. Ishmael's father was a high priest and R. Ishmael consequently of high priestly lineage;[110] the Bavli even transmits a Baraitha according to which R. Ishmael officiated as high priest in the innermost Sanctuary.[111] Historically dubious as these puzzling pieces of information are, there can be no doubt that the editor(s) of Hekhalot Rabbati sought to make precisely this connection between the earthly and heavenly Temples,[112] for the ascent of the Merkavah mystic through the seven palaces/heavens imitates, or rather replays, the high priest's entering the Temple, from the vestibule through the nave to the Holy of Holies.

---

[110] t Hallah 1:10.

[111] b Berakhot 7a; almost verbatim in Hekhalot Rabbati, *Synopse zur Hekhalot-Literatur*, § 151.

[112] See the detailed analysis in Boustan, *From Martyr to Mystic*, pp. 102 ff., 252 ff.

The composition of the havurah fellowship is no less anachronistic than the setting of the scene in the Temple; it consists of a list of nine[113] names that are chronologically ill-fitting but almost identical with the names of the ten martyrs.[114] This latter connection, obviously, is the reason for the composition of the havurah and certainly not an attempt to provide historically accurate information. The same is true, I posit, for the peculiar makeup of the havurah during R. Nehunya b. Haqanah's instruction, one of the major scenes preserved in the Hekhalot literature. We are told (§ 203) that the havurah consists of an inner and outer circle: the inner circle includes only the ten "rabbis" listed previously, and the outer circle involves a much larger audience, referred to as "the entire multitude of the fellows"; whereas the former are allowed to sit down, together with R. Nehunya b. Haqanah, the latter must remain on their feet "for they saw pans of fire[115] and torches of light that separated them from us." Taking into consideration the deliberately pseudohistorical setting of the whole instruction scene, I find it pointless to try to discover here some kind of historical reality, lurking behind this description, of the true Merkavah mystics and their original practices (for example, of an inner circle of initiates and an outer one of more loosely affiliated fellows).[116] The scene is a fiction, and the editor is aware of it.

The following ascent account – more precisely, an ascent account that is repeatedly interrupted by other material and most likely composed of fragments of diverse literary origin – is presented as the contents of R. Nehunya b. Haqanah's instruction to the havurah:[117]

> R. Nehunya ben Haqanah sat and expounded[118] before them all the matters
>   pertaining to the Merkavah,
> descent and ascent (*yeridah we-'aliyyah*),
> how one who descends should descend
> and how one who ascends should ascend.

The first explicit answer to the *how* of the ascent (§ 204) is quite surprising in light of the carefully arranged setting of the havurah at the Temple gate. To begin with, R. Nehunya b. Haqanah does not say to the fellows of the havurah, as we might expect: If one of you, my dear friends, attempts to undertake the descent, do such and such; rather, he says: "if a person (literally: a man, a human being [*adam*]) wishes to descend to the Merkavah ..." – evidently referring back to the

---

[113] Of course, R. Ishmael has to be added here, so that altogether they are ten fellows in number.

[114] *Synopse zur Hekhalot-Literatur*, § 109, Mss. New York 8128 and Vatican 228.

[115] For the difficult reading according to the manuscripts, see *Übersetzung der Hekhalot-Literatur*, vol. 2, p. 148, n. 18.

[116] As has been suggested by, e.g., Gruenwald, *Apocalyptic and Merkavah Mysticism*, p. 162.

[117] *Synopse zur Hekhalot-Literatur*, § 203.

[118] Lit. "ordered, arranged" (*mesadder*).

more neutral "man" with the ladder in his house (§ 199). Here is clear evidence that this instruction originally had nothing to do with the havurah setting but was combined with it by the editor. Furthermore, the instructor tells the adept, quite surprisingly, to call Suriyah, the Prince of the Countenance (of whom we have heard already), and to adjure him 112 times with several versions of the divine name, most prominent among them Tutrusiay (with variations).[119] So, what we learn here is something completely new, namely, that the ascent is achieved by an adjuration (the technical term used is *le-hashbia'* – "to adjure, to conjure up"). To be sure, the adjuration is an important part of the Hekhalot literature – its main purpose being to bring an angel down to earth so as to force him, by magical means, to do the will of the adept – but we would not expect it as a major lever, as it were, in the Merkavah mystic's successful ascent. I have argued elsewhere that the prominent place it takes at the very beginning of Hekhalot Rabbati's ascent account makes it virtually impossible to distinguish neatly between the "heavenly journey" as one (and, as many scholars want it, early) layer of the Hekhalot literature and the "adjuration" as another (and later, presumably even degenerate) layer.[120] The ascent and the adjuration are intrinsically interlinked, and it makes little sense to separate them neatly and assign them to clearly distinguishable layers that belong to different stages of development within the Hekhalot literature.

The following paragraph (§ 205) emphasizes the magical character of this second ascent account. It is extremely important, we are told, that the adept counts 112 times when uttering the divine names, for if he leaves out even one name or adds another, "his blood will be on his head" (Jos. 2:19), that is, he will immediately die. Magic works only if executed properly. Accordingly, the successful mystic not only descends to the Merkavah, as might be expected, but he also "has power over the Merkavah (*sholet ba-merkavah*)." This again is unheard of, since nothing we have been told so far about the Merkavah mystic and the havurah has prepared us for such an unabashed wish for power over the Merkavah.

Paragraphs 206–218 report another important detail for a successful ascent: the names of the guardian angels at the entrances of the first six palaces. We are told that God (again called by the name Tutrusiay) sits within seven palaces (*hekhalot*), "a chamber (*heder*) within a chamber (*heder*)," and that each palace is guarded by eight angels, four to each side of the entrance door (§ 206). How precisely God's location is to be understood – in each of the seven palaces, or

---

[119] Presumably derived from Greek *tetras* ("four") and alluding to the four-letter-name of God, the Tetragrammaton.

[120] Peter Schäfer, "Merkavah Mysticism and Magic," in Peter Schäfer and Joseph Dan, eds., *Gershom Scholem's Major Trends in Jewish Mysticism: 50 Years After. Proceedings of the Sixth International Conference on the History of Jewish Mysticism* (Tübingen: J.C.B. Mohr [Paul Siebeck], 1993), pp. 64 ff. On the adjuration in general, see Rebecca M. Lesses, *Ritual Practices to Gain Power: Angels, Incantations, and Revelation in Early Jewish Mysticism* (Harrisburg, PA: Trinity Press International, 1998).

merely in the seventh palace? – remains open, but the most likely explanation seems to me that he is envisioned as sitting in the seventh palace, which is surrounded, in concentric circles, by the other six palaces.[121] God's location is not the main issue here; rather, our editor is primarily concerned with presenting the proper names of the guardian angels at the entrances of the palaces.[122] The editor does not even bother to tell us why these names are important, but we may safely assume that the mystic needs to know them in order to accomplish his ascent successfully.

Having carefully listed the names of the guardian angels of the first six palaces, the editor breaks off his account of the names (skipping the names of the guardians of the seventh palace) and instead gives a graphic description of the guardians of the seventh palace and their huge horses, which eat glowing coals from their mangers and drink from rivers of fire (§§ 213–215). Apparently, the lack of knowledge of the guardians' names and their horrible appearance does not impede the mystic: he suffers no harm, we are informed, but "descends" in peace (§ 216). But the climax of this (second) ascent account is rather counterintuitive: the mystics "witness an awesome and terrible vision (*re'iyyah*), something that is not to be found in any palace of kings of flesh and blood," yet what precisely they see, we are not told. Having achieved their goal, they immediately burst into praise of God (again by the name Tutrusiay), and the editor finds it more important to add that God "is gladdened by those who descend to the Merkavah," that in fact he "sits and awaits each and every one from Israel" (§ 216):

> When does he descend
> in wondrous pride
> and special authority,
> in the pride of elevation
> and (in the) authority of sublimity
> that rush forth before the throne of glory
> three times daily in the height,
> from the day the world was created and until now,
> for praise.

This paragraph is almost identical to § 200, where it is said that the mystic descends and *gazes* at the wondrous pride and other qualities that three times daily rush forth before the throne of glory. Hence, what is actually happening here, at the climax of the mystic's vision, is his witnessing and apparently joining in with the liturgy carried out in heaven. Observation of and participation in the heavenly liturgy seems to be the goal of the mystic's vision – not viewing the physical

---

[121] Like the arrangement of the seven heavens and seven netherworlds; see Schäfer, "In Heaven as It Is in Hell," pp. 273 ff.

[122] The scribe of Ms. Oxford even notices, correctly so, that for each palace 2 × 4 = 8 guardian angels are mentioned, except for the third (only 7) and the fifth palace (9).

features of God. And this is also the reason why God is so happy about the ascent of the mystic: he wants him to see what transpires in heaven around his throne, because, we may add, he wants him to report this to the earthly community of Israel (a subject with which we are well acquainted by now). And indeed, after extended praise of God as king (§ 217), the text returns to God's longing for the Merkavah mystic (§ 218):

> Tutrusiay, the Lord, the God of Israel,
> desires and awaits (the mystic)
> inasmuch as he awaits the redemption and the time of salvation
> that is preserved for Israel
> after the destruction of the second, (the) last temple:
> When will he descend, he who descends to the Merkavah?
> When will he see the pride of the heights?
> When will he hear the ultimate salvation?
> When will he see (what) no eye has (ever) seen?
> When will he (again) ascend
> and proclaim (this) to the seed of Abraham, his beloved?

God longs passionately and impatiently for the Merkavah mystic because he expects him to return[123] to earth and report what he has seen to the "seed of Abraham," that is, to the community of Israel. Again, what precisely it is that he has seen is only alluded to – "the pride of the heights," obviously the heavenly liturgy. More importantly, in referring twice to the redemption or salvation (God awaits the mystic as eagerly as he awaits Israel's redemption, and the mystic hears the "ultimate salvation" – *qetz yeshu'ah*) this paragraph clearly hints at the possibility that in fact the events around the throne of glory – the heavenly liturgy – together with its necessary counterpart on earth represent the salvation or even replace the redemption in the traditional sense of the word.[124] What the mystic sees in heaven and what he communicates to his fellow Jews on earth *is* redemption: when God and Israel are united in their liturgical exchange, redemption takes place. The traditional Messiah has become superfluous, or rather, the Merkavah mystic becomes the Messiah who announces the divine message to the people of Israel. This result tallies with what we have observed above about the Messiah and messianic expectation in Hekhalot Rabbati.

With § 219 begins yet another lengthy ascent account that apparently ends with § 237; that it is a distinct literary unit becomes clear from the fact that it presents itself in the second person singular (instead of the third person singular in the ascent account of §§ 204–218). This account directly addresses the prospective Merkavah mystic and instructs him about the seals he needs when en-

---

[123] Note again the reverse terminology: descent for the ascent and ascent for the descent.

[124] Accordingly, God's longing for the Merkavah mystic in the same way as he longs for Israel's salvation is not just meant as a comparison; actually, he longs for the Merkavah mystic because the message that he will bring to the people of Israel *is* the salvation.

tering the entrances of the heavenly palaces. We have not heard about seals as a prerequisite for a successful ascent before (further indication that the ascent account is an originally independent unit that was inserted here by an editor), and we are also not told what kind of seals our author/editor has in mind. But since the mystic is advised to take the seals in his hands and since names are to be written on them, they must be some magical device, presumably a tablet or a piece of parchment/paper. The mystic needs two seals, one for each hand, with two different names for each of the palaces (so altogether, one might conclude – although this is never made explicit – fourteen seals). In all cases, one of the two seals contains a name of God (beginning, at the first palace, with Tutrusiay) and the other one a name of his Prince of the Countenance (beginning, at the first palace, with Suriyah).[125] The seal with God's name must always be presented to the guardian angels at the right of the entrance gate and the seal with the Prince of the Countenance's name to the guardian angels at the left. If the mystic presents the correct seals, the guardian angels of the respective gates lead him to the next gate. We are not told what happens when the seals are incorrect, but we may safely assume that in this case the guardian angels will kill the mystic.

This procedure is described in quite stereotypical terms until the mystic has reached the fifth palace, has shown the proper seals, and can expect to be led to the guardian angels of the sixth palace – but in all the manuscripts of the *Synopse* the procedure breaks off here (§ 223, end: the text literally breaks off in the middle of a sentence) and is interrupted by some additional material about the irrational behavior of the guardians of the sixth palace and the recall of R. Nehunya b. Haqanah from his vision of the Merkavah in order to explain this irrational behavior (§§ 224–228). The instruction about the seals is resumed in § 229, where suddenly three seals are required for the sixth palace. The guardian angels of this sixth palace are Qatzpiel and Dumiel (with some confusion about who is placed to the right and who to the left of the entrance gate),[126] later supplemented with Gabriel (§§ 235 f.)[127] I have argued elsewhere that the interruption of the instruction about the seals and the insertion of the additional material in the manuscripts of the *Synopse* is the result of an editorial process in Hekhalot Rabbati and that the originally unbroken sequence from the fifth to the sixth pal-

---

[125] Both names are most prominent in Hekhalot Rabbati.

[126] In *Synopse zur Hekhalot-Literatur*, § 229, Qatzpiel is located at the right side of the gate, whereas according to § 233 this place of honor is allocated to Dumiel. Since Dumiel is clearly superior to Qatzpiel (and the more benevolent angel, whereas Qatzpiel – as his name, derived from *qetzef* ["anger, wrath"], says – is less inclined to let the mystic pass), he is the better candidate for the right side. § 230 tries to explain the contradiction by arguing that Dumiel was actually displaced by the envious Qatzpiel from his hereditary place on the right side of the gate but – since his name is derived from *dumah* ("silence") – let this happen.

[127] This is probably the reason for the three seals.

ace is preserved in a Genizah fragment that does not show any indication of the additional material peculiar to the final form of Hekhalot Rabbati.[128]

The editor of Hekhalot Rabbati uses the allegedly irrational behavior of the guardian angels of the sixth palace (they tend to let pass the mystics, who undertake their ascent without permission, and to kill the "real" mystics, presumably those undertaking their ascent with permission) to insert the famous and much discussed story about R. Nehunya b. Haqanah's recall from the Merkavah.[129] Nehunya b. Haqanah has frequently been portrayed as the enigmatic master of the mysteries of the Merkavah: when he hears about the decree against the rabbinic martyrs, he leads R. Ishmael down to the Merkavah (§ 108); he expounds before the members of the havurah "all the matters pertaining to the Merkavah" (§ 203) and he instructs R. Ishmael concerning the seals to be shown to the guardian angels at the entrance gates of the seven palaces (§ 206). Now we learn that he is actually engaged in a vision (*tzefiyyah*) of the Merkavah (§ 225). How he got there and what he sees we are not (yet) told (but see below): the members of the havurah just want him to come back, to sit with them, and to explain to them the strange behavior of the angels.

To achieve their goal, they prepare – in an extremely complicated procedure – a piece of fine wool in such a way that it is imbued with an almost unnoticeable, if at all valid, impurity and inflict this doubtful impurity upon R. Nehunya b. Haqanah by putting the piece of wool on his knees (§ 227). The very fact that they are able to apply the dubious impurity to R. Nehunya, that is, to touch him with that "impure" piece of wool, presupposes that the rabbi-mystic was physically present among them during his vision of the Merkavah. If this assumption is correct, the conclusion can hardly be avoided that Nehunya b. Haqanah's vision of the Merkavah must have been solely a mental experience, with his body still remaining on earth, among the members of the havurah. This is a far-reaching conclusion because nothing that we have heard so far about the ascent of the Merkavah mystic indicates that his ascent is meant to be a purely spiritual experience – an ascent of the soul without the body. In fact, R. Nehunya b. Haqanah's recall from the Merkavah is the only passage in the entire corpus of the Hekhalot literature that suggests such a distinction between the mystic's body and soul.[130] To put it differently, if we did not know the story about Ne-

---

[128] Peter Schäfer, "Ein neues *Hekhalot Rabbati*-Fragment," in idem, *Hekhalot-Studien*, pp. 96–103.

[129] See in particular Margarete Schlüter, "Die Erzählung von der Rückholung des R. Nehunya ben Haqana aus der *Merkava*-Schau in ihrem redaktionellen Rahmen," *FJB* 10 (1982), pp. 65–109; Lawrence H. Schiffman, "The Recall of Rabbi Nehuniah ben Ha-Qanah from Ecstasy in Hekhalot Rabbati," *AJS Review* 1 (1976), pp. 269–281; *Übersetzung der Hekhalot-Literatur*, vol. 2, p. 179, n. 1.

[130] With the possible exception of *Synopse zur Hekhalot-Literatur*, § 93 (above, p. 253). The most explicit reference to a purely spiritual experience can be found in one of the ascent apocalypses; see Ascension of Isaiah 6:13–16 (above, chapter 3, pp. 94 ff.), where it is explic-

hunya b. Haqanah, it would not occur to us that the mystic's ascent to heaven is envisioned as just a spiritual experience and not as a journey involving the entire person of the initiate, composed of body and soul. I would not, therefore, want to place too much emphasis on the Nehunya b. Haqanah episode, keeping in mind also that it is clearly a secondary redactional insertion in the instruction regarding the seals.[131]

The procedure so meticulously employed by the members of the havurah turns out to be successful (§ 227):

> Immediately they dismissed him [Nehunya b. Haqanah] from (his place) be-
>   fore the throne of glory
> (where) he had been sitting and seeing
> (the) wondrous pride
> and special authority,
> the pride of the elevation
> and the authority of sublimity
> that rush forth before the throne of glory
> three times day after day
> in the height,
> from the day the world was created and until now,
> for praise.

We recall that what R. Nehunya b. Haqanah has been encountering in heaven is precisely the experience promised to the successful Merkavah mystic (§ 200), whom God so impatiently awaits (§§ 216, 218). Hence, the master of the mysteries of the Merkavah is obviously released not from a vision of God but again from some kind of liturgical activity taking place in heaven, around the throne of glory.

Returning now to the seals of the guardian angels of the sixth palace, Dumiel and Qatzpiel, the narrator continues his ascent account. When the mystic has presented the correct seals, Qatzpiel brings a "stormy wind" (*ruah se'arah*) to him and has him sit down "in a wagon of radiance" (*qaron shel nogah*) – a clear reference to the "stormy wind ... surrounded by a radiance" in Ezek. 1:4 (§ 231). The successful adept becomes a kind of *Ezekiel redivivus*, but of a different order: whereas Ezekiel, standing on earth, sees the stormy wind and the radiance out of which the four creatures that carry the throne of God manifest themselves, our mystic is seated in a radiant wagon – the text carefully avoiding the term *merkavah* here, but the allusion is unmistakable – that will bring him to God's merkavah-throne in the seventh palace.

But the mystic has not yet reached the goal of his desire (our narrator displays quite a sense of suspense in approaching the climax of his account). Dumiel, the

---

itly stated that Isaiah's "spirit" is "taken up from him," that is, that he ascended in his spirit only and not in his body.

[131] With this observation I qualify my remark above, pp. 95, 111.

other guardian angel of the sixth palace, seizes a gift (*doron*) and walks in front of the mystic's wagon (§ 231). We are not (yet) told what this gift is; instead we learn that Dumiel invites the mystic to sit down next to him on the "bench of pure stone" at the entrance to the sixth palace. There, in an intimate scene, he explains to him what the mystic's prerequisites are to accomplish his ascent. The angel uses the same word for "prerequisite" that we encountered above (§§ 198, 199, 201) – *middah* ("quality") – but now he becomes much more specific. Now it is not just observance of the Noachide Laws, supplemented by certain other legal requirements, but the heavy weight of the full rabbinic curriculum: knowledge of the threefold canon of the Hebrew Bible (Torah, Prophets, and Writings), of Mishnah and Midrash, of Halakhot and Aggadot, of everything that goes back to Moses on Mount Sinai (§ 234). In other words, the entrance ticket to the seventh palace is nothing less than rabbinic erudition in its fullest sense of the word. If the mystic convinces Dumiel that he possesses these qualities, he orders Gabriel, the scribe, to write the following on a piece of paper, which he attaches to the mast of the mystic's wagon (§ 235):

> Such and such is the teaching of so-and-so,
> such and such are his deeds.
> He requests (permission) to enter before the throne of glory.

Apparently, the piece of paper summarizing Torah knowledge and the merits of the adept is the "gift" that Dumiel gives the mystic and that guarantees his entrance into the seventh palace. And indeed, the frightening guardian angels of the seventh palace capitulate and allow the mystic to pass (§ 236). Yet this is quite an unexpected turn – after all the instructions we have heard as to the proper seals that the adept must present to the guardian angels of all the seven palaces. Full knowledge of the Torah in the true rabbinic sense of the word does the trick – and not a single word, at the highest palace / heaven with God's throne, about seals with the proper names of God and his Prince of the Countenance. An editor of our text must have sensed this tension and added: "Nevertheless, he must show them [the guardian angels] the great seal (*hotam gadol*) and the awful crown (*keter nora*)" (followed by names of God). The "great seal" and the "awful crown" are well-known magical tools, consisting of names of God, that are explained in greater detail in a microform that is also part of Hekhalot Rabbati (§§ 318–321). Clearly, the editor who added this magical tool wished to emphasize that traditional rabbinic Torah knowledge is *not* enough to accomplish the ascent; magic is an essential part of it. In presenting, at the entrance of the seventh and last palace, not just two seals but the "great seal" and the "awful crown" – the epitome of magical seals – the mystic summons the most powerful weapon at his disposal against the threatening weapons of the guardian angels.

Now he is in, or more precisely, he is led in by the angels Dumiel, Qatzpiel, and Gabriel. They not only accompany him till the very last moment but sing before him and have him sit down together with the keruvim, the ofannim, and the holy creatures (§ 236). As we recall, the keruvim, ofannim, and the holy creatures are the bearers of the throne who play so prominent a role in Hekhalot Rabbati and whom God loves so much – but, as we have seen, not as much as Israel. So, being seated together with the bearers of God's throne is probably the highest honor that a human being can expect in heaven. However, what is conspicuously missing here, at the climax of our ascent account, is God. There is definitely no vision of God; God is not even mentioned, just his throne and the bearers of the throne. This is remarkable enough. And what does our mystic see? Our narrator, once again a master of suspense, does not leave us in the dark – or so he pretends:

> And he sees wonders and mighty deeds,
> pride and greatness,
> holiness and purity,
> terror, humility and honesty at that hour.

After all the efforts and dangers the mystic has taken upon himself to reach his desired goal, this is quite an anticlimax. He and we are left, at the very peak of the ascent account, as it were, with almost nothing – unless we wish to see in the terms used another hint of the liturgical activity taking place around the throne of glory (which remains vague but is certainly possible).[132] The editor did not bother to be more explicit. He ends his ascent account (§ 237) with another reference to the ladder and assures us of the fact that it is ultimately the members of the havurah – and not just hoi polloi – who have that ladder in their house and make adequate use of it.

Not content with the outcome of this heavenly journey, our narrator continues by adding yet another (fragment of an) ascent account (§§ 238–257). He combines this new account with the previous section by pointing to the fact that R. Nehunya b. Haqanah "forgot" to mention the proper seals for the entrance into the seventh palace (§ 238).[133] Nehunya b. Haqanah, rebuked by R. Ishmael for this dangerous omission, duly makes up for it and passes on to all the members of the havurah not the *seals*, as we would expect, but the *names* of the guardian angels of the seventh palace. This is a clear indication that we are indeed dealing with the fragment of a separate ascent account, inserted here by our editor/ narrator. So frightening are these names that the members of the havurah fall upon their faces when R. Nehunya utters them (§ 240). The list consists of eight names with gradually intensifying epithets and culminates in the name of the angel Anafiel (§ 241), another Prince of the Countenance, of whom it is said

---

[132] The term "pride" (*ge'awah*) also appears prominently in the other descriptions of what the mystic sees (*Synopse zur Hekhalot-Literatur*, §§ 200, 216, 218, 227).

[133] The seals are explicitly mentioned only in Mss. Munich 22 and Budapest 238, but it is clear that they are the necessary link with the preceding account.

that even the angels prostrate before him, with special permission from God (§ 242). Moreover, the names differ for the mystic's ascent and his descent: the list for the descent (§ 243) also consists of eight names – culminating again with Anafiel – each of which, however, is assigned a second name (so we count altogether sixteen names), probably pointing to the fact that the descent is even more dangerous for the mystic than the ascent. Here Anafiel is undoubtedly the highest and most important angel holding the key to the entrance into the seventh and final palace (§ 244). Now, having passed the guardian angels of the seventh palace and standing in the open door to the seventh palace, the mystic encounters the horrible sight of the multiple faces, wings, and eyes of the holy creatures (§§ 245 ff.). Their eyes in particular (counting altogether 512) frighten the poor adept because they are wide open and directly pointed at him (§ 247). Whatever the meaning is of these widely opened eyes,[134] the mystic is frightened to death and collapses into unconsciousness. But Anafiel and all the guardian angels of the seven palaces that he has passed support him and promise him (§ 248):

> Do not be afraid, son of the beloved seed,
> enter and see the king in his beauty.
> You shall be neither destroyed nor burned up.

And so it happens. The holy creatures cover their faces, the keruvim and ofannim turn away, "and he enters and stands before the throne of glory" (§ 250). Another climax and yet another disappointment – at least for the reader of this ascent account. Because, after the promising announcement that the mystic will "see the king in his beauty," what actually happens is that he "stands before the throne of glory," and again no vision of God is communicated. Instead, the mystic intones a hymn, and not just any hymn but the hymn that the throne of glory sings every day (§ 251). This hymn goes on and on, focusing on God as king (§§ 251–257). So we are again confronted with the fact that at the climax of the mystic's heavenly journey stands a liturgical act, no vision in the proper sense of the word. Since the mystic's hymn is identical with the hymn of the throne of glory, there can be no doubt that the mystic participates in the heavenly liturgy surrounding the throne of glory, or, more precisely, that the mystic participates in the liturgy performed by the throne, the "creature" (as we have seen, the throne becomes personified in Hekhalot Rabbati)[135] closest to God. And indeed, the

---

[134] The eyes, of course, are reminiscent of the eyes on the wheels' rims in Ezekiel (Ezek. 1:18). The strange phrase that they are "ripped open (as wide) as a large sieve of the ones who understand/winnowers" (see *Übersetzung der Hekhalot-Literatur*, vol. 2, p. 221, nn. 13 and 15) has been explained by Halperin as a reference to the vagina (*The Faces of the Chariot*, pp. 393–396). According to Halperin, the poor adept is actually "confronted with five hundred and twelve gigantic vaginas staring at him" (ibid., p. 395).

[135] See above, p. 254.

various ascent accounts combined by our editor/narrator within the framework of the havurah conclude with the praise of the throne of glory (§§ 267–268).[136]

In conclusion, all the fragments of ascent accounts presented in Hekhalot Rabbati have in common that they climax not in a vision – certainly not a vision of the physical appearance of God – but in a liturgical performance taking place in heaven and focusing on the immediate surroundings of the throne of glory. The mystic, having finally reached his desired destination, becomes part of and joins in with the liturgy of the angels. Standing directly before the throne of glory, he comes as close to these liturgical events as one can get. Yet this closeness is not a physical closeness to God; there is no trace whatsoever of a *unio mystica*, a mystical union in the physical sense of the word between the mystic and God. Rather, as I have argued elsewhere[137] – and I still can think of no better phrase to describe the phenomenon we are confronting here – what takes place in heaven is a *unio liturgica*: a liturgical union, or communion, of the Merkavah mystic with God.

Several of the ascent accounts and related texts make it abundantly clear that the heavenly liturgy is not conceived as an isolated act, limited to God's entourage in heaven with the mystic participating; on the contrary, it is seen as the combined effort of the angels in heaven and Israel on earth – with a clear preference, on the part of God, for Israel. However much God loves the bearers of his throne and the (personified) throne "himself," his true and overwhelming love is reserved for the community of Israel on earth. And this is precisely the message that the ascent accounts, the way they are set out in an overarching narrative by the editor of Hekhalot Rabbati, want to convey: God continues to love Israel, even though the earthly Temple is destroyed and the Merkavah mystic must ascend to heaven to visit God in the innermost chambers of the seventh palace/heaven, and it is only this love that matters. In fact, the confirmation of this love that the Merkavah mystic brings down to his fellow Jews on earth is the ultimate sign of salvation. Redemption in the traditional sense of the word recedes into the background. The Merkavah mystic becomes the harbinger of redemption if not the new Messiah himself, who brings the new Gospel of redemption to the people of Israel.[138]

---

[136] The heavenly praise of the mystic and the throne is interrupted by a fragment describing the test that the mystic undergoes at the entrance to the sixth (!) palace (*Synopse zur Hekhalot-Literatur*, §§ 258–259). It is clearly out of place here and also integrated in Hekhalot Zutarti (§§ 407–410); see below, pp. 298 f.

[137] Schäfer, *The Hidden and Manifest God*, p. 165.

[138] Since the material collected in the havurah account has clearly undergone some kind of Ashkenazi redaction, it may even be that the eschatology deployed in Hekhalot Rabbati has been influenced by the "presentic" eschatology so characteristic of the writings of the Hasidei Ashkenaz; on the latter, see Peter Schäfer, "The Ideal of Piety of the Ashkenazi Hasidim and Its Roots in Jewish Tradition," *JH* 4 (1990), pp. 9–23.

The following microforms in Hekhalot Rabbati are not of particular concern for our purpose. They consist of hymns praising God (§§ 269–276), a short piece about Metatron (§ 277) and, above all, units presenting magical tools to militate against the rabbinic and, even more so, the Merkavah mystical trauma of forgetting the Torah, that is, of forgetting the Torah curriculum that one has so laboriously studied. The latter begin with a piece in which Hekhalot Rabbati's hero, R. Nehunya b. Haqanah, adjures R. Ishmael with the "great seal and the great oath" (§§ 278–280). Again, this scene anachronistically takes place in the Temple and proves to be successful. It leads into the famous Sar ha-Torah ("Prince of the Torah") section (§§ 281–294) in which Israel, against the fierce opposition of the angels, receives the "mystery" (*raz*) of mastering the Torah in its fullest and, indeed, magical sense of the word: no longer does Israel acquire command of the Torah through the toil and labor of arduous study but through "the name of this seal and through the mentioning of my crown" (§ 289),[139] the well-known magical tools.[140] The Sar ha-Torah traditions (more material about the adjuration of the Prince of the Torah) continue with § 297 and are completed with § 306, the end of Hekhalot Rabbati in the majority of manuscripts.

Hekhalot Zutarti

If Hekhalot Rabbati proves to be a loosely edited text kept together more or less successfully by the attempts of an editor to integrate its most essential parts into a narrative framework (mainly of the havurah), this lack of "literary identity" applies all the more so to the "work" conventionally dubbed Hekhalot Zutarti ("The Lesser Palaces"). There is even less of a unified structure in Hekhalot Zutarti than in Hekhalot Rabbati; rather, the text presents a large number of different themes and literary genres that have been characterized, quite rightly, as "something of a hodgepodge."[141]

The macroform Hekhalot Zutarti covers the paragraphs 335–517 according to the *Synopse*, but the respective manuscripts vary considerably with regard to the microforms they include.[142] And again, Ms. New York 8128 in particular interpolates a great deal of distinct material[143] that is largely characterized by its pref-

[139] Some manuscripts: "awful crown."
[140] On this unit and related sections, see Schäfer, *Hekhalot-Studien*, pp. 269–272; idem, *The Hidden and Manifest God*, pp. 49–53; Halperin, *The Faces of the Chariot*, pp. 429–446.
[141] Scholem, *Jewish Gnosticism*, p. 83.
[142] See the chart in *Synopse zur Hekhalot-Literatur*, p. XXIV, and the detailed analyses in Peter Schäfer, "Aufbau und redaktionelle Identität der *Hekhalot Zutarti*," in idem, *Hekhalot-Studien*, pp. 50–62; idem, *Übersetzung der Hekhalot-Literatur*, vol. 3: §§ 335–597 (Tübingen: J.C.B. Mohr [Paul Siebeck], 1989), pp. VII–XXVII.
[143] But also Ms. Munich 22 (yet material of a different character); see the respective charts.

erence for magical traditions, which allows us to speak of a "magical redaction" of the New York manuscript.[144] The macroform is preceded by Hekhalot Rabbati in its largest extent and followed by the much better structured macroform Ma'aseh Merkavah ("The Work of the Chariot").[145] As mentioned above, I tend to believe that, in the chronological sequence of Hekhalot texts, the macroform Hekhalot Zutarti follows Hekhalot Rabbati, not the other way around, and that, as with Hekhalot Rabbati, a Babylonian redaction ought to be considered.[146]

The following major microforms are loosely combined in Hekhalot Zutarti.[147] The macroform begins with (1) various fragments of ascent accounts (§§ 335–374), followed by (2) extensive pieces only in Ms. New York 8128[148] about Shi'ur Qomah and Metatron (§§ 375–406). The third microform deals with (3) the test to be passed by the mystic and his ascent (§§ 407–424), with some obvious parallels in Hekhalot Rabbati, closing with paragraphs (§§ 425 f. and 427 f.), which lead into the following microforms.[149] Next comes a microform (4) about the mysterious book and the knowledge of the divine name (§§ 489–495), and then the macroform concludes with (5) a final microform that appears differently in the various manuscripts (§§ 498–499 in the majority of manuscripts, but with additional material particularly again in Ms. New York 8128).[150] I will review all the respective microforms in the order in which they appear in the manuscripts of the *Synopse*.

1. §§ 335–374: Ascent Accounts

The first microform of Hekhalot Zutarti begins with the programmatic paragraph (§ 335):[151]

> If you want to be singled out (*le-hityahed*) in the world
> so that the secrets of the world and the mysteries of wisdom
> will be revealed to you,

---

[144] *Übersetzung der Hekhalot-Literatur*, vol. 3, p. XIII; Herrmann and Rohrbacher-Sticker, "Magische Traditionen," pp. 101–149.

[145] See the overview in *Übersetzung der Hekhalot-Literatur*, vol. 3, pp. XXVII–XLI.

[146] *Übersetzung der Hekhalot-Literatur*, vol. 3, pp. XVI f.

[147] See the overview in *Hekhalot-Studien*, pp. 51–54, and in *Übersetzung der Hekhalot-Literatur*, vol. 3, pp. XVII–XXVII.

[148] With parallels, however, in the other manuscripts in different contexts.

[149] *Synopse zur Hekhalot-Literatur*, §§ 425 f., lead into §§ 489–495, the next microform in all the manuscripts (except for Ms. Munich 22), and §§ 427 f. into §§ 429–467, the cosmological Seder Rabbah di-Bereshit macroform, followed by Shi'ur Qomah and Metatron pieces (§§ 468–488), both in this connection only in Ms. Munich 22.

[150] Mss. Oxford 1531 and New York 8128 share §§ 501 and 512, whereas §§ 502–511 and 513–517 are preserved only in Ms. New York; Ms. Munich 22 adds yet another piece of Seder Rabbah di-Bereshit material (§§ 518–540).

[151] Only Ms. New York 8128 regards this paragraph, clearly erroneously, as the last paragraph of Hekhalot Rabbati instead of the beginning of Hekhalot Zutarti.

study this mishnah and be careful about it until the day of your passing.[152]
Do not (try to) understand what comes after you
and do not explore the words of your lips.
You should (try to) understand that what is in your heart
and keep silent (about it)
so that you will be worthy of the beauty (*yofiyut*) of the Merkavah.
Be careful with the honor[153] of your creator and do not descend to it (*tered lo*).
When you (however) have descended to it (*yaradeta lo*),
do not enjoy anything of it.
Your end would be to be expelled from the world.
The honor of God (is), conceal the matter,[154]
so that you will not be expelled from the world.

This paragraph is a sophisticated rereading of the famous mishnah in m Hagigah 2:1. Its very beginning, the enigmatic *le-hityahed*, may well be, as I have suggested elsewhere,[155] an allusion to the Mishnah's "One does not expound the Merkavah to a single one (*le-yahid*), unless he is wise and understands on his own." The meaning of the first sentence of Hekhalot Zutarti then would be: If you wish to be the single and unique one, to whom the mysteries of wisdom (that is, the Merkavah) can be expounded, study this mishnah, and so on. So from the outset it becomes clear that the "mishnah" presented in Hekhalot Zutarti is indeed the mishnah of Hagigah 2:1 and that this "mishnah" can be taught and studied. However, it is also made crystal clear that the message Hekhalot Zutarti's authors/editors are about to reveal is a very delicate matter that is transmitted as esoteric knowledge, to be kept secretly in one's heart. Furthermore, the introductory paragraph leaves no doubt that it understands m Hagigah in the Merkavah mystical sense as dealing with the ascent to the divine chariot: whoever follows the appropriate precautions will be worthy of the "beauty of the Merkavah," which can only mean that he will indeed see God's Merkavah. However, the expression "beauty (*yofiyut*) of the Merkavah" is unique in the Hekhalot literature and obviously a modification of the common phrase[156] "beauty (*yofi*) of the king,"[157] which is the goal of the mystic's heavenly journey in Hekhalot Rabbati. The Mishnah's warning about not impairing the "honor of the creator" by gazing at "what is above, below, before, and after" is understood here as a caveat against descending to the Merkavah: one should not do it, but our editor seems to take

---

[152] From the world. An alternative translation would be "until the day of your separation," in the sense of mystical-ascetic practices.
[153] With the double meaning here of *kavod* as "glory" and "honor."
[154] Cf. Prov. 25:2. The masoretic text reads: "It is the glory/honor of God to conceal a matter."
[155] Schäfer, *The Hidden and Manifest God*, p. 70, n. 90.
[156] Predominantly in Hekhalot Rabbati, but also in the passages in Hekhalot Zutarti that share traditions with Hekhalot Rabbati.
[157] An early hint, probably, as to the secondary character of Hekhalot Zutarti.

it for granted that one nevertheless does it, since he admonishes the adept not to enjoy it – meaning that he should keep his experience a secret.

What is left open in the introductory paragraph of Hekhalot Zutarti is the question as to who exactly descends to the Merkavah and what precisely he "sees." This question is answered in the following sections, leaving no doubt that the heroes of Hekhalot Zutarti are quite different from those in Hekhalot Rabbati. Instead of R. Nehunya b. Haqanah and R. Ishmael, so prominent in Hekhalot Rabbati, we are now primarily dealing with Moses and R. Aqiva: Moses clearly functions here as Aqiva's role model, and Aqiva functions as a role model for the intended audience, the Merkavah mystics. Moses is perceived as the first mystic who ascended to God – but not just, as the tradition has it, to receive the Torah; rather, he ascended because God wished to reveal to him the *names* that protect the initiates from *forgetting* the Torah (§ 336). We have encountered the Merkavah mystics' concern about forgetting the Torah in the Sar ha-Torah piece in Hekhalot Rabbati, but now the knowledge of the divine names that, among other things, guards against forgetting the Torah becomes the very center of the whole enterprise. Immediately after Moses's ascent, Aqiva is introduced as the one who followed his example (§ 337):

> This is the name that was revealed to R. Aqiva
> when he beheld the work of the Merkavah (*hayah mistakkel be-maʿaseh merkavah*).
> And R. Aqiva descended (*yarad*) and taught it to his students.
> He said to them:
> My sons, be careful with this name,
> (for) it is a great[158] name,
> it is a holy name,
> it is a pure name.
> For everyone who makes use of it[159]
> in terror (and) in fear,
> in purity, in holiness (and) in humility,
> will multiply the seed,
> be successful in all his endeavors,
> and his days shall be long.
> Blessed are you, Lord, who has sanctified us with his commandments
> on the sanctification of the name (*qedushat ha-shem*).

Le-histakkel ba-merkavah or *bitzfiyyat ha-merkavah*, to behold the Merkavah or the vision of the Merkavah, has been the aim of the heavenly journey in Hekhalot Rabbati, climaxing – as we have seen – in the mystic's participation in the heavenly liturgy. Now the same terminology is used, but almost in passing, as something that is taken for granted and needs no further explanation.

---

[158] "Great" according to Mss. Munich 22 and New York 8128, absent here in Ms. Oxford 1531.

[159] "It" according to Mss. Munich 40, Munich 22 and Dropsie 436.

Accordingly, instead of beholding just the Merkavah, Aqiva beholds "the work of the Merkavah," which seems to allude to a well-defined discipline. Also, quite conspicuously, Aqiva *descends* from the work of the Merkavah (*yarad*), whereas Moses (in § 336) *ascends* to God ('*alah*), using in both cases the "correct" rather than the reverse terminology so characteristic of Hekhalot Rabbati. This all points to an ascent account that, in comparison with Hekhalot Rabbati, seems to be secondary and less "original."

The text leaves no doubt as to the outcome of Aqiva's ascent: without bothering itself with a description of what happens in heaven it informs us quite laconically that he receives, just like Moses, the great and holy name – clearly that of God. Nor are we kept in the dark about the purpose of this name: it is meant to be used, *le-hishtammesh* in Hebrew, a word that has a distinctly magical-theurgical function.[160] Hence, it is made crystal clear from the outset that Hekhalot Zutarti's ascent is inextricably linked with magic and theurgy (to be sure, we did notice a certain overlap also in Hekhalot Rabbati,[161] but this overlap pales in comparison with that in Hekhalot Zutarti). The proper use of God's holy name guarantees numerous descendants, success, and long life. This is not particularly modest[162] – and again, differs considerably from Hekhalot Rabbati. Whereas in Hekhalot Rabbati the Merkavah mystic derives no personal advantage from his ascent but returns to the earthly community to assure it of the perpetual love of God, Aqiva teaches the name only to his students (a faint echo of Hekhalot Rabbati's havurah), who are obviously the only ones who benefit from the use of the name. From this perspective, the final blessing about the sanctification of the name, which alludes to the third benediction of the Eighteen Benedictions prayer,[163] seems particularly bold.

It is precisely in this context of the revelation of God's holy name to Moses and Aqiva that the editors of Mss. New York 8128 and Munich 22 have incorporated the story of the four rabbis who entered the *pardes*,[164] so well-known from the Tosefta, the Yerushalmi, and the Bavli.[165] Since they introduce the story,

---

[160] Schäfer, *Hekhalot-Studien*, p. 260.

[161] See above, p. 272.

[162] Note that numerous descendants (lit. the multiplication of his seed) were promised to Abraham (Gen. 22:17).

[163] Cf. m Rosh ha-Shanah 4:5.

[164] *Synopse zur Hekhalot-Literatur*, §§ 344–346.

[165] See above, pp. 96 ff. Mss. New York 8128, Oxford 1531, and Dropsie 436 quote just the first sentence of the story and then break off with "etc."; only Mss. New York and Munich 22 bring here the full version of the story, §§ 344–345 (Ms. New York after some additional material about the name: §§ 340–343). Moreover, only Ms. New York incorporates here the water test into the *pardes* story (§ 345). It is clearly out of place here and fits in much better with the version of §§ 407–410 in Hekhalot Zutarti (see below) and §§ 258–259 in Hekhalot Rabbati, which is independent of the *pardes* story. Another version of the *pardes* story is preserved in the macroform Merkavah Rabbah (§§ 671–672), again with only Ms. New York including the water test and, in addition, the tradition about Elisha b. Avuyah that has a parallel in b Hagigah 15b.

quite in contrast to the rabbinic sources, with "R. Aqiva said," it becomes immediately clear why our editors are so keen at quoting it here: R. Aqiva is their hero, and he was the only one who ascended and descended in peace (§ 345).[166] Whatever the original purpose of the four rabbis' entrance into the *pardes* might have been, for our editors it is obvious that the rabbis ascended to the Merkavah, that only Aqiva survived this adventure unharmed, and that he received there a revelation of the divine name.

Most of the following passages in this microform focus on the knowledge of the divine name (combined with fragments of Aqiva's ascent). When Aqiva ascended[167] to the Merkavah, he heard a heavenly voice from beneath the throne of glory speaking to him in Aramaic (§§ 348 f.). The message that Aqiva receives from the heavenly voice is unmistakably inspired by the first chapter of Ezekiel. It begins by telling him that God, even before he created heaven and earth, provided access (apparently for the worthy human being) to his *raqia'*, to enter and exit it (of course, unharmed, as Aqiva did with the *pardes*). We know that *raqia'* in the Hekhalot literature refers to the (seven) heavens through which the mystic ascends to the divine throne in the seventh heaven (*'arevot raqia'*) and that it is most likely derived from the "expanse" (*raqia'*) in Ezek. 1:22 ff., carried by the four creatures, on which stands God's throne. Instead of adverting the throne, however, our text invokes again the divine name, informing us that God "established (his) firm name in order to shape with it the whole world" (§ 348). So it is the name of God that is established in (or above) the *raqia'* and that is essential for the creation of the world: presumably, the one who knows the name knows all the mysteries of creation. And then the text continues to praise the human being who successfully undertakes the ascent (§ 349). This chosen human being is here called *bar nasha*, the Aramaic translation of how God addresses Ezekiel immediately after his vision in Ezek. 2:1 (*ben-adam*): he is able to ascend on high and to ride (*le-merkav*: an allusion to the merkavah) on the wheels (*galgalin*) – another reference to Ezekiel, this time not to chapter 1 but to the parallel in chapter 10, where the *ofannim* (Ezekiel's technical term for the "wheels") are identified as *ha-galgal* (Ezek. 10:13). It goes without saying that he is also able to descend unharmed, but what follows is quite striking in its details and, again, its allusions to Ezekiel. The chosen human being is able[168]

to explore the universe,
to walk upon dry ground,
to behold his [God's] radiance (*ziw*),
to dwell (?)[169] with his crown,

---

[166] Again with the correct and not the reversed terminology.
[167] Same.
[168] I follow Ms. Oxford 1531 but amend the text, in particular using the Genizah fragment T.-S. K21.95.B = G7 in *Geniza-Fragmente zur Hekhalot-Literatur*, pp. 86–95.
[169] The verb is unclear here; see *Übersetzung der Hekhalot-Literatur*, vol. 3, p. 19, n. 11.

to be transformed (?) by his glory (*yeqara*),[170]
to say praise,
to combine (?) letters,[171]
to say names,
to peer upwards and to peer downwards,
to know the meaning of the living
and to see the vision of the dead,
to walk in rivers of fire
and to know the lightning and the rainbow.[172]

In exploring the universe and walking on dry ground (probably an allusion to the story of the Red Sea, where the people of Israel walked on dry ground),[173] the adept has almost limitless powers. High up in heaven he beholds the radiance, obviously of the Glory of God known from Ezekiel.[174] Whether he literally "dwells" with the crown (that is, God's crown) – which is without precedent, either in Ezekiel or in the Bible as a whole – or whether the verb translated here as "dwell" is actually a corruption of *le-hishtammesh*, that is, *le-hishtammesh be-taga* ("to make use of the crown),"[175] is difficult to decide.[176] The latter fits in well with the combination of letters, the uttering of the name, and the mystic's knowledge of the living and the dead, and it reinforces the magical tone of the passage. And finally, the "rivers of fire" are taken from the "river of fire" in Dan. 7:10, which streams forth from before God's throne, whereas the lightning and the rainbow again refer to Ezekiel (1:13 and 1:28). Taken altogether, there can be no doubt that the passage presents a patchwork of biblical allusions, with a clear preference for Ezekiel. The mystic portrayed here is the new Ezekiel, who, unlike his predecessor, ascends to heaven and receives there his limitless magical-theurgical power.[177] This power, to be sure, is exclusively for him, not for everybody, and is certainly not meant to be bestowed upon all of Israel. Again, the highly individualistic and elitist attitude of our author/editor must be emphasized.

The next section (§§ 350 ff.) poses, uniquely in Hekhalot Zutarti and in the Hekhalot literature as a whole, the question of who can see God, or rather whether it is possible to see God at all. The answer is given (this is again highly unusual in the Hekhalot literature) in a sequence of three Bible verses. As I

---

[170] G7: "to investigate his glory."
[171] See *Übersetzung der Hekhalot-Literatur*, vol. 3, p. 20, n. 16.
[172] Wording "the rainbow" only in Ms. Munich 22 and G7.
[173] Ex. 14:22; 15:19.
[174] The text alludes here to the rabbinic concept of the "radiance of the Shekhinah" (*ziw ha-shekhinah*) and to the "glory" of God, mentioned two lines down: *yeqara* is the Aramaic equivalent of the Hebrew *kavod*, used in Ezekiel (1:28), the human figure sitting on the throne.
[175] A magical reinterpretation of m Avot 1:13; see below, p. 292.
[176] See *Übersetzung der Hekhalot-Literatur*, vol. 3, p. 19, n. 12.
[177] This has been noticed already by Scholem, *Jewish Gnosticism*, pp. 77 ff.

have argued elsewhere,[178] the first verse (Ex. 33:20) offers the thesis: "For man (*adam*) may not see me and live," followed by the antithesis (Deut. 5:21): "For man (*adam*) may live though God has spoken to him." The thesis is taken from Moses's encounter with God, in which Moses asks God to see his Glory (*kavod*) and God answers that Moses cannot see his face because "man may not see me and live." The antithesis refers to the revelation of the Torah on the mountain, with the people of Israel seeing the Glory (*kavod*) of God and hearing his voice out of the fire (Deut. 5:21); the quoted part of the verse is the people's conclusion: "we have seen this day that man may (indeed) live though God has spoken to him" (ibid.). So one can see and hear God – but the people are nevertheless afraid that they might die (verse 23: "For what mortal ever heard the voice of the living God speak out of the fire,[179] as we did, and lived?") and ask Moses to listen alone to God and to tell them what he has heard. And then comes the synthesis, so to speak, with a verse from Isaiah: "I saw my Lord seated upon a high and lofty throne [and the skirts of his robe filled the Temple]" (Isa. 6:1). Hence, there are visionaries who can see God on his throne: the prophet Isaiah saw him in the earthly Temple and, we might add, the Merkavah mystic is able to see him on his throne in the heavenly Temple. To be sure, not everybody can see him, but certain chosen individuals are granted a vision without the usual unfortunate consequences – that is, without dying.

Having answered his question affirmatively, we would expect our author/editor to tell us what it is that the chosen individual sees. But instead of providing a description of God's appearance on the throne, the text continues (§ 351): "What is his name?" followed by a long list of names (mainly *nomina barbara*). So again, the name of God is the crucial revelation for the Merkavah mystic, not the vision of God, or, to put it differently, the vision of God consists of the communication of his names. Nor does the participation in the heavenly liturgy – which we discovered to be the main message in Hekhalot Rabbati – play any significant role here. Our microform in Hekhalot Zutarti is conspicuously oblivious if not opposed to Hekhalot Rabbati's major concern.

Yet our editor insists. We do know, he continues (§ 352), that certain groups of people, not just chosen individuals, see God. The "highest holy ones," he begins his list, see him "like the appearance of sparks (*bazaq*)." The "highest holy ones," of course, are the angels, but what they see actually refers to Ezek. 1:14, where it is said of the holy creatures that they "darted to and fro with the appearance of sparks."[180] So in Ezekiel the appearance is the appearance of the holy creatures, whereas in Hekhalot Zutarti it is God as seen by the angels (or only the holy creatures?) who looks like "sparks." The second category is the prophets:

---

[178] Schäfer, *The Hidden and Manifest God*, pp. 57f.

[179] They drop the seeing here, as if this is too dangerous to be even repeated.

[180] In my chapter on Ezekiel I have translated *bazaq* as "sparks" in order to distinguish it from *baraq*, "lightning."

they, he argues, see God in a dream vision, "like a man (*adam*) who sees a vision of the night (*hezyon laylah*)." This is common biblical material.[181] The prophets are followed by the kings, but what they see remains unclear in all the manuscripts. Finally our heroes, R. Aqiva and Moses, reappear (in this sequence):

> But Rabbi Aqiva[182] said:
> He is, so to speak (*kivyakhol*), like us,[183]
> but he is greater than everything,
> and this is his glory (*kavod*)
> that is concealed from us.[184]
> Moses says to them, to these ones and those ones:[185]
> Do not investigate your words,
> but rather he [God] should be blessed at his place.
> Therefore it is said: Blessed be the glory of the Lord from his place
>   (Ezek. 3:12).

With this statement, Aqiva,[186] the human rabbi, goes much farther than any of his predecessors. He is the only one who knows that God looks like us, like human beings.[187] We know this, of course, from Ezekiel (1:26), where God is described as a "figure with the appearance of a human being (*adam*)," yet Aqiva does not gain this knowledge from expounding Ezekiel but, as the context in Hekhalot Zutarti clearly shows, from the experience of his ascent. And Aqiva even goes a decisive step further than Ezekiel in revealing that God is "greater than everything," that is, of enormous dimensions. Scholem is certainly right in suggesting that Aqiva refers here to what is known as the Shi'ur Qomah tradition, the knowledge of the measures of the divine body,[188] but this tradition is only alluded to and is by no means the essence of Hekhalot Zutarti's message.[189] Hekhalot Zutarti's Aqiva, as the context of his dictum shows, is much less concerned with the vision of God as such than it is with the revelation of the divine names and how this knowledge can be used.[190]

---

[181] See Job 33:15, and cf. Isa. 29:7; Dan. 8:1 f.

[182] "Aqiva" according to Ms. New York 8128, absent here in the other manuscripts.

[183] Or "as we are."

[184] Or "that he is concealed from us."

[185] To the angels, prophets, kings, and R. Aqiva.

[186] Although Aqiva is mentioned explicitly only in Ms. New York, it makes much sense to argue that the anonymous "Rabbi" in the other manuscripts is indeed no one other than Aqiva.

[187] Duly qualified, in the classical rabbinic manner, by *kivyakhol*; see on this term Bacher, *Exegetische Terminologie*, vol. 1, pp. 72 f.

[188] Scholem, *Jewish Gnosticism*, p. 79.

[189] It appears only in the section *Synopse zur Hekhalot-Literatur*, §§ 375–406, in passages unique to Ms. Mew York 8128; but see also § 419.

[190] One could even argue that the essence of the Shi'ur Qomah tradition is the knowledge of the names of God's limbs and not so much their vision.

In fact, even Aqiva immediately retracts at least part of his bold declaration when he adds that God's glory is actually concealed from us. This reservation is confirmed by Moses, who emphasizes that, whatever we may know about God, what really matters is his praise in the daily liturgy – even if we do not know where exactly he is or what he looks like.[191] Moreover, the text does not continue with Aqiva's discovery but rather with how the angels, or indeed the holy creatures, see God: we have heard that they see him like sparks, and now we are told that from their appearance we can infer God's appearance (§§ 353 ff.). Since the holy creatures appear like sparks (*bazaq*) and the rainbow (*qeshet*), they are the true reflection of God's appearance; in looking at them we may get some idea of what God himself looks like. Accordingly, the text gives us a comprehensive description of the holy creatures, followed by the makeup of the heavenly geography (§ 356) – from the hoofs of the holy creatures to the divine throne covered by a cloud and ultimately concealed from our probing eyes.[192] The throne is surrounded by myriads of angels; above them hover thunder and lightning, and finally, clearly the climax of the long passage, "the letters of his name in[193] the radiance of the rainbow (*qashta*) in the cloud." This is but another reference to Ezekiel (1:28), concentrating, as it were, Ezekiel's appearance of God's glory in the letters of his name.

Nevertheless, the author/editor of our text refuses to give up and makes yet another attempt to get closer to God's appearance. We are told that God's feet rest on all the components the heavenly inventory has to offer, but ultimately "on the face of the human being, on the wings of the eagle, on the claws of the lion, and on the horns of the bull," that is, on the holy creatures. And then follows the enigmatic sentence (which is more or less corrupt in all manuscripts): "the expression of the physiognomy of his countenance (*sever qelaster panaw*) is like the appearance of the wind and like[194] the creation of the soul that no creature can recognize."[195] Whatever the precise meaning of this passage – apparently it follows the same strategy of give-and-take that we have observed in most parts of this long section initiated by Aqiva's revelation – it clearly conveys the message that in the end, we know nothing reliable about God's appearance – at least nothing that can be put in words and communicated. It is not by coincidence that the passage ends with the eulogy: "Blessed be his *name* in eternity and in

---

[191] This is the traditional rabbinic interpretation of *mimqomo*, "from his place," in the Ezekiel verse; see, e. g., Sifre Numbers, § 103 (ed. Horovitz, p. 101); Pirqei de-Rabbi Eliezer, ch. 4 (ed. Warsaw 1851/52, reprint Jerusalem 1962/63, fol. 11b).

[192] Using Job 26:9 as a proof-text.

[193] Some manuscripts "like."

[194] Most manuscripts: "and at the creation of the soul"; Ms. New York 8128: "and as the form of the soul."

[195] On the variant readings in the manuscripts, see *Übersetzung der Hekhalot-Literatur*, vol. 3, p. 33 with n. 76.

all eternity" – and God's name is again the focus of most of the subsequent sections in our microform.

Paragraph 357 begins with another eulogy of the name and, more important, offers a concrete list of names (transmitted by Balaam, Moses, the angel of death, David, and Solomon)[196] to be used in an adjuration, followed by ever more lists of *nomina barbara* (§§ 358 f.). However, we are again reminded that the use and distribution of the name are not for everybody but solely for those chosen few of Aqiva's disciples (§ 360):

> He used to say:
> Who spreads (his) name, loses his name,
> and who does not study, deserves death.
> Who makes use of the crown, vanishes.
> Who does not know Qintamisa, shall be put to death,
> and who knows Qintamisa, will be desired in the world to come.

"He," of course, is R. Aqiva, and his warning is directed against the unwarranted and uncontrolled transmission of the name. Aqiva's warning is a deliberate remodeling of Hillel's famous dictum in m Avot 1:13: "Who spreads his name, loses his name, and who does not add, perishes. Who does not study, deserves death, and who makes use of the crown, vanishes."[197] In its new guise Hillel's dictum now refers not to the ambitious man who spreads his own name but to Aqiva's students, who spread the knowledge of God's name. Furthermore, whereas "using the crown" in Hillel's dictum denotes improper use of Torah knowledge, now the phrase refers to the improper use of the "crown" (that is, God's names) in its magical sense of the word.[198] Finally, the knowledge of one particular name seems crucial: we do not know what Qintamisa means,[199] but no doubt the knowledge or ignorance of this particular name decides the mystic's life or death.

After a section that is identical to the highly magical work Havdalah de-Rabbi Aqiva and that reemphasizes the importance of God's names (§§ 362–365),[200] we learn of yet another ascent of R. Aqiva (§ 366):

---

[196] With a reference to the fact that the explanation of God's ineffable name is in the Greek language (*Synopse zur Hekhalot-Literatur*, § 357 end).

[197] Our text leaves out "and who does not add, perishes" and instead adds the last passage about Qintamisa.

[198] Such as the *keter nora* ("awful crown") in Hekhalot Rabbati (*Synopse zur Hekhalot-Literatur*, §§ 236 and 318); see above, p. 278. As Scholem, *Jewish Gnosticism*, p. 80, puts it: "it is perfectly clear that the [Hillel's] statement has acquired a new theurgical meaning."

[199] Scholem, following a suggestion made by Shaul Lieberman, explains the word as a derivation from the Greek word *kainotomēsai/kainotomein*, "to introduce something new" (*Jewish Gnosticism*, pp. 80 f.).

[200] The section is preserved in all the manuscripts of the *Synopse zur Hekhalot-Literatur*; on the relationship between Hekhalot Zutarti and Havdalah de-Rabbi Aqiva, see *Übersetzung der Hekhalot-Literatur*, vol. 3, p. 43, n. 1.

R. Aqiva said:
I beheld and saw the whole universe,
and I have perceived it as it is.
I ascended in a wagon of fire
and contemplated the palaces of hail,
and I found … (?) sitting on … (?)

Despite the obvious parallel to Hekhalot Rabbati, where the adept enters the seventh palace in a wagon,[201] the setting and the outcome of Aqiva's ascent here are remarkably different: Aqiva first of all sees the universe, that is, the makeup of the cosmos. Second, there are no seven palaces here, as in Hekhalot Rabbati; instead he encounters "palaces of hail" (a phrase unique not only in Hekhalot Zutarti but in the entire Hekhalot corpus).[202] And finally, Aqiva does see something, presumably God, sitting on his throne – the name of God and of the object he is sitting on are incomprehensible in all the manuscripts – but, most conspicuously, there follows neither a description of God nor, as in Hekhalot Rabbati, a description of the mystic's joining in with the heavenly liturgy; rather, we are again bombarded with a list of names. There could be no better proof of the true focus of Hekhalot Zutarti.

The theurgical use of these names, propagated so forcefully by Hekhalot Zutarti, is (literally) sealed in a magical formula that reemphasizes the cosmic dimension of Aqiva's ascent (§ 367):

This is the spell (*isra*) and the seal (*hatma*)
by which one binds the earth
and by which one binds the heavens.
The earth flees before it
and the universe trembles before it.
It opens the mouth of the sea
and closes the hooks[203] of the firmament.[204]
It opens heavens and floods the universe;
it uproots the earth and mixes up[205] the universe.

---

[201] Hekhalot Rabbati, *Synopse zur Hekhalot-Literatur*, §§ 231, 232, 235, 236: just a "wagon," only in § 231 explicitly "a radiant wagon" (*qaron shel nogah*). But our "wagon of fire" (*nura*) is by no means simply the Aramaic translation of the Hebrew "wagon of radiance" (*nogah*), as Scholem, *Jewish Gnosticism*, p. 82, maintains. The "wagon of radiance" (*nogah*) in Hekhalot Rabbati is a deliberate reference to Ezek. 1:4, which is lost in the "wagon of fire" (*nura*) in Hekhalot Zutarti.
[202] It reminds us of the wall and the house of hailstones that Enoch sees in heaven (1 En. 14), although "hailstones" (*avnei barad*) are also common in the Hekhalot literature (see the concordance, s.v. *even*).
[203] Ms. New York 8128: "the waters of the firmament."
[204] The word *raqia'* is here "firmament" in the biblical sense of the word (Gen. 1) and not the technical term for the seven heavens.
[205] Scholem, *Jewish Gnosticism*, p. 83, translates "confuses."

The spell and the seal that Aqiva receives in heaven give him (and his students) unlimited power over the universe in its fullest cosmic dimension. What we encounter here is a complete reversal of the ascent accounts described in Hekhalot Rabbati: whereas the mystic in Hekhalot Rabbati needs the proper set of seals, with the divine name(s) engraved on them, in order to survive his ascent, in Hekhalot Zutarti the mystic brings back with him the ultimate and most potent seal (with the divine names), which gives him control over heaven and earth.

Most manuscripts conclude this first microform of Hekhalot Zutarti with yet another set of names (§§ 367, end, and 368, 373–374): the names of the rainbow,[206] the sword,[207] the four feet of the divine throne, the divine throne itself, and finally the fourteen letters that "stand opposite the crown."[208] Only Ms. New York incorporates here (beginning with §§ 367 and 368, and then §§ 369–372) some additional material:[209] some brief Shi'ur Qomah fragments (§ 367), but mainly descriptions of the appearance of the holy creatures, of the throne of glory, and finally of God sitting on his throne (§ 372). The latter is inspired by Ezekiel (God's glory is "like *hashmal*": Ez. 1:4, 26) and climaxes in God's crown with the "ineffable name" on it – again proof that it is God's name or names that occupy the editor of our microform, much more so than the actual description of his physical dimensions.[210]

2. §§ 375–406: Metatron

This microform contains material that has been added here by the redactor of Ms. New York 8128 (some of which appears at different places in other manuscripts, mainly outside of Hekhalot Zutarti).[211] Its focus is Metatron as the highest angel, the names of God, and, not least, Metatron's names (since he comes very close to God). The redaction of Ms. New York was obviously systematic and purposeful: we are familiar with the editor's emphasis on the magical use of the name(s), but the enormous role he assigns Metatron comes as a surprise, certainly in the context of Hekhalot Zutarti.[212] There can be little doubt that the patchwork of texts presented in this microform is the work of the later editor of

---

[206] Again alluding to Ezekiel.

[207] Alluding to Harba de-Moshe?

[208] Whatever the latter phrase means. The microform concludes with a clear division marker: a benediction.

[209] On the redactional details, see *Übersetzung der Hekhalot-Literatur*, vol. 3, p. 61, n. 9. We also need to take into consideration that the redactor of Ms. New York has a tendency to combine quite diverse material, not least from the circles of the Hasidei Ashkenaz; see ibid., p. XIII.

[210] Pace Scholem, who overemphasizes the Shi'ur Qomah context (*Jewish Gnosticism*, pp. 79, 83).

[211] See *Übersetzung der Hekhalot-Literatur*, vol. 3, pp. XIII f., XXI ff., and 71 ff.

[212] The major Metatron text in the Hekhalot literature is, of course, 3 Enoch, and our editor seems to quote 3 Enoch at least in one case (*Synopse zur Hekhalot-Literatur*, §§ 387 f.).

the New York manuscript and hence a secondary stage in the development of the macroform Hekhalot Zutarti.[213] I will restrict myself to following only the major movements of the microform.

As to be expected, the microform begins with R. Aqiva. After a rather fragmentary introductory paragraph (§ 375),[214] it starts with a brief Shi'ur Qomah text, labeling Metatron the "beloved servant" and the "Great Prince of the testimony" who passes on to Aqiva the secrets of the measurement of the divine limbs (§ 376). This is the first "real" Shi'ur Qomah piece in Hekhalot Zutarti, detailing the dimensions (in parasangs) of God's right and left eye, his throne, the distance between his right and left arm as well as between his right and left eyeball, his skull, and the diadem on his head. As I mentioned above, it is unique in this context in Ms. New York 8128, but Mss. Oxford 1531, Munich 40, and Munich 22 transmit certain passages of it in very distinct contexts (namely, following in all three manuscripts, quite remarkably, the macroform of Seder Rabbah di-Bereshit).[215] Hence, the incorporation of Shi'ur Qomah in Hekhalot Zutarti is a clear result of the editorial process carried out by the redactor of Ms. New York[216] and cannot be regarded as a cornerstone of Hekhalot Zutarti's message.

Not surprisingly, the microform continues with the names of God (§ 376) and the assurance that everybody who knows these names will have a share in the world to come and will be saved from all kinds of trials (§ 377). Interestingly enough, this promise changes suddenly, in the middle of the paragraph, from the third to the first person, revealing the immediate magical purpose of the formula, so typical of magical texts meant to be practiced by everybody who knows them (and not so much of our macroform Hekhalot Zutarti). This practical application of the name is followed by a long litany praising God as king (§§ 378–383). If we remember that precisely such praise was the climax of the Merkavah mystic's ascent in Hekhalot Rabbati,[217] we note again the shift taking place in Hekhalot Zutarti: from the heavenly liturgy as the climax of the mystic's "vision" to the revelation of God's names culminating in (almost the same) liturgical praise. It

---

[213] This does not mean that the microform can simply be excluded from an edition of Hekhalot Zutarti, as was the case in Rachel Elior's edition; on this, see *Übersetzung der Hekhalot-Literatur*, vol. 3, p. 71, n. 6.

[214] It remains unclear what the author means by "Princes of the countenance of the [Holy] Creatures," but this passage apparently served as a transition to the Prince of the Countenance par excellence, Metatron.

[215] Ms. Oxford, *Synopse zur Hekhalot-Literatur*, §§ 728–739 (§§ 714–727 Seder Rabbah di-Bereshit); Ms. Munich 22 §§ 468–488 (§§ 428–467 Seder Rabbah di-Bereshit), Ms. Munich 40 §§ 728–739 (§§ 714–727 Seder Rabbah di-Bereshit). Hence, the location within the structure of the macroforms is identical in Mss. Oxford and Munich 40, apart from the fact that a similar Shi'ur Qomah/Metatron piece appears in Ms. 40 also after 3 Enoch passages (§§ 939–973).

[216] On this, see Klaus Herrmann, "Text und Fiktion: Zur Textüberlieferung des *Shi'ur Qoma*," *FJB* 16, 1988, pp. 117 ff.

[217] See above, p. 280.

seems again as if the editor of our macroform has adopted some Hekhalot Rabbati *Vorlage* and used it to his own and quite different purpose.

Beginning with paragraph 384, the redactor of Ms. New York 8128 has assembled a corpus of loosely edited traditions focusing on the extraordinary position in heaven of Metatron. It starts with a depiction of the heavenly geography, more precisely the innermost circle around God, with Metatron in its center, followed by a description of Metatron's heavenly liturgy. Most notably, Metatron is called here *na'ar* ("youth"), with no further explanation, but it seems obvious that our author is inspired by the famous passage in 3 Enoch[218] (in other words, that the macroform 3 Enoch is presupposed here, and not the other way around). The heavenly geography culminates in God's hand resting on the head of the "youth, whose name is Metatron," making clear that this Metatron is indeed closest to God. To underline this unique position, we are told that Metatron's name is like God's name (§ 384) and that he is even called "the lesser YHWH, according to the name of his master" (§ 387).[219] This almost-identification of Metatron's name with God's name, and accordingly of Metatron with God, is further proof of our editor's dependence on 3 Enoch.[220] It makes sense, therefore, that it is Metatron, who reveals God's names (§ 384) – the same Metatron who serves "under the throne of glory"[221] (§ 385), who himself has seventy names (§ 387),[222] and who even helped poor Moses remember the Torah after Moses forgot it immediately on receiving it on Mount Sinai (§ 388).

With this unique position assigned to Metatron, it also comes as no surprise that Metatron, and only he, knows and utters the Tetragrammaton, the ineffable name of God. A dramatic scene (§ 390, with a parallel in § 399) describes how Metatron blocks the ears of the holy creatures with the "fire of deafness" so that even they cannot hear God – nor hear Metatron, uttering the ineffable name. This is doubly ironic: first, because there is no reason why the holy creatures, the bearers of the throne, should not hear God speaking: note that in Hekhalot Rabbati they were the most beloved creatures of God (next to Israel) and in constant dialogue with their master.[223] Now they are demoted not only in their re-

---

[218] *Synopse zur Hekhalot-Literatur*, §§ 3–5; see below, pp. 317 ff.

[219] Followed by the appropriate Bible verse Ex. 23:21: "For my name is in him."

[220] In fact, *Synopse zur Hekhalot-Literatur*, §§ 387 and 388, are identical with (and most likely quotations of) §§ 76 and 77 of 3 Enoch.

[221] Literally "under."

[222] See also *Synopse zur Hekhalot-Literatur*, § 389, on the peculiar names of Metatron. In the parallel § 396, even Moses is requested to pay heed to him because God's name is in him (Ex. 23:21). The anonymous angel in Exodus has become Metatron.

[223] Already in Ezekiel we learn that when they stood still and let their wings drop, "there was a sound from above the expanse that was over their heads" (Ezek. 1:25). This sound, of course God's voice, was mainly directed at Ezekiel, but there is no reason to believe that the holy creatures were unable to hear it.

lationship to Israel but also to the highest angel of all, Metatron.[224] And second, because the text hastens to continue with the revelation of precisely this or these secret name(s) that the holy creatures are not allowed to hear. It is not entirely clear who the addressee of this revelation is supposed to be: certainly R. Aqiva and his students, as in all the passages before, but it seems that in these sections of Hekhalot Zutarti a shift takes place from the closed circle of Aqiva's students to a much larger audience of initiates (but still, of course, of the people of Israel only): God has separated them from all the nations and granted them the insight "to know his great and awesome name" (§ 392).[225]

God's and Metatron's names become almost interchangeable, to such an extent that it is not always clear who is being addressed. Paragraph 397 begins with names of Metatron, inscribed on God's crown. Then follows a new version of m Avot 1:1: instead of the Torah that Moses received on Mount Sinai, he now receives the "great name" and transmits it to Joshua, the elders, the prophets, the members of the great assembly, and finally to Ezra and to Hillel, after which the name was concealed.[226] This is not only an odd retelling of the famous chain of transmission in Pirqei Avot, with the "name" substituting the Torah; what is most remarkable is the fact that the scribes of our manuscripts do not agree on whose name is meant: God's or Metatron's.[227] The same blurring of boundaries between God and Metatron is true for paragraph 400, where we learn that they (apparently God and Metatron) "from his [sic] loins downward they [sic] resemble one another, from his loins upward they do not resemble one another." This is a quotation from Ezek. 1:27 (in reversed order),[228] where it is said of the figure of the human being on the throne (God) that "from the appearance of his loins upward I saw the like of *hashmal*, and from the appearance of his loins downward I saw something with the appearance of fire." Hence, what in Ezekiel is reserved for God alone is here applied also to Metatron, arguing that God and Metatron resemble each other in the lower part of their bodies. The microform continues with long lists of names (§§ 400–402) that again seem to play deliberately with the blurring of boundaries between God and Metatron, his highest angel.

The next two paragraphs of the microform (§§ 403–404) mark the transition to the next microform (§§ 407–427). They are suddenly put in the mouth of R. Ishmael, who transmits a message from R. Nehunya b. Haqanah, his master.

---

[224] Whereas *all* the angels in Hekhalot Rabbati are subordinate to Israel.

[225] See also *Synopse zur Hekhalot-Literatur*, § 393, where they praise God that he has revealed his name not to the nations but to them alone.

[226] I have no explanation for the fact that of all the rabbis R. Abbahu (the Palestinian Amora of the third century, head of the school of Caesarea) is mentioned as the one who apparently gets hold of the name again.

[227] They vary between "my (presumably God's) name" and "his (presumably Metatron's) name"; see *Synopse zur Hekhalot-Literatur* and the translation in *Übersetzung der Hekhalot-Literatur*, vol. 3, pp. 122 f.

[228] Only the Genizah fragment G24 preserves the order in Ezekiel; see ibid., pp. 128 f.

Hence we are back to a pattern that was peculiar to Hekhalot Rabbati in particular[229] and one that is quite distinct from the setting we have encountered so
far in Hekhalot Zutarti. The last paragraphs of our microform (§§ 405–406) are
transmitted again in the name of R. Aqiva, but both of them are integrated in
a single manuscript (Budapest 238) also in the Sar ha-Torah piece of Hekhalot
Rabbati.[230] The first reemphasizes Metatron's unique position (telling us for the
first time in Hekhalot Zutarti that he is of human origin), whereas the second returns to the distinct role that Israel plays during the heavenly liturgy – a feature
that again was highly characteristic of Hekhalot Rabbati.

3. §§ 407–427: The Test of the Mystic and His Ascent

So we are back now to the language and themes of Hekhalot Rabbati – with
considerable adaptations, however, to the style of Hekhalot Zutarti – and this is
precisely what distinguishes the microform §§ 407–427 from previous microforms.[231] The microform begins, out of the blue, with the famous test imposed
on the mystic, which is also incorporated (not particularly convincingly either)
in Hekhalot Rabbati.[232] An angel with the name *hashmal*[233] chooses the worthy
mystic by submitting him to a test carried out by his fellow angels: when they
invite him to enter the sixth palace, he is expected to follow only their second
request; the poor adept who immediately follows their first request will be bru-
tally killed (§§ 407 and 258, respectively). This test is followed by another one,
according to which the sixth palace looks as if it is full of water that pours out
onto the mystic who is about to enter it. When the adept, who has survived the
first test, panics and asks, "This water, what is its nature?" he is exposed as unworthy and killed (§§ 408 and 259). Whatever the precise meaning of the tests
may be,[234] both seem quite arbitrary, and I am still convinced that the role of the
angels and of the danger implied is much less significant than the texts want us

---

[229] The only direct parallel, however, can be found in the macroform Maʿaseh Merkavah
(*Synopse zur Hekhalot-Literatur*, §§ 579–580).

[230] *Synopse zur Hekhalot-Literatur*, §§ 295–296.

[231] On this, see Schäfer, *The Hidden and Manifest God*, pp. 60 f., 65 f., 73 ff.

[232] *Synopse zur Hekhalot-Literatur*, §§ 258–259; see above, p. 281, n. 136. On the differences between the two versions in Hekhalot Rabbati and Hekhalot Zutarti, see the notes on the
respective paragraphs in *Übersetzung zur Hekhalot-Literatur*, vol. 2, pp. 238–241, and vol. 3,
pp. 145–148.

[233] An interpretation of Ezek. 1:27, where the *hashmal* radiates from the upper part of the
body of the human-like figure seated on the throne (that is, God).

[234] For the water test and the vast literature on this topic see Schäfer, *Hekhalot-Studien*,
pp. 244 ff. with n. 67; Ronen Reichman, "Die 'Wasser-Episode' in der Hechalot-Literatur,"
FJB 17, 1989, pp. 67–100; Christopher Morray-Jones, *A Transparent Illusion: The Dangerous
Vision of Water in Hekhalot Mysticism* (Leiden: Brill, 2002).

to believe (and most scholars suggest).[235] The real decision about who is worthy and who is not has been made long before the tests.

In their present editorial context the tests clearly function as a prelude to Hekhalot Zutarti's peculiar (as we will see) version of an ascent account. After having Aqiva quote some anonymous mystic (who is only in Ms. New York 8128 identified as Ben Azzai),[236] who unfortunately did not pass the water test, the microform moves on to a poorly edited ascent account (under the tutelage of Aqiva). It begins (§ 411) with a reference to the countenance of Jacob that shines before God in heaven and which is compared to the love of God's beloved people that approaches God on his throne. Quite clearly, Hekhalot Zutarti here takes up from Hekhalot Rabbati[237] the motif of Jacob's countenance engraved on God's throne and blends the individual mystic's ascent with the ascent, so to speak, of the people of Israel. In doing so it incorporates, in a rather odd and abbreviated way, Hekhalot Rabbati's motif of God's love for his people (and of the ascent as ultimately serving this purpose) into what still remains the ascent account of an individual.[238] But then we are already in the seventh palace, where the worthy mystic, with no further ado, is placed before the throne of glory. This again reminds us of Hekhalot Rabbati,[239] as does the continuation of the mystic's experience: despite the promising introduction – "he beholds and sees the kings in his beauty"[240] – there follows no description of this vision; instead, the mystic breaks out in a long litany praising God as king (as he does in Hekhalot Rabbati).[241]

Then the editor leads us a step back and presents a sophisticated section (§§ 413–417) about the names of the guardian angels at the entrances of the seven palaces and the seals that the mystic must show them. We are familiar with

---

[235] See my remarks in *Hekhalot-Studien*, pp. 255–257. On the dangers awaiting the Merkavah mystic during his ascent in general, see Johann Maier's classic article, "Das Gefährdungsmotiv bei der Himmelsreise in der jüdischen Apokalyptik und 'Gnosis,'" *Kairos* 5 (1963), pp. 8–40.

[236] As we know from § 345.

[237] *Synopse zur Hekhalot-Literatur*, § 164 (see above, p. 261).

[238] Another indication of Hekhalot Zutarti's dependence on Hekhalot Rabbati is the fact that God sits under clouds that "drip blood": compare § 215, where a cloud dripping blood is above the heads of the guardian angels of the seventh palace and their horses.

[239] *Synopse zur Hekhalot-Literatur*, § 236 (see above, p. 279).

[240] Ibid., § 412.

[241] In *Synopse zur Hekhalot-Literatur*, § 236, follows some vague reference to the heavenly liturgy, whereas § 249 (immediately after the worthy mystic's entrance into the seventh palace in § 248) presents another litany praising God as king. When Wolfson, *Speculum*, p. 117, argues that in § 412 "it is stated in very direct and unequivocal terms that the mystic (R. Aqiva) has a vision of God upon the throne" and that I ignore or rather suppress this important evidence, he misses my point: I am not claiming that there is no vision (I simply don't know). What I am saying is that instead of describing a vision of the king on his throne the author indulges in a long litany about the "king." Moreover, Wolfson does not pay any attention to the complex and complicated literary layers of the paragraphs under consideration.

this important prerequisite for a successful ascent from Hekhalot Rabbati,[242] but, unlike in Hekhalot Rabbati (where the mystic presented two seals: one with names of God and the other with names of the Prince of the Countenance), here the seals contain only names of God. Moreover, each entrance is assigned only one guardian angel (unlike the two angels in Hekhalot Rabbati), and Aqiva carefully specifies which angel (with his proper name spelled out) relates to which name of God. After this belated instruction we find ourselves again with the mystic in the seventh palace (§ 418), where suddenly a voice – presumably the voice of God – calls upon him, "Ask your request," the mystic answering (§§ 418 and 419):

> May it be your will,
> Lord, God of Israel,
> our God and God of our fathers …,[243]
> that I may find grace and mercy
> before the throne of your glory
> and in the eyes of all your servants,[244]
> and bind all of your servants to me (*we-tizzaqeq li*),
> in order to do so and so.

Here the "vision" of the mystic ultimately culminates in the request for a successful adjuration of the angels.[245] The mystic who made it up into the seventh palace has his wish granted that the angels be at his beck and call. Although we did encounter some magical implications in Hekhalot Rabbati's ascent accounts,[246] they are a far cry from what is going on here: the magical adjuration as the goal and climax of the heavenly journey. Despite the fact that this microform of Hekhalot Zutarti is much closer to Hekhalot Rabbati than the previous microforms, there can be no doubt that Hekhalot Zutarti's editor reworked his material in order to adapt it to his overall magical-theurgical message. The passage concludes with a quotation of Cant. 5:10–16, with small segments of the biblical text interrupted with the stereotyped word *tzeva'ot* (an ellipsis of *YHWH tzeva'ot*, "the Lord of hosts"). This is clear indication of a rhythmic structure that interprets the quoted segments of biblical verses as names of God and underlines the theurgical-liturgical function of the text.[247] There is no hint

---

[242] See above, pp. 274 ff.

[243] The text is interrupted here by an interpolation in Ms. New York 8128 – parallel to §§ 251 ff. in Hekhalot Rabbati – praising again God as king (but fragments of this interpolation are preserved in the other manuscripts).

[244] The angels who attend God's throne.

[245] On the magical formula of binding the angels to human beings (and forcing them to do their will), see Schäfer, *Hekhalot-Studien*, pp. 258 ff.

[246] See *Synopse zur Hekhalot-Literatur*, §§ 204 f., where the mystic adjures Suriyah in order to undertake the ascent; see above, p. 272.

[247] *Übersetzung der Hekhalot-Literatur*, vol. 3, p. 171, nn. 13 and 15.

whatsoever, pace Scholem's and Lieberman's reading,[248] of Cant. 5:10–16 as referring to the Shi'ur Qomah as the true essence of the mystic's vision in the seventh palace.[249]

After this follows a strange Ishmael piece (§§ 420–421) that is unique not only in Hekhalot Zutarti but in the Hekhalot literature in general; it is preserved in all the manuscripts of the *Synopse* as well as in a Genizah fragment (with major differences).[250] The first part (§ 420) refers to a mysterious angel known by the unintelligible name MGHShH but who is undoubtedly identical with Metatron. He stands at the first entrance to the "great palace" (G8), where he burns the mystic's hands and feet, and serves before the throne of glory, where he prepares the throne, dresses God with a special garment (the *haluq*, a shirtlike robe, known also from Hekhalot Rabbati),[251] adorns the *hashmal*, and opens the gates of salvation (the latter not in G8). In this framework, only G8 incorporates an adjuration that guarantees full knowledge of the Written Torah (in its three components) as well as of the Oral Torah. The second part (§ 421) is put in the mouth of the angel Anafiel, whom we also encountered in Hekhalot Rabbati.[252] In the manuscripts of the *Synopse* it is he who immediately fulfills the request of the worthy mystic and, moreover, kills the mystic's opponent who dares to slander him. This immediately reminds us of the praise of the adept in Hekhalot Rabbati (in the Gedullah hymns), where the angels are said to throw upon such a slanderer all kinds of sores and evil bruises (§ 84). In the Genizah fragment, however, this message is turned into just the opposite: there, Anafiel threatens not the mystic's opponent but the mystic himself who dares to adjure him. Whatever the rationale of the fragment's author,[253] the editors of the manuscripts in the *Synopse* do not follow his lead but, on the contrary, reemphasize the magical-theurgical message of Hekhalot Zutarti: they conclude the paragraph by praising R. Aqiva because God revealed himself to him – through the work of the Merkavah (*ma'aseh merkavah*) – "in order to fulfill his desire." For the editor of Hekhalot Zutarti, the "ascent" to the Merkavah is a discipline that guarantees successful magical adjurations.[254]

---

[248] Scholem, *Jewish Gnosticism*, pp. 36 ff., 76, 79–83, 118 ff.

[249] Martin S. Cohen, *The Shi'ur Qomah: Liturgy and Theurgy in Pre-Kabbalistic Jewish Mysticism* (Lanham, MD: University Press of America, 1983), pp. 19 ff.

[250] G8, fol. 2b, l. 34 ff.: *Geniza-Fragmente zur Hekhalot-Literatur*, pp. 97 ff. (dated before the middle of the eleventh century CE); see also Schäfer, *The Hidden and Manifest God*, pp. 65 f. German translation of the passage in *Übersetzung der Hekhalot-Literatur*, vol. 3, pp. 174–180.

[251] *Synopse zur Hekhalot-Literatur*, § 102.

[252] Ibid., §§ 241–248. He appears also in 3 Enoch; see in particular § 26.

[253] In *Hidden and Manifest God*, p. 66, I suggest that we encounter here, for the first time in a Hekhalot text, "implicit criticism of the practice of adjuration by the Hekhalot mystic."

[254] And this discipline is again by no means restricted to Aqiva, for the text continues conspicuously once more in the first person: "Thus my will, my desire, my wish and my entire request will be fulfilled. Amen, Amen, Amen, Selah."

This is precisely the message that the last paragraphs of our microform underscore (§§ 422–424): not only Aqiva, who explains the secret of the ascent to and descent from the Merkavah[255] (§ 422) but everybody who troubles himself with the ascent and descent is granted (by God) a benediction in heaven and on earth. A final admonition by R. Aqiva concludes the microform, stressing the disciplinary character ("this mishnah") of the use of the name and specifying some preparatory rituals (§ 424):

> R. Aqiva said:
> Everyone who wishes to learn this mishnah
> and to explain the name[256]
> shall fast for 40 days.
> He shall rest his head between his knees,
> until the fast has taken complete hold of him.
> He shall whisper to the earth but not to heaven,
> so that the earth will hear (it), but not heaven.
> If he is a youth,
> he should say it before he has an ejaculation.
> If he is a married man,
> he should be prepared for three days,[257]
> as it is said: Be prepared for the third day [do not go near a woman].
>   (Ex. 19:15)

The goal of this exercise is the use of the divine name. To be sure, the name was brought back by Aqiva from an ascent to heaven – and "everyone" is called upon to follow his example – but in fact, the "ascent" has been reduced to learning the correct "recipe" (that is, the mishnah, taught by R. Aqiva), and the preparatory ritual (consisting here of fasting and sexual abstinence) is needed for the proper learning, remembering, and performance of the adjuration. This ritual is reminiscent of very similar rituals used by the adept to bind himself to the Prince of the Torah in order to learn properly and not forget the Torah.[258] What makes our ritual unique is the fact that the mystic is instructed to rest his head between his knees and to whisper to the earth, which is nowhere else mentioned in the Hekhalot literature.[259] Since precisely this request – "He must ... put his head between his knees and whisper many traditional songs and hymns to the

---

[255] Note again the "correct" terminology: *'aliyah* for the ascent and *yeridah* for the descent.

[256] Lit. "and to explain the name in its meaning."

[257] That is, he should refrain from sexual intercourse for three days.

[258] For example, *Synopse zur Hekhalot-Literatur*, § 299 (with a longer list of requirements: washing one's clothes, taking a bath of immersion, going into seclusion for several days, eating only bread and drinking only water) and § 560 (fasting, eating only bread with salt, immersions, not looking at colors, casting the eyes to the earth, and so forth).

[259] *Synopse zur Hekhalot-Literatur*, § 560 (part of the macroform Ma'aseh Merkavah) has only the request to cast the eyes downward to the earth.

earth" – is mentioned in a responsum of the tenth-century Babylonian scholars Sherira and Hai Gaon as the prerequisite for an ascent to the Merkavah,[260] some scholars, following Scholem,[261] believe that we are here offered a rare glimpse into how the ascent was achieved by the enigmatic circles practicing it: through some kind of shamanistic repeating of hymns (presumably the Qedushah hymns mentioned in Hekhalot Rabbati) combined with ascetic practices until a state of ecstasy was achieved in which the mystic would undertake the heavenly journey in his mind while his body remained on earth (like R. Nehunya b. Haqanah in Hekhalot Rabbati).[262] The problem with this explanation, however, is the fact that not only is this passage unique in the Hekhalot literature (one would expect such important information to be placed much more prominently and not just as a passing remark)[263] but also that it is aimed at mastering the proper procedure of the adjuration and not of a heavenly journey. I continue to believe,[264] therefore, that the attempt to extrapolate from this passage the actual *practice* of the ascent as it was carried out by the enigmatic circle of Merkavah mystics remains highly speculative and unconvincing.[265] The main concern of our passage, in addition to the instruction in how to learn and repeat Aqiva's "mishnah," is to make sure that those who use it observe certain restrictions so that they do not endanger themselves and God's "world."

The following two paragraphs (§§ 425–426), put into the mouth of R. Ishmael,[266] lead into the next microform (§§ 489–495). They emphasize the esoteric nature of the revelation that is recorded now in a "book" – further indication of a secondary stage of development of the Hekhalot traditions that has become progressively more apparent in the latter passages of Hekhalot Zutarti.[267]

---

[260] Explicitly referring to Hekhalot Rabbati and Hekhalot Zutarti: B. M. Lewin, *Otzar ha-Geonim*, vol. 4/2 (Hagigah), part 1 (Teshuvot), Jerusalem 1931, p. 14; cf. also p. 61.

[261] *Major Trends in Jewish Mysticism*, p. 49; James R. Davila, *Descenders to the Chariot: The People behind the Hekhalot Literature* (Leiden: Brill, 2001), pp. 96 ff.

[262] *Synopse zur Hekhalot-Literatur*, §§ 225 ff. (see above, p. 276).

[263] According to b Berakhot 34b, R. Hanina b. Dosa put his head between his knees when he prayed for the recovery of Yohanan b. Zakkai's son. Resting the head between the knees during prayer seems to be an (old?) ritual to intensify the effect of the prayer that originally, however, has nothing to do with a mystical ascent experience. It seems, therefore, that it was Sherira/Hai Gaon who made this ritual a prerequisite for an ascent.

[264] See Schäfer, *The Hidden and Manifest God*, pp. 153 f.

[265] No less problematic, of course, is the attempt to identify the works mentioned in this responsum with the Hekhalot texts as we know them from our later medieval manuscripts.

[266] In dialogue with Suriyah, a feature characteristic of Hekhalot Rabbati and not of Hekhalot Zutarti; see above, p. 257.

[267] For the paragraphs 427 and 428, see above. p. 283, n. 149. Hekhalot Zutarti continues in the *Synopse zur Hekhalot-Literatur* with § 489.

4. §§ 489–495: The Book of the Mysteries of the Divine Names

All the sections of this microform, preserved again in most of the manuscripts,[268] revolve around the book of the magical names and the use of these names. Some (presumably later) editor of Hekhalot Zutarti integrated them into this macroform because they fit in very well with the overall magical-theurgical orientation of the macroform. The microform begins with a praise of God (§ 489), who, we are told quite unexpectedly, did not reveal his wisdom to human beings but instead to the angels, and left it to the angels to reveal it to human beings. This runs counter to all that we have learned so far – from the Hekhalot literature (in particular Hekhalot Rabbati) as well as from the classical midrash[269] – where God's desire to reveal his "wisdom" (that is, the Torah) to Israel goes against the angels' desire to keep it to themselves. So Hekhalot Zutarti distances itself again quite openly from Hekhalot Rabbati. Its emphasis on the importance of the angels is concordant, however, with the role it constantly ascribes to the higher angels (specifically Metatron), thus reinforcing the impression of a later redactional stage.[270]

The essence of the knowledge of the name(s) is concentrated now in a "book" that someone "finds" and sets about using. The preparatory rituals he must undergo are similar to those carried out by someone who wishes to adjure the Prince of the Torah – further indication that the knowledge of the name(s) is nothing but full knowledge of the Torah in an eminently magical sense. This is confirmed by the fact that the preparations are supposed to extend over forty days (similar to the forty days Moses spent on Mount Sinai) and focus on ritual purity: the adept should not look at people afflicted with leprosy or gonorrhoea, or at menstruating women, or eat anything prepared by women; he should don white clothes and take ritual baths, and if he happens to have a nocturnal pollution he needs to start the whole procedure all over again. When he is finally able to read the book he should not lift his eyes to heaven, for when he sees the face of the Shekhinah (!) he will immediately die. Here the straightforward use of the rabbinical term Shekhinah and the unequivocal ban on seeing the Shekhinah – after the much more sophisticated discussions in previous sections of Hekhalot Zutarti[271] – point again to a later development within the transmission process of the Hekhalot traditions.

---

[268] For details, see *Übersetzung der Hekhalot-Literatur*, vol. 3, p. 188, n. 1.

[269] See above, pp. 267, 282.

[270] To be sure, the idea that the angels revealed the Torah to Israel is quite old; see, e. g., Josephus, Ant. 15, 136; Acts 7:51–53; Gal. 3:19; Heb. 2:1–3, and the rabbinic opposition against it expressed through the frequent formula "not through the medium of an angel or a messenger" (see Schäfer, *Rivalität*, pp. 48 ff.). But I don't think Hekhalot Zutarti is in dialogue with this tradition.

[271] See above, pp. 288 ff.

Furthermore, the happy owner of the precious book is advised not to give it away for some earthly goods or to reveal the name to some unworthy individual (the well-known emphasis on the esoteric nature of the revelation, particularly in the later sections of Hekhalot Zutarti). The adept who follows this advice is praised in terms similar to the Gedullah hymns in Hekhalot Rabbati, except that now we are no longer dealing with a mystic who obtains his knowledge and power from an ascent to the Merkavah (§§ 81 ff.) but rather from the use of the names he reads in a book. He is able to perform miracles reminiscent of the book Sefer ha-Razim – he catches lions, dries up the sea, extinguishes the fire, and kills whomever he desires[272] – and a far cry from the community-oriented power of the hero of the Gedullah hymns (§ 490).

The following paragraphs mainly present variations of the praise of the name(s) and of their multifarious forms. The microform concludes with the promise that the "house in which this book will be deposited" will not suffer from fire, dearth, and all sorts of other disaster (§ 495). This is but another indication of a more widespread and practical use of the magical book – most likely, of course, Hekhalot Zutarti itself.[273]

5. §§ 498–517: The Magic of the Name

Most of the paragraphs of this last microform are unique in Ms. New York 8128 and are clearly the work of a later editor who felt encouraged by the previous sections to augment the macroform Hekhalot Zutarti with ever more material about the magical use of the names of God. It begins (§ 498, only in Ms. New York) with an exegesis of Ex. 34:5 f. that takes the biblical verse literally: when God came down in a cloud, Moses uttered the name of the Lord (the Tetragrammaton) and – this is the interpretation of our author/editor – *as a consequence of this* the Lord passed before him, whereupon Moses uttered the divine name again and praised God as "compassionate and gracious" toward his people of Israel. Hence, according to the author/editor of this section, the name that the initiates use in magical adjurations is indeed the name that Moses uttered on Mount Sinai.

Paragraph 499 mentions the mysterious name of twenty-two letters that we encountered for the first time in § 364 in this macroform. With paragraph 501[274] begin sections that are added only in Ms. New York.[275] They all deal with prac-

---

[272] See Mordecai Margalioth, ed., *Sepher Ha-Razim: A Newly Recovered Book of Magic from the Talmudic Period* (Jerusalem: Yediot Achronot, 1966), passim. A new edition of Sefer ha-Razim with a German translation and commentary is in preparation.

[273] Paragraphs 496 f. are duplicates of §§ 366 f.

[274] Paragraph 500 is added only in Ms. Munich 22 because it deals with the names that are recorded in the "great book" (although put in the mouth of R. Ishmael).

[275] With the exception of §§ 501 and 512, which are also preserved in Ms. Oxford 1531 (§ 501 also in Ms. Munich 22, although in a different context: § 542).

tical magic (adjurations of certain angels, dream interpretations) and focus on varieties of the name, the extraction of names from biblical verses, and in particular the names of fourteen (§ 513), seventy-two (ibid.), and forty-two letters (§ 516). Since Moses is regarded here as the first recipient of the name, it is only logical – although not without some comical implications (taking into account the importance of the holy creatures, not least in Hekhalot Rabbati) – that the holy creatures need to ask Moses for the ineffable name of God (§ 508). The microform finally concludes with yet another adjuration, using God's name, that is located at the holy ark in the synagogue (§ 517) – another far cry from the Temple-oriented setting of, most prominently, Hekhalot Rabbati.

Altogether, my analysis of the macroform Hekhalot Zutarti, as it is preserved in the manuscripts of the *Synopse*, has made abundantly clear that the editors have put great emphasis on the magical use of the divine names or, more precisely, that they are obsessed with the names of God. Even the ascent accounts in this macroform are adapted to this overarching message: Aqiva and his followers achieve, through their "ascent," knowledge of the divine names and their proper use – definitely not a vision of God in the traditional sense of the word or even a participation in the heavenly liturgy. The communal orientation, so striking in Hekhalot Rabbati, has given way to a much more personal, if not individualistic and egoistic, attitude in Hekhalot Zutarti. The power of the angels (in particular of Metatron), which was present but clearly muted in Hekhalot Rabbati, returns with new force, albeit for the sake and to the advantage of the adept who knows how to make use of it in his adjurations. Accordingly, the secret knowledge revealed to Aqiva becomes a "mishnah" that can be studied and ultimately develops into a book that contains all one needs to know in order to use it for ever more mundane magical purposes. These last layers of the macroform are clearly later stages of the literary development of Hekhalot Zutarti, most conspicuous in Ms. New York 8128. Scholem's optimism that "most of the book's [Hekhalot Zutarti's] content is devoted ... especially to theurgical instructions *of considerable age*"[276] – which in fact are drawn, in particular, from the (late) magical redaction of Ms. New York – cannot be corroborated.

Shi'ur Qomah

We have encountered some smaller pieces of Shi'ur Qomah fragments – the enigmatic tradition of God's gigantic body dimensions and the names attached to them – scattered over Hekhalot Rabbati and, particularly, the Ms. New York 8128 recension of Hekhalot Zutarti.[277] In addition to these fragments, we find two

---

[276] *Jewish Gnosticism*, p. 76; my emphasis.
[277] See above, pp. 262, 290, 294 f., 301.

larger Shi'ur Qomah units, one incorporated in the macroform Merkavah Rabbah (§§ 688–704),[278] and the other one only in Ms. Munich 40 in a very similar
unit that may or may not add up to a macroform of its own (§§ 939–953 or 978,
respectively).[279] It is doubtful whether "Shi'ur Qomah" was ever regarded as an
independent macroform within the corpus of the Hekhalot traditions. Clearly, a
variety of versions were circulating in the Middle Ages and were absorbed into
different contexts; any attempt to track down an alleged *Urtext* of Shi'ur Qomah
proves futile.[280] I will briefly survey the Shi'ur Qomah material as presented in
Merkavah Rabbah and Ms. Munich 40 (following the sequence in Ms. Munich,
but noting some important differences in the Merkavah Rabbah version).

The "macroform" begins with sections (§§ 939 ff.), which the editor of
Ms. New York 8128 has incorporated into the macroform Hekhalot Zutarti
(§§ 376 ff.). As in Hekhalot Zutarti, the originator of the revelation is Metatron,
but the recipient now is R. Ishmael, whereas the same material in Hekhalot
Zutarti was put into the mouth of R. Aqiva. The actual description of the Shi'ur
Qomah begins in paragraph 948.[281] The sequence of God's body parts, although
not completely identical in the Merkavah Rabbah manuscripts and the Ms. Munich "marcroform," follows a very similar pattern. It starts from below, with
the soles of God's feet, moves upward from the ankles, shanks, knees, thighs,
shoulders,[282] and neck to the head (its circumference, crown,[283] nose, tongue,
forehead, eyes),[284] and then downward from the shoulders to the arms, fingers,
palms, and toes. In each case the measurement of the particular limb is given in
astronomical figures and always in parasangs (*parsa'ot*), the Persian miles (X
myriads parasangs). The use of Persian miles as the unit of length instead of biblical measurements clearly points to the Babylonian cultural context rather than
Palestine as the place of origin of these traditions.[285]

---

[278] Embedded, not surprisingly, in traditions about the "great mystery" of the divine name
and Prince of the Torah traditions.

[279] In *Übersetzung der Hekhalot-Literatur*, vol. 4, pp. XXXI ff., we have treated §§ 939–978
as a macroform "Shi'ur Qomah" of its own, but the core of the Shi'ur Qomah material consists
of §§ 939–953. It is preceded in Ms. Munich 40 by 3 Enoch (§§ 882–938) and followed by traditions about the heavenly geography and Metatron (§§ 954 ff.) that the redactor of Ms. New
York has incorporated in Hekhalot Zutarti.

[280] The major proponent of an *Urtext* is Martin S. Cohen; see his *The Shi'ur Qomah: Texts
and Recensions* (Tübingen: J.C.B. Mohr [Paul Siebeck], 1985), pp. 3 ff., and our critique in
Übersetzung der Hekhalot-Literatur, vol. 4, pp. XXXVIII ff.

[281] Paragraph 695 in Merkavah Rabbah.

[282] Only in Merkavah Rabbah.

[283] The crown here only in Merkavah Rabbah; in the Ms. Munich 40 "macroform" it follows
at the very end, just before the quotation of the verses from Song of Songs.

[284] The eyes are specified with regard to the "white" and "black" in each eye and even the
eye sockets in Merkavah Rabbah. Merkavah Rabbah is more detailed and also includes the
curls, ears, eyebrows, cheeks, and lips.

[285] This fits in well with the explicit attribution of the Shi'ur Qomah traditions to R. Nathan
(§§ 951 and 700): R. Nathan (a Tanna of the fourth generation and contemporary of R. Yehudah

Moreover, in addition to the measurements of the individual limbs, their names are also given in great and exhausting detail (*nomina barbara*). The importance of the limbs' names is emphasized by the fact that the editor sometimes interrupts his description of the limbs and their names with lists of specific names: we learn, for example, that on God's heart are written seventy names and on his forehead seventy-two letters (§§ 948 and 949, respectively).[286] This is a clear indication that for the editor, in accordance with his overall obsession with the letters of God's name(s), the revelation of the names seems to be the most meaningful part of the Shi'ur Qomah tradition.[287] To make his point absolutely clear, he even explicitly tells us – in the middle of all these detailed measurements and names – that "we have in our hands no measurement (*middah*), but the names are revealed to us" (§ 949).[288] So, after all these endless and tiring lists of figures and names, the anticlimactic message is, the measurements do not really count.[289] What is crucial here is the knowledge of the appropriate names, because, we might add, the one who knows the names not only knows God but becomes master over heaven and earth.

Conspicuously, the only meaningful name among all the *nomina barbara* is the one that appears on God's crown, the name of Israel; furthermore, on the precious stone between the "horns" of the crown is engraved "Israel is my people" (§ 951).[290] This by no means coincidental emphasis on Israel is followed by a quotation of Cant. 5:10–16, where, according to our author/editor, Israel addresses – and describes – God's, their "beloved's" (*dodi*), body.[291] Hence, for the "macroform" Shi'ur Qomah in almost all of its manifestations there exists a strong correlation between the description of the divine body and the quotation of certain verses from the biblical book Song of Songs. This correlation has been used by several scholars, most notably Scholem, to establish three related claims: first, that the Shi'ur Qomah tradition emerged from exegesis of Song of Songs; second, that Shi'ur Qomah must be regarded as essential for Merkavah

---

ha-Nasi) immigrated from Babylonia to Palestine (hence his epithet *ha-Bavli*) and obviously serves to legitimate the (pseudepigraphical) attribution of our traditions to R. Ishmael (and Aqiva). See Cohen, *The Shi'ur Qomah: Liturgy and Theurgy*, p. 66, and Schäfer, *Übersetzung der Hekhalot-Literatur*, vol. 4, pp. XXXIX f.

[286] Paragraphs 696 and 698 in Merkavah Rabbah.

[287] As I have argued already in *The Hidden and Manifest God*, pp. 101 f.

[288] Paragraph 699 in Merkavah Rabbah. The same paragraph also in Hekhalot Zutarti (§ 356); see above, p. 291.

[289] The absurdity of the figures given is emphasized by the seemingly serious but actually highly ironical attempt to convert the divine parasangs into some comprehensible human measurements – which, however, also fail to make much sense (§§ 950 and 703).

[290] Paragraph 697 in Merkavah Rabbah.

[291] The Merkavah Rabbah version (§ 704) offers no link between Israel's name on the crown and the Song of Song verses. However, the redactor of Ms. New York 8128 apparently quotes the verses not according to their biblical sequence but according to the description of God in the Shi'ur Qomah passage.

mystical speculations; and third, that this Shi'ur Qomah tradition is a particularly old and venerable layer of the Hekhalot literature and proves the antiquity of a core element of Merkavah mysticism.[292]

As to the first claim, Scholem does not actually prove but rather presupposes it. The (indisputable) fact that most of the Shi'ur Qomah texts in the Hekhalot literature refer to Cant. 5:11–16 seems proof enough for him.[293] True, Song of Songs serves as some kind of proof text, mostly at the very end of the Shi'ur Qomah traditions, but this does not mean that these traditions *originated* in an exegesis of Song of Songs. On the contrary, there appears no link whatsoever between the Shi'ur Qomah speculations' focus on the measurements/names of God and the biblical Song of Songs. To be sure, both texts refer to God's limbs, but whereas Song of Songs indeed *describes* them (his head is "finest gold," his locks are "curled and black as raven," his eyes are "like doves," his cheeks "like beds of spices," his lips "like lilies," and so on), the Shi'ur Qomah does not describe anything but rather gives the figures of the limbs' gigantic sizes and, most important, their names. It is simply impossible to explain how these figures and names could have originated from an exegesis of Song of Songs.[294]

The second and third claims are even more problematic. Here are Scholem's opening reflections on the alleged link between the vision and the Shi'ur Qomah speculation:[295]

> At the end of his journey the Merkabah mystic beholds not only a vision of the world of the Merkabah and the throne of God, but also a vision of Him who sits upon that throne – a vision in which He appears to the mystic in "a likeness as the appearance of a man [Ezek. 1:26]." Whereas all the other visions are of things created, however high their rank, this final vision is of the divine glory itself. The doctrine which grew around this vision, the doctrine of the mystical "body of God," *Shiur Komah*, is of special importance in establishing the antiquity of some parts of the Hekhaloth writings.

---

[292] For the research history from Graetz (Heinrich Graetz, "Die mystische Literatur in der gaonäischen Epoche," *MGWJ* 8 [1859], pp. 67–78, 103–118, 140–153), Jellinek (Adolph Jellinek, *Bet ha-Midrasch*, vol. 6 [Jerusalem: Wahrmann Books, 1967], p. XXXXII f.), and Gaster (Moses Gaster, "Das Schiur Komah," *MGWJ* 37 [1893], pp. 179–185; 213–230 = id., *Studies and Texts in Folklore, Magic, Mediaeval Romance, Hebrew Apocrypha and Samaritan Archaeology*, vol. 2 [New York: Ktav, 1971], pp. 1330–1353) to Scholem (*Origins of the Kabbalah*, pp. 20 f.; *Jewish Gnosticism*, pp. 36–42; *On the Mystical Shape of the Godhead: Basic Concepts in the Kabbalah* [New York: Schocken, 1991], pp. 20 ff.) see Cohen, *The Shi'ur Qomah: Liturgy and Theurgy*, pp. 13 ff.; Schäfer, *Übersetzung der Hekhalot-Literatur*, vol. 4, pp. XXXVII ff.
[293] See Scholem, *Jewish Gnosticism*, p. 37, and in particular p. 39: "I have said that the Song of Songs – because it contained a detailed description of the limbs of the lover, who was identified with God – became the basic scriptural text upon which the doctrine of *Shiur Komah* leaned." See also Jellinek, *Bet ha-Midrasch*, vol. 6, p. XXXXII: "Denn der Ausgangspunkt des *Shi'ur Qomah*, wie es in Handschriften zu lesen ist, ist das Hohelied."
[294] As has been aptly observed by Gaster, *Studies and Texts*, vol. 2, p. 1333: "Denn Anlehnung an biblische Texte ist nicht immer zu gleicher Zeit auch Abhängigkeit von denselben."
[295] Scholem, *Jewish Gnosticism*, p. 36.

Almost everything in this programmatic paragraph is open for discussion, to say
the least. That the Merkavah mystic, at the end of his journey, beholds a vision
of God does not stand up to closer scrutiny of the texts; in fact, all our analyses
have shown that if the mystic does indeed see God, the authors/editors of the
ascent accounts have taken great pains not to reveal what he sees. More concretely, they seem to have been not at all interested in such visions but rather
placed the emphasis on other things such as the participation of the mystic in
the heavenly liturgy or the knowledge of the divine names. The link between the
alleged vision and Ezekiel's "likeness as the appearance of a man" is highly sug-
gestive – since it wishes to imply that the mystic indeed sees the glory of God
on his throne in human shape as Ezekiel describes him – but is nowhere made
in the Hekhalot literature,[296] not even in Aqiva's famous dictum in Hekhalot
Zutarti (§ 352).[297] And finally, that "around this vision" grew the doctrine of
Shi'ur Qomah is pure wishful thinking, since nowhere in the Hekhalot literature
is a direct link established between the mystic's vision at the end of his ascent
and the Shi'ur Qomah.

The springboard for the third claim is the quotation from Origen's commentary on the Song of Songs discussed above.[298] There, Origen restricts the teaching of the Songs of Songs, together with other biblical books, to a mature age
(probably thirty): although the Hebrew Bible as well as the Oral Torah in their
entirety belong to the rabbinic curriculum for "young boys," Genesis 1, Ezekiel
1 and 40–48, and the Song of Songs are deferred to the final stage of the curriculum. From this quotation Scholem concludes that Origen refers to the exegesis
of the Song of Songs as an esoteric doctrine – as is the case with Genesis 1 and
Ezekiel 1 (the well-known rabbinic disciplines of *ma'aseh bereshit* and *ma'aseh
merkavah*, respectively) – dealing in fact with Shi'ur Qomah, and that therefore
the Shi'ur Qomah speculations must be earlier than Origen (d. 253 CE) and actually "represent a second century Jewish tradition."[299]

This conclusion again is highly questionable. In his zeal to finally discover
the origins of the Shi'ur Qomah speculations, Scholem overlooks or ignores
the fact that the four biblical passages are not described by Origen as *esoteric*
in the technical sense of the term; rather, Origen simply declares that these passages are restricted to a student of mature age and postponed to the final stages
of the official curriculum. Just because we encounter Genesis 1 and Ezekiel 1
as esoteric disciplines in rabbinic Judaism, we cannot and should not infer that
Ezekiel 40–48 and the Song of Songs were also regarded by the rabbis as esoteric disciplines in precisely the same sense (Scholem's explanation for the last

---

[296] Ezek. 1:26 (*demut ke-mar'eh adam*) is not quoted in the Hekhalot literature.

[297] See above, pp. 289 f.

[298] Origen, "Commentarium in Cant. Canticorum Prologus," in *Patrologia Graeca*, ed.
Migne, vol. XIII (Paris, 1857), cols. 63 f.; see chapter 6 in this book, pp. 183 ff.

[299] Scholem, *Jewish Gnosticism*, p. 38; id., *Origins of the Kabbalah*, p. 20.

chapters of Ezekiel appears to be particularly weak). Nor should we automatically assume that Origen had the same reason in mind for all four passages that were subjected to rabbinical restrictions.

If it was *not* because of certain esoteric Jewish Shi'ur Qomah speculations attached to the biblical book Song of Songs that Origen included the Song of Songs in the biblical passages postponed by the rabbis to the very end of their students' curriculum, then why *was* it included? Here Scholem dismisses too easily the explanation that Song of Songs was interpreted by the synagogue as an allegory of the love between God and his people of Israel.[300] True, this allegorical interpretation of Song of Songs was considered legitimate and seems to have been quite widespread. But it remains equally true that the purpose of this allegory was precisely to distance the reader from too physical a notion of love by spiritualizing this love in terms of the unique *history* between God and his people (the Targum of Song of Songs is a case in point).[301] So Song of Songs could indeed be deemed dangerous, and not for nothing was its canonicity disputed up until the middle of the second century CE.[302] Too crude a reading of Song of Songs as describing sheer physical love (not necessarily between God and Israel but just between man and woman), I posit, was ample reason to place exegesis of the Song of Songs at the end of the curriculum, when the students were mature enough to bear the only too obvious meaning of the book, and this despite the rabbis' efforts to explain it away by elevating it to a higher, spiritual plane.[303] The alleged connection with Merkavah mystical Shi'ur Qomah speculations seems speculative and highly unlikely.

Let us now briefly survey the other pieces of evidence collected by scholars, again prominent among them Scholem, to prove the second-century CE provenance of the Shi'ur Qomah speculations.[304] Obsessed as he was with the newly discovered connections between Merkavah mysticism and "Gnosis," Scholem believed he found another major proof in the Gnostic teachings of Marcus (late second century CE), a student of Valentinus. This Marcus, Scholem claims, became acquainted with the oldest forms of the Jewish Shi'ur Qomah traditions in

---

[300] Scholem, *Jewish Gnosticism*, pp. 38 f.

[301] Philip S. Alexander, trans., *The Targum of Canticles*, with a critical introduction, apparatus, and notes (Collegeville, MN: Liturgical Press, 2003), pp. 13 ff.

[302] m Yadayim 3:5. Not by coincidence was R. Aqiva a fervent proponent of its canonicity.

[303] In fact, Lieberman's collection of rabbinic statements concerning Song of Songs as an "esoteric" text (in Appendix D to *Jewish Gnosticism*) proves just this and does not necessarily strengthen the view, as Scholem proudly proclaims, "of the Tannaitic origin of the *Shiur Komah* Gnosis (!)" (Scholem, *Jewish Gnosticism*, p. 40, n. 15). On the rabbinic exegesis of the Song of Songs, see now David Stern, "Ancient Jewish Interpretation of the Song of Songs in a Comparative Context," in: Natalie B. Dohrmann and David Stern, eds., *Jewish Biblical Interpretation and Cultural Exchange: Comparative Exegesis in Context* (Philadelphia: University of Pennsylvania Press, 2008), pp. 87–107; 263–272.

[304] A much more nuanced treatment of these sources can be found in Gedalyahu G. Stroumsa, "Form(s) of God: Some Notes on Metatron and Christ," *HTR* 76 (1983), pp. 269–288.

Palestine, their place of origin.[305] According to Marcus's complicated Gnostic system, as related by the Church Father Irenaeus,[306] the divine pleroma consisted at first of the Tetrad of Propator ("the unoriginated, unthinkable Father, who is without material substance, and is neither male nor female"), Sige ("Silence"), the female counterpart of Propator, and their offspring Nous ("Mind") and Aletheia ("Truth"). It is Sige who reveals Aletheia to Marcus ("I wish to show you Aletheia [Truth] herself. I have brought her down from the dwellings on high that thou might look on her unveiled and learn of her beauty and also hear her speak and admire her wisdom")[307] and who describes her as follows:[308]

> See, then, *Alpha* and *Omega* are her head on high; *Beta* and *Psi* are her neck; *Gamma* and *Chi* are her shoulders with hands; her breast is *Delta* and *Phi*; *Epsilon* and *Upsilon* are her diaphragm; *Zeta* and *Tau* are her stomach; *Eta* and *Sigma* are her private parts; *Theta* and *Rho* are her thighs; *Iota* and *Pi* are her knees; *Kappa* and *Omicron* are her legs; *Lambda* and *Xi* are her ankles; *Mu* and *Nu* are her feet. This, according to the magician, is the body of Truth; this is the shape of her character; this the impression of her letter. And he calls this character *Anthropos* (Man). He claims that it is the source of every word, the beginning of every sound, the expression of all that is unspeakable, and the mouth of taciturn Sige. This indeed is the body of Truth (*sōma tēs alētheias*).

This, Scholem argues, is the Gnostic Marcus's version of what he calls "the strictly Jewish, or more correctly Jewish-Gnostic, *Shiʿur Komah* fragment" in the Hekhalot literature[309] – powerful proof not only of the Jewish origin of such Gnostic traditions but also of the antiquity of the Shiʿur Qomah speculations in Merkavah mysticism with their description of God's limbs and the names attached to them. True, the parallel is striking, but so are the differences.[310] To begin with, the letters in Marcus's system are not *nomina barbara* assigned to the limbs but rather letters of the alphabet arranged according to the simple *'atbash* method; also, they do not seem to be names in the proper sense of the word but "generative forces"[311] out of which the limbs are composed.[312] Furthermore, there is no indication in Marcus's text of Aletheia being a gigantic figure. Finally, and most importantly, in equating the descriptions of Marcus and of the Shiʿur Qomah traditions, Scholem insinuates that Marcus is indeed referring to

---

[305] Scholem, *Mystical Shape*, p. 25.
[306] Adv. haer., I, 14:1 ff. (*St. Irenaeus of Lyons Against the Heresies*, trans. and annot. by Dominic J. Unger, with further revisions by John J. Dillon, vol. 1, book 1 [New York/Mahwah, NJ: Paulist Press, 1992], pp. 59 ff.).
[307] Ibid., I, 14:3.
[308] Ibid.
[309] Scholem, *Mystical Shape*, p. 27.
[310] Noticed also by Cohen, *Shiʿur Qomah: Liturgy and Theurgy*, p. 25.
[311] Cohen's apt phrase.
[312] It is conspicuous that the letters designate twelve body parts, which makes a correlation with the zodiac quite probable; see Niclas Förster, *Marcus Magus: Kult, Lehre und Gemeindeleben einer valentinianischen Gnostikergruppe: Sammlung der Quellen und Kommentar* (Tübingen: Mohr Siebeck, 1999), pp. 222 ff.

the body of God. But nothing could be further from the truth: Aletheia as the offspring of Propator and Sige is, no doubt, a very high aeon, but she is nonetheless created and must not be confused with Propator (and Sige). Hence, the differences are much greater than the similarities, and it seems highly unlikely that Marcus adapted here Jewish Shi'ur Qomah speculations similar to those preserved in the Hekhalot literature.

In fact, in adducing his collection of outside evidence, Scholem indiscriminately conflates the subjects of his sources, paying no attention to whether they address God or a heavenly figure. The few examples that indeed address God's body[313] discuss the well-known problem of anthropomorphism (that the Jews envision God as being of human shape, with hands, fingers, feet, and so on) and have nothing to do with the Shi'ur Qomah in a technical sense. The only exception seems to be the quotation from the Slavonic Enoch (2 Enoch), where Enoch says (to his sons): "You see the extent of my body similar to yours, and I saw the extent of the Lord without measure and without image and without end."[314] Scholem takes for granted that Enoch saw the Shi'ur Qomah of God, and it is true that Enoch claims to have seen the "extent of the Lord"; yet in the same breath he declares that God cannot be measured and cannot be seen.[315] This may be a deliberate paradox (I saw him, but in fact he cannot be seen because he is infinite) rather than the plain description of a gigantic God in Merkavah-mystical terms.

The final (and earliest) source quoted by Scholem again refers to heavenly figures, in this case to huge angels, and most definitely not to God. It is from the lost Book of Elchasai, preserved only in Christian excerpts,[316] that was written during the time of Trajan.[317] There, the Christian writer Hippolytus of Rome claims that the Book of Elchasai

---

[313] Justin Martyr, Dialogue with Trypho, chap. 114 (*The Ante-Nicene Fathers*, vol. 1, p. 256; Michael Slusser, ed., *St. Justin Martyr, Dialogue with Trypho*, transl. Thomas B. Falls, rev. Thomas P. Halton [Washington, DC: Catholic University of America Press, 2003], p. 170); Pseudo-Clementines, Homilies, 3:7, and 17:7 f. (*Die Pseudoklementinen I: Homilien*, ed. Bernhard Rehm, 3rd ed., Georg Strecker [Berlin: Akademie Verlag, 1992], pp. 59, 232 f.).

[314] 2 Enoch, chapter 13 (ed. Vaillant). The English version above is Scholem's translation (*Mystical Shape*, p. 29) from the French translation of the Slavonic original by Vaillant, *Le livre des secrets d'Hénoch*, p. 39. See also F. I. Andersen, "2 (Slavonic Apocalypse of) Enoch," in *OTP*, vol. 1, p. 162 (39:5).

[315] Apart from the fact that neither the limbs nor their names are mentioned in 2 Enoch; on this, see also Pieter W. van der Horst, "The Measurement of the Body: A Chapter in the History of Ancient Jewish Mysticism," in Dirk van der Plas, ed., *Effigies Dei* (Leiden: Brill, 1987), pp. 56–68; repr. 1990, in idem, *Essays on the Jewish World of Early Christianity* (Freiburg Schweiz: Universitätsverlag; Göttingen: Vandenhoeck and Ruprecht, 1990), pp. 123–135.

[316] Hippolytus, Refutatio omn. haer., IX, 13–17 and X, 29; Epiphanius, Panarion, 19 and 30.

[317] Gerard P. Luttikhuizen, *The Revelation of Elchasai* (Tübingen: J. C. B. Mohr [Paul Siebeck], 1985), p. 191, dates the book to the autumn of 116 CE.

had been revealed by an angel whose height was twenty-four schoenoi,[318] which makes 96 miles, and whose [breadth][319] was 4 schoenoi, and from shoulder to shoulder 6 schoenoi; and the tracks of his feet extend to the length of three and one half schoenoi, which make 14 miles, while the breadth is one and a half schoenos and the height half a schoenos.[320]

Here we have an angel with a body of gigantic dimensions given in exact figures – though not figures of the measurements of his limbs but of the dimensions of his body as a whole. Still, this comes close enough to the Shi'ur Qomah – with the major difference that this enormous body belongs to an angel and not to God.[321] The text continues to explain that this male angel was actually the "Son of God"[322] and had a female companion of equally gigantic size, identified as the Holy Spirit. We may safely assume that the identifications of the angels as the Son of God and the Holy Spirit stem from the Christian adaptation and that the original book had just a male and female angel of gigantic proportions. Whoever these angels might have been – Luttikhuizen discusses the possibilities of Michael, the heavenly Melchizedek, and the Son of Man in the Similitudes of 1 Enoch and concludes that the male angel in the original book was the eschatological savior (which made it easy for the Christian author to identify him with Jesus)[323] – there is nothing unusual in the Jewish tradition when it comes to gigantic angels.[324] For example, the two angels who accompany Enoch to heaven in 2 Enoch are "huge," the like of which he had never seen on earth;[325] similarly, the appearance of the Watchers "was like the appearance of a human

---

[318] The Greek *schoinos* is originally a land measure, used especially in Egypt; see Henry George Liddell and Robert Scott, *A Greek-English Lexicon*, rev. Henry Stuart Jones (Oxford: Clarendon Press, 1968), p. 1747, s.v. *"schoinos."*

[319] The word "breath" in the translation is obviously a misprint.

[320] Hippolytus, Refutatio omn. haer., IX, 13:2 (Greek text: Miroslav Marcovich, ed., *Hippolytus, Refutatio Omnium Haeresium* [Berlin: Walter de Gruyter, 1986], pp. 357 f.; transl. A.F.J. Klijn and G.J. Reinink, *Patristic Evidence for Jewish-Christian Sects* [Leiden: Brill, 1973], p. 115).

[321] A distinction also neglected by Joseph M. Baumgarten, "The Book of Elkesai and Merkabah Mysticism," *JSJ* 17 (1986), pp. 220 f.

[322] Refutatio omn. haer., IX, 13:3. In Epiphanius, Panarion, 19, 3:4 and 19, 4:1, he is called "Christ"; see *The Panarion of Epiphanius of Salamis: Book I (Sects 1–46)*, trans. Frank Williams (Leiden: Brill, 1987), p. 46.

[323] Luttikhuizen, *Revelation of Elchasai*, pp. 196 ff.

[324] Even Adam, according to the rabbinic tradition, was originally of titanic dimensions (the *adam qadmon*) and was only reduced in size as punishment for his sin in the Garden of Eden; see, e.g., Bereshit Rabbah 8:1; Pesiqta deRav Kahana 1:1 (ed. Mandelbaum, p. 2); b Hagigah 12a. On the danger of perceiving Adam as a second divine power, see Alan F. Segal, *Two Powers in Heaven*, Leiden: Brill, 1977, pp. 110–115. Moshe Idel wants to reconstruct remnants of a myth of the *adam qadmon* in 3 Enoch, although he repeatedly admits that he has found no traces of an explicit identification of Enoch or Metatron with the *adam qadmon*; see his "Enoch Is Metatron," *Immanuel* 24/25, 1990, pp. 220–240.

[325] 2 Enoch 1:4 (*OTP*, vol. 1, pp. 106 f.).

being, and their size was larger than that of large giants."[326] Also in 3 Enoch the highest angels are of vast size,[327] in particular Metatron, who says of himself: "I was enlarged and increased in size according to the measurement (*shi'ur!*) of the world in length and breadth."[328]

Hence, in view of this evidence, it seems more plausible to argue that originally it was heavenly figures in the Jewish tradition, mainly angels, to whom outsize dimensions were attributed. That God was conceived to be of such vast proportions may well have been a later development, fully manifest in the (late) Shi'ur Qomah traditions. Why the enormous angelic dimensions were transferred to God remains unclear and is a matter of speculation. However, the identification of the two angels in the Book of Elchasai with Jesus Christ and the Holy Spirit by Hippolytus (early third century) and Epiphanius (fourth century) may give us a clue. Could it be that, once the vast size of the angels was adopted by the Christians (and, worse, these angels became divine figures), the Jewish tradition came to insist that only God himself has gigantic dimensions, and no longer the angels – because the latter could become, all too easily, powerful competitors of the one and only God?[329] If this is the case, 3 Enoch (which nevertheless grants some angels, chief among them Metatron, this particular status) stands out as a counterexample. I will turn to this question in the following section.

3 Enoch

This survey of the macroform 3 Enoch focuses first on R. Ishmael's ascent to heaven (how does it happen, what does he see?), and second on the special role the angel Metatron plays in it. As to the date and provenance of the macroform, I adopt, without going into details here, the following results of previous research (by Scholem, Alexander, and others), as conveniently summarized in *Übersetzung der Hekhalot-Literatur*.[330]

3 Enoch belongs to the late phase of the Hekhalot literature; in fact, of the macroforms that make up its core – Hekhalot Rabbati, Hekhalot Zutarti, Ma'aseh

---

[326] 2 Enoch 18:1 (*OTP*, vol. 1, pp.130 f.). According to the gnostic Gospel of Peter the two angels at Jesus's empty tomb (Lk. 24:4; John 20:12) were reaching with their heads to heaven, and the resurrected Jesus was even "overpassing the heavens" (Edgar Hennecke and Wilhelm Schneemelcher, *New Testament Apocrypha*, English trans. R. McL. Wilson, vol. 1 [Philadelphia: Westminster, 1963], p. 186).

[327] The holy creatures (*Synopse zur Hekhalot-Literatur*, § 32), Keruviel (§ 33), Ofanniel (§ 39), Serafiel (§ 41).

[328] *Synopse zur Hekhalot-Literatur*, § 12; cf. also § 73.

[329] I take up here an idea first expressed by Cohen, *The Shi'ur Qomah: Liturgy and Theurgy*, p. 39, n. 64 (albeit without his attempt to maintain Scholem's second-century date for the Shi'ur Qomah – which is strange enough, in view of his convincing arguments against it in the body of his text).

[330] *Übersetzung der Hekhalot-Literatur*, vol. 1, pp. L–LV.

Merkavah, Merkavah Rabbah, and 3 Enoch – it is the latest. More precisely, I regard the redaction of the Bavli as the *terminus post quem* and a quotation from §§ 71–80 by the Karaite Kirkisani[331] as the *terminus ante quem*, which gives us a time frame from ca. 700 until ca. 900 CE for the final redaction of 3 Enoch. As to the place of its origin, Babylonia is the most probable candidate, not Palestine. Unlike its companions, 3 Enoch reveals strong affinities to apocalyptic and classical rabbinic traditions. In fact, it is fair to say that it deliberately reverts to ideas and patterns predominant in the apocalyptic and rabbinic literature; as I have argued elsewhere, the message in the earlier macroforms of the Hekhalot literature is "rerouted into more traditional paths and 'objectified,' ... acquires a greater distance."[332] Furthermore, with regard to its relationship to the other macroforms, 3 Enoch shows intimate familiarity with earlier ascent accounts, in particular in Hekhalot Rabbati.

1. Ishmael's Ascent

With this background in mind, let us now look at R. Ishmael's ascent, with which the macroform opens.[333] Note that we are back to Ishmael again, the main protagonist of Hekhalot Rabbati (instead of Aqiva in Hekhalot Zutarti). However, before the author begins his account of Ishmael's heavenly journey, most manuscripts of the macroform quote Genesis 5:24: "Enoch walked with God. Then he was no more, for God took him." This prelude clearly points to the real hero of the macroform: the mortal man Enoch who became the immortal angel Metatron.

Ishmael's ascent (§§ 1–3) appears to be quite uneventful. Although the technical terminology familiar from Hekhalot Rabbati is retained ("When I ascended [*'aliti*][334] to the height to behold in my vision the Merkavah [*le-histakkel bitzfiyyati ba-merkavah*])," the ascent is only a faint echo of what we encountered in Hekhalot Rabbati (or even Hekhalot Zutarti): no dangers, no threatening angels, no tests. Ishmael immediately makes his way through the first six palaces, reaches the entrance to the seventh palace, and speaks a prayer (§ 1) – not before God's Glory (*kavod*) or the king, as in the other macroforms, but before the Holy One, Blessed be He, as God is called in the classical midrash (but not in the Hekhalot literature). And what does he ask for? Not that God let him adjure his angels to do whatever he wishes (as in Hekhalot Zutarti) but that Qatzpiel[335]

---

[331] Philip S. Alexander, "The Historical Setting of the Hebrew Book of Enoch," *JJS* 28 (1977), pp. 158 f.

[332] Schäfer, *The Hidden and Manifest God*, p. 134.

[333] All translations from 3 Enoch follow, with some variations, Philip Alexander, "3 (Hebrew Apocalypse of) Enoch," in *OTP*, vol. 1, pp. 255 ff.

[334] Note, however, the "correct" verb for the ascent.

[335] The same Qatzpiel whom we encountered as the guardian angel of the sixth palace, to-

and his army not cast him from heaven. God grants his request and assigns to him Metatron the angel, the Prince of the Divine Countenance. This is how Metatron makes his entrance: immediately as the highest angel, summoned to support R. Ishmael in heaven.

Again without further ado, Ishmael enters the seventh palace and Metatron leads him to the "camp of the Shekhinah" (another rabbinic designation of God) and presents him "before the throne of glory so that I might behold the Merkavah (*le-histakkel ba-merkavah*)" (§ 2). Despite this familiar terminology, nothing familiar happens. Although Ishmael is already in the seventh palace, it is only now that the "Princes of the Merkavah" frighten him so that he collapses. God (again the Holy One, Blessed be He) rebukes them, calls him his beloved son and friend, and Metatron revives him. Nevertheless, it takes him an hour until he gathers his strength and is ready to sing a song of praise – though not before God but before the throne of glory. This description, which reduces the ascent account to a bare minimum, is much more reminiscent of the classical apocalypses than of the Hekhalot literature proper (in particular that the adept faints at the climax of his "vision" and needs an angel to be revived). The first microform ends with another attempt of the angels – addressed not to God but to Metatron, who is suddenly called, without further explanation, *na'ar* ("youth")[336] – to question Ishmael's presence in heaven. Only when Metatron explains to them that he is from the people of Israel and a descendant of Aaron (that is, a priest) do the angels conclude that he is "certainly worthy to behold the Merkavah." This phrase is similar to the one used in Hekhalot Rabbati[337] and Hekhalot Zutarti,[338] but whereas there the adept's worthiness depends on his passing the tests, here it is just his lineage, in particular his priesthood, that makes him a worthy candidate.[339]

This is, more or less, what we learn in 3 Enoch about Ishmael's ascent. There can be no doubt that his is a heavily pruned-back ascent, a far cry from the ascent accounts in Hekhalot Rabbati and Zutarti. The ascent is reduced mainly to the framework of the major narrative about Metatron and Ishmael's heavenly journey in the style of the ancient apocalypses. Immediately following his routine ascent the text moves to Metatron and his story. It is only much later that Ishmael gets some attention again (§§ 59–70), when, after several complicated and confusing sections about the angelic hierarchies, Metatron suddenly offers to give Ishmael a sightseeing tour of heaven (stereotypically introduced by "Come and I will show you ... I went with him, he took me by his hand, lifted me up

---

gether with Dumiel, in Hekhalot Rabbati; see above, p. 277. Again, we have here a faint echo of what happens in Hekhalot Rabbati.

[336] The explanation follows in § 6; see below, pp. 319 f.
[337] *Synopse zur Hekhalot-Literatur*, §§ 258 f.
[338] Ibid., §§ 407 f.
[339] Another echo of the apocalyptic literature, where the priesthood plays an important role.

on his wings and showed me"). Ishmael sees the letters with which heaven and earth were created,[340] the heavenly storehouses and marvels of the elements of nature,[341] the souls of the righteous,[342] of the wicked and the intermediate,[343] the souls of the fathers of the world,[344] the curtain before God's throne in which are woven all the generations of the world with all their deeds,[345] the stars and their names,[346] the souls of the angels who were burned because they did not sing the Qedushah properly,[347] and finally the right hand of God, which he conceals behind his back because of the destruction of the Temple and will bring out in the future when he redeems Israel.[348]

Clearly, what Ishmael sees here during his heavenly sightseeing tour has nothing to do with the ascent in the other Hekhalot texts, somewhat clumsily alluded to in the first paragraphs of the macroform. It is an imitation of the apocalyptic heavenly journey, with Ishmael as the visionary and Metatron as his *angelus interpres* ("angelic interpreter"). Ishmael does not see God on his throne but the marvels of heaven and, in particular, the history of the people of Israel – with each individual accountable for his deeds and history culminating in God's overwhelming mercy leading to the ultimate redemption. Even the Messiah appears in his double manifestation as the Messiah b. Joseph and the Messiah b. David,[349] but in the end it is God, and God alone, who redeems his people.[350]

2. Enoch Is Metatron

As we have seen, the outstanding importance of Metatron in this macroform has been made clear from the very beginning, as has the fact that Metatron is

---

[340] *Synopse zur Hekhalot-Literatur*, § 59.

[341] Ibid., § 60.

[342] Ibid., § 61: they hover above the throne of glory.

[343] Ibid., § 62.

[344] Ibid., § 63.

[345] Ibid., §§ 64 f.

[346] Ibid., § 66.

[347] Ibid., § 67.

[348] Ibid., §§ 68–70. With this the core of 3 Enoch ends. What follows (§§ 71–80) are mainly sections about Metatron (some of which summarize what has been said about him before); their affiliation to 3 Enoch is disputed. On the motif of God's right hand / arm, see in particular Michael Fishbane, "Arm of the Lord: Biblical Myth, Rabbinic Midrash, and the Mystery of History," in Samuel E. Balentine and John Barton, eds., *Language, Theology, and the Bible: Essays in Honour of James Barr* (Oxford: Clarendon Press, 1994), pp. 271–292; see also Rebecca Lesses, "Eschatological Sorrow, Divine Weeping, and God's Right Arm," in DeConick, *Paradise Now*, pp. 265–283. Lesses's essay suffers from a complete ignorance of the relevant literature in German, not only on 3 Enoch but also on God's mourning and weeping; for the latter, see Peter Kuhn, *Gottes Trauer und Klage in der rabbinischen Überlieferung (Talmud und Midrasch)* (Leiden: Brill, 1978).

[349] *Synopse zur Hekhalot-Literatur*, §§ 65 and 70.

[350] Ibid., § 69.

none other than the enigmatic antediluvian figure, the son of Jared and father of Methuselah, who lived 365 years, at which point he finally disappeared from the earth because "God took him" (Gen. 5:21–24). Now we learn more about him (§§ 4–40). After Ishmael has been admitted to the vision of the Merkavah (§ 3) nothing of what we would expect happens; rather, he turns to Metatron and asks for his name (§ 4). Metatron reveals that he has seventy names (which are listed much later, in § 76), that these names correspond to the name of God, and that God calls him *na'ar* ("youth"). Since this is not much of an answer, Metatron goes on to explain that he is indeed Enoch, the son of Jared, who was taken up by God into heaven because of the sins of the generation of the deluge and transformed into an angel (§ 5). When the other angels in heaven opposed the ascent of a human being, God rebuked them (§ 6):

> Who are you that you claim for yourself the right to interrupt me? I find more pleasure in him [Enoch] than in all of you, to be a prince and a ruler over you in the heavenly heights!

The angels have no choice but to give in and greet Enoch as the youngest member of their exquisite club – hence, this is Metatron's explanation for Ishmael, his name "youth."[351] After inserting some earlier material about the idolatry of Enosh and his generation and God's subsequent removal of his Shekhinah from the earth (§§ 7–8),[352] the editor reveals more details about Enoch's ascent to heaven. It is the angel Anafiel, we are now told, who took him up to heaven in a "fiery chariot with fiery horses" – the same Anafiel whom we encountered in Hekhalot Rabbati as the one who opens the gate to the seventh palace (§ 247), but the chariot and horses of fire are inspired by Elijah's ascent to heaven (2 Kings 2:11) and not by the Hekhalot literature. When the holy creatures and all the angels around the Merkavah smell the presence of "one born of a woman," God explains to them that this human being is "the choicest (*muvhar*) of them all," God's "sole reward" from his world under the whole heaven (§ 9). He is elevated immediately to the seventh heaven and stationed there to serve the throne of glory (§ 10). But before he can begin his service, a process of transfor-

---

[351] Whatever the "real" explanation might be. I am not convinced by the suggestion, made repeatedly by Orlov, that "youth" is used as a title in 2 Enoch in the same sense as *na'ar* in 3 Enoch; see Andrei A. Orlov, *From Apocalypticism to Merkabah Mysticism: Studies in the Slavonic Pseudepigrapha* (Leiden: Brill, 2007), pp. 141 ff. James Davila has ventured the interesting idea that, in fact, the title "youth" had originally nothing to do with Metatron but was attached to the figure of Melchizedek, the celestial high priest and divine mediator; see his "Melchizedek, the 'Youth,' and Jesus," in James R. Davila, ed., *The Dead Sea Scrolls as Background to Postbiblical Judaism and Early Christianity* (Leiden: Brill, 2003), pp. 248–274.

[352] On the Enosh traditions, see Peter Schäfer, "Der Götzendienst des Enosh: Zur Bildung und Entwicklung aggadischer Traditionen im nachbiblischen Judentum," in idem, *Studien zur Geschichte und Theologie des rabbinischen Judentums* (Leiden: Brill, 1978), pp. 134–152; Steven D. Fraade, *Enosh and His Generation: Pre-Israelite Hero and History in Postbiblical Interpretation* (Chico, CA: Scholars Press, 1984).

mation needs to take place, and this is described in great detail: he is infused with divine wisdom (§ 11), enlarged and increased in size to enormous dimensions, and equipped with seventy-two wings and 365,000 eyes (§ 12). Then God provides him with a throne similar to his own throne of glory, placed at the entrance of the seventh palace, and has a herald announce that he is appointed God's servant as prince and ruler over all the heavenly forces. All the angels and princes of heaven are admonished (§ 13):

> Any angel and any prince who has anything to say in my [God's] presence should go before him and speak to him. Whatever he says to you in my name you must observe and do.

So Metatron becomes God's representative in heaven, his deputy and second in charge. Since he understands not only all the secrets of creation but also the "thoughts of men's hearts" (§ 14),[353] we might even conclude that not only the angels but also human beings are well advised to turn to him as the deputy and representative of God.

His transformation not yet finished, God fashions for him a majestic robe and a kingly crown and calls him his "Lesser YHWH (*YHWY ha-qatan*) … because it is written: My name is in him (Ex. 23:21)."[354] He inscribes on Metatron's crown the letters by which heaven and earth were created (§ 16), and all the angels in heaven fall prostrate when they see his majesty and splendor (§ 18). And then comes the ultimate transformation (§ 19):

> At once my flesh turned to flame,
> my sinews to blazing fire,
> my bones to juniper coals,
> my eyelashes to lightning flashes,
> my eyeballs to fiery torches,
> the hairs of my head to hot flames,
> all my limbs to wings of burning fire,
> and the trunk of my body to blazing fire.

In order to be transformed from the human being Enoch into Metatron, the highest angel in heaven, Enoch's human existence must be annihilated and turned into an angelic being of fiery substance. This procedure is reminiscent of some of the apocalyptic texts I have discussed above,[355] but in none of these apocalypses does an angel come as close to God – not just in distance but also in his physical appearance and, above all, his rank – as does Metatron in the macroform 3 Enoch: he is enthroned (almost) like God, he looks (almost) like God, he has

---

[353] Quite similar to what is said about the adept in the Gedullah hymns in Hekhalot Rabbati (*Synopse zur Hekhalot-Literatur*, §§ 83 ff.), but whereas there the hero is a human being, here the hero is a human being turned into an angel.

[354] Using the well-known biblical proof text; see above, p. 296, n. 222.

[355] See pp. 76, 82 f., 97, 102.

(almost) the same name as God, he knows all the heavenly and earthly secrets, including the thoughts of human beings, and he is worshiped (almost) like God. In sum, he is the perfect viceroy, who acts on behalf of God and to whom God has given unlimited power.

The status and power assigned to Enoch-Metatron in 3 Enoch is unprecedented[356] – to such an extent that the editor of our macroform found it necessary to include some outspoken anti-Enoch material. Rabbinic Judaism was rather critical of attempts to elevate Enoch (some positive statements notwithstanding), apparently in reaction to the earlier pseudepigraphical Enoch traditions.[357] A case in point is a midrash in Bereshit Rabbah that the editor of Ms. Oxford 1572 inserted in paragraph 8:

> Enoch walked with God. And he was not,[358] for God took him (Gen. 5:24).
> R. Hama b. R. Hoshayah said: ("And he was not" means) that he was not inscribed in the books of the righteous but in the books of the wicked.
> R. Aibo said: Enoch was a hypocrite, acting sometimes as a righteous, sometimes as a wicked man. (Therefore) the Holy One, Blessed be He, said: While he is (still) righteous I will remove him from the world.
> R. Aibo (also) said: He judged (that is, condemned) him on New Year, when he judges the whole world.[359]

This is the perfect counter-narrative to 3 Enoch. The first explanation of Gen. 5:24 by R. Hama b. R. Hoshayah – a rather insignificant Palestinian rabbi, allegedly the son of R. Hoshayah (Rabbah), the Palestinian Amora of the first generation – quite nastily understands the biblical "he was not" (in the sense of "he was no more found on earth") as "he was not found in the books of the righteous"; that is, he was wicked. R. Aibo, a much later Palestinian Amora of

---

[356] Piet van der Horst has made the intriguing suggestion that Moses's dream vision related in Ezekiel the Dramatist's *Exagōgē* (quoted in the ninth book of Eusebius's *Praeparatio Evangelica*) ought to be regarded as an early – that is, second century BCE – version of Merkavah mysticism, more concretely of Enoch-Metatron's enthronement in 3 Enoch; see Pieter W. van der Horst, "Moses' Throne Vision in Ezekiel the Dramatist," *JJS* 34 (1983), pp. 21–29 (repr. in idem, *Essays on the Jewish World of Early Christianity*, pp. 63–71). But as van der Horst himself points out, the differences are greater than the similarities: in Ezekiel the Dramatist the hero is Moses, not Enoch or Metatron, and nowhere in the Hekhalot literature, let alone in 3 Enoch, does Moses play a role comparable to the role he plays in Ezekiel the Dramatist. Furthermore, unlike 3 Enoch, there is only one throne in Ezekiel, namely, God's throne, and Moses is asked to be seated on it alone (God leaves his throne). I therefore don't think that Ezekiel the Dramatist's drama, or what has remained of it, reflects an earlier stage of what would become Merkavah mysticism. On this, see also Martin Hengel, "'Setze dich zu meiner Rechten!' Die Inthronisation Christi zur Rechten Gottes und Psalm 110,1," in idem, *Studien zur Christologie: Kleine Schriften IV*, ed. Claus-Jürgen Thornton (Tübingen: Mohr Siebeck, 2006), pp. 338f. (originally published in 1993).

[357] See Reed, *Fallen Angels*, pp. 136ff.; see also Alexander, "From Son of Adam to Second God," pp. 108ff.

[358] Lit. for "then he was no more," as translated above.

[359] Bereshit Rabbah 25:1.

the fourth generation, makes him a hypocrite who wavers between righteousness and wickedness and has him finally be condemned – obviously because of his wickedness – quite fittingly on New Year.

Even more conspicuous is the addition that made it into most of the manuscripts of 3 Enoch. Following his transformation, Enoch is described as seated on his throne and judging the angels in heaven (§ 20). This fits in well with what we have heard before. But then suddenly Aher appears, the arch-heretic known from talmudic sources,[360] who sees Metatron in all his glory sitting on his throne and concludes from his majestic appearance that "there are indeed two powers in heaven!" Immediately God sends out the angel Anafiel to punish Metatron with sixty lashes of fire and to make him stand on his feet.[361] It has long been noticed that the close parallel in the Babylonian Talmud[362] may well have been the origin of this story and that the version in 3 Enoch is a secondary addition, aimed at minimizing Metatron's role.[363] Irrespective of when and by whom these stories were added – plainly contradicting the main message of the macroform – it remains remarkable that this message was deemed so dangerous that some editors could not resist the temptation of sneaking a counter message into the very core of 3 Enoch.

What, then, was so dangerous about Metatron's elevation to the "Lesser YHWH"? Scholars normally resort to the danger inflicted on Judaism as a "monotheistic religion."[364] This is true enough, but what precisely does it mean? "Monotheism" is a notoriously vague category that has never been monolithic and easy to define, neither in the Hebrew Bible nor in the subsequent Jewish tradition. I believe we can go a step further. Metatron was elevated by God to the highest angel in heaven, superior to all the other angels, and sharing with God all the divine attributes (name, size, throne, wisdom, and so forth). The uneasiness with which some (later) editors of 3 Enoch addressed this message serves only to reinforce its uniqueness. There is only one other figure on whom similar qualities are lavished: Jesus Christ. And indeed, some scholars have invested great effort into discovering some kind of heavenly *Makro-Anthropos* in the Second Temple period that prefigured the New Testament Jesus and that might be connected with Jewish speculations that came fully to the force in

---

[360] See above, p. 234.

[361] Aher is also punished, but almost in passing: he is denied repentance.

[362] b Hagigah 15a; see the detailed comparison of the Bavli and the Hekhalot versions above, chapter 7, pp. 234 ff. The parallel version in Ms. New York 8128 (*Synopse zur Hekhalot-Literatur*, § 672) comes even closer to the Bavli version than our text in the 3 Enoch manuscripts; see the synoptic translation in *Übersetzung der Hekhalot-Literatur*, vol. 1, pp. 46–48. See also the Metatron stories in b Sanhedrin 38a and b Avodah Zarah 3b.

[363] Philip Alexander, "3 Enoch and the Talmud," pp. 54–66; id., "3 (Hebrew Apocalypse of) Enoch," p. 268, n. a.

[364] See, e. g., most recently Alan Segal, "Religious Experience and the Construction of the Transcendent Self," in DeConick, *Paradise Now*, p. 29.

3 Enoch.[365] Others, most notably Daniel Boyarin, wish to go a step further and see in Metatron a representative of the so-called "binitarian" theology, that is, a theology, within the very heart of early (pre-Christian) Judaism, that develops the notion of two divine powers sharing among them the "divinity" (most prominently the hypostasized "Wisdom" and "Logos"). It is not the place here to discuss Jewish binitarianism, but whereas there can be no doubt in my view that pre-Christian Judaism (and not only Philo) was indeed sympathetic to such ideas and that the Christian adaptation of Wisdom and Logos speculations put an end to this sympathy,[366] I do not think that Metatron belongs to this illustrious company. It may be tempting to argue (as Boyarin does – and repeats like a mantra) that the original meaning of Metatron, the "youth," is the "younger God" versus the "Old of Days" in Daniel and hence identical with the "Son of Man" in Daniel and, indeed, the "Son of God" in the Prologue of the Gospel of John,[367]

---

[365] Stroumsa, "Form(s) of God"; Jarl E. Fossum, *The Name of God and the Angel of the Lord: Samaritan and Jewish Concepts of Intermediation and the Origin of Gnosticism* (Tübingen: J.C.B. Mohr [Paul Siebeck], 1985), pp. 266–291; April D. DeConick, "What Is Early in Jewish and Christian Mysticism?" p. 19; Davila, "Melchizedek, the 'Youth,' and Jesus," pp. 267 ff.; Idel, *Ben*, pp. 108 ff.

[366] See Daniel Boyarin, "The Gospel of the Memra: Jewish Binitarianism and the Prologue to John," *HTR* 94 (2001), pp. 243–284; idem, "Two Powers in Heaven; or, The Making of a Heresy," in Hindy Najman and Judith H. Newman, eds., *The Idea of Biblical Interpretation: Essays in Honor of James L. Kugel* (Leiden: Brill, 2004), pp. 331–370.

[367] See Boyarin, "The Gospel of the Memra," p. 253, n. 35; more explicit in "Two Powers in Heaven," pp. 353 f. There he resorts to "the late-ancient mystical text, known as the 'Visions of Ezekiel,'" where Metatron "is posited on the grounds of Dan 7:9 f." I am not sure what "late-ancient mystical" means here, but assuredly the Re'uyot Yehezqel are late and not particularly mystical (see the best analysis of this enigmatic text by Goldberg, "Pereq Re'uyot Yehezqe'el: Eine formanalytische Untersuchung," in *Mystik und Theologie des rabbinischen Judentums*, vol. 1, pp. 93–147). Boyarin then boldly connects that "late-ancient mystical text" with 3 Enoch and the Gospel of John: "This is the same figure who in other texts of that genre is called 'The Youth,' *na'ar*, i.e., that figure known by other Jews (e.g., the Fourth Evangelist) as the 'Son of Man'!" I presume by "other texts of that genre" he means 3 Enoch, although it is the only text that mentions the *na'ar* (unless he wants to follow Orlov; see above, p. 319, n. 351), and is certainly not of the same genre as the "Visions of Ezekiel." This hazardous combination of rather diverse pieces of "evidence" leads to the final conclusion (inspired by Segal, *Two Powers in Heaven*, p. 67, n. 24): "Putting together the bits and pieces that other scholars have constructed into a new mosaic, I would suggest that we have a very important clue here to follow. From the text in Daniel it would seem clear that there are two divine figures pictured, one who is ancient and another one who is young. 'Son of Man' here in its paradigmatic contrast with the Ancient of Days should be read as youth, young man. ... We end up with a clear indication of a second divine person, called the Youth (Son of Man), about whom it can be discussed whether he is *homoousios, homoiousios, homoion,* or *anomoion* with the first person." No wonder that soon after this excursion into the intricacies of Christian dogmatic speculations he succumbs to the temptation of calling the Ancient of Days "Father" and the Youth "Son" (ibid., p. 354). This is more or less repeated now in Daniel Boyarin, "The Parables of Enoch and the Foundation of the Rabbinic Sect: A Hypothesis," in Mauro Perani, ed., *"The Words of a Wise Man's Mouth Are Gracious" (Qoh 10,12): Festschrift for Günter Stemberger on the Occasion of His 65th Birthday* (Berlin: Walter de Gruyter, 2005), pp. 62 f. I will return to this problem in my forthcoming book, tentatively titled *The Unity and Diversity of God in Rabbinic Judaism*. See now

but there is no proof whatsoever for such a link between Daniel, the Gospel of John, and 3 Enoch. The title *YHWH ha-qatan* is unique to 3 Enoch and needs to be explained first and foremost within the parameters of the historical setting of 3 Enoch – unless one wants to claim that this particular tradition is much older than the rest of the material collected in 3 Enoch (which would be very difficult, to say the least) or to conjure up the chimera of "phenomenological" versus "historical" evidence.

If we take the rather late date of 3 Enoch seriously and do not ignore the chronological and geographic setting of the macroform,[368] the most obvious source of comparison is clearly the New Testament. There is every reason to believe that the Babylonian Jews knew the New Testament, either directly, through the Diatessaron (the "Harmony" of the four Gospels composed by Tatian, most likely in Syriac) or the New Testament Peshitta (the Syriac translation of the four separate Gospels), or indirectly, through the medium of Syrian Church Fathers such as Aphrahat or Ephrem;[369] after all, Syriac and Babylonian Aramaic are closely related Aramaic dialects. Hence, I would like to turn the tables and suggest that instead of seeing 3 Enoch's Metatron as part of the fabric from which the New Testament Jesus emerged[370] we try to understand the figure of Metatron as an *answer* to the New Testament's message of Jesus Christ. In this context, Guy Stroumsa has drawn our attention to the famous hymn in Paul's letter to the Philippians,[371] where it is said of Jesus (Phil. 2:6–11) that he

> (6) though he was in the form of God (*en morphē theou*),
> did not regard equality with God
> as something to be exploited,

---

also Mark S. Smith, *God in Translation: Deities in Cross-Cultural Discourse in the Biblical World* (Tübingen: Mohr Siebeck, 2008), pp. 294 ff.

[368] Acknowledged even by Segal, *Two Powers in Heaven*, pp. 63 and 65. Chester, *Messiah and Exaltation*, p. 68, makes the remarkable statement: "In contrast to the view that it [3 Enoch] represents a late stage of the Hekhalot tradition [in a footnote he refers to my *Hekhalot-Studien*], however, it has been argued with some plausibility that it is in important respects different from the other Hekhalot traditions, and stands much closer to those found in apocalyptic texts." No one would deny that 3 Enoch, in terms of style and content, is different from the other Hekhalot traditions and closer to the apocalyptic texts, on the contrary – but does this necessarily mean that 3 Enoch is *chronologically* close to the classical apocalypses?

[369] On this, see the discussion in my book, *Jesus in the Talmud* (Princeton, NJ: Princeton University Press, 2007), especially pp. 122 ff.

[370] James Davila also takes it for granted that we can use 3 Enoch (together with the other Enochic texts, in particular the Similitudes) as evidence for the makeup of the Jesus figure in the New Testament; see his "Of Methodology, Monotheism and Metatron: Introductory Reflections on Divine Mediators and the Origins of the Worship of Jesus," in Carey C. Newman, James R. Davila, and Gladys S. Lewis, eds., *The Jewish Roots of Christological Monotheism: Papers from the St. Andrews Conference on the Historical Origins of the Worship of Jesus* (Leiden: Brill, 1999), pp. 14 ff.

[371] Stroumsa, "Form(s) of God," pp. 282 ff.

(7) but emptied himself,
taking the form of a servant (*morphēn doulou*),
being born in human likeness.
And being found in human form,
(8) he humbled himself
and became obedient to the point of death –
even death on a cross.
(9) Therefore God also highly exalted him (*hyperypsōsen*)
and bestowed on him the name
that is above every name (*to onoma to hyper pan onoma*),
(10) so that at the name of Jesus
every knee should bend,
in heaven and on earth and under the earth,
(11) and every tongue should confess
that Jesus Christ is Lord,
to the glory of God the father.

If we read this text in light of the Metatron traditions in 3 Enoch, some striking parallels become apparent – and some no less conspicuous differences. Christ, though conceived of in the "form of God," did not insist on his equality with God but rather assumed the "form of a servant (or slave)" and hence of a human being. After he died, God exalted him, that is, raised him from the dead, gave him the name "above every name," whereupon all heavenly and earthly beings worshiped him and acknowledged him as the "Lord." The movement here is from the top down (from Christ's divine existence to his human form) and then again from the bottom up (from his human existence back to his original divine form). The latter movement is caused by God, exalting Jesus after his death and bestowing on him the most powerful name, that is, the name of the Lord. In Metatron's case there is only one movement, from the bottom up: he begins as a human being that, however, does not die but is exalted by God to heaven to assume there his angelic and almost divine function as God's deputy and viceroy, appearing in the form and with the attributes of God, bearing God's name, and worshiped by the angels. Ironically, it is in this state that he is called, together with the name of God, "servant." Hence, despite the similarities, the Metatron tradition suggests a dramatic reversal of the New Testament narrative. We do have a God-like figure, it posits, but this figure did not first originate in heaven and then relinquish its divinity in order to become human; on the contrary, this figure was fully human and chosen by God to be transformed into a divine being and to assume its function as God's servant and as the judge of angels and humans alike.

Another noticeable parallel appears in the letter to the Hebrews (Hebr. 1: 3–4):

(3) He [Jesus] is a reflection of God's glory (*apaugasma tēs doxēs*)
and the exact imprint of God's very being (*charaktēr tēs hypostaseōs autou*),
and he sustains all things by his powerful word.
When he had made purification for sins,

he sat down at the right hand of the majesty on high,
(4) having become as much superior to angels (*kreittōn genomenos tōn*
      anggelōn)
as the name he has inherited is more excellent than theirs.

Here Jesus is conceived as God's reflection and hypostasis – in a language obviously derived from the Jewish Wisdom speculation, as we know it in particular
from the female figure in Proverbs 8[372] – who returns to his divine origin after
having purified humanity from their sins. Upon his return to heaven, God assigns
to him a throne next to him and a special name (presumably the name of God).
Both these qualities mark him as superior to all the angels, and the text continues to stress precisely this superiority: God calls him alone "my son" (v. 5),[373]
the angels are asked to worship him (v. 6),[374] his throne is forever (v. 8),[375] he
will remain forever (v. 11),[376] and he is asked to sit at God's right hand (v. 13).[377]
The analogies and differences are very similar to those in the letter to the Philippians, though with a closer parallel here between Jesus's and Metatron's superiority to the angels.

So one could ultimately argue that Metatron indeed adopts the role of Jesus
Christ, yet without the mythical and – for the Jewish reader – unacceptable pack-
age deal of Jesus's divine origin and human birth, let alone his cruel death on
the cross. The savior quality of that divine figure, so dominant in the New Testament, is no doubt also present in the Metatron tradition: Metatron knows, and
apparently judges, all the secrets in the hearts of his former fellow humans on
earth (§ 14). This function of Metatron obviously stands in tension to the traditional role of the Messiah that does appear, as we have seen, in the latter part of
3 Enoch. But this tension seems to be deliberate (the macroform wants to have
it both ways: the traditional messianic expectation as well as Metatron's new
role), just as it was in Hekhalot Rabbati, where the Merkavah mystic assumed
Messiah-like qualities (and some editors, by adding more conventional apocalyptic material, tried to retain the customary messianic expectation). To some
extent, Metatron's powerful figure in 3 Enoch – responding, as I propose, to the
Christian message – completes and concludes the movement of the Merkavah
mystics: the ascent to heaven of some individuals has become unnecessary, or
rather was replaced by that unique human being who ascended to heaven and
then did not return but stayed there forever. With Metatron in heaven, there is no
longer any need to send human representatives to heaven to assure the earthly

---

[372] See Schäfer, *Mirror of His Beauty*, pp. 23 ff.; Wisdom as *apaugasma* in Wisdom of Solomon 7:26 (*Mirror of His Beauty*, p. 35).
[373] Referring to Ps. 2:7; 2 Sam. 7:14.
[374] Referring to Deut. 32:43 (only in the LXX, not in the Masoretic text).
[375] Referring to Ps. 45:6 (the throne there is God's throne!).
[376] Referring to Ps. 102:26.
[377] Referring to Ps. 110:1.

community of God's continual love for Israel. Not unlike the Christians, 3 Enoch claims, we now have our own representative forever in heaven to take care of us – until the end of time, when the Savior will return to us.

Summary

We have followed the convoluted ways of the Merkavah mystics as they appear in the macroforms Hekhalot Rabbati, Hekhalot Zutarti, Shi'ur Qomah, and 3 Enoch, with special emphasis on the various redactional layers of the respective microforms. The first Hekhalot Rabbati microform, the Gedullah hymns, focuses on the elevated status of the mystic, praising him as the chosen human being who undertakes his heavenly journey in order to see God on his throne in the celestial Temple. In achieving this goal he joins the rank of the angels and is placed at the right side of or, alternatively, opposite God's throne and observes what is happening in heaven: the liturgy of the angels and, more important, what will happen to the people of Israel in the future. In this capacity, the mystic carries the knowledge of Israel's future history with him and brings it back to the earthly community. So the purpose of his ascent is neither an end in itself nor does it aim at his personal gratification (there is no indication whatsoever of God's physical appearance, let alone of a union between the mystic and his master); rather, it is geared toward the community that has sent him up to heaven. However, in the Gedullah hymns – and this is one of the peculiar characteristics of the microform – the earthly community does not accept the mystic's knowledge unanimously. On the contrary, since he knows not only Israel's future history but also the social makeup of the earthly community, with all the hidden deeds and halakhic (im)purity of his fellow Jews, he is met with considerable opposition. Nevertheless, God approves of his mission and raises him to a quasi-messianic status, assigning to him the role of the messenger-angel Elijah as the precursor of the Messiah.

The Qedushah hymns describe the heavenly throne ritual, as performed by the angelic hosts, that culminates in the terrifying vision not so much of God but of the gown worn by God, covered with various manifestations of the divine name. Despite the emphasis put on the angels, it becomes clear that the Merkavah mystics as the representatives of all human beings are included in this vision.

The following microform, the Ten Martyrs Narrative, provides the counterpart to the Gedullah hymns. Whereas the Gedullah hymns highlight the superiority of the Merkavah mystic to his fellow Jews, the Ten Martyrs Narrative underscores his superiority to the outside enemy, the Roman Empire. Integrated into an ascent account, the Ten Martyrs Narrative in its Merkavah mystical garb aims at proving that R. Ishmael, one of the ten martyrs and the hero of Hekhalot Rabbati's ascent accounts, belongs to the rabbinical elite.

With the two apocalypses incorporated into Hekhalot Rabbati, the editor tries to make up for the apparent lack of the traditional concept of the Messiah in all the other microforms of Hekhalot Rabbati. In strong resemblance to the classical apocalypses, he reintroduces the Davidic Messiah as the leader of the final battle against the nations with the resuscitation of the dead and the Messiah's and Israel's ultimate victory.

Another set of Qedushah hymns and hymns of praise centers on God's preference for Israel over the angels. It begins by describing the extraordinary and at the same time destructive beauty of God's face and making clear from the outset that the angels cannot bear it. In stark contrast to the angels' inability, the hymns turn to Israel (that is, the community on earth and the Merkavah mystic as the earthly community's representative) and point out that God and Israel, during Israel's Qedushah prayer in the synagogues, look directly into each other's eyes, and that the Merkavah mystic witnesses this intimate exchange between God and his people in heaven – to reassure Israel of God's continuous love for them. In a dramatic scene, the mystic sees how God displays his overwhelming love to the image of Jacob engraved on his throne. In unambiguous terms, taking into consideration the unique status of the holy creatures in Hekhalot Rabbati and the praise lavished on them, the microform goes out of its way to emphasize Israel's superiority even to the holy creatures. When they court their master, in unmistakably sexual gestures, God rejects their courtship, because his real love is for Israel and not for the beloved creatures that carry his throne. Hence, in an almost ironical conclusion, the angels, who are known for their jealousy and rivalry toward Israel, must give in and acknowledge Israel's superiority.

The editor of Hekhalot Rabbati has collected under the umbrella of the macroform a number of ascent accounts or fragments of ascent accounts that are only loosely connected and often interrupted by other material. The first such account, the famous havurah account, restricts the ascent to the members of a fictitious rabbinic fellowship, the havurah, consisting of ten rabbis with R. Ishmael at their head (despite the editor's initial assertion that almost "anybody" can undertake the ascent) and set up in a no less fictitious Temple scenery. The second account, pretending to be the continuation of the first one, introduces strong elements of magical adjuration into the procedure of the ascent. The names of the guardian angels at the entrances of the heavenly palaces become the most important magical tool for achieving a successful ascent. Having reached his goal, the mystic – despite the promise that he will see an awesome vision – bursts into praise of God and joins in with the heavenly liturgy of the angels. The heavenly liturgy with its earthly counterpart replaces the redemption and makes the traditional Messiah superfluous.

The third account is focused on the magical seals, with the names of God and his highest angel, to be shown at the entrances of the heavenly palaces. In addition to the seals, however, the mystic must prove his Torah knowledge in the traditional rabbinic sense of the word. Fortified with both magical tools and Torah knowledge, the successful mystic reaches his goal – God on his throne in the upmost heaven – and takes his seat together with the highest angels and the holy creatures. But no description of God on his throne follows. Again, the anticlimactic message of this account is that the mystic participates in the heavenly liturgy. The ascent account is interrupted by the so-called recall of R. Nehunya b. Haqanah from his vision of the Merkavah, which is the only clear passage in the entire corpus of the Hekhalot literature that suggests a distinction between the mystic's body and soul: apparently, Nehunya b. Haqanah's ascent was solely a mental experience, with his body remaining among the members of the havurah on earth. I have suggested not overemphasizing this episode, which is not only unique but also interpolated by the editor into the instruction regarding the seals.

The fourth and last fragment of an ascent account provides the members of the havurah with the proper seals for the entrance into the seventh palace (left out in the previous account), supplemented with the names of the palace's guardian angels. Standing before the throne of glory, the mystic again intones a hymn – with no vision of God communicated.

The microforms assembled in Hekhalot Zutarti are even more diverse than those we encountered in Hekhalot Rabbati. The hero is now R. Aqiva, and the magical use of God's names takes center-stage. The ascent to the Merkavah reveals the name(s) that can be taught to Aqiva's students and used by them for magical purposes. Hence, Merkavah mysticism becomes an esoteric discipline – reserved for an elite – that ultimately takes shape in a book. Even the explicit question of whether one can see God resorts to God's name and in fact concludes that seeing God consists in knowing his name. The heavenly liturgy as the climax of the ascent in Hekhalot Rabbati does not play a significant role in Hekhalot Zutarti. The macroform's ascent accounts are saturated with the editor's predilection for God's names.

The Metatron microform in Hekhalot Zutarti is unique to the New York manuscript. Hence, it is most likely a later addition that apparently makes use of some form of the 3 Enoch macroform. As to be expected in Hekhalot Zutarti, it focuses on the names of God and of Metatron, whose name is like God's name. Often the names of God and of Metatron become interchangeable, and it is not always clear who is being addressed. In his exceptional status Metatron is elevated above all the other angels, including the holy creatures (who are even not allowed to hear God's ineffable name).

The brief microform containing a version of the famous water test followed by an ascent account presents a peculiar blend of Hekhalot Rabbati- and Hekhalot Zutarti-type material. Characteristic of the former is a long litany praising God as king as the ascent's climax, and characteristic of the latter is a successful adjuration of the angels as the culmination of the mystic's endeavors. For the editor of Hekhalot Zutarti, the ascent to the Merkavah has become a discipline, put down in a book, that guarantees successful magical adjurations. The circle of recipients of the message is broadened to include not only students of R. Aqiva but in fact anyone who is able to learn and understand the book. The ascent has turned into an adjuration (with the proper preparatory ritual applied to it) that is accessible to everybody who knows how to carry it out. The concluding two microforms of Hekhalot Zutarti continue and explain in greater detail the macroform's editor's emphasis on the book and the use of the names.

The same is true for the Shi'ur Qomah macroform, incorporated in the Merkavah Rabbah macroform and preserved as a macroform of its own in Ms. Munich 40: it reveals not only the size of God's limbs (given in Persian miles, and hence pointing to a Babylonian context) but also the limbs' names, with the latter clearly being presented as the crucial part of the Shi'ur Qomah tradition. In contrast to Scholem and his followers, I do not see any reason to believe that the Shi'ur Qomah tradition as we have it in the Hekhalot literature emerged from exegesis of the biblical Song of Songs; nor do I think it has been proved that it must be regarded as essential for Merkavah mystical speculations because it is a particularly old layer of the Hekhalot literature. Nowhere in the Hekhalot literature is the description of God's body directly linked to the vision of the Merkavah mystic.

3 Enoch, the last macroform discussed in the chapter, belongs to the latest layer of the Hekhalot literature, compiled in Babylonia some time between 700 and 900 CE. With its concern with the Shekhinah and the traditional Messiah, it rerabbinizes the Hekhalot literature, and with its focus on the heavenly journey of its hero accompanied by an *angelus interpres* (as opposed to the Merkavah mystical ascent account), it redirects Merkavah mysticism to classical apocalyptical patterns. Apart from Ishmael's truncated ascent, it is mainly occupied with Enoch, who was transformed into the highest angel, Metatron – the *na'ar* and *YHWH ha-qatan* – who becomes God's viceroy with unlimited power, elevated over and above angels and human beings alike. The opposition to the unprecedented authority assigned to Metatron (which even found its way into the macroform) serves only to underline his unique status. Against the recent trend in scholarship to connect 3 Enoch's Metatron with the Enoch of 1 and 2 Enoch and to see this amalgam of Enochic traditions as the hotbed of early Jewish as well as Christian binitarian speculations, I am inclined to locate 3 Enoch's (as well as the rabbis') Metatron in the cultural context of (late) Babylonian Judaism and to regard it as a response to the New Testament message of Jesus Christ.

Chapter 9

Conclusions

We have made a long journey through quite a diverse body of literature, from Ezekiel's vision of God in the open heaven through the ascent to heaven of a few chosen individuals (Enoch, Levi, Abraham, Isaiah, Zephaniah, and John), the communion of human beings and angels in the Qumran community, the ascent of the human soul to its divine origin in Philo, and the exegetical exercises of the rabbis as their vehicle for approaching God, to the experiences of the Merkavah mystics as described in the Hekhalot literature. In this concluding chapter I summarize the major phenomena, motifs, and concepts as they appear in the respective literary corpora, as far as possible with their communal setting in mind, and compare them with each other.

Ezekiel and the Ascent Apocalypses

Ezekiel's inaugural vision was composed of the determinants of the open heaven, the seer-visionary, his vision, and a revelation as the purpose of the vision. I will begin with the first component, the open heaven, which soon becomes the goal of the seer who sets off to leave his place on earth and conquer unknown territory. Whereas Ezekiel remains on earth, with God appearing above him in the open heaven (a motif that returns in some apocalypses and in particular in the New Testament), the ascent apocalypses have the seer actively ascending to heaven to seek God there. In the book of Ezekiel the seer is the priest Ezekiel, who was part of the elite that was exiled to Babylonia in 597 BCE, hence a fairly well-known historical figure. The visionaries in the ascent apocalypses, by contrast, are all biblical heroes of the past (with the exception of John in the New Testament Book of Revelation, clearly a contemporary figure) to whom, although they are portrayed as protagonists of the ascent and recipients of the divine revelation, the heavenly journey is ascribed by a much later author/editor. In other words, the ascent apocalypses are no doubt pseudepigraphical works that pretend to belong to a distant past but in fact are later creations that emerged from highly concrete (postbiblical) historical circumstances, far removed from the time in which the biblical heroes flourished.

But in Ezekiel and in the ascent apocalypses, the seers do not peer into or ascend to heaven on their own initiative; rather, they are all taken by surprise because something unexpected happens to them. Ezekiel, standing on the bank of the Chebar canal, is caught by the hand of God; Enoch, in the Book of the Watchers and in 2 Enoch, receives his vision in a dream after he has fallen asleep (although in 2 Enoch he wakes up and the dream turns into "reality"), whereas in the Similitudes he is carried off by a whirlwind, with no further details disclosed; Levi, too, has just fallen asleep when an angel invites him to enter heaven; and John, suddenly seeing a door open in heaven, is likewise invited to come on up. Abraham's case is particularly revealing: the biblical *Vorlage* recounting Abraham's sacrifice and God's promise – which take place when Abraham is fast asleep – is turned into an ascent, with the sacrificial birds ironically used as the vehicle for Abraham's and the accompanying angel's ascent to heaven. Isaiah is the only exception, since he remains with his body on earth, only his spirit being lifted to heaven to experience the vision.[1]

The heaven(s) that the visionaries see open or to which they ascend are all quite different. Whereas the Book of Ezekiel, the Book of the Watchers, and, interestingly enough, the Apocalypse of John (following the paradigm of Ezekiel) retain the old biblical cosmology with the one-tiered heaven above the earth (and the Netherworld beneath the earth), all the other apocalypses introduce a multilevel schema consisting of a variety of heavens that climaxes in the seven-heavens pattern (2 Enoch, Apocalypse of Abraham, Ascension of Isaiah, and probably also the Testament of Levi). It goes without saying that if the multilevel schema is employed, God resides in the uppermost heaven. This highest heaven is often explicitly described as the heavenly Temple (Book of the Watchers, Testament of Levi, Similitudes), but frequently the connection with the Temple can only be deduced from specific circumstances, such as the angelic liturgy taking place in heaven (of which the seer becomes part).

On seeing the heavens open or on ascending to heaven, the visionary is exposed to certain experiences that affect his behavior and sometimes even his appearance. In Ezekiel, God's sudden "hand" on the prophet clearly implies some violence in the experience, but there is no indication of any immediate response on the part of the prophet when having this vision, let alone of his physical or spiritual transformation. Only after the vision, when he is brought back to his fellow exiles, is he "bitter" – presumably because God had forced such an impossible mission on him. Within the ascent apocalypses, the most common and almost stereotypical reaction of the seer to what happens to him is horror, fear, and prostration. Enoch in the Book of the Watchers, from the moment he sees the first house in heaven, is filled with horror; his body trembles and shakes, and he falls on his face, remaining in this position until an angel puts him back on

---

[1] The missing beginning of the Apocalypse of Zephaniah does not allow us to speculate about the circumstances of Zephaniah's ascent. Clement of Alexandria's brief quotation, however, refers to a "spirit" that took Zephaniah up into the fifth heaven; see Wintermute, *OTP*, vol. 1, p. 508.

his feet and brings him to the door of the second house (the throne chamber in the heavenly Temple). Similarly, when the Enoch of the Similitudes sees God on his throne (chs. 60 and 71), he trembles and, with his body collapsing, falls on his face. Finally, the Enoch of 2 Enoch almost excessively acts out his horror and fear: he perspires from anxiety when he sees the first angels, he is terrified and trembles when he sees the heavenly hosts, he is even more frightened when the angels are about to leave him and, in despair, prostrates before them, again falling down when he captures a glimpse of God.

The same holds true for the other ascent apocalypses. In the Apocalypse of Abraham, Abraham's soul flees from him when he first hears God's voice, and he falls on his face. Abraham's body weakens and his spirit departs from him again when he sees the heavenly liturgy of the angels, and when at the peak of his experience he hears God's voice in the fire, he wants to fall down; but since there is no firm ground in the highest heaven, he must pull himself together and focus all his energy on joining in with the praise of the angels. Isaiah, ascending through the seven heavens with his angelic guide, falls prostrate and attempts to worship the angels sitting on thrones in the respective heavens. And finally Zephaniah, whose reaction is directed solely at the angels. When he sees the first angel (who turns out to be the accuser), his body weakens and he falls on his face; this behavior recurs with the second angel (who turns out to be Eremiel, almost God's equal), and Zephaniah falls on his face and worships him.[2]

Yet, most conspicuously, some apocalypses are not content with referring to the customary horror and fear of the seer as the appropriate response to his experience. They go much further and see in the transformation of the visionary into an angelic being the ultimate climax of such an experience. This trend begins with the Enoch of the Similitudes, where we hear for the first time that the weakening of the seer's body is accompanied by his transformation into something different, obviously an angel (ch. 71). Interestingly enough, the text emphasizes that it is Enoch's *spirit* that is transformed; he apparently remains, despite his transformation, in his enfeebled body. Furthermore, I do not think that this transformation as described in the Similitudes must be viewed as the peak of Enoch's heavenly experience,[3] for it is mentioned rather casually; what seems of greater importance to the author is the angel Michael's announcement that this Enoch is the Son of Man – obviously a reference to Dan. 7:13, where the "one like a human being" comes down with the clouds of heaven and is presented to the Ancient of Days. Enoch has now become, quite literally, someone who looks like a

---

[2] There is no noticeable reaction of the seer in the Testament of Levi and in the Apocalypse of John: John completely fades in importance compared with the new hero, the Lamb.

[3] As has been suggested by Chester, *Messiah and Exaltation*, pp. 64 ff. I also see no basis in the text for Chester's claim that Enoch undergoes a physical *and* spiritual transformation (ibid., p. 66), unless one wants to argue that what comes through in the Ethiopic translation actually means body and spirit.

human being but, in fact, is no longer a human being in the full sense of the word. He is something in between, either between a human being and a genuine angel or between a human being and God (that is, an angel), depending on how much importance one wishes to attach to the fact that he remains in his body.

The ambiguity with regard to the question of a full bodily transformation (in the sense that the seer gets completely rid of his human body) is intensified in 2 Enoch. True, Enoch becomes like one of the angels, "with no observable difference," but it remains unclear what precisely this angelification means and to what extent it affects his bodily existence. There can be no doubt, however, that the book comes very close to a complete bodily transformation of its hero.

The Ascension of Isaiah seems to take a more straightforward stance. Isaiah's transformation into an angel is the prerequisite for his ability to join in with the angels' praise of God, that is, to participate in the heavenly liturgy. But the real transformation occurs only in the seventh heaven, where he is stripped of his garment of flesh and receives a new, heavenly garment. The ultimate transformation, however, will take place only after his death, when he has become one of the deceased righteous. His transformation is not only temporary – he needs to return to his "garment of flesh" – but also of a lesser degree (in his ability to see God) in comparison to the postmortem transformation of the righteous. The author does not bother to convey whether the transformation affects the seer's body or not (he seems to take it for granted); he is more concerned with the distinction between the transformation into an angel and the ultimate transformation into a deceased righteous. Finally Zephaniah, too, before he reaches the destination of his journey – the place of the righteous souls – puts on an angelic garment, that is, he is transformed into an angel. Since we are dealing here with a deceased righteous, the status Isaiah so desperately wants to attain, we may safely assume that Zephaniah's transformation does indeed include his body. Again, as in several of the other apocalypses, the immediate effect of Zephaniah's angelification is his ability to understand the angels' language and to join in with their praises.

Despite its elaborate description of the hero's heavenly journey with his transformation into an angel, the Ascension of Isaiah is the sole apocalypse that presents the seer as physically present among his companions on earth during his journey, even disclosing details about his bodily functions (eyes open, lips silent). Moreover, it explicitly maintains that Isaiah's body remained on earth and that only his spirit was taken up into heaven, clearly contradicting its own main narrative. In modern psychology one might call this phenomenon a case of "cataleptic rigor," a state in which the seer's self has left him, whereas the shell of his body, seemingly inanimate, stays behind. Such a concept is completely alien not only to the other apocalypses but also to the remaining literature of Second Temple Judaism. Its sharp distinction between body and soul would seem almost to betray a certain Platonic or Neoplatonic influence – a strange combination indeed – and, not by coincidence, comes closest to what we encounter in Philo and – again, strangely enough – in one peculiar narrative of the Hekhalot literature (R. Nehunya b. Haqanah's recall from the Merkavah). But whereas Philo blatantly and persistently dismisses the body and sees in the soul's return to its divine origin the goal of all human existence, the Nehunya b. Haqanah story stands out,[4] like Isaiah's experience in the ascent apocalypses, as unique in the Hekhalot literature, creating a tension with the ascent accounts as described in the bulk of the Merkavah mystical texts (which never distinguish between the adept's body and soul). It would appear prudent, therefore, not to overemphasize the Isaiah and Nehunya b. Haqanah incidents and to refrain from using them as the appropriate yardstick for determining the character and circumstances of the ascent experiences in the apocalypses and the Hekhalot literature.[5]

The vision that greets the seer at the peak of his ascent is typically considered the climax of the whole adventure. Yet the accumulated evidence of Ezekiel and the ascent apocalypses suggests adopting a more restrained and modest position. Some apocalypses simply do not convey a vision (Apocalypse of Zephaniah) or plainly declare that the seer was unable to look or was prohibited from looking at God (Apocalypse of Abraham, Ascension of Isaiah), whereas others are merely content with invoking the traditional biblical imagery of God seated on his throne in the heavenly Temple (Testament of Levi), heavily influenced by Ezekiel and Daniel (Similitudes). What remains, however, of Ezekiel's boldly depicted human-like figure surrounded by fire, is the fire rather than the human-like figure. No one of his successors goes as far as Ezekiel in approaching the human-like figure on the throne of glory. The Book of the Watchers makes do with God's luminous raiment veiled in fire as the object of Enoch's desire, and the Apocalypse of John describes God on his throne in terms of brilliant jewels (the author is much more preoccupied with the figure of the "Lamb"). Only the author of 2 Enoch goes beyond this rather stereotyped arsenal when he compares

---

[4] On the possible additional case of one Gedullah hymn (*Synopse zur Hekhalot-Literatur*, § 93), see above, p. 253. These two cases are definitely not enough evidence to claim that it is characteristic of Hekhalot Rabbati that only the soul ascends and the body is left behind on earth (as Philip Alexander suggests; private communication). Hekhalot Rabbati is anything but a uniform document, and if at all we want to judge it as a whole, we would come to the opposite conclusion, namely, that the ascent of body and soul is taken for granted.

[5] The only other text that reveals a similar awareness of the distinction between the mystic's body and soul is the apostle Paul's second letter to the Corinthians – written in the second half of the first century CE, hence not long after Philo wrote his tractates – in which Paul boasts of having been "carried off (or snatched up: *harpagenta*) into the third heaven" or "paradise" (2 Cor. 12:1–5). This is obviously a report about an ascent to heaven, very much in the tradition of the apocalyptic ascent accounts. When Paul, however, goes on to expressly state that he does not know whether this exciting event happened "in the body" or "out of the body" (*eite en sōmati ouk oida, eite ektos tou sōmatos ouk oida*), we suddenly encounter an author who, apparently under the influence of contemporary Platonic ideas, seems to have lost confidence in the traditional biblical unity of body and soul.

God's face to red-hot iron emitting sparks. Despite this no doubt creative – if not particularly ingenious – idea, obviously inspired by a very profane forge, the primary message remains: God's appearance is one of burning and impenetrable fire. Moreover, the author or some manuscript scribes of 2 Enoch, having brought themselves to venture this comparison, immediately retract from it and declare that God's appearance cannot be described.

The vision is almost always followed by and completed with a divine revelation that explains the function and purpose of the vision. Ezekiel is sent back to his rebellious people to tell them that Jerusalem and the Temple will be destroyed but that there is nevertheless hope: the hope of restoration after Jerusalem's fall. Enoch in the Book of the Watchers conveys the message that the Watchers will be condemned forever because they defiled the earth. Levi learns that the priesthood he inaugurated will become corrupt until the day when the eschatological priest appears. The Enoch of the Similitudes discovers that he is the Son of Man who will bring peace to the earth; and the Enoch of 2 Enoch is instructed to write down voluminous heavenly books that he must teach his sons. The purpose of Abraham's vision in the Apocalypse of Abraham is the revelation of the future history of Israel with the destruction of the Temple at its center, whereas in the Ascension of Isaiah the eponymous prophet is supposed to give an account of his vision to King Hezekiah. Finally, the Apocalypse of John reveals the secrets of the eschaton as contained in the scroll that only the Lamb can open. In a considerable number of cases the critique of the earthly Temple and its priesthood plays a prominent role.

The concern for the future history of the people of Israel in general and the unavoidable destruction of the Temple in particular underlines the ultimate goal of the visionary's ascent and the revelation he receives: he and his community on earth are assured that God, despite the utterly bleak prospects for the future, with the worst scenario that can happen, the destruction of the Temple, is still up there in heaven, in his celestial Temple. The very fact that God summons a human being to ascend to his heavenly abode, in order to grant him a vision and a revelation, proves that God is still approachable, that the gap between God and his human creatures can still be bridged, even if he is absent from the Jerusalem Temple.[6]

With the ascent of the seer, his liturgical union with the angels culminating in his angelification, his vision of God, and the revelation addressed to his earthly community, the process is complete. The seer or visionary clearly undergoes a distinct and unique experience that forever changes his life; it is only reluctantly and grudgingly that he returns to his previous human existence, and, hav-

---

[6] On this, see also Martha Himmelfarb, "Revelation and Rapture: The Transformation of the Visionary in the Ascent Apocalypses," in John J. Collins and James H. Charlesworth, eds., *Mysteries and Revelations: Apocalyptic Studies since the Uppsala Colloquium* (Sheffield, UK: JSOT Press, 1991), pp. 79–90.

ing done so, he can hardly wait until he is allowed to return to the place of his desire. Transformed into an angel, he comes as close to God as possible, but the distance between him and God is always maintained, as is the distance between God and his angels. The seer's angelification (*unio angelica*) does not mean that he merges into an indistinguishable mass of angels; he keeps his personality and identity in relationship to the angels as well as to God (as so do the angels). If in the course of his transformation he forfeits his body, this is only temporary, since he must eventually return to his body and resume his earthly existence – until he becomes a deceased righteous (but there can be no doubt that even the deceased righteous retain their original identities). Hence, the transformed seer, in his angelicized state, at no time enters into a union with his God. In view of the accumulated evidence, therefore, I see no justification for the attempt of some scholars to extend the notion of angelification in the ascent apocalypses to that of the deification of the seer.[7] Neither is angelification identical with deification, nor does it necessarily lead to deification; the apocalypses do not blur the boundaries between God and his angels or the few human beings who are chosen to be transformed into angels during their lifetime.

Finally, addressing the thorny question of whether Ezekiel and the ascent apocalypses reflect the actual experiences of their authors or whether they are to be regarded as literary constructs – that is, fiction – I would again sound a note of caution. As far as Ezekiel is concerned, I have summarized Ezekiel 1 as the report and testimony of a prophetic experience, as something that actually happened to the prophet (or that the prophet imagined happening to him, or that the author of the book imagined as truly happening to the prophet Ezekiel). This is certainly possible, and I do not wish to exclude such a possibility. On the other hand, however, I am well aware that such a premise may be overly naïve and that we may in fact be dealing here with a thoroughly literary enterprise, in other words, with fiction. This latter stance has been taken by some scholars,[8] and indeed the sophisticated texture of Ezekiel's first chapter with its fabric of bibli-

---

[7] See, e. g., Morray-Jones, "Transformational Mysticism," pp. 13–26; Chester, *Messiah and Exaltation*, p. 80. Not by coincidence, Himmelfarb ("Revelation and Rapture," p. 86), having briefly surveyed the apocalypses, uses the term "deification" only in connection with the Greek magical papyri and even there plays down its significance: "In a system in which there are many deities, 'a godlike nature' probably means something not very different from taking one's place among the angels."

[8] See, e. g., James L. Kugel and Rowan A. Greer, *Early Biblical Interpretation* (Philadelphia: Westminster, 1986), pp. 17–19; Ellen F. Davis, *Swallowing the Scroll: Textuality and the Dynamics of Discourse in Ezekiel's Prophecy* (Sheffield, UK: Sheffield Academic Press, 1989); and Menahem Haran, "Observations on Ezekiel as a Book Prophet," in Ronald L. Troxel, Kelvin G. Friebel, and Dennis R. Magary, eds., *Seeking Out the Wisdom of the Ancients: Essays Offered to Honor Michael V. Fox on the Occasion of His Sixty-Fifth Birthday* (Winona Lake, IN: Eisenbrauns, 2005), pp. 3–19. I owe these references to my Princeton colleague Simeon Chavel.

cal language and imagery, particularly from Genesis and Exodus, makes such a suggestion very plausible.

The same is true in my view for the ascent apocalypses. They, too, draw to a large extent on language, ideas, and imagery taken not only from the Bible (Ezekiel, Daniel, and others) but also from other apocalypses as an inherent part of their "experience." Moreover, and more important, they come in the disguise of pseudonymity – a strong disguise, indeed, and a strong argument against the actual experience that they pretend to have undergone. As Martha Himmelfarb has aptly put it: "there are many mirrors between the experience and the text," and "[p]seudonymity is perhaps the darkest" of all these mirrors.[9] Yet again, neither of these two arguments is in itself sufficient to prove that the ascent apocalypses are "fiction": it may well be that such a premise, too, can be "unmasked" as overly naïve. Recently, Christopher Rowland has tried to steer a kind of middle course between the Scylla of literary fiction and the Charybdis of genuine experience. He proposes that for some ancient readers, the interpretation of Ezekiel 1

> involved seeing again what Ezekiel had seen. It may well have involved the resort to cross-referencing, but this contributed to a dynamic imaginative activity in which the details of Ezekiel's vision were understood by a complex interweaving of vision and textual networking.[10]

This sounds like a reasonable compromise between the alternative of fiction versus experience, a polarized view increasingly being perceived as sterile and unproductive. But how does such a "complex interweaving of vision and textual networking" actually work? The visionary sees what his predecessors have seen, and adds to this his own experience? But what if his own experience consists of little more than reconfiguring the textual network that he has received? This does not really lead us out of our impasse. It also does not help much when Rowland continues to argue that even if the literary approach proves to be correct, "this does not in itself mean that the experiences described are false but rather that this is what the mystic was expected to see."[11] I could not agree more – but no one I know of who advocates the literary approach has ever claimed that the experiences described in the ascent apocalypses are *false*. Falsehood is a completely inappropriate (not to say false) category. Invoking this category means that one fails to understand the concept of pseudepigraphy. The authors of the ascent apocalypses clearly believed that their heroes (that is, they themselves) had cer-

[9] Himmelfarb, "Revelation and Rapture," p. 88; see also eadem, *Ascent to Heaven*, pp. 110–114.

[10] Christopher Rowland, with Patricia Gibbons and Vicente Dobroruka, "Visionary Experience in Ancient Judaism and Christianity," in DeConick, *Paradise Now*, p. 48.

[11] Ibid., p. 53.

tain experiences, but this does not necessarily mean that these experiences were genuine experiences and not literary constructs.

When Rowland concludes that the apocalypses of Second Temple Judaism may provide "examples of those moments when human experience moves beyond what is apparent to physical perception to open up perceptions of other dimensions of existence ... different from a purely analytical or rational approach to texts or received wisdom,"[12] he finally lets the cat out of the bag and reveals his true agenda. For there exists hardly a more devastating critique in some scholarly circles preoccupied with "mysticism" than accusations of a "purely analytical or rational approach" to the sacred texts of Judaism and Christianity. *Horribile dictu*. The real agenda behind this accusation is the firm conviction that it is only "natural" to crave for "other dimensions of existence," since the new generation of scholars has, at long last, left the old rationalism behind (a prime example of which was, to be sure, Scholem) and has opened itself up again to the possibility of paranormal experiences. I do not think, however, that it makes much sense to play off an allegedly "rationalist" approach against a more genuine or natural "experiential" approach – and all the more so if the experiential approach turns out to be informed by a pronounced religious (if not New Age) attitude. The "rationalists," to whose cohort I gladly admit belonging to, do not wish to exclude categorically any possibility of genuine experience on the part of the visionaries; they just do not see much of such genuine experience coming through the "textual networking" of Ezekiel and the ascent apocalypses. We may be blind, but the accumulated efforts of our opponents have not (yet) made us see.

Hekhalot Literature

The body of texts no doubt coming closest to the ascent apocalypses is the Hekhalot literature. With this statement I explicitly respond to and reject the recent trend in scholarship to locate at least the "phenomenological" if not the immediate historical precursor of Merkavah mysticism in the Qumran community. It is in the Hekhalot literature that we find the clearest analogy to the frame of reference that was so characteristic of the ascent apocalypses: ascent, seer, vision, and purpose of the vision. My analyses have demonstrated that the Hekhalot literature presents an extremely complex web of different, competing, and even conflicting ideas and tendencies that cannot and must not be forced into the Procrustean bed of a harmonizing synthesis. But for the sake of a comparison between the Hekhalot literature and the ascent apocalypses, I will nevertheless venture some broader and more general observations.

---

[12] Ibid., p. 55.

The ascent as such becomes not only more important in the Hekhalot literature than in the ascent apocalypses, it also turns into a highly perilous adventure.
The mystic or adept is not called into heaven by God, accompanied and guided
by angels, but rather undertakes the ascent, as a rule, on his own initiative[13] and
accordingly is exposed to considerable dangers, of which precisely the angels
constitute the greatest and deadliest one, since it is their main task not to guide
him through the heavenly realm but to *prevent* the unworthy mystic from ac-
complishing the ascent. And even for the worthy mystic it can, in certain layers
of the Hekhalot literature, be extremely dangerous to look at God (or rather at
his gown, as the text has it, similar to the tradition of God's raiment in the Book
of the Watchers and the Similitudes). The territory that the mystic crosses during his journey emulates the fully developed seven-heaven scheme of the ascent
apocalypses as inspired by the imagery of the earthly Temple; so it becomes clear
from the outset that the mystic ascends through the heavenly halls or chambers to
the Temple in heaven, where God in the seventh heaven resides on his throne.

The notion of the worthy and the unworthy mystic entails a complicated set
of implications and consequences that are alien to the ascent apocalypses: who
is worthy and who is not, how does the worthy mystic prove his credibility, how
do the angels prevent the unworthy adept from entering, and so on? Coming
into play here is a variety of magical tools (seals, names) that are inextricably
woven into the fabric of the ascent accounts, yet the traditional rabbinic virtue of
Torah knowledge (in the broadest sense of the term) is also invoked. The heroes
of the ascent are not biblical figures of the remote past but famous rabbis (Ishmael and Aqiva in particular, or a larger and well-defined circle of the rabbinic
elite), but many Hekhalot texts – presumably the later ones – grant the privilege
of the ascent to almost anyone who proves worthy. If we take seriously the dis-
tinctively priestly coloring of some of the ascent apocalypses and the emphasis
on the heavenly Temple in almost all our relevant texts, the shift from priests
to rabbis in the Hekhalot literature clearly follows the pattern employed in the
classical rabbinic literature. Some texts excel in elevating the chosen mystic over
and above not only his fellow Jews but also the Roman emperor and the angels,
and even make him a precursor of the Messiah or a savior figure that renders
the traditional Messiah superfluous. The few apocalypses incorporated into the
Hekhalot literature at a later stage attempt to correct this idea and revert to a
more conventional eschatology.

The vision no doubt is the climax of the whole enterprise in the Hekhalot literature; at least, this is what we are made to expect following the long, convoluted, and in many cases fragmentary accounts, narratives, hymns, and prayers.

---

[13] This is indeed the main difference between the ascent in the Hekhalot literature and the
ascent apocalypses (see above, pp. 331 f.), as has been noticed already by Michael Swartz in his
cautious and well-balanced article, "The Dead Sea Scrolls and Later Jewish Magic and Mysticism," *DSD* 8 (2001), p. 190.

But more often than not I have concluded that in fact our skillfully charged ex-pectation is mercilessly dashed: instead of finally observing the mystic enjoying the vision of God, we are fobbed off with just another volley of endless litanies. Yet precisely this, I have argued, is the "content" of the vision according to the Hekhalot literature – not the image and features of God on his throne but the inclusion of the mystic in the heavenly liturgy.[14] I have proposed that for this experience we employ the phrase *unio liturgica*, liturgical union or communion, in contrast to the misleading phrase *unio mystica*, or mystical union, of the adept with God. This liturgical union of the mystic with the angels and, to a certain degree, also with God (occurring during the angels' and the mystic's joint praise of God) is one of the most important characteristics shared by the Hekhalot lit-erature and the ascent apocalypses.

My persistent and unrelenting insistence on the fact that the ascent accounts in the Hekhalot literature have little to say about what the mystic actually sees when he attains the goal of his desire – that it is, in a way, the phenomenon of the "empty vision" – has met with some not unexpected criticism. As an exam-ple, I quote Elliot Wolfson:

> I think Schäfer is absolutely right in pointing out that a prime reason for the ascent is the participation of the adept in the liturgy of the heavenly court. Indeed, the *yeridah la-merkavah* (entry to the chariot) that follows the ascent to the seventh palace is fun-damentally a liturgical act. But – and here is my critical point – participation in the angelic choir arises precisely by virtue of the mystic's entry to the realm of the chariot and consequent vision of the enthroned glory. One cannot separate in an absolute way the visionary and liturgical aspects of this experience; indeed, it might be said that in order to praise God one must see God.[15]

Sure enough, the mystic's participation in the angelic liturgy is a consequence of his entry into the realm of the innermost heavenly sanctuary with God seated on his throne, and the liturgical and visionary aspects of the adventure do belong together, but I fail to see the logic of the conclusion (or is it a premise?) "that in order to praise God one must see God." Is any praise of God the *consequence* of seeing God? Certainly not, unless one wants to adopt a pan-mystical stance whereby all kinds of liturgical activity presuppose a vision of God.[16] I am not saying that a vision of God is impossible in the Hekhalot literature, and I am even not arguing that the Merkavah mystic does not see God. I am just pointing out the fact that the editors of the Hekhalot literature do not trouble themselves

---

[14] One may call this a clear case of "apophaticism," as Philip Alexander suggests (private communication), but apophaticism is not reserved for mysticism; it is part and parcel of nega-tive theology in a much broader sense.

[15] Wolfson, *Through a Speculum That Shines*, p. 117; see also idem, "Yeridah la-Merkavah," p. 23.

[16] The sentence makes more sense the other way around: in order to see God one must praise God, that is, the only way to seeing God leads through praising God, and in this sense one could say that praising God is seeing God and seeing God is praising God.

with communicating the contents of any such a vision – whether or not there is one. I do believe, however, that this lack of communication does not result from some inability or timidity on the part of the authors or editors, let alone from the loss of some crucial passages in the course of the manuscript transmission; rather, I hold that our authors' or editors' reticence with regard to the visionary aspect of the ascent experience – or, to be more precise, regarding not just any kind of visionary aspect (since the Hekhalot literature is clearly full of "visual elements") but the peak of this visionary experience, namely, the vision of God on his throne – is part of their deliberate editorial strategy and hence their message: they do not *want* to emphasize the vision of God as the climax of the mystic's ascent; they are more interested in his becoming part of the liturgical performance in heaven and, moreover, in the ultimate message conveyed to him by God.

If we conclude that the mystic, at the peak of the heavenly liturgy, enters into a liturgical (comm)union with the angels and also with God – since God, at least in some texts, is not only the passive recipient of the liturgical performance but also its active participant – does this mean that the mystic in the Hekhalot literature undergoes a process of physical transformation or transfiguration into an angel (that is, of angelification) similar to the transformation of the seer in the ascent apocalypses? I am reluctant to go so far because, again, I do not think that this is what our authors and editors are interested in. They are untroubled by the problem of a possible distinction between body and soul (taking it for granted that the adept ascends and descends in his body *and* soul), nor are they concerned with Enoch's very peculiar case or with the postmortem destiny of the righteous (taking it for granted that their heroes are in principle meant to return to their earthly community).[17] The angelification of a human being in the strict sense of the term is not what they apparently wish to advocate.

Nor are they intent on proposing that the Merkavah mystic is going even a step further and experiencing a process of deification or quasi-deification, as has been suggested by Wolfson. Wolfson claims that according to "the major texts" in the Hekhalot corpus, "the mystic is said to be seated in the seventh palace before the throne of glory"; that this fact, which he calls the "enthronement of the mystic," results from his vision of God; and that therefore "one can speak of the enthronement as the quasi-deification or angelification that renders possible the mystical vision."[18] The evidence for the mystic's being seated that Wolfson has provided[19] is not only much less ample than he maintains,[20] I also fail to see

---

[17] With the exception, of course, of 3 Enoch.

[18] Wolfson, "Mysticism," p. 194.

[19] Not in the above mentioned article, but in "Yeridah la-Merkavah," pp. 22 ff.

[20] *Synopse zur Hekhalot-Literatur*, § 227 (Nehunya b. Haqanah sits before the throne of glory), § 233 (Dumiel has the mystic sit down on a bench of pure stone – which has nothing to do with being seated before God), § 236 (the angels sit the successful mystic down next to the keruvim, ofannim, and the holy creatures), § 411 (the angels sit the mystic down before the

the equation of being seated with "enthronement," let alone the equation of "enthronement" with "deification" or "divinization."[21] True, the fact that the mystic obtains a seat in the divine throne room is remarkable and assigns to him an elevated position probably above that of even (most of) the angels, but where is the enthronement? And even if some kind of enthronement takes place, what does this have to do with deification? It seems that Wolfson is influenced here by the (much more greatly elaborated) enthronement of Metatron in 3 Enoch – which indeed comes close to a deification – but the "ordinary" mystic is not Metatron, and the authors/editors of the Hekhalot literature have invested remarkably little energy in the mystic's "enthronement" or "deification." Moreover, if one wants to go for a deification of the mystic, then why not refer to the text, unique though it is, in Hekhalot Zutarti, where the angels have sat the mystic down on God's own lap,[22] a text that Wolfson does not quote? To be seated on God's lap is surely better than being seated on an angel's lap (which then signifies angelification?).[23] Unfortunately, however, the text in Hekhalot Zutarti continues with the mystic's request for an adjuration of the angels[24] – hardly appropriate behavior for a human being who has just been deified!

I should like to assert, therefore, that Metatron's enthronement and transformation in 3 Enoch is the only case in the Hekhalot literature of the angelification of a human being that even borders on deification. Of all the macroforms assembled in the Hekhalot literature, 3 Enoch is not coincidentally the one that comes closest to the ascent apocalypses. It seems that after the classical rabbinic period, some Jewish authors felt free not only to revert to the apocalyptic tradition but also to utilize it against their Christian opponents, who, after all, had usurped the early Jewish ascent apocalypses and converted them into Christian writings. It is against this background that Metatron begins to compete with Jesus Christ.

Turning now to the fourth and last constituent of the pattern established by Ezekiel, the purpose of the vision (or, more broadly, of the mystic's heavenly adventure) in the Hekhalot literature, we discover another remarkable similarity with the ascent apocalypses: concern for the future and well-being of the mystic's community, the people of Israel on earth. Both the ascent apocalypses and the Hekhalot literature underscore the fact that God is still there, up in heaven, that certain chosen human beings can approach him in his heavenly throne room, and that he is deeply concerned about Israel's destiny. But the Hekhalot litera-

---

throne of glory), and the Genizah fragment T.-S. K 21.95.C, fol. 2b, l. 13–17 (Metatron has the mystic sit in his lap and [?] on a seat before the throne of glory).

[21] As he puts it in "Yeridah la-Merkavah," p. 24.

[22] *Synopse zur Hekhalot-Literatur*, § 417.

[23] In addition to the Genizah fragment, where the mystic is seated on Metatron's lap, the only other microform in which the mystic is invited to sit on the lap of an angel is the David apocalypse (*Synopse zur Hekhalot-Literatur*, §§ 122 and 125), not the most characteristic of all Hekhalot texts.

[24] *Synopse zur Hekhalot-Literatur*, §§ 418 f.

ture, or rather, and more precisely, certain layers within the Hekhalot literature, go much farther than the ascent apocalypses. Extensive passages in Hekhalot Rabbati in particular emphasize again and again that God longs for the mystic to ascend to him, that Israel's Qedushah is more important to God than the Qedushah of his angels, that God is still full of love for Israel, that he loves his people even more than his angels, and that the mystic's vision and participation in the heavenly liturgy is the ultimate sign of Israel's salvation.[25]

I regard this insistence on God's continued love for Israel – with the necessary caveat concerning the multilayered character of the Hekhalot literature – as one of the most striking results of our survey. And it is here that Scholem, in my view, went farthest astray in his characterization of the Merkavah mystical experience, calling it "cosmocratorial mysticism" or, following Graetz, "Basileomorphism."[26] True, the God of the Hekhalot literature "is above all King, to be precise, Holy King,"[27] but I do not think that this is an expression of "Basileomorphism," a term presumably influenced by the idea of an (allegedly) ossified Byzantine court ritual.[28] Scholem's usual knack for distancing himself from Graetz's prejudices has obviously forsaken him here. Nor do I think that Merkavah mysticism is permeated by "a complete absence of any sentiment of divine immanence" and that there is, furthermore, "almost no love of God"[29] – quite the contrary. The upshot of this claim is revealing and deserves to be quoted in full:

> Ecstasy there was, and this fundamental experience must have been a source of religious inspiration, but we find no trace of a mystical union between the soul and God. Throughout there remained an almost exaggerated consciousness of God's *otherness*, nor does the identity and individuality of the mystic become blurred even at the height of the ecstatic passion. The Creator and His creature remain apart, and nowhere is an attempt made to bridge the gulf between them or to blur the distinction. The mystic who in his ecstasy has passed through all the gates, braved all the dangers, now stands before the throne; he sees and hears – but that is all.[30]

One can easily see that Scholem, having denied Merkavah mysticism (almost) any trace of divine immanence and love, is drifting to his pet subject: the lack of the notion of *unio mystica*. I can endorse almost everything that he says with

---

[25] This communal orientation is almost completely abandoned in Hekhalot Zutarti, with its emphasis on the individualistic and disciplinary aspect of the enterprise.

[26] Scholem, *Major Trends*, pp. 54 f.

[27] Ibid.

[28] For a detailed and more cogent analysis of the imperial (Roman and Sasanian) court ritual background of the Hekhalot literature, see Philip Alexander, "The Family of Caesar and the Family of God: The Image of the Emperor in Early Jewish Mystical Literature," in Loveday Alexander, ed., *Images of Empire: The Roman Empire in Jewish, Christian and Greco-Roman Sources* (Sheffield, UK: Sheffield Academic Press, 1991), pp. 276–297.

[29] Scholem, *Major Trends*, p. 55.

[30] Ibid., pp. 55 f.

regard to the distinction between the mystic and God and the mystic's persisting identity and individuality. But in his zeal to make clear this point, Scholem grossly overshoots the mark. I therefore share Wolfson's unease in particular with the last quoted sentence: that the seeing and hearing of the mystic "is all" that happens. This is indeed a distressing example of an overly minimalist approach.[31] Although I would not wish to argue, with Wolfson, that Scholem "forgets" the following enthronement and deification of the mystic, I agree that he does forget the most important part of the whole exercise: the confirmation of God's continuous love for Israel, the message that God still cares for his people on earth. Of course, in the Hekhalot literature there is no trace of the classical notion of God's immanence on earth. This has become impossible, because the (Second) Temple has been destroyed and because it does not appear as if God will be able to return to his earthly Temple any time soon. But this is precisely the message: that God, enthroned in the Holy of Holies of his heavenly Temple in the seventh heaven, this "transcendent" God, can still be approached – to be sure, by only a few chosen mystics, but he can indeed be approached, and the gulf between him and his creatures can be bridged. God's transcendence turns into a new and unexpected immanence.[32]

Such a message obviously presupposes not only the destroyed Temple but also the admission that this deplorable situation may continue into the foreseeable future – and beyond. If we take seriously the late formation of the Hekhalot literature toward the end of the rabbinic or even during the post-rabbinic period, we must also take into account the claim of a Christian Church firmly establishing itself in Palestine as the preeminent power – and underscoring this power with a plethora of Christian churches that rendered futile any Jewish hope for rebuilding the Temple. This applies equally to the Jews of Palestine and the Jews of Babylonia, and so it little matters where we wish to locate our Merkavah mystical texts. The Temple was lost to the Christians, who claimed that they were the new Israel and the new spiritual Temple, a claim that made a rebuilding of the Temple and a resumption of its sacrifices superfluous. It is under the impress of these historical circumstances that the Merkavah mystics set out on their journey into the heavenly Temple so as to rediscover their God there, to unite with the angels in their heavenly liturgy – and then to return to their earthly community with the divine assurance of love and redemption.

---

[31] Wolfson, "Mysticism," p. 194.

[32] A striking example of the lasting and, in this regard, unfortunate influence of Scholem can be seen in Nickelsburg's commentary on 1 Enoch in which he, with a few generalizing strokes, emphasizes the transcendent otherness and inaccessibility of God in 1 Enoch 1–36, similar, so he believes (following Scholem), to Merkavah mysticism, and even concludes that whereas "Enoch's ascent and vision of God are prologue to his commissioning, [f]or the later mystics, the vision of God was an end in itself" (Nickelsburg, *1 Enoch 1*, p. 261). That is what happens when one ignores twenty years or so of research on Merkavah mysticism and just conjures up old stereotypes.

As to the question of actual experience versus literary fiction, the Hekhalot literature has become one of the major battlefields of modern research addressing this problem. As I have noted already, the Hekhalot literature differs from the ascent apocalypses in that its protagonists assume a much more active stance: they are not the passive recipients of divine rapture but take matters into their own hands. Nevertheless, with its rabbinic heroes of the time of the Mishnah – mixing them up most anachronistically in the circle of the havurah – the Hekhalot literature invokes a "mythic past" [33] rather than describing concrete historical circumstances. Hence, as in the ascent apocalypses, the decidedly pseudepigraphical character of the Hekhalot literature speaks strongly in favor of their being literary creations rather than reflections of actual experiences. This obviously holds true for R. Ishmael, R. Aqiva, and R. Nehunya b. Haqanah, the most famous protagonists of the ascent accounts – since it would clearly be naïve to assign to them the "original" mystical experience that only later develops into "literature" – and it becomes increasingly evident with the growing tendency, in later layers of the Hekhalot literature, to extend the circle of initiates further – to include even the rabbis' students and ultimately everyone who knows the rules of the game.

One could, of course, argue that in fact some unknown authors – and hence protagonists of the "real" mystical experience – hide behind the heroes of the past. But all attempts to uncover the original mystical circles behind the literature, the circles of adepts that were actually engaged in the practices described in the literary corpus that has been preserved, these attempts have still not led us very far. Either they impose on the multifarious and polymorphic body of the Hekhalot literature a uniform concept that does little justice to its diversity (such as David Halperin's theory of the authors of the Hekhalot literature as the disenfranchised *'ammei ha-aretz*, who rebelled against the rabbinic elite),[34] or they apply only to certain segments of the Hekhalot literature (such as Michael Swartz's theory of the "secondary elites" of scribes that addresses primarily the Sar ha-Torah traditions in the Hekhalot literature),[35] or they use models of religious experience whose applicability to the Hekhalot literature is at the very least debatable (such as James Davila's shamanic model, taken from preliterate societies).[36] The practitioners of the ascent and the sociohistorical grounding of their "experiences" have largely eluded us.

Again, this is not to say that with regard to the Hekhalot literature, too, the dichotomy between "literature" and "experience" has definitely been solved in favor of the former. It may even be that this dichotomy is a false and mislead-

---

[33] Himmelfarb, *Ascent to Heaven*, p. 143.

[34] Halperin, *The Faces of the Chariot*, pp. 437 ff.

[35] Michael D. Swartz, *Scholastic Magic: Ritual and Revelation in Early Jewish Mysticism* (Princeton, NJ: Princeton University Press, 1996), pp. 209–229.

[36] Davila, *Descenders to the Chariot*.

ing one and that the very fact of establishing it inhibits its solution. Yet if one wishes to make this claim, one needs to take seriously the literary character of the Merkavah mystical experience as presented in the Hekhalot literature. And this literary character with its endless and stereotypical recitations, repetitions, allusions, and cross-references – in all the layers of the Hekhalot literature – is so predominant that it seems hopeless to discover and expose an "experiential core" behind the literary veil.[37] Whatever there may have been of an original experience, it has coagulated into literature, and it is precisely this literature that becomes the focus of attention: Merkavah mysticism is described over and over again as an esoteric discipline that can nevertheless be studied, that is written in a book, and that can be taught to one's students. Reading and reciting the experience of the ascent has *become* the ascent, or, to put it in terms of our dichotomy, reciting the literature *is* the experience.

This reading and reciting of the Hekhalot *literature* was neither a uniform nor a timeless venture but a process refracted through the kaleidoscopic lens of a variety of literary forms and configurations of the Hekhalot literature, at different historical moments, that is, at different places and different times. And it is this internal literary development of the Hekhalot literature, the diversification of its literary layers, structures, and rhetorical devices, *anchored in specific historical moments*, that needs to be evaluated and further described. I made this assertion very early on in my preoccupation with the Hekhalot literature,[38] and I have been misunderstood as trying to obstruct if not outright prevent through rather boring "philological"[39] and literary exercises access to what really matters in our dealings with the Hekhalot literature – the mystical experience behind that literature.[40] Far be it from me to do so. But I still do not see how the laborious and time-consuming work of philological and literary analysis can be circumvented – as a matter of fact, a fair portion of it has been done in the Berlin Hekhalot project, particularly in the introductions to the volumes of the Hekhalot translation – and I note with gratification that the pendulum has begun to swing

---

[37] Unless one wants to see in R. Nehunya b. Haqanah's ascent and in the havurah account the very core of the Merkavah mystical "experience."

[38] Schäfer, "New Testament and Hekhalot Literature," pp. 34 f. = id., *Hekhalot-Studien*, p. 249.

[39] Another non-PC word that has become stigmatized.

[40] See, e. g., Ithamar Gruenwald, *From Apocalypticism to Gnosticism: Studies in Apocalypticism, Merkavah Mysticism and Gnosticism* (Frankfurt am Main: Peter Lang, 1988), p. 179 f.:
If we follow Schaefer without making any concessions or compromises, the emphasis in our study of the *Hekhalot* literature has to shift from the contents of works to fragments of information variously grouped together in several manuscripts. ... [W]e have to limit ourselves to relatively small units which, because of the uneven editorial work to which they were subjected, only inadvertently reflect the original compositions. Eventually, the manuscripts at our disposal are more like a veil that blurs our vision of the Merkavah mystics rather than a vehicle that supposedly can carry us back into the very circles of those mystics.
See also Idel, *Kabbalah: New Perspectives*, p. 27.

back toward this approach, opening it up even further to the material conditions of the literary and cultural production of what has come to be assembled under the heading "Hekhalot literature."[41] It is becoming ever more apparent that such an approach (the "new textualism" in the newly emerging field of the history of the book)[42] will lead us, geographically and culturally, into the realm of the late antique/early medieval Byzantine and Babylonian cultural context(s) in the broadest sense of the word.

Qumran

The Qumran literature describes an experience sui generis, equally remote in many respects from both the ascent apocalypses and the Hekhalot literature. Of the four components of Ezekiel's taxonomy there is no ascent, (almost) no seer, (almost) no vision, and very little concern for the future (at least for *all* of Israel). As for the ascent, even if the joint worship of angels and human beings takes place in heaven (and not on earth), the earthly community does not ascend to heaven in the technical sense of the term; rather, what counts is the liturgical communion with the angels and not how it comes about. Only the author of the Self-Glorification Hymn envisions himself as being elevated to heaven, but we never learn how he got there; his ascent as such plays no role. And with regard to the Songs of the Sabbath Sacrifice – the backbone of the alleged underground connection between the mystical experiences of the Qumran and the Hekhalot communities in recent scholarship – the performative act of reciting the songs during the community's worship must serve as bridge between heaven and earth, that is, as proof of the claim that the Qumran sectarians indeed ascend to heaven in order to unite with the angels. I do not want to exclude this possibility, but if it is indeed the case, then the focus of the songs lies elsewhere.[43] In particular, I see no basis for the increasingly popular idea that the community's "ascent" in the songs is the prototype for the Merkavah mystic's ascent in the Hekhalot literature.

As for the seer, unlike the ascent apocalypses and the Hekhalot literature, the Qumran texts are not concerned with the individual or the individual serving as

---

[41] See Boustan's programmatic statement in "The Study of Heikhalot Literature," pp. 133, 136.

[42] See, e.g., D. F. McKenzie, *Bibliography and the Sociology of Texts* (London: British Library, 1986); R. Chartier, *The Order of Books* (Cambridge: Polity Press, 1994); and most recently the Christian test case presented by Anthony Grafton and Megan Williams, *Christianity and the Transformation of the Book: Origen, Eusebius, and the Library of Caesarea* (Cambridge, MA: Harvard University Press), 2006.

[43] See also Wolfson's caveat: "The extant sources do not demonstrate conclusively that the recitation of the hymns facilitated the translation of the worshippers to heaven and their translation into angels" ("Mysticism," p. 201).

the community's representative. The only exception is again the unknown hero of the Self-Glorification Hymn, a fact that underlines the peculiarity or even anomaly of the hymn within the larger corpus of the Qumran literature. The bulk of the Qumranic texts centers on the community at large, and not on the individual. And there is even less concern for the vision. The visionary element in the songs concentrates on the animated architecture of the Temple and, related to it, on the angels. Moreover, the songs' radical reinterpretation of Ezekiel 1 transfers the appearance of God to the angels and God's voice to the angels' telling silence, hence ultimately substituting the angels for God. Even in the Self-Glorification Hymn there is no trace whatsoever of the author's desire to see God; he is completely, and proudly, content with his place among the angels.

It is difficult ascertaining precisely to what extent the Qumran texts envision the members of the community as being transformed into angels. We definitely and most conspicuously do find the idea of the *unio liturgica* – the liturgical union or, better, the communion of humans and angels. This feature connects the Qumran evidence with the ascent apocalypses and the Hekhalot literature. But how far beyond this do the Qumran texts go? Is it just a joint enterprise, or are the sectarians physically transformed into angels, that is, do they undergo a process of angelification (*unio angelica*) similar to that of the seers of (some of) the ascent apocalypses and Enoch-Metatron in 3 Enoch? If they imagine their joint worship as taking place not just on earth but actually in heaven (in the Hodayot and the Songs of the Sabbath Sacrifice), it seems only natural that such an idea would also include their physical transformation, but unfortunately, the texts are rather vague here. Since we have the precedent of the ascent apocalypses, I am inclined to see the angelification as a realistic option (with the angelification of the individual in the ascent apocalypses transferred to the community in Qumran). Yet still a caveat is in order. The only explicit case of an angelification remains the Self-Glorification Hymn, which, not by coincidence, comes closest to the ascent apocalypses.

These findings inevitably exclude the notion of a union with God, whether of the Qumran community at large or of that chosen individual speaking in the Self-Glorification Hymn. We must not confuse "communion" with "union" – not with regard to human beings and angels, and even less so with regard to human beings and God. Philip Alexander has made this clear with admirable lucidity:

> Where does Qumran stand on this issue [the question of a mystical union with God]? The position there seems to be unequivocal: there is no absorption into God. The highest transformation that the mystic can undergo is into an *angel*, not into *God*, and angels are definitely not God. The Scrolls do indeed use language which at first sight dangerously blurs the boundary between God and the angels (e. g., by applying the same term 'Elohim apparently indiscriminately to both), but closer inspection shows that in fact the distinction is rigidly maintained: our authors evince a deep consciousness of the

difference between God and the angels, even the highest of the angels. The angels are outside the Godhead.[44]

Despite this unambiguous clarification, Alexander nevertheless intimates that the hero of the Self-Glorification Hymn, in taking "his seat in heaven above the angels," achieves "a classic component of mysticism: ... communion or union with the divine."[45] To be sure, Alexander does not explicitly say that the hero of the Self-Glorification Hymn unites with the divine, but he apparently blurs the boundaries. This becomes clear also from the fact that he ponders the possibility not just of the hero's angelification but even of his "apotheosis" and that he declares, precisely in this connection, the "communion *or* union with the divine"[46] to be a "classic component of mysticism." Here Alexander softens his earlier definition of mysticism, which distinguishes so carefully between "communion" and "union."[47]

Finally, if there is no vision of God in Qumran, there is also no purpose to the vision. But of course there *is* a purpose to the whole exercise of humans entering into a close relationship with angels, howsoever and to whatever extent achieved. And here the Temple-critical approach, with the sacrifice shifted from the polluted Temple in Jerusalem to the celestial Temple and with the angels in heaven officiating as the legitimate priests and high priests, connects (some of) the Qumran texts again with the ascent apocalypses and disconnects them quite dramatically and blatantly from the Hekhalot literature. This, in my view, is one of the most significant results of our survey and one that can hardly be neutralized by the strained efforts of some scholars to turn the Hekhalot literature into a document deeply imbued with priestly ideology.

The Rabbis

My survey of the relevant passages in the classical rabbinic literature (Tosefta and Mishnah Megillah, Mishnah and Tosefta Hagigah, with their respective parallels in the Yerushalmi and the Bavli) led to the unequivocal conclusion that the rabbis were preoccupied with the *exegesis* of certain passages perceived as dangerous, and not with ecstatic experiences. There is no ascent in our rabbinic sources, no seer, no vision, and no revelation as payoff of the vision. Or, to be

---

[44] Alexander, *The Mystical Texts*, p. 105.

[45] Ibid., p. 90.

[46] My emphasis.

[47] Ibid., p. 8. He even goes a step further and also includes the Songs of the Sabbath Sacrifice in this "union with the divine" scenario: "All this [the communion turned union in the Self-Glorification Hymn] can easily be integrated with the Sabbath Songs. ... One could imagine the Self-Glorification functioning as a sort of introit to the Sabbath Songs ... or possibly as coming after Song 13" (ibid., p. 91 with n. 8).

more precise, the seer turned rabbi receives his revelation through proper exegesis of the Bible and discovers his God in the Torah. It is only in the Bavli that we could make out traces of Merkavah mystical (in the technical sense of the word) influences that, however, were immediately neutralized and rerabbinized by the Bavli editor.

Such emphasis on the fundamentally exegetical character of the rabbinic approach to the biblical texts in question – as opposed to an experientially oriented enterprise – has again elicited objections from certain scholars. As he did in the case of the ascent apocalypses, Elliot Wolfson in particular emphatically and programmatically wishes to demolish the (in his view) sterile distinction between "exegetical activity" and "ecstatic experience." He claims that these two domains "were not, and cannot be, held in absolute distinction"[48] and that "the effort on the part of some modern scholars to distinguish sharply between an 'exegetical mysticism' and an 'experiential mysticism' in early Jewish Merkavah speculation is to a degree overstated."[49] True, he admits, "[s]tudy of Ezekiel's vision ... does not in and of itself constitute an ecstatic vision of the chariot," but still, "given the literary and conceptual continuity linking apocalyptic and Hekhalot [literature?], it is difficult to maintain that the rabbis who lived in the period of the Mishnah were not cognizant of heavenly ascensions to the throne when they spoke of expounding the chariot."[50] The key word for Wolfson, following Rowland, is the desire also of the rabbis to "reexperience" what they have come across in the Bible and related texts.[51] "Exegesis," Wolfson argues, is never "devoid of any experiential component," and, therefore, we are well advised "on the one hand, not to characterize rabbinic exegesis of the chariot as fundamentally nonmystical ... and, on the other, to recognize the midrashic underpinning of ecstatic visions."[52] Summarizing Wolfson's approach, Boustan grants him that "he rightly emphasizes the generative relationship [!] between discursive and embodied practices in the formation of mystical experience."[53]

Unfortunately, these bold statements are not bolstered by any rabbinic evidence that connects the exegetical and experiential aspects of the enterprise. Resorting to the outdated stereotype of an unbroken continuity between the ascent apocalypses, the rabbis' dealings with Ezekiel 1, and the Hekhalot literature – a very Scholemian concept, to boot – fails to do the trick. Of course the rabbis were "cognizant of heavenly ascensions to the throne when they spoke of expounding the chariot," but they did everything in their power to mitigate the dangers attendant to such heavenly ascents, even and especially when they

---

[48] Wolfson, *Speculum*, p. 121.
[49] Ibid., p. 122.
[50] Ibid., p. 123.
[51] Ibid.
[52] Ibid., p. 124.
[53] Boustan, "Study of Heikhalot Literature," p. 145.

could not refrain (in the Bavli) from Merkavah mystical experiences. It was least of all in the rabbinic exegeses that we were able to discover any traces of the rabbis' physical and bodily "reexperiencing" the complex web of literary allusions taken from the Bible and related documents. That ultimately the rabbinic exegesis of the chariot, in Wolfson's view, turns out to be "mystical" is all the more surprising if we remember his definition of "mysticism" vis-à-vis the Qumran evidence.[54]

Philo

Standing out as the truly exceptional phenomenon of our survey is Philo. Evoking once again Ezekiel's schema, Philo provides us with an ascent, a seer, a vision, and, most important, a transformation of the seer. But the meaning of these components has dramatically changed. Cladding his biblical *Vorlage* in the garment of Platonic philosophy, Philo for the first time distinguishes unequivocally between body and soul, a distinction that was alien to (or problematic for) most of the other texts that we have discussed. Accordingly, the ascent for Philo is not the ascent of body and soul but solely the ascent of the soul:[55] anyone who renounces the temptations of the body can undertake such an ascent, but it is in fact solely reserved for the prophets and true philosophers (including Philo).

Nor does the vision conform to the pattern that we are familiar with from the ascent apocalypses and the Hekhalot literature. When the soul returns to its divine origin, after its death or during the lifetime of certain chosen individuals, it does not "see" God in order to receive a message; rather, it becomes overpowered by the divine essence and is transformed into something completely new, a different – though for the one who undertakes the journey during his lifetime only temporary – state of existence. Achieving this new state, the individual soul loses its individuality and unites with the divine. This "merging" of the human soul in the divine may be called, in the true sense of the phrase, *unio mystica*. It certainly comes closest to what is captured under the terms "divinization" or "deification."

Moreover, since here the revelation and its corresponding message as the purpose of the traditional vision are relinquished, Philo's "vision" – resulting in the complete transformation of the "seer's" soul – becomes a truly and uniquely

---

[54] Wolfson, "Mysticism," p. 187; see above, p. 19. To state my point clearly, I am not advocating an axiomatic dichotomy between "midrash" and "mystical experience" – I am aware that mystical texts can be heavily exegetical and that exegetical texts can have mystical components – but I would like to see more of this cherished mystical element in rabbinic exegesis; see also above, pp. 338 f.

[55] Hence, quite ironically, when Scholem speaks of the ascent of the soul in Merkavah mysticism, he is influenced by Philo (and by what he called Gnosticism).

individualistic experience. It is only a very special individual who, during his lifetime, can achieve the desired goal of uniting his soul with the divine and bringing to ultimate perfection his human existence. This is what human beings are supposed to do, but unfortunately very few specimens of the human race attain this goal. Hence, Philo's program is deeply elitist and not particularly concerned about the destiny of the community. True, the philosopher is part of his community and it is his task to lead its members to perfection, but in reality only very few chosen members of the community are capable of realizing this goal. It is also in this regard that Philo is far removed from the ascent apocalypses, Qumran, the rabbis, and the Hekhalot literature.

Mysticism

As to be expected, it turns out that the phenomena collected and described under the headings "Ezekiel," "Ascent Apocalypses," "Qumran," "Philo," "The Rabbis," and "Merkavah Mystics" are greatly diverse and resist the modern scholar's desire to subsume them under a single all-embracing category. Ezekiel's open heaven differs from the ascent in the ascent apocalypses, and the ascent in the ascent apocalypses differs from the ascent of the Merkavah mystic in the Hekhalot literature or from the elevation among the angels of the Self-Glorification Hymn's hero, not to mention the differences with Philo's ascent of the soul and with the rabbis' careful and cautious exegesis of Genesis 1 and Ezekiel 1. What nevertheless unites all these variegated efforts that are reflected in their respective bodies of literature is the craving of their authors to bridge the gap between heaven and earth, between human beings and heavenly powers, between man and God. In most cases, moreover, it is the attempt to *restore* the lost relationship of some ancient and originally whole past: because the Temple as the natural venue for the encounter between God and his human creatures on earth has been destroyed or polluted or usurped by a competing community; because the soul, severed from its divine origin, has been entombed in its human body; or because, after the termination of prophetical revelation, the Torah has become the only vehicle for approaching God. So, at stake in our sources – a wide range of discrete forms and implementations notwithstanding – is the attempt to get (back) to God as close as possible, to experience the living and loving God, despite the desolate situation on earth with all its shortcomings and catastrophes.

The experience of the living and loving God is reserved for the individual (with the conspicuous exception of the Qumran sectarians' communal enterprise), and here the spectrum fluctuates between the two poles of the unique and chosen individual and everyone who fulfills certain conditions. Yet in most cases, this experience is not for the sake of the individual or an end in itself but community-oriented, that is, the individual is deemed worthy of experiencing

God for the sake of his community on earth. There are only a few exceptions to this rule, namely, the individual who sallies forth on his last journey and the soul returning to its place of origin. Furthermore, the communities that the seer represents are highly diverse: from Ezekiel's exiled Israelites to the various geographically as well as chronologically distinct communities standing behind the ascent apocalypses, to the Qumran sectarians, to Philo's Alexandrian brand of Judaism, to the rabbinic elite in Palestine and Babylonia, and through to the elusive circles behind the Hekhalot literature that we try to localize in the cultural realm of Byzantine and Babylonian Judaism.

If at all, it is this experience of the living God (that is, the God who is physically present, and approachable, in his heavenly sanctuary) and the loving God (that is, the God who still loves his people of Israel on earth) that binds our sources together and that might be called their recurrent theme or even common denominator. But this does not mean that we are able to pursue our common denominator in a linear development that "originates" with Ezekiel, unfolds and accumulates progressively through the various stations that we have reviewed, and finally climaxes in the Hekhalot literature. The variety of sources, motifs, and emphases clearly does not allow for such a harmonious and ultimately simplistic view; in a certain sense we must be capable of bearing the polymorphic and even chaotic evidence that our sources confront us with. Not least, the romantic quest for "origins" has turned out to be a futile and methodologically misguided exercise.

Finally, do our findings add up to something that could adequately be captured under the heading "mysticism"? One could argue that precisely this craving for the experience of a living and loving God – with its retention, in most cases, of the individual's corporality and, even more important, the individual's personal identity and integrity, thus preventing a mystical *union* with God – that precisely this experience constitutes the particularly *Jewish* form of mysticism in contrast to other forms, not least the Christian variety. I admit that I still have some sympathy for such a claim – even after all that has been said in the pages of this book – and be it only for heuristic purposes. But the craving for the living and loving God and the experience that he still exists obviously applies to so many more texts that we have not included in our survey that we run the risk of voiding the category of "mysticism" and ultimately rendering it meaningless by confusing mysticism with religion. We should also not forget that what we call mysticism has no equivalent in any of the languages in which our sources are preserved.

That said, should we share the scathing criticism recently uttered by Boaz Huss, who maintains that the categories of mysticism in general, and that of Jewish mysticism in particular, are based on Christian theological concepts that, in the wake of Western imperialist and colonialist efforts, have been imposed on non-Western societies and religions?[56] These are generalizations, I am afraid, behind which the chimera of an essentialist approach again raises its head – this time not of a pan-mystical essentialism but of an essentialism that identifies mysticism with Christian theology (based on a superficial concept of mysticism as well as of theology). Yet despite such qualms, we should take seriously the possibility that the *history of research on mysticism* – Jewish and non-Jewish alike – is deeply imbued with Christian theological assumptions and biases. These implications should indeed warn us against being too enthusiastic about adopting the category of mysticism within a Jewish context. Against this background, mysticism turns out to be an inappropriate category to prove that the Jewish religion exhibits the same characteristics as its Christian counterpart (apart from the fact that the apologetic attitude of this approach is highly problematic in itself). Furthermore, the universalistic and ahistorical tendencies inherent in such a concept of mysticism run counter to everything that our survey has yielded. In the end, however, the answer to the question of whether or not mysticism remains a meaningful category for the period under consideration – that is, before the rise of Kabbalah in Western Europe – becomes largely a matter of taste. I would not want to promote a ban on the use of the term "mysticism" – similar to how other scholars have been trying to exorcize the use of the term "magic," interestingly enough for much the same reasons – since bans smack strongly of political correctness and are hardly conducive to promoting uninhibited scholarly discourse. Yet I do hold that the term and its conceptual parameters are of limited benefit for our understanding of the phenomena that we have discussed.

---

[56] Huss, "Mystification."

Bibliography

Abegg, Martin G. "4Q471: A Case of Mistaken Identity?" in J. C. Reeves and J. Kampen, eds., *Pursuing the Text: Studies in Honor of B. Z. Wacholder on the Occasion of His Seventieth Birthday*. Sheffield, UK: Sheffield Academic Press, 1994, pp. 136–147.

—. "Who Ascended to Heaven? 4Q491, 4Q427, and the Teacher of Righteousness," in C. A. Evans and P. W. Flint, eds., *Eschatology, Messianism, and the Dead Sea Scrolls*. Grand Rapids, MI: William B. Eerdmans, 1997, pp. 61–73.

Alexander, Philip (S.). "The Rabbinic Lists of Forbidden Targumim." *JJS* 27 (1976), pp. 177–191.

—. "The Historical Setting of the Hebrew Book of Enoch." *JJS* 28 (1977), pp. 156–180.

—. "3 (Hebrew Apocalypse of) Enoch," in Charlesworth, *OTP*, vol. 1, pp. 223–315.

—. "3 Enoch and the Talmud." *JSJ* 18 (1987), pp. 40–68.

—. "The Family of Caesar and the Family of God: The Image of the Emperor in Early Jewish Mystical Literature," in Loveday Alexander, ed., *Images of Empire: The Roman Empire in Jewish, Christian and Greco-Roman Sources*. Sheffield, UK: Sheffield Academic Press, 1991, pp. 276–297.

—. "Response," in Peter Schäfer and Joseph Dan, eds., *Gershom Scholem's Major Trends in Jewish Mysticism: 50 Years After*. Tübingen: J. C. B. Mohr (Paul Siebeck), 1993, pp. 79–83.

—. "From Son of Adam to Second God: Transformations of the Biblical Enoch," in Michael E. Stone and Theodore A. Bergren, eds., *Biblical Figures Outside the Bible*. Harrisville, PA: Trinity Press International, 1998, pp. 87–122.

—. "The Enochic Literature and the Bible: Intertextuality and Its Implications," in Edward D. Herbert and Emanuel Tov, eds., *The Bible as Book: The Hebrew Bible and the Judaean Desert Discoveries*. London: British Library and Oak Knoll Press, 2002, pp. 57–69.

—. "Mysticism," in Martin Goodman, ed., *The Oxford Handbook of Jewish Studies*. Oxford: Oxford University Press, 2002, pp. 705–732.

—, trans. *The Targum of Canticles*, with a critical introduction, apparatus, and notes. Collegeville, MN: Liturgical Press, 2003.

—. *Mystical Texts: Songs of the Sabbath Sacrifice and Related Manuscripts*. London: T. & T. Clark International, 2006.

Altman, Alexander. "Qedushah Hymns in the Early Heikhalot Literature." *Melilah* 2 (1946), pp. 1–24 (in Hebrew).

Andersen, F. I. "2 (Slavonic Apocalypse of) Enoch," in Charlesworth, *OTP*, vol. 1, pp. 91–221.

Arbel, Vita Daphna. *Beholders of Divine Secrets: Mysticism and Myth in the Hekhalot and Merkavah Literature*. Albany: State University of New York Press, 2003.

Aune, David E. *The Cultic Setting of Realized Eschatology in Early Christianity*. Leiden: Brill, 1972.

Bacher, Wilhelm. *Die exegetische Terminologie der jüdischen Traditionsliteratur*, part 1: *Die bibelexegetische Terminologie der Tannaiten*. Leipzig: Hinrichs'sche Buchhandlung, 1899 (repr. 1965, Olms, Hildesheim).

Baillet, M. *Qumrân Grotte 4.3 (4Q482–4Q520)*, DJD 7, Oxford: Clarendon Press, 1982.

Barton, J. M. T. "The Ascension of Isaiah," in H. F. D. Sparks, *The Apocryphal Old Testament*. Oxford: Clarendon Press; New York: Oxford University Press, 1984, pp. 775–812.

Baumgarten, Joseph M. "The Book of Elkesai and Merkabah Mysticism." *JSJ* 17 (1986), pp. 212–223.

–. "The Qumran Sabbath Shirot and Rabbinic Merkabah Traditions." *RdQ* 13 (1988), pp. 199–213.

Becker, Hans-Jürgen. *Die großen rabbinischen Sammelwerke Palästinas: Zur literarischen Genese von Talmud Yerushalmi und Midrasch Bereshit Rabba*. Tübingen: Mohr Siebeck, 1999.

Beckwith, Isbon T. *The Apocalypse of John: Studies in Introduction with a Critical and Exegetical Commentary*. New York: Macmillan, 1919 (repr. 1967, Baker Book House, Grand Rapids, MI).

Berchman, Robert M. *From Philo to Origin: Middle Platonism in Transition*. Chico, CA: Scholars Press, 1984.

Black, Matthew (in consultation with James C. Vanderkam). *The Book of Enoch or 1 Enoch: A New English Edition*, with commentary and textual notes. Leiden: Brill, 1985.

Block, Daniel I. *The Book of Ezekiel: Chapters 1–24*. Grand Rapids, MI: William B. Eerdmans, 1997.

Boustan (Abusch), Ra'anan S. "Sevenfold Hymns in the *Songs of the Sabbath Sacrifice* and the Hekhalot Literature: Formalism, Hierarchy and the Limits of Human Participation," in James Davila, ed., *The Dead Sea Scrolls as Background to Postbiblical Judaism and Early Christianity: Papers from an International Conference at St. Andrews in 2001*. Leiden: Brill, 2003, pp. 220–247.

–. "Angels in the Architecture: Temple Art and the Poetics of Praise in the *Songs of the Sabbath Sacrifice*," in Ra'anan S. Boustan and Annette Yoshiko Reed, *Heavenly Realms and Earthly Realities in the Late Antique Religions*. Cambridge: Cambridge University Press, 2004, pp. 195–212.

–. *From Martyr to Mystic: Rabbinic Martyrology and the Making of Merkavah Mysticism*. Tübingen: Mohr Siebeck, 2005.

–. Review of Vita Daphna Arbel, *Beholders of Divine Secrets: Mysticism and Myth in the Hekhalot and Merkavah Literature*. *JAOS* 125 (2005), pp. 123–126.

–. "The Emergence of Pseudonymous Attribution in Heikhalot Literature: Empirical Evidence from the Jewish 'Magical' Corpora." *JSQ* 13 (2006), pp. 1–21.

–. "The Study of Heikhalot Literature: Between Mystical Experience and Textual Artifact." *Currents in Biblical Research* 6 (2007), pp. 130–160.

Box, G. H., and J. I. Landsman. *The Apocalypse of Abraham*. London: SPCK, 1919.

Boyarin, Daniel. "The Gospel of the Memra: Jewish Binitarianism and the Prologue to John." *HTR* 94 (2001), pp. 243–284.

–. "Two Powers in Heaven; or, The Making of a Heresy," in Hindy Najman and Judith H. Newman, eds., *The Idea of Biblical Interpretation: Essays in Honor of James L. Kugel*. Leiden: Brill, 2004, pp. 331–370.

–. "The Parables of Enoch and the Foundation of the Rabbinic Sect: A Hypothesis," in Mauro Perani, ed., *"The Words of a Wise Man's Mouth Are Gracious" (Qoh 10,12): Festschrift for Günter Stemberger on the Occasion of His 65th Birthday.* Berlin: Walter de Gruyter, 2005, pp. 53–72.

Brockhaus Enzyklopädie in Zwanzig Bänden, vol. 13. Wiesbaden: F.A. Brockhaus, 1971.

Buber, Martin. "Zu Jecheskel 3:12." *MGWJ* 78 (1934), pp. 471–474.

Burkhardt, Helmut. "Inspiration der Schrift durch weisheitliche Personalinspiration." *ThZ* 47 (1991), pp. 214–225.

Charles, R. H. *A Critical and Exegetical Commentary on the Revelation of John,* vol. 1. Edinburgh: T. & T. Clark, 1920 (repr. 1975).

Charlesworth, James H., ed. *The Old Testament Pseudepigrapha,* vol. 1: *Apocalyptic Literature and Testaments,* London: Darton, Longman and Todd, 1983; vol. 2: *Expansions of the "Old Testament" and Legends, Wisdom and Philosophical Literature, Prayers, Psalms, and Odes, Fragments of Lost Judeo-Hellenistic Works,* Garden City, NY: Doubleday, 1985.

Chartier, R. *The Order of Books.* Cambridge, MA: Polity Press, 1994.

Chester, Andrew. *Messiah and Exaltation: Jewish Messianic and Visionary Traditions and New Testament Christology.* Tübingen: Mohr Siebeck, 2007.

Cohen, Martin S. *The Shi'ur Qomah: Liturgy and Theurgy in Pre-Kabbalistic Jewish Mysticism.* Lanham, MD: University Press of America, 1983.

–. *The Shi'ur Qomah: Texts and Recensions.* Tübingen: J. C. B. Mohr (Paul Siebeck), 1985.

Collins, John J. *Daniel: A Commentary on the Book of Daniel.* Minneapolis, MN: Fortress Press, 1993.

–. *The Scepter and the Star: The Messiahs of the Dead Sea Scrolls and Other Ancient Literature.* New York: Doubleday, 1995.

–. "A Throne in the Heavens: Apotheosis in Pre-Christian Judaism," in John J. Collins and Michael Fishbane, eds., *Death, Ecstasy, and Other Worldly Journeys.* Albany: State University of New York Press, 1995, pp. 43–58.

–. *Apocalypticism in the Dead Sea Scrolls.* London: Routledge, 1997.

–. *The Apocalyptic Imagination: An Introduction to Jewish Apocalyptic Literature,* 2nd ed. Grand Rapids, MI: William B. Eerdmans, 1998.

Colson, F. H., and G. H. Whitaker. *Philo, with an English Translation,* 10 vols. London: William Heinemann; Cambridge, MA: Harvard University Press, 1929–1998.

Cross, Frank Moore. *Canaanite Myth and Hebrew Epic: Essays in the History of the Religion of Israel.* Cambridge, MA: Harvard University Press, 1973.

Davidson, Maxwell J. *Angels at Qumran: A Comparative Study of 1 Enoch 1–36, 72–108 and Sectarian Writings from Qumran.* Sheffield, UK: JSOT Press, 1992.

Davila, James R. "Prolegomena to a Critical Edition of Hekhalot Rabbati." *JJS* 45 (1994), pp. 208–226.

–. "Of Methodology, Monotheism and Metatron: Introductory Reflections on Divine Mediators and the Origins of the Worship of Jesus," in Carey C. Newman, James R. Davila, and Gladys S. Lewis, eds., *The Jewish Roots of Christological Monotheism: Papers from the St. Andrews Conference on the Historical Origins of the Worship of Jesus.* Leiden: Brill, 1999, pp. 3–18.

–. "The Dead Sea Scrolls and Merkavah Mysticism," in Timothy H. Lim, ed., *The Dead Sea Scrolls in Their Historical Context*. Edinburgh: T. & T. Clark, 2000, pp. 249–264.

–. *Liturgical Works*. Grand Rapids, MI: William B. Eerdmans, 2000.

–. *Descenders to the Chariot: The People behind the Hekhalot Literature*. Leiden: Brill, 2001.

–. "Melchizedek, the 'Youth,' and Jesus," in James R. Davila, ed., *The Dead Sea Scrolls as Background to Postbiblical Judaism and Early Christianity*. Leiden: Brill, 2003, pp. 248–274.

–. "The Ancient Jewish Apocalypses and the *Hekhalot* Literature," in April D. DeConick, ed., *Paradise Now: Essays on Early Jewish and Christian Mysticism*. Leiden: Brill, 2006, pp. 105–125.

Davis, Ellen F. *Swallowing the Scroll: Textuality and the Dynamics of Discourse in Ezekiel's Prophecy*. Sheffield, UK: Sheffield Academic Press, 1989.

de Jonge, Marinus, ed. (in cooperation with H. W. Hollander, H. J. de Jonge, and Th. Korteweg). *The Testaments of the Twelve Patriarchs: A Critical Edition of the Greek Text*. Leiden: Brill, 1978.

de Lange, Nicholas R. M. *Origen and the Jews: Studies in Jewish-Christian Relations in Third-Century Palestine*. Cambridge: Cambridge University Press, 1976.

DeConick, April D., ed. *Paradise Now: Essays on Early Jewish and Christian Mysticism*. Atlanta, GA: Society of Biblical Literature, 2006, and Leiden: Brill, 2006.

–. "What Is Early Jewish and Christian Mysticism?" in eadem, ed., *Paradise Now: Essays on Early Jewish and Christian Mysticism*. Leiden: Brill, 2006, pp. 1–24.

Dillon, John M. *The Middle Platonists. A Study of Platonism 80 B.C. to A.D. 220*. London: Duckworth, 1977 (rev. ed. with a new afterword 1996, Cornell University Press, Ithaca, NY).

Dillon, John M., and Wilhelm H. Wuellner, eds. *The Transcendence of God in Philo: Some Possible Sources*. Protocol of the Sixteenth Colloquy, 20 April 1975, Center for Hermeneutical Studies in Hellenistic and Modern Culture. Berkeley, CA: Center for Hermeneutical Studies, 1975.

Dimant, Devorah. "The Apocalyptic Interpretation of Ezekiel at Qumran," in Ithamar Gruenwald, Shaul Shaked, and Guy Stroumsa, eds. *Messiah and Christos: Studies in the Jewish Origins of Christianity Presented to David Flusser on the Occasion of His Seventy-Fifth Birthday*. Tübingen: J. C. B. Mohr (Paul Siebeck), 1992, pp. 31–51.

Duhaime, Jean. *The War Texts: 1QM and Related Manuscripts*. London: T. & T. Clark International, 2004.

Dupré, Louis. "Mysticism," in Mircea Eliade, ed., *The Encyclopedia of Religion*, vol. 10. London: Collier Macmillan, 1987, pp. 245–261.

Elior, Rachel. "From Earthly Temple to Heavenly Shrines: Prayer and Sacred Song in the Hekhalot Literature and Its Relation to Temple Traditions." *JSQ* 4 (1997), pp. 217–267.

–. "The *Merkavah* Tradition and the Emergence of Jewish Mysticism: From Temple to *Merkavah*, from *Hekhal* to *Hekhalot*, from Priestly Opposition to Gazing upon the *Merkavah*," in Aharon Oppenheimer, ed., *Sino-Judaica: Jews and Chinese in Historical Dialogue*. Tel Aviv: Tel Aviv University, 1999, pp. 101–158.

–. *The Three Temples: On the Emergence of Jewish Mysticism*. Oxford: Littman Library of Jewish Civilization, 2004 (originally published in Hebrew, 2002, Magnes, Jerusalem).

–. "Ancient Jewish Calendars: A Response." *Aleph* 5 (2005), pp. 293–302.

–. "The Foundations of Early Jewish Mysticism: The Lost Calendar and the Transformed Heavenly Chariot," in Peter Schäfer, ed., *Wege Mystischer Gotteserfahrung: Judentum, Christentum und Islam/Mystical Approaches to God: Judaism, Christianity, and Islam*. Munich: Oldenbourg, 2006, pp. 1–18.

Eshel, Esther. "4Q471B: A Self-Glorification Hymn." *RdQ* 17/65–68 (1996), pp. 175–203.

Eshel, Esther, Hanan Eshel, Carol Newsom, Bilhah Nitzan, Eileen Schuller, and Ada Yardeni, eds. *Qumran Cave 4*, vol. 6: *Poetical and Liturgical Texts*, part 1. Oxford: Clarendon Press, 1998.

Even-Shemuel, Yehudah. "Messiah Aggada," in idem, *Midreshe Ge'ulla*, 2nd ed. Jerusalem: Mosad Bialik, 1953–1954, pp. 326–327.

Finkelstein, Louis, ed. *Siphre ad Deuteronomium*. Berlin: Jüdischer Kulturbund, 1939.

Fishbane, Michael. "Arm of the Lord: Biblical Myth, Rabbinic Midrash, and the Mystery of History," in Samuel E. Balentine and John Barton, eds., *Language, Theology, and the Bible: Essays in Honour of James Barr*. Oxford: Clarendon Press, 1994, pp. 271–292.

Fletcher-Louis, Crispin H. T. *All the Glory of Adam: Liturgical Anthropology in the Dead Sea Scrolls*. Leiden: Brill, 2002.

Fohrer, Georg. *Ezechiel*, mit einem Beitrag von Kurt Galling. Tübingen: J. C. B. Mohr (Paul Siebeck), 1955.

Ford, J. Massyngberde. *Revelation: Introduction, Translation, and Commentary*. The *Anchor Bible*. New York: Doubleday, 1975.

Förster, Niclas. *Marcus Magus. Kult, Lehre und Gemeindeleben einer valentinianischen Gnostikergruppe: Sammlung der Quellen und Kommentar*. Tübingen: Mohr Siebeck, 1999.

Fraade, Steven D. *Enosh and His Generation: Pre-Israelite Hero and History in Postbiblical Interpretation*, Chico, CA: Scholars Press, 1984.

Gafni, Isaiah. "Rabbinic Historiography and Representations of the Past," in Charlotte E. Fonrobert and Martin S. Jaffee, eds., *The Cambridge Companion to the Talmud and Rabbinic Literature*. Cambridge: Cambridge University Press, 2007, pp. 295–312.

García Martínez, Florentino, and Eibert J. C. Tigchelaar, eds. *The Dead Sea Scrolls: Study Edition*, 2 vols. Leiden: Brill, 1997–1998.

Gaster, Moses, "Das Schiur Komah," *MGWJ* 37 (1893), pp. 179–185, 213–230 = idem, *Studies and Texts in Folklore, Magic, Mediaeval Romance, Hebrew Apocrypha and Samaritan Archaeology*, vol. 2. New York: Ktav, 1971, pp. 1330–1353.

Ginzberg, Louis. *Legends of the Jews*, vol. 1. Philadelphia: Jewish Publication Society, 1909 (repr. 1947).

Goldberg, Arnold. "Der Vortrag des Ma'ase Merkawa: Eine Vermutung zur frühen Merkawamystik," in idem, *Mystik und Theologie des rabbinischen Judentums: Gesammelte Studien I*, ed. Margarete Schlüter and Peter Schäfer. Tübingen: Mohr Siebeck, 1997, pp. 1–15 (repr., originally published in *Judaica* 29 [1973], pp. 4–23).

–. "Rabban Yohanans Traum: Der Sinai in der frühen Merkavamystik," in idem, *Mystik und Theologie des rabbinischen Judentums: Gesammelte Studien I*, ed. Margarete Schlüter and Peter Schäfer. Tübingen: Mohr Siebeck, 1997, pp. 16–35 (repr., originally published in *FJB* 3 [1975], pp. 1–27).

–. "Einige Bemerkungen zu den Quellen und den redaktionellen Einheiten der Grossen Hekhalot," in idem, *Mystik und Theologie des rabbinischen Judentums: Gesammelte Studien I*, ed. Margarete Schlüter and Peter Schäfer. Tübingen: Mohr Siebeck, 1997, pp. 49–77 (repr., originally published in *FJB* 1 [1973], pp. 1–49).

–. "Pereq Re'uyot Yehezqe'el: Eine formanalytische Untersuchung," in idem, *Mystik und Theologie des rabbinischen Judentums: Gesammelte Studien I*, ed. Margarete Schlüter and Peter Schäfer. Tübingen: Mohr Siebeck, 1997, pp. 93–147.

Graetz, Heinrich. "Die mystische Literatur in der gaonäischen Epoche." *MGWJ* 8 (1859), pp. 67–78, 103–118, 140–153.

Grafton, Anthony, and Megan Williams. *Christianity and the Transformation of the Book: Origen, Eusebius, and the Library of Caesarea.* Cambridge, MA: Harvard University Press, 2006.

Greenberg, Moshe, *Ezekiel 1–20: A New Translation with Introduction and Commentary*, Garden City, NY: Doubleday, 1983.

Grimm, Jacob, and Wilhelm Grimm. *Deutsches Wörterbuch*, vol. 11.3, ed. Karl Euling. Leipzig: Hirzel, 1936.

Gruenwald, Ithamar. *Apocalyptic and Merkavah Mysticism*. Leiden: Brill, 1980.

–. *From Apocalypticism to Gnosticism: Studies in Apocalypticism, Merkavah Mysticism and Gnosticism*. Frankfurt am Main: Peter Lang, 1988.

Hall, Robert, "Isaiah's Ascent to See the Beloved: An Ancient Jewish Source for the *Ascension of Isaiah*?" *JBL* 113 (1994), pp. 463–484.

Halperin, David. *The Merkabah in Rabbinic Literature*. New Haven, CT: American Oriental Society, 1980.

–. "A Sexual Image in Hekhalot Rabbati and Its Implications," in Joseph Dan, ed., *Early Jewish Mysticism: Proceedings of the First International Conference on the History of Jewish Mysticism*. Jerusalem: Hebrew University of Jerusalem, 1987, pp. 117–132.

–. *The Faces of the Chariot: Early Jewish Responses to Ezekiel's Vision*. Tübingen: J.C.B. Mohr (Paul Siebeck), 1988.

Hamacher, Elisabeth. "Die Sabbatopferlieder im Streit um Ursprung und Anfänge der jüdischen Mystik." *JSJ* 27 (1996), pp. 119–154.

Haran, Menahem. "Observations on Ezekiel as a Book Prophet," in Ronald L. Troxel, Kelvin G. Friebel, and Dennis R. Magary, eds., *Seeking Out the Wisdom of the Ancients: Essays Offered to Honor Michael V. Fox on the Occasion of His Sixty-Fifth Birthday.* Winona Lake, IN: Eisenbrauns, 2005, pp. 3–19.

Harari, Yuval. "What Is a Magical Text? Methodological Reflections Aimed at Redefining Early Jewish Magic," in Shaul Shaked, ed., *Officina magica: Essays on the Practice of Magic in Antiquity*. Leiden: Brill, 2005, pp. 91–124.

Hengel, Martin. "'Setze dich zu meiner Rechten!' Die Inthronisation Christi zur Rechten Gottes und Psalm 110,1," in idem, *Studien zur Christologie: Kleine Schriften IV*, ed. Claus-Jürgen Thornton. Tübingen: Mohr Siebeck, 2006, pp. 281–367.

Hennecke, Edgar, and Wilhelm Schneemelcher. *New Testament Apocrypha*, English trans. R. McL. Wilson, vol. 1. Philadelphia: Westminster, 1963.

Herman, Emily. *The Meaning and Value of Mysticism*. London: Clark, 1922.

Herrmann, Klaus, "Text und Fiktion. Zur Textüberlieferung des *Shi'ur Qoma*." *FJB* 16 (1988), pp. 89–142.

–. "Re-Written Mystical Texts: The Transmission of the Hekhalot Literature in the Middle Ages." *BJRL* 75 (1993), pp. 97–116.

Herrmann, Klaus, and Claudia Rohrbacher-Sticker. "Magische Traditionen der New Yorker Hekhalot-Handschrift JTS 8128 im Kontext ihrer Gesamtredaktion." *FJB* 17 (1989), pp. 101–149.

Himmelfarb, Martha. *Tours of Hell: An Apocalyptic Form in Jewish and Christian Literature*. Philadelphia: Fortress Press, 1985.

–. "Heavenly Ascent and the Relationship of the Apocalypses and the *Hekhalot* Literature." *HUCA* 59 (1988), pp. 73–100.

–. "Revelation and Rapture: The Transformation of the Visionary in the Ascent Apocalypses," in John J. Collins and James H. Charlesworth, eds., *Mysteries and Revelations: Apocalyptic Studies since the Uppsala Colloquium.* Sheffield, UK: JSOT Press, 1991, pp. 79–90.

–. *Ascent to Heaven in Jewish and Christian Apocalypses.* New York: Oxford University Press, 1993.

–. "Earthly Sacrifice and Heavenly Incense: The Law of the Priesthood in *Aramaic Levi* and *Jubilees*," in Ra'anan S. Boustan and Annette Yoshiko Reed, eds., *Heavenly Realms and Earthly Realities.* Cambridge: Cambridge University Press, 2004, pp. 103–122.

–. "Merkavah Mysticism since Scholem: Rachel Elior's *The Three Temples*," in Peter Schäfer, ed., *Wege Mystischer Gotteserfahrung: Judentum, Christentum und Islam / Mystical Approaches to God: Judaism, Christianity, and Islam.* Munich: Oldenbourg, 2006, pp. 19–36.

–. "Temple and Priests in the Book of the Watchers, the Animal Apocalypse, and the Apocalypse of Weeks," in Gabriele Boccaccini and John J. Collins, eds., *The Early Enoch Literature.* Leiden: Brill, 2007, pp. 219–235.

Hitzig, Ferdinand. *Der Prophet Ezechiel.* Leipzig: Weidmann, 1874.

Hoffmann, David, ed. *Midrash Tanna'im.* Berlin: H. Itzkowski, 1908–1909.

Hollander, H. W., and M. de Jonge. *The Testaments of the Twelve Patriarchs: A Commentary.* Leiden: Brill, 1985.

Hölscher, Gustav. *Hesekiel, der Dichter und das Buch: Eine literarkritische Untersuchung.* Giessen: A. Töpelmann, 1924.

Horbury, William. *Herodian Judaism and New Testament Study.* Tübingen: Mohr Siebeck, 2006.

Horovitz, H. S., and I. A. Rabin, eds. *Mechilta d'Rabbi Ismael.* Jerusalem: Bamberger and Wahrman, 1960.

Huss, Boaz. "The New Age of Kabbalah Research: Book Review of Ron Margolin, *The Human Temple*; Melila Hellner-Eshed, *A River Issues Forth from Eden*; Jonathan Garb, *Manifestations of Power in Jewish Mysticism*." *Te'oriyah u-Viqqoret* 27 (2005), pp. 246–253 (in Hebrew).

–. "The Mystification of the Kabbalah and the Myth of Jewish Mysticism." *Pe'amim* 110, 2007, pp. 9–30 (in Hebrew).

Idel, Moshe, *Kabbalah: New Perspectives.* New Haven, CT: Yale University Press, 1988.

–. "Enoch Is Metatron." *Immanuel* 24/25 (1990), pp. 220–240.

–. "The Contribution of Abraham Abulafia's Kabbalah to the Understanding of Jewish Mysticism," in Peter Schäfer and Joseph Dan, eds., *Gershom Scholem's Major Trends in Jewish Mysticism: 50 Years After.* Tübingen: J. C. B. Mohr (Paul Siebeck), 1993, pp. 117–143.

–. *Ben: Sonship and Jewish Mysticism.* London: Continuum, 2007.

Inge, William Ralph. *Christian Mysticism: Considered in Eight Lectures Delivered before the University of Oxford.* London: Methuen, 1899.

Isaac, E. "1 (Ethiopic Apocalypse of) Enoch," in Charlesworth, *OTP* 1, pp. 5–89.

James, William. *The Varieties of Religious Experience: A Study in Human Nature.* London: Longman, Green, 1902.

Janowitz, Naomi. *The Poetics of Ascent: Theories of Language in a Rabbinic Ascent Text.* Albany: State University of New York Press, 1989.

Jastrow, Marcus. *A Dictionary of the Targumim, the Talmud Babli and Yerushalmi, and the Midrashic Literature,* 2 vols. New York: Pardes, 1950.

Jaubert, Annie. "The Calendar of Qumran and the Passion Narrative in John," in Raymond E. Brown and James H. Charlesworth, eds., *John and Qumran.* London: Geoffrey Chapman, 1952, pp. 62–76.

–. "Le calendrier des Jubilés et de la secte de Qumrân: Ses origines bibliques." *VT* 3 (1953), pp. 250–264.

Jellinek, Adolph. *Bet ha-Midrasch,* vol. 6. Jerusalem: Wahrmann Books, 1967.

Jones, Rufus M. *Studies in Mystical Religion.* London: Macmillan, 1909 (repr. 1923).

–. *New Studies in Mystical Religion.* London: Macmillan, 1927.

Kadushin, Max. "Introduction to Rabbinic Ethics," in Menahem Haran, ed., *Yehezkel Kaufmann Jubilee Volume: Studies in Bible and Jewish Religion Dedicated to Yehezkel Kaufmann on the Occasion of His Seventieth Birthday.* Jerusalem: Magnes, 1960, pp. 88–114.

Kaplan, Lawrence. "Adam, Enoch, and Metatron Revisited: A Critical Analysis of Moshe Idel's Method of Reconstruction." *Kabbalah* 6 (2001), pp. 73–119.

Karrer, Otto, and Herma Piesch, eds. *Meister Eckeharts Rechtfertigungsschrift vom Jahre 1326: Einleitungen, Übersetzung und Anmerkungen.* Erfurt: Kurt Stenger, 1927.

Kee, H. C. "Testaments of the Twelve Patriarchs," in Charlesworth, *OTP,* vol. 1, pp. 775–828.

Keel, Othmar. *Jahwe-Visionen und Siegelkunst: Eine neue Deutung der Majestätsschilderungen in Jes 6, Ez 1 und 10 und Sach 4.* Stuttgart: Katholisches Bibelwerk, 1977.

Klijn, A. F. J., and G. J. Reinink. *Patristic Evidence for Jewish-Christian Sects.* Leiden: Brill, 1973.

–. "2 (Syriac Apocalypse of) Baruch," in Charlesworth, *OTP,* vol. 1, pp. 615–652.

Klinzing, Georg. *Die Umdeutung des Kultus in der Qumrangemeinde und im Neuen Testament.* Göttingen: Vandenhoeck and Ruprecht, 1971.

Knibb, Michael A. (in consultation with Edward Ullendorf). *The Ethiopic Book of Enoch: A New Edition in the Light of the Aramaic Dead Sea Fragments,* vol. 2: *Introduction, Translation and Commentary.* Oxford: Clarendon Press, 1978.

Knohl, Israel. *The Messiah before Jesus: The Suffering Servant of the Dead Sea Scrolls.* Berkeley and Los Angeles: University of California Press, 2000.

Krebs, Engelbert. *Grundfragen der kirchlichen Mystik dogmatisch erörtert und für das Leben gewertet.* Freiburg: Herder, 1921.

Kugel, James L., and Rowan A. Greer. *Early Biblical Interpretation.* Philadelphia: Westminster, 1986.

Kuhn, Heinz-Wolfgang. *Enderwartung und gegenwärtiges Heil.* Göttingen: Vandenhoeck and Ruprecht, 1966.

Kuhn, K. H. "The Apocalypse of Zephaniah and an Anonymous Apocalypse," in H. F. D. Sparks, *The Apocryphal Old Testament.* Oxford: Clarendon Press, 1984, pp. 915–925.

Kuhn, Peter. *Gottes Trauer und Klage in der rabbinischen Überlieferung (Talmud und Midrasch).* Leiden: Brill, 1978.

–. *Offenbarungsstimmen im antiken Judentum: Untersuchungen zur Bat Qol und verwandten Phänomenen.* Tübingen: J. C. B. Mohr (Paul Siebeck), 1989.

Kuyt, Annelies. *The "Descent" to the Chariot: Towards a Description of the Terminology, Place, Function, and Nature of the Yeridah in Hekhalot Literature.* Tübingen: J.C.B. Mohr (Paul Siebeck), 1995.

Langermann, Y. Tzvi. "On the Beginnings of Hebrew Scientific Literature and on Studying History Through 'Maqbilot' (Parallels)." *Aleph* 2 (2002), pp. 169–189.

Lauterbach, Jacob Z., *Mekilta de-Rabbi Ishmael*, 3 vols. Philadelphia: Jewish Publication Society, 1933–1935.

Lesses, Rebecca. *Ritual Practices to Gain Power: Angels, Incantations, and Revelation in Early Jewish Mysticism.* Harrisburg, PA: Trinity Press International, 1998.

–. "Eschatological Sorrow, Divine Weeping, and God's Right Arm," in April D. DeConick, ed., *Paradise Now: Essays on Early Jewish and Christian Mysticism.* Atlanta, GA: Society of Biblical Literature, 2006, pp. 265–283.

Levy, Jacob. *Wörterbuch über die Talmudim und Midraschim*, 4 vols., 2nd. ed. Berlin: B. Harz, 1924 (repr. 1963, Wissenschaftliche Buchgesellschaft, Darmstadt).

Lewin, B.M. *Otzar ha-Geonim*, vol. 4/2 (Hagiga), part 1 (Teshuvot). Jerusalem, 1931.

Lichtenberger, Hermann, *Studien zum Menschenbild in Texten der Qumrangemeinde,* Göttingen: Vandenhoeck and Ruprecht, 1980.

–. "Auferstehung in den Qumranfunden," in Friedrich Avemarie and Hermann Lichtenberger, eds., *Auferstehung – Resurrection. The Fourth Durham-Tübingen Research Symposion: Resurrection, Transfiguration and Exaltation in Old Testament, Ancient Judaism and Early Christianity.* Tübingen: Mohr Siebeck, 2001, pp. 79–91.

Liddell, Henry George, and Robert Scott. *A Greek-English Lexicon*, rev. Henry Stuart Jones. Oxford: Clarendon Press, 1968.

Liebes, Yehuda. *Torat ha-Yetzirah shel Sefer Yetzirah.* Jerusalem: Schocken, 2000.

Luttikhuizen, Gerard P. *The Revelation of Elchasai.* Tübingen: J.C.B. Mohr (Paul Siebeck), 1985.

Luzzatto, Samuel David. *Erläuterungen über einen Theil der Propheten und Hagiographen.* Lemberg: A.I. Menkes, 1876 (in Hebrew).

Mach, Michael. *Entwicklungsstadien des jüdischen Engelglaubens in vorrabbinischer Zeit.* Tübingen: J.C.B. Mohr (Paul Siebeck), 1992.

Maier, Johann. *Die Texte vom Toten Meer*, vol. 2. Munich and Basel: Ernst Reinhardt Verlag, 1960.

–. "Das Gefährdungsmotiv bei der Himmelsreise in der jüdischen Apokalyptik und 'Gnosis.'" *Kairos* 5 (1963), pp. 8–40.

–. *Jüdische Auseinandersetzung mit dem Christentum in der Antike*, Darmstadt: Wissenschaftliche Buchgesellschaft, 1982.

–. "Zu Kult und Liturgie der Qumrangemeinde." *RdQ* 14 (1989/90), pp. 543–586.

–. "*Shire 'Olat hash-Shabbat.* Some Observations on Their Calendric Implications and on Their Style," in Julio Trebolle Barrera and Luis Vegas Montaner, eds., *The Madrid Qumran Congress*, vol. 2. Leiden: Brill; Madrid: Editorial Complutense, 1992, pp. 543–560.

Mandelbaum, Bernard, ed. *Pesikta de Rav Kahana*, 2 vols. New York: Jewish Theological Seminary of America, 1962.

Marcoulesco, Ileana. "Mystical Union," in Mircea Eliade, ed., *The Encyclopedia of Religion*, vol. 10. London: Collier Macmillan, 1987, pp. 239–245.

Marcovich, Miroslav, ed. *Hippolytus, Refutatio Omnium Haeresium.* Berlin: Walter de Gruyter, 1986.

Marcus, Ralph. "A Sixteenth Century Hebrew Critique of Philo." *HUCA* 21 (1948), pp. 29–37.

–. *Philo*, Supplement II, *Questions and Answers on Exodus*, trans. from the ancient Armenian version of the original Greek. Cambridge, MA: Harvard University Press; London: William Heinemann, 1961.

Margalioth, Mordecai. *Sepher Ha-Razim: A Newly Recovered Book of Magic from the Talmudic Period*, Jerusalem: Yediot Achronot, 1966 (in Hebrew).

Margulies, Mordecai, ed. *Midrash Wayyiqra Rabba*, 5 vols. Jerusalem, 1953–1958.

Marshall, John W. *Parables of War: Reading John's Jewish Apocalypse*. Waterloo, ON: Wilfrid Laurier University Press, 2001.

–. "Who's on the Throne? Revelation in the Long Year," in Ra'anan S. Boustan and Annette Yoshiko Reed, eds., *Heavenly Realms and Earthly Realities in Late Antique Religions*. Cambridge: Cambridge University Press, 2004, pp. 123–141.

McGinn, Bernard. *The Foundations of Mysticism*, vol. 1: *The Presence of God: A History of Western Christian Mysticism*. London: SCM Press, 1992.

McKenzie, D. F. *Bibliography and the Sociology of Texts*. London: British Library, 1986.

Meyer, Marvin W., and Richard Smith, eds. *Ancient Christian Magic: Coptic Texts of Ritual Power*. San Francisco: HarperCollins, 1994.

Milik, Józef T., ed. (with the collaboration of Matthew Black). *The Books of Enoch: Aramaic Fragments of Qumrân Cave 4*. Oxford: Clarendon Press, 1976.

Miller, James. *Measures of Wisdom: The Cosmic Dance in Classical and Christian Antiquity*, Toronto: University of Toronto Press, 1986.

Mizrachi, Noam. "*Sh'elat ha-ziqqah ben shirot 'olat ha-shabbat le-sifrut ha-hekhalot: hebetei lashon we-signon*," *Megillot* 7 (2008), pp. 263–298.

Momigliano, Arnaldo D. "Greek Culture and the Jews," in M. I. Finley, ed., *The Legacy of Greece: A New Appraisal*. Oxford: Clarendon Press, 1981, pp. 325–346.

Morray-Jones, Christopher. "Hekhalot Literature and Talmudic Tradition: Alexander's Three Test Cases." *JSJ* 22 (1991), pp. 1–39.

–. "Transformational Mysticism in the Apocalyptic-Merkabah Tradition." *JJS* 43 (1992), pp. 1–31.

–. "The Temple Within: The Embodied Divine Image and Its Worship in the Dead Sea Scrolls and Other Early Jewish and Christian Sources." *SBL.SPS* 37 (1998), pp. 400–431.

–. *A Transparent Illusion: The Dangerous Vision of Water in Hekhalot Mysticism*. Leiden: Brill, 2002.

Neis, Rachel. "Embracing Icons: The Face of Jacob on the Throne of God." *Images* 1 (2007), pp. 36–54.

Neusner, Jacob. *The Tosefta Translated from the Hebrew: Second Division Moed (The Order of Appointed Times)*. New York: Ktav, 1981.

Newsom, Carol A. "The Development of *1 Enoch* 6–19: Cosmology and Judgment." *CBQ* 42 (1980), pp. 310–329.

–. *Songs of the Sabbath Sacrifice: A Critical Edition*. Atlanta, GA: Scholars Press, 1985.

–. "Merkabah Exegesis in the Qumran Sabbath Shirot," *JJS* 38 (1987), pp. 11–30.

–. "'Sectually Explicit' Literature from Qumran," in William H. Propp, Baruch Halpern, and David N. Freedman, eds., *The Hebrew Bible and Its Interpreters*. Winona Lake, IN: Eisenbrauns, 1990, pp. 167–187.

Nickelsburg, George W. E. "Enoch, Levi, and Peter: Recipients of Revelation in Upper Galilee." *JBL* 100 (1981), pp. 575–600.

–. *Jewish Literature between the Bible and the Mishnah*. Philadelphia: Fortress Press, 1981.

–. *1 Enoch 1: A Commentary on the Book of 1 Enoch, Chapters 1–36, 81–108*, Minneapolis, MN: Fortress Press, 2001.

Niehoff, Maren R. "What Is in a Name? Philo's Mystical Philosophy of Language." *JSQ* 2 (1995), pp. 220–252.

–. "Did the *Timaeus* Create a Textual Community?" *GRBS* 47 (2007), pp. 161–191.

Nietzsche, Friedrich. *Die Geburt der Tragödie aus dem Geiste der Musik*. Leipzig: E. W. Fritzsch, 1872.

Nitzan, Bilhah. "Harmonic and Mystical Characteristics in Poetic and Liturgical Writings from Qumran." *JQR* 85 (1994), pp. 163–183.

–. *Qumran Prayer and Religious Poetry*. Leiden: Brill, 1994.

Origen. *The Song of Songs: Commentary and Homilies*. Westminster, MD: Newman Press; London: Longmans, Green and Co., 1957.

Origène. *Commentaire sur le Cantique des Cantiques*, vol. 1: *Texte de la Version Latine de Rufin*, introduction, traduction et notes par Luc Brésard et Henri Crouzel, avec la collaboration de Marcel Borret. Paris: Cerf, 1991.

Orlov, Andrei A. *The Enoch-Metatron Tradition*. Tübingen: Mohr Siebeck, 2005.

–. "God's Face in the Enochic Tradition," in April D. DeConick, *Paradise Now: Essays on Early Jewish and Christian Mysticism*. Atlanta, GA: Society of Biblical Literature, 2006, pp. 179–193.

–. *From Apocalypticism to Merkabah Mysticism: Studies in the Slavonic Pseudepigrapha*. Leiden: Brill, 2007.

Otto, Rudolf. *Mysticism East and West: A Comparative Analysis of the Nature of Mysticism*, trans. Bertha L. Bracey and Richenda C. Payne. New York: Macmillan, 1932 (repr. 1957, Meridian Books, New York).

The Oxford English Dictionary, 2nd ed., prepared by J. A. Simpson and E. S. C. Weiner, vol. 10. Oxford: Clarendon Press, 1989.

Pennington, A. "The Apocalypse of Abraham," in H. F. D. Sparks, *The Apocryphal Old Testament*. Oxford: Clarendon Press, 1984, pp. 363–391.

Reed, Annette Yoshiko. *Fallen Angels and the History of Judaism and Christianity: The Reception of Enochic Literature*. New York: Cambridge University Press, 2005.

Reeg, Gottfried, ed. *Die Geschichte von den Zehn Märtyrern*. Tübingen: J. C. B. Mohr (Paul Siebeck), 1985.

Regev, Eyal. *Sectarianism in Qumran: A Cross-Cultural Perspective*. Berlin: Walter de Gruyter, 2007.

Rehm, Bernhard, ed. *Die Pseudoklementinen I: Homilien*, 3rd ed. Georg Strecker. Berlin: Akademie Verlag, 1992.

Reichman, Ronen. "Die 'Wasser-Episode' in der Hechalot-Literatur." *FJB* 17, 1989, pp. 67–100.

Roberts, Alexander, and James Donaldson, eds. *The Ante-Nicene Fathers: Translations of the Writings of the Fathers down to A. D. 325*, vol. 1: *The Apostolic Fathers – Justin Martyr – Irenaeus*, rev. A. Cleveland Coxe. New York: Charles Scribner's Sons, 1925.

Rohr, Ignaz. *Der Hebräerbrief und die Geheime Offenbarung des Heiligen Johannes*, 4th ed. Bonn: Peter Hanstein, 1932.

Rowland, Christopher. *The Open Heaven: A Study of Apocalyptic in Judaism and Early Christianity*. London: SPCK, 1982.

–, with Patricia Gibbons and Vicente Dobroruka. "Visionary Experience in Ancient Judaism and Christianity," in April D. DeConick, ed., *Paradise Now: Essays on Early Jewish and Christian Mysticism*. Atlanta, GA: Society of Biblical Literature, 2006, pp. 41–56.

Rubinkiewicz, Ryszard. "Apocalypse of Abraham," in Charlesworth, *OTP*, vol. 1, pp. 681–705.

Runia, David T. "Redrawing the Map of Early Middle Platonism: Some Comments on the Philonic Evidence," in André Caquot, Mireille Hadas-Lebel, and Jean Riaud, eds., *Hellenica et Judaica: Hommage à Valentin Nikiprowetzky*. Leuven: Peeters, 1986, pp. 85–104.

–. *Philo and the Church Fathers: A Collection of Papers*. Leiden: Brill, 1995.

–, trans. *Philo of Alexandria: On the Creation of the Cosmos According to Moses*, with an introduction and commentary. Leiden: Brill, 2001.

Sandmel, Samuel. *Philo of Alexandria: An Introduction*. Oxford: Oxford University Press, 1979.

Schäfer, Peter. *Rivalität zwischen Engeln und Menschen. Untersuchungen zur rabbinischen Engelvorstellung*. Berlin: Walter de Gruyter, 1975.

–. "Der Götzendienst des Enosh. Zur Bildung und Entwicklung aggadischer Traditionen im nachbiblischen Judentum," in idem, *Studien zur Geschichte und Theologie des rabbinischen Judentums*. Leiden: Brill, 1978, pp. 134–152.

–, ed. *Synopse zur Hekhalot-Literatur*. Tübingen: J. C. B. Mohr (Paul Siebeck), 1981.

–, ed. *Geniza-Fragmente zur Hekhalot-Literatur*. Tübingen: J. C. B. Mohr (Paul Siebeck), 1984.

–. "New Testament and Hekhalot Literature: The Journey into Heaven in Paul and Merkavah Mysticism." *JJS* 35 (1984), pp. 19–35 = idem, *Hekhalot-Studien*, pp. 234–249.

–, ed. *Konkordanz zur Hekhalot-Literatur*, 2 vols. Tübingen: J. C. B. Mohr (Paul Siebeck), 1986–1988.

–. *Hekhalot-Studien*. Tübingen: J. C. B. Mohr, 1988.

–. "Zum Problem der redaktionellen Identität von *Hekhalot Rabbati*," in idem, *Hekhalot-Studien*, pp. 63–74.

–. "Ein neues *Hekhalot Rabbati*-Fragment," in idem, *Hekhalot-Studien*, pp. 96–103.

–. "Handschriften zur Hekhalot-Literatur," in idem, *Hekhalot-Studien*, pp. 154–233.

–. "The Ideal of Piety of the Ashkenazi Hasidim and Its Roots in Jewish Tradition." *JH* 4 (1990), pp. 9–23.

–. *Übersetzung der Hekhalot-Literatur*, 4 vols. Tübingen: J. C. B. Mohr (Paul Siebeck), 1987–1995.

–. *The Hidden and Manifest God: Some Major Themes in Early Jewish Mysticism*. Albany: State University of New York Press, 1992.

–. "Merkavah Mysticism and Magic," in Peter Schäfer and Joseph Dan, eds., *Gershom Scholem's Major Trends in Jewish Mysticism: 50 Years After. Proceedings of the Sixth International Conference on the History of Jewish Mysticism*. Tübingen: J. C. B. Mohr (Paul Siebeck), 1993, pp. 59–78.

–. *Judeophobia: Attitudes toward the Jews in the Ancient World*. Cambridge, MA: Harvard University Press, 1997.

–. "Diversity and Interaction: Messiahs in Early Judaism," in Peter Schäfer and Mark R. Cohen, eds., *Toward the Millennium: Messianic Expectations from the Bible to Waco*. Leiden: Brill, 1998, pp. 15–35.

–. "Ekstase, Vision und *unio mystica* in der frühen jüdischen Mystik," in Aleida and Jan Assmann, eds., *Schleier und Schwelle: Archäologie der literarischen Kommunikation V*, vol. 2: *Geheimnis und Offenbarung*. Munich: Fink, 1998, pp. 89–104.

–. *Mirror of His Beauty: Feminine Images of God from the Bible to the Early Kabbalah*. Princeton, NJ: Princeton University Press, 2002.

–. "In Heaven as It Is in Hell: The Cosmology of *Seder Rabbah di-Bereshit*," in Ra'anan S. Boustan and Annette Yoshiko Reed, eds., *Heavenly Realms and Earthly Realities in Late Antique Religions*. Cambridge: Cambridge University Press, 2004, pp. 233–274.

–. "From Cosmology to Theology: The Rabbinic Appropriation of Apocalyptic Cosmology," in Rachel Elior and Peter Schäfer, eds., *Creation and Re-Creation in Jewish Thought: Festschrift in Honor of Joseph Dan on the Occasion of his Seventieth Birthday*. Tübingen: Mohr Siebeck, 2005, pp. 39–58.

–. "Communion with the Angels: Qumran and the Origins of Jewish Mysticism," in Peter Schäfer, ed., *Wege Mystischer Gotteserfahrung: Judentum, Christentum und Islam / Mystical Approaches to God: Judaism, Christianity, and Islam*. Munich: Oldenbourg, 2006, pp. 37–66.

–. *Jesus in the Talmud*. Princeton, NJ: Princeton University Press, 2007.

Schäfer, Peter, and Hans-Jürgen Becker, eds. *Synopse zum Talmud Yerushalmi*, vol. II/5–12: *Ordnung Mo'ed – Traktate Sheqalim, Sukka, Rosh ha-Shana, Besa, Ta'anit, Megilla, Hagiga und Mo'ed Qatan*. Tübingen: Mohr Siebeck, 2001.

Schäfer, Peter, and Klaus Herrmann. *Übersetzung der Hekhalot-Literatur*, vol. 1: *§§ 1–80*. Tübingen: J. C. B. Mohr (Paul Siebeck), 1995.

Schiffman, Lawrence H. "The Recall of Rabbi Nehuniah ben Ha-Qanah from Ecstasy in Hekhalot Rabbati." *AJS Review* 1 (1976), pp. 269–281.

–. "*Merkavah* Speculation at Qumran: The 4QSerekh *'Olat ha-Shabbat*," in Jehuda Reinharz and Daniel M. Swetschinski, eds., with the collaboration of Kalman P. Bland, *Mystics, Philosophers, and Politicians: Essays in Jewish Intellectual History in Honor of Alexander Altmann*. Durham, NC: Duke University Press, 1982, pp. 15–47.

Scholem, Gershom. *Jewish Gnosticism, Merkabah Mysticism, and Talmudic Tradition*, 2nd ed. New York: Jewish Theological Seminary, 1965 (first published 1960).

–. *Major Trends in Jewish Mysticism*. New York: Schocken, 1974 (repr.).

–. *Origins of the Kabbalah*, ed. R. J. Zwi Werblowsky. Philadelphia: Jewish Publication Society; Princeton, NJ: Princeton University Press, 1987.

–. *On the Mystical Shape of the Godhead: Basic Concepts in the Kabbalah*. New York: Schocken, 1991.

Schlüter, Margarete. "Die Erzählung von der Rückholung des R. Nehunya ben Haqana aus der *Merkava*-Schau in ihrem redaktionellen Rahmen." *FJB* 10 (1982), pp. 65–109.

Segal, Alan F. *Two Powers in Heaven*. Leiden: Brill, 1977.

–. "Religious Experience and the Construction of the Transcendent Self," in April D. DeConick, ed., *Paradise Now: Essays on Early Jewish and Christian Mysticism*. Atlanta, GA: Society of Biblical Literature, 2006, pp. 27–40.

Segal, Moshe Z., ed. *Sefer ben Sira ha-shalem*. Jerusalem: Bialik Institute, 1958.

Sellin, Gerhard. "Gotteserkenntnis und Gotteserfahrung bei Philo von Alexandrien," in Joachim Gnilka et al., eds., *Monotheismus und Christologie. Zur Gottesfrage im hellenistischen Judentum und im Urchristentum*. Freiburg: Herder, 1992, pp. 17–40.

Siamakēs, Kōnstantinos. *Hierōnymou De viris illustribus*. Thessalonike: Kentro Byzantinōn Ereunōn, 1992.

Slusser, Michael, ed. *St. Justin Martyr, Dialogue with Trypho*, transl. Thomas B. Falls, rev. Thomas P. Halton. Washington, DC: Catholic University of America Press, 2003.

Smith, Mark S. *God in Translation: Deities in Cross-Cultural Discourse in the Biblical World*. Tübingen: Mohr Siebeck, 2008.

Smith, Morton. "Ascent to the Heavens and Deification in 4QMᵃ," in Lawrence H. Schiffman, ed., *Archaeology and History in the Dead Sea Scrolls: The New York University Conference in Memory of Yigael Yadin*. Sheffield, UK: JSOT Press, 1990, pp. 181–188.

–. "Two Ascended to Heaven – Jesus and the Author of 4Q491," in James H. Charlesworth, ed., *Jesus and the Dead Sea Scrolls*. New York: Doubleday, 1992, pp. 290–301.

Sparks, H. F. D. *The Apocryphal Old Testament*. Oxford: Clarendon Press, 1984.

Sokoloff, Michael. *Dictionary of Jewish Palestinian Aramaic of the Byzantine Period*. Ramat-Gan: Bar Ilan University Press, 1990.

Stern, David. "Ancient Jewish Interpretation of the Song of Songs in a Comparative Context," in Natalie B. Dohrmann and David Stern, eds., *Jewish Biblical Interpretation and Cultural Exchange: Comparative Exegesis in Context*. Philadelphia: University of Pennsylvania Press, 2008, pp. 87–107, 263–272.

Stern, Sacha. "Rachel Elior on Ancient Jewish Calendars: A Critique." *Aleph* 5 (2005), pp. 287–292.

Stone, Michael E. "Aramaic Levi in Its Contexts." *JSQ* 9 (2002), pp. 307–326.

Stroumsa, Gedalyahu G. "Form(s) of God: Some Notes on Metatron and Christ." *HTR* 76 (1983), pp. 269–288.

Strugnell, John. "The Angelic Liturgy at Qumran – 4Q Serek Šīrōt 'Olat Haššabbāt," in *Congress Volume: Oxford 1959*. Leiden: Brill, 1960, pp. 318–345.

Suter, David. "Fallen Angel, Fallen Priest: The Problem of Family Purity in 1 Enoch 6–16." *HUCA* 50 (1979), pp. 115–135.

Swartz, Michael D. *Mystical Prayer in Ancient Judaism: An Analysis of Ma'aseh Merkavah*. Tübingen: Mohr Siebeck, 1992.

–. *Scholastic Magic: Ritual and Revelation in Early Jewish Mysticism*. Princeton, NJ: Princeton University Press, 1996.

–. "The Dead Sea Scrolls and Later Jewish Magic and Mysticism." *DSD* 8 (2001), pp. 182–193.

–. "Mystical Texts," in Shmuel Safrai Z"L, Zeev Safrai, Joshua Schwartz, and Peter J. Tomson, eds., *The Literature of the Sages*, part 2. Assen: Royal Van Gorcum and Fortress, 2006, pp. 393–420.

Ta-Shma, Israel M. "The Library of the Ashkenazi Sages in the Eleventh and Twelfth Centuries." *QS* 60 (1985), pp. 298–309.

Théry, G. "Édition Critique des Pièces Relatives au Procès d'Eckhart Contenues dans le Manuscrit 33ᵇ de la Bibliothèque de Soest." *AHDL* 1 (1926–1927), pp. 129–268.

Underhill, Evelyn. *Mysticism: A Study in the Nature and Development of Man's Spiritual Consciousness*, 12th ed. London: Methuen, 1930 (repr. 1967; first published 1911).

Unger, Dominic J., trans. (with further revisions by John J. Dillon). *St. Irenaeus of Lyons Against the Heresies*, vol. 1, book 1. New York/Mahwah, NJ: Paulist Press, 1992.

Urbach, Ephraim E. "The Traditions about Merkabah Mysticism in the Tannaitic Period," in Ephraim E. Urbach, R. J. Zwi Werblowsky, and Chaim Wirszubski, eds., *Studies in*

Mysticism and Religion Presented to Gershom G. Scholem on His Seventieth Birthday. Jerusalem: Magnes Press, 1967, pp. 1–28 (in Hebrew).

Vaillant, André. *Le livre des secrets d'Hénoch*. Paris: Institut d'Études Slaves, 1952.

van der Horst, Pieter W. "Moses' Throne Vision in Ezekiel the Dramatist." *JJS* 34 (1983), pp. 21–29 (repr. in idem, *Essays on the Jewish World of Early Christianity*, pp. 63–71).

–. "The Measurement of the Body: A Chapter in the History of Ancient Jewish Mysticism," in Dirk van der Plas, ed., *Effigies Dei*. Leiden: Brill, 1987, pp. 56–68 (repr. in idem, *Essays on the Jewish World of Early Christianity*, pp. 123–135).

–. *Essays on the Jewish World of Early Christianity*. Freiburg Schweiz: Universitätsverlag; Göttingen: Vandenhoeck and Ruprecht, 1990.

van der Woude, A. S. "Fragmente einer Rolle der Lieder für das Sabbatopfer aus Höhle XI von Qumran (11QŠirŠabb)," in W. C. Delsman et al., eds., *Von Kanaan bis Kerala: Festschrift J. P. M. van der Ploeg*. Kevelaer: Butzon and Becker; Neukirchen-Vluyn: Neukirchener Verlag, 1982, pp. 311–337.

van Uchelen, Nick A. "Ethical Terminology in Heykhalot-Texts," in Jan W. van Henten et al., eds., *Tradition and Re-interpretation in Jewish and Early Christian Literature: Essays in Honour of Jürgen C. H. Lebram*. Leiden: Brill, 1986, pp. 250–258.

VanderKam, James C. *Enoch and the Growth of an Apocalyptic Tradition*. Washington, DC: Catholic Biblical Association of America, 1984.

–. "The Origin, Character and History of the 364 Day Calendar: A Reassessment of Jaubert's Hypotheses." *CBQ* 41 (1979), pp. 390–411.

Vermes, Geza. *The Dead Sea Scrolls in English*, 3rd ed. Sheffield, UK: JSOT Press, 1987.

Versnel, Henk S. "Some Reflections on the Relationship Magic-Religion." *Numen* 37 (1991), pp. 177–197.

Vogt, Ernst. *Untersuchungen zum Buch Ezechiel*. Rome: Biblical Institute Press, 1981.

von der Osten-Sacken, Peter. *Gott und Belial: Traditionsgeschichtliche Untersuchungen zum Dualismus in den Texten aus Qumran*. Göttingen: Vandenhoeck and Ruprecht, 1969.

Weinberg, Joanna, ed. *The Light of the Eyes: Azariah de' Rossi*, trans. from the Hebrew with an introduction and annotations. New Haven, CT: Yale University Press, 2001.

Wevers, John William. *Ezekiel: Based on the Revised Standard Version*. London: Nelson, 1969 (repr. 1982, William B. Eerdmans, Grand Rapids, MI).

Wewers, Gerd A. *Hagiga: Festopfer*. Tübingen: J. C. B. Mohr (Paul Siebeck), 1983.

Williams, Frank, trans. *The Panarion of Epiphanius of Salamis: Book I (Sects 1–46)*. Leiden: Brill, 1987.

Winston, David. "Was Philo a Mystic?" in Joseph Dan and Frank Talmage, eds., *Studies in Jewish Mysticism: Proceedings of Regional Conferences Held at the University of California, Los Angeles and McGill University in April, 1978*. Cambridge, MA: Association for Jewish Studies, 1982, pp. 15–39.

–. *Logos and Mystical Theology in Philo of Alexandria*. Cincinnati, OH: Hebrew Union College Press, 1985.

–. "Philo and the Contemplative Life," in Arthur Green, ed., *Jewish Spirituality*, vol. 1: *From the Bible throughout the Middle Ages*. New York: Crossroad, 1987, pp. 198–231.

Wintermute, O. S. "Apocalypse of Zephaniah," in Charlesworth, *OTP*, vol. 1, pp. 497–515.

Wolfson, Elliot R.. "*Yeridah la-Merkavah*: Typology of Ecstasy and Enthronement in Ancient Jewish Mysticism," in R.A. Herrera, ed., *Mystics of the Book: Themes, Topics, and Typologies*. New York: P. Lang, 1993, pp. 13–44.

–. "Mysticism and the Poetic-Liturgical Compositions from Qumran: A Response to Bilhah Nitzan." *JQR* 85 (1994), pp. 185–202.

–. *Through a Speculum That Shines: Vision and Imagination in Medieval Jewish Mysticism*. Princeton, NJ: Princeton University Press, 1994.

–. "The Image of Jacob Engraved upon the Throne: Further Reflection on the Esoteric Doctrine of the German Pietists," in idem, *Along the Path: Studies in Kabbalistic Myth, Symbolism, and Hermeneutics*. Albany: State University of New York Press, 1995, pp. 1–62.

Wordsworth, William. "Tintern Abbey," in *The Pedlar. Tintern Abbey. The Two-Part Prelude*, ed. with a critical introduction and notes by Jonathan Wordsworth. Cambridge: Cambridge University Press, 1985.

Zaehner, Robert C. *At Sundry Times: An Essay in the Comparison of Religions*. London: Faber and Faber, 1958.

Ziegler, Konrat, and Walther Sontheimer., eds. *Der Kleine Pauly: Lexikon der Antike*, vol. 3. Munich: Deutscher Taschenbuch Verlag, 1979.

Zimmerli, Walther. *Ezekiel 1: A Commentary on the Book of the Prophet Ezekiel, chaps. 1–24*. Philadelphia: Fortress Press, 1979.

Source Index

Hebrew Bible

Genesis

1	30–31, 181, 185, 209, 211, 212, 293n204
1:2	208, 234
2	181
1:6 ff.	42
1:7	58, 107n84, 208
1:14–17	177n6
1:26	81
1:26 f.	44
1:27	44n61, 163
1:28	39n33
2:21	173
5	53
5:21–23	53
5:21–24	319
5:23	77
5:24	77, 176, 316, 321
5:32	74
6:1–4	54
7:14, 21	39n33
8:19	39n33
8:21	69, 140
9:12	89
9:12 f.	47
11:26–29	87
12:1	170
15	87, 89
15:2	90
15:9	89
15:10	89
15:11	90
15:12	165
15:17	90
15:18–21	90
17:1	42n56, 91

22:2	37n14
22:17	286n162
28:3	42n56
34	68
35:11	42n56
35:22	179
37:20	39n33
38	179
38:7	161
43:14	42n56
48:3	42n56
49:9	109
49:10	109

Exodus

3:2–6	45
3:2	57n11
6:3	42n56
7:9	89
7:19 f.	89
8:1	89
8:12	89
12	109n88
14:22	248n31, 288n173
15:11	147
15:19	288n173
19 f.	45, 56
19:6	109n89
19:16 ff.	107
19:9	45, 50
19:18	188, 206
19:20	45
20:13	251n38
20:16	45
20:18	45
20:19	45

21:9	106n78
21:11	106n78
21:12	106n78
21:14	106n82
23:21	296n219, 296n222, 320
24	43n59
24:2	166
24:10	43, 89, 134, 172
24:12	167
26:31–33	136n88
28	106n79
28:4 ff.	140
28:17–21	106
28:20	40n41
28:21	106
28:31	139n102
28:32	140
28:39	88n9
30:22–29	82n114
30:35	137n96
31:4	135n74
32:1–20	179
32:21–25	179
32:35	179
33	44, 45, 46n64, 80n104
33:9	46
33:11	46
33:17–23	156
33:18	156
33:20	46, 63n41, 80, 289
33:22 f.	46
33:23	91
34:5 f.	305
36:35	136n88
39:22	139n102, 140
39:27	140
39:28	88n9
40:34 f.	48n68

Leviticus

2:13	137n96
9:23	48n68
15:13	34
16:2	136n88
16:4	61
16:17	169n69
18	214
18/20	30, 181, 211

21:13	232n77
21:17–21	122
22:24	232
26:6	39n33

Numbers

5:1–4	121
5:3	121
6:24–26	179
10:8	216n8
12:7	63n41
12:8	44n60
14:10	48n68
16:19	48n68
18:19	137n96
19:17	34
27:20	240n115
28:9 f.	131

Deuteronomy

4:11 f.	107
4:15	44n60
432	210, 212, 223
4:32a	209, 210
4:32b	209, 210
4:32c	209
5:4	188
5:21	289
5:23	289
23:2–3	251n40
23:10–15	121
23:15	121
26:15	129n40
30:20	168n63
32:11	208
32:43	326n374
33	167
33:2	239, 248

Joshua

2:19	272

1 Samuel

1:15	168
4:4	39n34

2 Samuel

6:2	39n34

7:14	326n373
11:12	179
13	179
22:10	35n7

1 Kings

2:19	249
6:2	248n27
6:3	59, 59n25, 136n82
6:5	59, 132
6:23–28	39
6:29–35	136n85
7:23–39	41
7:50	248n27
8:11	48n69
8:13	141
19:11 f.	239, 47n64
19:12	138
22:19–23	62
22:19	44n62, 248

2 Kings

2:11	84, 176, 319
19:15	39n34
20:18	129n41

Isaiah

3:1–5	231
3:1–7	231, 241
3:3	225n46
6:1	34, 44, 289
6:2	39, 108, 229
6:3	79, 108, 136, 254, 259, 261, 263, 266
11:1	109
11:10	109
14:14	224
14:15	224
28:16	115
29:7	290n181
35:9	39n33
37:16	39n34
40:18	44n60
40:25	44n60
41:4	108
41:8 f.	72n77
42:1	37n14, 72n77
44:6	108

48:2	239
48:12	108
53	148
53:3 f.	148
53:4–7	109n88
62:8	248
63:8	125n31
63:9	125, 125n31
66:1	231

Jeremiah

1:2	34
1:9	44
1:12	137n94
1:17	137n94
3:14	234, 236
3:22	234, 236
14:21	70n68
17:12	70n68
25:34	264n92

Ezekiel

1	27, 30–31, 104n65, 176–182, 185, 187, 193, 200, 207, 211–212, 214, 231, 289n180
1:1	36
1:1 f.	35n3
1:2	35
1:3	35
1:4–26	229, 241
1:4	227, 229, 293n201, 294
1:5	108
1:6	107, 229
1:7	137n94
1:9	137n94
1:10	108, 229
1:12	137n94
1:13	107, 134, 288
1:14	134n72, 229, 289
1:15	138, 229
1:16	40n41, 89
1:17	137n94
1:18	79, 108, 280n134
1:20	138
1:22	57, 107, 134
1:22 ff.	137, 287
1:23	137n94

1:24	91, 138, 191
1:24 f.	138
1:25	138, 191, 254, 296n223
1:26–28	105
1:26	73n79, 88, 89, 135n76, 137, 227, 294, 309, 310n296
1:26 f.	103n63, 241
1:27	61, 138, 227, 228, 229, 241, 297
1:27 f.	229
1:28–3:15	48
1:28	58, 89, 101, 134, 138, 140n111, 191, 228, 240, 288, 288n174, 291
2:1	226, 287
2:2	104
2:4	48
2:7	50
2:9 f.	108
2:10	108
3:1	108
3:7	50
3:11	48
3:12–15	48
3:12	49n75, 268, 290
3:12 f.	138, 191
3:14	58, 104
3:15	34
3:16 ff.	49
3:22	37n18
3:22 f.	35n3
3:23	48n70
3:26	59
4:13	34
8:1	37n18
8:3	37, 104
8:3 f.	35n3
8:16	248n27
8:41	248n27
10	135n76, 137, 176, 178, 181
10:2	138
10:9	40n41
10:13	287
10:14	40n40, 229
11:1	104
11:3	52
11:14	52
11:15	51
11:16	51
16:2	179
22:1	36
28:13	40n41, 74n86, 106n79
40–48	51, 184
40:1	37n18
40:1 f.	37
40:2	35n3, 37, 128
40:48	136n82
41	136
41:18	136
41:25	136
43:3	50
44:18	88n9
46:4 f.	131

Hosea
13:15	264n92

Amos
4:13	215
7:7	44
9:9	44

Nahum
2:10	264n92

Habakkuk
2:17	112

Zechariah
3:6	88n9

Malachi
3:1	252n41
3:2–5	252
3:5	251n37
3:23	352n42

Psalms
2:7	37n14, 326n373
11:7	192n68, 193
15:1	192, 193
16:5 f.	124n27
16:11	191, 192
24:3	192, 193

34:9	5
45:6	326n375
45:16	129n41
65:5	193
68:5	79n101, 224, 248n28
73:26	124n27
80:2	39n34
84:5	192, 193
96:12	188
99:1	39n34
101:7	202
102:26	326n376
104:3	134n69
104:25	39n33
110:1	249, 326n377
118:9 (LXX)	159n23
118:16 (LXX)	159n23
118:17 (LXX)	159n23
118:25 (LXX)	159n23
118:28 (LXX)	159n23
118:42 (LXX)	159n23
118:57 (LXX)	159n23
118:67 (LXX)	159n23
118:74 (LXX)	159n23
118:81 (LXX)	159n23
118:101 (LXX)	159n23
118:114 (LXX)	159n23
118:139 (LXX)	159n23
118:147 (LXX)	159n23
118:160 (LXX)	159n23
118:169 (LXX)	159n23
119:18	128
140:14	192, 193
142:6	124n27
148:7	188n52
148:8	215
148:9	188n52
148:14	188n52
116:15	196

Proverbs

8	326
8:5	326
8:6	326
8:8	326
8:11	326
8:13	326
8:22	160

10:35	223
25:2	284n154
25:16	196, 233

Job

1:6–12	62
2:1–6	62
25:2	57n13
25:3	229
26:9	291n192
33:15	290n181
37:18	42
38:7	124, 125
40:15–24	200
41:1–34	200

Song of Songs

1:10	189, 190n57
1:4	197, 199, 200, 200n119, 201n120, 237
4:11	226
5:9–16	262
5:10–16	300, 301, 308
5–16	309
5:10	239
5:11	230

Ecclesiastes

5:5	197, 234, 234n82

Daniel

1:4	129n41
7	44, 60, 73, 105, 241
7:9	44, 61, 73, 89, 103n63, 105, 230
7:9 f.	60
7:10	61, 62, 73n81, 74n86, 75, 136n86, 229, 288
7:13	249n32, 333
7:13 f.	73
7:14	109
7:22	118n14
7:27	109, 118n14
8:1 f.	290n181
10:13	141n116
10:20 f.	117
10:21	141n116
11:30	117

12:1	117, 141n116
12:2 f.	161
12:3	42, 125n30

Ezra

4:36	101
10:15	42n56

1 Chronicles

28:11	136n82
28:18	135n76

2 Chronicles

7:1	48n69
3:14	136n88
4:22	248n27
32:27	264n92

Apocrypha and Pseudepigrapha

Sapientia Salomonis

7:26	162
9:1	159n27

Jesus Sirach

3:21 f.	221n27
24:23	159n24
49:8	135n76, 178n11

3 Maccabees

6:18	36n11

1 Enoch

1–36	27, 54, 345n32
1–5	54
4:20	105
4:21	105n73
6–11	54, 63, 65
9:1	119n17, 126
9:4	70n68
12–16	54, 55
12	55
12:1–2	55
12:4	95
13	55
14	27, 55, 65, 229, 293n202
14:5	56
14:8 ff.	72
14:9	59n25
14:10	107
14:13	64
14:13 f.	72

14:18	101, 107n84
14:20	101
14:22	81
14:24	58n17, 72, 81
15:1	63, 95
16:4	63
17–19	54, 63
20–36	54, 63
20:8	101
22:1	80, 82
22:5	81
22:8	82
36 ff.	83
37–71	28, 72
37:2	83
39:3	72
39:6	72
39:8	72
39:14	72
40:2 f.	126
40:9	126
46:1	73
46:4–47:4	73
47:3	73n81
56:2	83
60	73
60:1	73
71	74
71:1	74
71:2	229n64
71:3 f.	75
71:6	229n64
71:8	75

71:8 ff.	126		12:8	89
71:9 f.	119		12:10	90
			13 f.	90
2 Enoch			15:1	90
1:1	77		15:2	90
1:4	314n325		16:1	90
1:5	101		17:1	91, 92
1:8	78		17:8–21	91
10:2	229		18	92
13	313n314		18:1 f.	91
18:1	315n326		18:11	92n27
20:1	78		18:14	92
21	79		25:1 f.	93
21:2	79		27	87
21:4	79		27:1	93
21:5	79		29	87
21:9	106n78		29:1–13	93n29
21:11	106n78			
21:12	106n78		*Apocalypse of Zephaniah*	
22:1	79, 80, 82, 105		2	100
22:4	106		3	100
22:5	81		3:2	99n49
22:8	82		4	100
22:9	101		5	100
36 ff.	83		6	100
37:2	83		6:8	100
56:2	83		6:11	100, 105n74
60	333		6:13	105n74
71	333		6:17	101
			7	101
2 Baruch			8:1	101
22:1	104n65		9:1	102
55:3	101		9:3	102
63:6	101		9:5	102
			10:12 f.	111n92
Apocalypse of Abraham			11	102
8:1–3	87		12	102
9	87			
9:5	89		*Ascension of Isaiah*	
9:6	87		1–5	93
9:9	87		6–11	93
10:2	88		6:8	94
10:3	88		6:9	94
10:4	88		6:13–16	94
10:8 f.	88		6:15	94
11:1	88		6:17	94, 95
11:2	105n74		7:25	96
12:6	89		8:5	95

8:7	95
8:14	97n40
8:16 f.	96
8:13	96
9:2	97
9:9	97
9:27	97
9:33	97
9:37	97, 98
9:38	97, 98
10	98
10:2	98n42
11:32	98

Testament of Levi

2:5 f.	194n79
2:6	36, 68
2:10	36, 68
3:4–6	141
3:4	68

5:1	36, 70
8	70
8:2	70
8:3	71
8:4	70
8:16 f.	71
9:9	71
9:10	71
14:1	71
14:5	71
18:2	71
18:6	36, 71
18:8	71
18:10	71

Testament of Judah

24:2	36

Testament of Isaac

5:21–25	229

Qumran

1QpHab

XII:7 f.	112n1

1Q17–18

	126n33

1QS

VI, 4–6	114n5
VI, 19	115
VI, 22	115
VIII, 4–10	115n7
VIII, 4	115
VIII, 5	128
IX, 3–5	114n4
IX, 3	114
IX, 5 f.	115
XI, 5–8	127

1QSa (1Q28a)

II, 3–10	120n18

1QSb (1Q28b)

III, 5 f.	130n42

III, 25 f.	129n38
IV, 22–28	129

1QM

I, 9–12	117
VII, 3–7	120, 121
VII, 4	121
VII, 6	120
VII, 7	121
XII, 1–5	119
XII, 5	120
XII, 7–9	118
XV, 14	118
IX, 1 f.	118n15
IX, 10 ff.	119
IX, 14–16	119

1QH[a]

XI, 19–23	123
XI, 22 f.	125
XIV, 12 f.	125
XIV, 13	129
XIV, 28	130
XIX, 10–14	123n23

XIX, 14	125	20 ii-21–22	137n94, 138nn99–100
XXIII, 6	125	22	141n113
XXVI	146, 149nn151–155	23 i	139nn102, 103
		23 ii	140nn107, 110
2Q19–20			
	126n33	*4Q427 (4QHᵃ)*	
		7, col. I	146, 147n141,
3Q5			148nn143–144, 146–
	126n33		148, 149nn151–155,
			150nn162, 164
4Q176a+b			
	126n33	*4Q471ᵇ*	
		1–2	146, 147n141,
4Q216–224			148nn143–148, 150n162
	126n33		
		4Q482	
4Q400			126n33
1 i	132n52		
2	132n55	*4Q491*	
		11, col. I	146n135
4Q401			
14 i	132n55	*4Q491ᶜ*	
		1	146, 147, 148nn144–147,
4Q403			149, 149nn150, 158,
1 i	133nn61–66, 134n68		150nn162, 165
1 ii	134nn70–71, 73,	1–2	146
	135n75		
		11Q12	
4Q405			126n33
14–15 i	136nn81, 84		
15 ii-16	136n86	*11Q17*	
19	136nn89–93	IX	140n106

Philo

De Abrahamo		*De Congressu Eruditionis Gratia*	
58	172n82	14	164n48
80	155n9, 171n80		
		De Ebrietate	
De Cherubim		30 f.	160n30
27	173n87	152	168n66
De Confusione Linguarum		*De Fuga et Inventione*	
95–97	172n84	12	159n21
95	155n9	166–168	169n70
97	155n9		
146 f.	158n19		

De Gigantibus

14	162n40
30 f.	162n38
49	172n81

De Migratione Abrahami

34 f.	173n85

De Mutatione Nominum

11 ff.	156n11

De Opificio Mundi

19 f.	158n20
24	159n21
69	163n44
70 f.	171n79
146	162n42

De Plantatione

64	168n65

De Posteritate Caini

12	168n63
28	155n9

De Praemiis et Poenis

39 f.	171n80
40	156n11

De Sacrificiis Abelis et Caini

78	163n46, 164n47

De Sommiis

I, 75	158n20
II, 13	164n52
II, 185	169n69
II, 231	169n69
II, 232 f.	169n68

De Specialibus Legibus

I, 32	156n11
I, 34	156n12
I, 35	156n13
I, 41	156nn14, 15
I, 45	157n16
I, 46–49	156n17
I, 81	158n20

De Vita Mosis

II, 127	158n20
II, 288	167n60

Legum Allegoriarum

I, 108	161n35
II, 31 f.	173n88
II, 85	173n88
III, 69	161n33
III, 72	162n37
III, 110 f.	166n58

Quaestiones et Solutiones in Exodum

II, 29	166n59, 167
II, 40	167n61

Quis Rerum Divanarum Heres Sit

63	169n72
69 f.	170n74
230 f.	163n44
259	165n54
263–65	165n56

Quod Deus Immutabilis Sit

31 f.	158n19
92	164nn49, 50
143	164n51

New Testament

Matthew

3:16 f.	37n13
10:2	103n59
26:64	249

Mark

1:10 f.	37n13
3:17	103n59
14:62	249n33

Luke
3:21 f.   37n13
6:14   103n59
22:30   107n82
22:69   249n33
24:10   315n326

John
1:29   109n88
1:32–34   37n13
1:36   109n88
1:51   37n15
20:12   315n326

Acts of the Apostles
7:51–53   304n270
7:55 f.   36
7:56   104n65
10:11   104n65
10:11 ff.   36

2 Corinthians
12:1–5   335n5

Galatians
3:19   304n270

Philippians
2:6–11   324

Hebrews
1:3–4   325
2:1–3   304n270

Revelation
1:1   103n56
1:4   103n56
1:8   108n87
1:9   103nn56, 60
1:10   104n66
1:12 ff.   104n66
1:13–16   105n70
1:13   103n63
2   103n61
3   103n61
4   103
4:1   104
4:1 ff.   37n12
4:11   110
5   103, 108
5:1   108
5:2   108
5:5   108
5:6   109
5:7   109
5:9   109
5:12   110
5:13   110
6   104
19:9   104n67
20:11   105n69
21:6   108n87
22:3 f.   105n69
22:8   103n56
22:13   108n87

Josephus Flavius

Bellum
2:129–132   114n5

Antiquitates
15:136   304n270

Rabbinic Literature

Mishna
Berakhot
2:1   253n47

Rosh ha-Shanah
4:5   286n163

Megillah
4:6   177nn5, 7
4:10   179nn14, 16, 211

Hagigah
2:1   30, 180, 185, 209n164,
               210n168, 211, 215, 218,
               219nn15, 19, 222, 225,
               284
2:2   225

Avot
1:1   297
1:4 ff.   225
1:13   288n175, 292
2:8 f.   187n50
3:14   264n92

Middot
4:5   205n141

Niddah
2:5   200n116

Yadayim
3:5   311n302

Tosefta

Berakhot
4:18   195n83

Hallah
1:10   270n110

Megillah
3 (4):28   177n8, 179, 211
3 (4):31–38   179n17
3 (4):34   179n18, 211

Hagigah
2:1   182n29, 185, 186n41,
               247
2:2   195n80
2:3 f.   197n94
2:5   208n159
2:6   204n136, 206n145
2:7   209n163, 210n168

Talmud Yerushalmi
Bikkurim
2:1/3, fol. 64c   205n141

Sheqalim
6:1/26, fol. 49d   207n154

Yoma
1:1/37, fol. 38d   216n9

Rosh ha-Shanah
2:5/2, fol. 58a   57n15

Megillah
1:12/9, fol. 72b   216n9

Hagigah
2:1/1–2:1/33, fol. 77a–c   214n1
2:1/7, fol. 77a   215n5,
                            218n12
2:1/8, fol. 77a   206n144,
                            219n16
2:1/9 f. fol. 77a   188n51
2:1/12, fol. 77a   191n63
2:1/13, fol. 77a/b   208n160
2:1/14, fol. 77b   196n89,
                            219n21
2:1/15, fol. 77b   197n99
2:1/15 end –2:1/17, fol. 77b 221n23
2:1/15 f., fol. 77b   199n111
2:1/18, fol.77b   197n99
2:1/18, fol. 77b – 2:1/29,
    fol. 77c   221n24
2:1/20 f., fol. 77b   189n56
2:1/30, fol. 77c   221n27
2:1/33 f., fol. 77c   209n163
2:1/42, fol. 77c   204n137

Sota
8:3/22, fol. 22d   207n154

Horayot
3:3/37, fol. 47d   216n9

Talmud Bavli
Berakhot
7a   258n68, 270n111

34b	303n263
62a	248n31

Shabbat

64a–b	205n142

Pesahim

26a	205n141

Betzah

9a	200n117

Megillah

25a–b	179n17

Hagigah

11b–13a	223n33
11b	209n163, 222n31, 223n32
12a	314n324
12b	141n115, 224n37
13a	224n39, 225n47, 227n52, 228n55, 258n68
13b–14a	229n63
13b	229n62
14a	230nn70–71
14b–15a	232n76
14b–16a	231n73
14b	188n51, 194n78, 196n90, 197n99, 202n128
15a–b	236n99
15a	197n99, 208n160, 233n80, 234n87, 322n362
15b	97n39, 197n99, 237n101, 238n102, 286n165
16a	239n108, 240n111

Sanhedrin

38a	322n362
56a	251n39

Avodah Zarah

3b	322n362

Zevahim

13a	216n9

Hullin

91b	261n79

Niddah

17b	200n116

Midrash

Sifre Numbers

§ 75	216n9
§ 103	291n191

Sifre Deuteronomy

§ 10	192nn66, 69
§ 47	192n66
§ 306	125n29

Midrash Tannaim

p. 6	192nn66, 69

Bereshit Rabbah

1:1	159n25
1:3	134n69
1:5	182n28, 222n29
1:10	222n28
1:15	222n30
2:4	208n160, 233n81
8:1	314n324
25:1	321n359
65:21	125n29
68:12	261n79
82:2	261n79

Wayyiqra Rabbah

4:1	248n31
16:4	190n59
20:10	204n138
30:2	192n66
23:13	205n142

Shir ha-Shirim Rabbah

1:28	200n119
1:53	190n57

Pesiqta de-Rav Kahana

27:2	192n66

Midrash Tehillim

11:6	192nn66, 69

Targum

Fragment Targum

Gen 28:12   261n79

Pseudo Jonathan

Gen 28:12   261n79

Hekhalot Literature

§§ 1–3	316
§ 1	246n14, 316
§ 2	317
§§ 3–5	296n218
§ 3	319
§§ 4–40	319
§ 4	319
§ 5	319
§ 6	317n336, 319
§§ 7–8	319
§ 9	319
§ 10	319
§ 11	320
§ 12	315n328, 320
§ 13	320
§ 14	128n35, 320, 326
§ 15	236n92
§ 16	320
§ 18	320
§ 19	320
§ 20	235n90, 236nn92, 94, 246n15, 322
§ 26	301n252
§ 32	315n327
§ 33	315n327
§ 39	315n327
§ 41	315n327
§ 58	230n68
§§ 59–70	317
§ 59	318n340
§ 60	318n341
§ 61	318n342
§ 62	318n343
§ 63	318n344
§§ 64 f.	318n345
§ 65	318n349
§ 66	318n346
§ 67	230n68, 318n347
§§ 68–70	318n248
§ 69	318n350

§ 70	318n349
§§ 71–80	318n348
§ 73	315n328
§ 76	296n220, 319
§ 77	296n220
§§ 81–93	245
§§ 81–276	244
§§ 81–306	244
§ 81	245n13, 247, 253, 254, 254n51, 259n71, 268
§§ 81 f.	248, 305
§ 82	249, 250, 250n35
§ 83	250
§§ 83 ff.	320n353
§ 84	250, 301
§ 85	250
§ 86	251
§ 91	250
§ 92	248n30, 253n46
§ 93	246n18, 253, 253n45, 276n130, 335n4
§§ 94–106	254, 259, 259n71, 260
§ 94	135n78, 254, 254n51, 259n71, 264n92
§ 95	254, 259n71
§ 96	254
§ 97	254
§ 98	254
§ 99	135n79, 254
§ 101	255, 260n73
§ 102	198n107, 255, 301n251
§§ 103 f.	255
§ 104	259
§ 106	256
§§ 107–121	256, 268
§ 108	276
§ 109	195n84, 271n114
§ 120	258n66
§§ 122–126	258
§ 122	343n22

§ 123 — 258, 258n65
§ 125 — 343n23
§§ 125 f. — 258
§ 126 — 258
§§ 130–138 — 258
§ 139 — 258n66
§§ 140–145 — 258
§§ 146–151 — 258n68
§ 151 — 270n111
§§ 152–197 — 259
§ 152 — 259
§ 154 — 135n78, 259n71, 264n92
§ 155 — 259n71
§ 156 — 259
§ 157 — 259
§ 158 — 259n72
§ 159 — 198n108, 259, 263
§§ 159 ff. — 98n44
§ 160 — 260
§ 162 — 92n22, 135n80, 260
§ 163 — 260, 263, 268
§ 164 — 260, 261, 266, 268, 299n237
§§ 165 f. — 262
§ 167 — 262
§ 168 — 262
§ 169 — 98n44, 262
§§ 170 ff. — 263
§ 174 — 264
§§ 178–188 — 265n94
§§ 178 ff. — 265n94
§ 179 — 265
§§ 181 f. — 265
§ 183 — 265
§§ 183 f. — 98n44, 266
§ 184 — 265
§ 188 — 268
§ 189 — 98n44, 265
§ 190 — 267
§§ 190 f. — 267n101
§ 192 — 267n102
§ 195 — 268
§ 197 — 268n104
§§ 198–267 — 244
§ 198 — 268, 268n105, 278
§ 199 — 268n105, 269n106, 272, 278

§ 200 — 269, 269n108, 273, 277, 279n132
§ 201 — 268n105, 269, 269n108, 270, 278
§ 202 — 270
§§ 202 ff. — 95n34
§ 203 — 95, 195n85, 271, 276
§§ 204–218 — 274
§ 204 — 271, 271n117
§§ 204 f. — 300n246
§ 205 — 272
§§ 206–218 — 272
§ 206 — 96n37, 272, 276
§§ 206 ff. — 96n36
§§ 213–215 — 273
§ 215 — 299n238
§ 216 — 273, 277, 279n132
§ 217 — 274
§ 218 — 274, 277, 279n132
§ 219 — 274
§§ 219 ff. — 96n36
§ 223 — 275
§§ 224–228 — 275
§ 225 — 198n109, 246n16, 276
§§ 225 ff. — 95, 253n49, 303n262
§ 227 — 276, 277, 279n132, 342n20
§ 228 — 95
§ 229 — 275, 275n126
§ 230 — 96n36, 275n126
§ 231 — 277, 278, 293n201
§ 232 — 293n201
§ 233 — 96n36, 270, 275n126, 342n20
§ 234 — 268n105, 278
§ 235 — 278, 293n201
§§ 235 f. — 275
§ 236 — 278, 279, 292n198, 293n201, 299nn239,241, 342n20
§ 237 — 274, 279
§§ 238–257 — 279
§ 238 — 279
§ 240 — 279
§§ 241–248 — 301n252
§ 241 — 279
§ 242 — 280
§ 243 — 280

§ 244	280	§§ 353 ff.	291
§§ 245 ff.	280	§ 356	291, 308n288
§§ 246 f.	255n56	§ 357	292, 292n196
§ 247	280, 319	§§ 358 f.	292
§ 248	280, 299n241	§ 360	292
§ 249	299n241	§§ 362–365	292
§ 250	102n54, 280	§ 364	305
§§ 251–257	280	§ 366	292
§ 251	135n80, 280, 300n243	§§ 366 f.	305n273
§§ 258–259	281n136, 286n165,	§ 367	293, 294
	298n232	§ 368	294
§ 258	298	§§ 369–372	294
§§ 258 f.	317n337	§ 372	294
§ 259	298	§§ 373–374	294
§§ 267–268	281	§§ 375–406	283, 209n189
§§ 269–276	282	§ 375	295
§ 277	282	§ 376	295
§§ 278–280	282	§ 376 ff.	307
§§ 281–294	282	§ 377	295
§§ 281–306	267n103	§§ 378–383	295
§§ 282–306	244	§ 384	296
§ 289	282	§ 385	296
§§ 295–296	298n230	§ 387	296, 296n220
§ 297	282	§§ 387 f.	294n212
§ 299	302n258	§ 388	296, 296n220
§ 303	246n20	§ 389	296n222
§ 306	282	§ 390	296
§§ 307–314	245	§ 392	297
§§ 315–317	245	§ 393	297n225
§§ 318–321	245, 278	§ 396	296n222
§ 318	292n198	§ 397	297
§§ 322–334	245	§ 399	296
§§ 335–517	282	§§ 400–402	297
§§ 335–374	283	§ 400	297
§ 335	283	§§ 403–404	297
§ 336	285, 286	§ 403	246n17
§ 337	285	§§ 405–406	298
§§ 340–343	286n165	§§ 407–410	281n136, 286n165
§§ 344–345	286n165	§§ 407–424	283, 297
§§ 344–346	286n164	§§ 407–427	298
§ 345	286n165, 287, 299n236	§ 407	298
§ 346	97n39, 238n103	§§ 407 f.	317n338
§ 348	287	§ 408	202n131, 298
§§ 348 f.	287	§ 409	202n131
§ 349	287	§ 410	202n131
§§ 350 ff.	288	§ 411	299, 342n20
§ 351	289	§ 412	299nn240, 241
§ 352	289, 310	§§ 413–417	299

§ 417	343n22
§ 418	300
§§ 418 f.	343n24
§ 419	290n189, 300
§§ 420–421	301
§ 420	301
§ 421	301
§§ 422–424	302
§ 422	302
§ 424	302
§§ 425–426	303
§§ 425 f.	283, 283n149
§ 427	303n267
§§ 427 f.	283, 283n149
§§ 428–467	295n215
§ 428	303n267
§§ 429–467	283n149, 295n215
§§ 468–488	283n149, 325n215
§ 489	303n267, 304
§§ 489–495	283, 283n149, 303
§ 490	305
§ 495	305
§§ 496 f.	305n273
§§ 498–499	283
§ 498	305
§ 499	305
§ 500	305n274
§ 501	283n150, 305, 305n275
§§ 502–511	283n150
§ 508	306
§ 512	283n150, 305n275
§§ 513–517	283n150
§ 513	306
§ 516	306
§ 517	306
§§ 518–540	283n150
§ 534	265n95
§ 542	305n275
§ 556	199n113
§ 560	302nn258, 259
§§ 579–580	298n229

§ 579	246n17
§ 591	248n30
§ 623	128n35
§ 634	135n78, 264n92
§§ 671–672	286n165
§ 672	235n89, 238n104, 322n362
§ 673	97n39, 238nn104, 105
§ 686	135n78, 264n92
§ 687	135n78, 264n92
§§ 688–704	307
§ 695	307n281
§ 696	308n286
§ 697	308n290
§ 698	308n286
§ 699	308n288
§ 700	307n285
§ 703	308n289
§ 704	308n291
§§ 714–727	295n215
§§ 728–739	295n215
§ 772	141n119
§§ 882–938	307n279
§§ 939–353	307, 307n279
§§ 939–973	295n215
§§ 939–978	307, 307n279
§§ 939 ff.	307
§ 948	307, 308
§ 949	308
§ 950	308n289
§ 951	307n285, 308
§ 954 ff.	307n279

Hekhalot Genizah Fragments

T.-S. K 21.95.A	
fol. 1b	195n86
T.-S. K 21.95.B	
fol. 2a–b	238n103, 287n168
T.-S. K 21.95.C	
fol. 2a	198n108
fol. 2b	342n20

General Index

Aaron 43, 63n41, 82, 82n113, 113,
 115–116, 122, 128–129, 140, 166,
 172, 216n8, 317
Abaddon 123
– *see also* Netherworld
Abbahu (R.) 297n226
Abihu 43, 166, 172, 204–205
Abraham 28, 42n56, 45, 102, 165,
 169–170, 171n80, 187, 216–217, 267,
 274, 286n162, 331–332
– angelification of 28
– early life of 87
– *see also* Abraham, apocalypse of
Abraham, apocalypse of 28–29, 86–93,
 105n74, 111, 333, 335–336
– Abraham's sacrifice to God 89–90
– appearance of the angel Iaoel to Abraham 88–89
– changing form of the angels in 90
– description of his ascent to heaven in
 90
– God's voice like a fire in 91–92
– issues of idolatry in 92–93
– parallels to Hekhalot literature 92
– song of with Iaoel in 91–92
– tension between the spoken word and
 the vision in 87–88
Abulafia 17n67, 19
adam 38, 43–46, 73, 80, 88, 134, 204,
 206, 206nn148, 150, 207, 269, 271,
 287, 289–290, 310n296
– *adam qadmon* 314n324
Adam 53, 173, 314n324
Aher (Elisha b. Avuyah) 189, 196–197,
 199–201, 219–222, 231, 234–237,
 238n104, 239, 241, 246, 286n165, 322
– fate of 236–237
– punishment of 235, 322n361
Aibo (R.) 321–322

Aletheia 171n80, 312–313
Alexander Lysimachus 154
Ammi (R.) 214, 225, 225n45
Amos 44
Anafiel 236, 279–280, 301, 319, 322
angelification 19–20, 28–30, 81n107,
 133, 153, 334, 336–337, 342–343,
 349–350
Antiochus IV Epiphanes 60, 117n13
Aphrahat 324
apophaticism 341n14
Aqiva (R.) 9n30, 11, 22, 32, 97, 177,
 185–186, 190n59, 195–200, 202–203,
 212, 214–221, 230–235, 237–241,
 242n116, 247, 256, 285–287, 290–295,
 297–304, 306–307, 307n285, 310,
 311n302, 316, 329–330, 340, 346
Aquinas, Thomas 5, 5n13
Aravot 79, 79n101, 223–224, 248,
 265n97
Archangels 68–69, 75–76, 78–79, 101,
 119, 126, 141, 149, 149n157
– *see also* Eremiel, Gabriel, Michael,
 Phanuel, Raphael
ascent account(s) 65, 72, 93–94, 203,
 235, 238, 244, 271–275, 277, 279–281,
 283, 286, 294, 299, 300, 306, 310,
 316–317, 327–330, 335, 335n5,
 340–341, 346
ascent apocalypse(s) 19–20, 22, 27–33,
 53, 65, 67, 96, 98, 102–104, 108,
 110–111, 116, 126, 128, 151, 153,
 174–175, 213, 224, 276n130, 331–333,
 335, 337–344, 346, 348–354
Assi (R.) 225–226
Azazel 90

Bacchanalia 170, 174
Baruch 36

Bathsheba 248

battle, final 29, 113, 116–122, 126, 150–151, 258, 328

– see also eschatology

Behemoth 200–201

Belial (Prince of Darkness) 117

Ben Azzai 190n59, 196, 199–200, 202n131, 208n162, 219, 299

Ben Zoma 196, 199–200, 203n134, 206–209, 212, 219–220, 231, 233–234, 241

"binitarian" theology 33, 110–111, 323, 330

– binitarianism 323

cherubs 39, 39n34, 41, 57–59, 66, 136–138

– see also keruvim

Christianity 7–8, 16, 69, 94n31, 103n55, 155, 339

chrysolite 40, 40n41, 59, 60, 88–89, 105n74

Church Fathers 155, 324

communion: military communion with angels 116n11, 120, 190

– liturgical communion with angels 29, 92, 116, 120, 122–125, 128, 132, 144, 146, 149–152, 175–176, 281, 331, 348–349

– see also "communion"/"union" distinction

"communion"/"union" distinction 8n27, 18, 124, 349–350, 350n47

Corybants 170–171, 174

cosmology 16, 181, 210, 210nn171, 172, 223–224, 258n68, 332

creation 7, 30, 42, 44, 76, 159, 168, 172, 180–185, 201, 208–211, 215, 222, 227, 240, 267, 287, 320

– cycle of Merkavah creation stories on 220–222

– "work" of 31, 180–182, 187, 206–210, 212, 214–215, 218, 221n25, 222–224, 226, 231, 234, 240–241

– see also ma'aseh bereshit

Daniel 33, 44–45, 60–62, 62n38, 72–74, 88n8, 105, 108, 110, 117, 118n14, 184, 229, 229n65, 231, 268, 323–324, 335, 338

David 102, 108–109, 147, 179, 230, 249, 257n62, 258, 292, 343n23

Davidic Messiah

– see Messiah, Davidic

deification 8, 19–20, 150–151, 168, 337, 337n7, 343, 345, 352

– of Moses 168

– quasi-deification 342

Dinah 68

Dumiel 270, 275, 275n126, 277–279, 316n335, 342n20

Eckhart, Johannes (Meister Eckhart) 4, 4n8

ecstasy, state of 3, 6, 8, 17n67, 30, 64, 165, 169–170, 170n76, 173–174, 303, 344

– Corybantic frenzy 171, 173

– see also Corybants

elders

– see Israel, elders of

Eleazar b. Arakh (R.) 186–188, 188n51, 190, 193, 195–196, 196n88, 206, 211, 216–217, 219–220, 226, 226n48, 231, 237, 240

Eleazar b. Azarya (R.) 231

Eleazar b. Pedat (R.) 240

Elihu 200

Elijah 46n64, 84, 102, 138, 176, 237, 252, 319, 327

Elisha 189

Elisha b. Avuyah

– see Aher (Elisha b. Avuyah)

Enoch 12, 13n45, 15n53, 20, 27–28, 33, 53–54, 83n115, 84, 86, 102, 107, 331, 342

– angelification of 81–85

– fear of 79, 79n102

– as a mediator between angels 55

– as Metatron 318–327

– as one who "walks with God," 53–54, 316

– as the "scribe of righteousness," 95

– as the Son of Man 76, 84

– symptoms of shock displayed by 64–65

– transformation of into an angel 28, 33, 235
– *see also* Enoch, vision of
Enoch, vision of 70, 72, 293n202, 313, 332–334, 345
– of angels 74–75, 77–79, 79n102, 119, 314, 335–336
– anticlimax of the vision 80–81
– climax of the vision 60–63, 80–81
– Enoch's reaction to the scene of heaven 63
– function of the angels in 62–63
– function of the heavenly Temple in 65–67, 67n55
– of God in heaven 55–58, 61, 76, 78–80, 80nn104, 105
– of the hailstones and the cherubs 57–58
– of the houses 58–59, 59n25, 293n202
– of the last judgment 74
– meaning of 63–64
– and the schema of the seven heavens 77–79
– of the throne 59–60, 60n27
– of the wall in heaven 56–57
Enoch-Metatron traditions 12, 12n44, 13n45, 19–20, 33, 349
Ephrem 324
Epiphanius 315
Er 161
Eremiel (Remiel) 29, 101, 105n74, 111, 333
eschatology 66, 70, 105n69, 123, 129, 181, 340
– eschatological battle 29, 116–117, 121–122, 151, 184
– eschatological priest 28, 36, 71, 84, 336
– eschatological savior 314
– eschatological Temple 51, 65–66, 70, 128, 184
– "presentic" eschatology 123, 281n138
– speaker of the Self-Glorification Hymn 150
exegesis 30–33, 155, 169, 175–176, 178, 183–185, 187–194, 195n82, 201, 201n121, 205–213, 215, 217, 220, 222, 225–226, 228, 231, 233–234,

239–241, 305, 308–311, 311n303, 330, 350–353
Ezekiel, vision of 35–39, 53, 56–58, 61, 63–65, 108, 176, 178, 178n11, 191, 331–332, 336, 343
– archaic imagery used to describe God in 42–43, 43n59, 50–51
– auditory aspects of 42–43, 48, 53
– the chrysolite throne in 40, 40n41, 59–60, 89
– climax of 43–44
– coordination of the wheels and creatures by the spirit in 41
– divine favor in 50
– effects of the vision on Ezekiel 52
– Ezekiel's eating of the scroll 48
– Ezekiel's feelings of afterward 49–50, 50n77, 52
– glory of God revealed in 47–49, 49n76, 51
– God's appearance to Ezekiel in 44–48, 310
– stages of 38–44
– termination of 49
Ezra 297

Fallen angels (Nefilim) 54–55, 63–64

Gabriel 63n42, 75–76, 79, 108, 117, 119, 119n17, 275, 278–279
Gaius Caligula 154
Gedullah hymns 245–254, 256–257, 301, 305, 320n353, 327
Greek mystery cults 1–2

Hagar 164n48
Hai Gaon 303, 303n263
Halakhah 17, 22, 214–218, 231
– Qumranic 22
Hama b. Hoshayah (R.) 321
Hananyah b. Hakinai (R.) 195–196, 212, 219
Hananyah b. Teradyon (R.) 256
hashmal 38, 43, 47, 105, 137–138, 227–229, 241, 268, 294, 297–298, 298n233, 301
– etymology of 38n21
Hasidism, in medieval Germany 10

havurah 95, 195, 268, 270–272, 276–277, 279, 281–282, 286, 328–329, 346, 347n37
hayyot 38–39, 40n40, 41, 57, 107, 134–135, 135n76, 137, 137n94, 263, 265
– *see also* holy creatures
heavens (seven) 68n58, 77–79, 88, 94–96, 141, 144, 153, 193n70, 210, 223, 243, 273n121, 287, 293n204, 333
Heraclitus 161
Herod 150n163, 175
Hezekiah 94, 336
high priest(s) 36, 61, 66–67, 82, 82n113, 106, 106n79, 112–113, 113n2, 129, 130n42, 139–142, 145, 145n129, 151n167, 152, 169n69, 175, 205, 228n61, 232–233, 241, 253, 270, 319n351, 350
Hillel 292, 292n198, 297
Hippolytus of Rome 313–315
Hiyya (R.) 219, 224–225
holy creatures 224, 255, 255n56, 259–260, 262–268, 279–280, 289, 291, 295n214, 296–297, 306, 319, 328–329, 342n20
– *see also* hayyot
Holy of Holies 27, 39, 59, 61, 63–64, 66, 68, 75–76, 81, 84, 115–116, 119, 128–129, 132–134, 136–137, 143–144,169n69, 205, 243, 248, 270, 345
Holy Spirit 94, 96–98, 165, 314–315

Iaoel 28, 88–89, 91–92, 92n27, 105n74, 111
– clothes of 89
– sapphire-like body of 89
ice 42, 42n49, 57–60, 75, 107, 107n84, 134, 206
Irenaeus 312
Isaac 45, 71, 102, 164, 169, 267
Isaiah, ascension of to heaven (Vision of Isaiah) 29, 44, 86, 93–99, 102, 108, 111, 332–336
– angelic state of 97–98
– Christian origin of 94, 94n31
– Isaiah's account of 94–95

– Isaiah's place in the heavenly hierarchy 97
– Isaiah's vision of God 98, 98n42
– journey of Isaiah through the seven heavens 96–98
– message of 98–99
– similarity of to the havurah account in Hekhalot literature 95
Ishmael (R.) 11–12, 22, 33, 95, 214–215, 245–246, 256–258, 268, 270, 271n113, 276, 279, 282, 285, 297, 303, 305n274, 307, 307n285, 315–318, 327–328, 346
Israel 28–29, 32–34, 35n3, 36–37, 43, 47–48, 50–51, 64, 70–71, 86, 93, 98, 106, 106nn79, 81, 108–109, 111, 114–117, 128–129, 142, 184, 187–188, 200, 223–224, 230, 232, 234, 248–250, 250n35, 252, 255–256, 258, 261, 263, 267, 274, 274n124, 281–292, 296–297, 299–300, 305, 308, 311, 317, 327–328, 336, 343–344, 348, 354
– elders of 43, 104, 106–110, 166, 172, 197
– God's love for 345
– Jacob as representative of 262
– and the Qedushah 260–263, 266–268, 328
– redemption of 76, 84, 125n31, 318
– superiority of to angels 98, 125, 262, 297n224, 304n270

Jacob 42n56, 45, 68, 102, 136, 171n80, 256, 261–262, 266–268, 299, 328
Jehoiachin 34–36
Jerome 155, 184n35
Jerusalem 16, 34, 37, 100, 104, 105n69, 106, 112, 117, 120–121, 131, 141, 155, 231
– eschatological Jerusalem 128
– New Jerusalem 106n78, 111
– and the priesthood 66–67, 69, 132
Jesus Christ 29, 33, 37, 97, 103–104, 106n82, 109, 111, 151, 151n169, 249, 314–315, 315n326, 322, 330, 343
– as the "Chosen One," 93, 93n29
– as the Lamb 109, 111
– as a reflection of God's glory 324–326
– *see also* Son of Man

"Jewish thought," 26, 26n94
Joachim (son of Asaph) 95
John , vision of (Revelation) 29, 86,
  103, 103n55, 105n69, 111, 332–333,
  335–336
– appearance of the Messiah in 109
– inaugural vision of 104–105
– the Lion of Judah and the Root of
  David described in 108–109
– praise of the Lamb in 109–110
– vision of precious stones and the splendor of God 105–106, 106nn76, 79
– vision of the scroll 108
– vision of the Son of Man 103–105
– vision of the throne 105, 105n69,
  107–108
– vision of the twenty-four elders
  106–107
John the Baptist 37
John XXII (Pope) 4n8
Jonathan the Maccabee 112
Joseph ha-Kohen (R.) 190–192, 220
Josiah 34

Kabbalah 10, 10n34, 18, 18n72, 21–22,
  44n61, 355
– relationship of to Jewish mysticism 27
keruvim 39, 57, 255, 259–260, 263, 268,
  279–280, 342n20
– *see also* cherubs
Kybele 170

"lapis lazuli" (*sappīr*) 43n57
leprosy 121, 217–219, 250, 304
"Lesser YHWH," 33, 235–236, 296, 320,
  322
Levi 28, 36, 67–72, 82, 84, 86, 194n79,
  252, 331–332, 336
– *see also* Levi, visions of
Levi, visions of 28, 68–70, 332, 335
Leviathan 200–201
Logos, the 33, 158–160, 162–163,
  165–166, 169n69, 171–174, 323
lunar calendar 113, 113n2
Lupinus 256

ma'aseh bereshit 180, 207, 310
– *see also* creation, work of

ma'aseh merkavah 12n44, 13, 186, 190,
  219, 219n19, 225, 243, 244n5, 250,
  283, 285, 298n229, 301, 302n259, 310,
  315–316
– *see also* Merkavah, the, "work of"
Maccabees 112, 117
magic 2, 2n1, 243, 251n37, 252n44, 272,
  278, 286, 355
– magical seals 278, 328–329, 340
– practical magic 305–306
Mar Shemuel 233n78
marble stones 107, 202–203
– Aqiva's warning concerning 230,
  234–235, 241, 242n116
Marcus (Gnostic) 311–313
Meir (R.) 221, 237, 241
Merkavah, the 30–31, 95, 111, 135n76,
  137, 143–145, 145n129, 177–184,
  186–188, 190–191, 193–201, 201n123,
  203, 206, 208–212, 214–227, 229,
  231–232, 236–243, 253
– "work of the," 31, 186–188, 190, 210,
  212, 219, 222–223, 225–227, 250,
  285–286, 301
Messiah 36–37, 76, 103, 111, 252,
  257–258, 258n70, 274, 281, 318,
  326, 328, 330, 340
– Davidic Messiah 109, 113, 129,
  230, 258, 318, 328
– Elijah as precursor to 327
– Messiah of Aaron 113, 129
– new Messiah 32
– priestly Messiah 113, 129, 150
– Qumranic Messiah 151n169
Metatron 92, 231, 245, 254, 254n53, 258,
  258n68, 282–283, 283n149, 294–298,
  301, 304, 306–307, 307n279, 314n324,
  315–318, 330, 342n20, 343, 343n23
– adoption of the role of Jesus by 326
– encounter of with Aher 234–237,
  238n104, 241, 246
– Enoch as Metatron 318–327, 349
Methuselah 53, 83, 319
Michael 63n42, 75–76, 81–82, 119,
  119n17, 149, 149n157, 333
– as the heavenly Melchizedek 314
– as heavenly Prince 117, 141
– sacrifices offered by 142

Middle Platonism 154, 154n1
Miriam 63n41
monotheism 322
- "monotheistic religion," 322
Moses 43, 45–48, 50, 57n11, 63n41, 80,
    80n104, 89, 91, 122, 126, 156–157,
    163, 165–169, 172–174, 188–190,
    211, 240n115, 278, 285–286, 289–292,
    296–297, 304–306, 321n356

Nadab 43, 166, 172, 204–205
Nebuchadnezzar 34, 224, 241
names, divine 32–33, 255n56, 272,
    275, 278, 285, 288–290, 292,
    294–297, 300, 304–306, 307n278,
    308–310, 312, 313n315, 319,
    328–330, 340
Nathan (R.) 307n285
Nefilim 54–55
- *see also* Fallen angels
Nehunya b. Haqanah (R.) 95, 111, 245,
    246n16, 253, 256, 268, 270–271,
    275–277, 279, 282, 285, 297, 303, 329,
    335, 342n20, 346, 347n37
Neoplatonism 19, 154
Netherworld 98, 123–124, 181, 210, 221,
    221n27, 224, 273n121, 332
- *see also* Abaddon, She'ol
Noachide Laws 251, 269, 269n109, 278
Nous 162–163, 165–166, 168, 312

ofannim 78n100, 79, 135, 135n76,
    137–138, 224, 255, 259–260, 263,
    268, 279–280, 287, 342n20
Origen of Caesarea 183–184, 184n35,
    310–311

Papias 103
pardes 198, 202–204, 208, 208n162, 212,
    220–221, 231–235, 237–238, 238n106,
    247, 286–287
Paul 324–325, 335n5
Peter 37
Phanuel 75–76, 119
Philo of Alexandria 30, 77n91, 154–155,
    155nn5, 6, 323, 331, 335, 335n5,
    352–354
- on Abraham 171n80

- on the ascent of the soul/mind
    168–169
- on the athlete's and philosopher's
    approaches to their bodies 161–162
- on the body/soul distinction 160–164,
    175
- concept of God 155–160
- identification of wisdom and Logos
    159–160, 162
- on immutable tranquility 172, 172n81
- on the inability of the soul to view God
    171–172
- on Moses 165–168
- philosophical influences on 154,
    154n2, 157n18
- prominent role of wisdom (*Sophia*) in
    his work 159–160, 162–164, 169, 173
- on the soul's journey 170–174
- on the soul's vision of God 164–174
Plato 30, 154–155, 157n18, 161, 162n39,
    170, 170n76
priesthood 15, 28, 66, 70–72, 82, 109,
    109n89, 112, 114, 122, 132, 143,
    317n339, 336
priest(s) 14–15, 28, 36, 66–71, 84, 109,
    113–116, 128–130, 132, 137n96,
    139–143, 145, 145n129, 151–153,
    169n69, 175, 179, 184n35, 216n8,
    232–233, 240, 252, 336, 340, 350
Propator 312–313

Qatzpiel 275, 275n126, 277–279,
    316–317
Qedushah hymns 254–257, 259–268,
    303, 327–328

rainbow 47–48, 89, 104–105, 106n77,
    190–191, 240, 288, 288n172, 291, 294
Raphael 63n42, 75–76, 119, 119n17
Rav 215, 217–220
Joseph (R.) 226–227
religion, evolutionary model of 7
- and mysticism 6–7, 9
Remiel
- *see* Eremiel
righteous 63, 68–69, 72–74, 76, 93,
    101–102, 105n69, 199, 208, 223,
    230, 318, 321, 334, 337, 342

– deceased 29, 97–111, 161
– seven classes of in heaven 96, 191–194, 72
romanticism 21
– German 21

sacrifice 68–69, 89, 109, 114–115, 131, 139–146, 152–153, 175, 232, 256, 332, 345, 350
Samnas (scribe) 94
sapphire (blue corundum) 43n57
"sapphire brick" (*livnat ha-sappir*) 43–44, 89, 172
"sapphire stone" (*even-sappir*) 43–44, 74n86, 88–89, 105
Sariel 63n42, 119, 119n17
Self-Glorification Hymn 17, 19–20, 30, 146, 149–153, 348–350, 350n47, 353
sexual relations 30, 68, 71, 180–184, 201n122, 206, 211, 214–215, 218
Shemuel b. Nahmani (R.) 230
She'ol 98, 123, 224
– *see also* Netherworld
Sherira Gaon 303, 303n263
Shim'on b. Netan'el (R.) 190–192
Shi'ur Qomah 32–33, 244, 244n4, 262, 283, 283n149, 290, 290n190, 294–295, 295n215, 301, 306–307, 307nn279, 285, 308–315, 315n329, 327, 330
Sige 312–313
solar calendar 15n53, 113, 113n2, 131
Solomon 248, 292
Songs of the Sabbath Sacrifice 13, 14nn48, 50, 16–17, 19, 30, 130, 133, 135, 147, 149, 150n167, 152, 348–349, 350n47
Son of Man 33, 36–37, 45, 72–73, 73n82, 103–105, 106n79, 109–110, 226, 249, 314, 323, 323n367
– Enoch as the Son of Man 76, 84, 333, 336
spirit 3, 5, 7, 36, 38, 40–41, 48, 48n71, 71, 71n70, 74–75, 76n89, 88, 90, 94–95, 97, 104, 111, 120–121, 123, 138, 276n130, 332–334
– divine Spirit 165
– of holiness 114
– Holy Spirit 94, 96–98, 165, 314–315

– Spirit of God 36–37, 207–208, 234
"Star from Jacob," 36
student/teacher relationships 216, 219–220, 225–226
Suriyah 257, 268, 272, 275, 300n246, 303n266

Tabernacle 44–45, 48, 50, 63n41, 82, 136n88, 169n69
Tarfon (R.) 216–217
Temple, the celestial/heavenly 133n67, 137, 139, 141–144, 152–153, 327, 336, 350
– desecration of 28, 92–93
– the earthly Temple 28, 59, 61, 65–67, 67n55, 69, 84, 86, 116, 130, 141–142, 142n119, 243, 281, 289, 336, 340, 345
Ten Martyrs 195, 256–257, 259, 268, 271, 327
Terah 87, 93
Tiberius Julius Alexander 154

unio angelica ("angelification" of humans) 153, 337, 349
unio liturgica (liturgical comm/union of the Merkavah mystic with the angels/God) 29, 32, 92, 96, 153, 281, 341, 349
unio mystica (unification of the human with the divine) 1–4, 6, 6n15, 9, 17–19, 24, 32, 153, 168n64, 281, 341, 344, 352
– influence of Neoplatonic philosophy on 19

vision of God 8, 27–28, 30, 32, 34, 37, 43, 47–48, 51, 53, 55, 58n17, 62, 70, 72–74, 79n102, 81, 84, 91, 98–99, 101, 111, 138–139, 145, 151–153, 168, 174, 193, 223, 240, 248–249, 255, 277, 279–280, 289, 290, 299n241, 306, 310, 329, 331, 336, 341–342, 345n32, 350

Yehoshua (R.) 189, 193, 193n75, 195, 195n82, 207–209, 219, 231, 234, 241
Yehudah (R.) 177–179, 195
Yehudah ha-Nasi (R.) 195, 215, 219–220, 227–228, 228n54, 237
Yehudah b. Pazzi (R.) 215, 223

Yitzhaq Nappaha (R.) 227–228
Yohanan b. Nappaha (R.) 225, 230, 240
Yohanan b. Zakkai (R.) 186–196, 206,
    211–212, 219–220, 224–227, 231, 240,
    303n263
yored (la-) merkavah, yoredei merkavah
    20, 144, 239, 243, 247, 252, 268

Zephaniah, apocalypse of 29, 86, 99–102,
    105n74, 111, 111n92, 332n1, 333–335

– description of the ascent of the dead
    soul in 99–100
– hierarchy of heaven in 102
– journey of Zephaniah 100
– mistaking of an angel for God in
    100–101
– Zephaniah in Hades 101
– Zephaniah's angelic garment 101–102
Zera (R.) 225

9 780691 142159